D. A. Codling

Nov. 1965.

(s)

Educational Psychology

THE STUDY OF EDUCATIONAL GROWTH

J. M. STEPHENS

THE JOHNS HOPKINS UNIVERSITY

REVISED EDITION

HOLT, RINEHART AND WINSTON
NEW YORK

Preface to the Revised Edition

THE PUBLICATION of this second edition has made it possible to include some important new materials and to bring about other improvements. A chapter on the group processes and social development has been included and the whole topic of personal adjustment has been greatly enlarged. Almost all chapters have been rewritten to bring them into line with important recent material. Along with these additions, there has been some rearrangement of topics based partly on the suggestions of many instructors who have kindly reported their experience.

This edition is accompanied by a student workbook and an instructor's manual. Most of the notes intended primarily for the instructor have been transferred to the latter publication. This manual includes an extended list of suggestions for films, suggestions and material for classroom demonstrations, and some 800 objective examination questions organized by chapters. The student workbook includes materials for the extended study of an individual child, a large number of exercises and questions for discussion, questions for self-testing, and the student materials for classroom demonstrations.

The chart which follows on page xvi may prove useful to readers who wish to make certain cross comparisons. In its horizontal dimension, the chart shows the organization of the book in relation to aspects of growth (dependent variables) and the vertical dimension treats some characteristics of growth as well as factors affecting growth (independent variables). The reader who wishes to compare various aspects of growth with respect to (say) constancy, or factor analysis, can readily do so. The Instructor's Manual contains additional suggestions for the use of this chart.

J. M. S.

Baltimore, Md.
March, 1956

Preface to the First Edition

THIS TEXT IS ESSENTIALLY a study of educational growth or development. It is a study of the nature of such growth; of the forces which affect it; and of the means of facilitating it. This growth is considered chiefly from the view point of the teacher, it being assumed, of course, that the reader will consider himself as a teacher or prospective teacher. The teacher, actual or prospective, is encouraged to regard himself as one element in a very complex pattern of forces, all affecting educational growth. He is shown his position in the pattern. He is introduced to the other forces and told what to expect of each—either in the way of help, of neutral tolerance, or of active interference. He is then introduced to his own specialized role in the process and is shown the various tools he may use in carrying out his task.

Emphasis on the Teacher as a Theorist

The text is addressed to two prospective teachers within the same individual. It is addressed to the teacher-practitioner and to the teacher-theorist. The emphasis on the teacher-practitioner, of course, is in no way surprising. The emphasis on the teacher as a theorist, on the other hand, may be somewhat unusual and may call for an explanation.

Throughout the book, the theoretical needs of the teacher are shown to be very real. The teacher cannot contemplate such a complex process as education without forming opinions. He is bound to generalize and to seek to introduce some order into the separate facts of education. These opinions and generalizations formulated by the teacher may have far-reaching practical consequences, especially if they come to be widely held. The future of education, in fact, may depend more on the careful and accurate forming of views than on any ordinary increase in pedagogical skill. Conversely, inept theorizing may be just as disastrous as lack of practical competence.

The requirements of the teacher-practitioner and of the teacher-theorist are both very real and very important. They are, however, somewhat different, and the differences in these requirements are nowhere more strik- ing than in the matter of caution versus confidence. There are times, unquestionably, when the teacher-practitioner should not be assailed by doubts or qualifications, when he should carry out with confidence and with decision any course of action that he has undertaken. At these times, any large measure of doubt, uncertainty, or hesitation may seriously re- duce his effectiveness.

The hesitation or uncertainty which might work against the practi- tioner presents no handicap to the theorist. On the contrary, caution, admission of uncertainty, willingness to withhold judgment are of the utmost importance when the teacher-theorist is forming his opinions about the nature of the educational process. The teacher-theorist, there- fore, must receive training in this very necessary practice of entertaining doubts and qualifications. A certain amount of such training, by the way, is not only necessary to enable the teacher to formulate dependable opinions, but is also invaluable in helping him develop into a mature and well-rounded person. As part of his own progress toward maturity, the teacher must learn to be happy and reasonable efficient, even in a world as full of uncertitude as our own. And if he is to look honestly and steadily at the complex and little-understood process of education, then he must be prepared to tolerate a measure of uncertainty that is very large indeed.

To meet these conflicting demands of confidence versus caution, I have simply made use of the opportunities of the moment. When considering factors beyond the control of the teacher, for instance, I have emphasized caution, complexity, and the need for suspended judgment. I have felt that this approach was quite safe in a field where little direct action is possible for the teacher anyhow. In suggesting specific pedagogical tech- niques, on the other hand, I have frequently made very definite recom- mendations, choosing the risk of being in error rather than the certainty of being indefinite. This separation of emphasis, however, is by no means clear-cut. Even in discussing specific teaching practices, I have felt free, on occasion, to point out that the advice offered here does not represent the truth in any complete and final stage.

From among the hundreds of people to whom I am deeply indebted, I select a few to whom it is an especial pleasure to express my gratitude. Such gratitude is due to the editors of the series for much encouragement and for scores of helpful suggestions; to a large number of students, assist- ants and colleagues who, during some twenty years, have helped work the course into shape; to my daughters Dorothy and Doreen Stephens for much reading and rereading and for some extremely forthright criticism; to Mrs. Lois L. Sim for long and tiring labor during a period completely bereft of reinforcement; and above all to my wife who, in addition to the expected encouragement and censoring of my weirder notions, also took on almost complete responsibility for the more vexatious details, granting to them assurance of adequate attention and to me the opportunity of concentrating on the simpler phases of the project.

All the illustrations especially drawn for this text were prepared by Mr. John O'Rourke. It is a pleasure to express my appreciation for the excellent work he has done.

J. M. S.

The Johns Hopkins University
January 10, 1951

Contents

PART ONE: **Psychology and the Study of Educational Growth**

1. **The Content and Scope of Educational Psychology**   3

Educational Development: Its Nature, Prevalence, and Importance — THE TEACHER AND OTHER FORCES RESPONSIBLE FOR DEVELOPMENT — ROLE AND VALUES OF EDUCATIONAL PSYCHOLOGY — Aid in Directing the Process of Development — Aid in Adjusting to Other Forces Responsible for Development—Aid in Understanding the Nature of Educational Growth—Additional Roles of Educational Psychology — POSSIBLE LIMITATIONS OF EDUCATIONAL PSYCHOLOGY — Possible Limitations Arising from the Nature of Teaching — Possible Limitations Arising from the Nature of Science — Possible Limitations Arising from the Nature of Psychology

2. **Understanding Educational Development: Procedures and Pitfalls**   20

The Need for Care in Reaching Conclusions about Education — The Pitfall of Wishful Thinking—Systematic Study: Values and Limitations—PROCEDURAL ERRORS: FREQUENT IN CASUAL STUDIES, RARE IN SYSTEMATIC STUDIES — Too Few Cases — Using Selected Cases — Lack of Precision in Observing, Measuring, and Describing Data — No Control Group: In Casual Studies and in Systematic Studies — EMPIRICAL RELATIONS IN UNDERSTANDING EDUCATION — Establishing Empirical Relations — Methods of Securing Differences in the Inde-

pendent Variable — PITFALLS IN INTERPRETING
EMPIRICAL RELATIONS — Accepting the First Plausi-
ble Hypothesis which Presents Itself — Important General
Types of Alternate Hypotheses — Alternate Hypotheses in
Experimental Investigations — Alternate Hypotheses in
Causal-comparative Investigations — Interpreting Empirical
Relations: Resumé

3. Locating and Using Published Research   47

LOCATING PUBLISHED INFORMATION — Texts and
Handbooks — Bibliographical Sources — The Problem of
Desultory Reading — EXAMINING AND ORGANIZING
THE RESULTS OF RESEARCH — Ignore the Unessentials
— Probe Behind the Author's Interpretations or Conclusions
— Frequency Distributions — Using Averages — Coefficients
of Correlation — The Statistical Significance of the Results
— Results of Several Investigations Combined — Criticism
of the Individual Reports

PART TWO: **Physical and Mental Growth:
The General Pattern of Forces**

4. Physical Growth and the Problem of Health   71

PHYSICAL DEVELOPMENT — Height — Rate of Growth
and Sexual Maturity — Weight — Proportion — Empirical
Factors of Body Build — Typical Changes in Proportion in
Growing Children — PHYSICAL EFFICIENCY — Health
— Physiological Efficiency — Tests of Physical Performance
— Motor Skill — The Regulators of Growth — Present
Status as an Indication of Later Status

**5. Growth in Intelligence and in the General Use of
Symbols**   106

THE NATURE OF INTELLIGENCE — The Problem of
Definitions — Definitions Aimed at Clarifying the Meaning
of Intelligence — A Down-to-earth View of Intelligence —
INTELLIGENCE AS MEASURED BY TESTS — Individual Intelligence Tests — Group Tests of Intelligence —
Factor Analysis of Intelligence-test Performance — Test-
measured Intelligence: Resumé — Cautions in Administering Tests — INDIVIDUAL DIFFERENCES IN INTELLI-

GENCE — Children Who Are Normal or Above Normal — Children Who Are Below Normal — Cautions in Interpreting High and Low IQ's — THE CONSTANCY OF INTELLIGENCE — The Constancy of Brilliance — The Constancy of Deficiency — The Study of the General Population — THE COURSE OF INTELLECTUAL GROWTH — Early Growth in Motor Control — Growth in Language — Growth in General Intelligence

6. Growth in Scholastic Achievement   **144**

MEASURING ACHIEVEMENT — Tests to Fit Objectives — Informal Tests — Formal Essay Tests and Their Advantages — Disadvantages of the Essay Test — Types of Short-answer Tests—Standard Tests and Their Advantages — Disadvantages of the Standard Test — Use of Common Sense in Deciding upon Tests — THE STUDY OF ACHIEVEMENT — TEST RESULTS — Factor Analysis — Individual Differences in Achievement — The Constancy of Achievement — GROWTH IN ACADEMIC ACHIEVEMENT — Adult Achievement in Scholarly Pursuits — The Advantages of Deferred Practice — PREDICTING SCHOLASTIC ACHIEVEMENT — Intelligence and Achievement: Two Theories — General versus Special Achievement — Intelligence and Achievement: Results — Previous Achievement as a Predictor — Specialized Aptitude Tests

7. Mental and Physical Growth: The Role of Non-scholastic Factors   **181**

PHYSIQUE AND HEALTH IN RELATION TO MENTAL GROWTH — Body Size — Facial Features — Basal Metabolism — Disease and Physical Defects — HYGIENE IN RELATION TO ACADEMIC DEVELOPMENT — Use of Drugs — Fasting — Loss of Sleep — Ventilation — Lighting — SEX DIFFERENCES IN MENTAL GROWTH — Intelligence — Problem Solving — Achievement — DIFFERENCES IN RESIDENCE AND FAMILY BACKGROUND — The General Cluster of Differences — Alternative Explanations for the Cluster of Differences — Environment, Heredity, and the Scientific Attitude — The Influence of the Environment on Educational Growth — Test Favoritism — Selective Influences — Direct Inheritance — THE MAJOR GROUP DIFFERENCES — Regional Differences — Social and Economic Status—Size of Family—Race, Nationality, or Culture Group — Educational Significance of Nonscholastic Factors

PART THREE: **Physical and Mental Growth: The Teacher Enters the Pattern of Forces**

8. Theories of General Behavior   233

Disagreement in Psychology — THE INTERRELATIONS AND ORIGINS OF CURRENT THEORIES — Three Different Views of Behavior — Prelude to Present-day Controversies — ASSOCIATION THEORIES: EMPHASIS ON REACTION TO THE ENVIRONMENT—Connectionism or Modern Associationism — Behaviorism — FIELD THEORIES: EMPHASIS ON THE ORGANIZED NATURE OF EXPERIENCE — Gestalt Psychology — Topological Psychology — PURPOSIVE PSYCHOLOGY: EMPHASIS ON GOALS AS DETERMINERS OF BEHAVIOR — Psychoanalytic or Freudian Psychology

9. Theories of Learning   265

EXPLANATIONS EMPHASIZING A CHANGE IN THE PSYCHOLOGICAL SITUATION ACTING ON THE PERSON — The Lewinian Approach — The Approach of Classical Gestalt Psychology — EXPLANATIONS EMPHASIZING A CHANGE IN THE LEARNER — Principle of Substitution: Conditioned Response Learning — The Principle of Effect: Trial-and Error Learning — Comparative Advantages and Disadvantages of Substitution and Effect — Theories which Combine Substitution and Effect — Sign Learning: Learning Through Changes in Cognitions— DIFFERING POSITIONS WITH RESPECT TO SPECIFIC ISSUES—Relation to the Nervous System — The Problem of Need or Motive — The Problem of the Permanence or Change in Learning — WHAT TO DO ABOUT THE CONTROVERSIES — The Problem of a Personal Decision — Controversial Theories as a Basis for Educational Reform

10. Utilizing Motivation and Experience   294

The Role and Importance of Motivation — Motivation Used by the Teacher — THE EFFECTIVENESS OF DIFFERENT MOTIVES — Intention to Learn — Ego-involvement—Frequent Tests — Objective Knowledge of Results — Failure (and Blame) versus Success (and Praise) — Social Factors — A Standard to Be Attained — Intrinsic versus Extrinsic Motives — Utilizing Existing Interests and Activity Already in Progress — The Urge for Achievement — Manipulation, Curiosity, and Play — Reducing Distraction — Motivating Students: The General Problem — TYPES OF PRACTICE OR ACTIVITY — Reading or Listening — Drill — FACTORS AFFECTING THE EFFICIENCY OF PRACTICE — Sensory Avenue — Amount of Material — THE COURSE OF PRACTICE — Observed Graphs of Learning — Conditions Making for Special Types of Graphs — Plateaus and Their Causes — Cessation of Growth — Practical Uses of Graphs of Learning — Cautions in Interpreting the Role of Practice

11. Providing Guidance and Reinforcement   330

Interrelation between Reinforcement and Guidance —Arranging for Reinforcement — Arranging for Guidance or Conditioned-response Learning — Classroom Adaptions of Conditioned-response Guidance — The Overlapping of Guidance and Reinforcement — Limitations of Guidance — THE DIFFERENT TREATMENT OF WEAK AND OF STRONG TENDENCIES — Dealing with Weak Tendencies — Dealing with Strong Tendencies — Identifying Weak and Strong Tendencies

12. Meaningful Relations in Learning and in Problem Solving   351

The Value of Structure in Experience — THE USE OF MEANING AND STRUCTURE IN PRESENTING NEW MATERIAL — In Teaching Meaningful Material — In Teaching Arbitrary Material — Learning by Wholes — MEANING AND INSIGHT IN THE APPLICATION OF REINFORCEMENT — The General Role of Insight — Enhancing Insight — Supplying Ready-made Insights — MEANING AS A PRIME GOAL OF TEACHING — Use of Standard Mechanisms of Learning — Special Problems in the Development of Meanings and Understanding — MEANINGFUL RELATIONS IN THINKING AND PROBLEM SOLVING — General Processes in Problem Solving — The Problem of "Set" — Providing Guidance in Problem Solving

13. Reducing Interference and Confusion   387

Learning Is Seldom Neatly Channeled — PRIMARY TASK CIRCUMVENTED BY EXTRANEOUS LEARNING — Extraneous Methods of Reducing Negative Reinforcement — Significance for Personal Adjustment — The Use of Properly Graded Tasks — PRIMARY TASK ACCOMPLISHED, BUT WITH EXTRANEOUS SIDE EFFECTS — The Dual Action of All Stimulation and Reinforcement — Dealing with the Dual Action of Stimulation and Reinforcement — The Role of Extraneous Stimuli — Extraneous Learning May or May Not be Desired — The Problem of Extraneous Learning in Teaching Abstract Concepts — The Spread of Reinforcement or Effects — Special Problems in Teaching a Fixed Series of Tendencies — Current Learning as Affected by Earlier or Later Learning — REDUCING THE EFFECT OF INTERFERENCE — Avoiding the Conditions that Produce Interference — Use of Distributed Practices — Values and Limitations of Spaced Practices — Reasons for the Superiority of Spaced Practices

14. Teaching for Permanence and Transfer   417

THE PERMANENCE OF LEARNING — The Relation between Interference and Forgetting — Methods of Measuring Retention — Speed of Learning and Degree of Retention — The Course of Retention — Factors Affecting Retention — TEACHING FOR TRANSFER — General Ideas Regarding Transfer — Illustration of Positive Transfer — General Prevalence of Transfer — Transfer in School Situations — High-school Subjects and College Success — Factors Affecting Amount of Transfer — Theories of Transfer — What to Expect from Transfer — NOTE ON METHODS FOR EFFICIENT STUDY

15. Administrative Influences: Their Powers and Limitations   454

STATISTICAL EVIDENCE ON ADMINISTRATIVE FACTORS — Size of School — Cost and Quality of the Schools — Selection and Training of Teachers — Reducing the Teacher's Working Load — The Student's Time in School and in Study — The Philosophy of Organization of the School — REACTING TO UNPALATABLE EVIDENCE

PART FOUR: **Personal and Social Growth**

16. Personal and Social Adjustment: Basic Needs and Processes   477

Needs and Drives — TYPICAL NEEDS AND THEIR ASSOCIATED DRIVES — Physiological Needs — Social Needs — The Need to Manipulate or Explore — Ego Needs — Need for Achievement — The Need for Security — Catalogues of Needs Are Merely Illustrative — Possible Relation between Needs — TYPES OF FRUSTRATION — Conflicts Not Involving the Need for Esteem — Conflict Which Involves the Need for Esteem — Roundabout Enhancement of Self-esteem — PERSONAL ADJUSTMENT AS ACTUALLY OBSERVED — Common-sense Definitions of Personality — Operational or Working Definitions — THE MEASUREMENT OF PERSONAL ADJUSTMENT — The Interview — The Questionnaire or Inventory — Projective Techniques — Rating Scales — Man-to-man Scales — Social Distance — Performance Tests — Using the Different Tests of Personality — DIFFERENCES AND PATTERNS IN PERSONAL TRAITS — Individual Differences — Basic Patterns of Personality — Suggested Factors or Dimensions in Personality — Factor Analysis — Differences within the Individual — The Constancy of Personality — Age Changes in General Personality

17. Adjustment in Major Aspects of Personality   518

EMOTIONAL DEVELOPMENT — Anger and Aggression — Fears and Worries — Joy or Happiness — Affection — INTERESTS, ATTITUDES, IDEALS — Recreational Interests — Interests as an Index of Maturity — Vocational Interests — Attitudes — Prejudice — ETHICAL BEHAVIOR AND CONDUCT — Simple Conformity — Ideas of Right and Wrong — Performance on Objective Tests — Delinquency — The Nature of the Delinquent and His Background — Reducing Delinquency

18. Social Patterns: Individual Reaction and Group Processes   549

The Development of Social Behavior — Social Sensitivity and Responsibility — Being Accepted by Others — Social Participation — Friendships — GROUPS AND GROUP

PROCESSES — Spontaneous Groups — Leadership in Spontaneous or Accidental Groups—THE WORKING GROUP AND ITS TASKS — Reaching a Decision — Keeping Conformity within Bounds — Maintaining Satisfactory Group Relations — Achieving an Effective Solution — Effectiveness of the Group Process in Problem Solving — THE GROUP-CENTERED CLASSROOM — Advantages and Disadvantages of the Group-centered Approach

19. Personal and Social Adjustment: Major Forces and Interrelations   582

Physique, Health, and Personality — Physical Disability — Intelligence in Relation to Personality Adjustment — Achievement in Relation to Personal Adjustment—MAJOR FORCES IN PERSONAL AND SOCIAL ADJUSTMENT — Sex Differences in Personal Traits — Family Background — The Environment within the Family — Identification and Understanding between Parent and Child — Need for Caution in Interpreting the Role of the Family — General Community Differences — National and Racial Groups—Motion Pictures, Radio, Television, and Comics — The School as a General Force

20. Guiding Personal and Social Growth: The Problem and the Goals   618

TEACHING FOR ADJUSTMENT: DOUBTS AND DIFFICULTIES TO BE FACED — Fears of Limited Success — Fears of Working in the Wrong Direction — Handicaps in the Traditional Approach of the School — THE BROAD GENERAL GOALS OF PERSONAL DEVELOPMENT — The School Should Not Cause Harm to Personality Development — Balance between Drive and Control — Acceptance of Reality — Maturity — Frustration Tolerance

21. Improvement in Adjustment and Attitudes: Mental Hygiene in the Classroom   639

MAKING REALITY EASIER FOR THE CHILD TO FACE — General Acceptance of the Child — Role of Basic Needs (Maslow's Hierarchy) — Securing Partial Outlet for Drives in Some Acceptable Manner — Protection against Undue Stress — The Problem of Failure — TRAINING IN SOLVING PROBLEMS OF PERSONAL ADJUSTMENT — Direct Practice — Transfer — GUIDANCE AND REIN-

FORCEMENT OF WEAK AND OF STRONG TEND-
ENCIES — Weak Tendencies — The Importance of Praise
and Early Success — Changing Techniques as Tendencies
Get Stronger — Welcoming Opportunities to Develop Frus-
tration Tolerance — The Direct Approach; Classes in Ad-
justment — THE SPECIAL PROBLEM OF ANGER AND
AGGRESSIVE TENDENCIES — Reducing the Need for
Anger or Aggression — Anger Should Not lead to Success —
Providing Acceptable Outlets for Aggression — One's Own
Aggressive Needs and the Aggressive Needs of Others —
THE SPECIAL PROBLEM OF FEAR — Reducing or Pre-
venting Unnecessary or Undesirable Fear — Dealing with
Existing Fears — Emotional Adjustment: The Teacher's
Opportunities and Limitations — DEVELOPING SO-
CIAL ADJUSTMENT — Social Acceptance — Leadership
— Changes in Attitudes and Prejudice

22. The Teacher and His Own Adjustment — 682

The Satisfactions of Teaching — The Frustrations of Teaching — Dealing with the Frustrations: General — Dealing
with Specific Frustrations — Making the Most of Teaching

Index — 699

GENERAL SURVEY OF EACH TYPE OF GROWTH *Study of Growth by:*	A. GROWTH IN PHYSIQUE AND HEALTH	B. GROWTH IN GENERAL INTELLECT	C. GROWTH IN ACADEMIC SUBJECTS	D. PERSONAL AND SOCIAL GROWTH
General Impression or Speculation 1	82–83, 88, 90, 97	106–09, 119		477–96, 505–07, 532–34, 538–40, 556–60, 626–36, 639–51, 659–70
Inspection of the Tests 2	91, 94–95	109–15, 119	145–58	496–503, 529, 552–53, 598
Factor Analysis of Test Results 3	84–86	115–19	158–59	459, 505, 507–08, 525, 532, 540, 587–88, 591, 596
Individual Differences 4	74–75, 79–80, 91, 94–95	120–25	159–60	503–04
Constancy of Each Aspect of Growth 5	99–100	126–29	160–61	509–10, 530, 560–61, 598–99
Relations between Different Aspects of Growth: Physical 6	———→	182–87	184, 187–92	540, 582–87
Intellectual 7	182–87	←— —→	169–73	122, 540, 585–87
Academic 8	184, 187–92	169–73	←— —→	540, 587–90
Personal and Social 9	540, 582–85	122, 540, 585–87	540, 587–90	←———

INDEPENDENT VARIABLES:
FORCES DETERMINING GROWTH
Nonscholastic Forces

General 10		195–204	195–204	604–05, 674–75
Age or Maturity 11	75–78, 80–82, 86, 88–90, 92–98, 130	129–37	161–68	510–12, 518–39, 549, 557, 560, 630–35
Sex 12	75–77, 80, 86, 93, 95–98	192	193–95	520–21, 523–24, 525, 526, 527, 528, 555, 583, 590–92
Community 13	207–08	198, 200, 208–09	200–01, 208	600–02, 621–22
Culture Group 14		214–16	215, 216	602–03
Social Class 15	210	209–14		535, 536, 592, 594–96
Family Environment 16		199, 201, 214		539–40, 584, 596–600, 621–22
Heredity 17	228	197, 204–07	205	593–94, 621

Scholastic Forces	PHYSIQUE AND HEALTH	INTELLECT	ACADEMIC	PERSONAL AND SOCIAL
Motivation 18			290–310, 364–65, 387–96, 409, 428	692
Experience or Practice 19	93		310–24, 400, 410–13	620, 651–52, 658–59, 660–64, 666, 672–73
Reinforcement 20			331–35, 338–46, 365, 387–96	655–57
Guidance 21			335–46, 365–66, 378–81	654–55, 656–57, 670–71, 693
Meaning and Insight 22			351–83, 409, 423, 427, 440–41	653, 661, 664
Reduction of Interference 23			387–413	
Reduction of Forgetting 24			417–31	
Transfer 25			431–45	652–53, 665–66
Administrative Improvements 26			454–69	467–68, 605

PART **one**

Psychology and the Study
of Educational Growth

1

The Content and Scope
of Educational Psychology

EDUCATIONAL PSYCHOLOGY is the systematic study of educational growth or development. In the study of educational psychology we try to ascertain the nature of educational growth, to learn its typical features, and to understand the forces which affect it.

Educational Development: Its Nature, Prevalence, and Importance

As used here, educational development is a very broad term covering a great deal of ground. Roughly it includes growth in all the things the school is concerned about. If the school should be concerned chiefly about reading and arithmetic, educational growth would mean chiefly growth or change in these subjects. If the school, on the other hand, is concerned about health, personality, attitudes, general intellect, and social relations, then educational growth would include growth in all these traits.

For the teacher, development, and particularly educational development, constitutes an ever-present phenomenon. The students with whom he deals are changing continually. These students become larger and stronger and change markedly in physical appearance. With this changing physique come changing needs and urges and powers. The personality as a whole is by no means static but grows and develops in various ways. The student's interests, his intellect, and his mastery of academic matters also grow and develop in many directions and in complex fashion.

3

It is, of course, upon this laborious and ever-present development of the human youth that civilization and humanity depend. Without this gradual development during the long period of dependence and relative weakness, the human species could never meet the complex demands placed upon it. Our ability to adjust to the demands of life lies in the fact that we enter the world in a very undeveloped state. Our success in meeting these demands is also due to the further fact that we have the power of maturing and fitting into a pattern of life that will "work" in our particular environment. All in all, our way of life depends on this initial lack of development, on the fact that development takes place, and on the flexibility of development.

The Teacher and Other Forces Responsible for Development

Educational development results from many different forces. We may think of an ocean liner proceeding toward its berth, acted on by the thrust from its propellers and its own internal forces, affected also by the wind, by the current or tide, and by the auxiliary pressures exerted by the tugboats which have been called to its assistance. The resulting motion is a product of all these forces. A change in one of these forces would change the over-all picture, but would not change it completely. The other forces would continue to exert their own particular influence, and a change in one of these would exert only its proportional share.

The pattern of forces acting on the ocean liner is rather simple compared to the complicated pattern of forces which combine to produce educational development. The forces responsible for this development include the thrust from such internal forces as the genes and other biological factors deep within the child. Pressures from the home also affect educational development, often in very drastic fashion. The general community clearly has its effect on the child's educational progress. So, too, do the church, the "street," and the culture group to which he belongs.

The school, then, is far from the only force which affects educational development. On the contrary, it is only one of many forces which act on the child in a complicated, though not always harmonious, pattern. The teacher can make no more serious mistake than that of assuming that he and his school are the only factors which determine the student's educational progress. The other forces are always there. Many of them were established and active long before the teacher entered the picture. And when he does enter the picture he cannot expect that these other forces will obligingly retire in his favor.

Although the teacher and his school are only one item in a complex pattern of forces, they are nevertheless the most deliberate and conscious of all the forces. The school is perhaps the only force which knows, in any precise fashion, just what should be accomplished in the way of educational growth. Some of the other forces, such as the genes, may be completely blind. There is, indeed, something awesome in the thought of these powerful but blind forces that push persistently on the organism, perhaps urging him toward the harbor, but perhaps toward the shoals. Still other agencies may have a vague general idea of the desired goal and may exert their efforts in ways calculated to achieve that goal. The general community and the home, for instance, may have rather definite general standards in many matters, and may apply powerful forces impelling the student toward those goals. Very often, however, those goals are shadowy and vague and the efforts taken are sporadic and clumsy in the extreme.

There is a danger, of course, that we may exaggerate the school's insight and deftness in seeking the goals of educational development. We must not think of the school as the shining opposite of the less deliberate forces. It is blind enough, groping enough, clumsy enough upon occasion. It is far from all that it might be in the matter of intelligent direction to a deliberate goal. But if it is not the bright example of all that the other forces lack, it is still somewhat different. If it is not always intelligent and deft in pushing the student toward those goals, it is at least more deliberate, and it certainly works with more insight into the relation between its efforts and its goals.

Role and Values of Educational Psychology

It has been said that the teacher is intricately involved in the process of educational development. What, more specifically, are the responsibilities of the teacher with respect to this development?

1. The teacher stimulates educational growth, and to a certain extent directs and manages it.
2. The teacher must deal with the other forces which affect educational development, adjusting his own efforts to the influences which they exert.
3. Over and above the immediate demands of the practical work to be accomplished, the teacher is bound to try to understand the phenomenon of development. He must deal with it as an intriguing and challenging intellectual problem.

It is not too much to expect that the study of educational psychology should help the teacher to discharge each of these three important responsibilities.

Aid in Directing the Process of Development

An understanding of the basic nature of development and of the mechanisms by which that development proceeds should be of value to anyone who is responsible for any part of the process. We state this as something which should be so. We must not take it as a truism, however, no matter how obvious it may sound. Indeed the facts may turn out to be disappointing. It may well be possible that an understanding of the process does not lead to increased efficiency in directing the process. On this we must keep an open mind. Meanwhile, however, we can proceed on the hope that everything we can learn about the process will help us in its direction.

Educational psychology should help the teacher by providing a description of the various tools that are available for his use. It tells him of the tools or mechanisms through which teachers have acted on students since teaching first began. Teachers have always *stimulated* or *motivated* children. They have provided for practice, guidance, and reinforcement, and have used the more specific tools to be discussed in later sections of this book. The teacher should therefore know something of the nature of these tools and how to apply them. He should know their strengths and their limitations, and the conditions under which each may be used.

Aid in Adjusting to Other Forces Responsible for Development

It is not enough for the teacher to understand only the tools which he uses in his daily work. He must also know something of the many other forces which combine to affect the course of educational development. Indeed, the position of the teacher as the most conscious and deliberate of these forces confers on him a very special responsibility. The school, being the most conscious and deliberate member of the group of forces, must adjust its efforts to the action of the other forces in the group. The teacher is something like the pilot of the ship who must deal with the blind forces of the tide and the wind, and who must manage the forces under his control so as to produce the desired combination of all of them. The teacher, always working with the forces of biological maturation and the forces of home influence and of community pressures, must take account of these extraneous forces and apply his efforts accordingly.

But if the teacher is to make an intelligent adjustment to these extraneous forces, he must know something of their nature and of their contribution to educational development. It is only through knowing something of the tide and its vagaries that the ship's pilot can take steps to exploit it or to counteract it. It is only through knowing something of the role of biological maturation, and of the influence of the home, that the teacher can make the most intelligent use of his own efforts.

Educational psychology, as the systematic study of all the forces responsible for educational development, should be of considerable use in aiding the teacher to take the extraneous forces into account and to adjust his efforts to these forces in the most efficient manner.

At the very least the teacher must be aware of the degree of development which his students have attained. In making his plans and in carrying out his decisions he can never ignore the general course of development. He must ask if the child is ready to attempt this topic in arithmetic, or to understand that concept in history. In dealing with a bad case of negativism or obstinacy, he must consider whether or not the student will merely grow out of the negativistic attitude, or whether some actual training must be applied to supplement the normal course of growth. At every turn he is faced by the question of whether or not the stage of development is propitious for the task to be undertaken. If it should happen that the stage of development is not propitious but that the task must be faced anyhow, then the teacher must seek special measures which will ensure success in spite of the unfavorable circumstances.

So far we have assumed that the other forces are always allies. We have been prepared to let them do our work for us, when they will, and to cooperate with them under any circumstances. Unfortunately, however, these other forces are not always allies. There are times when the normal development, induced by other forces, presents new problems for the teacher and creates tasks for him to solve. Because of normal development, for instance, the child's need for adventure may endanger the larger goals of safety and health. Here, then, the normal development of the need for adventure is something which the teacher must counteract. Thus, because of the normal development of his need for the approval of the gang, the youth may behave in a way that will lose him the approval of the larger community. Here, again, normal development, instead of properly assuming new tasks, may readily become a problem with which the teacher must contend.

Aid in Understanding the Nature of Educational Growth

Development as a Challenge to the Intellect. Because he is so inextricably wrapped up in the process of development, the teacher has good reason to understand its course and mechanisms. But there are other reasons for understanding this process. Even if the teacher were not partly responsible for the process of development, he would still observe it almost constantly. Even when he can do nothing about these continual changes, and when he need do nothing about them, he can and must watch them as they take place. He can and must watch the dramatic physical changes in the student. He can watch the growing need for independence struggling with the fluctuating demands for guidance, direction, and advice. He can watch the scorner of girls and women become the awkward blushing gallant.

In watching the process of development, the intelligent observer must be led to speculate, to inquire, and to seek to understand. Even when understanding will not affect his daily work, he must still seek it as an intellectual need. Most people, and certainly most intelligent people, cannot observe a complicated process for a long period of time without wanting to know more about the process, about its inner workings, and the forces which make it function. Indeed, if we should know of one who had such a process under his scrutiny and who made no effort to understand it, we should feel a little sorry for him, regarding him as something less than alert.

It is a great mistake to assume that all need for understanding springs directly from a practical need. True enough, increased understanding often does lead to practical gains, and it is often directed to that end. Farmers do speculate about soils and planting times. The sailor does work out general rules for predicting weather conditions. The chef does estimate the food preferences of various groups. Salespeople do try to formulate rules regarding seasonal demands for various things. And these things all help in the vocations in question. But the tendency to theorize is not limited to practical matters. The sailor also theorizes about the mental processes of porpoises. The farmer forms opinions about the relative intelligence of pigs and turkeys. The clerk works out elaborate theories about the taxi-hailing gestures of people in front of his shop. Even when it will be of no practical value, it is natural for many people to work out general principles and reach conclusions regarding processes under their scrutiny.

In the same way, teachers, whether they have given systematic study to the problem or not, are almost bound to form opinions on the effect of skipping grades, on the advantages or disadvantages of being an only child, on the relative value of summer school versus regular school attendance, on the effect of infected tonsils on achievement.

The teacher's opinions on such subjects are not to be considered lightly. In the long run, the course of education may be more influenced by his opinions than by his teaching skill. In the long run, erroneous opinions may be more harmful than lack of skill. If this is true, it may be more important that the teacher increase his ability to reach correct conclusions about education than it is for him to increase his mastery of the art of teaching.

Not only will the teacher form opinions about educational development, but he will be expected to do so. Parents will consider him an authority on many matters. Over and over again he will be asked, "Will it hurt Mary to skip a grade?" "Will Johnny change from a dull to a bright boy as he enters his teens?" "Has Sam too many extracurricular activities?"

Educational psychology, as the systematic study of educational growth, should aid the teacher greatly in reaching valid conclusions about the nature of educational growth. It presents the views on these matters that have arisen from investigations and from careful and prolonged study. It is most important that the teacher compare his views on these complicated matters with the results of investigations and with the opinions of people who have given much thought to the problems. We do not wish to suggest that the opinions of specialized students are always right. We are keenly aware of the conflicting results of experiments. But the prospective teacher should decide this point after he has considered the opinions of the specialized students and not before.

All in all the study of educational psychology should help the teacher in many ways. It should give him a much clearer picture of the phenomenon of educational development, and this is the dramatic process within which his work is intertwined. It is the process which he seeks to direct, and which he must always take into account either as an ally or as an occasional antagonist. It is the process which he must always scrutinize and seek to understand.

Additional Roles of Educational Psychology

General Psychology Adapted for Teachers. In addition to its chief purpose of explaining educational development, educational psychology may serve other roles(1).[1] To a certain extent it may represent that part

[1] Numbers in parentheses refer to specific references cited at the end of chapters.

of general psychology which is of especial importance to teachers. Since teachers deal with people, clearly there are many aspects of general psychology which they should know. There might be some value then in going over the entire field of general psychology, in selecting the topics which appear to be of most importance to teachers, and in presenting those topics in a special text.

This view of educational psychology was very prevalent some years ago(2) and understandably so, since at that time the only psychology we knew was general psychology. The tradition still prevails to a certain extent, and one of the secondary purposes of this text is to present some of the topics of general psychology that are most clearly related to education. These topics are drawn from the problems of perception and sensation as well as motivation and learning.

Psychological Advice on Specific Educational Problems. In picking up a textbook on educational psychology, one might expect to find in it the psychologist's answers to the specific practical problems which confront the teacher. A book completely arranged in this fashion would be organized around those practical problems. We would have a list of such problems, and in connection with each problem the advice of the psychologist.

There is a great deal of justification for such a view of educational psychology. As yet, however, this approach has not been used at all widely(3), although most texts, including this one, fill this need to a certain extent. By the use of the subject index the student can find the relevant information bearing on each of a large number of practical problems. This information appears in its scientific setting, however, as an integral part of the story of development and not as an answer to an isolated problem.

In the two additional views just discussed, educational psychology appears as an applied science. In these views the principles of general psychology are to be applied to the practice of education in much the same way as the principles of physics are applied to the practice of engineering.

Such an approach can no longer be considered the whole story of educational psychology, nor even the most important part of that story. Not only is educational psychology the application of a science to an art, but, even more important, it is by now also a special field of study. It is the psychological study of the phenomenon of educational growth. In this sense educational psychology is not so much an application of psychology as a special division of psychology. It is the division of psychology which seeks to understand the phenomenon of educational growth, just as social psychology is the division of psychology which seeks to understand social phenomena.

The large and growing body of information regarding educational growth has come not only to constitute a separate field of psychological study, but it is also important enough to contribute to the more general field of psychology. It may well turn out that educational data, properly analyzed and integrated, will form the key for a larger understanding of many social phenomena. The school, after all, is our closest approximation to a laboratory in which many kinds of social behavior may be studied. The school provides opportunities for experimentation and for careful observation of group behavior that are seldom found in other situations.

Possible Limitations of Educational Psychology

Possible Limitations Arising from the Nature of Teaching

There are some tasks or arts in which the written or spoken word may be of great value. In making a cake or a window box, for instance, a set of directions may solve many of our problems. Tetlow(4) tells of a Hudson Bay trader stationed in the wilds who had delivered his wife of a baby and, when asked how he managed, had replied, "I had a book." The war stories give us other accounts of surgical operations carried on by laymen with the aid of a book. But there may be different kinds of tasks, or arts, in which written instructions are of less value. In learning to dance, for instance, or in coming to feel at ease at a party, or in learning to create a favorable impression on people we meet, we may profit little from written or spoken instructions. Success in these latter tasks may depend more on original "aptitude" or on experience.

It is, of course, dangerous to suggest that one profession is largely dependent on book learning and that a second profession is chiefly dependent on aptitude and experience. We all agree that both information, on the one hand, and experience plus aptitude, on the other hand, count in all difficult undertakings. Professions vary, however, in the relative importance of these factors. Engineering, for instance, will serve as an illustration of a profession in which information and a mastery of formulas is of especial importance. Painting or oratory, on the other hand, represent professions in which original aptitude and experience are at a distinct premium.

One may illustrate the difference between the professions as follows:

Let us suppose we had a bridge to build and that we were given our choice of such a famous engineer as Brindley, possessing all the knowledge of his craft available in his time, or of a recent graduate of a good modern engineering school, possessing the knowledge currently available. Brindley had outstanding aptitude and a great deal of experience. In spite of that, we should probably choose the young man from the engineering school. We know nothing of his aptitude. His experience is very limited. But he has a store of technical information learned from books and lectures, and this we would consider to outweigh completely Brindley's superiority in other respects.

Let us now suppose, on the other hand, that we have a picture to paint and we have our choice between Raphael and the most recent graduate of a good school of art. The young graduate must have information of which Raphael was completely ignorant. Much technical information must have been gathered in all these years. Yet we should undoubtedly choose the old master, believing that his aptitude and experience would more than make up for his lack of information.

It is impossible to decide once and for all whether teaching is more like painting or oratory, or more like engineering. We shall undoubtedly find proponents on both sides of the argument(5, 6, 7). But, even if we cannot be sure of the final answer, we must admit the possibility that teaching is more art and less applied science.

If it should ultimately appear that teaching is largely an art and less an applied science, we should have to face certain conclusions. We should have to admit that we can get relatively little help from books and lectures and other media of information, and must depend largely on natural aptitude, experience, and person-to-person supervision.

Possible Limitations Arising from the Nature of Science

We shall not try to settle here the question of whether educational psychology is "entitled" to be called a science. But we can be sure that it is afflicted with all the limitations which apply to science. And science has many limitations. Contrary to popular impression, for instance, science does not always make a decision for us. It may readily leave us with a decision to be made and offer no help in making that decision. To make the decision we must look to something beyond science. What the scientist can usually do is to tell us the relation between two things. He can say, if you do such and such then this will follow. But someone must decide whether or not we wish "this" to follow. Suppose a geneticist should tell us that by sterilizing 5 percent of the population we could reduce the number of feeble-minded children by 25 percent. What shall we do about it? The problem is by no means settled by this piece of scientific information. Moreover, it is not likely to be solved completely by further scientific information. We would ultimately have to decide between the rights of some individuals to lead a normal life and to have children, and the right of society to rid itself of a portion of the burden of feeble-mindedness. We would also have to consider the claims of religion. This decision refers to values and rights and in so doing becomes a question of philosophy and ethics.

The same limitations of science are apparent in our own field of educational psychology. The psychologist may determine that one third of the present population of high-school age cannot follow the current high-school curriculum. Such information does not automatically point to any single program of action. While it may be useful or even indispensable in settling the problem, it does not tell us what we should do about it. In the face of a problem such as this we could do several things. We could change the curriculum. We could maintain the present curriculum and refuse admittance to those who could not follow it. Which should we do? There is no automatic answer to this problem. Different courses of action would bring about different consequences. We should have to decide which of these consequences we prefer. And this decision, like the other, could not be made on a purely scientific basis.

We must admit, of course, that there are times when there is no problem in deciding what to do, once we know the facts. If we know that a certain procedure will save a life, boost achievement, or prevent a neurosis, we know at once what to do. In a very large number of problems, however, the decision is not so simple.

In summing up, we may say that while science is often indispensable in the solution of a problem, and while sometimes the information provided by science is the key to the solution, still there are many cases where all the scientific information in the world will not relieve us of the necessity of making a choice.

Possible Limitations Arising from the Nature of Psychology

Educational psychology, we have said, has all the limitations of science. Unfortunately, it has a good many limitations on its own account that some other sciences do not have. Psychology is not as yet a highly integrated science. Like other sciences it possesses a vast number of facts. But, unlike many of the older sciences, it has not been able to integrate this multitude of facts into any closely knit pattern.

Every science has these two aspects. On the one hand, it has a vast number of individual facts, and on the other hand, it has a relatively small number of principles by which these facts are described. In the ideal situation as many facts as possible are described by the smallest possible number of principles.

The ideal situation, mentioned above, is approached by some of the older sciences such as physics or astronomy. Let us review the classical illustration. The position of a planet is observed on a great many different nights. Each of these observations is in a sense a fact. The total observations would add up to a vast number of facts. Very early, wise men saw that the various positions of any planet could be described by a single statement or equation or law. This is a great convenience as well as a great achievement. Instead of having many specific things to remember, we need only remember one general statement. It is like remembering a simple rule instead of memorizing a railway timetable.

This is, of course, a very simple illustration of generalization in science. If we went no farther than this we should have one formula for one planet. We would have another formula to describe the various positions of another planet. The next step is to find a single formula or principle which could be used to describe the positions of all the planets, thus reducing the number of principles needed to describe all the facts. Historically this second step was accomplished and was followed by the great and brilliant feat of showing that one *single* formula would describe not only the positions of the planets, but also such seeming unrelated phenomena as the action of the tides and the behavior of falling bodies.

We have stressed the *convenience* of simple generalizations which relieve us of the necessity of remembering a vast array of detailed facts. The *convenience* of these generalizations is, of course, not their sole virtue. They also satisfy an intellectual hunger. Most people get a great satisfaction from the realization that many seemingly diverse things can be attributed to the same general principle. They get a mild thrill in making such generalizations for themselves. For instance, a man may conclude that "Teaching is just another form of salesmanship." He has reduced these two seemingly separate activities to one type of activity. Achieving this generalization makes him feel good.

This point, however, is irrelevant to our main argument and we shall not push it too far. Our chief concern is to show that justifiable generalizations are of great convenience and that a science becomes more useful as it gathers more and more data under fewer and fewer principles.

When we apply this test to psychology we find that it is very rich in individual facts. These facts are reported in investigations which pour in at the rate of some five thousand a year. On the other side of the shield, however, psychology is less adequate. To express these many facts, psychology requires a relatively large number of principles. As yet, psychology has not had its Newton—or at least none whom other psychologists will acknowledge as a Newton—to integrate the large number of existing facts under a relatively few general principles.

We must point out, in passing, that a good deal is being done to bring about some synthesis. The efforts range from brilliant intuitions resulting in rather loose generalizations such as those of Freud, to painstaking attempts to fit psychological data to mathematical curves, as illustrated by the work of Hull(8).

Because psychology needs so many principles to describe its facts, the prospective teacher is in a less favorable position than the prospective engineer. When the engineer, for instance, has to decide how much impact his structure will withstand, he can turn to fairly well-established laws which enable him to compute these values. Of course, if he is wise, he will make his structure much stronger than the results suggested by his calculations. But he will have a fairly precise idea of what he is doing. There are few cases, on the other hand, in which the teacher can turn to such definite equations and secure answers to a wide area of problems. If a teacher, for instance, wishes to know to what extent he should encourage extracurricular activities, or whether or not Susie will "grow out of" her nail-biting habit, he can turn to no general law but must look for specific investigations on the subject.

The haphazardness of educational psychology is nowhere more glaringly illustrated than in the case of the psychologist planning his own course. He wishes to arrange his instruction as scientifically as possible. Can he begin with a few general principles and a handbook of constants and proceed as an engineer might in designing an airplane? Most certainly he cannot. He must look up the answers to a whole host of questions from a whole host of specific investigations. From these investigations he can find something about the interests of students, about their ideas regarding the nature or the value of psychology. He can find a list of professorial mannerisms which most annoy students. He can find out what happens when students are permitted to attend or not as they please. Likewise, he can determine if achievement is affected by seating positions, or if frequent quizzes are desirable, or whether the discussion method is superior to the lecture method, or how students prepare for objective examinations as opposed to essay examinations.

All these and many more questions can be answered. But the answers cannot be derived from any single set of principles. Nor does there seem to be any small group of forces behind all the phenomena involved. We get the picture of a hodgepodge group of questions, and it appears that the answer to each comes from its own principle.

Thus, whereas the student of applied physics learns a relatively few general laws from which a myriad of specific facts may be deduced, the student of applied psychology must be prepared to get the answers to his problems by consulting specific investigations bearing on those problems. Suggestions for locating and using these investigations are presented in Chapter 3.

Summary

In our discussion of educational psychology we shall review some of the facts that are frequently learned in general psychology, and we shall offer some psychological advice on educational problems. Most of the time, however, will be spent in trying to understand the nature of educational growth—the phenomenon in which the teacher is most vitally interested.

Although educational psychology is no magical solution for all educational problems, the prospective teacher cannot afford to overlook it. The serious teacher must study everything which has a reasonable chance of increasing his proficiency. He cannot wait for guarantees. He must also understand his profession and must be as well versed as possible in whatever there is to be known about the nature of educational growth.

Unfortunately, educational psychology is bound to be limited in its value. No scientific discussion can settle all educational problems. Even after the most exhaustive scientific treatment, there is much to be left to a consideration of rights and values. In addition to this defect, inherent in any science, the science of psychology may not be able to do as much for the profession of education as other sciences, say physics, are able to do for such a profession as engineering. This limitation may arise partly from the fact that education is not entirely an applied science, and partly from the fact that psychology is still relatively unwieldly as a science.

These possible limitations, of course, must be faced and accepted. They should not, however, cause us to throw up our hands in utter discouragement. On the contrary, a knowledge of these limitations should lead us to make up for them whenever we can. Knowing that science, for instance, does not answer all questions, we must be prepared to deal with **values** and to exercise shrewd judgment. Knowing that psychology lacks a neat set of integrated principles, we must be prepared to solve many of our problems by an appeal to specific investigations.

SPECIFIC REFERENCES

1. Blair, G. M. Educational Psychology, Its Development and Present Status. *Univ. of Ill. Bull.,* 1948, 46, No. 13.
2. Gates, A. I., A. T. Jersild, T. R. McConnell, and R. C. Challman. *Educational Psychology.* Macmillan, 1942, Chap. 1.
3. Watson, G. B., and R. B. Spence. *Educational Problems for Psychological Study.* Macmillan, 1930.
4. Tetlow, H. *We Farm for a Hobby and Make It Pay.* New York: Morrow, 1938.
5. Bagley, W. C. Teaching as a Fine Art. *Educ. Method,* 1930, *9,* 456-461.
6. Adler, M. J. Liberalism and Liberal Education. *Educ. Rec.,* 1939, *20,* 422-436.
7. Childs, J. L. Philosophy and Educational Research. *Adv. Sch. Digest,* 1939, *4,* No. 6.
8. Hull, C. L. *Principles of Behavior.* Appleton-Century-Crofts, 1943.

SUGGESTIONS FOR FURTHER READING

There are a great many texts that cover essentially the same ground as this one. You may be interested in looking over one or more of them. Especially when you find some idea difficult to grasp, it may pay you to consult an additional text. Often a slightly different approach may help you "unsnag" a difficult problem.

1. Bernard, H. W. *Psychology of learning and teaching.* McGraw-Hill, 1954.
2. Blair, G. M., Jones, R. S., and Simpson, R. H. *Educational psychology.* Macmillan, 1954.
3. Coladarci, A. P. *Educational psychology* (Readings). Dryden, 1955.
4. Commins, W. D., and Fagin, B. *Principles of educational psychology.* Ronald, 1954.
5. Cronbach, L. J. *Educational psychology.* Harcourt Brace, 1954.
6. Ellis, R. S. *Educational psychology.* Van Nostrand, 1951.
7. Fox, C. *Educational psychology.* International Universities Press, 1951.

8. Garrison, K. C., and Gray, J. S. *Educational psychology*. Appleton-Century-Crofts, 1955.
9. Laycock, S. R. *Teaching and learning*. Toronto: Copp Clark, 1954.
10. Morse, W. C., and Wingo, G. M. *Psychology and teaching*. Scott Foresman, 1955.
11. Mursell, J. L. *Psychology for modern education*. Norton, 1952.
12. Remmers, H. H., Ryden, E. R., and Morgan, C. L. *Introduction to educational psychology*. Harper, 1954.
13. Seidman, J. M. *Readings in educational psychology*. Houghton Mifflin, 1955.
14. Skinner, C. E., ed. *Educational psychology*. Prentice-Hall, 1951.
15. Smith, H. P. *Psychology in teaching*. Prentice-Hall, 1954.
16. Sorenson, H. *Psychology in education*. McGraw-Hill, 1954.
17. Trow, W. C. *Educational psychology*. Houghton Mifflin, 1950.
18. Wheat, H. G. *Foundations of school learning*. Knopf, 1955.
19. Witherington, H. C. *Educational psychology*. Ginn, 1952.

Exercises and Questions for Discussion

1. List six or seven of the outstanding characteristics in your own make-up. List some characteristics that give you satisfaction (for instance, your thoughtfulness for your parents); some that bother you (for instance, your tendency to giggle too much); and still others that you regard with indifference (your great dislike for asparagus).

For each of these traits, try to make a rough guess of the probable forces that have been at work. What is your guess about the probable role of heredity, of early family background, of the community, specific individuals in the community, the general school environment, the teachers you have known, the books you have read or the shows you have seen?

Do you think the influence of the school or the teacher could have been more effective? How?

To have helped you in the way that you needed, what additional equipment would the teachers have required? More knowledge of you as a person? More interest in you as a person? More knowledge of your home background? More ordinary understanding of young people? More specialized understanding of psychology? Of sociology? Would better training for teachers be the answer?

How sure do you feel about your answers to this question? Do you think you *ought* to feel sure, or that you ought to have doubts? If you do have doubts about the dependability of your answers, what is the basis for those doubts?

Return to this question after you have studied the chapter on Procedures and Pitfalls (Chapter 2).

2. Make a list of the items of information you think you would like to get from a course such as this. From your reading of the text so far, which of these

items do you think you may get? Which may still be lacking? What can you do to obtain the desired information that will not be supplied by this course?

3. From the point of view of the classroom teacher, what is the main difference between psychology and philosophy? Between psychology and physics?

4. List some important problems in education that do not fall within the field of educational psychology.

5. Recall some of the better teachers that you have known and try to decide on the traits that made them good teachers. Do you think that they acquired those traits by careful study? Think of the poorer teachers that you knew. Could they have eliminated their harmful traits by more study?

2

Understanding Educational Development: Procedures and Pitfalls

_____

The Need for Care in Reaching Conclusions about Education

EDUCATION is a very familiar process. It has been under observation for a long period of time. On the surface it seems to be a fairly simple process. It has little of the mystery of lightning or of atomic fission or of cardiac surgery. It is a process, moreover, that has been managed at times by rather ordinary people. True enough, some of these rather ordinary people may have obtained very mediocre results. But they have not produced disasters. All in all we can hardly declare educational ideas to be out of bounds for amateurs. We can hardly claim that here we have a process so complicated, so delicate, and so dangerous that the ordinary person cannot hope to understand or manage it. We can hardly contend that the specialist is the only one who can reach valid conclusions about the nature of the educational process.

Without for a moment ignoring the familiar and common-sense nature of education, we must realize, however, that there are few fields in which it is easier to go astray and which are so permeated by misconceptions. These misconceptions, moreover, are found not only among laymen and among people who have given the matter only casual thought. They are found also among people who have long been familiar with educational problems and who have given those problems moderate study.

To illustrate the treacherous ground on which we tread when we study the very familiar process of education, let us suppose that someone has shown that people with more education earn much more money than people with less education. In the face of these facts it seems to be the most natural thing in the world, among educators and laymen alike, to assume that further education leads to more earning power. And yet this conclusion is by no means justified. It is only one of several possible conclusions which could be drawn from the facts.

It is quite possible that those who secured more education were fortunate enough to have more ability and more money behind them in the first place, and it is further possible that these advantages of greater ability and greater financial backing may have led to greater earnings anyway. Until we can dispose of this second hypothesis, we should not take it for granted that education leads to greater earnings.

The Pitfall of Wishful Thinking

Educators are not the only people who have to worry about the pitfall of wishful thinking. It is a pitfall which plagues investigators in very many fields. But it is especially hazardous to those who would attempt to understand the nature of education.

Education Calls for Faith, Emotion, and Enthusiasm. The professional educator must have considerable faith in the educational process. He is intimately involved in the process. He must hope and believe that it will accomplish great things. His motive and his drive depend largely on a warm and enthusiastic conviction that education is an important route to human betterment. Teaching is often such a warm, emotional, enthusiastic process. It calls for devotion and commitment to a given course of action. It is possible that a cold, analytic attitude of suspended judgment would prevent the teacher from stimulating students and would make for poor rapport.

These convictions and emotional commitments which may be so necessary in the practice of education are obvious handicaps in the careful and precise study of education. Enthusiastic feelings or warm hopes should not influence our decision as to what is so. Our faith in education, for instance, encourages us to believe that schooling will enable a person to earn more money. But this faith should be put aside when we try to reach a sober conclusion on this or on any other problem. To take another example, suppose that in the course of a long journey we come to a bridge which appears to be precarious. Our problem is to decide whether or not the bridge is safe. Now in making that decision we should not be influenced by our desire to cross the bridge. We should make our decision on the basis of sober measurement and cold logic. A decision based on hopes and desires and hunches could lead to disaster.

In our profession we should be infused with a sense of good will. We must *prefer* to believe good things about education. We must prefer to believe that education is most effective when the teacher is kind and conscientious and has a driving concern for the welfare of his students. We hope that he will do his best work when he is a leader rather than a despot. We must prefer to believe that things will be best when the teacher is well paid and well regarded in the community and when he takes his place on a par with other professions. We must hope that the school will be most efficient when the teacher works in a democratic framework of enlightened administration and supervision. We must prefer to believe these things. But if we insist on being guided by our preferences in these matters, we should stay out of the scientific arena. For in any branch of science we must be prepared to face unpalatable, unflattering, and downright discouraging facts. The biologist, for instance, must hope that penicillin will not become any less effective as the years go by. If the evidence points to that grim conclusion, however, he must face this discouraging fact in spite of his high hopes for human welfare. In our own field, we must face similar unpalatable facts. We must not only tolerate, but must actually seek out unpleasant and unflattering explanations and give these unwelcome explanations a fair trial before the tribunal of logic and experimentation.

For the enthusiastic practitioner, this necessary detachment may come hard. He may show an understandable impatience for possible explanations which minimize his importance or which cast doubt on the convictions he is dedicated to express. This impatience, necessary perhaps for the successful practitioner, and understandable in all men of good will, nevertheless pushes us relentlessly toward the pitfall of wishful thinking.

The Possibility of Calculated Risks. To understand a process, we must try to put our feelings and wishes in cold storage for a time, and having done so, we must try to face the facts with an open mind. But although we must face facts, we need not become the slaves of facts. Facing the facts in a cold and scientific way, for instance, we may come to the conclusion that there is only one chance in three of crossing the bridge safely. So great may be our need, however, that we may elect to try to cross it in spite of the adverse scientific picture. Or, to take another example, our urgent desire that our child shall rise above a life of invalidism should not blind us to the risks of the operation necessary for his cure. But once those risks have been calculated and faced, our feelings may properly urge us to take the risk. Similarly, in the field of education our hopes and ideals may properly push us beyond our understanding. Our cold understanding, for instance, may show that there is very little chance for a significant gain from this course in world brotherhood. Our need may be so great, however, and the alternatives so disastrous, that we will take that slim chance in spite of the pessimistic picture presented by cold science.

Systematic Study: Values and Limitations

For most of us, the systematic study of problems is markedly uncongenial. Faced with a problem, or with a set of interesting facts, we much prefer to make our decision on the basis of general impression, casual observation, and even more casual speculation. If this does not yield an answer that makes us feel comfortable, we may resort to a conference in which we compare our casual observations and speculations with those of other people. Sometimes this is a mere pooling of ignorance. Sometimes it yields a residuum of truth. In either case we are relying basically on casual impression.

Stop for a moment and consider some of the opinions that you yourself have reached either on your own or through discussion. Undoubtedly you have formed many opinions on the differences between high school and college, on the customs of different communities, on the relative attractiveness of people of different nationalities, and on the merits of different school subjects. Some of these opinions you may hold very strongly. Others you will admit are merely hunches or feelings. But strong conviction and tentative hunch alike were undoubtedly reached by the method of general impression.

In answering educational questions by means of casual impression, we encounter a number of serious pitfalls. One of these, the pitfall of wishful thinking, we have already examined. The others are to be considered below.

Systematic study of educational problems (or the *scientific* study of education) is chiefly an attempt to deal with the pitfalls that afflict casual impression. In adopting the scientific method then, or in using the systematic approach, we do not free ourselves from the need of worrying about these various pitfalls. Worrying about pitfalls is, in fact, the essence of the scientific method. In adopting this method we merely pledge ourselves to search painfully and in detail for one pitfall after another.

As a matter of fact, we may have to make some effort not to expect too much from such words as systematic or scientific. Scientific has come to mean "good" or "accurate" or "unanswerable." By saying our results are based on science we can often silence our opponents and we may even bludgeon them into acquiescence.

Not only has science come to mean a good or desirable thing, it has also come to mean an all-or-none thing. To many people science is some mysterious treatment to which a study is subjected and thereby becomes immediately purged of all its errors, just as sterilizing a dish or instrument will kill all microbes at one fell swoop.

Science, of course, is neither of these things. In the first place, it is not always the *best* way to inquire into a subject. On many important human matters such as duty, filial devotion, or the pangs of remorse, we can get a much better picture from the disciplined intuitions of the poets and philosophers than from scientific studies. It is quite possible that education is, as yet, such a subject. Perhaps it can be studied most profitably by consulting the disciplined intuitions of shrewd men who have pondered the problems over a long period of time.

In the second place, it is equally wrong to suppose that science purifies its investigations in an all-or-none fashion. Science merely uses some well-known precautions to guard against specific errors. Not all studies, moreover, use all these precautions. Some may employ a great many precautions and thereby eliminate many errors. Others may employ only a few. No study eliminates all possibility of error.

Searching for Errors in Casual and in Systematic Answers. Any proposed answer to an educational question, any conclusion that is offered to us, contains some possibility of error. Before we accept it we should examine it to see if it may contain some error that may invalidate it. Before we "buy" this conclusion, before we commit ourselves and our students to this new program, we should satisfy ourselves that it is free from any defect that would render it unsafe or undependable. Notice, by the way, that we stress those defects which will make the conclusion unwarranted or undependable. There is a vast difference between defects which merely offend our sense of elegance and those other defects which may spell disaster.

In looking at conclusions based on general impression, we shall not be surprised to find many errors that may invalidate the conclusions. In looking at conclusions based on systematic studies, we shall not expect so many serious errors, but we may still encounter some. Any conscientious investigator can point to the errors in his previous systematic studies. If he can't, his colleagues can.

Procedural Errors: Frequent in Casual Studies, Rare in Systematic Studies

The procedural errors which we are about to consider may frequently invalidate the conclusions reached by the method of general impression. In the systematic, published studies that we read, however, it will be seldom that one of these errors will play a significant part.

To see this contrast, let us consider a mistaken notion, based on casual impression, and, at the same time, let us see how the systematic investigator would deal with the problem. Let us suppose that a teacher has come to the conclusion that rich children do not get along well in school. This is a fairly prevalent view. It seems, moreover, to have some justification from common sense. It happens, however, to be wrong.

Since the opinion stated is in error, the procedure by which it was reached must be faulty at one point or another. Let us consider some of the mistakes which may have led to this erroneous view.

Too Few Cases

We cannot establish a general rule on only a few observations. Only the most uncritical person would advance the opinion that all sorrel horses were fast just because he knew one sorrel horse who won a race. Equally unscientific is the man who distrusts all Armenians because he was once cheated by one. Such people are more renowned for their vigorous prejudices than for their critical judgment.

Our teacher, presumably, has based his conclusion on more than one rich child. It is altogether probable, however, that he has not stopped to ask himself how many such children he has observed. Many such conclusions are based on very few illustrations, perhaps not more than five or ten.

Avoiding the Pitfall. The systematic investigator, on the other hand, knows very definitely that he must have enough cases to rule out mere chance. To take care of this need he does several things. He does the obvious thing of securing a large number of cases. He tries to observe a large representative sample of rich children. He also uses some statistical tests, described in the next chapter, to see whether his results could have come from pure chance. In recent years especially, it would be very unusual for a systematic study to fall into this particular pitfall.

Using Selected Cases

Our teacher may have based his conclusions, not on all the rich children he has taught, but on a few striking cases he happened to notice and happened to remember. We are much more likely to observe and to remember striking or incongruous things. A minister's son who grows up to be an ordinary youth will not attract our attention. Let the son develop a wild streak, however, and he will be noticed, and the irony or incongruity will receive comment. A cobbler's wife who is ordinarily well shod would elicit no unusual attention. A cobbler's wife going barefoot, however, intrigues our fancy and becomes the basis for a proverb.

It is very difficult to avoid depending on these unusual or outstanding cases. Stop and ask yourself about the relation between brain and brawn. Do you not find yourself thinking of several brilliant men who were physically feeble? Yet these men are by no means typical. They are merely the newsworthy cases who become attended to, written up, remembered, and incorporated into a legend.

The tendency to remember and utilize the dramatic incident is always with us. The tendency to select favorable cases, however, does not affect us until we begin to formulate some sort of opinion or theory. As soon as our opinion or hunch does begin to take form we will be very much on the lookout for illustrations which support our theory. These we pounce upon with glee and treasure up in our memories. If we should come upon evidence which runs counter to our theory we are less likely to be impressed by it and certainly less likely to remember it.

Avoiding the Errors of Selection. The systematic investigator is by no means free from these tendencies. His imagination will be intrigued by the unusual or incongruous case. He will experience the same fervor when he comes across an illustration which bolsters up his theory.

Knowing that he is heir to these ills, the systematic investigator takes steps to counteract them. In investigating the achievement of rich children, for instance, he would not merely observe the rich children he happens to come across but would make a systematic search for rich children, using some objective standard of wealth. He would either study all the rich children in a given sample or would select cases at random, thereby preventing any special chance of selecting the dramatic or incongruous cases.

Knowing that memory is untrustworthy and biased, the systematic investigator makes an effort to record all data. He leaves practically nothing to memory. Sometimes the data are automatically recorded, as when we make a sound movie of a classroom scene. At other times the information may be written in examinations or tests taken by the students, and these may be preserved. When information is not automatically recorded, the investigator takes notes on what was done and what was observed.

Lack of Precision in Observing, Measuring, and Describing Data

The casual observer very seldom uses precise methods in making observations or measurements. He may not have the necessary apparatus or tests, or he may not have the training necessary to use them. He may not be aware of the necessity for care in these matters. Whatever the reason, very few of us go to much trouble in making the observations on which we base our casual opinions. Ordinarily, for instance, the casual observer would not set up a criterion for "rich" or a scale of wealth, or even a standard for "doing well in school." He would merely go by general impression. Some children would be classified as coming from rich homes and others as coming from homes of moderate income. Similarly, some children would be thought of as doing well in school. Others would be judged as doing poorly. In neither case, however, is there likely to be any clear-cut standard for rich or for doing well in school.

For extreme cases this method of general impression may do very well. There are some families whom everyone would consider rich. There are some children whom everyone would consider poor scholars. But for the in-between cases, the method of general impression is very treacherous. There are some families which one observer would class as wealthy and which other observers would consider to be only moderately well off. There are some children who at one time might seem to be good students and at other times very poor students.

Need to Use Consistent Measuring Devices. To take care of these in-between cases and to ensure some consistency, the systematic investigator uses some objective test or scale. He uses some definite criterion of "wealthy" which he applies to all children and which he uses from one day to another. He also measures school performance on some definite scale. As far as possible, these criteria or scales are made so they will not be influenced by the investigator's bias or by a whim of the moment.

At times the systematic investigator uses measuring devices which are very elaborate indeed. When you think of science you undoubtedly think of very elaborate apparatus and equipment. Some of this equipment is for the purpose of measuring and recording differences in a precise and objective manner. Elaborate equipment, however, is not always necessary for systematic investigations. It is necessary that the observations be as precise as possible, and that any standards of measurement which are used shall be objective and consistent. Investigators are often able to fulfil these conditions with very simple devices.

Need to Make Precise Statement of Results. The systematic investigator aims not only at precise measurement but also tries to express his results in a precise or definite form. He would not merely say that rich children tend to be poor students, if that should be true. He would also give the percentage of "rich" children who make poor grades as compared with the percentage of "poor" children who make poor grades. Or he would give the average grade for rich children and the average grade for poor children. He may also make use of the more elaborate devices described in Chapter 3.

No Control Group: In Casual Studies and in Systematic Studies

You read the following statement: "Twenty-three percent of all the men in Sing Sing were disciplinary problems in school." For the time being lay aside your critical tendencies and ask yourself what conclusion that statement points toward. The statement suggests, and was intended to suggest, that the number of erstwhile disciplinary problems among the clientele of Sing Sing is unusually high. By "unusually high" we mean a greater proportion than one would find in the general male population or in some other comparison group. But what is the proportion among the general population? As far as the statement is concerned we merely have to guess. The statement implies that the proportion in the comparison group is much less than 23 percent. It is most important, however, that the corresponding proportion in the comparison group should not be left to guesswork. The significance of the whole statement depends on it. It may well be that 23 percent of the unmentioned comparison group were also disciplinary problems. It is not at all impossible that 23 percent of *all* males were disciplinary problems in school. If one listens to the alleged exploits recounted by most male adults one might think that 23 percent is a very low estimate indeed. If the percentage of disciplinary cases in the comparison group is anywhere near 23 percent, the statement loses its significance. It merely means that the Sing Sing population is normal in this respect.

The use of a nebulous or indefinite comparison group is a favorite trick of amateur statisticians or outright propagandists. For these people, the trick is a type of mental sleight of hand. They focus our attention on one definite group (Sing Sing prisoners) for which they give definite figures and then, while we are still interested in the Sing Sing group, they hurry past the comparison group without giving us a chance to take a good look at it.

The untrained investigator may neglect, innocently enough, to specify his comparison group or fail to give definite information about it. In so doing he may lead his listeners to reach an unjustifiable conclusion. We are told, for instance, that 35 percent of all the reading clinic cases in Beloit school were of Polish extraction. If we are not unusually critical we may conclude that Polish children, more than other children, have trouble with reading. Actually, of course, 35 percent of the *good* readers in Beloit school also may have been of Polish extraction. Until we know the figures for this comparison group (good readers or nonreading-clinic cases) we cannot attach any meaning to the statement.

Consider another illustration. The newspaper announces that over a given period of time, 30 percent of all persons apprehended for traffic violations had traces of alcohol in their blood. You know there is a joker in this. But what will your less critical friend think? To him it will appear that alcohol is connected with traffic violations. That may very well be, but not on the strength of this statement. Here again there is an unspecified comparison group. The traffic violators are being compared, by implication, with some other group. We should, of course, compare them with some group innocent of traffic violations. We should clearly specify or describe this group. We should also show what percent of this group showed traces of alcohol. For all we know, 30 percent of the safe drivers may also have had something to drink.

Avoiding the Pitfall. As we have pointed out, this error is exceedingly prevalent in casual studies. Most systematic investigators, on the other hand, are clearly aware of this problem and go to great lengths to provide an adequate control group. Unfortunately, however, you may still come across some published studies in which no control group has been used. In looking at any conclusion, whether based on casual impression or on a systematic study, you would be wise to ask yourself whether or not the conclusions are based on the comparison of at least two groups.

Empirical Relations in Understanding Education

Very often we may be convinced that two events are related or connected in some way, but may still feel unable to make sense out of the relation. We cannot work out the underlying causal pattern. We may notice, for instance, that as soon as Train 47 crosses the bridge, a light in one of the windows of a certain house goes out. We have observed this on a number of nights and we are sure that the two things go hand in hand. We have no certainty, however, about the nature of the connection. This connection is the sort of thing we mean by an *empirical* relation. It is there, but, as yet, is unexplained or unanalyzed.

There are many such unexplained empirical relations. There are relations between seasons of the year and incidence of murder, between intelligence and city of birth, between intelligence and month of birth.

These crude, unexplained empirical relations prove little or nothing as they stand. At this stage they tell us nothing about the forces at work, and they provide us with no dependable conclusions. Very often, however, they do serve as a most important first step in reaching a real understanding. They often arouse our curiosity and, more important, perhaps, they set the nature of the problem for us. They present a picture that calls for further understanding, and they point the way for achieving that further understanding.

Establishing Empirical Relations

To establish an empirical relation between month of birth and intelligence, we must have at least two groups of people. These groups must differ systematically in month of birth. By *systematically* we mean that, whatever the differences within each group, there are clear-cut differences between the groups. These groups must also differ significantly in intelligence. They must differ in intelligence more than we would expect on the basis of pure chance.

To establish even a crude empirical relation between alcoholic intake and ability to drive, we must again have at least two groups. These groups must differ systematically (from group to group) in alcoholic intake and must also differ significantly in ability to drive. To establish an empirical relation between home background and reading we must have two or more groups which differ systematically in home background, and we must show that these groups also differ significantly in reading ability. To establish even a loose empirical relation between (x) watching TV horror stories and (y) emotional disturbance, we must again have two or more groups that differ systematically in one of these traits and that also differ significantly in the other.

From all this it is easy to see the necessity of a control or comparison group. The whole idea of an empirical relation hinges on corresponding differences between groups, and with only one group such differences would be out of the question.

In each case there are two kinds of differences. Typically there are differences or variations that we arrange for, or create, or bring about in some way. There are also differences or variations in what we look for. To see if there is an empirical relation between home background and skill in reading, for instance, we will actually seek out differences in home background, or arrange for these differences in one way or another. There is no gamble or uncertainty about this difference. Having made sure of this difference, we next look to see if there are also any differences or variations in ability to read. But regarding this difference we cannot be sure. We may find some variations or we may not.

The difference or variation that we create, or arrange for, or make sure of at the outset of the investigation is called the *independent variable*. Variation in this trait (home background) is *independent* of the outcome of the investigation. This difference is ensured before we start. In contrast, the difference or variation that we look for, that may or may not appear, is called the *dependent variable*. The appearance of this difference depends on the outcome of the investigation.

Methods of Securing Differences in the Independent Variable

Let us suppose that we want to see if there is an empirical relation between (x) watching TV horror shows and (y) emotional disturbance. There are two alternative methods by which we can secure differences in time spent in looking at TV horror shows (independent variable). We can actually schedule a heavy diet of such shows for one group of children, and schedule fewer horror shows or no horror shows for another group, or other groups. In this case, the differences are under our control. This we call the *experimental method*. Using a different method, we could merely look around and find some children who already spend much time with such shows and other children who see these shows seldom or not at all. Then we merely sort our children into two groups on the basis of the TV habits they now exhibit. This is often called the *causal-comparative* method. We shall also refer to it occasionally as the *statistical* method.

When investigating the drinking-driving problem we have the same choice in our methods of securing differences in the independent variable. We ourselves could deliberately assign the amount of alcohol to be consumed. Preferably on the basis of random numbers, we could give some people no alcohol, others ½ ounce, others 1 ounce, still others 1½ ounce, and so on. This would be the *experimental* method. To use the *statistical* or *causal-comparative* method, we would merely look around until we found people who had already taken different amounts of alcohol for reasons of their own.

Sometimes, of course, we do not have this choice between the causal-comparative and the experimental methods. It would be difficult, for instance, to create home backgrounds at will. It would be even more out of the question for us to decide that this individual is going to be a boy and that other a girl. We are equally powerless to arrange for age differences to suit ourselves. When these factors form the independent variable, the experimental method cannot be used. We are forced to employ the causal-comparative method and to make use of differences that already exist.

Pitfalls in Interpreting Empirical Relations

Suppose that our investigator, by one method or the other, has secured sizable groups that differ in the exposure to TV horror shows. He finds that these groups also happen to differ significantly in emotional disturbance. That is to say, he has established an empirical relation between (*x*) a diet of horror shows and (*y*) emotional disturbance.

Or, to take another example, suppose that a careful investigator, avoiding the pitfalls that face the casual observer, has studied the relation between (*x*) parental income and (*y*) school achievement, and has found that children from wealthy homes get along somewhat better in school. This empirical relation, notice, is the reverse of that suspected by the teacher who relied upon general impression.

Accepting the First Plausible Hypothesis which Presents Itself

Whenever we encounter an interesting or baffling problem it is natural to accept the first reasonable explanation that occurs to us. Take the case of horror stories and emotional disturbance. Point out that empirical relation to your friends, and most of them, if they accept the fact that the relation exists, will immediately jump to the conclusion that horror stories actually produce emotional disturbance.

In considering the empirical relation between family income and school attainment, it may occur to us that in wealthy homes there are better facilities for study. Here is a reasonable, plausible hypothesis which could explain the relation. And unless we are on our guard, many of us would promptly accept it as *the* explanation. Here is one good explanation, we might think. Why look any further?

But, of course, we should look further. Not to do so would be like trying to solve a crime by convicting the first person who seemed a likely suspect. If we thought further we might come up with other suspects just as impressive. Similarly, in trying to make sense out of an empirical relation, we might, if we thought further, come up with several rival explanations, each perfectly plausible and each capable of explaining the relation.

Listing All Plausible Hypotheses. If we are to avoid risk of a serious mistake in interpreting empirical relations, we must do two things. We must be sure to list all the plausible hypotheses that we can think of. Each hypothesis that could possibly explain the relation should have its day in court. Second, we must make sure that each hypothesis, no matter how plausible, is given some sort of test. Some investigations will contain "built-in" tests which will enable us to eliminate many of the hypotheses we might think of. In some investigations, however, we are merely given a rough empirical relation with no built-in devices by which we can test rival hypotheses. In that case we might have to search around for some new means of testing each hypothesis. Often the test will call for a supplementary investigation that we are not in a position to carry out. In that case we will have to face the fact that the issue is not settled and that we merely have a hypothesis which appears plausible but is still untested.

This process of "thinking up" plausible hypotheses is the least systematic of the scientist's tasks. There is no rule or method which will guarantee that we have covered all the ground. Hypotheses may be good guesses or brilliant intuitions. Success in thinking of them depends on a wide variety of things including, perhaps, luck. It may also depend on familiarity with the material, familiarity with other sciences, fertility of imagination, ingenuity, and ability to see elusive relations.

It also depends on many other intangible qualities. Surprisingly enough, lack of familiarity with materials has, in some instances, helped people think of the hypothesis which finally proved to be right. While this seems paradoxical at first glance, it appears more reasonable after some reflection. Looking for the right hypothesis is like looking for a lost ball. In the great majority of cases the ball will be found by the man who has a pretty good idea where it is. It may happen, however, that our man is mistaken. When this is so, his mistaken idea may so restrict his area of search that he is less likely to find the ball than someone who has no knowledge of where it may be.

The fact that we secure hypotheses in such an unsystematic way should not disturb us. Every hypothesis must be tested. Consequently, a far-fetched or fantastic hypothesis can do no harm as long as we realize that no importance must be attached to it until it has been tested. The only harm that a fantastic hypothesis can do is to increase our labor by giving us one more hypothesis to test. It is for this reason alone that we suggest limiting ourselves to plausible hypotheses. If we did not have to be concerned about limitations of time, energy, and patience, there would be much to say in favor of including all hypotheses no matter how implausible. In many cases the true hypothesis may come from a very unlikely source.

The rule then is (a) catch all the hypotheses you can; (b) retain for testing all those that seem to have a reasonable chance of passing the test. The chance of passing should be reasonable enough to justify the time and effort of making the test. In deciding which hypotheses have a chance of passing the test, there is nothing definite to go on. You must always face the risk that the hypothesis you discard without a test may have been the most adequate.

Let us see how this rule works in trying to explain the educational superiority of children from richer homes. First, we list all the hypotheses we can think of. The following plausible hypotheses suggest themselves:

1. Children in better homes have better facilities for study.
2. Richer parents have, on the average, more ability than poorer parents, and the children of the former inherit this superior ability.
3. Children in better homes are better fed and receive better medical care.
4. Children in better homes have fewer worries or emotional troubles.

A great many implausible hypotheses may also occur to us. Someone may suggest, for instance, that rich parents must have had considerable luck to enable them to get rich, and perhaps the children inherit that luck, or that school officials, feeling the need of keeping the proletariat in its place, force the teachers to give better marks to children from wealthy homes. This latter hypothesis is rather cynical and sordid. But do not dismiss it on that account. Dismiss it only if it seems too farfetched or implausible. Indeed, we may decide that both these hypotheses are too improbable to justify a test. In thus dismissing them we must realize that we run a risk. If we *did* test these hypotheses we might find that one of them was correct. But since we cannot test all hypotheses we must draw the line somewhere.

Important General Types of Alternate Hypotheses

Our main job then is not to be swept off our feet by some persuasive "explanation" that dominates our minds when we first encounter an empirical relation. This dominating "explanation" or hypothesis may have been suggested by the author, or it may have struck us as being obvious or self-evident. But in any case it is there, ready to take over, unless we can see some rival or alternate possibilities.

It is true that there is no single rule for digging up hypotheses that will prove fruitful in explaining relations. There are a few general types of hypotheses, however, that are frequently in order. In our search for rival hypotheses, we would be wise to think quickly of the various types to be described below.

You may notice, by the way, that the items we list as types of alternate hypotheses or rival hypotheses are often described as types of error. And obviously an investigator would be in error if he had proposed a certain conclusion and had failed to deal with one of these important rival hypotheses.

Alternate Hypotheses in Experimental Investigations

In experimental investigations, it will be remembered, the investigator himself determines the treatment each person is to receive. He decides who shall get the drug and who shall not; or who shall study under this method and who shall study under that. Preferably, he makes these decisions by drawing random numbers, or by tossing a coin.

Failure to Restrict the Differences to the Independent Variable. Suppose we give one group of men an alcoholic drink. Another group receives no such drink. We now proceed to test both groups in ability to drive. In such an experiment we run a very definite risk. The groups differ not only in the independent variable (amount of alcohol taken), but they also differ in the fact that members of one group know they have been drinking and the members of the other group know they have not been drinking. This knowledge in itself may act by suggestion on driving ability. It may lead some people to be more cautious. Other people, however, may feel gay and reckless merely from the idea of drinking. Either of these conditions may affect driving ability and so distort our experiment.

In almost any experiment we run the risk that in arranging for differences in the independent variable we will also do something else to the people involved, and this something else may affect the dependent variable. In our experiment on horror programs, for instance, we will find it most difficult not to do many different things to our two groups. We may select one group of children at random from a classroom and send them off to a series of TV shows, leaving a comparable group in the regular classroom. Obviously we may have set in motion a large number of forces. The selected group may be suspicious, or elated, or may feel superior. The group left behind may be resentful, or rejected, or may feel that they are less worthy in some way. Any one of these factors, completely unrelated to the viewing of horror stories, could have an effect on emotional disturbance. The difference which we charge up to the diet of horror stories could really be due to one of these incidental features.

When we consider the results of an experimental investigation, we should, tentatively at least, consider this hypothesis: The differences found in the dependent variable (emotional disturbance) are not due to the differences in the independent variable (horror shows) but to other incidental differences (suspicion in the experimental group) created while setting up the differences in the independent variable.

Systematic Steps for Avoiding the Pitfall. We say we should give tentative consideration to the long-winded alternate hypothesis enunciated above. Often, however, after very slight scrutiny we will find that the experimenter has built certain controls into his investigation and that these controls would force us to give up our hypothesis. In these days, for instance, any experimenter would be sure to try to eliminate the influence of suggestion in his experiment on alcohol. If some of his people thought they were drinking alcohol, he would make sure that the rest also thought they were drinking alcohol. He would do this by giving everyone the same kind of drink (or injection) as far as quantity and taste were concerned. By the same token, many investigators would take steps to be sure that both groups of children saw a TV program of some sort, and that both (or neither) thought they were taking part in an experiment.

Often we will find that the experimental investigator has taken steps to avoid this pitfall, and thus has ruled out our alternate hypothesis.

Often, but not always. Every day, some bright young student finds some loophole or weakness in earlier experiments, thought to be error-free at the time they were completed. Even today, when investigators should be able to profit from the glaring errors of the past, you will occasionally find published experiments which could be explained by the uncontrolled operation of one of these incidental effects.

Suppose the investigator has failed to control all these incidental differences (power of suggestion) that could produce the differences in the dependent variable (driving skill). In that case you have two plausible but rival hypotheses to explain the differences in driving skill. It is just as if you have good reason to suppose that it was Bill who committed the murder and also good reason to believe that it was Tom. So long as things remain this way, you must admit your uncertainty. Bill alone may be guilty. Tom alone may be guilty. Both may be guilty. You just don't know. At this stage, you had better not hang either. Similarly, so long as both hypotheses are tenable, you cannot tell which is true. It may be the alcohol. It may be the suggestion. It may be both. You just don't know. You had better not accept either as established.

Alternate Hypotheses in Causal-comparative Investigations

In using the causal-comparative method or statistical method, the investigator does not bring about the differences in the independent variable (amount of alcohol taken, amount of time spent in viewing TV horror shows). On the contrary, he merely locates people who already differ in the independent variable. He then sorts them according to the differences he finds. By these means he is able to get two groups who differ systematically in the alcoholic intake or in the TV viewing habits.

This method, by its very nature, invites its own alternate hypotheses. As in the experimental method, these represent pitfalls or sources of error that face the investigator.

The Hypothesis of the Common Cause. Suppose that we had used the statistical or causal-comparative method to determine the relation between drinking and ability to drive. We have found people who already differ in the amount of alcohol taken. We now test them on ability to drive and find that they also differ significantly in this respect. We now have a rough empirical relation between drinking and driving. At this stage, many people will immediately and definitely accept one plausible hypothesis and will assume that this hypothesis has been established. They will assume that we have *proved* that drinking leads to poor driving. If we are to be cautious, however, we cannot accept this as proved until we rule out any rival hypotheses equally capable of explaining the empirical relation.

In statistical investigations we must always consider the hypothesis of the common cause. We did not cause the differences in drinking. There must have been some other forces at work to bring about these differences. Let us consider the probable nature of these forces.

Why do these people differ in the amount of alcohol imbibed? Why have some of these men taken a lot of alcohol and others only a little or none at all? There may be many reasons. The heavy drinkers may be less cautious or they may have more worries or they may have a sense of unworthiness from which they wish to escape. Thus, the groups vary not only in the amount of alcohol taken but also in the traits or factors which led to drinking. *The same thing (excessive worry) which causes a man to drink may also cause him to be a poor driver,* and the worry may cause poor driving even if he does not drink. Thus, alcohol may not be a cause of poor driving, but merely an index of some other trait which causes both drinking and poor driving. The worry is a *common cause* for both drinking and unskillful driving.

We face precisely the same problem when we use the causal-comparative or statistical method to investigate the effect of horror shows. When we use the statistical method, the differences in TV viewing habits do not come from our action. These differences must come from some other force or forces that lead some children to see many horror stories and others to see few or none. When we start listing possible reasons for this difference we can see many that may act as a common cause. Indifferent parents, for instance, or lack of other recreation may lead to excessive TV viewing in general. Parental indifference or lack of supervision again may lead to an unusual concentration on horror stories. In each case, the very factor responsible for excessive exposure to horror stories could, in and of itself, directly produce the emotional disturbance. It is not at all implausible to suppose that indifference of parents, lack of normal recreation, or lack of normal supervision could increase a child's emotional disturbance even if he never saw a horror story.

This pitfall in statistical investigations appears in a great many sociological investigations. We may wish, for instance, to see if marriage (independent variable) has any influence on mental health (dependent variable). Obviously the experimental method is out of the question. We cannot arrange to have people marry or not marry according to our decision, or just by drawing lots. Hence we must use the statistical method. We must find one group of people who have married and another group of people who, for one reason or another, have not married. We observe the people in both groups and find the married group to have significantly better mental health. Here again we have an empirical relation and, if we are not careful, we may find ourselves jumping to the conclusion that marriage promotes mental health. In doing so, however, we fail to consider the possibility of a common cause. There must be some reason for marrying or not marrying. A person may fail to marry, for instance, because of dominating or jealous parents, or because of some physical unattractiveness, or because of a fear of making important decisions. Any one of these factors could prevent marriage. And, more important, any one of these factors could lead to poor mental health even apart from marriage. Here again marriage (the independent variable) may have nothing to do with mental health. Marital status may merely be an index of the traits which do lead to poor mental health. Both variables may merely be two separate results of a single common cause.

Methods of Avoiding the Pitfall of the Common Cause. Whenever we encounter an empirical relation that is based on the causal-comparative method, we should stop for a moment and ask if some common cause could be responsible. In many systematic studies, however, we will find that the investigator foresaw the possibility of a common cause and has so arranged his investigation that the common cause is ruled out. Suspecting parental domination as a common cause, for instance, he may have been careful to match his married and unmarried people with respect to the parental attitude. Whenever he had an unmarried person from a rigid or dominating home, he would try to find a married person from a similar home. In the same way he would match up a married person from a permissive home with an unmarried person from a similar home. In this way he would make sure that the two groups did not differ systematically with respect to parental domination. This being so we could forget about the possibility (hypothesis) that it is the difference in parental domination that causes the difference in mental health.

Matching is one method by which we can *control* a factor, or *hold* it *constant,* and thus eliminate it as a potential common cause. When matching is impossible or inconvenient, we may prefer to use some method of *correcting for* the influence of the common cause. Let us suppose that the mental health of our married group is 18 points higher than the mental health of our unmarried group. Let us also suppose that the two groups have not been matched on parental permissiveness and that the married group averages 10 points ahead on this trait. Now we must be able to estimate the extent to which mental health would be increased by 10 points of permissiveness. Suppose our calculations show that 6 points of mental health could be produced by this difference in permissiveness. So we correct our total difference of 18 points by subtracting the 6 points that could be produced by the common cause (permissiveness). The remaining 12 points of difference in mental health represents the role of marriage after we have allowed for the influence of this particular common cause. The two most frequent devices used to make a correction of this sort are *partial correlation* and *analysis of covariance*.

Notice that the investigator can only take care of those common causes that he suspects and that he can observe or measure. It is only by thinking of possible common causes in advance of the investigation, and by taking specific steps to control them or correct for them, that they can be ruled out. Notice too that each common cause is a problem in its own right. In taking care of parental domination, we do not automatically take care of physical handicaps.

The Hypothesis of Reversed Causality. In jumping to the conclusion that marriage leads to mental health, we not only ignored the possibility of a common cause, but we also ignored the possibility that the causal arrangement may be the direct opposite of what we imagine. It may be that mental health leads to marriage. Our empirical relation can be explained just as well by this "reverse" hypothesis as by the first hypothesis we so hastily adopted.

Whenever we encounter an empirical relation that is based on the causal-comparative method we should check to see if this "other way around" hypothesis is plausible enough to consider. Sometimes we will find that it is not, and we may dismiss it as soon as we think of it. We find, for instance, that boys are more obstreperous than girls. Reversed causality suggests that being obstreperous causes one to be a boy! This hypothesis need not keep us very long.

In many investigations, in contrast to the illustration just given, we will find that the hypothesis of reversed causality is quite plausible and that it deserves serious consideration. It is quite possible, for instance, that some emotional quirk in children leads to a fondness for horror shows. When we hear of an empirical relation between exercise and health, we must not jump to the conclusion that exercise causes health. Perhaps it is the good health that leads one to exercise.

Methods of Avoiding the Pitfall of Reversed Causality. The pitfall of reversed causality has not received the attention that it deserves. It is found, for instance, that there is more aggressive behavior on the part of children who are frequently punished at home. Even in elaborate published discussions, it is suggested that because of this empirical relation, we can conclude that punishment leads to aggressive behavior. Of course we should conclude nothing of the kind. Such an empirical relation could merely mean that aggressive children are more likely to be punished.

Although this pitfall is all too frequently ignored, it is still true that many investigators do foresee it and take steps to rule it out. Typically this is done by matching the groups on the *dependent* variable at the outset of the investigation. Suppose we measure the emotional adjustment of a group of children at the beginning of the year and again at the end of the year. At the end of the year, we find out who has been watching horror stories and who has not. We find one "watcher" who had an emotional adjustment score of 63 at the beginning of the year. We search through the group of "nonwatchers" until we find another child with a similar initial score. These make a pair. We find as many pairs as possible made up of two children who differ in their viewing habits but who do not differ in initial emotional adjustment. Now we will have two groups who started the year with no systematic difference in emotional adjustment. We can hardly say that it was the difference in emotional adjustment that led to the difference in the television programs seen.

Interpreting Empirical Relations: Resumé

The following outline summarizes the first steps to be taken in scrutinizing an empirical relation. It is assumed, of course, that you are satisfied that the relation has actually been established.

Empirical Relation: Children from more punitive homes are found to be significantly more aggressive.

Chief Explanatory Hypothesis Under Consideration. (This could be the explanation suggested by the investigator, or it could be an obvious explanation that had occurred to you): Punishment in the home leads to aggression in children.

1. *Question*: Was the empirical relation established by the experimental method, or by the causal-comparative method?

If *experimental,* consider the following alternate hypothesis:

2. In producing the differences in the amount of parental punishment (independent variable), the investigator also produced differences in the general parental attitude, and it was this latter difference that produced the observed differences in aggression.
3. Is this hypothesis plausible enough to justify further thought?
4. If plausible, does the report present any evidence to rule out this hypothesis?

If *causal-comparative,* consider the hypothesis of the *common cause.*

5. Some other factor (marital discord, or rejection by the community) caused excessive parental punishment and excessive aggression in children.
6. Is this hypothesis plausible enough to justify further thought?
7. If plausible, does the report present any evidence to rule out this hypothesis?

If *causal-comparative* also consider the hypothesis of *reversed causality.*

8. The relation could be due to the fact that aggressive children are more likely to be punished.
9. Is this hypothesis plausible enough to justify further thought?
10. If plausible, does the report present any evidence to rule out this hypothesis?

The formal steps just outlined must not be taken to represent the be-all and end-all of scientific caution. In any specific investigation you may easily suspect other hypotheses that would have to be tested and eliminated before you could accept the interpretation that had been proposed. The hypotheses stressed in the outline merely happen to be some formal classes or types of hypotheses that are crucial, and that are frequently ignored in casual study and occasionally ignored in more systematic study.

So long as any plausible alternate or rival hypothesis is still in the field, you cannot, of course, accept any proposal or conclusion as having been established. So long as there is one other suspect who is still a plausible candidate for the crime, you cannot be sure that your favorite suspect is guilty. You have no choice but to consider the whole question still in doubt. In all this, by the way, do not feel that you are being mean and destructive. By the same token, do not feel triumphant or superior when you discover alternate hypotheses that are not ruled out. You are not out to tear the other fellow down, or to show that you are smarter than he is. You are merely asking, "Has it really been shown that *x* leads to *y*? Do we have dependable evidence that would justify us in urging parents to go easy on punishment? Shall we throw out our old procedures and adopt new ones on the strength of this evidence?" It is the truth or dependability of the conclusion that is under consideration, not the skill or competence of the investigator. You are not asking, "Is this mechanic a scoundrel?" but, "Do I care to trust myself in this airplane?"

In many published studies, of course, you will find that the investigator has been clearly aware of these pitfalls or alternate hypotheses, and that he has provided built-in devices to take care of them. Often, indeed, the whole investigation has been organized around the problem of dealing with all these pitfalls or alternate hypotheses. When this has been done with perfect success you are forced to accept the author's proposed interpretation. You agree that an empirical relation has been established. The author proposes one hypothesis to account for this relation. He considers every other plausible hypothesis that has been proposed, or that you can think of, and shows that each of these has been ruled out by precautions that he has incorporated into his study. As far as you are concerned, then, there is an established relation for which there is—so far—only one plausible explanation. For the time being, you must agree. This is science at its exciting best.

Summary

Although education is a very familiar process, it is still full of pitfalls for the student who seeks to understand its essential nature. Such a student must first of all avoid the pitfall of wishful thinking. He must not let his hopes and feelings determine his convictions regarding the nature of education. The serious student will do well to consider the steps taken by the systematic investigator to protect himself against the more frequent sources of error.

The systematic investigator knows most of the more common mistakes which people may make when they attempt to work out a theory. He tries to take care of these common errors by using enough cases to rule out coincidence, by adopting some system so that he will observe and remember cases which go against his theory as well as cases which support it. He will also use precise methods of making measurements and observations and will describe his results in a definite and precise manner.

By taking care of these matters, and by using a control or comparison group, the investigator can often establish a valid *empirical relation*.

In attempting to get the causes behind this empirical relation, the investigator encounters many pitfalls. In an *experiment*, for instance, he may give a drug to one group to see if this affects mental output. In giving the drug, however, he may inadvertently frighten the students or arouse some apprehension. And any difference in output may come from the apprehension and not from the drug itself. He must avoid this pitfall by making sure that both groups have the same amount of apprehension. He usually does this by giving both groups pills of the same appearance. Only half the pills, however, contain the drug. The others merely contain sugar and baking soda, or some other indifferent substance.

When the investigator uses the *statistical* or *causal-comparative* method, he encounters even greater pitfalls. He wishes to find if marriage affects mental health. He cannot use the experimental method here. He cannot administer marriage to one group and leave the other group unmarried. He can only utilize the differences in marriage which he happens to find. If he finds any relation between marriage (independent variable) and mental health (dependent variable) he must consider at least three explanations:

1. The difference in marital status may have caused the differences in mental health.
2. The same factors (undue caution or parental domination) which caused the differences in marriage may have directly caused the differences in mental health.
3. Poor mental health may have kept people from getting married.

Or, summing up, whenever we find a *statistical* relation between the independent variable (X) and the dependent variable (Y) we must realize that X may have caused Y, or that Y may have caused X, or that both may be caused by the factors which produced the original differences in X.

Suppose it is the first explanation that the investigator wishes to test. He must eliminate the other two possible explanations. The second explanation can be eliminated by making the groups comparable in caution or in parental domination. The third explanation is hard to eliminate by statistical methods. At times, however, it can be rejected on the grounds of common sense.

It is by taking these various pitfalls into account and by devising ways of avoiding them that the systematic investigator attempts to improve on the method of general impression.

SUGGESTIONS FOR FURTHER READING

1. Cohen, M. R., and Nagel, E. *An introduction to logic and scientific method.* Harcourt Brace, 1934.

   Chapter 16, Part 5, of this book discusses many of the pitfalls of statistical investigations from the point of view of the professional logician. The whole book is an excellent treatment of the logical aspects of science.

2. Tyler, Leona E. *The psychology of human differences.* Appleton-Century-Crofts, 1947.

   Chapter 10 discusses correlation and also provides a very easily understood discussion of the pitfalls in statistical research.

3. Barr, A. S., Davis, R. A., and Johnson, P. O. *Educational research and appraisal.* Lippincott, 1953.

   Pages 296–305 provide some excellent advice for the interpretation of empirical relations. The entire book is useful for a more technical understanding of the problems involved in educational research.

Exercises

1. Here are some actual studies described in very brief fashion. Each description is followed by *one* plausible hypothesis which could be used to explain the facts. You are to advance other or alternative hypotheses or guesses which could also be used to explain the facts. Do not just ask questions. List positive hypotheses that are plausible enough to deserve a test.

Example:

In a questionnaire filled in by 1300 problem children in the Iowa schools, some 21 percent reported that their fathers were seldom home in the evenings.

One Hypothesis: Habitual absence of the father contributes to problem behavior of the child.

Alternative Hypotheses:

(1) It is possible that 21 percent of *nonproblem* children would also report frequent absence of the father; (2) even if the number for nonproblem children is less than 21 percent, it is still possible that some other condition, such as a nagging mother, caused the father to be absent and also caused the child to be disturbed; (3) it is possible that the problem behavior of the child caused the father to stay away in the evening. (Note: Some of the following questions may call for only one or two alternative hypotheses.)

a. In the Illinois Statewide High School Testing Program, the students were asked to indicate if they had taken the test previously. The 708 students who had taken the test before excelled the other students by some eight points.

One Hypothesis: Previous experience helps boost the score.

b. Of the 500 consecutive admissions to a children's clinic for emotional problems, 12.5 percent were found to be children whose birth was desired or "planned for" by the parents.

One Hypothesis: "Planned-for" children are liable to emotional maladjustment.

c. From a nationwide test given to 304,000 high-school seniors, the averages for each state were found. There was a correlation of 0.6 between the average of the state and the amount each state spent on teachers' salaries.

One Hypothesis: More money for teachers will boost the attainment of students.

2. Distinguish between the experimental and the statistical or causal-comparative methods as the terms are used in this text.

Which pitfalls are especially bothersome in the experimental method? In the statistical or causal-comparative method?

3

Locating and Using Published Research

I N THE FIELD of educational psychology, as we pointed out in Chapter 1, there are a great many isolated facts that have not yet been neatly incorporated into a single text or handbook. Many of the isolated facts, moreover, may have considerable importance for your particular problems. Suppose, for instance, that you are thinking of a system of optional attendance, under which students attaining a certain grade need not attend class unless they wish. Being thoroughly convinced that you should profit by the experience of others, you try to find out what is already known about this system. It is possible, of course, that you may have a summary already at hand in connection with some course you are taking. But you cannot depend on this and you may have to make a detailed search. Very often such a search is very rewarding. Tucked away in technical journals and in handbooks, there is much valuable information bearing on many practical problems. This important information can be available to you if you learn to find your way around in the educational and psychological literature.

Locating Published Information

Texts and Handbooks

You cannot be sure, of course, that your topic will be treated in the first text that you pick up. Texts are always worth a try, however. They

47

are convenient sources. If your topic is treated in a text, moreover, you will often find that it is discussed in its general context and is discussed in relation to similar problems. It may also be interpreted in a helpful way.

For these reasons, a quick look for promising texts should often be your first step. Just how to find promising texts or handbooks, of course, may be quite a problem in itself, and it is one that cannot be solved in general for all questions that you may have occasion to answer. There are a great many general leads, however, which will apply to a large number of questions. Before you go very far afield, for instance, you will want to take a quick look at the "Suggestions for Further Reading" at the ends of some of these chapters. Common sense will suggest many other leads. If your question has to do with truancy, for instance, you would immediately think of books on child guidance, delinquency, or problem children. If the question has to do with favorable lighting conditions, you would naturally think of books dealing with the school plant, school administration, with industrial psychology, or applied psychology.

When you decide what sort of text might prove to be a promising lead, the next problem is to find some texts in that field. Here, of course, you will turn to the subject index of the card catalogue in the library, or to the *Cumulative Book Index* which is available in most libraries. Look under your general topic or under a synonym for it. Ordinarily you will be surprised by the number of books that you can choose from. Make a point of selecting the more recent publications, since these may incorporate the valuable information of the earlier publications. Obviously, too, it is only the more recent publications that can summarize the recent researches. Consult several of these more recent texts. One may have much more information than another. Make good use of the subject index to track down the special problem you have in mind.

One excellent handbook which treats a variety of educational subjects is the *Encyclopaedia of Educational Research*, edited by W. S. Monroe (Macmillan, 1950).

Bibliographical Sources

The use of textbooks, handbooks, and encyclopaedias is to be encouraged. Such sources give us an excellent start. The good ones summarize earlier investigations in their historical and scientific setting and present the results in an integrated and intelligible pattern. All in all, they provide an excellent jumping-off place.

But they provide only a jumping-off place. We cannot expect to find a complete answer to our problem from these general sources. In the first place, even a recent book is somewhat out of date by the time it is published. In the second place, these books, treating as they do many topics, seldom provide a complete treatment of any one.

Review of Educational Research. For complete information on any topic, we should consult several of the bibliographical sources. Although the best source varies from topic to topic, there are a few which are exceptionally valuable for a large number of topics. For the teacher, probably the most useful of all is the *Review of Educational Research,* published five times a year by the American Educational Research Association. Each of these issues summarizes the research on a single topic, with most topics treated once every three years. Research on *Teacher Personnel,* for instance, was summarized in June, 1955, and in June, 1952. A subject index, published in 1944 (Volume 14), covers the first twelve volumes. A list of all the topics covered to date is found in the back pages of each issue. A folder containing the same information may be obtained from the Association. Select the topic most likely to include your problem. Begin with the most recent summary, and work back to earlier summaries.

Annual Review of Psychology. This series, begun in 1950, provides a yearly review of the more important psychological topics. Some topics will be covered once every two years. The student of educational psychology will probably be most interested in the sections on child psychology, learning, individual differences, personality, social psychology (group processes), measurement, counseling, educational psychology, problem solving, and thinking. There is a fair subject index at the back of each volume. This may prove especially useful if you are not sure which chapter is most likely to treat your topic.

Psychological Bulletin. This journal is published six times a year. Almost every issue contains a summary of one or more psychological topics. This journal differs from the *Annual Review* in that it employs no regular system for covering each topic. You cannot tell in advance which topics will be treated. The summaries in the *Psychological Bulletin,* moreover, may be devoted to highly specialized topics. These summaries are likely to cover a period of years and are often quite complete.

Since there is no regular system for covering different topics, the only thing to do is to get out each bound volume, starting with the most recent, and quickly look through the table of contents.

The summaries to be found in the *Psychological Bulletin,* naturally enough, stress psychological rather than educational problems. There is a good deal of overlapping, however, and you will find summaries on such problems as "Learning During Sleep?" (1955), "Social Class and Personality" (1952), "Infant Care and Personality" (1949), "Transfer of Training" (1948), "Measurement of Attitudes" (1948), "Leadership" (1947), and "Law of Effect" (1947).

The summaries to be found in the *Review of Educational Research, The Annual Review of Psychology,* and in the *Psychological Bulletin* vary in completeness. Occasionally you may obtain a fairly complete answer from the summaries alone. More frequently, however, the summaries will merely provide you with a marvelous list of references to individual investigations, and you will have to consult these to reach your answer.

Make careful notes of the precise titles of the journals. Often students wander into the library asking vaguely for "The Psychology Journal," or "The Education Journal." Actually there are a large number of journals in both fields, some of which have rather similar names. There is a *Journal of General Psychology* and also a *Journal of Genetic Psychology.* There is a *Journal of Educational Research* and a *Review of Educational Research.* There is a *Journal of Psychology,* an *American Journal of Psychology,* and a *British Journal of Psychology.* So, when copying down references, be careful of the titles of the journals and be sure to get them straight. To be safe, copy down the title exactly as given. If the abbreviation reads, *J. genet. Psychol.,* do not change it to *J. gen. Psychol.* or to *J. gen. Psych.* These are quite different journals.

Education Index. The three bibliographical sources just discussed should be used for all they are worth. It is possible, however, that they may not go far enough. For one thing, your problem may be a "maverick" that cannot be neatly classified within one of the standard topics. For another thing, the last treatment of your topic may be several years old. In any event, it is wise to supplement these bibliographical sources by consulting the *Education Index.* Use this just as you would use the *Readers' Guide to Periodical Literature.* Start with the most recent copy that you can find and work back to the cumulative bound volumes. Look up your problem or a synonym for it in the alphabetical index. Here, of course, you will merely get references to specific studies.

Psychological Abstracts. Psychological Abstracts, begun in 1927, is published once every two months. Each issue contains a brief summary of articles which appear in other journals. These summaries are numbered serially through the year, the first summary appearing in the January-February issue being number *1* and the last summary in the year being (say) *6023.* The summaries are identified by volume and number. For instance *28:813* would refer to article number *813* in volume *28.*

The separate bi-monthly issues provide an excellent means of keeping in touch with psychological work, and the student with special interest in this field will be well rewarded for thumbing through an occasional issue. These separate numbers, however, are not especially useful as bibliographical sources. It is the special subject index published every year that is useful for this latter purpose. There is an author index as well as a subject index. This index is found at the back of each bound volume and it is a gold mine of references.

To use this helpful bibliographical source, start with the last complete or bound volume that you can find. Look up your topic, or a synonym, in the subject index. If you are interested in optional attendance, for instance, you might look under *attendance,* hoping to find a subhead, *attendance, optional.* This entry is followed by a number, say *1121,* which refers to the abstract number (*not* the page number) in this same volume. Look up the abstract. It will give you the reference to the complete article or book. Ordinarily, it will also give you a brief description, and from this you can usually tell whether it is worth your while to look up the original article. As a rule, it is *not* wise to depend exclusively on the abstract for all your information. If it seems that the information may have a bearing on your question, you should consult the original.

Miscellaneous Sources. The five general bibliographical sources just discussed will prove most useful for general purposes and for current materials. In addition you will find fairly regular summaries of special fields in many specific journals. Both the *Elementary School Journal* and the *School Review* (secondary education), for instance, publish annual summaries in different fields. Many of the specific articles which you later come across will also contain lists of other articles dealing with the same topic.

The Problem of Desultory Reading

It is inevitable, of course, that in the process of opening a thick volume in search of a smaller article, you will find yourself reading a great deal that has no direct bearing on your problem. Curtail this tendency to some extent, especially if you are faced with some deadline. Don't be too angry with yourself, however, for being led astray by these tempting, irrelevant articles or book reviews. Such desultory reading can certainly be overdone and even at the best is bound to interfere with the main endeavor. All things considered, however, it is not too high a price to pay for the boon of intellectual curiosity. Once in a while, moreover, you come across something which is of great value and which you could not have found in any other way.

These very simple suggestions should give you a fair introduction to the published material. In most cases, this will be about as far as you need to go and about as far as you will have time to go. If it is important that you cover the published material in really thorough fashion, you should consult the more elaborate discussions listed at the end of this chapter. The books by Alexander, by Monroe and Shores, and by Good and Scates should prove excellent for this more ambitious purpose. Beyond this, you may find yourself going to the stacked volumes of the journals and thumbing through volume after volume of likely publications. This, of course, is a joy in itself and it will bring many interesting surprises and much information that you would never encounter in any other way. Compared to the more systematic procedures, however, it is not an efficient method of locating material.

Examining and Organizing the Results of Research

So far you will have spent much of your time, perhaps most of it, in merely collecting a large number of references. In copying out these references from the bibliographical sources, you may have used a separate sheet of paper for each, or perhaps a medium-sized card for each. (Different people prefer different methods. Cards are easier for sorting, papers make for easier filing.) At any rate, you have a number of these references, and now you start your examination of the original sources.

Ignore the Unessentials

Learn to be selective. In the first place, a brief glance may show you that the article as a whole does not live up to the promise in its title. Seeing the actual article, you may conclude that it has no bearing on your problem. Make an appropriate notation on your card, or paper, and go on. In the second place, every article, no matter how useful it is in general, is bound to contain many details which are irrelevant to your

purposes. Many of these details are supplied to enable another investigator to rework the data or to repeat the entire investigation. These details may include the address of the investigator, an elaborate description
of the apparatus or of the tests used, and the names of the schools involved. Ignore these details unless you can see how they might affect
your interpretation of the results.

Probe Behind the Author's Interpretations or Conclusions

If the research contains any help for the solving of your problem,
that help will come from the factual results. These in turn, as we point
out in Chapter 2, must be interpreted in the light of the methods used.
The author's own interpretation or conclusion may provide a most
useful guide or starting point. But do not rely exclusively on this interpretation. Use it as a first hypothesis and then go on to a study of the
results. See if there are any other reasonable hypotheses that might
provide a rival explanation of the results.

To study the results, of course, you will often have to deal with tables
and graphs. Give them as much attention as your mathematical background will permit. It is difficult to suggest just how much detail you
ought to consult when you are looking at the results. Ordinarily, you
will not want to look at the individual scores or observations. Rather
than do this you will seek out some convenient summary of the data.

Frequency Distributions

One very useful means of summarizing data is the *frequency distribution.* You have probably encountered these distributions many times.
Almost any textbook or journal article in the field of education is likely
to contain distributions such as these. Consequently, at this point, we
need only give one example to serve as a brief reminder.

In distributions such as those in Table 3-1 we can see the results in
fairly compact form, and yet we can see something of the range of the
results. Looking at the distribution for age 7, for instance, we can see
that one child is somewhere between 132 and 135 centimeters tall,
whereas two children of this age are between 128 and 131, and four are
between 124 and 127, and so forth. We can get similar information from
the distributions of the other age groups. Results such as these are
sufficiently compact to enable us to see the general pattern in one "eyeful," yet they are sufficiently detailed to see the range and the overlapping
of the results. Looking at a distribution such as this, for instance, we

TABLE 3-1

Frequency Distributions for Children of Different Ages

Height in Centimeters	Age 7	Age 8	Age 9
140–143			2
136–139			5
132–135	1	5	10
128–131	2	10	27
124–127	4	23	20
120–123	16	24	11
116–119	32	17	4
112–115	20	7	1
108–111	11	4	
104–107	3		
Number of Children	89	90	80
Mean Height	117.2	122.7	128.4
Median Height	117.3	122.8	128.5

could never get the mistaken notion that *all* seven-year-old children have a height of approximately 117.2 centimeters, or that all eight-year-olds are 122.7 centimeters tall. On the contrary, we see in most compelling fashion that there is a wide range in the heights of all age groups. Many of the seven-year-olds, in fact, are taller than the average eight-year-old. A few of the seven-year-olds are taller than the average nine-year-old. These ranges and overlappings, so important in our later discussions, are brought out in unmistakable fashion in distributions such as these. Look for them and use them whenever they are presented.

Interpreting Graphs of Frequency Distributions. Frequency distributions are often presented in graphical form by the use of *frequency polygons* or *histograms*. These devices, too, are probably very familiar to you. At this stage, in fact, it is only necessary to remind ourselves briefly of some of the characteristics of such graphs and to clear up a few of the misconceptions that are often encountered.

Figure 3-1 is a graphical representation of the results in the first two columns of Table 3-1. The results for the third column can also be placed on this same graph, but putting too much into a single graph makes it hard to read.

Graphs, when you are used to them, make it even easier to take in the general trend of the results in one glance. These graphs, for instance, show how the children from each age group tend to "pile up" at one point. They also show how the two groups overlap.

Danger of Confusing the Two Dimensions. When you first looked at these graphs, did you have some feeling that, paradoxically, the seven-

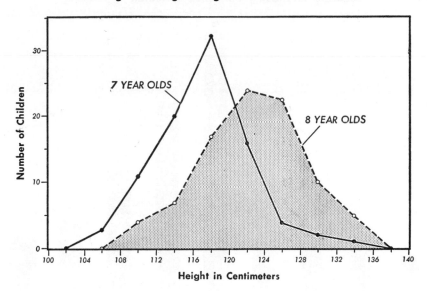

FIGURE 3-1. *Frequency Polygon Showing the Distributions of Heights for Two Groups*

year-olds are actually *taller* than the eight-year-olds? If so, you are probably confusing the two dimensions of a frequency distribution. You are assuming that "up means tall," and since the graph for the seven-year-olds reaches a higher point, you assume that they must be taller. This is a very understandable misconception. Actually, in most of the graphs we encounter "up" does mean a higher score or a higher temperature or a higher price. But in a frequency distribution the dimensions are reversed. In these distributions it is distance to the right which means greater height. Distance in the vertical direction merely means more people (or observations). The fact that there is a high peak in the graph for seven-year-olds merely means that *many* children of this age reached a certain height, whether that height represented a tall child or a short child.

To get this point clearly in mind, try to visualize how frequency distributions are constructed. Getting down to earth in almost ridiculous fashion, let us suppose that we have a large number of men and that each man knows what his height is. Using numbers to the nearest inch, these heights are written down on a series of placards. Now the men are told to "fall in," each man lining up behind the placard which indicates his height. In a typical group of men, the results would be very much like those in Figure 3-2, except that here the even numbers have been omitted.

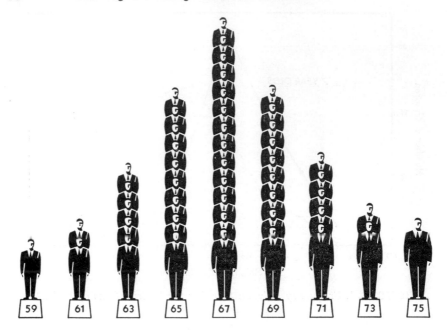

FIGURE 3-2. *Frequency Distribution Produced by Assembling Men According to Height*

Notice in Figure 3-2 the tall men are not toward the top of the picture but are toward the right. A high point in the figure does not mean tall men but merely a large number of men. It is a graph *of* frequency *on* height.

The Shape of Frequency Distribution Curves. It happens that many distributions of height are very similar to the so-called normal curve. This familiar bell-shaped curve plays an important part in satistics. It is a theoretical curve showing the expected distribution of such things as pure chance errors of different sizes. It also happens to give a very good picture of certain biological differences such as height.

Unfortunately this useful curve has been the subject of considerable confusion. Many people have assumed that any symmetrical distribution is thereby normal. Many people also assume that all distributions either are normal, or nearly normal, or ought to be normal. All these assumptions are wrong. A distribution can be quite symmetrical and yet fail to follow the precise path demanded by the equation of the normal curve. Second, many distributions depart widely from the normal curve and there is no reason why they should not. Such distributions, when we encounter them, should cause us no worry or concern.

A FREQUENCY DISTRIBUTION OF INCOME

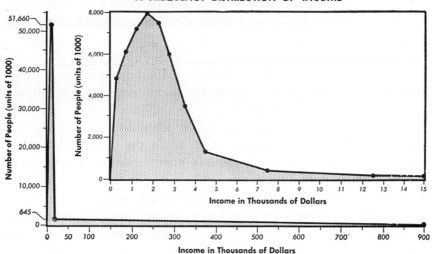

Income in Thousands of Dollars

A FREQUENCY DISTRIBUTION
OF AGE IN A STATIC SOCIETY

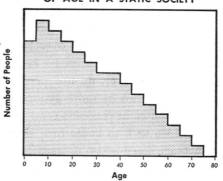

Age

HYPOTHETICAL FREQUENCY DISTRIBUTION
OF DAYS SPENT IN JAIL

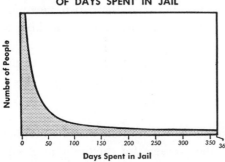

Days Spent in Jail

A BI-MODAL DISTRIBUTION OF ABILITY
TO TASTE THE CHEMICAL P.T.C.*

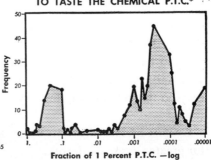

Fraction of 1 Percent P.T.C. —log

FIGURE 3-3. *Distributions Departing from the Normal Curve*
* Redrawn by permission from J. Cohen, and D. G. Ogdon, "Taste Blindness to Phenyl-thio-carbamide and Related Compounds," *Psychol. Bull.,* 1949, *46,* 490-498.

In Figure 3-3 there are several frequency distributions which are markedly different from the normal distribution. The first, a distribution of income, is markedly nonsymmetrical (or *skewed*), but the mode, or high point, is still between the extremes. Distributions showing a definite skewness are very often observed. In the second graph, a distribution of age, the mode is actually at the lower extreme. This is an unusual degree of skewness, but it has been reported in other distributions, especially where social pressure may be applied, as in the distribution of days spent in jail. The last graph shows a distribution with two separate modes. This is encountered very seldom, but it can still occur. The distribution shows the ability to taste a certain chemical. The double mode suggests the presence of two different groups, the "tasters," those clustering around 0.0005, and the "nontasters," those clustering around 0.5.

Using Averages

Frequency distributions enable us to see how the results vary from student to student and how the two groups overlap. This sort of information is most important and should always be kept in the back of our minds. These distributions, however, do not permit us to make precise or numerical comparisons of two or more groups. They merely enable us to see *in general* how the eight-year-olds tend to pile up to the right of the seven-year-olds. If we wish to know how much the average eight-year-old exceeds the average seven-year-old, we will have to get our results into more compact form. And to do this we use *means* or *medians* or some other measure of central tendency. The mean and the median heights for the different age groups are given at the bottom of Table 3-1. We will not go into the difference between these two measures. Ordinarily, either one will serve our purposes when we are looking at the results of investigations. These averages are the kind of numbers you can copy down or remember. Ordinarily, you will be forced to put your faith in these highly simplified averages even though you know they do not tell the whole story.

Graphs of Averages. Just as frequency distributions may be graphed for greater ease of interpretation, so the averages for the different groups are frequently graphed to form some sort of curve of growth, or learning or forgetting. These graphs, being most familiar, are very easy to interpret. We give two or three here merely for the sake of review.

Figure 3-4 is the graph of the *averages* in Table 3-1.

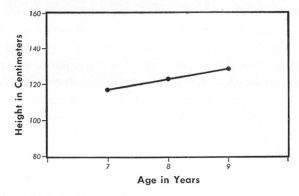

FIGURE 3-4. *Graph Showing Average Height for Children of Different Ages*

Figure 3-5 is an imaginary and erroneous graph showing what one teacher *thought* to be the relation between parental income and attainment of children (see Chapter 2). The actual relation is suggested in Figure 3-6.

Coefficients of Correlation

The *slope* of such graphs tells us whether or not there is any relation between age and height of children, or between parental income and school grades. At times, investigators will also use a number to describe this relationship. This number is called a *coefficient of relationship* or a *coefficient of correlation* and is represented by the symbol r. An r of 1.00 would mean a perfect positive one-to-one relation. It would suggest a very steep slope in the graph. It would mean that as the groups increase one unit in wealth they also increase one unit in school grades. An r of this size is very unusual. It represents, for instance, the correlation between increase in the temperature of a gas and increase in volume of the gas. A coefficient of .90 is not perfect, but is very high. It is the relation which we would expect between students' scores in two halves of the same test. An r of .60 is only a moderate correlation. It is positive but far from perfect. Correlations of this size are obtained between the intelligence of children and the intelligence of parents. An r of .20 represents only a slight resemblance or relation. An r of this order may be obtained when such traits as height and intelligence are correlated. This means that on the average tall people are slightly, but only slightly, more intelligent than short people.

Not all correlations are positive. Theoretically, r may range from 1.00

through 0.00 to −1.00. An r of 0.00 means complete absence of relation. Negative correlations, of course, mean negative or inverse relations. A negative relation is found between the pressure on a gas and the volume of a gas. The *greater* the pressure, the less the volume becomes. In this instance r would be close to −1.00. In educational materials we never get such extreme negative relations although moderate negative relations may be found between chronological age and the achievement of pupils within a given grade. This means that, within a given grade, the older the pupil the less his achievement.

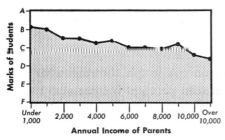 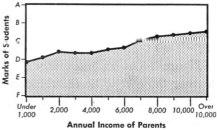

FIGURE 3-5. *Graph Showing a Nega-tive Relation between Achievement of Students and Income of Parents*

FIGURE 3-6. *Graph Showing a Posi-tive Relation between Achievement of Students and Income of Parents*

The Statistical Significance of the Results

When you encounter recent descriptions of experiments you will not read very far before you come across some reference to the *significance* of the results. At this point many students throw up their hands and feel that a subject like this must be completely beyond them and that they had better abandon the whole project. Now, in all truth, the prob-lem of significance is a tricky subject if you insist on going into it in all its details. The basic idea is not so difficult, however, and it would be wise to try to master this basic idea and then take the highly technical problems more or less on faith.

Suppose we investigate the backgrounds of some eighty delinquent boys and find that 30 percent of them come from broken homes. Being aware of the need for a control group, we are also careful to investigate the background of a comparable group of nondelinquent boys, and here we find only 22 percent from broken homes. It is at this point that the critical reader becomes concerned about the problem of significance. He suggests, "Eighty boys make up a rather small sample and this differ-ence is not very large. Suppose you forget all about delinquency and just draw eighty names out of a hat and then draw another eighty names out of the same hat to form a second group. Now examine the number of broken homes in these two groups. You might easily find that one of these groups had a larger number of broken homes just on the basis of chance or *sampling.*" Or, suppose that we have measured the attainment of (say) 140 eleventh-grade students who have been studying under optional attendance and a similar group of 140 students who have been studying under required attendance. We find the average gain of the *optional* group is 73.4 whereas that of the *required* group is 68.1. Again our critic is worried about the significance of the difference. Again he suggests that two groups of 140 students drawn entirely at random from a single large population, all of whom had been treated alike, might reveal differences of this size.

Factors Affecting Uncertainty. It is, of course, impossible to be completely sure that our sample tells the true story for the larger unobserved group that the sample is supposed to represent. There is always bound to be some uncertainty. But that uncertainty can be more or it can be less. It can range from close to zero, at the one extreme, to a very large measure of uncertainty, at the other.

There are several things which will affect the uncertainty we feel about the average of our sample. One of the most obvious is the number of cases or observations in our sample. If our average is based on only a few people, or on only a few observations, we are likely to be very uncertain about its representativeness. As we add more and more cases, however, the less and less our uncertainty becomes. If we add *enough* cases, of course, our sample will come to contain all the cases in the larger group, thereby ceasing to be a real sample, and at this point our uncertainty would be zero. Here then, we have a neat inverse relation; the larger the sample, the less is our uncertainty.

The second factor which affects our uncertainty is the matter of *variability* or *fluctuation.* Suppose, for instance, that I draw a *random* sample of only ten apples from a large bin and find that each and every one of the apples weighs almost exactly 6 ounces. After drawing, let us say, even four apples and finding them all to be the same weight, I might begin to form a "hunch" about the apples in that bin. I might begin to wonder if they all may be exactly 6 ounces, which would mean, of course, that the average would be 6 ounces. That hunch would be very tentative or uncertain. If I were betting that 6 ounces was the average weight for all the apples in the bin, I would want substantial odds. But after I draw six more apples at random and find each and every one of them is 6 ounces, I would feel even more confident that the average of all the apples was 6 ounces. If still betting, I would demand less stringent odds.

Now, suppose I begin to encounter some variation in the weight of the apples I draw at random. Immediately my uncertainty begins to increase. If I had some slight confidence that I knew the average weight of all the apples in the bin, then the appearance of this variation or fluctuation would cause my confidence to decrease. This rule holds in almost all cases. A random sample, which shows little variation within itself, inspires a fair confidence that the average of the sample represents the average of the group from which it is drawn. A random sample, however, which includes a wide range of different measures, is bound to inspire less confidence, or to invoke more uncertainty. Our uncertainty regarding the significance of the average of a sample has a direct relation to the variation, or variance within the sample. The greater the variance, the more our uncertainty.

It is possible to use a simple formula to express our uncertainty regarding the average of a sample:

$$\text{Amount of uncertainty regarding the average} = \frac{\text{Variance of observations}}{\text{Number of observations}}$$

It happens that one good measure of variance of a sample is σ^2. Consequently we could write our formula:

$$\text{Uncertainty regarding the average} = \frac{\sigma^2}{N},$$

using N to stand for number of observations. In order to make this number more comparable to some other standard statistical formulas, many people prefer to take the square root, getting:

$$\text{Uncertainty (or } \textit{Standard Error}\text{) of the Average} = \frac{\sigma}{\sqrt{N}}.$$

If we get a standard error for each of two averages, we can easily obtain a standard error for the difference between these two averages. If we are uncertain about either average, we are clearly uncertain about the difference between them. Consequently, the standard error of the difference is ordinarily larger than the standard error of either of the averages.

Critical Ratio. When we know the size of the difference and the standard error of the difference, we are in a position to determine the significance of the difference. We merely ask whether the difference is large in comparison with its standard error. We get the clearest idea of this relation by dividing the difference by its standard error. This ratio,

$$\frac{\text{Difference}}{\text{Standard Error of Difference}} \text{ is often called the } \textit{critical ratio.} \text{ As a rule}$$

of thumb, we say that a critical ratio ought to be at least 2.5 or 3.0 before we can be reasonably confident that the difference in our samples actually indicates a genuine difference in the larger groups from which our samples are drawn.

This explanation of the general problem of significance is far from precise. It is something like the "intuitional geometry" which you may have studied in high school. It is merely intended to help you make sense of the matter of significance in a very loose and general way. When you come to study statistics in a more formal course, you will find that the ideas underlying the standard error are based on many precise assumptions that we have not mentioned here. When you do begin the more systematic study of statistics, therefore, you must hasten to throw away the temporary crutch provided by this loose and intuitive approach.

The critical ratio, discussed above, will be used in many early studies that you consult. In more recent investigations, however, you will find refinements of this concept, such as the t test. When we have groups of twenty-five cases or more, t is practically identical with the critical ratio. Under any circumstances it is not so necessary that the student understand the precise methods of interpreting these newer measures. Whenever they are used the author usually supplies the interpretation. He usually gives the t value and then points out whether or not it is significant at the 1 percent level, or at the 5 percent level. If it is significant at either of these levels we can accept it on faith, and feel fairly confident that the difference which he reports is not due to random fluctuations in sampling.

The **F** *Test.* The F test is also used very frequently in modern investigations. If we were merely comparing two groups, F and t would be about the same thing. The F test, however, enables us to test the significance of a whole cluster of differences. It could be used, for instance, if we were comparing the weight of the apples in several different bins, and if we wanted to find out whether or not any of the bins were different from any of the others. If we find that there is some general, over-all difference, then we could use t to test the difference between each pair of bins.

The author who uses F, like the one who uses t, will almost always tell you whether or not it is significant. If he reports that the F value is significant at either the 1 percent or the 5 percent level, you can assume that there is some difference in his cluster of averages which cannot be attributed to sheer chance.

Chi Square. In some investigations you may find that the author uses χ^2 (Chi square) to test the significance of his results. This is frequently used when the subjects in the investigation are not measured but are merely classified. If I wish to find out, for instance, whether certain body builds are prone to certain diseases, I might use χ^2 to tell me whether or not the relations I get could be attributed to chance. Here again, the author who uses this device will probably tell you of its significance.

Actual Significance as Opposed to Statistical Significance. There is a danger of reading too much into statistical significance. This measure does nothing more than tell us whether or not the results reported could be due to random fluctuations in sampling. It does not tell us whether or not the results are of the kind that we must take seriously or that we must do something about. Suppose, for instance, we learn that a random sample of children born in June turn out to have an average IQ of 101.6, whereas a random sample of children born in January have an average IQ of only 99.8. Suppose we learn, further, that this difference of 1.8 has a standard error of 0.3. The difference, being six times its standard error, is highly significant in a statistical sense. It is most unlikely, that is to say, that the difference would vanish if we examined the two large groups from which the samples were drawn. But is the difference significant in a practical sense? Most of us would think not. A difference of this order is not worth worrying about. To how much trouble would you go merely to increase your IQ by 1.8 points?

Results of Several Investigations Combined

Before coming to a conclusion about your problem, try to get the results of several investigations into one table, as in the following illustration:

Investigation	Number of Cases	Grade Level	Gain of Group with Required Attendance	Gain of Group with Optional Attendance	Superiority of Required Attendance Group
Brown (1947)	86	7–9	68.1	73.4	−5.3 *
Margolis (1944)	114	9	44.6	47.7	−3.1
Estay (1943)	72	8	75.0	81.8	−6.8 *
Etc.					
Etc.					

* Difference was significant at the 5 percent level.

An extended table, such as this example, enables us to see the over-all results of several investigations all in one place. By running the eye down the last column, we see a general trend in which the required group is at a disadvantage. Such trends, based on a large number of investigations, are much more convincing than the isolated results of several separate investigations.

It is not often, by the way, that a group of experiments comes out as consistently as those in the illustration. Sometimes, indeed, the results are diverse. They may refuse to follow a single trend and may fail to provide a definite answer to our question. In that case we must accept the fact that there is no clear-cut experimental answer to our problem.

Criticism of the Individual Reports

In the preceding section we have suggested that you may have to take certain things on faith. Do not overdo this, however, and do not take things on faith as a matter of general principle. Many of the studies which you consult may have serious errors. Go over them critically, looking for the pitfalls that were stressed in Chapter 2. Try to distinguish between those errors which may seriously affect the results and those lesser errors which merely detract from experimental elegance. There are many errors which would not affect our interpretation of the results. Do not worry about an error just because it is an error. Worry about it only if you can see some way in which it might alter our interpretation of the results.

Obviously, research is not a simple, all-or-none process. Even with extensive training and careful direction, many investigators still fall into some of the serious pitfalls that beset their path. With all its liability of error, however, and with all its qualifications and cautions, it is clearly worth the tremendous effort involved. To use its products you must be prepared to seek through complex and deceptive storehouses. You must be prepared, too, for occasional disappointment and for considerable uncertainty. But once having tasted the satisfaction of knowing whereof you speak, it is unlikely that you will ever again be content with easy surmise or with the glib expressions of good will which so often pass for educational truth.

Summary

Educational psychology has many more individual facts than can be incorporated into a single text. For this reason it is necessary for the student to be able to run those facts down and make use of them when they are located.

To locate information, make use of any recent handbooks that would

seem to treat the subject. But supplement this with the running biblio-
graphical sources designed to keep us up to date on various questions.
The *Review of Educational Research,* the *Psychological Bulletin,* the
Education Index, the *Annual Review of Psychology,* and *Psychological
Abstracts* should prove most useful in this respect.

In reading the material after it is located, learn to be selective. Concentrate on the results and use the other material only enough to give
meaning to the results. Do not shy away from tables, frequency distributions, or graphs. With some practice you will find these to be marvelous
sources of organized information. For more precise comparisons, or for
numbers to remember, you will have to depend on averages and such
matters as coefficients of correlation.

Whenever we see that two groups differ in a certain score, we must
ask whether or not a difference of that size could come about from sheer
random differences in sampling. To check on this, make use of the tests
of significance ordinarily reported. In the more recent investigations,
the author will ordinarily report whether or not the difference is significant. If it is significant at the 1 percent level or the 5 percent level, we
can assume that it is not merely due to coincidence or to the quirks of
sampling.

SUGGESTIONS FOR FURTHER READING

1. Dahl, Myrtle H., ed. *The implications of research for the classroom
   teacher.* Joint yearbook, Amer. Educ. Res. Assoc., and Dept. Classrm.
   Teach., National Education Assoc., 1939.

   Chapter 3, The interpretation and evaluation of research (Maeh-
   ling, Hilda, and Rankin, P. T.), is an excellent brief description of
   the whole general problem.
2. Tyler, Leona E. *The psychology of human differences.* Appleton-
   Century-Crofts, 1947.

   Chapter 3 of this book gives a very clear account of sampling and
   the troublesome problem of significant differences.
3. Alexander, C., and Burke, A. J. *How to locate educational information
   and data.* Teachers College, Columbia University, 1950.
4. Monroe, W. S., and Shores, L. *Bibliographies and summaries in education to July, 1935.* H. W. Wilson, 1936.

   Valuable aids in finding necessary research. Alexander and Burke
   cover the general problem. Monroe and Shores give specific sources
   for early material.

5. Good, C. V., and Scates, D. E. *Methods of research.* Appleton-Century-Crofts, 1954.

   Chapter 3, like the two preceding references, will prove most useful in locating published material. The entire book is a technical treatment for potential research workers, but is also useful for understanding existing research.

   The following books are also directed to research workers but will prove useful to the reader of research:

6. Barr, A. S., Davis, R. A., and Johnson, P. O. *Educational research and appraisal.* Lippincott, 1953.

7. Whitney, P. L. *Elements of research.* Prentice-Hall, 1950.

8. The National Society for the Study of Education. *The scientific movement in education.* Thirty-seventh Yearbook, Part II, 1938.

Exercises

1. Prepare a bibliography (including some journal articles) on any educational topic that interests you.

2. Summarize two of the articles that make some use of tables, graphs, and estimates of significance.

PART two

Physical and Mental Growth:
The General Pattern of Forces

In Part Two of this book we consider the nature and measurement of physical, intellectual, and academic growth. We also consider the normal course of such growth and the various nonscholastic forces which play a part in such growth.

Essentially, these chapters of Part Two place the child in the teacher's hands. They say, in effect, "Here are some of the traits on which you will be working. Here are the forces that have already been at work and which will continue to affect the student while he is in your charge. Here is the type of growth that ordinarily occurs in these traits. From here on it is up to you."

4

Physical Growth
and the Problem of Health

THE PHYSICAL GROWTH of the child is one of the most dramatic processes that comes under the teacher's eye. The physical changes which take place almost force themselves upon our attention. To see these changes in broad outline we do not have to give elaborate tests or to make elaborate comparisons. We have only to look about us, to observe the children in first one grade and then another, to see an older and a younger brother together, or to watch the changes which take place in any one child.

Although we can hardly fail to notice the dramatic physical changes which take place in school children, we can all too readily overlook their significance. We can notice the loss of the two front teeth and still fail to realize how that loss may affect the youngster who has undergone the change. We may not know whether the loss is most likely to bring enhanced prestige or an embarrassed feeling of being conspicuous. We may notice the adolescent with his gangling arms and legs, protruding from inadequate garments, and we may still be unaware of the complex mixture of pride and diffidence that goes along with these shifts in proportion.

Along with the more obvious physical changes there are many that are subtle or hidden. Without special instruments we would not observe the important changes in physiological efficiency. Hidden glandular changes, too, follow a complex pattern of subtle interaction, the increased activity of one gland stimulating some of its fellows and inhibiting others. In a more practical field, immunities to disease develop or break down, and the response to different diseases changes its pattern.

These physical and physiological changes, whether obvious or hidden, have great significance for the teacher. In the first place the healthy functioning of the physical organism is a prime goal of education. True enough, the teacher has neither the sole responsibility nor even the chief responsibility in this area. The teacher can do much less than the home, the physician, or the community clinic. But the teacher has much residual responsibility, and in the discharge of that responsibility he should have some understanding of the general course of physical development.

At the very least the teacher must be conscious of the health hazards actually presented by the school, since very often the school does act as a possible health hazard. It bring large numbers of children together in close quarters, thus facilitating the ready transfer of germs, vermin, and parasites. It requires of children many "unnatural" activities such as sustained visual attention or prolonged periods of sitting still. By the same token, it deprives them of much of the vigorous physical activity which would be natural under more primitive conditions. Under unfavorable circumstances the school may subject children to poor illumination, poor ventilation, or to conditions which induce poor posture. Under most conditions the schools will impose emotional and intellectual strain, and some of these may have unfortunate physical consequences.

Some of these hazards, of course, can be avoided while others are inevitable to some extent. With regard to the avoidable hazards, the course of the teacher is clear. He should eliminate them. The inevitable hazards, he can keep at a minimum. If he is to conduct school, he cannot prevent children from congregating in closed spaces, but he can reduce the exposure of the majority of children to germs or vermin. If he is to teach, he cannot avoid producing some intellectual and emotional strain. He should make every effort, however, to avoid any more strain than is necessary for legitimate academic goals. He must be on the alert, moreover, to detect strain that is reaching the danger point, and this he must eliminate no matter how necessary it may seem for academic purposes.

It is not enough, of course, that the teacher merely refrain from interfering with the health of the children. Whenever possible he must also take positive steps to increase the physical well-being of the students. Typically the teacher and the school do this in at least three ways. Ordinarily the school provides a good deal of physical training, exercise, and organized sport, intended, among other purposes, to facilitate physical development and to improve health. The school also provides health information and seeks to have the children learn more about diet, first aid, and healthful practices in general. Finally the teacher is on the alert to detect danger signals. He notices symptoms such as a rash, a squint, a persistent cough, or an unusual loss of weight and refers these to the school nurse, the physician, or to the student's parents. There are excellent manuals such as that of Rogers(1) which point out the things to be looked for. Every teacher ought to be familiar with one of these manuals and ought to keep it close by for ready reference.

The physical development of the child has still another significance for the teacher. The child's physical growth is an excellent illustration of growth in general. The pattern of development so readily observed in physical development provides an excellent schema or framework for understanding the other kinds of growth which we will study later. If the general pattern of physical growth is understood, and the pattern is kept in mind, the more subtle forms of growth will also become easier to comprehend. Looking at physical growth, we shall see immediately and in unmistakable fashion many of the characteristics which we shall later laboriously discover in other aspects of growth. In physical growth, for instance, we shall see that constancy in the midst of change which is typical of so many kinds of growth. We shall see the child changing in his physical appearance, but we shall also see that he remains identifiable and recognizable. We shall see in his general over-all appearance something which identifies him as the same but different child we knew years ago. Looking at physical growth, we shall see both changes in size or quantity or amount, and we shall also see changes in proportion, or quality, and this feature too we shall see when we study other aspects of growth. Looking at physical growth, we shall see that various parts of the body mature at somewhat different rates. We see that the child's head grows only moderately after birth whereas his shoulders and hips grow several times as large. Whiskers, on the contrary, grow hardly at all in early life but begin to develop rapidly in adolescence. These differences in age at maximum growth also appear in the development of the intellect and the emotions. But perhaps, most important, in our survey of physical growth we see that the organism remains intact. The different rates of growth are never such as to violate his organic unity. And this unity, in spite of diversity, is also characteristic of the other aspects of growth.

Physical Development

People vary widely in all aspects of physical development and, indeed, in all aspects of every sort of development. In Figure 4-1, for instance,

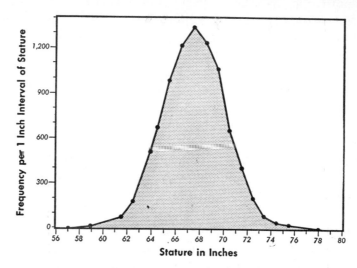

FIGURE 4-1. *Frequency Graph Showing the Distribution of the Height of Adult Males.* Redrawn from *An Introduction to the Theory of Statistics* by Yule and Kendall. Courtesy of Charles Griffin and Co., Ltd., Publishers.

we see a frequency distribution of height of adult males in the British Isles. Here we notice heights ranging from 59 inches to 78 inches. This range of half a yard or so is quite extensive, but, of course, still within very definite limits. The distribution also shows complete coverage between the extremes. Name any height between 59 and 78 inches, and a man can be found to meet that height. There are no abrupt gaps between short men and average men, or between average men and tall men. Instead, we find a steady increase in the number of men as we move from the short to the average, and then a steady decrease in numbers as we

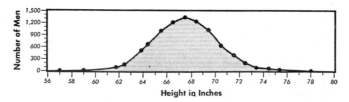

FIGURE 4-2. *Frequency Graph Showing the Effect of Reducing the Vertical Scale*

move from the average to the tall. Do not worry about the proportion of the two scales, by the way. A frequency distribution can be tall and slender, or short and squat, and still tell precisely the same story. Figure 4-2, for instance, is exactly the same as Figure 4-1 as far as information is concerned. The difference in general appearance is due to the arbitrary selection of the scales to be used and is quite unimportant.

Height

Individual Differences in Height. The wide variation in height which is found in adult men is also found in children of both sexes and of all ages. Figure 4-3a shows this variation in the height of boys ranging in age from six to eighteen. Because of the smaller number of cases, these graphs are not so smooth as the graph for the height of adult men. Nevertheless the general form is very similar. For each age group we find a single mode or peak. This mode is located somewhere between the extremes and is flanked by a decreasing number of children toward the extremes.

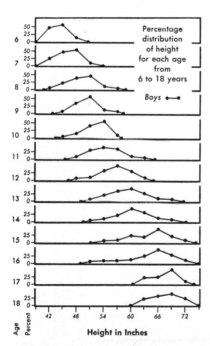

FIGURE 4-3a. *Percentage Distribution of Height of Boys at Different Ages.* Redrawn by permission from Baldwin (2).

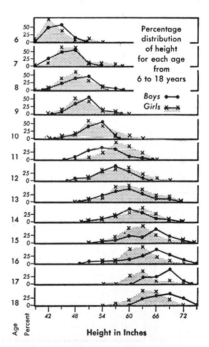

FIGURE 4-3b. *Percentage Distributions of Height for Boys and Girls of Different Ages.* Redrawn by permission from Baldwin(2).

In Figure 4-3b we see a similar set of graphs for girls, superimposed in phantom on the graphs for the boys, for the sake of comparison. The graphs for the girls are much the same as those for the boys. At most ages, the boys and girls extend over approximately the same range. By age eleven, however, the girls tend to pile up somewhat to the right of the boys, indicating a slightly higher average for the girls at this age. By the age of fifteen, on the other hand, the trend is reversed, and the boys begin to pile up to the right of the girls.

The graphs also indicate marked overlapping from age to age. Notice that the tallest six-year-olds equal the height of the shortest eleven-year-olds and that the tallest eleven-year-olds exceed the shortest eighteen-year-olds. Some children entering grade one will be as tall as some of the children in grade five or six. Some of the larger children in grade six will be as tall as the shortest of the high-school graduates.

With a very few exceptions, most of the differences in height are to be regarded as normal. In the face of such wide differences it is ridiculous, of course, to set arbitrary height standards for each age or to expect each child to approximate an arbitrary average as he moves from grade to grade.

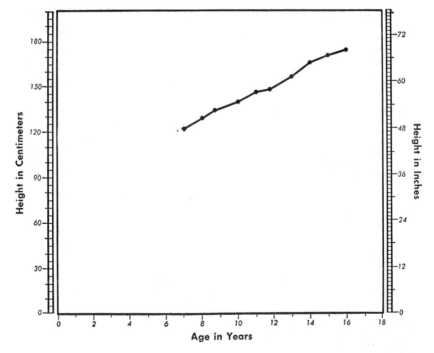

FIGURE 4-4. *Growth in Height for One Boy.* Redrawn by permission from Baldwin(2).

Changes in Height with Age. The graphs in Figures 4-3a and 4-3b give one of the truest pictures of the changes in height with age. In these graphs we see that the distributions move gradually toward the right as the children become older. But we also see that this movement to the right is a gradual and imperfect process. The difference from one age level to the next is never so great as the differences within each age group.

But the growth represented in Figures 4-3a and 4-3b is the growth of a group of children. What does the growth of one child look like? A graph for an individual child is shown in Figure 4-4. Here we find an over-all increase throughout the years, but we also find marked irregularities. Some part of those irregularities, of course, may be due to slight errors of measurement. Part may be due to accidents such as illness during any one year. To some extent, however, the irregularities may represent the true story. Perhaps children really do grow largely by fits and starts. Perhaps a slight gain is followed by a period in which that gain is consolidated, so to speak.

In Figure 4-5 we see an idealized growth curve of an individual boy and girl. The solid line is based chiefly on repeated measurements of a

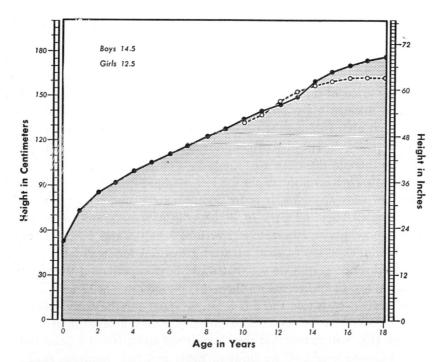

FIGURE 4-5. *Composite Growth Curve Showing Changes in Height for Selected Groups of Boys and Girls.* Data from Baldwin(2) and Shuttleworth(3).

large group of boys who happened to show a typical adolescent spurt at about the same time (14.5 years for this group). The broken line is based on similar measurements of girls who grew most rapidly at 12.5 years of age. Notice, by the way, that the two curves are almost indistinguishable prior to age 11. For both sexes, the curves for the first six years of life are taken from one group of children(2) whereas the curves for six years on are based on a different group(3), but this does not spoil their value as a generalized or idealized picture of growth.

Notice the extremely rapid growth in the early years. The child has attained one quarter of his ultimate height by the time he is born, and one half of that final height by the time he is three years of age. With the exception of the adolescent spurt, the rate of growth decreases fairly steadily. The child continues to grow, of course, but the increase is less from year to year.

The adolescent spurt, already mentioned, is observed in a great many children. That spurt is brought out clearly in Figure 4-5, because each curve is made up only of children who showed such a spurt and showed it at the same time. Most individual growth curves similarly show a short period in which there is more growth than in the recent past. This period of sudden "shooting up," of course, has long been recognized in the lore of common knowledge.

Figure 4-5 shows the period of adolescent spurt for the greatest number of boys and girls. The period of fourteen to fifteen years is the *most frequent* period of maximum growth of boys. Similarly the period from twelve to thirteen is the *most frequent* period of rapid growth of girls. Notice that about the age of twelve the girls in this group forge ahead of the boys. By the age of fourteen, however, the boys overtake the girls, and from then on the average of the boys is clearly higher.

Although Figure 4-5 shows the period of rapid growth for the largest number of boys and girls, it is by no means the period of most rapid growth for all boys and girls. In Figure 4-6 we see a graph for a group of girls who experienced greatest growth at age 10.5 and a second graph for girls who experienced their greatest growth at the age of 14.5. From the second set of graphs we see that some boys experienced the greatest increase at age 12.5 whereas for others this period came at 17 years of age. Notice that in each case there is a larger spurt for the early maturing people (A) than for the people who experience their greatest increase at a later age (B). Notice, too, that the time of the spurt is not a good index of the ultimate height of the student. Early and late maturing students end up at approximately the same height, the differences in these particular graphs being very slight in view of the small size of the sample.

Early maturing boys, however, tend to develop a somewhat less masculine figure than later maturing boys.

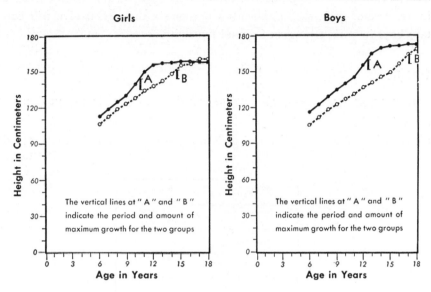

FIGURE 4-6. *Separate Growth Curves for Early and Late Maturing Individuals.* Data from Shuttleworth(3).

Rate of Growth and Sexual Maturity

Height, of course, is only one aspect of maturity, although it correlates fairly closely with several other indices(4). Apart from height, sexual maturity is probably the most dramatic indication of the progress toward adulthood. We find that the period of most rapid growth coincides fairly closely with the onset of sexual maturity. The period between fourteen and fifteen years is the most frequent period of rapid growth for boys and it is the time when most boys report the first seminal emission. Similarly, it is between twelve and thirteen that most girls experience the greatest increase in height and this is the most frequently reported age of first menstruation.

As might be expected, onset of sexual maturity varies widely from one person to another. For girls sexual maturity may occur at any time be tween ten and seventeen years. Among a great many girls in grade four it is possible that one may be sexually mature. From a great many girls in grade eleven, there may be one who has not yet reached the menarche. Each grade between four and eleven will probably contain some girls who have reached this degree of maturity and some who have not. The range for boys is probably equally wide. Judging from body hair, change of voice, and the other secondary sex characteristics that are typically used as indicators of the onset of puberty in boys, we can assume that, as in the case of girls, each grade from five or six through twelve will contain boys in various stages of sexual maturity.

Weight

Individual Differences in Weight. Differences in weight, like differences in height, are quite marked at all ages. Figure 4-7 shows frequency distributions for both boys and girls for each age from six to eighteen.

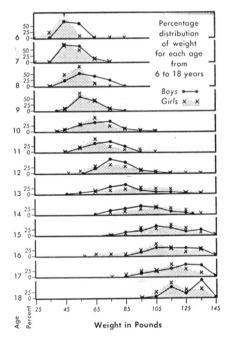

FIGURE 4-7. *Percentage Distributions of Weight for Boys and Girls of Different Ages.* Redrawn by permission from Baldwin(2).

Here we see, for both sexes, a wide range of weights at each age. Indeed, some children at age six are heavier than other children at age sixteen. The distributions are not so symmetrical as those for height, but they do show the familiar tendency to pile up toward the middle part of the range.

Age Changes in Weight. The change in weight of a group of children is shown very accurately in Figure 4-7. Such a figure shows both the gradual increase from year to year and the wide overlapping at each age. The changes in weight for an individual child, of course, are a different matter. A sample curve for one child is shown in Figure 4-8. Such marked

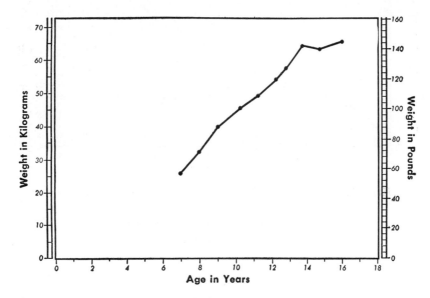

FIGURE 4-8. *Growth in Weight for One Boy.* Redrawn by permission from Baldwin(2).

fluctuations in weight are easy to understand and may be due to a variety of causes. An idealized curve, eliminating the irregular fluctuations, is shown in Figure 4-9. Notice that this curve differs somewhat from the curve for height. The child begins to acquire his adult weight at a much later age. Whereas the child of three has attained half his adult height, he has attained only one sixth of his adult weight. It is not until he is twelve or thirteen that he will reach half his adult weight.

It is obvious, of course, that weight has none of the stability that we can attach to height. Except for the very old, it is hard to think of a reversal in the curve for height. Such reversals, however, are not uncommon in curves for weight. Again, we can expect the teens or early twenties to see the end of growth as far as height is concerned, but we know only too well that increases in weight, far from coming to a halt in the early twenties, may continue to a distressing extent all through middle age.

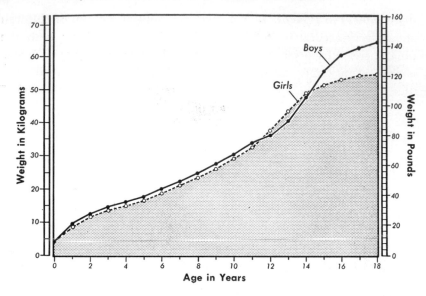

FIGURE 4-9. *Composite Growth Curve Showing Changes in Weight for Selected Groups of Boys and Girls.* Data from Baldwin(2) and Shuttleworth(3).

Proportion

People differ not only in height and weight but also in proportion. This phenomenon has been familiar and important for a long time and is still the subject of much careful inquiry. At any age we find a wide range of body build. Such a range is illustrated by Figure 4-10 showing three boys all aged fourteen years. Between these boys there are marked differences in height and also in weight. But more striking than these differences are the extreme variations in body build. The labels given to each figure are taken from Sheldon(5) and refer to the part of the embryo which seems to contribute most to the individual's build. At a very early stage of its development, the embryo is made up of three different kinds of cells. The cells of the endoderm are in the interior of the spherelike embryo, and these give rise to the digestive and the respiratory system. On the outside of the sphere are found the cells of the ectoderm, and these give rise to the skin and nervous system and sense organs. Inserted between the inner and outer surfaces of the embryonic sphere, we find the mesoderm from which arise the bones, the muscles, the heart, and kidneys.

Using these different parts of the embryo as key points in his system of classification, Sheldon assumes that the *endomorph,* with his bountiful supply of fat and viscera, is dominated by the endodermal layer of the embryo. The *mesomorph,* on the contrary, with his heavy muscles, sturdy bones, and rugged build, is thought to be dominated by the mesodermal cells of the embryo. Finally, the *ectomorph,* with his small fragile bones, his stringy muscles, and his slight build, is assumed to have been affected by the ectoderm of the embryo. The probable origin of the different

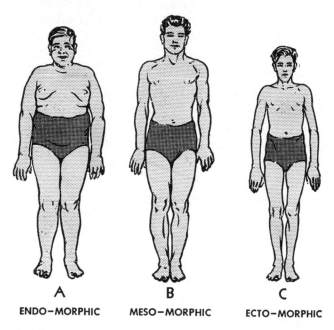

A   **B**   **C**
ENDO-MORPHIC   **MESO-MORPHIC**   **ECTO-MORPHIC**

FIGURE 4-10. *Three Boys Aged Fourteen Showing Extreme Differences in Somatotype.* Reproduced from "Adolescent Changes in Body Build," by Bayley and Tuddenham, Chapter III in *Adolescence,* Forty-third Yearbook of the National Society for the Study of Education, 1944. Courtesy of the Society.

types should not be taken too seriously. The labels themselves, however, will probably be in common use for some time and may as well be mastered.

Somatotypes and Their Components. It would be a mistake to assume that each person must be either an endomorph or a mesomorph or an ectomorph. Sheldon has been most careful to point out that most people are mixtures of different builds. One person, for instance, may be mostly endomorph but may also have some of the characteristics of the mesomorph or the ectomorph. It is customary to rate each person on each characteristic, employing a 7-point scale for the purpose. Thus a somatotype of 6-2-1 would mean that the individual had very many of the characteristics of the endomorph, a trace of the mesomorph, and a minimum of the characteristics of the ectomorph. A somatotype of 4-4-4 would mean that a person was about average with reference to each of these traits.

Obviously the theory of somatotypes is quite elaborate and comprehensive. In its extreme form, as we shall see, it is still under scrutiny and there is much disagreement about its adequacy. Whatever the final decision, however, this theory has emphasized the fact that wide differences in body build are perfectly normal. Along with other work, the emphasis on somatotypes has made us suspicious of height-weight norms that are expected to hold for all students. To guard against this error, devices such as the Wetzel Grid(6) have been worked out whereby each child can be assigned to a growth channel that represents normal progress for one of his build. A marked departure from this channel would be cause for some concern. A departure from the average of all children, however, would cause little or no anxiety provided weight for one of his build is within reasonable limits. Even here, however, we must remember that the channels are somewhat arbitrary(7, 8).

Empirical Factors of Body Build

Kretschmer and Sheldon got their types or components from general observation and from theory. A different group of investigators believe that this is an undependable approach. They ask, "How do we know that there is a single thing such as muscularity? Is it not possible that a man may have muscular shoulders and puny legs? Could a woman be endomorphic with respect to her calves but ectomorphic with respect to her neck?"

General Approach of Factor Analysis. To get an empirical answer to questions such as those just raised, many people make use of factor analysis. This technique is also important in other areas of psychology. We may as well give the general approach the attention that it needs before considering the actual factors that have been reported. This process, by the way, is discussed again in Chapter 5 in connection with intelligence tests. If it is difficult to see how factor analysis makes sense when applied to physical measurements, you might consult the section on intelligence. It may be easier to grasp the process in a different context.

The factor analyst begins by finding out which traits or measurements go together and which do not. In determining such relations, the basic tool, of course, is the coefficient of correlation, considered earlier. To discover factors in physical make-up, for instance, we measure a large number of people in a great many different dimensions. We then find the correlations between each of these things. We find out whether the man who has the longest spine also has the longest thigh and whether the man with the most slender neck also has the most slender waist. We also find correlations between things that we might not expect to go together. Is it possible, for instance, that men with slender waists tend to have heads that are longer than average? Could heavy shoulders go with broad palms?

From the group of correlations we can see measurements that seem to go together and others that seem to have no relation to each other. We might find, for instance, that shoulder muscle, arm muscle, shoulder width, and palm width are all closely related to each other, but that no other measurement is closely linked with any of these. Here then we have a little clique or cluster or *factor*. A man who has a high score on one of these will also have better than average score on all. Knowing about his shoulder muscles, for instance, we could get a fairly good idea of the other three items in the cluster. This knowledge of shoulder muscle, however, would tell us practically nothing about such other measurements as calf muscle, foot width, or arm length.

When definite clusters or factors appear in a table of relationships, we usually give them names. The naming, of course, is not a very precise matter. The cluster we suggested, for instance, might be called shoulder-arm heaviness. We note that it has little to do with arm *length,* or with *heaviness* in the lower part of the body. But this naming process is quite arbitrary. Other people looking at this same cluster might think of a different name.

The method of factor analysis will tell us whether or not there is such a general thing as muscularity, or stockiness, or spindliness that appears in all parts of the body. It might also reveal factors, such as our fictitious shoulder-arm heaviness factor, that may not be suspected on the basis of theory or common sense. These factors, when they appear, also guide our speculations about the underlying mechanisms. Why do four of these things always go hand in hand? Are they all controlled by a single gene? Or by a closely related group of glands? Or is it the type of work one does that affects these four measurements and leaves the other measurements relatively unchanged? In suggesting speculations such as these, our factors can point the way to useful investigations. Finally, if we can establish dependable clusters or factors, we can reduce the number of separate things with which we have to deal.

The process of factor analysis has been applied to a great many problems in psychology and we shall refer to it over and over again in the different sections of this book. The process as actually carried out is much more precise and much more complex than our fictitious example would suggest. For a more accurate idea of this important technique, read one of the more comprehensive treatments listed under Suggestions for Further Reading. Some of these call for a fair knowledge of mathematics. Others demand only elementary statistics.

Factors in Body Build: Results. In the studies of factor analysis(9, 10, 11) we find some support for the theory of somatotypes. The endomorph-ectomorph dimension, for instance, applies to almost all body measurements. If a man has the capacious endomorph chest, he is likely to have the plump endomorph thigh. If he has the ectomorph's lean neck, he is likely to have the ectomorph's spindly legs. If his arms and shoulders place him midway between the ectomorph and endomorph we can expect the rest of his body to conform to this same midway status.

The mesomorph-ectomorph dimension seems to be equally general(12). Knowing a man's general status on this dimension we could expect that most of the separate measurements of his body will also have that same status. We can be less sure, however, that the endomorph-mesomorph dimension is completely general. From the fact that a man's waist is more endomorph than mesomorph, we cannot be sure that his shoulders and head will also be of the endomorph type. One factor analysis(12) has brought out a fourth type called the *omomorph*. This is something like the mesomorph except that the stockiness and muscularity is confined to the upper trunk. Hips and lower limbs are slender and not well muscled.

Typical Changes in Proportion in Growing Children

In a later section we shall ask whether or not an individual child tends to fluctuate with respect to his body type. Does he change from endomorph to mesomorph or does he retain membership in his earlier type? Meanwhile we are concerned with the typical changes in proportion that hold for most children. If we follow a composite or typical child through his first twenty years, for instance, what changes in proportion shall we observe? Obviously, the simple height-weight ratio will change. The newborn child has only 8 or 10 pounds distributed over his 20 inches of length. The eighteen-year-old has some 140 pounds packed away within or around his 70-inch frame. Other marked changes in proportion also occur with age. Many of these are illustrated in Figure 4-11. To the left we see the infant whose head comprises one quarter of his total height, and whose legs make up only one third of his total height. His head is as wide as his chest and almost as wide as his shoulders. The head of course will grow, but will grow much less than the rest of the body, and much of that remaining growth will have occurred by the age of three. The trunk grows very rapidly at first, gradually slowing down in later years. The legs contribute more and more to total height. Whereas at birth the legs make up only 33 percent of the total height, by the age of three they constitute some 43 percent and by the age of fourteen or fifteen (for boys) the legs represent 48 percent of the total height. From fourteen on, the ratio of leg length to total length remains approximately constant, with a slightly greater increase on the part of the trunk.

The change in proportion is almost endless. The trunk loses its flat sides and acquires a waist. Both sexes acquire hips and shoulders, but obviously in different ratios, especially during the teens. The average seventeen-year-old girl has about the same hip width as her taller, heavier twin brother, but there is a marked difference in shoulder width. For every ten inches of height gained between the ages of eleven and seventeen, the boys grow 1½ inches of hip and 2½ inches of shoulder.

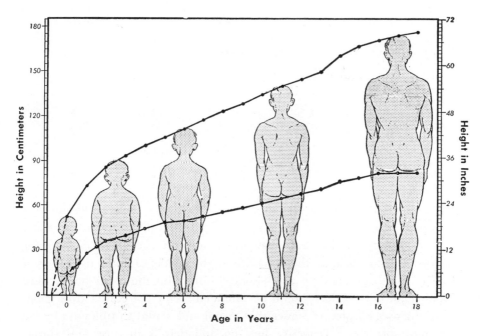

FIGURE 4-11. *Changes in Stature and in Proportion from Birth to Age Seventeen*

In gaining those same 10 inches of height, however, the average girl will grow about 2 inches of hip and only 2 inches of shoulder. Of course girls are less likely to gain 10 inches of height between the ages of eleven and seventeen.

Physical Efficiency

Health

Much more important, of course, than height, weight, or proportion is the matter of health and physical efficiency. The amount of serious physical illness or deficiency is not well known for the whole country. In a complete survey(13) of one county in Kansas, however, it was found that 9 percent of boys and 4.8 percent of girls were suffering from a physical disability of some sort. Of these handicapped children, 6.5 percent did not attend school. The types of difficulty most frequently reported are given in Table 4-1. The different surveys reported there

TABLE 4–1

Percentage of Different Groups Having Certain Defects

	Elementary School Students	Junior and Senior H.S. (Various Groups)	College Students	Men of Military Age (World War II)
Visual defects	19	6–12	11	15
Hearing defects	2	1–2	—	4
Dental defects	33	18–83	70	12
Nose and throat	19	2–6	20	3
Tuberculosis	—	——	0.5	2
Heart & blood vessel	1	1–5	1	5
Underweight	21	6–18	28	7
Overweight	—	——	6	
Hernia	—	——	0.3	5
Diabetes	—	——	0.2	—
Syphilis	—	——	0.3	2

are not strictly comparable, of course, since they cover different age groups. The different surveys were also conducted for different purposes. The examiners of the draft registrants, for instance, were looking for serious defects such as those which might render a man useless as a soldier. The examiners of the school children, on the other hand, were looking for defects that should be attended to for the child's own good.

In the over-all picture we see that visual and dental troubles are by far the most prevalent. Defective hearing and defects in nose and throat come next in frequency, with heart trouble being serious for two of the groups. The diagnosis of overweight or underweight is very difficult. The extreme figure for the college students may be due partly to the fact that in 1939 the examiners allowed only 10 percent departure from the average. Since that time, people have been less disturbed by fairly wide variations from the average.

Changes with Age. In some respects the school years are the healthiest of the whole life span. Looking at the death rate curves in Figure 4-12, for instance, we find that for children under one year there are some

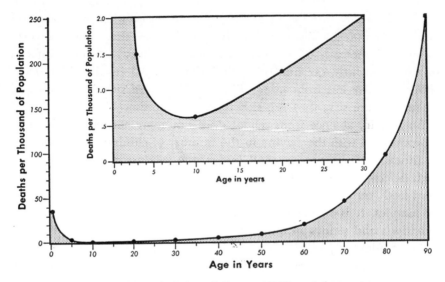

FIGURE 4-12. *Death Rates at Different Ages*

thirty-five deaths per thousand children. For children from one to four this rate drops to 1.6 per thousand. But during the elementary-school period the rate drops still further, reaching a low of 0.7 per thousand for children between the ages of five and fourteen. For the high-school and college years the death rate doubles, reaching a value of 1.4 per thousand, which is also the rate among children from one to four. From this age period, of course, there is a continual rise at an increasing rate. All in all, the period from five to twenty represents the low dip of the curve.

Death rates, of course, tell only one part of the story. The death rate can be very low and yet the health picture may be far from bright. If we follow a thousand young men through their eighteenth year, for instance, we will find only one or two deaths in the whole group, but we will find that some 280 of these thousand young men have defects which render them ineligible for military service. This is a formidable figure for the group which includes most of our high-school graduates. True enough, this figure of 28 percent, high as it is, proves to be lower than the rejection rate for older men. Some 44 percent of thirty-year-olds and 68 percent of forty-six-year-olds were rejected.

During the school period itself, there is an over-all decline in the percent of children who are absent because of illness. Prior to age 10, about 70 percent of children miss one day or more during the year because of illness. By the age of eighteen this figure has declined to 40 percent. This over-all decline does not hold for all diseases. Prior to age 10, there is a fairly steady increase in absence due to measles, chicken pox, and other communicable diseases. This increase is more than offset, however, by marked decreases in the incidence of colds, digestive upsets, infected tonsils, bronchitis, ear infections, and the like. All in all, older school children suffer less from minor diseases. They are sick less often and, when they are sick, they are sick for a shorter time(14, 15).

But, again, absence from school does not represent the whole story. As contrasted with the decline in the number of children absent because of illness, we may note a small but steady increase in the presence of such defects as enlarged thyroid, especially among girls, decay of permanent teeth, certain types of visual defects, and such skin conditions as acne or pimples. It is during the teens, too, that we are most apt to see tuberculosis and serious mental derangements.

As we might expect, Sheldon and his followers believe that somatotype has a great deal to do with the type of illness to be expected. The endomorph must worry about circulatory troubles. The mesomorph has more than his share of accidents, and, as an adult, of ulcers. The ectomorph must deal with a sensitive skin and chronic fatigue.

Physiological Efficiency

In addition to being as free as possible from recognizable defects, a student should have a body that can rise to the many demands that are likely to be placed upon it. The student should be able to take part in strenuous physical activity and feel no ill effect. No student would be considered healthy, no matter how few defects were tallied against him, unless his body could readily do his bidding in all sorts of vigorous activity.

One measure of physiological efficiency is the ability to recover from strenuous exercise. To test this ability, a student is required to run up several flights of stairs, say a total of 60 feet or so, or to step on and off a 20-inch stool some thirty times a minute for 4 or 5 minutes. At the conclusion of the exercise his pulse, blood pressure, and breathing are observed to see how rapidly they return to normal. Gallagher and Brouda(16) have constructed a standard recovery index using pulse rate after exercise. To understand this index let us assume that a boy has been stepping on and off the 20-inch stool for 5 minutes. One minute after he has finished this exercise we count his pulse for 30 seconds, getting (say) 80 beats (160 per minute). Two minutes after the exercise we again count his pulse for 30 seconds getting, say, 70 counts. At 3 minutes after the exercise the count has gone down to 60 (or 120 beats per minute). The index of recovery is

$$\frac{\text{Number of seconds of exercise} \times 100}{\text{Total number of pulse counts} \times 2} = \frac{30000}{(80 + 70 + 60) \times 2} = 70.2$$

This number (70.2) is just about average for high-school boys. In one group of boys the index number ranged from 90, which means a very rapid recovery, down to 40 or lower, which means a very poor recovery. In order to attain an index of 90, the boy's pulse rate 2 minutes after the exercise would have slowed down to 56 beats per minute. The index of 40 means that the boy still had a pulse of 120 beats per minute, 2 minutes after the exercise had ceased.

The complete distribution of the recovery indexes is shown in Figure 4-13. Here we see the typical distribution in which most of the boys pile

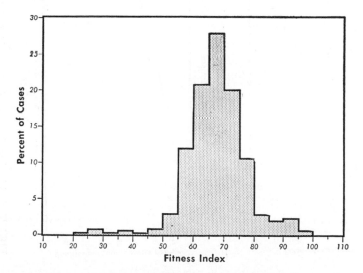

FIGURE 4-13. *Distribution of Degree of Recovery from Strenuous Exertion (Adolescent Boys)*. Redrawn by permission from Gallagher and Brouda(16).

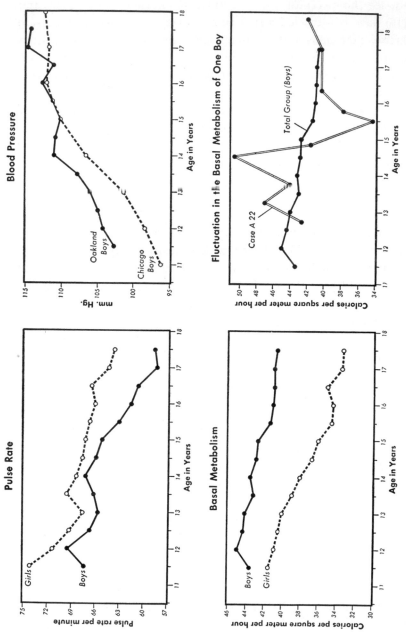

FIGURE 4-14. *Age Changes in Physiological Factors.* Redrawn from "Physiological Changes in Adolescence," by Shock, Chap. 5 in *Adolescence*, Forty-third Yearbook, National Society for the Study of Education, 1944, Part I. Courtesy of the Society.

up almost midway between the extremes. Most of the boys recover at an average rate, leaving a few with an exceptionally good recovery and another small number with very poor powers of recovery.

We must not regard this particular distribution of differences as fixed and settled for all time. Fortunately, powers of recovery can be greatly increased. Gallagher and Brouda(16) report that the boys with low recovery scores will show very definite improvement after a program of graduated exercises. As might be expected, the boys who already have a high index will show less improvement from exercise. Thus, after a period of exercise the range of the differences will be reduced, although a considerable distribution will inevitably remain. Such experiments, of course, should be repeated using a control group who receive no training. In many traits we find that those at the bottom of the scale tend to improve anyhow.

Age Changes in Various Physiological Factors. Apart from the influence of specific exercise, there are regular changes in the basic mechanisms involved in strenuous exertion. Some of these regular changes are shown in Figure 4-14. Here we see a fairly steady decline in pulse rate, counteracted somewhat by an increase in blood pressure. There is also a decrease in oxygen consumption. These three curves, of course, are based on repeated measurements of a *group* of students and thus indicate average changes. No one student can be expected to follow these fairly smooth regular changes. To bring out this fact, the metabolism changes of one exceptional boy have been superimposed on the average curve for a group of boys. Here we see wide fluctuations from time to time. Although this one graph represents an exceptional swing, we should not be surprised to find definite fluctuations in the physiological rhythm of any one student.

So much for the basic mechanisms involved in strenuous exertion. How do these mechanisms respond to exertion for students of different ages? In general, both thirteen-year-old boys and thirteen-year-old girls adapt to strenuous exertion chiefly by a very rapid increase in pulse rate, and secondarily by an increase in blood pressure and in rate of oxygen consumption. The seventeen-year-old boy, on the other hand, relies much less on increase in pulse rate, and much more on increased blood pressure and oxygen consumption. The older girl shows no compensating increase in blood pressure but does show an increase in oxygen consumption. All in all, the younger student, relying as he does on a more flexible mechanism, responds more quickly to the demands of exertion and also returns to normal more quickly after the exertion is over.

Tests of Physical Performance

As a more natural or more direct measure of physical efficiency, specialists have devised many performance tests(17). One such test, described by Cureton(18), is illustrated in Figure 4-15. In this test the

University of Illinois Motor Fitness Test

FIGURE 4-15. *University of Illinois Motor Fitness Test.* Reproduced by permission from Cureton(18).

emphasis is placed on the big-muscle groups and on the vigorous activity of the whole body. The expected performance for college freshmen appears beside each illustration.

Wide differences in physical skill or capacity are to be expected. At the college level, for instance, 36 percent of one group of freshmen "failed" the Cureton test, 24 percent passed conditionally, whereas 40 percent passed satisfactorily. Among other college groups 24 percent were unable to jump an obstacle waist high, 26 percent were unable to chin themselves five times, 3 percent being unable to chin themselves once. In one midwestern college 64 percent were unable to swim 50 yards, and 13 percent were unable to swim across the tank(18). In an eastern college group only 2 percent were unable to swim at all.

Most of the standards just described seem quite moderate. It would seem most desirable that almost all students should attain such minimum competence. Over and above these minimum standards we would welcome wide ranges in proficiency. We can hope, for instance, that almost all our students will be able to swim 100 feet or so. Beyond that minimum, however, we can expect a great variation in competence, ranging from those who just achieve the minimum to those who can swim 25 or 30 miles. It is probable that some students have more capacity for this sort of thing than others. In general, the mesomorph will excel in tests of physical fitness whereas the endomorph is almost always handicapped. The ectomorph is unpredictable(19). He does well in some things but not in others(20).

Growth in Physical Performance. Some representative age changes in physical performance are shown in Figures 4-16 and 4-17 and in the insets. These graphs are drawn from two separate investigations and refer to four different types of activity. One of the investigations followed the children from age 7 to 17 whereas the other obtained successive measures from age 13 to 17. In each case all scores are shown as fractions or percents of male scores at age 17. Thus the performance of boys at age 17 is always 100. The performance of girls at age 17, or of boys younger than seventeen, is expressed as a percent of the score of seventeen-year-old boys.

From the graphs in Figures 4-16 and 4-17, the differences between the sexes stand out very clearly. In both investigations and in all tests of athletic power the boys are ahead of the girls at all ages and are especially ahead during the later years of adolescence. The girls are closest to the boys in speed of running and farthest behind in the distance throw. We notice that in many traits the girls show little improvement after the age of thirteen whereas the boys continue to improve up to the age of sixteen or seventeen.

Undoubtedly these marked sex differences are due partly to sheer physical make-up and partly to practice or motivation. The shorter, lighter girl, with her different distribution of tissue, should not be expected to keep up with her more powerfully built brother. The fact that girls so often fail to improve after thirteen, however, suggests lack of participation as an additional cause of the lower performance. During high school, girls seem anxious to avoid physical education. In grade seven about 7 percent of both boys and girls present medical excuses to escape gymnasium. By grade twelve the figure for boys has not changed

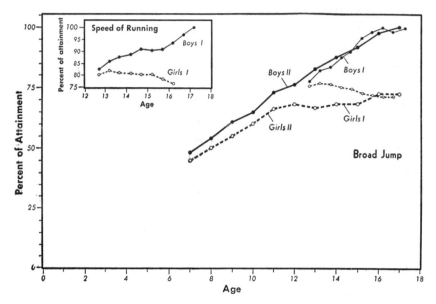

FIGURE 4-16. *Performance of Boys and Girls of Different Ages in the Broad Jump and in Speed of Running (Inset)*

but as many as 24 percent of girls now present medical excuses. Some of this, of course, may reflect a direct increase in physical troubles on the part of girls. Some of it, however, may reflect lack of interest.

Progress toward maturity proceeds at different rates for different traits. By the age of six, for instance, the child has acquired over 60 percent of his ultimate height, but only 30 percent of his mature weight and only 20 percent of his mature strength. By the age of thirteen he has acquired almost 90 percent of his height, 85 percent of his speed of running, but still only 70 percent of his weight and of his ability to "jump and reach." With the exception of speed, the most rapid increase in several track events comes after the age of fifteen.

In considering averages such as these, it is most important to remember the wide spread of performance at each age level. This variation in physical performance is somewhat related to the differences in physiological and sexual maturity. At any given age, for instance, the postpubescents make a higher score than the prepubescents of the same age, and, in general, physical performance correlates more closely with physiological age than with chronological age.

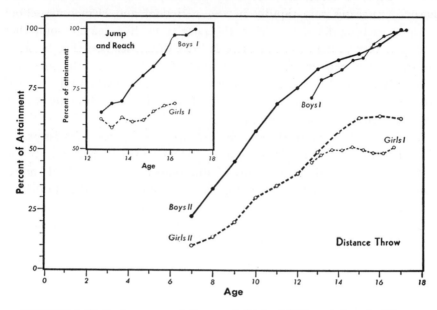

FIGURE 4-17. *Performance of Boys and Girls of Different Ages in Throwing a Ball and in the Jump-and-Reach Test. In Figures 4-16 and 4-17 the performance is represented as the percent of the attainment of eighteen-year-old boys.* Data for Group I are from Anna Espenschade, "Motor Performance in Adolescence," Monogr. Soc. Res. Child Develpm., 1940, 5, No. 1. Data for Group II are from Figures 24 and 25, J. E. Anderson, *The Psychology of Development and Personal Adjustment,* Holt, 1949.

Motor Skill

The performances just discussed emphasize strength, endurance, and the ability to control the movements of the whole body. True enough, skill is an important item, but that skill is used along with strength. There are many other motor performances, however, in which strength is of less importance, but which demand much in the way of speed, dexterity, and precision or coordination. In general, the things we call *motor skill* refer to tasks emphasizing sheer reaction time, tapping, rapid manipulation of levers or cranks, delicate use of fingers as with tweezers or small bolts, steadiness, a good eye with a rifle, and over-all control as opposed to awkwardness(21).

In most skills that have been measured there is a steady increase throughout the school period. As is well known, large muscle skills, involving the use of the whole arm, for instance, mature more rapidly than small muscle skills as shown in rapid movements of the fingers. Sheer speed, or reaction time (as in pressing a key as soon as a light flashes), increases very rapidly in the preschool and elementary-school period, reaching the best speed by the early teens. Boys may be somewhat ahead at very young ages, but there is little difference between the sexes by the age of ten or so. In many tests of coordination the girls are definitely ahead. In general, sex differences are not marked especially if we observe over-all scores on a battery of several tests such as steadiness, two-hand coordination, spool packing, and the like.

When it comes to teaching penmanship, sewing, use of scissors, or similar tasks, there is no single best age to start. Among children of any given age, there will be widespread differences. For each child, more-over, we can say that the longer we wait, the more likely the child is to rise to the demands of the activity. The improvement is gradual, and there is no sudden increase in basic skill. Consequently the decision of when to teach these skills is one which calls for over-all judgment. There is nothing in the scientific literature to point to any age period and say, "This is the time."

The Regulators of Growth

We have seen many different kinds of changes take place in the child's physique as he grows up. This complex pattern is chiefly due to the action of some of the important endocrine glands. A portion of the pituitary gland, for instance, is thought to be the great instigator of growth. This gland also acts on other glands, particularly the sex glands, and stimulates them to action. The sex hormones thus released act on other tissues inducing many of the changes we have noticed. One of the most important functions of the sex hormones is to act back on the pituitary and thus reduce its productivity. Through this complex "feed-back" or "servo-mechanism" the growth process is brought to a halt within reasonable limits. If the sex hormones fail to reduce the activity of the pituitary soon enough, giantism may result.

The role of the sex hormones is far from simple. Both boys and girls produce both types of sex hormones. It is in the over-all pattern of the production of these two hormones that the two sexes differ. As far as the male hormones (the androgens) are concerned, there is a steady increase on the part of both boys and girls, the boys being constantly ahead and, naturally enough, increasing their lead slightly with the years. But the differences are never phenomenal. By the age of fourteen, for instance, the boys produce only about 25 percent more androgens than the girls do. For the estrogens, or female hormones, however, the story is very different. For the first 10 years there is little if any difference between the sexes. After age 10, however, the boys continue their slow increase in estrogen production whereas the girls increase their production tenfold or more. It is this vast increase in estrogen production on the part of the girls which chiefly differentiates the two sexes.

The combination of the two hormones in each individual may have many peculiar results. The frequent appearance of acne or pimples in the adolescent, for instance, has been attributed to the conflicting influence of these two powerful agents.

Present Status as an Indication of Later Status

As we have seen in sample graphs presented earlier, there are marked fluctuations in the growth curves of individual children. This is particularly true for weight curves, since a child may actually lose weight from one period of measurement to another, but it is also true, to some extent, of many other aspects of growth.

Regression toward the Average. Repeated measurements of growing boys and girls have shown that the extremely tall or extremely short children seldom maintain their extreme status at all times. The child who is the very tallest of a group of nine-year-olds will not necessarily be the very tallest of the group at the age of twelve or thirteen. He will tend to move in a little closer to the average at this time. The same is true for the extremely short children at any given time of measurement. Many of these will not hold their extreme position for future measurements but, like their extremely tall opposite numbers, will move in toward the average of the whole group.

This *regression,* or movement toward the average, comes largely from the way chance elements combine or pile up. To be the very tallest in a group, a child must, of course, be basically tall. But he must also have a few chance elements in his favor if he is to exceed another child who is also basically tall. There is a fair chance that this tallest youngster is at the top of his growth spurt, and that he was favored in the inevitable errors of measurement. Now we cannot expect that he will always have the breaks from these chance factors. In subsequent measuring periods, some of the children who profited from chance factors in the first measurement will find those chance factors neutral or against them. All in all, it is difficult to maintain an extreme position especially when that extreme position may be partly due to chance errors of measurement or to chance swings in the cycle of growth.

A Fair Degree of Constancy. Apart from the typical regression toward the average, there is a fair degree of constancy in the growth of children. True, the tallest children do tend to regress toward the average, but they seldom regress *to* that average, and it is very seldom indeed that they regress below it. Although the very tall child will not maintain his extreme status he will remain taller than the average. Children who are above or below average at one period of life will tend to remain somewhat above or below average throughout the growth period.

Naturally enough, in the prediction of height, the adolescent growth spurt makes for complications. This spurt, it will be remembered, occurs at different ages for different people. Thus we may have two thirteen-year-old boys both of whom are above average height, and yet one of these boys may have completed his spurt and the other may not have begun. Obviously it would be risky to predict that these two boys would both have the same height as adults.

Because of the complications introduced by the adolescent spurt, it is much safer to predict adult height from a student's height at age 8 or 9 than age 12 or 13. That is to say, there is a higher correlation between height at age 8 and adult height than between height at age 12 and adult height.

The constancy of physique is clearly important in the theory of somatotypes. Sheldon and his followers believe that the somatotype is determined early in one's development. Diet may produce an emaciated endomorph or an obese ectomorph, but the basic skeletal structure is unchanged. Some investigators doubt that this rigorous constancy can be expected to persist throughout life(22). Over three or four years, however, a fair amount of constancy is observed(10), and with respect to such things as fat deposits in various parts of the body we find a fair degree of constancy during the entire school period(23).

Summary

Good health and adequate physical development are among the most important educational goals. Certainly the teacher must be careful not to interfere with health and, on the positive side, he can take steps to encourage exercise, to provide health information, and to report any danger signals he may observe.

The various aspects of physical development give us our most dramatic evidence of the wide individual differences to be found among children. These differences are most obvious in height and weight, but they are also found in health, in physiological efficiency, and in ability to perform ordinary physical tasks.

Among children of any given age we will find wide differences in all aspects of physical development. On the average, however, there are some fairly regular changes. Height increases very rapidly in the early years, half of the student's adult height being attained by the age of three. The increase is fairly steady except for a definite preadolescent spurt which takes place anywhere between twelve and seventeen years of age for boys and between ten and fifteen years for girls. Sexual maturity is attained about the time of this spurt.

Weight does not increase as rapidly as height does. The child of three who has attained half his adult height has attained only one sixth of his adult weight. The ratio between height and weight has always attracted much attention. The most systematic workers in this field have suggested the existence of three basic types but have also pointed out that each of us is probably somewhat of a mixture of all three types. Factor analysis gives partial support to this suggestion of three types. Knowing about these natural differences in body build, we should be cautious in applying a simple height-weight scale to all children. General body proportion shows marked change with age. As the infant matures his legs become longer with respect to his trunk. His body becomes larger with respect to his head, and finally he (or she) approaches the typical adult figure for his or her sex.

The widespread prevalence of physical defects has caused much concern to educators and laymen alike. At most ages, eyes and teeth account for most of the defects. Hearing defects and diseases of the nose and throat are also important, especially in the earlier years. Measured by absence from school, the health of children increases fairly steadily during the school period. Older children are sick less often and sick for a shorter period of time. The death rate is at its lowest level during the elementary-school period and is doubled during high school and college. Even this latter rate, however, is very low compared to the sharply rising rates after the college period.

About the beginning of adolescence there is a reduction in flexibility of response to vigorous exercise. After strenuous exertion older children return more slowly to normal circulation and respiration. This reduced flexibility is accompanied by an increase in blood pressure.

Performance in various athletic tasks increases fairly steadily, boys regularly excelling girls, especially in later adolescence. Except for speed of running the most marked improvement in many track events comes after the age of thirteen or fourteen (for boys). A fair number of college freshmen cannot swim, cannot chin the bar more than once or twice, and can get around an ordinary obstacle course only with marked effort.

Growth and physical change, affected as it is by a complex interaction of glands and hormones, shows a fair degree of consistency. A very tall boy at the age of nine will be above average as an adult, although he will not stand out as markedly at that age.

SPECIFIC REFERENCES

1. Rogers, J. F. What every teacher should know about the physical condition of her pupils. *U.S. Office of Education Pamphlet No. 68*, 1945.
2. Baldwin, B. T. The physical growth of children from birth to maturity. *Univ. Iowa Stud. Child Welfare*, 1921, *1*, No. 1.
3. Shuttleworth, F. K. The physical and mental growth of girls and boys age six to nineteen in relation to age at maximum growth. *Monogr. Soc. Res. Child Developm.*, 1939, *4*, No. 3.
4. Nicolson, A. B., and Hanley, C. Indices of physiological maturity: derivation and interrelationships. *Child Develpm.*, 1953, *24*, 3–38.
5. Sheldon, W. H., and others. *The varieties of human physique; an introduction to constitutional psychology.* Harper, 1940.
6. Miller, K. D. Wetzel grid as a performance classifier with college men. *Res. Quart.*, 1951, *22*, 63–70.
7. Kallner, A. Growth curves and growth types. *Annales Padiatrici*, 1951, *177*, 83–102.
8. Garn, S. M. Individual and group deviations from "channel-wise" grid progression in girls. *Child Develpm.*, 1952, *23*, 193–206.
9. Howells, W. W. Factors of human physique. *Amer. J. phys. Anthrop.*, 1951, *9*, 159–191.
10. Hammond, W. H. The determination of physical type in children. *Hum. Biol.*, 1953, *25*, 65–80.
11. Howells, W. W. A factorial study of constitutional types. *Amer. J. phys. Anthrop.*, 1952, *10*, 91–118.
12. Sills, F. D. A factor analysis of somatotypes and their relationship to achievement in motor skills. *Res. Quart.*, 1950, *21*, 424–437.
13. Barker, L. S., and others. The frequency of physical disability in children: a comparison of three sources of information. *Child Develpm.*, 1952, *23*, 215–226.

14. Collins, S. D. A general view of the causes of illness and death at specific ages. *U.S. Publ. Health Reports,* 1935, *50,* 237–255.

15. Wilson, C. C., and others. A study of illness among grade school children. *U.S. Publ. Health Reports,* 1931, *46,* 1801–1823.

16. Gallagher, J. R., and Brouda, L. Physical fitness—its evaluation and significance. *J. Amer. med. Ass.,* 1944, *125,* 834–838.

17. Hewitt, J. E. Achievement scale scores for high school swimming. *Res. Quart.,* 1949, *20,* 170–179.

18. Cureton, T. K. The unfitness of young men in motor fitness. *J. Amer. med. Ass.,* 1943, *123,* 69–74.

19. Bookwalter, K. W., and others. The relationship of body size and shape to physical performance. *Res. Quart.,* 1952, *23,* 271–279.

20. Willgoose, C. E., and Rogers, M. L. Relationship of somatotype to physical fitness. *J. educ. Res.,* 1949, *42,* 704–712.

21. Fleishman, E. A. A factorial study of psychomotor abilities. Personnel and Training Research Center, Lackland AFB, *Res. Bull.,* 1954, No. 54, 15.

22. Hunt, E. E. Human constitution: an appraisal. *Amer. J. phys. Anthrop.,* 1952, *10,* 55–73.

23. Reynolds, E. L. The distribution of subcutaneous fat in childhood and adolescence. *Monogr. Soc. Res. Child Developm.,* 1950, *15,* No. 2.

SUGGESTIONS FOR FURTHER READING

1. Carmichael, L., ed. *Manual of child psychology.* Wiley, 1954.
   Chap. 5. Physical growth. (Thompson, Helen)
   Chap. 11. The adolescent. (Horrocks, J. E.)
   Includes material on physical growth as well as general development.

2. Shuttleworth, F. K. The adolescent period: a pictorial atlas. *Monogr. Soc. Res. Child Developm.,* 1949, *14,* No. 59.

3. Walker, H. *Health in the elementary school.* Ronald, 1955.
   A helpful book, directed to the classroom teacher.

4. Jensen, K. Physical growth. *Rev. educ. Res.,* 1952, *22,* 391–420.
   Useful as a compact account of work that is going on and as a source of specific references.

5. Stolz, H. R., and Stolz, Lois M. *Somatic development of adolescent boys.* Macmillan, 1951.
   A careful follow-up of a group of boys over a period of years. A complete account of bodily development during adolescent years.

6. Sheldon, W. H. *An atlas of men.* Harper, 1954.

7. Sheldon, W. H. *Varieties of delinquent youth.* Harper, 1949.

   For illustrations of different somatotypes and for Sheldon's views on the relation of somatotype to delinquency and disease.

8. Eysenck, H. J. The logical basis of factor analysis. *Amer. Psychologist,* 1953, *8,* 105–114

9. Adcock, C. J. *Factorial analysis for nonmathematicians.* Cambridge University Press, 1955.

   Eysenck and Adcock present nontechnical accounts of the general principles of factor analysis. For more complete accounts consult Cattell, Thomson, or Vernon (below).

10. Cattell, R. B. *Factor analysis; an introduction and manual for the psychologist and social scientist.* Harper, 1952.

11. Thomson, Sir G. H. *The factorial analysis of human ability.* Bickley, Kent, Eng.: University of London Press, 1950.

12. Vernon, P. E. *The structure of human abilities.* Wiley, 1950.

13. Munn, N. L. *The evolution and growth of human behavior.* Houghton Mifflin, 1955.

    Physical growth gives a clear illustration of the continuity of development that is found in other aspects of growth. Munn's book provides a clear account of this continuity in behavior. Chapter 10 also gives a detailed account of motor development.

14. Jones, H. E. *Motor performance and growth.* University of California Press, 1949.

    Comprehensive report of the author's investigations.

15. *Review of Educational Research,* 1953, Vol. 23, pp. 453–507.

    These sections treat the prevalence of various handicaps, their educational significance, and methods of dealing with them. The following handicaps are covered:

    Auditory and speech, pp. 453–475 (DiCarlo, L. M., and Amster, W. W.)

    Visual, pp. 476–491 (Meyerson, L.)

    Orthopedic, pp. 492–507 (Hollinshead, M. T.)

16. *Midcentury White House Conference on Children and Youth.* Health Publication Institute, 1951.

    An interesting collection of charts and graphs including graphs on health and disability in children.

17. Zahl, P. A., ed. *Blindness.* Princeton University Press, 1952.

    A source book on many phases of this handicap.

18. National Society for the Study of Education. *Adolescence.* Forty-third Yearbook, Part I, 1944.

An important collection of articles on physical and physiological changes during this period.

Exercises and Questions for Discussion

1. All the children in an eight-year elementary school are lined up according to height. Would it be possible to find two children standing next to each other who differ by as much as two years in age? more than three years?

2. To what extent and under what conditions can you tell how tall a student will be when he reaches his full growth?

3. List some of the physical abilities (e.g., swimming 80 feet) that you think almost every student should possess. Would you differentiate between the standards for boys and for girls? For each skill indicate the age at which the standard might be attained.

4. Discuss the teacher's responsibility in the matter of ventilation; in lighting.

5

Growth in Intelligence and in the General Use of Symbols

IT IS MOST IMPORTANT for the teacher to know something about the nature of intelligence and about the various systematic investigations designed to throw light on this subject. As everyone suspects, there is a very close relation between intelligence and the scholastic growth which the teacher is expected to induce. The two are so closely intertwined, in fact, that it would be foolish to try to understand academic growth without considering the nature of intelligence.

Over and above its bearing on academic achievement, intelligence is most important in its own right. One of the greatest boons the teacher could confer on humanity would be to foster, to detect, and to unleash the intellect of his students. Whether or not the teacher can greatly alter the intelligence of a child is a question we shall consider later on. But whatever the answer to that question, we can be sure right now that the teacher can detect intellect and can guide people of different intellectual endowments into more efficient use of their talents. In this way the intelligence of the group will become more available and more effective, whether or not it ever actually increases.

The Nature of Intelligence

The Problem of Definitions

"When *I* use a word," Humpty Dumpty said in a rather scornful tone, "it means just what I choose it to mean—neither more nor less."

"The question is," said Alice, "whether you can make words mean different things."

"The question is," said Humpty Dumpty, "which is to be master—that's all."

A definition may be used to serve either one of two purposes. It may be used to clarify a term, perhaps giving us some insight into the phenomenon described by the term. If I ask for a definition of science, for instance, I may want a definition which will make me feel that I know more about science. I may welcome such a definition as, "Science is the orderly arrangement of human knowledge," or, "Science is the attempt to make the chaos of the external world conform to some systematic categories of thought." Such definitions sound good and may make me feel, "Yes, that is what I mean."

The other purpose of a definition is to delimit a term, to make sure that everyone concerned understands the particular way in which a term is to be used. According to this latter purpose, a definition of democracy, for instance, would not be intended to give me a warm glow of understanding. It would, on the contrary, merely tell me which of the many meanings often associated with the term we are going to use in this particular discussion. The best illustrations of definitions of this sort come from the field of physics. An "ohm," for instance, may be defined as the resistance offered by a column of mercury 14.4521 grams in mass, of a constant cross-sectional area, and a length of 106.3 centimeters. Now this gives me precious little insight into the inner nature of an ohm. But it does enable me to identify an ohm when I come across one.

Definitions Aimed at Clarifying the Meaning of Intelligence

A great many definitions of intelligence belong to the "clarifying" type first described. Intelligence has been defined as (a) the ability to carry on abstract thinking, (b) the ability to adapt to new situations, (c) the ability to adjust to environment, (d) as intellect plus knowledge, and as (e) a biological mechanism by the effects of which a complex group of stimuli are brought together to act on behavior in a unified way.

Perhaps the most systematic work along this line was done by Spearman(1). Spearman held that intelligence is essentially the perception of relations, especially the perception of difficult or subtle relations. He believed that when two objects or ideas are present we immediately see the relation between them. When an object is presented along with a relationship, we immediately think of the related object. The more intelligent person will see more relations. He will see relations which are too subtle for other people. He will see them more quickly. Also, when he sees a group of relations he will be more impressed by unique and intrinsic, or essential, relations and less impressed by frivolous or incidental relations. Of all the relations between "bat and ball," for instance, he will be especially concerned with the essential relation of striking and being struck. He will not be impressed by the fact that both words begin with "b" or that both have weight or that boys play with them.

These definitions just discussed are the kind of definitions which most of us like. They are the kind of definitions which, by a few words, try to elucidate a phenomenon or give us insight into the phenomenon and send us away with a feeling of understanding.

A Down-to-earth View of Intelligence

Definitions such as those just described do very well when we merely intend to discuss the subject of intelligence. They can be somewhat misleading, however, when we set out to consult a specific investigation. Suppose, for instance, that we are about to consider an investigation in which the intelligence of boys and girls has been compared. What ideas shall we associate with this word intelligence as we read the study? Would it be safe to assume that intelligence means the ability to do abstract thinking or the ability to adjust to the environment? This might be going too far. Actually we cannot be sure that the intelligence that we shall read about actually measures these things. Maybe somebody *hoped* it would, but that is a different matter.

In interpreting the results of tests actually given, we may prefer to be exceedingly cautious and to stay as close as possible to the things we can be sure of. What can we be "sure of" in connection with this intelligence our investigator has studied? The thing he actually observed was performance on a particular test. We can say with considerable confidence, "On this test that was used, there was no significant difference between the scores of the boys and the girls." If we accept this we are on fairly safe ground. As we move farther and farther from this statement, however, we are depending more and more upon inference and surmise.

Facing a problem such as this, many people hold that we should *start* with the known thing that we can agree on, and move beyond it cautiously, one step at a time, being clearly aware of the inferences we are making as we progress. According to these people, we should first of all identify intelligence as the sort of thing that is revealed by a specified group of tests. Having done that, we can look at the tests and see what general traits they seem to measure. When we read that these two groups differed, or did not differ, in intelligence, we should say, "We know that the two groups got identical, or different, scores on the Brant Mental Level Test. From the results of other investigations we believe that this instrument measures chiefly speed, ability to deal with verbal relations, and numerical ability."

This latter approach is the one you are urged to take here. In reading about investigations of intelligence, try to keep in mind that, basically, this means intelligence-test score. Later we shall try to see what intelligence-test score seems to mean. This approach is all the more workable in the field of intelligence since the different tests in this area are very similar. When we come to understand what one test means, we shall also have a fair idea of what the others mean.

Intelligence as Measured by Tests

Individual Intelligence Tests

The most influential development in the history of intelligence testing was the work of Alfred Binet in the early years of the twentieth century(2). Prior to Binet's work, many psychologists had tried to find a single touchstone test, a simple "open sesame," which would provide an index of intelligence. It seemed natural, for instance, to suppose that the key might be in the size of brain or the speed of neural reaction or in some other single item. Perhaps, from our modern vantage point, these approaches seem somewhat simple or naive. At any rate they missed fire and were abandoned.

Binet's approach was the direct opposite of that of his predecessors. Instead of trying to find a single index of intelligence, he went to the other extreme and deliberately searched for a multiplicity of indexes. He reasoned that if we are looking for a *general* intelligence we will have to see how it manifests itself in a great variety of activities. In our search for general intelligence we must be careful not to base a decision on only one or two performances as these might not be representative of a person's general ability.

Binet's first sample of performances included such simple items as pointing to the nose, eyes, and mouth on request; drawing a picture of some simple object; repeating short sentences; and telling the last name.

It also included more difficult tasks such as distinguishing between closely related abstract terms (pity–justice). In general the items were not chosen from any scholastic subjects. True, older children were expected to be able to read, but no item was chosen from the detailed facts of history or geography or mathematics. No special training was presumed. Indeed, we can say that practically every child tested by Binet would have encountered the experience necessary to give him proficiency on these tests. Such, at least, has been the hope of Binet and his successors.

Another important aspect of the Binet tests was their emphasis on age. Binet found that age was one of the most convenient methods of describing and defining the level or the difficulty of his tests. Some items, for instance, could be performed by most four-year-old children but by very few three-year-olds. These tasks were said to be at the four-year level. Any child who could perform these tasks and only these, would be said to have the same ability as the typical four-year-old. This would be true no matter what his actual chronological age.

The Binet tests, with this emphasis on variety and on age as a criterion of ability, have been greatly expanded, enriched, and refined by many other investigators. The chief improvements have been made by Professor Terman of Stanford University. The early "Stanford Revision of the Binet" (Stanford-Binet), published in 1916, remained the great standard intelligence test for twenty years. In 1937 it was further extended, recalibrated, and expanded. In this revision many tasks are presented. The presentation is either oral or by gesture or by print. The age level of each task is carefully worked out. Copying a complex design from memory, for instance, is a ten-year-old task. Pointing to the mouth on request is a three-year-old task. Naming a simple object such as chair, bed, or house, is a two-year-old task. Repeating a series of numbers which has been read aloud such as 6, 9, 4, 8, 2, 7 is assigned to the ten-year level.

These test items are, for the most part, highly verbal, and hence are unsuitable for people who are not at home in the language. For such people, nonlanguage tests have been devised. Such tests may use form boards, puzzles, pictures, or diagrams. The pictures may be imperfect and require completion. They may constitute a series of items with one discordant element to be crossed out. They may represent the materials with which the subject is to carry out directions given by gesture or example.

During the years there have been many modifications and versions of the Binet tests. The Wechsler-Bellevue Intelligence Scale, for instance, was designed to measure the intelligence of adults. Like the Stanford-Binet, this contains subtests in such things as detecting similarities in words, vocabulary, general information, repeating numbers, arranging pictures, completing pictures, assembling objects that have been taken apart, and mastering a simple code. It is possible to get separate scores for the group of subtests dealing with words and for the group of subtests that emphasize manipulation rather than language. The fact that a person may do much better on some subtests than others may be some indication of mental deterioration or other mental difficulties. This test, originally devised for adults, has been extended downward to produce the Wechsler Intelligence Scale for Children (WISC). This is intended to be used for children as young as five years, although there is some question that it is really applicable to the five-year-old.

Group Tests of Intelligence

The Binet tests and many of the nonlanguage tests can be given to only one child at a time. Most of them must be given by a trained tester. They are, therefore, slow and costly. When large numbers of children are to be tested, we usually employ a group test. These group tests may be either highly verbal tests or nonlanguage tests.

It is the verbal group test which has been used most widely. Most of the statements which we will make later on will be based on the results of these verbal group tests. Although these tests are undoubtedly painfully familiar to every reader of this text, we give a few arbitrary examples just as a reminder.

Arithmetic.
  Select the correct answer for each of the following questions:
  Mr. Johnson planted 85 acres in five days. What was his daily average?
  (a) 8.5 acres   (b) 10 acres   (c) 17 acres   (d) 21 acres
Broken Sentences.
  In these sentences the words have been jumbled up. Decide whether the original sentence was true or false.
  Freight to used are carry trucks. True   False
Completion.
  Select the best word to complete the following sentences:
  The wife of a marquis is called a —.
  (a) marchioness   (b) duchess   (c) queen   (d) princess
Number Series.
  Find the pattern in the series of numbers and select the number which should come next.

6   9   7   10   8   ——

(a) 8   (b) 9   (c) 11   (d) 13

In addition to these few samples, the reader will remember many other items. Since World War II, for instance, block counting has been used a good deal. In this test, a drawing of an incomplete pile of blocks is shown, and the student is asked to determine how many blocks are actually there. Tests of ability to see similarities in complex designs are also used fairly frequently.

Mental Age and the IQ. Like the original Binet tests, many of the later individual and group intelligence tests are calibrated in terms of age. Whenever a student succeeds on a certain item, or gets a certain score, we can look in a *table of norms* and find the age level of that item or that score. Suppose, for instance, our student has taken a group test and has correctly answered forty-two items. We look up 42 in a table of norms for this particular test and find that it corresponds to a mental age of nine years and four months. What does this mean? It means that, by actual trial, 42 is the typical score made by children who are nine years and four months old. Our student, then, makes the score that is typical of the child of nine years four months. He can do the tasks which the average child of nine years four months can do. We say that his mental age is nine years four months.

Notice that the mental age is determined entirely by the student's performance on some test. It has nothing to do with his actual age. As yet, we have completely ignored the actual chronological age of the student in our illustration. And yet we know that his mental age is nine years four months. His chronological age may be six years or it may be twelve or it may just happen to be nine years four months.

It is most important to realize that mental age is determined entirely by the performance on a test and by a table of norms. It is important because we are likely to have a great deal of confidence in such a thing as age. After all, age is one of the most substantial things about a person. However much his health or his success or his temperament may fluctuate, his age goes on most steadily. It is not something which can fluctuate violently from day to day. If we are not careful we are likely to invest mental age with this same comforting stability. We are likely to think of it as a very substantial something which moves along steadily. And this would be most misleading. Far from having the comforting stability of chronological age, the mental age will fluctuate as markedly as the test score does.

When we have found out the mental age that describes the score of our student, we are bound to compare it with his actual age. On this test, for instance, our student is performing at the level of the nine-year-four-month-old child. If his actual chronological age happens to be in the neighborhood of nine or ten years, this should cause us no surprise. Things are about as we might expect them. Suppose, however, that the child is only six years old chronologically and is still performing at the level of the typical child of nine or more. In this case, of course, we have a very bright child. It may have happened, on the other hand, that the child who was tested was considerably older than nine years. If he had been twelve years old, for instance, and was still performing at the level of a nine-year-old, we would consider him a dull child.

Obviously the relation between a child's actual age and his mental age provides a good index of his general brightness. It is to make that index more precise and systematic that the *intelligence quotient* or familiar IQ is used. The IQ is the ratio of the child's mental age to his chronological age. It is given as follows:

$$IQ = \frac{MA}{CA} \times 100$$

A child with an MA of nine years four months and a chronological age of six years would have an IQ of:

$$\frac{9 \text{ years } 4 \text{ months}}{6 \text{ years}} \times 100 \text{ or } \frac{112 \text{ months}}{72 \text{ months}} \times 100 \text{ or } 156.$$

Now work out the IQ of a twelve-year-old child with the same MA. It should be 78.

A nine-year-old child with a mental age of nine years and four months has an IQ of:

$$\frac{112}{108} \times 100 \qquad \text{or } 104.$$

The IQ is simply an index of relative standing. A high IQ means that the child is doing as well as children somewhat older than he is. A low IQ means that he is doing no better than a somewhat younger child. The IQ, of course, has no *absolute* meaning. Unless we also know the chronological age, the IQ gives us no index of the level of work the child should attempt. If I tell you that Sam has an IQ of 120, you only know that he is somewhat in advance of his years. You have no idea of his absolute standing. He may be a ten-month-old baby who is performing as well as the typical child of one year. He may be a five-year-old showing the same achievement as a typical six-year-old, or he may be a ten-year-old who performs at the level of a child two years older.

Limitations of Mental Age Scales. As long as children are still growing, the mental age index proves to be of great value. It helps give some meaning and some common-sense status to the arbitrary test scores. For older students and for adults, however, the concept of mental age is less valuable. Although most of us have a fair picture of the mental prowess of a two-year-old in contrast to the one-year-old, few of us have a comparable picture of the difference between the twenty-one-year-old and the twenty-two-year-old. Perhaps, indeed, there is no difference—a matter we will discuss in a later section. At any rate the concept of mental age loses its value for people in the later teens and beyond.

Since the concept of mental age is of little use for older high-school students or college students or adults, some other device is necessary to give meaning to the scores of these people. Most of these devices show how any one person stands in relation to some group average. In the Wechsler tests, and in the tests used in the armed services, a score of 100 means that a person is just average. A score of 115 means that this person is one standard deviation above the average. A score of 85 would mean that he is one standard deviation below the average. There is no necessary reason, of course, why one standard deviation should be represented by 15 points. This number was chosen, somewhat arbitrarily, because it gives a distribution very similar to the older and better known IQ. The Wechsler Intelligence Scale for Children, by the way, also uses such a deviation score for younger children, even though, with these children, we could get an MA and from that, a regular IQ. As we might expect, these two ways of getting a score do not always show perfect agreement. With children the Wechsler tends to give somewhat lower IQ's than the Stanford-Binet(3). The deviation score, moreover, does not provide for extremely low IQ's (below 40) or extremely high IQ's (above 160).

Instead of using a deviation score that is translated into numbers resembling IQ's, many people prefer a direct ranking system. Suppose, for instance, that a certain college student got 137 items correct on the American Council Psychological Examination (a very popular intelligence test). What does that mean? We look up the table of norms and find that 137 corresponds to a *percentile rank* of 92. This latter number means that my student excelled 92 percent of all the students who were used to standardize the test. A second student gets a score of 86 items.

This gives him a percentile rank of 26, meaning that he excelled the scores of 26 percent of the standardization group.

Factor Analysis of Intelligence-test Performance

In an attempt to get a down-to-earth idea of the kind of intelligence which is actually investigated, we have surveyed very briefly the general types of intelligence tests. But this leaves us with a very diffuse and sketchy picture of the nature of intelligence-as-measured-by-tests. We feel the need of a neater, more compact, and systematic view of this ability to get a high score on intelligence tests. We cannot carry around a picture of all the concrete tests that have been used. We need a few general, abstract descriptions.

In our attempt to get a more systematic picture of intelligence-test performance, we could, of course, merely inspect a variety of tests and decide on the basis of common sense what they seem to measure. We will get a much more precise idea, however, if we use the technique of factor analysis which is described in Chapter 4. It was in connection with intelligence-test performance, as a matter of fact, that the techniques of factor analysis were first developed. After they were developed in this field they were applied to other problems such as body build, personality, and a whole host of other phenomena.

The Possibility of a General Factor in Intelligence. In the study of intelligence there has been a great deal of interest in the possibility of a single general factor that may underlie all aspects of intelligence. The interest in a general factor comes partly from common sense, logic, or theory, and partly, perhaps, from accidents of history. In our common sense discussions, we often assume that intelligence is a single thing. We ordinarily consider that a person is intelligent in general or not intelligent in general. The earlier investigators, it will be remembered, actually tried to find a single test that would reveal this thing called intelligence. Some of our interest in a single, general factor, however, may also come from the fact that the man who first developed the techniques of factor analysis was an enthusiastic believer in the existence of a general factor. The early work in factor analysis, as a matter of fact, had many of the attributes of a vigorous and spirited controversy between Spearman and all comers(4).

Suppose we give a group of students an intelligence test made up of the four subtests arithmetic (*a*), broken sentences (*b*), completion (*c*), and number series (*n*). We then work out correlations between these subtests. We find that the correlation between c and n, for instance, is .72. If a student does well in c then he also does fairly well in n. If another student does poorly in c, we can be reasonably sure he will do somewhat poorly in n. Suppose we find that the whole set of correlations is as follows:

c and n	.72		
c and b	.63	n and b	.56
c and a	.54	n and a	.48	b and a	.42

Here we find that there is some correlation or resemblance between all subtests but that there is much more resemblance between some pairs than between others. To explain this cluster of relations we could call upon either the theory of the *general factor* or upon the rival theory of *group factors*. In its extreme form the theory of group factors would say that there is one thing that links c and n and something quite different that links c and b. The theory of the general factor, on the other hand, would say that it is the same thing (g) that links all the pairs, but that subtest c happens to have a lot of g, n has somewhat less, b still less, and a least of all.

This whole issue is something like the situation we might face if we had to speculate about the conversational interests of four club members C, N, B, A. We "clock" C, for instance, and we observe that 72 percent of the time that he is engaged in conversation N is also taking part in that conversation. We notice that B is present in 63 percent of the conversations. In the same way let us consider each of the resemblances previously listed as the extent to which any two of the men converse with each other. Here we could imagine either that the bond between C and N was one thing, say interest in fishing, whereas the bond between C and B was something else, say politics. We could imagine a separate common interest for each of the six pairs. Or we could imagine that it was the same topic, interest in baseball, that linked each pair, but that this interest was strongest in C and weakest in A. Suppose, for instance, that 90 percent of C's leisure conversational interests revolve around baseball, that 80 percent of N's interests concern this subject, and that the corresponding figures for B and A are 70 percent and 60 percent respectively. Under these circumstances there would be a 72 percent chance, (.90) (.80), that whenever C and N get together they would both happen to be interested in baseball. Similarly we would find that C and B would happen to share this interest on 63 percent of their meetings, and that each of our observed common interests could be calculated precisely from the extent of each man's interest in baseball. The whole cluster of relations could be explained by this one common interest. Prevent these men from talking about baseball and the cluster of relations would vanish. The men would spend no more time together than would any four club members drawn at random.

Resemblances between tests almost never fall into the nice neat pattern that appears in our cluster of relations. If they did, there would be less likelihood of controversy. It would be most convenient to imagine that a single common factor was at work. But typically we find that a small group of tests will have more in common than we could explain by the presence of *g*. Subtests *n* and *a,* for instance, might really go together to the extent of .60 instead of the .48 that comes from the presence of *g*. Where does this additional resemblance come from? These two tests must have something in common over and above the general influence of *g*. Seeing that *n* is number series and that *a* is arithmetic we might guess that this additional something they have in common has to do with the emphasis on numbers. Such a factor which is present in a smaller *group* of tests (in this case a group of two), but not present in all tests, is called a *group factor*.

Multiple-factor Theories of Intelligence. In most investigations of intelligence tests, we find that we cannot get along entirely on the basis of *g*. We almost always have to bring in some group factors. Now it has occurred to some theorists that, since we need group factors anyway, perhaps we could get along with group factors alone. Perhaps the group factors might not only supplement the general factor but might actually replace it. Perhaps the group factors should be called upon, not only to explain the excess relationship between tests, but to explain the entire relationship.

The possibility of doing away with *g* altogether resulted in a vigorous controversy. On the one side were the followers of Spearman who believed that the resemblance between tests should be explained primarily in terms of *g* and only secondarily in terms of group factors. On the other side were those who believed that all the observed relationships should be explained primarily in terms of group factors. According to these latter theorists, a general factor was to be introduced only to supplement the group factors. This controversy involved some very intricate mathematical problems which go beyond the scope of this book.

The group-factor approach is represented in Thurstone's classical investigation(5). Thurstone gave a battery of many separate tests to some 250 students. In this battery he included tests which, from *common sense,* would seem to involve ability to abstract, ability to deal with words, to deal with space, with numbers, ability to reason with numbers, ability to reason with words, to reason about space, to memorize lists of words or items, and several other abilities. He then determined the resemblances between these various tests and tried to estimate how many group factors would be required to account for the resemblances he found.

It appears that the following tests have a resemblance which could be due to a single group factor: number code test, adding test, subtracting test, multiplication test, division test, filling in the missing entries of a table of figures, estimating the approximate size of the answer in computation, and the test in arithmetical reason. It seems safe to assume that the thing which these tests have in common is the use of numbers. This assumption is strengthened by the fact that there was only one test in which numbers seem to be involved which did not fit into this group. Thurstone, moreover, suggests that this apparent exception did not involve numbers so much as logic.

By a similar treatment, Thurstone has isolated six other factors which altogether account for a good deal of the total resemblance. The complete list of factors follows:

1. Ability to deal with space.
2. Ability to perceive details which are imbedded in irrelevant material (perhaps similar to finding a given word in a page of print).
3. Numerical ability (discussed above).
4. Dealing with verbal relations.
5. Dealing with isolated words. (Constructing many small words out of a large word. Rearranging letters so as to spell words and the like.)
6. Ability to memorize (word-number pairs, etc.).
7. Inductive reasoning. (Ability to find the rule or principle involved in tasks.)

These factors seem to account for most of the relationships. There is less definite evidence for a factor of deductive reasoning and for a factor of solving problems which must be solved in a certain way as, for instance, working out a problem in mathematics in which we must use arithmetic and cannot use algebra. It is interesting to note that the group factors or abilities which came out of the investigation were not precisely the same as those which seemed, from casual inspection, to be going into the investigation. Thurstone found, for instance, no single ability to reason with numbers, though he put in tests which he thought would reveal such an ability or factor if it were present.

The factors that Thurstone reported in 1937 seem to hold up when studied by newer techniques(6). Thurstone's earlier suggestion that g may not be necessary, however, has not held up completely. Thurstone(7) and others(8, 9) find that, over and above the resemblance that can be explained by the group factors, there is a "second-order" resemblance that should be attributed to a general factor of some sort. This does not mean, of course, that all investigators agree with Spearman on the nature of this general factor or on the relative part that it plays.

Test-measured Intelligence: Resumé

In view of all this, what can we say about the nature of the abilities that are needed to get a high score on these tests? First of all, of course, the high-scoring person must have had *some* experience with the materials in the test. There is no evidence, however, that he must have had more than an average, or more than a minimum, amount of such experience. The high-scoring person has been unusually successful (a) in seeing the essential relations between the things, (especially ideas and symbols) that he has encountered, and (b) in remembering the relations and perhaps some of the details. He is very good (c) in "catching on" to the essential task in each test, and (d) he can use what he remembers to solve the task in very rapid fashion.

Our summary deals, of course, with the kind of intelligence that will most often come through the typical intelligence test. Naturally there are also many tests dealing with specialized aspects of intelligence such as reasoning ability or creative intelligence(10, 11). In one sense, moreover, we could include almost any aptitude test as a test of *some kind* of intelligence. Of these, of course, there are very many. They cover aptitudes for clerical, mechanical, musical abilities, and for skill in the graphical arts. Some of these, such as the Differential Aptitude Tests, provide separate scores in eight different areas that have most significance for vocational counseling.

Another test that departs from the beaten path is the Davis-Eells Test of General Intelligence. In this battery there is an attempt to break away from the highly academic, verbal emphasis and from the possible bias in favor of middle-class children. The items consist chiefly of illustrated practical problems, and the student is required to show his comprehension of the issues involved and of the most fruitful solutions. For detailed discussions of these specialized tests, consult one of the texts, such as that of Freeman, given under Suggestions for Further Reading.

Cautions in Administering Tests

The individual tests of intelligence are rather complex and should be administered only by someone thoroughly trained in the process. The group tests, on the other hand, are relatively simple and can be given by any teacher who will take the trouble to familiarize himself with the directions that come with the test. Even here, however, a few precautions are in order. As many people have suspected, rapport is important. Young children especially are more likely to do well if the test is given by someone they know. A general atmosphere of cordiality also helps.

There is considerable evidence that test score can often be raised by practice or by deliberate coaching(12). This increase may be as much as seven IQ points. As it happens, simple practice does about as much good as deliberate coaching, and one practice does about as much good as a number of practices. Because of these facts we can iron out the inequities by making sure that all students have a brief practice just before the real test. This will place all students almost on a par with those who have been coached or who have had earlier experience.

Individual Differences in Intelligence

In the discussion of individual differences in physical characteristics, it was pointed out that there is a continuous range of differences in height, for instance, from the very short to the very tall. Between the two extremes there is no height that can be named that does not describe some person. Specify the height, and someone can be found to meet that height.

This continuous range seems obvious when we discuss height. It has seemed far less obvious, however, to many people when they came to discuss intelligence. In the latter discussion people are quite willing to argue as to whether or not one man falls into one category of intelligence, say genius, or whether or not a second man can be classified as feeble-minded. In discussing intelligence we are not so likely to see that it is merely a question of *how* intelligent the person is. When it comes to intelligence we are more likely to assume that people can be classified into neat groups which are clearly distinct from each other.

Actually, of course, there are no separate or distinct classes of intellect. As is shown in Figure 5-1, the distribution of intelligence quotients is continuous. There are no gaps or blank places. Put your pencil down on any IQ along the baseline of the graph, and you will find that there are some people that have that IQ. Put your pencil on an IQ of 50 and then run it up until it meets the curved line. You do not go very far, but you do go some distance. This means that there are at least a few people who have that IQ. Put your pencil on an IQ of 90 and run it up to the curved line and you find that this IQ describes a lot of people. But whether few or many, at every point along the range of IQ's you will find some people.

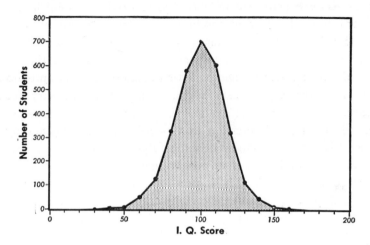

FIGURE 5-1. *Distribution of IQs on the L-M Revision of the Stanford-Binet Test.* Data from Q. McNemar, *The Revision of the Stanford-Binet Scale,* Houghton Mifflin, 1942. Table 2.

The distribution of IQ's shown in Figure 5-1 is typical of most such distributions. This particular distribution is based on the results from the 1937 revision of the Binet test(13). The revised test was given to some twenty-nine thousand children and the IQ's which were obtained were used to plot the graph. The graph has a single mode and is also symmetrical, the mode being almost midway between the extremes. Although in most respects it follows the general shape of the normal distribution, actual calculation shows that it is a trifle too peaked to be considered a precise fit to that curve(13).

Although it is impossible to find breaks or gaps in the actual distribution of intelligence, many people feel better if they can break the range of intelligence into sections and apply names or labels to the sections. Naturally, as a reasonable student, you should try to get beyond this wish and should try to be at home with the concept of a continuous gradation. Meanwhile, however, you will hear other people talking about certain arbitrary groups and it may be helpful to look at the more commonly mentioned classifications.

Children Who Are Normal or Above Normal

180 IQ and Over. This is an unusual degree of intelligence, a level attained by less than one person in a million(14). It is probably the level of intelligence which permits the brilliant achievements of such men as Leibnitz, Goethe, John Stuart Mill, Macaulay, Galton, and others. We say "permits such achievement" because it would be foolish to expect every person of 180 IQ or over to become a Goethe or a Leibnitz. While people of this IQ may have enough intelligence for this outstanding success, there is no reason to suspect that they will have the zeal, the opportunity for study, the good luck, or the energy reserve and enormous capacity for grueling physical and mental labor necessary for such eminence.

There is a general impression that people of such outstanding mentality are likely to be peculiar in some respect. Mrs. Hollingworth, who spent much of her busy life in observing gifted children, suggests that there is some basis for this impression. She reports that unusually brilliant children often suffer a certain amount of isolation. They may readily lose contact with more ordinary children and may come to live in a world intellectually apart. They literally come to use a different and more adult and technical vocabulary than their contemporaries. They may become intolerant of less gifted people, and since they find other people unable to follow their reasoning, they may come to tell others what they think the latter would appreciate or understand rather than what is so. They tend to withdraw from other children and to seek the company of older people or to play solitary games, sometimes inventing new and difficult games. Such children may resent or resist authority and tend to worry greatly over ethical problems.

In spite of these few difficulties which are, perhaps, inherent in unusual intelligence, we must not assume that gifted children are peculiar in all respects. In a vast number of personality traits they are, if anything, a little superior to normal children(15). They also excel in such things as art judgment, musical memory, and in many kinds of mechanical skill(16).

165–180 IQ. As we have mentioned before, there is nothing magic about any of the arbitrary boundary lines. Consequently, we would expect the people just below 180 IQ to be very similar to those just above. The range 165–180 IQ may be regarded as near genius. People of this degree of intelligence are rare and are exceedingly brilliant. Like those with IQ's over 180, they are likely to feel isolated.

130–165 IQ. As we pass below the 165 IQ mark we begin to leave the area in which only a very rare person may be found. About this point we begin to encounter substantial numbers of people. Some 3 percent of the total population have IQ's between 130 and 165. An army of one million men would call up thirty thousand people of this degree of intelligence, whereas the same army would draft (or at least examine) only one single person over 180 IQ. In this IQ range you will find the majority of children enrolled in special classes or special programs for the gifted(17, 18).

Students between 130 and 165 IQ represent the top half of college graduates, ranging from those who were just above the average of such graduates (130 IQ) through the honors group and those who may later be listed in *American Men of Science* (140 IQ), to those who secure honors in a topnotch graduate medical school or graduate law school (150 IQ).

If we wish a verbal description for the group from 130 to 165 IQ, we may say that people in this group range from the definitely superior to the very bright. Speaking rather loosely, we may say that these people use the same language as ordinary people but use it remarkably well. They are not out of touch with the rest of us. Mrs. Hollingworth suggests that this is the most comfortable range of intelligence.

110–130 IQ. This range of intelligence includes a large number of people. In general, an IQ of 110 represents the *average* high-school graduate, whereas 130 IQ represents the *average* graduate of one of the more selective colleges.

90–110 IQ. This is usually thought of as the *normal* group. It comprises about 45 percent of the population. This group hardly needs description. The people in it range from those who have just been able to finish grade school (90 IQ) to those who have completed high school (110 IQ).

Children Who Are Below Normal

The boundary lines which we have drawn so far have not been very significant. It rarely makes any difference whether or not a man is classified in the potential genius group or merely in the bright group. He can do what he can do, and our classification rarely affects his opportunities. True, some schools may exclude students who are below an arbitrarily established IQ, or some employers may have minimum IQ standards. These standards, however, even if they are rigidly enforced, do not ordinarily place a great restriction on the people to whom they apply. There are usually other schools, and there are usually other places or types of employment.

Unlike the boundary lines in the upper part of the scale, the boundary lines between the normal and various degrees of the subnormal, on the other hand, have great practical significance. The decision as to whether a person falls on this or that side of a "boundary" line may determine whether he is to live in the world as an "officially" normal person or to be greatly protected and restricted by society.

It is the restriction or protection applied by society which makes the lower boundary lines so important. Obviously, there are some people with whom society must take a hand. Unprotected or unrestricted they would be prey to the unscrupulous or a menace to the rest of us. Often when society does take a hand it does so in all-or-none fashion. That is to say, a child is not usually restricted in proportion to his defect. He does not attend a special class, for instance, in proportion to his deficiency. He either attends or does not attend. Similarly, he is either committed to an institution or not committed. In rare cases, he is either sterilized or not sterilized.

These things that society must do, or may do, for some people are often drastic, sometimes unpleasant, and usually carry some stigma or suggestion of disgrace. Consequently, the decision as to whether or not a person needs some special treatment is a very important decision, and any boundary which may mark off those who can get along in some sort of way from those who must be taken in hand should be set with a great deal of care. Fortunately such decisions are usually made by shrewd specialists who do not adhere rigidly to an arbitrary boundary in making their decisions. Any boundary set up, however, is very likely to exert a great deal of influence, especially among unthinking people.

Perhaps as much as 3 percent of the population falls below 70 IQ. This is a very large proportion. If such people were evenly distributed there would be at least one to a classroom. Of this total group, often classified as *feeble-minded,* there are a great many for whom some special provision must be made. This special provision may range from mere extra coaching or additional assignments to commitment to an institution. These children are especially likely to have trouble when they are required to deal with abstractions. They may show less handicap in mechanical or motor skills, but ordinarily do not excel in these traits(19).

45–65 IQ. Children of this range of intelligence are often labeled morons. With great effort such children may learn to read in a mechanical sort of way but with very little comprehension. As adults such people may be trained to help around a farm, to do simple sewing, to do rough painting, or simple carpentry.

25–45 IQ. This is the imbecile group. Reading or writing or arithmetic are beyond the level of children in this group. With patient teaching, adults at this level may learn to wash dishes, to do very simple cooking, to herd chickens or sheep, or to do simple sewing. Such adults rarely exceed the mental ability of average children of six or seven years.

Below 25 IQ. The name idiot is properly applied to people of this level of intelligence. For children of this group, little learning is possible. Under favorable circumstances adults of this degree of deficiency have been taught, after five to eight days of instruction, to pick one or two kinds of fruit, to scrub or dust, to saw wood, or to run very simple errands. These are the exceptions, however. Many idiots cannot dress themselves or keep themselves ordinarily clean. Some of them have to be fed. Fortunately only a few children are born with such limited IQ. One type of idiocy, mongolism, appears in only three out of two thousand in the case of mothers under thirty. The rate rises sharply to one out of a hundred births for mothers over forty-five.

Cautions in Interpreting High and Low IQ's

Very often the IQ gives an excellent indication of a child's standing with respect to his age mates. We must not attach too much precision to these measures, however, and we must remember that some extrinsic or accidental factors may play a part. It is easier to get an extremely high IQ or an extremely low IQ, for instance, on the Stanford-Binet (1937) than on the Wechsler. It is also easier to get an extremely high IQ on the 1937 revision of the Stanford-Binet than on the 1916 revision. Some studies(20) have also shown that it is easier to get a low IQ at the age of eleven than at the age of six. These fluctuations and uncertainties need not worry us too much, however, so long as we regard the IQ as an approximate index and not as a measure having unquestioned precision.

The Constancy of Intelligence

Before attaching any great significance to this intelligence we have been discussing, we may well ask whether or not it is a genuine characteristic of the individual. Is intelligence something a person carries with him from one situation to another? Is a person who is intelligent at one time also intelligent at another time? Or does the intelligence that we reveal depend entirely on the situation in which we find ourselves? Do the gifted continue to be gifted and do the dull remain dull?

To avoid misunderstanding and unnecessary contention let us make it perfectly plain that the IQ can be changed. We have seen that the apparent IQ can be changed by such a device as coaching. As we shall see, it can also be changed by improvements in the environment. Our question, then, is not whether the IQ is susceptible to change, but whether under ordinary circumstances it does in fact remain fairly constant or fluctuate widely from one situation to another.

The Constancy of Brilliance

Contrary to popular impression, the gifted child, *on the average,* turns out to be a gifted and accomplished adult(21), and the genius of history is discovered to be a precocious and gifted child(22). We say "on the average" because there are many, many exceptions. Some of these exceptions come from the *regression effect* described in Chapter 4. The outstanding position, for child or adult, is a precarious or "chancey" position. A great many ingredients go into the recipe that produces a child labeled as gifted. Some of those ingredients may involve luck or good fortune and we cannot expect these to persist indefinitely. At any rate, not all gifted children will go on to distinction as adults. Conversely, not all geniuses of history will have come from the ranks of child prodigies.

With due regard to the exceptions, we find that most of the brilliant men for whom we have childhood records turn out to have been exceedingly brilliant children. Even such alleged dullards as Scott and Darwin were estimated to have childhood IQ's of 165. Of 282 eminent men only 3 (Massena, Vaughan, and Fontaine) were estimated to have childhood IQ's as low as 100. The rest ranged from 105 to 190 with an average of approximately 140.

The childhood attainments of some of these men were phenomenal. John Stuart Mill studied Greek at the age of three. When six years old he wrote a history of Rome. Between the ages of nine and thirteen he completed one book of an epic intended as a sequel to Homer's *Iliad*.

Goethe began the study of Latin at the age of seven and within a few months was able to write compositions in that language. At eight and a half his Latin exercises were those used for the last year in the *Gymnasium*—an educational level perhaps comparable to our first year of college.

The Constancy of Deficiency

When we turn to the opposite end of the scale we also find some constancy together with a regression toward the norm. Many investigators have followed the progress of feeble-minded children into adulthood. The results of one of the pioneer studies are shown in Figure 5-2.

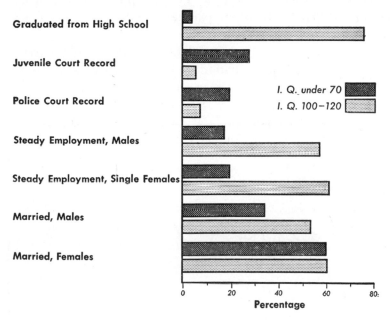

FIGURE 5-2. *Adult Performance of Two Groups Having Different Childhood IQs.* Data from Baller. Figure redrawn by permission from F. K. Shuttleworth, "The Adolescent Period." Monogr. Soc. Res. Child Develpm., 1938, 3 No. 3 (Serial No. 16), Fig. 267.

Most studies(19, 23) show, first, that many such people make fairly adequate adjustment. Most are married. In some studies this is true for 80 percent. Many have children, and the intelligence of the children is, on the average, only slightly below normal. Since the pioneer investigations made in the early 1930's, the employment picture has improved.

As many as 80 or 90 percent are employed. Only a few constitute serious social problems.

Obviously the outlook for people of low IQ is not completely bleak. But neither is it completely normal. Most are employed but at the unskilled level. Not all get into trouble, but the rate is still much above average. Court records, though not universal, are frequent. The death rate is higher than normal, and death by violence is greatly above the average.

The Study of the General Population

From our study of the very bright and the very dull we observe (a) that there is some tendency for the extremes to regress toward the average; (b) that the regression is never complete, the dull remaining below the average for the most part, and most of the bright students remaining well above the average.

When we study the general population, instead of the extremes, we also notice considerable fluctuation in individual scores. On one test a child may have an IQ above average, showing that he is somewhat above

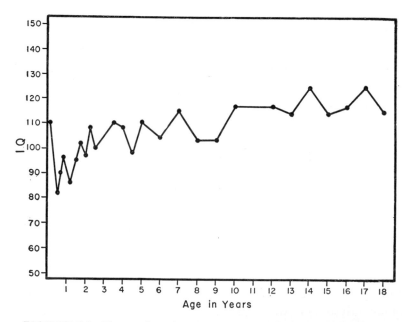

FIGURE 5-3. *Fluctuations in IQ for One Child Over an Eighteen Year Period.* Redrawn by permission from Nancy Bayley, "Consistency and variability in the growth of intelligence from birth to eighteen years," J. Genet. Psychol., 1949, 75, 165-196.

his age group. The next time he is tested he may have an IQ that is average or even below average, showing that he has lost out with respect to his age group. The fluctuations for one child over a long series of tests are shown in Figure 5-3.

The marked fluctuations appear while the child is still young. With increasing maturity the IQ tends to settle down. Between tests given at age 2 and repeated at age 5, the correlation is only .30 or .40. Tests given at ages 4 and 7, however, will correlate to the extent of .60 or .70, and tests given at ages 9 and 12 will correlate .85 or higher(24, 25).

In general, any given child, especially a young child, may show marked fluctuations. A child obtaining an IQ of 105 now and tested a year later could get an IQ as high as 135 or as low as 75. This is possible but it is extremely unlikely. Over half the changes will be less than 5 IQ points. Half the changes, of course, will be more than 5 points, and about one quarter will be more than 10 points. Marked changes are more likely to occur when the child is young or the interval between tests is long. They are also more likely to occur in very bright children. Apparently it is easier for a bright child to tumble from his precarious position than for a dull child to rise suddenly to new heights.

The Course of Intellectual Growth

Most children tend to keep their relative place with respect to their age mates. If a child is slightly ahead of the age group at one time he will probably be slightly ahead at another time. But how does the whole age group move? Can we plot the intellectual progress of the group average during the growing-up process?

Early Growth in Motor Control

The intellectual development of the young infant is shown chiefly in his increased mastery of his own muscles and of the simple objects in his immediate environment. At the age of four weeks his accomplishments are limited to such things as turning his head, moving his arms in uncoordinated windmill fashion, and watching nearby objects for a short period of time(26). It is not until he is two months old that he can hold his head erect in a wobbly sort of way, or watch a person move around the room. At this age, his fingers may move in seeming exploration when they come in contact with his body. When lying on his back, he kicks his legs vigorously, and when placed face downward, he tries to draw his legs up under him as if trying to crawl.

Control of the head improves continuously and by the age of three months the average child can hold his head erect quite steadily and will turn it at the sound of a voice. His other activities also seem more purposeful and coordinated. Now as he looks at objects, he reaches toward them. True, he seldom grasps the object even if he does touch it, but he will grasp an object that is carefully placed in his palm. About this age he makes stepping movements when he is held in the upright position.

By the age of six months the child's coordination has vastly improved. Now when he sees a rattle he reaches for it, grasps it, and uses it to bang on the table. If it falls he follows it with his eyes and tries to grasp it again. He still cannot grasp small pellet-sized objects, although he may reach in their general direction. Among his other accomplishments, a child of this age can sit unsupported for a short time. He seems to anticipate, or get set for, sounds or other stimuli that are frequently repeated. He watches nearby objects in a systematic manner, moving his eyes frequently from one part of the object to another.

By nine months the child can support his weight on his legs but cannot balance himself in the standing position. In the sitting position he is quite active, often leaning forward and then sitting up straight. By this time he grasps small objects using the thumb and index finger instead of the whole palm. He can manage two larger objects at the same time.

At the end of the year, motor control is highly developed. The infant now walks when supported. He is much more dexterous with his hands. He can transfer objects from hand to hand, place them in the hand of an adult, and even thrust or throw them from him. Manipulation appears more elaborate, more purposeful, as if he were trying to make the toy rattle or the marble roll out of the cup.

The two-year-old masters fairly complex tasks. He may be able to put his shoes on. He uses a spoon with moderate success, and he can scribble with a crayon. These accomplishments represent distinct advances in prolonged, purposeful, and intricate motor control.

Growth in Language

After the first year of life, it is language development which provides the most interesting index of intellectual growth(27). Some language, of course, is in evidence before the end of the first year. Apart from enthusiastic crying, the first sounds uttered by an infant are probably incidental grunts accompanying swallowing or other simple alimentary functions. These may occur in the first ten days after birth. Perhaps the next step in the attainment of language is the more flexible use of his skill in crying. By the age of one month he begins to cry differently for different reasons. Perhaps the difference is merely in intensity or vigor, but to the alert mother or nurse one cry can signify pain whereas another may mean hunger or boredom. We do not know what the child is *trying* to express by these various ways of crying, but he does achieve a sort of differential communication which comes to make sense to those around him. And this is a rudimentary form of language.

About this same time or shortly afterward he utters sounds which are more formed or structured than the early grunt. These early utterances have enough vocal quality to lead investigators to analyze them into the type of vowels or consonants employed. No investigator at the present time, however, assumes that this simple chatter is used in a meaningful way.

Between two and four months the infant progresses from simple syllables to sustained babbling and cooing. There is no suspicion now that these sounds are mere incidental accompaniments of other functions. These vocalizations seem intentional and social in character. True enough they are to be heard when the infant is alone, but they are especially likely to be set off by the presence of other people and especially by affectionate attention. Before the year is half over some of the sounds seem to be clearly associated with pleasure as the infant expresses his happiness or satisfaction by enthusiastic crowing or cooing. At this time the babbling often seems to be clearly directed to the person who is playing with him or talking to him. Apart from its lack of meaning, the jargon has many of the attributes of talk.

Before the end of the first year the babbling will include syllables which can be recognized by the eager parents or nurse. At this time the familiar "da-da" or other double syllables may occur, although it is most improbable that this expression is associated with any one person or even with any general situation. Since it is an expression, however, which gets dramatic and interesting results, it may readily come to be repeated very frequently. At this time the infant also shows some comprehension of words such as "bye-bye." Toward the end of the first year these syllables may be spoken upon request or in imitation of his elders. Within the next few months he will pick up one or two additional words, repeating them upon request and spontaneously using them in more and more appropriate fashion. He will also react appropriately to "no, no." At eighteen months he will apply the correct name to a few persons or objects (or even pictures) that are pointed out. He will also point out objects that are named by someone else.

By the time he is a year and a half old, the child has passed through the stages of incidental grunting, of tentative vocalization, of sustained babbling, of the enunciation of recognizable syllables, of the use of reduplicated syllables, of the pronouncing of syllables upon request, and has come to the stage of consistently using several simple words, giving them their conventional meanings. The next step is the use of two or three words in combination, and this is usually accomplished by the end of the second year.

From the end of the second year, language development takes several forms. There is first of all the enormous growth in the number of words used and understood. Starting with the very considerable vocabulary of some 270 words at the age of two, the child progresses to an understanding of some 16,000 words by the age of seven. Adequate use of the language also calls for the mastery of different parts of speech. It is not enough that the child can name a large number of objects. He must also be able to indicate actions, and this, of course, he is soon competent to do. Very soon he must be able to react appropriately to the difficult abstract ideas contained in prepositions. He must be able to distinguish between "on the table" and "under the table," and this very subtle distinction he comes to make in his third year. Pronouns, too, are especially complicated and abstract, with one person sometimes being "me" and at other times being "her" or "you." The three-year-old makes some progress in using the personal pronouns but it is in the fifth or sixth year that the most marked growth is seen in this respect.

In discussing the active use of speech we must not neglect the quality of the articulation. A very important aspect of language growth consists of this progress from a babble, which is clearly understood by the mother but by no one else, through baby talk which, though amusingly mispronounced, is still intelligible, to regular pronunciations typical of the community.

By the age of eighteen to twenty months trained observers agree to some extent on the vocalizations of children(28). One investigator(27) found that she was able to understand only 26 percent of the vocalizations of children of eighteen months. For children only six months older, however, the percentage of understandable statements increased to 67, and by the age of three years over 90 percent of the remarks were understandable. These figures, shown in the top line of Figure 5-4, refer, of course, to the comprehensibility of the speech and not to its accuracy. The four-year-old's statement that "The tain goes under the Chismas tee," might be perfectly intelligible to many adults but is still far from accurate. The accuracy of articulation lags far behind, as is shown in the lower line of Figure 5-4. Even at the beginning of the first grade, a fair number of children will mispronounce a good many words.

In addition to mastering more words, more complex words, and more abstract words, the child comes to use longer and more complex sentences. From the single-word "sentences" used by the child of eighteen months, we find slow but regular progress. The *average* sentence of the three-year-old may contain three or four words. This means, of course,

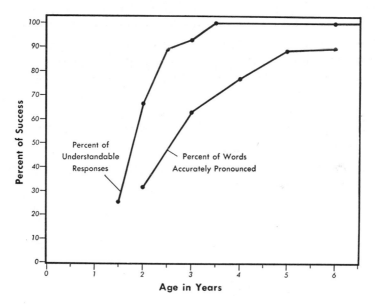

FIGURE 5-4. *Growth in Comprehensibility and Accuracy of Speech.* Data from McCarthy(27, p. 514).

that some of the sentences are much longer. For the five-year-old, sentences of four or five words are a fair average, and this is about the level to expect of the child when he enters the first grade. The length of sentences used continues to increase all through school, especially in written compositions. Children in grade three write sentences with an average length of some ten words, whereas students finishing high school use sentences of almost double that length.

The use of compound or complex sentences is even more significant than sheer length of sentence. Correct use of a compound or complex sentence suggests a grasp of relations between ideas, as well as the ability to express a single idea. Very few children under the age of three use anything but simple sentences, perhaps with an additional phrase thrown in. By the age of three, however, as many as 6 or 7 percent of the childish statements are in the form of either complex or compound sentences.

As sentences become longer and more involved, there is much greater opportunity for grammatical error. It is not surprising, then, to find as many as two grammatical errors per sentence in the written compositions of fourth-grade children. By the beginning of high school this error rate has dropped to about one per sentence. It is not surprising that the length and complexity of the unit of speech is a better index of intelligence than the size of the vocabulary.

Along with the changes in the form of the language there are changes in the content. There is a rapid increase between two and three in the number of words dealing with distance, space, or with numerical relations(29). Ability to tell time appears about the age of four or five and increases rapidly even with no formal instruction(30).

Growth in General Intelligence

The kinds of development already discussed will reappear, of course, in a study of intelligence-test performance, since the typical intelligence test uses items which involve language use, language comprehension, and motor control. In Table 5-1 we show the type of item that can be mastered by children of different ages. The table shows several kinds of development. In the first place there is a change in the quantity or amount of the task, as in the *number* of digits that can be repeated after one repetition or in the *number* of words that are understood. In the second place there is an increase in the complexity of the tasks that can be performed, as in drawing a diamond rather than a circle. Finally, there is an increase in the subtlety of the language relations called for. At the outset the child is merely asked to name the objects. Later he is asked to describe those objects in terms of their structure, in terms of their function, and in terms of their relation to other objects. Later he is able to deal with abstract qualities, and still later he points out relations between abstract qualities.

Some students, in observing this progression of the intellect, have been intrigued with the fact that beyond the age of three the growth is chiefly quantitative. After the age of three the child copies more complicated figures, uses longer sentences, repeats a longer series of digits, and perceives more subtle relations. After this age we find relatively few powers that are completely new. Certainly it is true that the three-year-old has made enormous strides along the road to intellectual maturity. His 1000-word vocabulary, his short sentences, and his simple abstract concepts may cause us to smile in patronizing fashion, but in relation to his beginning, or to the three or four halting words that can be learned by the chimpanzee(31), his accomplishments are astonishing indeed.

TABLE 5–1

Typical Examples of Abilities of Children of Various Ages

Age in Years	Motor Skill	Repeating Digits Just Heard	Vocabulary: Number of Words Understood	Names of Objects and Qualities	Common Sense
16			40,000	Shows difference between "laziness" and "idleness."	
14			38,000	Defines "charity" "defend."	
13					
12		7 digits	32,000	Defines words like "lecture" "skill" "brunette."	
11				Tells how *snake, cow,* and *sparrow* are alike.	
10		6 digits	26,000		
9					
8			23,000	Tells how *baseball* and *orange* are alike *and* different.	Knows what to do upon finding a lost child.
7				Tells how *wood* and *coal* are alike.	
6	Copies a diamond	5 digits	16,000		Knows what to do when "you break something that is not yours."
5	Copies a square			Tells what *shoe* is made of.	
4	Makes an X	4 digits		Points to picture of "something we wear on feet."	
3	Copies a circle	3 digits			Knows what to do when thirsty.
2		2 digits	270	Points to picture of a shoe.	

To get systematic changes in test score, we can adopt either of two methods, or, perhaps, a combination of the two(32). We can use the *longitudinal method,* following a group of children through from an early age, and testing the same person as he grows older. Or, at any one time, we can test a number of people at each age level. This is called the *cross-sectional approach.* Both methods have their disadvantages. The longitudinal method takes time and patience and implies the willingness of people to submit to test after test. Each test also gives the person some practice and this practice may add to his score. The cross-sectional approach, on the other hand, also has its difficulties. The ten-year-olds we get today may be drawn from a different group than our six-year-olds. The differences we observe may be due not only to age but to the fact that in one community the dull seventeen-year-olds have left school leaving only the bright seventeen-year-olds to be tested. Or, with another community, the bright nineteen-year-olds may have moved to the city, leaving only the average or below to be tested.

Follow-up Studies. So far the follow-up studies have given us growth curves up to the age of nineteen or so. And up to this point we find annual increases in total test score. We cannot say, of course, that the rate of growth is constant because it is impossible to know that a gain from, say, seventy to eighty items on a test is the same as a gain from fifty to sixty items on that test. But we do know that there is *some* growth each year until the twentieth year at least(33, 34). Beyond the age of nineteen we have only indirect evidence for very highly selected groups. Ordinarily, for instance, college students obtain a higher score on intelligence tests in their senior year than in their freshman year(35, 36). But as yet we have no idea whether most of that increase takes place in the first year or so (i.e., in the years under twenty) or whether there is a fairly continuous increase up to the age of twenty-two. Beyond the age of twenty-two or so we do not find many regular follow-up studies. Occasionally, however, the same people are tested in college and again twenty or thirty years later(37, 38). In these cases there is little loss and there may be a gain. Since typically we only have two tests ten to thirty years apart, we cannot tell whether there was an early gain after college followed by a gradual decline or whether the people remained at a stationary level. We must also remember that these tests are based on the select group that attended college during the 1920's.

Cross-sectional Studies. A great many cross-sectional studies have been carried out. These agree with the longitudinal studies in showing a continued increase up to twenty years or so. The cross-sectional studies, however, show little increase during the twenties and most cross-sectional studies show a definite average decline after the age of thirty(33, 39). This decline is quite gradual, however, and does not appear in all subtests. Typically there is no loss in vocabulary(40) and there may be some gain beyond the fifties in this trait. General information may also hold up through the years. The decline is most likely to be noted in arithmetic, block counting, coding. Many people have called attention to the handicap that a speed requirement may impose on older people. There may also be a decline in tests that stress visual perception (block counting, motor control) and in tests that require the older person to steer his way through a great many complexities(41).

Summary

Intelligence is a most important topic both for its bearing on achievement and in its own right. It has been difficult to define intelligence in a way that will make it meaningful and will at the same time correctly indicate the definite limitations of the scientific use of the term. It must be remembered that the intelligence actually studied has been only that kind of intelligence which our tests will measure.

Individual tests were developed early in the twentieth century. Binet hit upon the fruitful approach of using a variety of tasks, each one geared to a definite age level. The improved versions of the Binet tests involve many tests in one or more alternate forms. Other individual tests such as the Wechsler also use a variety of tasks. Group tests were developed later but have become even more familiar than the individual tests. For elementary-school children, both individual and group tests use the concept of mental age to give meaning to their scores. When the score has been translated into a mental age, this figure can be divided by the actual chronological age to give an IQ. For older students the mental age is less useful and here percentile ranks or standard scores are more likely to be used.

The factor analysis of intelligence tests has suggested the presence of verbal, numerical, spatial, and other factors in most intelligence tests. This is in line with the impressions gathered from a more casual analysis.

Individual differences in intelligence are very much like individual differences in height. There are a few very dull people, a steadily increasing number of people as we move toward the average, and then a steadily decreasing number as we move out toward the genius class. In this continuous range of talent, people have inserted arbitrary divisions. Students above 180 IQ, for instance, may be considered in the potential genius class, whereas those of 165–180 IQ may be considered the exceptionally bright. Below these high levels we find the college honors group (140 IQ), and the average high school graduate (110 IQ). The range from 90–100 IQ includes the normal group containing some 45 percent of people. Students below 65 or 70 IQ are often described as feeble-minded. This class includes the upper level moron who can learn elementary school tasks, but with difficulty, the imbecile who can learn simple manual tasks, and the idiot who, even as an adult, seldom exceeds the intelligence of a child of two or three. These arbitrary groupings are subject to change and should not be taken too seriously nor used exclusively in making decisions.

Under most conditions, the IQ remains fairly constant. There are many exceptions, however. Any drastic change in the environment may affect the IQ. The IQ of infants may fluctuate widely. And, in line with the regression phenomenon, very dull children turn out to be dull adults, but not quite so dull as they were. Brilliant adults have outstanding childhood records, but not quite so promising as the adult performance.

The intellectual development of the young infant shows itself in the attainment of motor skill and in the achievement of elementary vocalization. After the age of twelve or eighteen months this development shows itself more and more in the mastery of words and in the comprehension of ideas that are increasingly complex. As he moves through the grades the student is able to understand more words, and he is more able to deal with abstract ideas and with subtle relations between words.

Language ability plays a large part in intelligence test performance. Even apart from its significance in general intelligence, language growth is of great importance to the school. Development of ability to communicate with others and to understand and to appreciate language is one of the great tasks of the school. Rudimentary use and comprehension of words can be seen about the end of the first year. By the end of the second year, the child has learned to understand as many as 250 or 300 words and can use some of them in the form of short sentences. At the age of three years, sentences average three or four words in length. By the time the child enters school, he will make frequent use of sentences of four or five words and will occasionally use sentences that are much longer. By the age of three, the first complex or compound sentence appears. Intelligibility and accuracy of utterance increase steadily through this preschool period. By the time the child enters school, most of his words will be intelligible but many of them will not be articulated with precise accuracy.

Growth in intelligence-test score can be measured either by follow-up studies or by a cross-sectional method. By both methods we find an increase into the college period but with diminishing returns. After the age of thirty, the cross-sectional studies show a decline in most, but not all, subtests. The few follow-up studies show little if any decline prior to the age of fifty.

SPECIFIC REFERENCES

1. Spearman, C. E. *The nature of "intelligence" and the principle of cognition.* London, Macmillan, 1923.
2. Varon, Edith J. The development of Alfred Binet's psychology. *Psychol. Monogr.,* 1935, *46,* No. 207.
3. Koch, Helen I.. Child psychology. *Annu. Rev. Psychol.,* 1954, *5,* 1–26.
4. Cureton, E. E. The principal compulsions of factor-analysts. *Harvard educ. Rev.,* 1939, *9,* 287–295. (See for humorous account of the early controversies.)
5. Thurstone, L. L. *Primary mental abilities.* University of Chicago Press, 1938.
6. Zimmerman, W. S. A revised orthogonal rotational solution for Thurstone's original Primary Mental Abilities Test battery. *Psychometrika,* 1953, *18,* 77–93.
7. Thurstone, L. L. Theories of intelligence. *Sci. Mon.,* 1946, *62,* 101–112.
8. Kelley, T. L. *Crossroads in the mind of man.* Stanford University Press, 1928.
9. Vernon, P. E. *The structure of human abilities.* Wiley, 1950.
10. Marron, J. E. The search for basic reasoning abilities: a review of factor analytic studies. *USAF hum. Resour. Res. Cent. Res. Bull.,* 1953, No. 53, 28.
11. Matin, L., and Adkins, Dorothy C. A second-order factor analysis of reasoning abilities. *Psychometrika,* 1954, *19,* 71–78.
12. Maxwell, J. Educational psychology. *Annu. Rev. Psychol.,* 1954, *5,* 357–376. (See for a review of earlier work.)
13. McNemar, Q. *The revision of the Stanford-Binet Scale.* Houghton Mifflin, 1942, p. 18.
14. Hollingworth, Leta S. *Children above 180 IQ Stanford-Binet.* World, 1942.
15. Lewis, W. D. Some characteristics of very superior children. *J. genet. Psychol.,* 1943, *62,* 301–309.
16. Wilson, F. T. Some special ability test scores of gifted children. *J. genet. Psychol.,* 1953, *82,* 59–68.
17. Witty, P. Educational provision for gifted children. *Sch. & Soc.,* 1952, *76,* 177–181.
18. National Society for the Study of Education. *The education of exceptional children.* Forty-ninth Yearbook, Part II, 1950.
19. Kirk, S. A., and Kolstoe, O. P. The mentally retarded. *Rev. educ. Res.,* 1953, *23,* 400–416.
20. Fraser-Roberts, J. A., and Mellone, Margaret A. On the adjustment

of Terman-Merrill IQ's to secure comparability at different ages. *Brit. J. Psychol.*, Statistical Section, 1952, *5*, 65–79.

21. Terman, L. M., and Oden, Melita. *The gifted child grows up.* Genetic Studies of Genius, Stanford University Press, 1947, Vol. IV.

22. Cox, Catharine M. *The early mental traits of three hundred geniuses. Genetic Studies of Genius,* Stanford University Press, 1926, Vol. II.

23. Charles, D. C. Ability and accomplishment of persons earlier judged mentally deficient. *Genet. Psychol. Monogr.*, 1953, *47*, 3–71.

24. Bayley, Nancy. Consistency and variability in the growth of intelligence from birth to eighteen years. *J. genet. Psychol.*, 1949, *75*, 165–196.

25. Carmichael, L., ed. *Manual of child psychology.* Wiley, 1954, Chap. 10, The environment and mental development (Jones, H. E.)

26. Gesell, A. L., and Thompson, Helen. *The psychology of early growth.* Macmillan, 1938.

27. Carmichael, L., ed. *Manual of child psychology.* Wiley, 1946, Chap. 10, Language development in children (McCarthy, Dorothea)

28. McCurry, W. H., and Irwin, O. C. A study of word approximations in the spontaneous speech of infants. *J. Speech Hearing Disorders,* 1953, *18*, 133–139.

29. Martin, W. E. Quantitative expression in young children. *Genet. Psychol. Monogr.*, 1951, *44*, 147–219.

30. Springer, Doris. Development in young children of an understanding of time and the clock. *J. genet. Psychol.*, 1952, *80*, 83–96.

31. Hayes, Cathy. *The ape in our house.* Harper, 1951.

32. Bell, R. Q. Convergence: an accelerated longitudinal approach. *Child Develpm.*, 1953, *24*, 145–152.

33. Jones, H. E., and Conrad, H. S. Mental development in adolescence. *Yearb. Nat. soc. Stud. Educ. 43* (I), 1944, 146–163.

34. Thorndike, R. L. Growth of intelligence during adolescence. *J. genet. Psychol.*, 1948, *72*, 11–15.

35. Flory, C. D. The intellectual growth of college students. *J. educ. Res.*, 1940, *33*, 443–451.

36. Sister M. Florence Louise. Mental growth and development at the college level. *J. educ. Psychol.*, 1947, *38*, 65–82.

37. Garrison, S. C. Retests on adults at an interval of 10 years. *Sch. & Soc.*, 1930, *32*, 326–328.

38. Owens, W. A., Jr. Age and mental abilities: a longitudinal study. *Genet. Psychol. Monogr.*, 1953, *48*, 3–54.

39. Nyssen, R., and Delys, L. *Contribution à l'étude du problème du*

déclin intellectuel en fonction de l'âge. Archiv. de Psychol., 1952, *33,* 295–310.

40. Corsini, R. J., and Fassett, Katherine K. Intelligence and aging. *J. genet. Psychol.,* 1953, *83,* 249–264.

41. Clay, H. M. Changes of performance with age on similar tasks of varying complexity. *Brit. J. Psychol.,* 1954, *45,* 7–13.

SUGGESTIONS FOR FURTHER READING

1. Freeman, F. S. *Theory and practice of psychological testing.* Holt, 1955.

2. Anastasi, Anne. *Psychological testing.* Macmillan, 1954.

3. Cronbach, L. J. *Essentials of psychological testing.* Harper, 1949.

   Any one of the three books just listed will give an excellent account of the various intelligence tests.

4. Goodenough, Florence L. *Mental testing.* Rinehart, 1949.

   A comprehensive account of the history, theory, and applications of testing. The treatments of the history and of the underlying assumptions of testing are especially valuable.

5. Terman, L. M., and Merrill, Maud A. *Measuring intelligence.* Houghton Mifflin, 1937.

   The "bible" for those who use the Stanford Revision of the Binet Tests. Should be consulted for details of the test and for the methods of standardization.

6. Tyler, Leona E. *The psychology of human differences.* Appleton-Century-Croft, 1947.

   Chapter 15 is devoted to factor analysis of intelligence and other traits. Easier than the basic texts but by no means simple. Chapters 8 and 9 give a brief and readable account of the feeble-minded child and the gifted child respectively.

7. Anastasi, Anne, and Foley, J. P. *Differential psychology.* Macmillan, 1949.

   Chapter 15 covers factor analysis. Chapters 16 and 17 treat the feeble-minded and the bright child respectively. These treatments, like those of Tyler, are recommended as the "next step" beyond the discussion in this textbook.

8. Carmichael, L., ed. *Manual of child psychology.* Wiley, 1954.

   Chap. 8. The measurement of mental growth in children (Goodenough, Florence L.).

   Chap. 9. Language development in children (McCarthy, Dorothea).

Chap. 10. The environment and mental development (Jones, H. E.).

The first section of this chapter provides an excellent discussion of the growth and constancy of intelligence.

Chap. 16. Gifted children (Miles, Catharine C.).

Chap. 17. Psychological sex differences (Terman, L. M., and Tyler, Leona E.).

Chap. 18. Psychopathology of childhood (Benda, C. E.).

A detailed account of feeble-mindedness.

9. The National Society for the Study of Education. *The Education of Exceptional Children*. Forty-ninth Yearbook, Part II, 1950.

10. Hollingworth, Leta S. *Children above 180 IQ. Stanford-Binet*. World, 1942.

11. Terman, L. M., and others. *Genetic studies of genius*. Stanford University Press.

This is a series of volumes providing a very elaborate account of an enormous project on the development of gifted people.

Vol. I. Terman, L. M., and others. *Mental and physical traits of a thousand gifted children*. 1925.

Vol. II. Cox, Catharine M. *The early mental traits of three hundred geniuses*. 1926.

Vol. III. Burks, Barbara S., Jensen, Dortha W., Terman, L. M., and others. *The promise of youth*. 1930.

Vol. IV. Terman, L. M., and Oden, Melita. *The gifted child grows up*. 1947.

Exercises and Questions for Discussion

1. "When about to consider a series of investigations regarding intelligence, we must remember that the intelligence we will be reading about is only the kind of intelligence that will come through the tests used by the investigators."

Such statements have proved irritating to a great many people. Advance some reasons to account for this fact. Is the statement partially untrue? If it is true, try to rephrase it to make it less disturbing.

2. Write a note on "The Mental Age: Its Advantages, Limitations, and Hazards." Contrast the MA and the IQ. What does one measure tell you that the other does not?

3. A child gets 38 items right on a group test of intelligence. You want to express this as an MA. What additional information should you seek? the student's CA? his IQ? a table of norms for that test? his school grade? his effort?

4. List some of the abilities that would help a student get a high score on an intelligence test.

5. What is a *group* factor in intelligence? How does it differ from a general factor? from a specific factor?

6. According to certain critics, when psychologists talk about intellectual growth they really mean linguistic growth. Is there any basis for this charge? How much importance should be attached to language and the use of symbols in calculating the growth of intelligence?

7. Some writers have claimed that a child has reached the halfway mark in his intellectual development by the age of three. Discuss this contention.

8. Two of your friends are having a violent argument about the constancy of the IQ. Do you think you could state the actual facts in a way that should prove satisfactory to both parties? Try it.

6

Growth in Scholastic Achievement

THERE IS NO NEED to emphasize the teacher's responsibility for scholastic growth. As the word scholastic implies, this has traditionally been the area with which we have a unique and special concern. True enough, we cannot ignore the other aspects of development. As we are told so often, we deal with the whole child, and we must be concerned about his physical welfare and his personal and social development.

Most people would deplore emphasis on academic matters that excludes all other facets of development. Hardly anyone, however, would advocate any real neglect of academic skill. For one thing, the fuller life that we visualize for each child will be impossible unless he has some skill in the intellectual and scholastic arts. His ability to express his personality and to enjoy rich and complex social relations depends to a large extent on his mastery of such academic matters as reading and self-expression, and on a mastery of the more commonly mentioned ideas of history and literature. His ability to satisfy his more primitive needs likewise depends to a large extent on his competence in many scholastic subjects.

Skill in scholastic matters, whether important as an end in itself or important as a means of attaining more complete self-realization, is not only one of the school's responsibilities but it is a unique responsibility. If the school should falter in this area, no other agency stands ready to step into the breach. In this area the school and the school alone is responsible for any academic attainment the child may acquire.

Measuring Achievement

The problem of measurement is unusually important for teachers. In our profession the results of our efforts are seldom self-evident. Unlike the machinist, or carpenter, or farmer, or financier, we cannot merely look and see what we have been doing. Like the ocean navigator, on the contrary, we must go to some trouble to find out where we are. Continually we must apply some measure or test or indicator to see if our students are getting anything out of the lesson. We must, likewise, test and measure to find out if we can safely leave this topic or safely begin a new project. All in all, we are seldom free from the necessity of measuring or appraising the achievement of our students.

The problem of measuring achievement is so critical for the teacher that he should take additional work in the subject either through the independent study of one of the references at the end of this chapter or through a systematic course in tests and measurements. Consequently, this section will in no way tell the teacher everything he needs to know about the problem of testing achievement. On the contrary, it will merely attempt to help him organize his very general ideas on the subject, and to ensure enough general understanding to follow the remaining sections of the text.

Tests to Fit Objectives

Any test that is used should be chosen to fit in with the educational objectives. The test is intended to show how the students stand with respect to those objectives. Unless the tests are selected with the objectives in mind, they cannot be expected to function as they ought(1, 2, 3).

Before deciding on a test, try to visualize your objectives in some concrete terms. After all, the test you select will place the children in situations which call for concrete activities, and it will be easier to decide on the suitability of the test if you can also reduce the objective to concrete terms. Be honest in this endeavor. Do not insist on using inspiring and high-sounding objectives. Do not be afraid of practical down-to-earth goals. High-sounding goals are likely to be a bit vague and hard to reduce to the point where they can be tested. Suppose, for instance, the goal, when all dressed up in its formal language, states that your student should show a generous willingness to help worthy social activities. It sounds good, but before you can test it you must visualize this in more concrete form. What does it mean? Perhaps it means that the student should give up something he really likes in order to contribute to the Community Fund. That is just one fairly concrete illustration. Others equally concrete may suggest themselves.

To visualize the objective in concrete fashion, it may help to think of some practical situation and then ask yourself how the student should act in that situation. For instance, you are asked to develop in the student a genuine appreciation of the best in music. To reduce this to concrete terms, you try to think of the way the student would be expected to behave in a specific situation. As one illustration you may visualize the student having a chance to go to the symphony or to a ball game, and you hope that once in a while he will choose the symphony. You may visualize him looking over the television section in the newspaper and choosing between two programs presented there.

Most objectives can be expressed by a cluster of concrete illustrations. In fact, if you can find no concrete situation which illustrates the objective, perhaps you should turn a suspicious eye on the objective. If it does not suggest any concrete illustration perhaps it does not mean much. As soon as you have reduced an objective to concrete terms the problem of testing is simplified. Ideally, all you have to do is to put the student in the situation you have in mind and see how often he behaves the way the objective calls for. Give him a chance to select several kinds of recreation and see whether he chooses the concert or the western. Have him keep a "log" or diary of his television viewing and see what he has been choosing.

Such a direct test, if it were free from extraneous pitfalls, would be ideal from the point of view of *validity*.[1] Such a test would actually measure the objective you are interested in and would thus be valid for your purposes. Often, however, the direct test is not feasible. It may be too cumbersome. It may take too much time or money. Perhaps the student, knowing he is under scrutiny, will not turn to his real choices on the radio. Perhaps, indeed, the direct test may be dangerous. We dare not put the student in a burning building, for instance, to see if our fire drill will be effective. When the direct test is not feasible, it is necessary to think up some substitute for the real situation and see how the student reacts to that substitute situation. We say, "Let's pretend the building is on fire." We give him a catalogue of musical records and ask him which he would choose if he had the money.

[1] The three terms, *validity, reliability,* and *objectivity* have become words to conjure with in the field of testing. As indicated above, a test is valid to the degree that it measures what it purports to measure. It is reliable insofar as it will give consistent measures of the same thing. It is objective insofar as all persons marking it will arrive at the same score. The terms *reliability* and *objectivity* will be dealt with in a later part of this chapter.

As we move away from the direct test, the problem of validity becomes more vexing. We become less and less sure that the substitute test really gets at the objective we have in mind. But the problem of validity should still be faced. We should ask ourselves if the test *seems* to cover the sort of thing we had in mind when we started teaching this unit. Sometimes test constructors try to go much further. They try to make a more direct test of the objectives, expensive and cumbersome as that more direct test may be, and then find the correlation between the less direct (but more feasible) test and the elaborate direct test. But obviously this is a tricky business. For the most part we must depend on common sense or *face validity*. We must try to include situations which seem to be like the situations we had in mind when we stated the objective(4).

Informal Tests

General Impression. Undoubtedly as a teacher you will form some opinion of your students merely on the basis of your casual contacts with them. You may not be able to put your finger on a score or a grade, but you have an impression that this student is good and that student is mediocre.

The general impression of one person, of course, is most undependable, and for many objectives it should not receive serious consideration. You would be foolish, for instance, to rely on sheer general impression to decide whether a student could type rapidly enough to hold down a job. For other objectives, on the other hand, general impression may be a perfectly valid measure. One of your objectives may be that the student should make a favorable impression on people. In that case your general impression is a most valid measure. Since you are only one person, however, and since you are interested in the impression he makes on *people,* your single impression is not a very *reliable* measure. It may not reflect what other people think. A composite of the impressions of several different people would be much better.

This whole problem of ratings and scales of general impression is discussed in more detail in the section on personal and social growth. Meanwhile, remember that general impression, supplemented by certain safeguards, is a perfectly legitimate index of some phases of educational development.

Oral Tests. For some objectives, oral tests are absolutely essential. For instance, we may want to see how well the student can pronounce French, or how well he reads out loud, or how well he can express himself in oral composition. For these objectives there is no valid substitute for the oral test.

In addition to being essential for some objectives, the oral test is useful for other objectives. In teaching geography, for instance, the oral test is not essential. We could determine the student's mastery by some other means. But for testing minor objectives in geography, the oral test is extremely convenient. To employ an oral test, we merely need to ask a question. There is no elaborate preparation of physical materials. The oral test also permits us to teach while we test. Any mistakes which appear in an oral test can be remedied on the spot, and this, as we shall see, is most wise from a pedagogical point of view.

Oral tests, of course, have obvious disadvantages. For a large number of students a program of extensive oral tesing is unwieldy in the extreme. It takes an enormous amount of time to get around to an oral test for each of forty or fifty students. In addition to being unwieldy, the oral test has all the disadvantages of the formal essay test, to be discussed in the next section.

Formal Essay Tests and Their Advantages

A fair amount of the day-in and day-out testing will be accomplished by the casual oral tests interspersed throughout the teaching and by the many other incidental student activities which contribute to the teacher's general impression. But these must be supplemented by more formal evaluations, often in the form of pencil-and-paper tests.

In considering these tests we soon run into the traditional quarrel between the claims of the essay test as opposed to the short-answer test.

For some objectives there is no substitute for the essay test. If we wish, for instance, to determine the student's proficiency in written composition, the only logical thing to do is to have him write. Anything else is clearly a substitute, and as such it is of questionable validity or at least of undetermined validity(5, 6).

Even when proficiency in English composition is not the entire objective, it may well be an important secondary objective. Very often we may be convinced that the student's ability to organize and to express his ideas about a subject is one of several indexes of his knowledge of the subject. Especially for some subjects at the high-school and college level, we may feel that this ability to express himself is an essential feature of his mastery. We may believe that a student who cannot make intelligent statements about the function of the law courts, for instance, falls short of an adequate understanding of that function. We may believe that in these subjects it is not enough that the student can nod his head at the right places. He must also be able to communicate his ideas.

Under ideal conditions, the essay examination tests not only the student's ability to make intelligible statements but also his understanding of the relations between the parts of the subject matter. It enables him to organize ideas into a structure if that is within his power. It permits him to differentiate between the major and minor points.

On the more mechanical side, the essay examination permits the student to express the subtle qualifications he feels while answering a question. It permits him to escape the frustration we often feel when we are called upon to make a "yes" or "no" answer. Often we feel that the problem cannot be answered by an unqualified "yes" or an unqualified "no." When taking an essay examination we are free to insert any qualifications that seem important.

The essay examination makes guessing less attractive. True it does not preclude guessing. But if he is to guess in the essay examination the student must choose from a large number of possibilities. In the typical essay question the student who is completely ignorant would have difficulty in his task of choosing one of an infinite number of alternatives. In the short answer test, on the contrary, a student who is completely ignorant need only choose between two or five or ten alternatives.

When students are told to expect an essay examination, they study in one way. When they expect a short-answer test they study in a different way. For the essay test they try to work out broad general principles, to outline, to organize the material under main headings and subordinate headings. They try to see the broad picture first, and then they try to fit the details into that broad picture. At least that is what they report(7, 8, 9, 10). When preparing for the short answer test, on the other hand, students look for identifiable, testable bits of information. They look for isolated concrete facts that could be worked into a question and try to memorize these. We must not assume, of course, that the method used in preparing for essay tests is always the method which gets best results. On that point there is considerable doubt(11). Finally, the essay examination has one very practical advantage. It takes less labor to construct. True enough it should take some time and thought. But it does not involve all the arduous detail that is typical of the short answer test.

Disadvantages of the Essay Test

The essay question may leave the student in doubt as to how much the teacher or examiner wants. He may not know how thorough the answer should be. He may wonder about the amount of detail. He is probably in doubt about the sheer quantity of the answer. This uncertainty is a great handicap. After the examination is over the students often wail, "If I had known that you wanted all that detail." There is also the opposite difficulty in which the student writes far more than is necessary. This, however, is less likely to come to the student's attention and is less tragic when it does. It merely imposes excess work on the student and teacher.

Because of the time required to answer a single essay question, it is seldom possible to include many such questions in a single examination. This means poor sampling of the material on which the examination is based. Of all the multitude of topics covered in the course, we can ask questions about only five or eight. Regarding the mastery of the others, we can tell nothing except by inference. The student who just happened to be prepared on a few of our questions shows up in an unduly favorable light. The student who just happened to miss those items in his preparation is unfairly handicapped, and is aware of the fact.

It happens that both the difficulties just mentioned can be remedied to some extent by the use of a large number of "spot" questions. When using these "spot" questions, the examiner specifies that the student is to write only a few lines or a sentence or so, or he includes a sample answer illustrating the amount of detail that is expected. By stressing short answers, it is possible to present a large number of such questions. Spot questions, of course, do not offer the opportunity for organization of ideas or for extended exposition. But they do embrace some of the other advantages of the essay questions.

Style May Mask Content. The essay examination offers a clear invitation to extended literary composition, and this is a two-edged sword. It shows us how the student can express himself about the material. But it also permits the method of expression to take the stage, so to speak. When marking the paper you may be completely swept off your feet by the style and the smoothness of the expression. Or you may be unfavorably impressed by the awkwardness of the exposition. In either case it may be hard to disregard the English and to examine the mastery of sheer content. You may mark the paper almost entirely on the manner of expression and on such mechanics as spelling, penmanship, typing, or punctuation.

Students, of course, are not slow to take advantage of the fact that style may prevail over content. The temptation to "bluff" is always present. For some people it is very easy to write persuasive nonsense and to carry the reader along by the sheer sound of the words. To an astounding extent, moreover, such people often get away with it. Few of us are able to disregard the presentation when we are really probing for hard facts.

Essay Tests Highly Subjective. It is well known that different teachers will assign different scores to the same answer paper of an essay exam. This is true, not only in such subjects as English or history, but it is also true in subjects like geometry or physics. In many subjects vast ranges appear between the lowest and highest score assigned to the same paper. In such a case the student's final score will depend not so much on what he has written as on who has read his paper.

The fluctuations from teacher to teacher can be reduced somewhat by prior discussion between teachers, by briefing, and by the joint marking of a few sample papers. When a great many essay papers have to be marked, this preliminary work is clearly worth while. Under ordinary circumstances, however, it may be impossible to have more than two people read the same paper. An agreement between two people is reassuring. Disagreements may be dealt with by resorting to a third reader, or by a detailed review on the part of the original readers. A second reader should be the rule for any examination in which there is a great deal at stake. For less critical routine examinations, this extra trouble is not feasible.

Ideally, of course, a test should be so arranged that the student's score will be the same no matter who marks it. Such a test is said to be objective, and this characteristic of *objectivity* receives much attention in discussions of specific tests.

The lack of objectivity in marking an essay examination may be made worse by our general attitude toward the student. If our general opinion of him is high, we are apt to give him credit for a dubious answer. Otherwise we might fail him on that question. To guard against this danger, examining agencies often go to a great deal of trouble to be sure that the examiner will not know whose paper he is reading. The individual teacher can adopt similar precautions on a smaller scale. For instance, you can have the students write their names on the back of the last page of the examination booklet, and you can make a point of not looking at this name until the paper has been marked. Or, as a more elaborate device, you can prepare a list of symbols or numbers on a sheet of paper and pass that around. Each student signs his name opposite a symbol which he selects and records. He uses the symbol to sign the examination. You do not consult the "key" until after the papers are marked.

Inconsistency between the marks assigned by different teachers is not the only problem of essay examination. There is also the fact that one teacher is not entirely consistent with himself. Suppose a teacher has graded a group of one hundred papers and has recorded the grades on a separate piece of paper. A day or so later he grades the same papers again. Would he get 100 percent agreement? It would be most unlikely. A great many things work to change the grades. The teacher's mood fluctuates from time to time. Certainly his standards shift from one time to another. This shift in standards may be haphazard, or the standards may gradually relax or gradually rise. It is, in fact, very difficult not to let our judgment change as we read paper after paper. An answer that seemed terrible as we began to read may seem more acceptable after a steady diet of poor papers. Conversely, a paper which seemed almost brilliant might appear less exceptional if it were reread after a long succession of equally exciting answers.

Several suggestions have been made to help guard against these difficulties and to help alleviate these sources of error. First, it may help to read all the answers to question 1 before looking at any student's answer to question 2. Go right through the pile, marking only question 1. Then come back to question 2, and so forth. In reading question 1, moreover, it may be better not to strive for unrealistic precision. Sort the papers into four or five or six piles of different levels of excellence. After you have finished, make a point of rereading the first few papers in each pile to see if your standards changed while you were reading the answers. If you can force yourself to be unusually conscientious, you might profitably read many of the papers a second time.

It may be objected that the procedures just suggested call for a great many mechanical details which will interrupt the main activity. Actually the interruptions imposed will probably prove a most welcome respite from the extremely arduous and agonizing task of marking papers and of facing the bitter truth that they so often seem to force upon us.

Finally, there is one very practical, earthy disadvantage of the essay test. Obviously, from what has been said, it is extremely laborious and vexatious to mark. Marking these tests is time consuming and wearying. We are seldom free from a host of important but perplexing decisions and redecisions.

Considering the advantages and disadvantages of the essay test, we can see that it is neither all good nor all bad. It is necessary for testing the ability to organize and to present the course material. It is likely to be misleading as a test of straight factual content. It is also an awkward and laborious method of testing such content.

Types of Short-answer Tests

The short-answer, or objective, tests take many forms. Several of the forms have been illustrated in the chapter on intelligence testing. There we saw an example of the true-false test which has merely two alternatives. We also saw the multiple-choice test and two kinds of completion tests. In one of these completion tests the student had to decide which of four possible answers provided the best completion of the statement. In the other test he was not given a group of alternative answers from which he had to choose, but was free to make any choice that appealed to him.

The matching test is also of the short-answer type. In the following illustration, for instance, the student selects an important export of, say, Australia, and enters the number of the product in the appropriate parentheses.

Matching Questions

Country	Important Export
( ) Australia	1. Wine
( ) Brazil	2. Coffee
( ) Canada	3. Fish
( ) France	4. Mutton
( ) Malaya	5. Wood pulp
( ) Newfoundland	6. Linen cloth
( ) USA	7. Oil
( ) Venezuela	8. Rubber
	9. Musical instruments
	10. Automobiles
	11. Diamonds

There should be more items in one list than in the other, else the last item would take care of itself.

Similar items are often placed together to form a separate part or subtest. Sometimes the items in each part are all of approximately the same difficulty. In such a case the test is often timed, and the score consists of the number of items answered correctly in a given time. This, of course, is essentially a *speed* test. In other tests the items increase in difficulty, and the student's score is indicated by the most difficult item he can answer. Students are usually given unlimited time for these tests. Such tests are called *power* tests.

Advantages and Disadvantages of Short-answer Tests

In discussing the essay test we have already, by implication, treated the good points and the defects of the short-answer tests, since the advantages of one are almost identical with the defects of the other. Thus, in contrast to the defects of the essay test, we find that the short-answer tests provide excellent sampling, since a very large number of separate questions can be used. They offer no advantage to the glib bluffer. They are almost perfectly objective in that they would be marked in exactly the same fashion by any number of people. Since they are so objective they can be marked by a clerical assistant or, when the test is so designed, by a machine.

Along with its advantages, the short-answer test presents many limitations. There is clearly no demand that the student organize his ideas. Typically, moreover, we avoid asking him to deal with any items where there is any real possibility of a difference of opinion. To overcome these difficulties to some extent, some authors suggest that the student should be asked to justify his answers. If he marks an item false, for instance, he may be asked to alter the statement so as to make it true(12).

There are other disadvantages. Although the short-answer test discourages the persuasive bluffer, it provides a wonderful opportunity for the test-wise student who wishes to guess. He can readily do some legitimate guessing about items that are somewhat familiar. More serious, perhaps, he can also use some extraneous clues that often distinguish between true and false items. In constructing short-answer tests we must be on our guard not to provide some "giveaway" by which the student can guess the correct answer even when he knows nothing of the subject. If we are not careful we will find that many of our false statements are unduly categorical or flat-footed, making much use of such words as *only, alone, no, none, nothing, always, never, cause.* Our true statements are more likely to be qualified. Unless we are careful, these true statements will bristle with such words as *may, most, should, some, often, generally.* After we have finished constructing such a test we should go over it and alter some of the items so as to be sure that both kinds of giveaway words appear with equal frequency in true statements and in false. For additional help in this matter consult one or more of the books listed under Suggestions for Further Reading.

The short-answer tests do not lend themselves to the measurement of complex or speculative material, although with some effort and ingenuity they can be constructed to get at these matters. On the whole, however, the test constructor who is committed to the use of the short-answer test will find himself looking for smaller, more factual nuggets for his test. At any rate students expect this sort of thing to predominate in such tests, and consequently they prepare for them by looking for isolated, clear-cut, factual statements which can be memorized.

Finally, the short-answer test is extremely laborious to construct. Many hours may be given to the selection of items, to the phrasing of the statements, to the selection of alternate choices, to the sequence of correct choices, and to the many detailed tasks involved in printing answer sheets and preparing simple keys.

Standard Tests and Their Advantages

Standard tests are the ready-made, printed kind which you buy in a neat package. They are undoubtedly very familiar. With one or two exceptions they are of the short-answer type, and consequently most of what we have said about the general short-answer tests will be applicable. The exceptions consist of the *quality scales* such as the handwriting scales. In these we find standard samples of handwriting varying in excellence by fairly regular steps. The number assigned to these samples has been determined by the pooled judgments of a large number of people. The student has only to place a sample of his own handwriting on the chart and to decide which of the standard specimens is most like his own.

The standardized short-answer tests have many advantages over the test which the teacher may be able to "whip up" on the spur of the moment. They are better constructed. Much thought is given to the sampling, to the wording, to the precautions against extraneous clues. The printing is usually excellent, the directions clear. The tests are designed so that marking is greatly simplified. Most present-day tests, in fact, are designed so that they can be scored by machine if that should be desired.

The standardized tests are typically more *reliable* than the homemade tests. That is to say they will tell the same story with more consistency. Administered to a group of students twice in succession, they would give about the same standing to each student on the two different occasions. The makers of standard tests are very conscious of this matter of reliability and try out their tests before putting them in final form. If, in preliminary form, the test does not give about the same results from time to time, it is made more reliable, chiefly by adding more items to reduce the influence of chance. All this trouble and care, of course, is ordinarily beyond the power of the classroom teacher, who has neither the time nor the training to go in for this sort of refinement in his homemade test.

Norms. Like intelligence tests, the standard achievement tests provide norms with which the progress of a class may be compared. The preliminary forms of the standard tests are given to a large number of children of different ages and in different grades. From these results tables are constructed which show the scores of the average child of six years, of six years and one month, of six years and two months, and so forth. Consequently, if we know that a child has answered eighty items correctly on a test of reading, we can look in the table and find that this is the typical score of a child who is, say, ten years and eight months. We say then that the child has an *educational age* (EA) in reading of 10-8. If he has also taken a standard test in arithmetic we can determine his raw score on the arithmetic test and again look up the norms for that test and determine his educational age in arithmetic. Obviously a child can have a different educational age for each subject. In some comprehensive test batteries we can also get a total score and use this total score to read off his composite or over-all educational age.

Knowing a student's educational age, we can decide whether he is advanced, retarded, or normal with respect to children of his chronological age. To make this comparison more precise we can compute his educational quotient (EQ) in the same way that we computed the IQ.

Norms are not always given as educational ages. They may appear instead as *grade scores*. Knowing, for instance, that our student got eighty items right in the reading test, we can look this up in a table of grade norms. Suppose we find that this corresponds to a grade of 5-6. This means that 80 is the score of the typical child who has spent six months in grade five. This information helps give some meaning to the raw score of 80. In the minds of some people this may be a more definite "anchor point" than an educational age, since, for some people, the performance to be found in a given grade may seem more uniform than the performance to be expected of a given age group. At any rate, both kinds of norms can be used, and both kinds are provided by most standard tests.

In addition to age norms and grade norms, many tests provide percentile norms and tell us the population on which the norms are based. The use of these percentile norms was discussed in the section on intelligence testing.

Disadvantages of the Standard Test

The great disadvantage of the standard test is the fact that it may not fit the local program. The history questions may not represent the history taught in our community. The geography and civics may likewise fail to fit our curriculum. It is unlikely that a test designed to serve the whole nation will adequately sample the curriculum of each local community.

For some subjects, of course, the objectives of most communities are roughly comparable. Standards for skill in reading, in ordinary computation, or in spelling are fairly consistent throughout all communities, and with these subjects there is little difficulty with varying objectives. In many other subjects, on the other hand, the variation in objectives may be very real and very important.

It is most important that the standard tests be selected to fit the objectives which the school wishes to stress. Otherwise the normal or desirable process may be reversed. If a test is selected which does not fit in with the objectives of the school, it may readily happen that the teachers, knowing what is stressed on the tests, will consciously or unconsciously emphasize these things. Because of such tendencies, the objectives stressed in the test and the actual objectives stressed in the classroom will never remain very far apart. If the test is not selected to fit the objectives of the school then we shall find that the actual day-by-day objectives of the school are becoming rearranged to fit the test(2).

In our anxiety to set our own objectives, we must not make a fetish of individualism. We should, in fact, welcome the opportunity to compare the standing of our children with the children of the nation on any objective that is fairly common to all communities. There may be times, indeed, when our need to compare our schools with other schools may justify the use of standard tests, even though there are slight discrepancies between the objectives of the tests and the objectives we have set forth.

If you do decide to use a standardized test, you will profit a great deal from the use of the reference sources listed at the end of this chapter. You can also find check lists of the points to look for when considering the purchase of a test(13).

Use of Common Sense in Deciding upon Tests

When contemplating the many methods of measuring scholastic achievement, the most important thing is an open-minded approach. There are many valuable instruments available for your use. Do not force yourself to use one instrument exclusively for all purposes or all objectives. Occasionally, within the privacy of the teacher's lounge, of course, you will argue the relative merits of this test versus that test, as if one type were good for all purposes and the others useless for any purposes. Like other forms of relaxation, such arguments are amusing and do no harm provided they are not taken seriously. You would not engage in a serious argument trying to decide whether a mechanic should use a screw driver *or* a pair of pliers. Obviously, each is excellent for one purpose but awkward, clumsy, or useless for another. So with different types of tests. Use each for the work it can best do. Try not to become the devotee of a single device.

The Study of Achievement-test Results

Tests of various kinds have been given to many hundreds of students of different ages, sexes, and conditions of life. The results have been reported in score upon score of articles. Let us see what we can learn about the kind of achievement or scholastic attainment that such tests can reveal.

Factor Analysis

It is, perhaps, not to be expected that scholastic achievement will resolve itself into a small number of factors. Certainly we would be surprised to learn that achievement was a single unitary thing and that one single factor determines achievement in arithmetic, spelling, manual training, and civics. We expect that a student's achievement in one area will differ considerably from his achievement in another area. On the other hand we are prepared to believe that there may be something in common between the different areas.

The early investigations carried on chiefly in England(14, 15, 16) came out with a general school factor plus special factors for verbal ability, for numerical ability, and for such manual abilities as writing or drawing. This general school factor is not the same as general intelligence since it shows up chiefly in school marks. Perhaps it is something like studiousness or willingness to work at the tasks of the school. French's(17) summary of work done in this country suggests a larger number of factors but, in general, tends to confirm the earlier English work. In one study or another, for instance, he finds factors that have been labeled "school grades," "performance in school subjects," "attentiveness," and "carefulness." These are somewhat akin to the school factor, although here we have a suggestion of a group of different factors.

French's summary also suggests a cluster of separate factors each of which emphasizes *speed* of some sort. These run through several different school subjects. There is a factor of speed in oral reading or in oral spelling, and a separate factor of speed in writing. *Perceptual speed* calls for the ability to locate the word or phrase you are seeking on a page of print. *Word fluency* refers to the rapid listing of words, however meaningless. By *ideational fluency* we mean the ability to evoke a large number of ideas in a hurry. Here again there is no suggestion that the ideas should be good or relevant. They have to be different and to come rapidly. *Fluency of expression* also emphasizes speed but with the restriction that the material produced must meet some sort of standard.

Over and above these wide-ranging factors, we have factors dealing with specialized subject matter. There appears to be a "culture" factor, for instance, made up of fine arts, music, and literature. This is distinct from a social studies factor. There may also be a foreign-language factor, but as yet this has been investigated chiefly with respect to German. There is no all-inclusive mathematics factor but factors identified in intelligence tests (numerical, spatial) also reappear in analyses of achievement tests.

Individual Differences in Achievement

The striking individual differences to be found in physique and in intelligence are also to be observed in measures of achievement. Even in the same grade, where we might expect some uniformity, we find vast ranges in achievement. Figure 6-1 plots the differences in reading to be found in a typical junior high school. These graphs show the range in

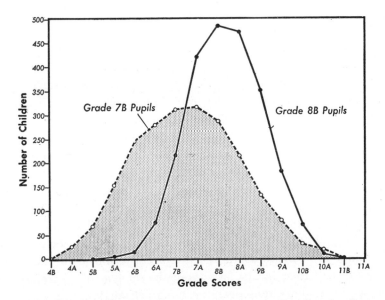

FIGURE 6-1. *Distribution of Grade Scores in Reading for Pupils in Grades 7B and 8B*

reading ability for grades 7B and 8B. Here we notice not only a wide spread of ability in each grade but a great amount of overlapping. By looking at the extremes and peaks of each graph we can see that on the average 8B pupils read better than 7B. But we find some pupils in 7B who exceed the average of the 8B pupils, and we also find some 8B pupils who fall below the average of the 7B class. In both grades we find some pupils reading at each grade level from 5B to 11.

The range of differences reported for these middle years holds for all levels. Six-year-olds, on entering school, will show verbal skill ranging from below that of the typical four-year-old to above that of the average eight-year-old(18). In many measures of achievement given to high-school seniors we will find some students who fall below elementary-school norms. Amazingly enough, we may also find as many as 10 percent of these high-school seniors exceling the typical college senior(19).

The Constancy of Achievement

We have shown that the child who profits greatly from general experience over a period of years will, in most cases, tend to profit almost equally well from the next dose of general experience. We now ask the same question with regard to the specialized experience of the school. Will the student who has gotten along well in one grade continue to get along well in subsequent grades? Here, again, we exclude any marked or systematic change in the type of schooling.

The chief device used for the study of the constancy of achievement has been the coefficient of correlation. This coefficient tells us to what extent a student who had one rank (say five) in grade ten also has the same rank in grade twelve. A high correlation means there was little change in rank. A low correlation means that rank in one school grade is not much of an indication of rank in another school grade.

All things considered, the correlations are rather high. When carefully constructed objective tests are used, we may expect a correlation of .80 or thereabouts between a student's achievement as a college sophomore and his achievement in the same subject during his senior year. The same correlation holds roughly for achievement at the high-school level. A student who is well ahead of his class in grade ten English will also be ahead of his class in grade twelve English. Most students who are below average will continue to be below average. The correlations to be found between two achievement tests, in fact, are about the same as the correlations between two intelligence tests over the same period(19, 20).

Under circumstances that are less ideal, the constancy of achievement drops appreciably. Over a very long interval, for instance, there is less constancy than over a short interval. The use of less reliable tests will also reduce the correlations. At the college level, for instance, there is a correlation of .60 between the grades a student receives as a sophomore and the grades he receives as a senior. This is to be contrasted with the correlation of .80 based on objective tests.

As might be expected there is also less constancy between one educational level and another than there is within one level. In general, the correlations between grades in elementary school and grades in high school may be as low as .50(21, 22). This is also the relation we can expect between a student's performance in high school and his attainment in college(23) and, for that matter, between college performance and success in graduate school(24, 25, 26). This matter is discussed again later in this chapter, when we consider the general problem of predicting scholastic attainment.

Growth in Academic Achievement

The general pattern of academic growth is familiar to each of us. We can get a rough picture of that growth by visualizing the activities of children in different school grades. We see the children in grade one just beginning to read short and simple sentences. We picture them learning to count, to make crude marks on paper, and to express themselves orally in more connected fashion. In grades two and three we visualize the same children reading connected material of some difficulty, and reading much of it with very little help. In these grades, too, the students can write and spell simple words. In many schools they will have mastered the more simple tasks in arithmetic.

In later grades, the growth in academic matters takes two forms. First, there is an increase in the difficulty of the tasks which can be performed. The children in the upper grades, for instance, can read more difficult material, can perform more difficult operations in arithmetic, and can spell harder words. Second, there is an increase in the number of tasks that can be performed at any given level of difficulty. Students in the upper grades can read more material, as well as harder material. Within a given time they can do more exercises in arithmetic and can spell a larger number of words.

The increase in the *number* of academic tasks which can be accomplished is shown in Figure 6-2. This graph shows the total composite score on the Stanford Achievement Test for each grade. This general test covers several different subjects, including arithmetic, reading, spelling, social studies, and elementary science. The resulting score is thus an index of over-all general attainment. The graph of those composite scores gives us a picture of growth in average general attainment.

The growth shown in Figure 6-2 follows a familiar pattern. It represents smooth continuous increase, from a low of 14 points in grade two to an average score of 70 in grade eight. There are no sudden starts or stops. Each year the students perform a little better than the previous year.

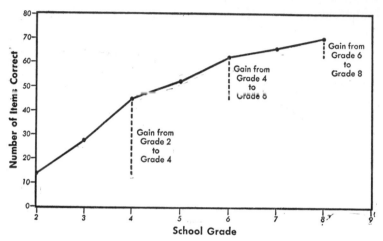

FIGURE 6-2. *Growth in Total Test Score on the Stanford Achievement Test.* Redrawn by permission from Agatha Townsend, *Educational Records Bulletin,* No. 52.

Although the growth on this group of tasks is continuous, we cannot pretend that it is perfectly regular. Like the graph of physical growth, it shows the familiar phenomenon of decreasing returns. In the two years between grades two and four, the growth is 30 items on the test. In the next two years, this growth is only 17 points, and in the two years between grades six and eight, the growth drops to 8 points. In other words, although the students push steadily ahead, they do so at a decreasing rate. Although they gain something every year, they gain more in the early years than in the later years. Here is a suggestion of the same leveling off which we noticed in the graphs of physical growth.

The trend for average attainment which is shown in Figure 6-2 is by no means unique. When we study growth in narrower fields of attainment we find much the same picture. Figure 6-3, for instance, shows some early data for speed of silent reading. Here again we notice continuous growth and also the tendency to level off. In this matter of speed of reading, indeed, the leveling off process is very marked. The increase from grade six to grade eight is very slight. Indeed there is much to suggest that in the realm of sheer mechanics (matching written and spoken words), for instance, as opposed to understanding or comprehension, there is little increase beyond grade four(27).

This slowing up of educational growth after the early grades has caused a great deal of concern. Before becoming too pessimistic, however, we should keep a few points in mind. In the first place this phenomenon

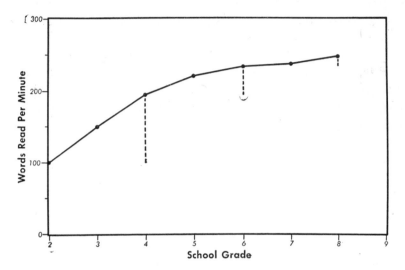

FIGURE 6-3. *Growth in Speed of Silent Reading.* Data from Gray, W. S., A Study of the Emphasis on Various Phases of Reading Instruction in Two Cities. *Elem. Sch. J.* 1916, *17,* 178-186. Courtesy University of Chicago Press.

of diminishing returns, although frequently noticed, is not completely universal. In appreciation of English poetry, for instance, we find definite evidence of increasing returns. On the Abbot-Trabue test there is little growth prior to grade nine. From that point on the curve rises at an *increasing* rate showing more growth in college than in high school. It is also possible that growth in complex mathematics would show no leveling off for some years. In the second place, it is possible that much of the apparent leveling off to be seen in the later years may be due to inequalities in the test scale. It is seldom true that all the items in a test are equally hard. And when this is the case, the gains of the more advanced students always *appear* to be less. Suppose, for instance, students in several grades take a test which is made up of both easy items and hard items. Suppose, further, that the students in grade three get twenty-six items correct. Naturally they will get many of the easy items correct and few of the hard items. The students in grade four also get these twenty-six easy items correct and now set out to surpass their younger colleagues. But the easy items have been largely used up. Consequently the superiority of the grade four people can be shown only by doing additional items from among the more difficult group. To some extent, in other words, the lower gains of the older groups may come from the fact that their gains are carved out of more difficult material. They are simply operating at a more difficult part of the scale.

Finally, curves presented merely represent the growth that takes place under average conditions. Rather than setting the limits of academic attainment, these various graphs should be considered as a comforting base line from which we can operate. With ordinary effort and application on the part of teacher and student, a certain slow but regular growth can be expected. As the student moves from grade to grade his mastery of academic matters will also increase fairly steadily, although, for the most part, at a diminishing rate. This average steady growth which appears so regularly can be used by the conscientious teacher as a point of departure for higher reaches of attainment.

Adult Achievement in Scholarly Pursuits

Recently there has been considerable interest in the age at which adults achieve their greatest creative achievement(28). In all fields, of course, there is a wide range of ages at which men have accomplished their best work. Some men shine forth in early youth. Others do not show their best powers until late middle age. In spite of this wide range, however, there tend to be periods at which outstanding achievements are more likely to occur. For many fields this most productive period is in the early thirties. Men who contribute an outstanding idea or technique or work of art at this early age do not ordinarily cease to contribute, but many of them do their most important work in this earlier period.

It is interesting that extremely youthful achievement is more likely to occur in some fields than in others. Great poets typically show their powers well before the age of thirty, often before twenty-five. Typically, composers of instrumental music also develop before thirty and an unusual number of chemical discoveries have been made before this age. The early thirties is the most productive period for mathematicians and physicists, for short-story writers, for the composers of vocal solos and symphonies, and for practical inventors. There are some exceptions, however. It is in the later thirties that we find the most productive work for geologists, astronomers, and physiologists, for logicians and general philosophers, for the writers of tragedies, and for the operatic composers. And for novelists and metaphysicians the most fruitful years do not come until the early forties.

The Advantages of Deferred Practice

The academic growth that we observe in the schoolroom comes from two important forces. During the time that a child is in school he is being acted on by the experiences he encounters in the school. During that time he is also growing older. Probably both the experience and the increased maturity contribute to his increased attainment. It is easy to see how the school experience may contribute to his academic growth. The contribution of increased maturation may not be so obvious but, upon a little reflection, it is seen to be a force which must be taken into account.

The influence of this increasing maturity is illustrated in an incident from the life of Alexander Bain(29) the famous nineteenth-century English psychologist. As a young boy Bain showed a precocious ability in algebra, mastering the early portions of this subject by the age of nine or ten. At this point he began the study of geometry, but to his great disappointment he found the subject beyond his powers. Later, however, at the age of fourteen or fifteen he returned to the study of geometry and found that the subject gave him no trouble whatever.

It seems reasonable to suppose that Bain's difficulty with geometry at the age of nine or ten came not from lack of experience with mathematics but chiefly from sheer lack of maturity. Conversely, his success at age fourteen cannot be attributed to systematic study in the meantime but must be credited to sheer increased maturity supplemented by any skill that may have transferred from his nonmathematical studies.

A similar process was observed by the writer in a rural school that had just been opened up. This school was located in a frontier community, and some of the settlers had been there for years. By the time the school was started two of the students were twelve years old whereas several were just six years old. The others ranged between these extremes. None of these children had been to school. None could read connected material, although the older children could pick out a few words in the mail-order catalogue. All started in the first reader. By the end of the term, however, the students were no longer in the same class. The six-year-olds had gone through a normal term of reading. During this same term the twelve-year-olds had gone through seven or eight *terms* of reading, although naturally their achievement was somewhat uneven. Here one term of practice was much more productive when applied to twelve-year-olds than when applied to six-year-olds.

Neither of the incidents just reported, of course, provides good scientific information. Only a few cases are involved. Many other things, such as incidental practice or increased motivation, may have accounted for the superior performance of the fourteen-year-old Bain or of the twelve-year-olds in the frontier school. Any satisfactory scientific evidence must come from systematic investigations.

For really careful work in this field, of course, we must resort to experiments with animals. The drastic curtailment of experience would be impossible in dealing with human subjects. Many such experiments with animals have suggested a strong maturational factor. A group of tadpoles "grew up" under an anesthetic and were thus deprived of all experience. Within half an hour, however, they could swim just as well as their fellows who had had practice throughout their development. Half an hour of practice at the end of four days was as effective as the previous four days of practice at an earlier age. In a similar experiment Cruze(30) started young chicks on a maze-learning problem at various intervals after hatching. During the time they were waiting to begin the task, the chicks were kept in a very restricted environment and had no experience with anything resembling a maze. Cruze found that chicks which began the maze at four days learned more readily than those which began at one, two, or three days of age. Biel(31) also found that rats twenty-nine days old were more proficient in such an unnatural task as learning to swim through a water maze than other groups learning the task at the age of nineteen and sixteen days respectively.

Although it would be unthinkable to deprive young children of all experience, there have been many experiments in which practice in one specific task has been withheld from some children for a time. These children were then given practice in this task and we can see how this deferred practice compares with practice provided at an earlier age. One infant beginning stair climbing at the age of forty-six weeks rapidly caught up to her twin sister who had started practicing some six weeks earlier. The same was true for skill in piling blocks. Similarly, children who have received late practice in speed of tapping, or keeping time to music, tend to overtake comparable children who began their practice at an earlier age. Two-year-olds who had been practicing cutting along lines with scissors and buttoning clothes for twelve weeks were overtaken in one week by children who began practice at a later age(32). This also holds true for memorizing and for skill in a simplified game of quoits(33).

The results from these studies of relatively simple types of behavior point rather clearly to one conclusion: within the period of childhood, deferred training is more economical than early training. If we wait until a child is a little older we may accomplish in two weeks what would take six weeks if the practice begins now.

The investigations just discussed have been concerned with fairly simple functions. It would not be wise to assume that maturation is equally effective for all skill. McGraw(34) holds that maturation is only self-sufficient, or nearly self-sufficient, for those traits such as walking (or locomotion) which have always been essential for survival. For traits such as roller skating, or skillful balancing, which are not deeply ingrained in the survival needs of the race, maturation is by no means sufficient and must be supplemented by a considerable amount of practice. Even for these traits, however, the practice will be more effective if not begun at too early an age.

Readiness for Various School Tasks. Readiness, of course, includes much more than sheer physiological maturity. A child of eight may be more ready to undertake a certain academic task partly because he is more mature in a physical sense, but he may also be better prepared because of his general experience and from his experience in related subjects. His interests and motivation may also develop. Altogether we may find that by waiting a few months or a year before undertaking a given topic, we will subject a child to much less frustration and that each hour of later practice may be much more effective. Indeed if we wait long enough we may find that maturation plus the incidental experience of school has done the job for us. Courtis(35) reports an investigation in which some spelling words were taught and other equally difficult words were left untaught. It turned out, however, that there was as much gain on the untaught words as on those taught. Sheer maturation plus the transfer from other school experience made the teaching not only easier, but unnecessary.

Probable Disadvantages from Deferred Practice. It is true that we may get more efficient results by waiting until a child is older before starting him out on a new subject. But we must not let that fact alone be the sole factor in affecting our decision. In spite of the technical increase in efficiency, there may be important practical reasons for beginning the study at an early, although less efficient, age. It is probably true, for instance, that a child will learn to read more rapidly at the age of eight than at the age of six, but think of the enjoyment he will lose between the ages of six and eight! During those two years he could have attained some skill in reading, and this skill may have brought him a great deal of satisfaction. The same principle may hold true for many other subjects.

In discussing the education of young children, the saving of time may not be a very compelling argument. The six-year-old has much time at his disposal. Consequently we may not be greatly disturbed to know that he will take much longer to learn to read at age six than at age eight. The excess time required at age six may not represent any real social, economic, or personal loss.

There is another practical matter which must be faced. If a child has gotten along for several years without a skill, he may feel less and less need for the skill. He may find ways of being comfortable without the skill, and these adjustments or rationalizations may reduce his need when the skill is about to be taught.

Just as interest in such things as reading may wane if undeveloped, so other competing interests may grow. The range of interests for a young child is not so wide as that of an older child. Learning to read may be fun for a young child who has less interest in sports, business, romance, or small talk. An adult, on the other hand, may begrudge the time taken from these more engrossing enterprises. For him, learning to read is a chore to which he must drive himself at the cost of considerable effort.

It is also important to remember that the gains to be had from deferred practice do not continue indefinitely. If we wait *too long* we will get less rather than more from our deferred practice. For some tasks, moreover, the age for most efficient learning may come fairly early. In learning acrobatic dancing, for instance, or in learning to speak a foreign language, it may be important to begin at a fairly early age. In these activities deferred practice may be a handicap. It is also possible that practice in other complex functions, such as becoming adjusted to the social environment, might be more effective if begun early.

Predicting Scholastic Achievement

There are many times when it is important to be able to estimate a student's chances for reasonable success in any program. This information could be useful in helping him select one program from several alternatives and it could also be useful in preparing him to meet probable difficulties.

In the predicting of academic attainment great emphasis has been placed upon the intelligence test. Indeed, in its early stages at least, the intelligence test was chiefly a test of scholastic aptitude, and much of the justification for intelligence tests has come from their presumable ability to select those students who should do well in school.

Intelligence and Achievement: Two Theories

There are two different reasons for suspecting that intelligence might be a good index of subsequent achievement. The first view assumes that intelligence is a real measure of capacity. In a very real sense, intelligence is supposed to represent how much a student can "hold." The second view regards intelligence as merely a measure of a very general sort of achievement. According to this view, intelligence tests are useful because (a) they show what a student has attained in the haphazard curriculum of life, and (b) a student's success in this haphazard curriculum could give us some idea of his probable success in the more specialized curriculum of the school.

Intelligence as Capacity. The idea that intelligence is a true measure of capacity is very old. It is often associated with the belief that the capacity measured by intelligence is essentially an inherited capacity. This second idea, however, though very prevalent, is not a necessary aspect of capacity. Presumably one's capacity could change with experience, but could still represent a limit at any given moment.

The emphasis on intelligence as capacity has led to the development of the *accomplishment quotient*. As we have seen, a student's intelligence can readily be expressed as an age score (MA) indicating, according to this view, his capacity. His achievement in any given subject can also be indicated as an age score (EA) showing his actual attainment. By turning these into a ratio $\frac{EA}{MA}$ we can get an AQ or accomplishment quotient. In this ratio we assume that the MA and the EA were obtained at the same time so that CA would be the same in both cases. If not, it would be necessary to use the formula $AQ = \frac{EQ}{IQ}$. In this latter formula the influence of the different CA's would be eliminated.

To those who regard intelligence tests as precise measures of true capacity, the AQ indicates at a glance whether or not a student is working up to capacity. A student with an AQ of less than 100 would be achieving below his capacity. A student with an AQ of 100 would be just up to his capacity, whereas a student with an AQ over 100 would be achieving beyond his capacity. If capacity is interpreted at all literally, an AQ over 100 would be impossible.

Intelligence as Achievement in General Tasks. In contrast to the view just considered, we may prefer not to think of intelligence as a precise measure of capacity and certainly not as capacity that comes entirely from inheritance. True enough, as we shall see, we may find that intelligence is greatly influenced by heredity, but we need not assume this at the outset.

When we look at the tasks that we ask a child to perform while he is taking an intelligence test, we see that we are really testing him on the words he has *learned* to use, on the motor skill he has *acquired,* and on the various relations he has *come* to comprehend. In other words, we find ourselves actually measuring achievement in defining words, naming objects, following directions, and a host of other tasks. Whatever our hopes or intentions, our test is really a test of an exceedingly general sort of achievement.

General versus Special Achievement

Realizing the fact that intelligence tests inescapably turn out to be achievement tests, is there any point in trying to distinguish between intelligence tests and other kinds of achievement tests? Or more important, is there any satisfactory method of distinguishing between intelligence tests and the other kinds of achievement tests? As it happens, there are some very real differences between the two types of tests, in spite of the fact that both are achievement tests. In the first place, as we have seen, the items on an intelligence test are chosen from a wide variety of tasks. We seldom or never see an intelligence test made up entirely of questions in arithmetic or entirely of questions in history or science. Items used in an intelligence test, on the contrary, usually cover many different subjects. Some of the tasks may involve arithmetic, others are highly verbal. Some may call for a very ordinary knowledge of history while others may demand a familiarity with baseball or with moving pictures.

In the second place the tasks found in an intelligence test must be fair to all-comers. They must be tasks which everyone has encountered, and which everyone has had a chance to master. They must not be tasks which people encounter only in a special environment. They must not be problems which one would come across only in a highly specialized course.

Putting these two facts together we can say that intelligence tests are clearly achievement tests, but *they are tests of achievement in the ordi-*

nary, everyday tasks which one encounters in the casual day-by-day experience of everyday life.

The regular achievement tests, in contrast to intelligence tests, have neither of these restrictions. The maker of an achievement test need not sample a wide variety of fields. Indeed most frequently he selects his items entirely from one subject, such as music or history or algebra. The maker of an achievement test, moreover, does not try to select items which could be answered on the basis of casual, general experience. Indeed, he is more likely to seek items which would be encountered only in a specialized course such as Latin or geography. Typically he makes a point of concentrating on these specialized tasks and makes a deliberate effort to avoid items which could be mastered by one who had never studied the subject.

This, then, is the practical, down-to-earth distinction between achievement tests and intelligence tests. Whatever the underlying theory, whatever the *intentions* or the *hopes* of the person who makes the tests, this is what he comes out with: the intelligence test is an achievement test stressing a wide variety of tasks which everyone encounters in casual experience. The regular scholastic achievement test, on the other hand, is a test of achievement on those tasks which are encountered in more specialized, scholastic experience.

According to this latter view, intelligence tests could still be excellent predictors of achievement. But their value in this respect comes from the simple assumption that a child's ability to master a wide variety of general tasks may turn out to be a good index of his ability to master some more specialized tasks. A good index, but probably not a perfect index! According to this view, for instance, there is no reason why an AQ cannot exceed 100. There is no reason, that is to say, why a sudent's "achievement" cannot exceed his "intelligence." According to the down-to-earth view, an AQ of 120 would merely mean that the student gets along better on some of the specialized tasks of the school (achievement) than he does on the more general haphazard tasks of everyday life (intelligence). It is to be expected that some studiously minded people will be more successful in the classroom than in the unorganized curriculum of life. They may have more of a flair for remembering events in history than for remembering the information they pick up in casual experience. Such students will obtain a higher score on an achievement test in history than on a test of general intelligence.

Conversely, according to this view, we would not be unduly disturbed about a student whose achievement falls below his intelligence, whose AQ, that is to say, is markedly below 100. Some students are bound to have more of a flair for mastering the tasks which they come across in the street or in the home or in the movies than for mastering the experiences of the school. Such students, by definition, will secure a higher score on an "intelligence" test than on an "achievement" test.

Intelligence and Achievement: Results

Theoretically it is reasonable to suppose that a student's ability to master the tasks of everyday life should be a good index of his ability to master the specialized tasks of the schoolroom. But is this theory correct? How does it actually work out?

For the elementary school we can get a fairly accurate idea of the typical relations from a study of Table 6-1. At the left of the table we see a range of correlation coefficients running all the way from −.10 to .99. The numbers under "Reading" tell us how many correlations between reading and intelligence fall in each interval. For instance, of the forty-six correlations between reading and intelligence, none happen to fall between .90 and .99, but six are somewhere between .80 and .89, seven between .70 and .79, and so forth. The median shows the average correlation for each subject.

TABLE 6-1

*Correlations between Intelligence and Achievement
in Different Subjects at the Elementary-school Level*

Size of Correlation	Reading	Spelling	Arithmetic	Handwriting
.90—.99			2	
.80—.89	6	2	1	
.70—.79	7	3	6	
.60—.69	12	7	2	
.50—.59	5	5	10	
.40—.49	4	4	6	1
.30—.39	4	5	6	1
.20—.29	6	3	1	1
.10—.19		2		
.00—.09	2	1		3
−.10— −.01				1
No. of Correlations	46	32	34	7
Median r	.60	.51	.55	.08

A study of this table suggests several trends. We notice, for instance, (a) that different investigators have come up with widely different answers, (b) that *on the average* the relation might be represented by a correlation between .50 and .60, and (c) that there is some suggestion that there is a closer relationship between intelligence and reading than between intelligence and any other subject.

Similar tables for the secondary schools and the colleges would tell about the same story as those at the elementary-school level. At all levels, there is wide variation from one investigation to another. At all levels, there is some tendency for the correlations to cluster. At all levels, intelligence correlates somewhat more highly with English than with other subjects. In contrast to this complete agreement at all levels, however, we find a somewhat lower over-all or average correlation at the high-school and college level. Whereas the over-all average for the elementary schools is between .50 and .60, that for the higher levels(23, 26) is between .40 and .50. Such a difference, of course, is not very large, and, in view of the wide range of correlations at all levels, it is certainly not very dependable.

This higher correlation at the elementary-school level may be due in part to the fact that we probably have better tests for both intelligence and achievement at this level. Remembering our down-to-earth method of distinguishing between intelligence and achievement, moreover, we are not surprised by either of the slight trends just noticed. We would expect to find a somewhat closer relation between intelligence and English than between intelligence and other subjects. We would also expect to find higher correlations in the elementary school. According to our down-to-earth distinction, intelligence is merely an index of our mastery of everyday nonscholastic tasks. And those nonscholastic tasks are more closely connected with English, with talking, and listening than with most other school subjects. Similarly, there is more resemblance between the tasks of everyday life and the elementary-school curriculum than between those everyday tasks and the curriculum at the higher levels. At the elementary-school level the difference between specialized school experience and generalized experience is much less than at the higher levels.

When intelligence-test results are used to predict general college achievement, we often get better results from the more verbal tests(36).

Previous Achievement as a Predictor

If a student has had no experience or very little experience in the specialized work of the school, we might readily use his "achievement" in the general tasks of the world as our best predictor. When we know about his actual performance in school, however, we might prefer to use this as an index of future attainment. The chief flaw in this reasoning lies in the frequent lack of reliability in many tests of achievement, and in the further fact that the tasks at one educational level may be radically different from those at another.

Whatever our expectations, we find that at most levels previous academic success is about as good as any other predictor, or perhaps a little better than any other. At the college level, where this problem of selection is especially acute, high-school grades give a somewhat better prediction than any other index(26, 37). They become even more effective when relative standing in high school is used. Objective tests of high-school attainment also provide a good basis for selecting college students(38).

At the graduate level, we find that the best prediction usually comes from college grades in the major subject. This is not always so(39), however, and many graduate schools place considerable emphasis on advanced versions of the typical intelligence test.

Specialized Aptitude Tests

It has often been assumed that advanced professional courses in engineering, medicine, nursing, law, business, and accounting call for rather specialized aptitudes. Accordingly, there has been a considerable effort to devise special aptitude tests for these areas. For the most part, however, such tests have not been quite so useful as college grades coupled with a more general intelligence test(24, 25, 40, 41). At the college level such special aptitude tests have been used chiefly for added help in predicting success in special fields such as language or mathematics. Here again their value, over and above the help provided by more general measures, is somewhat dubious(42, 43).

Summary

The student's growth in academic subjects is a unique responsibility for the teacher, since the teacher's failure in this area would seldom be rectified by any other agency. The student's status in these subjects is seldom obvious and must be revealed by a deliberate testing program made up of informal tests, such as impromptu oral quizzes, or involving more formal tests. The type of test used should fit the teaching objective which the teacher has in mind. No test is perfect for all objectives. Each has advantages and disadvantages.

The traditional essay test is excellent for testing ability to organize ideas about the subject and permits the student to express subtle qualifications in his answers. It does not tempt the student to guess the right answer. On the other side of the shield, the essay test permits only limited sampling of the course content. Although it discourages sheer guessing between two or three answers, it does permit bluffing. Such tests are also highly subjective and are exceedingly laborious to mark.

The short-answer tests are of several types: the true-false, the multiple-choice tests, completion tests, and matching tests. These tests are in many ways the complement of the essay tests. They are strong where the essay test is weak. Standard tests are of the short-answer type, and these more carefully made tests have several advantages. They supply norms with which we can compare our students and from which we can compute educational ages and grade scores. They are excellent technically and ordinarily are more reliable than homemade tests. They also lend themselves to mechanical methods of scoring. With so many excellent testing procedures available, no teacher should become the exclusive champion of any one device.

The study of achievement test results reveals a few general factors below the college level. These include a general school factor, and factors involving numerical ability, verbal ability, several kinds of fluency, and cultural interests. At the college level, fewer general factors have emerged. Achievement tests show wide individual differences within the same age level and within the same grade.

Academic development, like general intellectual development, shows itself both in the increasing difficulty of the tasks which can be mastered and in the greater number of tasks mastered at any level of difficulty. Composite achievement test score shows a steady increase throughout the grades, with a suggestion of diminishing returns in the later grades. In many early investigations, the rate of silent reading changed little after grade six or seven. The same continuous rise with a hint of diminishing returns appears in such specific subjects as arithmetic and spelling.

The performance level of adults remains high in subjects such as reading but falls off in the less used subjects of history, geography, and the more esoteric aspects of arithmetic. The brilliant academic or scientific productions of adults are most likely to occur in the early thirties, but may continue, of course, throughout life.

As the child gets older he becomes increasingly able to master academic tasks and to profit from the experience in the schoolroom. Would there not be an advantage, then, in having him defer his scholastic study as long as possible? In a sense, yes. There may be a few subjects, of course, such as acrobatic dancing or learning a foreign language where the older child is under a handicap. But for most academic subjects the older child has the advantage. Against this technical advantage, however, we must set the valuable experience the child will miss while he is waiting to begin his instruction. We must also realize that the time of the young child is not especially crowded, and that there may be no great tragedy in having him spend two years at age six in learning something that he could learn in six months at the age of ten.

In predicting academic achievement for one level, we can use either previous academic achievement, general intelligence, or special aptitude tests. Previous academic achievement may have a slight advantage.

There has been a good deal of confusion about the theoretical relation between intelligence and achievement. At one time people held that intelligence indicates capacity whereas achievement indicates actual accomplishment. The accomplishment quotient formalized this relation. Intelligence was hereditary and achievement was acquired. It is wiser to think of intelligence tests as being really achievement tests which measure the student's mastery of the ordinary everyday tasks he encounters in his casual daily life. Achievement tests, on the other hand, are measures of the student's mastery of the tasks he encounters within the schoolroom or the specialized class.

Empirical studies show that a student who is good in mastering the casual tasks of everyday life is also fairly good in mastering the more specialized tasks of the school. The correlations cluster around .50 and .60 for the elementary school and between .40 and .50 for high school and college. At all levels intelligence correlates more highly with English and reading than with other subjects.

SPECIFIC REFERENCES

1. Wrightstone, J. W. Frontiers in educational research: in the measurement of aptitudes and achievement. *J. educ. Res.,* 1947, *40,* 389–396.
2. Dexter, L. A. Examinations as instruments of, and obstacles to, general education. *Sch. Rev.,* 1947, *55,* 534–541.
3. Rulon, P. J. On the validity of educational tests. *Harv. educ. Rev.,* 1946, *16,* 290–296.
4. Davis, F. B. *Utilizing human talent.* American Council on Education, 1947.
5. Freeman, F. N. The monopoly of objective tests. *Educ. Forum,* 1946, *10,* 389–395.
6. Sims, V. M. The essay examination is a projective technique. *Educ. psychol. Measmt.,* 1948, *8,* 15–31.

7. Class, E. C. The effect of the kind of test announcement on students' preparation. *J. educ. Res.*, 1935, *28*, 358–361.

8. Douglass, H. R., and Talmadge, Margaret. How university students prepare for new types of examinations. *Sch. & Soc.*, 1934, *39*, 318–320.

9. Meyer, G. An experimental study of the old and new types of examination: II. Methods of Study. *J. educ. Psychol.*, 1935, *26*, 30–40.

10. Terry, P. How students review for objective and essay tests. *Elem. Sch. J.*, 1933, *33*, 592–603.

11. Vallance, T. R. A comparison of essay and objective examinations as learning experiences. *J. educ. Res.*, 1947, *41*, 279–288.

12. Jones, S. Process testing—an attempt to analyze reasons for the students' responses to test questions. *J. educ. Res.*, 1953, *46*, 525–534.

13. Rinsland, H. D. Form for briefing and evaluating standardized tests. *J. educ. Res.*, 1949, *42*, 371–375.

14. Ormiston, Mary. The bearing of general and special abilities upon scholastic success at the beginning and end of a secondary school career. *Brit. J. educ. Psychol.*, 1939, *9*, 164–173 and 213–223.

15. Vernon, P. E. Educational abilities of training college students. *Brit. J. educ. Psychol.*, 1939, *9*, 233–250.

16. Burt, Sir C. The relations of educational abilities. *Brit. J. educ. Psychol.*, 1939, *9*, 45–71.

17. French, J. W. The description of aptitude and achievement tests in terms of rotated factors. *Psychomet. Monogr.*, 1951, No. 5.

18. Cook, W. W. Individual differences and curriculum practice. *J. educ. Psychol.*, 1948, *39*, 141–148.

19. Learned, W. S., and Wood, B. D. *The student and his knowledge.* Carnegie Foundation for the Advancement of Teaching Bull. No. 29, 1938.

20. Townsend, Agatha. Some aspects of testing in the primary grades. *Educ. Rec. Bull.*, 1944, No. 40, 51–54.

21. Adams, F. J. Predicting high-school and college records from elementary-school test data. *J. educ. Psychol.*, 1938, *29*, 56–66.

22. Traxler, A. E., and Selover, Margaret S. Relationship of elementary-school achievement tests to achievement tests taken in the secondary school. *J. educ. Res.*, 1942, *36*, 161–167.

23. Eysenck, H. J. Student selection by means of psychological tests. *Brit. J. educ. Psychol.*, 1947, *17*, 20–39.

24. Harrell, W. Predicting success of law school students. *Amer. Law. Sch. Rev.*, 1939, *9*, 290–293.

25. Hoffman, W. S. Rank in college and the medical school. *Sch. & Soc.*, 1938, *47*, 314.

26. Garrett, H. R. A review and interpretation of investigations of factors related to scholastic success in Colleges of Arts and Science and Teachers Colleges. *J. exper. Educ.*, 1949, *18*, 91–138.

27. Triggs, Frances O. The development of measured word recognition skills, grade four through the college freshman year. *Educ. psychol. Measmt.*, 1952, *12*, 345–349.

28. Lehman, H. C. *Age and achievement.* Princeton University Press, 1953.

29. Bain, A. *Autobiography.* London, Longmans, 1904, p. 7.

30. Cruze, W. W. Maturity and learning ability. *Psychol. Monogr.*, 1938, *50*, 49–65.

31. Biel, W. C. Early age differences in maze performance in the albino rat. *J. genet. Psychol.*, 1940, *56*, 439–453.

32. Hilgard, Josephine R. Learning and maturation in preschool children. *J. genet. Psychol.*, 1932, *41*, 36–56.

33. Hicks, J. A. The acquisition of motor skill in young children. *Univ. Iowa Stud. Child Welfare*, 1931, *4*, No. 5, 1–80.

34. Carmichael, L., ed. *Manual of child psychology.* Wiley, 1946, Chap. 7, Maturation of behavior (McGraw, Myrtle B.).

35. Courtis, S. A. The rate of growth makes a difference. *Phi Delta Kappan*, 1949, *30*, 316–323.

36. Merrill, R. M., and Heathers, Louise B. A comparison of the Wechsler-Bellevue and the ACE tests on a university counseling center group. *J. consult. Psychol.*, 1953, *17*, 63–66.

37. Consand, J. P. Admissions criteria: a review of the literature. *Calif. J. second. Educ.*, 1953, *28*, 12–21.

38. Dolansky, Marie P. "The Essential High School Content Battery" as a predictor of college success. *J. educ. Psychol.*, 1953, *44*, 361–365.

39. Jenson, R. E. Predicting scholastic achievement of first-year graduate students. *Educ. psychol. Measmt.*, 1953, *13*, 322–329.

40. Stuit, D., and others. *Predicting success in professional schools.* American Council on Education, 1949.

41. Hendrix, O. R. Predicting success in elementary accounting. *J. appl. Psychol.*, 1953, *37*, 75–77.

42. Kinzer, J. R., and Kinzer, Lydia G. Predicting grades in advanced college mathematics. *J. appl. Psychol.*, 1953, *37*, 182–184.

43. Peters, H. C. The prediction of success and failure in elementary foreign language courses. *J. appl. Psychol.*, 1953, *37*, 178–181.

SUGGESTIONS FOR FURTHER READING

For General Discussions of Tests and Testing

1. Mursell, J. L. *Psychological testing*. Longmans, 1947.
2. Stephenson, W. *Testing school children, an eassy in educational and social psychology*. Longmans, 1949.
3. Remmers, H. H., and Gage, N. L. *Educational measurement and evaluation*. Harper, 1943.
4. Greene, H. A., Jorgensen, A. N., and Gerberich, J. R. *Measurement and evaluation in the elementary school*. Longmans, 1942.
5. Greene, H. A., Jorgensen, A. N., and Gerberich, J. R. *Measurement and evaluation in the secondary school*. Longmans, 1943.
6. Thomas, R. M. *Judging student progress*. Longmans, 1954.
7. Greene, E. B. *Measurements of human behavior*. Odyssey, 1952.
8. Odell, C. W. *How to improve classroom testing*. Longmans, 1953.
9. Simpson, R. H. *Improving teacher-learner processes*. Longmans, 1953.
10. Traxler, A. E., and others. *Introduction to testing and the use of test results in public schools*. Harper, 1953.
11. Torgerson, T. L., and Adams, Georgia S. *Measurement and evaluation*. Dryden, 1954.
12. Ross, C. C., and Stanley, J. C. *Measurement in today's schools*. Prentice-Hall, 1954.

For Help in Constructing Tests

13. Adkins, Dorothy C. *Construction and analysis of achievement tests*. U.S. Printing Office, 1947.
14. Weitzman, E., and McNamara, W. J. *Constructing classroom examinations; a guide for teachers*. Science Research Associates, 1949.
15. Remmers, H. H., Ryden, E. K., and Morgan, C. L. *Introduction to educational psychology*. Harper, 1954, Chap. 12.
16. Bean, K. L. *Construction of educational and personnel tests*. McGraw-Hill, 1953.

For Help in Locating and Selecting Tests

17. Hildreth, Gertrude H. *A bibliography of mental tests and rating scales*. Psychological Corp., 1939.
18. Hildreth, Gertrude H. *A bibliography of mental tests and rating scales—1945 supplement*. Psychological Corp., 1946.

19. Buros, O. K. *The fourth mental measurements yearbook.* Gryphon, 1953. (Use this issue to obtain references to earlier yearbooks.)

For Discussions of Essay versus Objective Tests

20. Monroe, W. S. Educational measurement in 1920 and in 1945. *J. educ. Res.*, 1945, *38*, 334–340.
21. Scates, D. E. Fifty years of objective measurement and research in education. *J. educ. Res.*, 1947, *41*, 241–264.
22. Findley, W. G., and Smith, A. B. Measurement of educational achievement in the schools. *Rev. educ. Res.*, 1950, *20*, 63–75.

For General Discussions of Academic Growth

23. Stuit, D., and others. *Predicting success in professional schools.* American Council on Education, 1949.
24. Lehman, H. C. *Age and achievement.* Princeton University Press, 1953.
25. Courtis, S. A. The rate of growth makes a difference. *Phi Delta Kappan,* 1949, *30*, 316–323.

Exercises and Questions for Discussion

1. Discuss the problem of validity in tests. Why is validity so important? Why is perfect validity frequently unobtainable?

2. List several points you should look for in selecting a standard test.

3. Would you expect to find individual differences in a grade-six class where the students have been promoted according to fairly strict academic standards? Justify your answer.

4. What do you think of intelligence tests as a means of predicting a student's performance in school or college? Under what conditions is the intelligence test a good basis for prediction? When is it less valuable?

5. When achievement is measured in terms of the number of test items that can be completed, we find a certain similarity between the growth curves of achievement and for height or strength. In what respects are these curves similar? Is there any "moral" for teachers in this similarity? Does it call for pessimism, optimism, a change in plans, or what?

7

Mental and Physical Growth:
The Role of Nonscholastic Factors

In OUR EXAMINATION of physical well-being, of intelligence, and of academic attainment we have seen something of the nature of each type of growth and have examined the general course that each follows. Later we shall discuss the things the teacher can do to promote such growth. Before taking this latter step, however, we shall consider the part played by forces outside the school. The teacher, after all, is only one member of a complex pattern of forces. The experiences that he provides for the student can never occur in isolation. They take on much of their meaning in terms of the student's family. The family in turn belongs in some way to the community, and that community is a part of a larger regional environment. Much of this nonscholastic environment, moreover, is largely or almost entirely beyond the control of the teacher. The teacher can do little or nothing about the geographical region of his students, about the size of the community, or even about the quality of the community. He can do little to change the economic status of the home. In many respects, even the status of the child within the home will evade his influence. All in all, although the teacher may influence some of these things as a citizen or as a voter, his position as a teacher gives him no unique control. As a teacher, he must take many of these hereditary and environmental forces as he finds them. If they are good, he may take advantage of them. If they are bad, he must contend with them and counteract them as best he can. But he cannot change them.

Physique and Health in Relation to Mental Growth

Obviously, one aspect of growth can act as a force to influence another. As we have pointed out in Chapter 6, intellectual and academic growth can be intimately related. In the same way it is possible that physical growth may be an important nonscholastic factor in the development of intelligence and in academic progress. Let us consider, then, how growth in physique and in health can affect these other aspects of educational growth.

To many people, it seems that physical and mental superiority never go together. The stereotype put out by the newspaper cartoonist never depicts an intelligent football player, a healthy child genius, or an attractive intellectual woman. To him and to his readers, the football player must be dumb, the intelligent child must be a frail wispy creature, and the intellectual woman must be excessively "plain," to say the least.

When people first began to study the problem systematically they were impressed by the falsity of the general impression. Indeed the conclusions of early systematic investigations seemed to constitute a swing of opinion to the opposite extreme. Not content with merely showing that brilliant people were of average health, it was suggested that geniuses, for the most part, had exceptional physical endowment. Sir Francis Galton contended that the eminent men whom he studied would provide the material for a formidable football team. This view later received vigorous support from L. M. Terman and from Mrs. Leta S. Hollingworth, who also rejected the idea of the frail genius. The group studied by these investigators seemed not only the physical equals of normal children but actually superior in both size and health.

As might be supposed, the discrepancy between general impression and the early systematic studies produced a flood of investigations. As early as 1940 some two hundred and fifty separate studies were reported on the relation of physical and mental status. So many investigations have been carried out, in fact, that the answer for many aspects of the problem seems no longer in doubt. And, needless to say, the truth has been found to be somewhere between the two extremes.

Body Size

On the whole, intelligence and achievement have only a very slight relation to height. Whatever relation there is, however, turns out to be positive. On the average, tall people are ever so slightly more intelligent than short people. The average correlation from a great many studies is about .20. A correlation this low means, of course, a tremendous amount of overlapping. There will be many tall people of low intelligence and many short people who are bright. It is only on the average that this very slight relation holds. Other physical measurements, such as weight and girth, also correlate slightly with intelligence and achievement, but with lower correlations than we find for height.

Size of Head or Brain. From general discussion one would gather that intelligence and head size, or certainly brain size, are intimately related. Actually this is not the case. Of course, if we compare one species with another we do find that, on the average, ability to learn increases with the development of the brain. Within our own species, however, there is almost no relation. Head size or brain size is no more closely related to intelligence or achievement than is height or weight.

If not sheer size, what aspect of the brain does control intelligence? It is extremely difficult to say. From a whole series of brain operations(1, 2, 3), it appears that the loss of considerable amounts of brain tissue in certain areas will bring about only very slight change in general intelligence, or may bring about no change whatever. We must remember, of course, that practically all the patients observed must have had some defect, such as a brain tumor or a disturbance of personality, prior to operation. People who are perfectly normal do not ordinarily undergo brain surgery.

Facial Features

Judgments of intelligence based on photographs are of little or no value. This is true whether the judgments are made by naive observers or by people who profess to be character analysts. We should add that perhaps it would be easier to judge intelligence by looking at the person himself than by looking at the photograph. Changes in expression, the liveliness of the attention, and the general manner may prove more revealing than sheer proportion of features. It is interesting to note, by the way, that when observers set out to select the best looking photographs—ignoring the matter of intelligence—they tend to select intelligent people. When looking at photographs, that is to say, you are more likely to find intelligent people if you look for beauty than if you look for intelligence(4).

Basal Metabolism

The general energy level at which the individual operates is reflected in the basal metabolism or in the rate at which oxygen is consumed. This metabolic rate is largely governed by the thyroid gland and can be speeded up by the administration of thyroxin. It would be natural to suppose that general bodily activity or energy would affect intellectual performance. This supposition is especially plausible when we remember the great emphasis placed on speed in the measurement of intelligence. Remembering this emphasis, we might readily expect that the high-strung, hyperthyroid person would have a great advantage over the slow, lethargic, more indolent competitor.

This very plausible expectation received considerable support from early investigations. Some of the earliest and most dramatic evidence came from a study of cretinous children. These cretins are so lacking in thyroid function as to be physically deformed. Typically they are heavy, dwarfed individuals with coarse, dry skin. The mentality of such children is usually of a very low order. If such cretins are treated at an early age, and if the treatment is continued for a long time, a very definite physical and mental improvement will result.

Does this rather marked relation hold for more normal people? Apparently not in any consistent way. The great majority of the investigations show practically zero correlation between intelligence and metabolic rate(5). An examination of all people who have low metabolism would reveal a wide range of intelligence, from the very dull to the very bright. The same would be true for people with a high metabolic rate. The average intelligence of the two groups would be very similar.

Like so many other questions, this matter is by no means settled. There is some suggestion, for instance, that there may be a positive relation for children under the age of fourteen or so. It would not be surprising, moreover, if there were such a relation during the period of more rapid growth, even though that relation failed to persist into later adolescence. We must wait for further evidence on this matter.

Disease and Physical Defects

There is a superficial or over-all relation between physical well-being and intelligence or scholastic achievement(6). This relation is especially marked in the case of crippled children and children who have defective vision or defective hearing. There are, of course, many types of crippled children and many types and degrees of sensory defect. Naturally we might suspect different results for these different groups. Children who are crippled because of some impairment of the brain or central nervous system (spastic birth paralysis or chorea), for instance, have a lower intelligence than children crippled through accident or through diseases such as tuberculosis or poliomyelitis. The average IQ for the former group is about 70 whereas the averages for the other groups range from 85 to 92(7).

These relations are most clear-cut in the case of children who have some serious handicap. These handicaps show up more in achievement than in intelligence. Slight visual defects within the so-called normal range may have some adverse effects on reading, although this matter is in dispute. Other subjects, however, show little or no effect(8).

It is the crippled child and the child suffering from sensory defects who is most likely to do poorly on the intellectual and scholastic tests. Other defects do not show nearly as much relation to intelligence or achievement. An examination of children suffering from pronounced dental decay, infected tonsils, heart disease, tuberculosis, or malnutrition will show them to be only slightly behind healthy children in intelligence or achievement(9, 10). With such slight difference, of course, we are bound to find that many of the children with defects are far ahead of the average for the healthy children. It is only on the average that the children with the defects fall slightly behind.

Explaining the Relations between Physique and Intellect. Whenever we find that reduced achievement goes hand in hand with some physical defect, it is most natural to jump to the conclusion that the physical defect is the cause of the poor achievement. This may well turn out to be true, but before finally deciding upon such a simple and direct relation we should examine other hypotheses. It is always possible, for instance, that the differences come entirely from the unsuitability of our tests. After all, it is difficult to be sure that a child with poor hearing or poor vision has had a fair chance in taking a test. We must also be on the lookout for some common cause. Slum life, for instance, may increase the risk of physical defect. Slums may also limit the IQ and may be apt to produce the intellectual defect even without the intervention of some physical handicap. We must also consider the possibility that limited intelligence may lead to accident or poor health.

Of these alternative hypotheses, there has been little work done on the idea of reversed causality—the hypothesis that limited intelligence or attainment may lead to physical ailments. The common cause has been investigated, however, and there is evidence that some of the relation between physical defect and intelligence is due to the common influence of heredity and family background. Crippled children, for example, are more likely to come from the less fortunate environments. Children from such environments, moreover, are not likely to do so well on our tests. Consequently the poor background (or heredity) may cause both the physical defect and the poor test score. To get some evidence on this point, investigators have compared crippled children with their noncrippled brothers and sisters. The investigations reveal little if any difference between crippled and noncrippled children within the same home. On the average, both are below normal in intelligence(7). If the crippled condition actually affected the intelligence, the children with the defect should receive a lower score than their brothers and sisters.

The Correction of Physical Defects. The correction of physical defects, of course, is a most important end in itself, and, as has already been stated, the teacher should do everything within his competence to cooperate in such a program. If the hypothesis of direct causality is true, moreover, this correction of a defect should lead to a definite increase in academic attainment. This is what we should expect from the hypothesis. In actual fact, what are we likely to find? We find a wide variety of results. In one very careful investigation(11) hard-of-hearing children showed no scholastic improvement after being provided with hearing aids. Later experiments, however, show more promise(12) and there is some evidence that elaborate preschool training of deaf and hard-of-hearing children will permit them to attend regular schools instead of the residential schools(13). As yet there is little to suggest that children with mild visual defects will do any better after being provided with glasses(14).

There is further confusion from the experiments on the administration of glutamic acid to dull children. Some studies report marked improvement(15) whereas others report no gains(16). There is also some conflict in the reports on the administration of thiamine(17).

Intelligence may be affected by some prenatal conditions and by conditions existing about the time of birth. Mongoloid idiocy, for instance, is very rare in infants born of mothers under thirty (1.5 mongoloids for every ten thousand births) but rises to twenty-nine cases per ten thousand births for mothers over forty and to ninety cases per ten thousand births in mothers over forty-five(18).

The removal of tonsils, once the great panacea for retarded children, has proved to be disappointing as a means of improving scholastic performance. Children undergoing the operation do not gain any more than other children who needed the operation but who did not receive it. The experiments on diet are somewhat complicated. Several of the more elaborate investigations were aimed, not only at dietary gains, but at the improvement of the whole community life. These investigations report improvement in scholastic work(19). Other investigations have concentrated on diet, and these have found that the improved diet brought about gains in weight but failed to induce any change in intelligence(20, 21).

All in all, it appears that improvements in health and physical efficiency should be encouraged for their own sake. Nothing can be more justifiable than the attempt to bring about greater health in children and to reduce the handicap imposed by physical defect. We should not be overconfident, however, that such improvement will automatically help the teacher in his academic tasks. The relation between health and intellect is by no means marked or dependable. Indeed some students of the problem suggest that the mechanisms responsible for the intellect are in some way protected from all but the most extreme ravages of disease.

Hygiene in Relation to Academic Development

Hygiene, of course, is not intended primarily to bring about increased academic attainment. It is intended chiefly to improve the health and physical well-being of the child. Although there is no clear evidence as to the health gains to be had from these hygienic procedures(22), still we cannot afford to take any risks. So long as there is a reasonable hope that children will profit from attention to health rules, just so long must we continue to practice and to recommend those health rules.

Aside from the main question of the relation of hygiene to actual physical well-being, it is also in order to ask whether or not there is any relation between mental and academic efficiency and the various health practices.

Use of Drugs

General Effects of Alcohol. For teachers of young children, alchohol is not a serious problem, particularly in most sections of the United

States where alcohol is not considered a normal accompaniment of a meal. Teachers at the high-school or college level, however, may well wish to know something of the effects of alcohol on the mental and academic performance of students.

The social evils resulting from the immoderate use of alcohol are, of course, too well known to require any discussion here. A discussion of the permanent effect of alcohol on the tissues or organs of the body is also out of place here, although we may note that the harmful physiological effects may have been exaggerated in the past.

Almost all psychological functions are impaired by alcohol. Taking any considerable dose of alcohol, especially before a meal, lessens one's ability to discriminate between letters on a chart, to distinguish between sounds, to see a large number of letters in one eyeful, to name colors rapidly, to put marks through all the "e's" on a page of print, to react to a signal quickly, to perform tasks calling for simple motor coordination, to sew, to string beads, to type, to throw darts at a target, to remember poetry studied, to solve problems in arithmetic, to judge intervals of time, or to judge one's own success in performing tasks. It is this last deficiency, by the way, which is one of the most serious. Poor performance by itself is bad enough, but inferior performance coupled with the delusion of competence may be a prescription for disaster(23, 24).

Differential Effects of Alcohol. Alcohol affects younger children more than older children or adults. This is true even when the dosages have been somewhat equalized. It reduces complicated functions such as learning an artificial language more than simple functions such as learning to withdraw the finger at a signal. It has more effect on ability to distinguish between two objects or sounds than on ability to detect the presence or absence of any object or sound. There has been some suggestion, in fact, that alcohol may actually increase one's ability to detect the presence of light or to hear a slight noise.

All in all, no one could justify the use of alcohol in the schoolroom or as an aid in learning. Many people, of course, may remark that no sensible person would advocate such use of alcohol. The more reasonable endorsers of alcoholic beverages consider them as an aid to relaxation, sociability, or perhaps gaiety and not as aids for the more exacting tasks of the working day.

The investigation of the influence of alcohol has proved to be most complex and has provided excellent illustrations of the pitfalls that plague the experimenter. In any experiment on the influence of drugs, the subject may be affected not only by the drug but also by the mere knowledge or suspicion that he is getting a drug. A subject can readily get some reaction from the mere knowledge that he is about to drink alcohol and to take a test. To take care of this factor we must use some control drug which the subject cannot distinguish from alcohol, and this, as may well be imagined, has proved to be difficult. And it is only when this control is accomplished that we will have two groups, both *thinking* that they are getting alcohol but only one group actually getting it. Under these conditions the reaction to the idea would be the same for both groups, and any difference in reaction could be attributed to the physiological effect of alcohol.

Benzedrine Sulphate. This drug, once widely available, may readily become a problem for the teacher. It is considered to be a "pep pill" that will boost one's score on a test or examination. As a matter of fact, most people actually do perform slightly better on an intelligence test after taking some twenty milligrams of benzedrine. The gain, however, is very slight and is in no way large enough to offset the very definite physiological risks that may accompany the prolonged use of a new drug.

Caffeine. Caffeine occurs naturally in coffee and tea and at times it has been included in some commercial soft drinks, although recently this practice has been discouraged. Taken in fairly large quantities, caffeine helps many people obtain a higher score on tests in which speed is an important item. Unfortunately the quantity sufficient for this effect is also sufficient to be injurious to the health if the practice becomes frequent or habitual.

Tobacco. Tobacco has been a troublesome drug to investigate because of the difficulty of securing a control which the subject could not distinguish from real tobacco. The few experiments which have overcome this difficulty suggest that ordinary smoking has little immediate influence on mental performance. For nonsmokers there may be a slight decrease in efficiency. For habitual smokers there seems to be either no change or if anything a slight increase in ability. Any difference observed is very small and of questionable significance.

Fasting

Data on fasting have been based on the records of only a few people(25, 26). Those records, however, cover fasts extending to one month in length. There is a slight decrease in some mental powers such as in arithmetical computation. In some physiological capacities there may be a slight improvement.

Loss of Sleep

The experiments in this field have been carried out on college students or other people in the early twenties. For this reason we cannot be sure that the results will apply to young children. Most of the experiments have investigated the influence of a prolonged period of sleeplessness. We have fewer data regarding the results of a slight reduction in each night's sleep.

A period of forty-eight hours of wakefulness brings about relatively little decrease in score on intelligence tests. There is some evidence, however, that a great deal of effort is used to overcome the loss of sleep. It is hard to eliminate this high motivation, as most people in such an experiment act as if they are on a "dare."

After a period of seventy-two or a hundred sleepless hours there is a noticeable, but not a large, decrease in mental performance, and any performance whatever is made with great effort. There is great difficulty in standing without swaying. Many students, after one hundred hours of wakefuless, reported dizziness or headaches or gave evidence of hallucinations(27).

Ventilation

Obviously, air conditioning and ventilation have a tremendous effect on comfort, and the comfort of our students (and our own comfort) is a justifiable goal. The effect of these factors on output or learning, however, is fairly complex.

Strangely enough the oxygen or carbon dioxide content of the air can be ignored as far as comfort in the typical classroom is concerned. Under ordinary conditions it would be almost impossible for the oxygen to fall low enough, or the carbon dioxide to rise high enough, to affect one's sense of well-being.

When motivation is high, ventilation has little if any effect on mental output. If poor ventilation cuts down performance it is because people just quit trying, and not because they are less able to work. Under experimental conditions, people even try as hard when ventilation is poor, but they feel as if they were accomplishing less. Under nonexperimental conditions, poor ventilation may lead to more dilatory work and to greater frequency of interruption. When loafing or dallying are prevented, however, most people are just as efficient under conditions of poor ventilation as under favorable conditions, though they are far less happy.

Within ordinary limits, the oxygen or carbon dioxide content of the air has little or no effect on production. Acute oxygen deprivation, such as aviators may encounter, markedly decreases efficiency. Long continued deprivation, such as might be felt by certain Andes miners who live at seventeen thousand feet, appears to reduce mental speed to a marked extent. Under ordinary conditions, however, the teacher can forget about oxygen and carbon dioxide.

Lighting

There is some evidence that careful attention to school lighting will have a moderate effect on the attainment of the students(28). Good lighting has become so cheap and so easy to obtain, however, that we may be tempted to overdo the matter. The levels suggested in Table 7-1 are much lower than those often provided. The minimum for each task is based on experimentation(29). The suggested level provides a generous margin for safety. Actually, for people of normal vision, we will not get any better performance from the suggested levels than from the minimum levels. By setting our sights on the suggested levels, however, we can be reasonably sure that we will not fall below the minimum safe levels.

TABLE 7-1

Minimum and Suggested Illumination Levels for Various Tasks

| | Number of Foot Candles | |
Sample Task	Minimum Level	Suggested Level
Reading legible print (such as in this book)	3–6	10–15
Reading a newspaper	7	15–20
Doing exercises in arithmetic	9–10	20–30
Etching or setting fine type (6 point) by hand	20–22	30–40
Threading a needle	30	40–50

Along with sheer level of illumination, of course, we must be careful to avoid glare and to secure a fairly even distribution of light. Visual fatigue is markedly increased when lights or bright spots are directly in the student's field of vision. This even distribution can be most readily obtained by use of daylight or by the use of indirect artificial lighting. A single small source of undiffused light is bound to produce glare and sharp contrasting shadows.

Sex Differences in Mental Growth

Intelligence

Sex differences in health and physical efficiency are discussed in Chapter 4. At this point we wish to consider the differences between boys and girls in intelligence and in achievement. Most of our comparisons, as it happens, will be in the field of achievement. Comparisons in general intelligence are almost impossible because of the way the original intelligence tests were constructed. In the original preparation of these tests it was anticipated, naturally enough, that some test items would be easier for boys and that others would be easier for girls. In the desire to be fair to both sexes, the test constructors eliminated items in which the boys markedly exceeded the girls, or vice versa. Insofar as this effort was successful, it would have the effect of making the average score for the two sexes comparable. Obviously a test so constructed can be of little use in determining whether one sex exceeds the other in general intelligence.

Variability. Although the two sexes are almost bound to have the same average score on our existing intelligence tests, they are not bound to have the same spread or variability. At one time, moreover, it was thought that there were more male geniuses and more male idiots. This excess of males at the extremes was, in turn, linked up with a neat theory of evolution. According to this theory the males, being clearly more expendable, were used as nature's experiments. Most of the time these extremes were definite freaks and failed to survive. Once in a great many generations, however, some of these freaks would be able to exploit some new condition and would serve as a link for a modified species. Although this greater male variability may hold for many traits, it is not at all well established for intelligence. Any piling up at the extremes that was earlier observed was probably due to selection. A male idiot is more likely to be caught being an idiot. So is a male genius.

Subtests of Standard Intelligence Tests. Although the sexes are equal on the total test score of intelligence tests, they are by no means equal on each part of the test. Almost universally, girls get a much higher score on the language part of the test and the boys a higher score on the parts dealing with arithmetic or mathematics. Girls are more apt to be ahead in word fluency and in speed of reading than in size of vocabulary. **Girls** often excel in memory.

Problem Solving

In the various tests of problem solving, especially when some originality is demanded, boys are somewhat ahead(30). Boys are especially likely to excel when one must adopt a radically different approach to solve the problem. When students are given a series of problems to solve and when one general approach proves effective every time, boys and girls will adopt that approach with equal readiness. Suppose now the problem is changed and a new approach is necessary. Girls are less likely to abandon the old approach(31). In general the girls may be more cautious and careful and thus be at a disadvantage when the solution calls for daring(32).

Achievement

In general achievement at the elementary-school level, girls tend to surpass boys of the same age. This trend has appeared fairly regularly(33). Several people, in fact, suggest that boys ought to start school half a year or so older than girls to give them a chance to compete on equal terms(34). The sorry showing of boys at this stage of development has been held to account for the high incidence of stuttering and other disorders in males.

The early superiority of the girls may come partly from their linguistic prowess. Certainly girls show this superiority in language at an early age. They talk before boys do. They are ahead of boys in their use of complex sentences. One investigator(35), by the way, suggests that part of this superiority may come from the fact that little girls are often treated with more affection by their parents. Be that as it may, the linguistic superiority is there by the time school age is reached and is maintained throughout high school and college.

During the elementary school the boys may begin to catch up in mathematics and the content subjects. In general at this level they are ahead of the girls in scientific information although they are not always ahead in the matter of scientific attitude(36). By high school, however, they are clearly ahead on most aspects of science. In the science talent search, for instance, there are two or three boys chosen for every girl, and the girls who are chosen do not come off as well on the tests. At the high-school level boys are also clearly ahead in mathematics.

The different performances of the two sexes are shown quite clearly in the graphs in Figure 7-1. Tests given at the college level show men to be ahead in the natural sciences and women to be ahead in language, literature, and fine arts. The graphs also show the wide range of scores for each sex and the tremendous amount of overlapping. In spite of the definite difference in the averages, we find many men excelling the average woman in the arts and many women excelling the average man in the sciences.

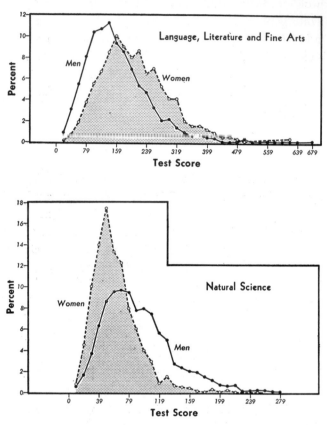

FIGURE 7-1. *Comparison of Men and Women in Different Tests at the College Level.* Redrawn by permission from Learned and Wood(39).

Teachers' Marks. Whatever they may do on objective tests of achievement, girls are unquestionably more successful than boys in getting good marks from teachers. Girls get higher marks from teachers than they would get on standard achievement tests, while boys get lower marks from teachers than they would get on achievement tests(37).

At the elementary-school level, both men teachers and women teachers favor girls(38). The number of men teaching in elementary school is, of course, not large. But the men who do teach in elementary school are just as likely as women to give girls higher marks than boys and to give the girls higher marks than they would get on standard tests.

In high school, women teachers undoubtedly give higher marks to girls than to boys of the same intelligence. The data regarding men teachers, however, are not clear. In one school system the men as well as the women favored the girls over boys of equal intelligence. In another school system the men favored the boys. In this later study, however, the boys and girls were not of the same intelligence.

Girls appear to be able to surpass the boys in getting good marks, especially from women teachers, even when they cannot surpass the boys in getting high scores on achievement tests. Why should this be? Several reasons have been advanced, but none of these has been definitely established.

1. Teachers, both men and women, consider girls to be more industrious, cooperative, persevering, dependable, and ambitious than boys, although they consider the boys to be more original and to show more leadership. Perhaps the qualities in which the girls excel are more important in getting good marks from teachers than in doing well on achievement tests.

2. Girls are known to surpass boys in linguistic skill and in handwriting and spelling. These qualities are obviously more important in teachers' essay examinations than on the short-answer objective tests.

Causes of Sex Differences in Achievement. Quite probably both inheritance and training work together to produce the differences which the sexes show in achievement. The linguistic superiority of the girls shows itself so consistently that it seems not all due to training. As girls grow older, however, their natural tendency toward linguistic ability is increased by the fact that adults expect them to do well in that field and by the fact that so many other forms of activity are less available to girls than to boys.

Differences in Residence and Family Background

The differences we are about to consider deal fairly regularly with the student's ancestry or with his home or with the larger group to which he belongs. This fact makes for great complexity in trying to understand the basic forces that may be involved. Difficult as it is to interpret the roles of sex and health, we shall find it even more vexing to try to decide which of many forces may be at work when a rural child falls behind his city cousin or when a physician's child gets a higher score than the child of a day laborer. The true explanation for such differences may lie deep in the cultural pattern that surrounds the child. It may lie in differences in training practices or genetic stock. It may even lie in the peculiarities of our measuring instruments.

The General Cluster of Differences

First of all, let us try to get a brief, over-all look at the general cluster of group differences in health, intelligence, and achievement. Then we shall consider the possible interpretations of these differences. With these possible interpretations in mind, we shall proceed to examine the group differences in greater detail.

On the average, who does well on our various tests, and who tends to come off poorly? In the United States, the Westerner, on the average, tends to excel the Southeasterner in health, intelligence test score, and achievement. The urban child is ahead of his country cousin, again on the average. Modern "Suburbia" is ahead of "Dogpatch." The children of professional groups excel the children of day laborers. Children from small families do better than children from large families. White children, on the average, surpass Negro children. The child of Dutch or Scottish ancestry gets a higher score than the child of Greek or Mexican ancestry.

Alternative Explanations for the Cluster of Differences

To take one example, how could we explain the fact that the city child gets a better score on our tests than the child from the country? It is clear that there could be several reasons. Right away we probably suspect that the city children may have had *better training* and may have attended better schools. Over and above this actual schooling we may suspect that the general urban environment has been more stimulating and exacting and that this *more stimulating environment* has kept the city children on their toes. Both of these explanations suggest that city life actually does contribute to a high test score. But there are other explanations which refuse to grant the city any such advantage. Many people point out that the tests we are talking about were made by city people and that, even with the best of intentions on the part of the authors, they may include a *test bias* in favor of the city children. The question, "What is the thing to do when you find your house on fire?" for instance, may be more geared to city children than to rural children. There is another hypothesis which also denies that the city actually produces any advantage. This explanation or hypothesis claims that the city drains off an unfair share of bright people. Members of certain professions may find a more adequate outlet for their training in the city. There is, then, a sort of *selective migration* by which an undue proportion of clever adults are enticed into the city, bringing their children with them. But why is it that the children of these bright parents are also bright? Here we could fall back on the idea of the better training or more stimulating environment provided by these parents. But we could also suppose that *direct inheritance* may account for the superior intelligence of these children.

Environment, Heredity, and the Scientific Attitude

It has been difficult in the past to discuss heredity and environment in a sober, objective fashion. Whenever we talk about the influence of environment on intelligence, or about the possibility of direct inheritance, we often run into violent feelings and sometimes encounter closed minds. It is often almost impossible to convince students or the public that we are merely about to examine the evidence for and against each of a group of "possible" explanations, that we are merely going to give each its day in court with no previous commitments as to guilt or innocence. Very often as soon as we say "Let's look at the evidence regarding environmental influences," someone will exclaim, "Oh! So you belong to *that* camp!" Similarly, an attempt to gather the data with respect to heredity will bring down an accusation of "rightist" or reactionary partisanship.

As students of psychology we must regard this violent emotion as understandable but troublesome. It is understandable because the issues involved have terrific implications for humanity in general and for educators in particular. If one should show that intelligence, to take one example, were almost *entirely* a matter of heredity, we would be faced with a rather gloomy picture. The fact that it would be gloomy, of course, has no bearing on its probable truth. It is natural that people will resent a gloomy picture, however, and that they will try to argue it away.

It is extremely difficult to be completely objective when important human values are at stake. Nevertheless in our examination of the evidence bearing on these hypotheses we shall try to put our emotions and hopes and even our loyalties to one side. We shall not ask if this conclusion is pretty, or comforting, or a boost for our profession. At this stage, we shall ask merely whether the conclusion seems justified by the evidence at hand. Above all we shall not take the position of deciding between two contestants. We shall not ask, "Do we give the award to heredity *or* to environment?" We shall look at the claims of each of the hypotheses. There may be some awards that none may get. And there may be some award for each.

The Influence of the Environment on Educational Growth

There is much to suggest that an infant will fail to develop intellectually if he is denied the forceful human contacts found in the typical home(39). The kind of care found in an excellent hospital or orphanage apparently does not suffice. Here we find close attention to health and comfort. Nor is there anything that one could call neglect. Yet inevitably there can be little sustained, affectionate interaction between the child and one adult. And this condition, especially if prolonged through one or two years(40), has been held to induce mental retardation. This whole matter has been vigorously challenged(41), however, and is the subject of some controversy.

Extremely Unusual Environments. The most extreme cases of environmental deprivation are found in the accounts of children reared in clothes closets or, like the alleged case of Caspar Hauser, in dungeons. Presumably this extreme degree of isolation came after early infancy. Here, of course, the immediate effects are devastating. Many aspects of development are almost at zero level. This effect is not permanent, however, and in the few cases studied, the unfortunate child rather rapidly overtakes his more normal age-mates.

Children reared by animals, on the other hand, do not always shake off this early training. Zingg(42) reports some thirty cases of individuals who were supposed to have lived a substantial part of their youth with animals or to have lived as isolated savages. Some of these, like the fabulous Romulus and Remus or Kipling's Mowgli, were apparently stolen and suckled by wolves. Others were found running with animals and seemed to feel at home with animals but were not considered to have been brought up from infancy by animals. Most of these children were not brought into human society until over eight years of age. By this time the imprint of their early years seemed almost permanent. This seemed especially so with regard to food preferences and general living habits. Several ate and drank like animals, lapping liquids or gnawing food on the floor. Ten of the thirty were reported to refuse for a long time to wear clothing. Six were reported as indifferent to heat or cold. The degree of adaptation to human society varied.

Of all the children reported by Zingg, perhaps the best authenticated cases are those of two girls recovered from a wolf den at the age of two and eight respectively. Apparently both had been living with the wolves since infancy. Of these, the younger showed some promise of adaptation and actually seemed to act as a pioneer for the older girl. The younger child died, however, within a year after her recovery from the wolves. The older child lived to the age of seventeen. During this time she was induced to abandon her wolfish eating habits, to wear clothes, to use some fifty words, and to run simple errands.

Obviously these interesting accounts do not constitute ideal experiments. Some of these children had spent some time in human homes before living with animals. In coming to conform to the animal environment, they were clearly successful in shaking off the effects of that earlier human environment. For older children, the effects of both environments could not have been irreversible(43).

A Change to a Better Environment. If a poor environment is responsible for retardation, and if the effects are reversible, an improvement in the environment should lead to a higher test performance.

This straightforward approach to the study of environment has been used for a good many years(44, 45, 46), and almost uniformly we find that children who are moved from a poor environment to a better environment can be depended upon to show an increase in IQ. These facts are not likely to be disputed. There is some dispute, however, over the amount of change that can be expected. Much of the controversy regarding the extent of the environmental influence was set off by a series of studies at the University of Iowa(46). These studies reported considerable gains on the part of young children who were moved to a better environment. True, the actual gains reported do not seem markedly out of line with those of the earlier investigators. Perhaps much of the controversy was caused by the implication that the actual ancestry of children seemed to play no part whatever. When very young children from different parents were adopted into a good environment and lived there for some time, the children of feeble-minded mothers could not be distinguished from the children of normal mothers.

Whatever the outcome of the controversy on the many details of the problem, there can be little doubt on the main points. Young children who are moved from a poor to a good environment will obtain a higher score on our tests after they have been moved. The younger the child at the time of transfer, the more marked the change will be. This comforting fact, so obviously in line with common sense, seems clearly established by the data.

Attendance at a Nursery School. At the present time it is impossible to say whether or not the stimulation and directed experience of a nursery school tends to raise the test score of children. Much work has been done in the field but the question is highly controversial. A substantial section of the thirty-ninth Yearbook of the National Society for the Study of Education was given over to the problem. Of the eleven investigations reported in that yearbook, seven found no significant gain on the part of the nursery school children, whereas four studies did find a significant gain(47). Many of these investigations and much of the controversy has been stimulated by the very promising results reported from the University of Iowa. The Iowa investigations cover two kinds of nursery-school populations. On the one hand there are children from a select professional group attending a nursey school attached to a university. The gains reported for these groups are still the subject of controversy. On the other hand we have children from a very unstimulating orphanage environment who are enrolled in a nursery school. The gains reported for these groups have been accepted after the most searching analysis by critics. Of course, we would feel better if similar results were reported by a number of independent investigators. But for the present we should assume that children from limited and dull environments will do better on tests when they have some nursery-school experience(39).

Identical Twins Reared Apart versus Identical Twins Reared Together. A pair of identical twins is occasionally (but rarely) separated at birth. Such twins have identical heredities but grow up in somewhat different environments. Are they any less similar for having experienced those different environments? Are they, in other words, less similar than other identical twins who have been reared together?

By an elaborate investigation, involving great expense and patience, Professor Newman has managed to collect records of some twenty pairs of twins who were separated at an early age and who, upon examination, appeared to be identical. If we take the average differences between each of these twenty pairs we find that the separated twins are less similar than the twins reared together. The average difference in IQ for the separated twins is 8.2 while that for identical twins reared together is about 5.0 points. In achievement quotients we find an even greater difference on the part of identical twins reared apart. From studies of this type we would conclude that the environment has at least a moderate effect on intelligence and a more marked effect on achievement.

Parents and Adopted Children. There is a small but positive correlation between the quality of the home and the later intelligence of children adopted into that home. This correlation could not be due to hereditary factors, and it seems reasonable to suppose that it is due to the action of the environment. There is a slight possibility that more intelligent parents may be able, in one way or another, to select more intelligent children. When we compare two children both adopted into the same home, for instance, we find a clear resemblance. There is much more resemblance than between an adopted and an unadopted child in the same home(48). This *additional* resemblance could be due to some selective process during adoption.

Cumulative Effects of Environment. The longer the child lives in a good environment the more he moves in the direction of the environment(49). The longer a child lives with bright parents the brighter he becomes. The longer he lives in an unfavorable environment, the more he falls behind the national norms. At first glance, this may seem to be convincing evidence of the effects of the environment. We must remember, however, that a boy's resemblance to his father in height(50) and in beard color will also increase as the boy grows older. In other words, part of this increased resemblance may come from the maturation of adult patterns really established by heredity.

The Influence of the Environment: Résumé. As we have seen, it is not an easy thing to get a dependable estimate of the influence of the environment. In spite of these difficulties, however, it seems clear that a superior environment could well induce a superior performance on our tests of intelligence and achievement, and that a less fortunate environment could bring about a serious handicap.

Test Favoritism

A quick look at the group that does well on our tests of intelligence or achievement immediately makes us suspicious of the tests themselves. The intelligence tests and the achievement tests most widely used in this country were largely constructed by white, urban, professional workers. It would be miraculous if the people who constructed the tests had not unconsciously included material which would be more familiar to children of their own class or group. Davis(51) has presented many data to show that much of the content of the typical intelligence test does not have any significance in the everyday life of children outside the "middle" class. Shimberg(52) has also shown that the urban-rural differences would actually be reversed if the items in an intelligence test were supplied by rural teachers and if the norms were based on the scores of rural children. It was in an attempt to get rid of the middle-class bias in traditional intelligence tests that the Davis-Eells Tests of General Intelligence were developed. It was thought that, with an emphasis on practical problems presented in picture form, some of the handicap for the lower class groups would be removed.

The possibility of test favoritism or test handicap is clearest perhaps in observing children of foreign birth or extraction. Since many of our tests are highly verbal, it would be amazing if many immigrant groups were not under a severe handicap. This possibility is supported by the fact that many immigrant groups come closer to our norms when tested on performance tests or nonverbal tests.

In addition to the language handicap experienced by some foreign groups, there are other more subtle attitudes which may well act as a handicap. The emphasis on speed, for instance, may easily be a handicap to some national groups who do not share our jittery way of doing things. There are some groups who can comprehend the need of haste in certain practical situations but to whom the idea of making marks on paper at breakneck speed must seem ridiculous in the extreme. There are also some cultures, especially perhaps tribes of American Indians, in which it is bad form to be too eager to show off all one knows. Any child in whom this reluctance was thoroughly ingrained would be at a disadvantage in taking a group intelligence test.

Selective Influences

Certain jobs and communities may not only help to create intelligence and achievement. They may also attract those who are already capable or who have already achieved. This hypothesis could account for the superior intelligence of people in certain professions, and, as we pointed out earlier, it could account for part of the superior performance of city children. Not only does the city often provide better schools, but it also tends to drain off some of the more able young folk from the rural areas. There is some evidence for this selective migration from country to city. Smaller communities tend to lose an undue share of their bright young people(53, 54). The young people who leave the smaller communities are more likely to be drawn from the more able high-school students. During the depression, of course, this trend was partially offset by the migration of "relief" clients to the larger cities. But over a period of years the city has taken more than its share of the brighter people.

This hypothesis of differential heredity must be considered even when we contemplate such flagrantly undesirable environments as those found in the "Dogpatch" communities. As Goodenough(55) asks, "Why is the environment so unfavorable?" The cultural environment that we live in was created by our ancestors. It is quite possible that the parents who prefer or who tolerate this primitive or peculiar life are less intellectually minded than parents who seek more civilized surroundings. If this is so, the children may inherit this lack of intellectuality directly from the parents.

It may be more difficult to see how hereditary factors could account for the differences found between different parts of the country. It must be remembered, however, that for the most part the high scores came from the more recently developed regions. These regions were settled by the pioneers who had the foresight to see the possibilities of the new country and who had the ability and resourcefulness to get there. In more recent times some of these regions have attracted successful people who have been looking for a pleasant place to live.

At one time it was thought that the superior intelligence of the northern over the southern Negro could be explained by a similar kind of selective migration. It was suggested that the more intelligent Negro would be the first to leave the restrictions of the south and to seek the somewhat greater freedom and the nominal equality in the north. And if the intelligent Negro left and the dull Negro stayed, we should soon have a difference of intelligence in favor of the northern Negro. Actually, however, the tests conducted so far(56) reveal no such selective factor. The children of Negroes emigrating from the south have about the same intelligence as those remaining behind.

Although selective migration will not explain the difference between northern and southern Negroes, it may explain the difference between some of the national groups emigrating to this country.

The groups in this country are only samples of the larger groups from which they come. They probably do not represent the larger groups perfectly. An emigrant group always has some reason for emigrating. Sometimes it is the sturdy and courageous, the independent, who leave and the more timid who remain. Sometimes it is the failures and "remittance men" who move out, just one jump ahead of the sheriff, while the successful ones remain. Moreover, the reasons which lead people to emigrate from one country may not be the same as those which are in effect in another country. The rise of a Hitler may send us a large number of intellectuals from Germany. The demand for cheap labor may send us many peasants from Sicily. Under the circumstances, if we compare the Germans *who happened to come here* with the Sicilians *who happened to come here,* we might find that the former have a higher average. But that would not mean that the average German in Germany was more intellectual than the average Sicilian in Sicily.

Results of tests(57) given to Europeans in Europe suggest that there is less difference in the parent populations than in the samples to be found in the United States. The difference between German and Italian children in Europe, although present, is not always consistent. There is hardly any difference, for instance, between the intelligence of Roman children and children of Hamburg.

Direct Inheritance

To show that environmental advantages and test favoritism could account for many of our differences is not to show that heredity plays no part whatever. There are many differences to be explained, and, indeed, much of the variation will remain unexplained after we have made the most of all the plausible hypotheses we can come by.

Comparisons of Identical and Fraternal Twins. Some of the best investigations of the influence of heredity come from the use of identical twins. Such twins form from 20 to 30 percent of all twin births. They are always of the same sex and typically show marked physical resemblance. They result from the splitting of a single fertilized egg at a very early stage of development. In this split, the genes are divided evenly, so that each twin has exactly the same genetic constitution. As far as heredity is concerned, these twins are identical.

When such twins are given intelligence tests we find a remarkable intellectual similarity(58, 59). The average difference in IQ between two members of a twin pair is only about 5.0 points—which is the average difference we observe between two tests given to the same person. Two identical twins are as much alike as one person is like himself! When the resemblance is measured by a coefficient of correlation, we find it to be about .90, which again is close to the correlation between two tests given to the same person.

It would be most unscientific, of course, to credit heredity with all the resemblance between identical twins. These twins ordinarily grow up in a remarkably similar environment. Whatever happens to one is most likely to happen to the other. They are close companions. Much of their experience is gathered together. To "control" this influence of the similar environment, investigators have used fraternal twins, selecting fraternal twins of the same sex. Fraternal twins arise from two separate sperms and two separate eggs. They are merely sibling pairs (brother-brother, sister-sister, or brother-sister) that happen to be conceived at the same time. Consequently, as in the case of ordinary brothers and sisters, their genetic resemblance is much less than that of identical twins. The environment, however, is a different matter. Theoretically, the environment of a pair of same-sex, fraternal twins should be just as similar as the environment of a pair of identical twins. This claim has been contested(21), but the difference in the similarity of the environments is probably very slight. All in all, as far as environment is concerned, fraternal twins should show as much intellectual resemblance as identical twins. Do they? By no means. Whereas the resemblance of identical twins is approximately .90, the resemblance of same-sex fraternal twins is closer to .60 or .65. The difference between .90 and .65 would have to be credited to the greater hereditary resemblance of identical twins.

The very general results given for intelligence tests (and they are very rough averages of the results of several investigations)(60), also holds for achievement tests. Identical twins clearly show more similarity in scores on achievement tests, and this greater similarity is attributable to heredity.

Comparisons of Parent-offspring with Parent-foster Child. There is a fair resemblance between the intelligence test score of parents and the score of their children. On the average, the parents who score high will have children who score high. This resemblance produces a correlation of .55 or .60(61). Such a resemblance, of course, could be due either to inheritance or to the common environment or to both. In order to test the influence of heredity, we must in some way "control" the environment or hold its influence constant. To do this, investigators have used adopted children, preferably children who were adopted into the home at a very early age. As far as environment is concerned, foster parents should exert as much influence on their foster children as real parents exert on their offspring. If intellectual resemblance comes from intimate association, such resemblance should appear between parents and foster children. It does not appear, however. The correlation between the intelligence of parents and of foster children is only about .20. From this comparison it appears that the greater hereditary similarity of parents and offspring must boost the intellectual similarity from .20 to .55 or .60. These differences are illustrated in Figure 7-2.

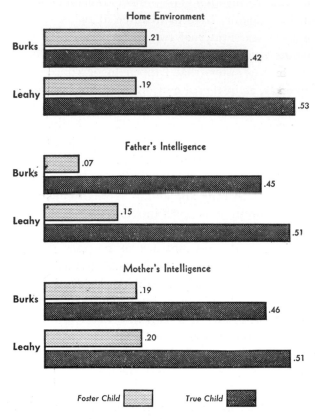

FIGURE 7-2. *Comparison of Parent-Offspring Resemblance with Parent-Foster-Child Resemblance.* Reproduced from Jones(21). Redrawn by permission from L. Carmichael, *Manual of Child Psychology,* John Wiley & Sons, Inc., 1946.

As a converse of this pattern, it appears that children as they grow older come more and more to resemble the true parents with whom they no longer live. Consider, for instance, a child of seven who was adopted at birth. His IQ at this age has considerable relation (r = .35) to the education of his true mother with whom he has never lived. It has almost no relation (r = .07) to the education of the foster mother with whom he has lived for seven years(21).

Heredity: General. Heredity unquestionably has a considerable influence on intelligence and on achievement. When other factors are held constant and heredity is allowed to vary, we find that intelligence and achievement also vary. Let us accept this as an apparent fact. But let us not rush off to assume that heredity is the only factor that affects mental development, or that it is the most important factor.

The Major Group Differences

The forces we have been considering may be at work in any of the differences between groups that we may observe. These forces, however, are never seen in their pure form. On the contrary, they can be investigated only by indirect means that call for considerable effort. The superficial groupings, in contrast, are readily observed and every teacher will frequently be aware of the major group or region from which any student comes.

Regional Differences

Within the United States as we move from one region to another we tend to find differences in health, intelligence, and achievement. The map in Figure 7-3, for instance, shows wide discrepancies in the percentage of men free from recorded physical defects. In general the West and

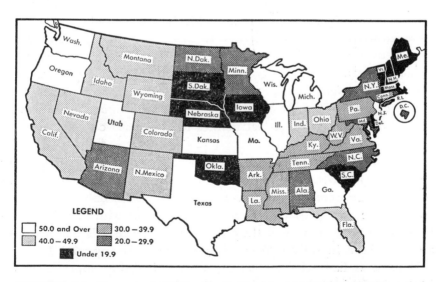

FIGURE 7-3. *Percent of White Draft Registrants Having No Recorded Defects. Data are based on white (all races except Negro) registrations between April 1942 and March 1943.* Reproduced by permission from Selective Service System, Med. Statist. Bull. No. 3. Washington, Government Printing Office.

the eastern edge of the Great Plains do well, whereas defects pile up in the North Central Plains and in New England. The extreme Southeast (Georgia and Florida) is healthy. The rest of the East is only fair.

In intelligence and achievement we also find regional differences. This fact was first brought out by the extensive intelligence-test program of World War I. New England, the Pacific Coast, and the Rocky Mountain states had higher average scores than the rest of the nation. The southeastern states were lower than the average(62). The more extensive data from the testing program of World War II have not yet been completely analyzed. Preliminary reports on white soldiers, however, show that there is a difference between Northern and Southern soldiers drawn from comparable occupations(63). For the thirty-three occupations compared, the Northern soldiers were higher in all but two. In certain nation-wide achievement tests, regional differences have also appeared(64, 65). Probably the best sample of college males comes from the Selective Service Qualifying Tests. Here we find that New England still has a high place but the western states, although still high, have been nudged out of their position by the Middle Atlantic States. The West is almost equaled by the North Central States. The Southeast is low(66).

To account for these differences many people call attention to the differences in environment. The states that obtain the highest intellectual and academic scores are those which spend the most on schools as we can see from Figure 7-4. Certainly this is one possible explanation. Through selective migration, however, it is also possible that one region could attract, and retain, one kind of people and another region could attract or retain a different group. A state that happened to have intelligent people might well spend more on education and on other intellectual enterprises. As yet both of these hypotheses must be considered as possible explanations. As yet neither has been proved.

Rural-urban Differences. On our present tests city children regularly obtain a higher average score than rural children, and the larger the city, the higher the score. This difference, of course, holds only for the average. But the average differences remain and persist with surprising uniformity. City children excel their country cousins in this nation. They are also ahead in Ireland(67) and in France, Germany, and Italy(57).

Here, as we have seen, we can invoke test favoritism, superior schooling, and selective migration. In support of the latter hypothesis it has been noted that rural-urban differences are more marked when movement to and from the city is easy(21). So far as we know, all three forces may be at work.

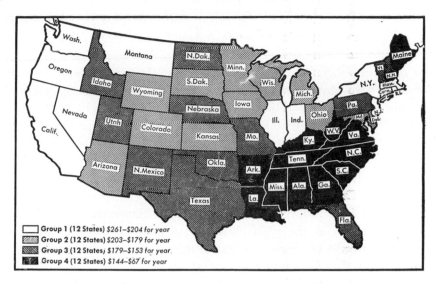

FIGURE 7-4. *Average Per-pupil Expenditure by States.* Reproduced from "Facts—on federal aid," Washington. Courtesy of the National Educational Association, Publishers.

Wide-awake versus Backward Community. Children who live in extremely primitive or backward communities almost always obtain lower average scores on our tests. This is true for Gypsy children and for children who spend a large part of their lives on canal barges. It is true for the children who live in the slum areas or marginal areas of our cities. It is also true for the children who live in the isolated "Dogpatch" hollows of the Appalachian Mountains, where cultural life is at a very low ebb and where schools may be kept open as little as sixteen months in an eleven-year period.

Here the superficial facts are pretty well established but of the forces we have considered, it is quite impossible to tell which ones may be at work. It is interesting to note that achievement may be affected less than intelligence(68). Perhaps in the more progressive communities there is less emphasis on the traditional subject matter stressed by achievement tests.

Social and Economic Status

One of the features of family life that has been most frequently investigated is that of general socioeconomic status (SES). This term refers to a cluster of factors, including occupation, income, and cultural features of the home. In some scales of SES there is a strong emphasis on intellectualness or "bookishness," the rating being affected by such things as the number of books in the home and interest in art or music.

SES, of course, has some general relation to the concept of social class that one hears so much about nowadays. But the two are not precisely the same. Two physicians, for instance, may have the same income and the same amount of education, and yet one could belong to the "upper-upper" class, whereas the other may belong to the "lower-middle" class. Membership in these classes is not determined chiefly by profession, income, or education. To belong to the upper class, one should come from a family that has been established in the community for several generations. The income of the family, irrespective of its amount, should come largely from property or from substantial investments. The family must have access to the good clubs. Its members are sought after as trustees for worthy enterprises. It is such things rather than sheer income, or profession, that determine one's social class.

In general the healthier, bigger, and more robust children tend to come from the families higher up in the social scale(69). Many physical defects, poor teeth, poor hearing, lameness, and tuberculosis are more frequent in the lower income brackets. In one study, however, under-nourishment was more frequent in the children of the well-to-do(70).

TABLE 7-2

Intelligence Ratings of Children from Various Occupational Groups

	Intelligence Quotients *		Percentile Rank † College Students
	Children 2—5½	Children 10—14	
Professional	116	118	60—65
Semiprofessional and managerial	112	112	57
Clerical and skilled trades	108	107	50—54
Semiskilled and minor clerical	104	103	45
Rural owners	99	92	45
Slightly skilled	95	101	45
Day laborers	94	97	35

* From Terman & Merrill. *Measuring intelligence*, p. 48. Courtesy Houghton Mifflin Co.

† From various studies reported by Jane Loevinger, "Intelligence as Related to Socioeconomic Factors," *Yearb. nat. soc. Stud. Educ.*, 39 (I), Chap. V, 1940.

It is not only in the matter of health that nature smiles on the "upper classes." The children of these groups also tend to excel on intelligence tests (Table 7-2), on achievement tests(71) and on the sort of adult achievement that gets one into "Who's Who"(72).

Although trends such as these turn up in investigation after investigation, we must not exaggerate their significance. In the first place the relation, although considerable, is never very large. The correlations are about .3 or .4. This means that many children from the lower SES groups are very bright and that many children from higher income homes are very dull. The results hold only for the average. In the second place, in absolute numbers, more bright children will come from the lower SES groups than from the higher brackets. True, a higher *proportion* of the upper group will obtain high scores. But there are many more children in the ordinary SES groups to draw from and the larger numbers will more than make up for the smaller proportions.

SES represents a complex pattern, of course, and we must not assume that all aspects of this pattern are equally effective. Sheer income seems to count for relatively little. Education of parents has perhaps the clearest relation to the test score of the children. The amount and quality of language usage in the home is also a good index of both the language usage and the IQ of the children(73, 74). We also find lower test scores for children who grow up in homes in which two languages are used or in which the language in the home differs from that in the community(75). This handicap of the bilingual child, although perhaps not universal, appears in immigrant families in the United States and in bilingual homes in Wales.

As we have seen, the profession of the parent is closely related to the intelligence of the child and is even more closely related to the intelligence of the parents themselves (Figure 7-5). Results from both world wars show a definite relation between civilian occupation and intelligence test score(63). These differences in intelligence also appear in students who are preparing for different occupations.

On the Selective Service Qualification Test(66), college students preparing for engineering averaged much higher than college students preparing for other professions. After that, in order of merit, we find majors in mathematics and the physical sciences, in the biological sciences, in the social sciences, in the humanities, in general arts, in agriculture, in business and commerce, and last, we blush to admit it, majors in education. Our problem of adjusting to this last harsh fact, by the way, is discussed in Chapter 22. Meanwhile, forgetting about our own professional worries, we can see a definite selection effect of the different professions. Under present conditions it is the scientific and engineering professions that are attracting an unusual proportion of bright young men.

These results from military testing programs, of course, are based en-

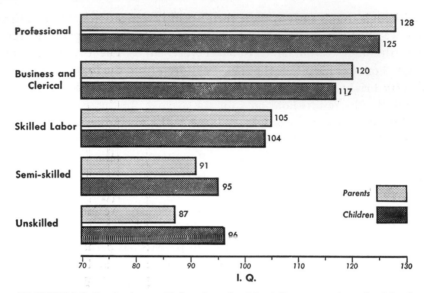

FIGURE 7-5. *Profession as Related to the IQ of Parents and to the IQ of Their Children.* Reproduced from Jones(21). Redrawn by permission from *Manual of Child Psychology* by L. Carmichael, John Wiley & Sons, Inc., 1946.

tirely on males. Other investigations based on both men and women, however, show the same general trend(76).

Suggested Explanations for SES Differences. The differences we have discussed could be explained by any one of our standard hypotheses. There is some evidence for selection in that people about to enter the professions show the same differences in intelligence that we find on the part of people actually in the professions. If different professions attract different degrees of intellect, could that intellect be transmitted to the children by direct inheritance? There is some evidence to support this hypothesis. The intelligence of orphanage children has a clear relation to the profession of their dead parents(77). Here the only link would be early training or direct inheritance.

It is obvious that, on the average, the environment of the higher SES groups may be more intellectual and may include more elaborate training programs. It is also true that the so-called middle class attach great importance to schools and to educational matters. Middle-class parents take education very seriously. Whereas many lower-class parents pay little attention to schools one way or another, the middle-class parent, mothers especially, cannot take such a free and easy attitude. To a greater extent than her lower-class neighbor, she keeps an eye on the school, often feeling quite critical of what she finds. At the same time, however, she urges regular attendance(78) and defends the school against the complaints brought home by the children(79). Obviously the middle-class parent is greatly "involved" in schools and schooling, and with an attitude such as this we can expect much more motivation toward intellectual and academic proficiency.

Although there are many arguments about the hypotheses of *superior training, selection,* and *direct inheritance,* these arguments seem mild in comparison to the fierce fight raging around *test favoritism.* It is natural to suspect, as we have pointed out, that existing tests should favor middle-class or upper-class students. This matter has been brought into sharper focus by the classical study of Eells and his associates(80, 81). From an elaborate system of testing which included a variety of tests, Eells found differences in the averages of different social groups. He found, however, that these differences came mostly from the fact that the upper SES groups made higher scores on the verbal part of the test. With the low SES groups we find about equal scores on verbal and nonverbal items. As we move up the SES scale, however, we find the higher SES groups doing better on the verbal than on the nonverbal tests. According to Eells it is this special flair for verbal tests on the part of the middle class that does the trick.

Eells' interpretation of his results has been challenged by Tyler(82) and others(83). Tyler holds that the units in the verbal and nonverbal parts of the test were not equal and that when we equate for this, the higher SES groups excel in the nonverbal tests in about the same way that they excel in the verbal tests. And from other sources(84) there is some suggestion that the higher SES groups also do better on performance tests designed to minimize cultural differences.

Clearly this is a complex problem and one that, by its very nature, is difficult to solve. The simple-minded way to get an unbiased test, of course, would be to discard any item on which we find class differences in performance. But this would commit us in advance to the conclusion that there are no class differences. No one, of course, actually adopts this simple-minded approach and there have been many ingenious efforts to break into the circle that seems to confront us. In spite of those efforts, however, we must consider the problem unsolved. Lacking convincing evidence we must be prepared to encounter a wide diversity of opinion, ranging from those who consider that existing tests reflect genuine differences between classes to those who consider that the social classes are equal in capacity and that any differences in performance, or in rewards received, must come from unconscious bias or outright prejudice on the part of school people(85).

While waiting for a scientific answer to this complex problem we can take to heart the extreme danger that we as teachers, espousing middle-class values, may be unduly harsh(37) and cold when we deal with those who have been brought up to accept quite other values. In urging our values, we should avoid an attitude of condemnation. To condemn these children for their lack of scholarly application may be like scolding a deaf child because he fails to respond to your question.

Size of Family

Many investigations between 1920 and 1950 reported somewhat lower intelligence for children from large families. This tendency was much more marked in England than in the American Midwest(86) and there is now some evidence that it may no longer hold in the British Isles(87). The phenomenon may appear or vanish as fashion swings from small families to large. When the relation prevailed, many people were disturbed at the prospect of "breeding out our brains." This seemed likely if bright people had few children and dull people had many. Whatever the underlying relation, this particular worry seems unjustified. If anything there has been a gradual increase in intelligence over the past thirty years rather than the predicted decline(21).

Whenever this relation does appear it could be explained either by more favorable environment in the small family(88) or by the fact that the more intellectual people go in for smaller families. In the latter case, we should expect the relation to decrease or disappear whenever larger families become more popular with the higher SES groups.

The only child constitutes the lower limit of a small family. Typically he does exceptionally well on our tests of intellect and achievement. He is especially precocious or "old-fashioned" in the use of language. His personality or social adjustment, as we shall see in a later section, does not appear to suffer.

Race, Nationality, or Culture Group

It will be impossible in this discussion, unfortunately, to state exactly what we mean by racial or national or other such differences. These are very difficult distinctions. Is the difference between Chinese and Japanese a racial difference or a national difference? Shall we consider French-speaking Canadians and English-speaking Canadians as of the same nationality? Is the difference between Jews and non-Jews a racial or a religious or a cultural difference?

All these are questions for the anthropologist and not for the psychologist. The psychologist merely encounters groups of people who belong to different census groups or who have different labels, such as Norwegian, Indian, Chinese, or Jewish, attached to them. Frequently he observes differences in physique, intelligence, or achievement. Whenever he finds such differences he has tried to explain them, trying out the classical hypotheses that we have stressed so much.

White-Negro Differences. There have been many comparisons of the intelligence(59) and achievement(89) of white and Negro children(90) and of white and Negro adults(91), using both verbal and nonverbal tests and comparing groups with little and with much education. The vast preponderance of these results shows the white group to have a higher average score. There is, of course, a tremendous amount of overlapping and many Negro children obtain very high scores(92). In contrast to this trend it is frequently reported that very young Negro infants often exceed the white norms(93). This may suggest a different rate of maturation or, possibly, a more permissive attitude in Negro homes, giving the infant more freedom to explore his environment(94).

To account for the general trend of the differences, we can readily invoke any of the traditional hypotheses. Certainly when these results were gathered many Negro children lived and attended school under very unfavorable circumstances. To support the environmental hypothesis we have Klineberg's evidence(56) based on Negro children who moved from southern areas and settled in New York. He found that the children who had lived in New York a long time made higher scores on the tests than children who had just recently arrived. This superiority of the long-time residents may readily be due to the superior schooling they received.

Test favoritism seems especially plausible as an explanation of Negro-white differences. All the arguments showing the effect of that bias for lower SES groups apply with even more force in explaining the lower scores of Negroes. The actual evidence, however, is less clear-cut. In some cases, the white superiority is even greater on "culture-free" tests(83).

Finally, undemocratic as the suggestion may seem, we cannot yet conclude that the possibility of direct inheritance has been completely removed. Even when environments are roughly comparable, rural Negro groups in Ontario, Canada, obtain a lower score on our tests than rural white children in the same community(95). In this comparison, of course, test favoritism is not completely ruled out, but its influence should be reduced. In general we should consider direct inheritance as by no means established but still deserving, and in need of, further tests.

North European—South European. In a number of investigations, American children descended from German, British, or Scandinavian groups obtain higher average scores than children descended from Southern European families. European children tested in their own countries, however, show no such clear-cut trends. Much more is known about the performance on intelligence tests than about performance on the achievement tests.

Other Frequently Tested Groups. A large number of comparisons of Jewish and non-Jewish groups shows very little difference between the average performance(96). If anything, the average of the Jews slightly surpasses that of the non-Jews(59). Chinese and Japanese groups in this country are fairly close to the average for the American population. This is especially true when nonlanguage tests are used. One study(97), however, finds a lower average for the Japanese children who lived in the relocation camps during World War II. Mexican children often fall below the American norms(98). For children of American Indians the data are conflicting. The early studies reported a somewhat lower average for these groups. Several more recent investigations, however, report no such differences(99, 100, 101), or complex differences(102).

Here again the traditional hypotheses will apply. In many cases we find marked differences in the districts inhabited by different groups. Test handicap is clearly possible, and selective migration may well have been a factor in the case of many groups.

Educational Significance of Nonscholastic Factors

The factors just considered are the forces which the teacher cannot alter by direct action. But they are the forces which he is bound to encounter. If they are good he can exploit and utilize them. If they are bad, he must contend against them. In either case they are important forces, and they should be faced.

Do not be surprised or disillusioned if you find that the approach which worked well with one group fails to elicit as much growth from another group. Do not give up, either. Start from where you are and work from that point. But you cannot make a realistic start from where you are unless you honestly survey the situation and accept the evidence that presents itself.

Above all remember that these differences hold for group averages only. Not all children of physicians are bright. Not all children of laborers are dull. Some white children are far below normal in intelligence. Some Negro children are very brilliant. Whenever we compare two groups such as those we have described, we get the sort of overlapping indicated in Figure 7-6. Here we find the distributions of the intelligence

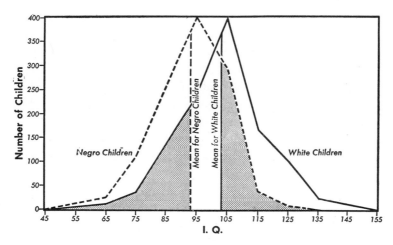

FIGURE 7-6. *Distribution of the IQ's of White and Negro Children Aged 8 and 9 Years.* Data from Lacy(103) by permission of the University of Chicago Press.

of a group of Negro children and a group of white children of the same age and in the same grade. (Both groups are in grades one, two, and three.) This figure clearly shows the wide range of intelligence in each group. In both groups we find children with IQ's as low as 55 and as high as 125. It is only on the average that the white children pile up to the right of the Negro children. For IQ's above 100 we find more white children than Negro children. This *general* or *average* difference between the groups is indicated by the two perpendicular lines which show the mean or averages of the two groups. Obviously, however, this difference in the averages, significant as it is, does not tell the whole story. It would be a great mistake to think of all the white children as having an IQ of about 103 and all the Negro children having an IQ of about 94. The shaded area to the right shows a large number of Negroes (about 20 percent of all Negroes) who have an IQ higher than the average white child. The shaded area to the left includes the white children who have lower IQ's than the average Negro child. About 27 percent of the white children are in this group.

Whenever we compare two different groups, national, racial, geographical, economic, or what have you, we find, first, these widespread differences within each group and, second, a great amount of overlapping. In view of this, it is useless to consider the class or group to which individuals belong when thinking about their intelligence. If we are considering the prospective ability of an *individual child* it will not help to inquire whether he is colored or Chinese, or whether he comes from Utah or Florida. If he is a colored child his intelligence may be anywhere from 20–160, and if he is white or Chinese this is equally true. Whenever it is important to sort *individuals* according to intelligence, we may as well forget about race, nationality, family background, or place of residence.

It is only when we have to deal with fairly large groups of people that average differences in intelligence have any significance. The fact that a man is a laborer tells us nothing about his intelligence. But the fact that this group is an unselected group of laborers tells us that more members of that group will be below 100 IQ than would be the case if we had a typical group of accountants.

In spite of the care taken by the investigators, we must always be on the alert for some important factor that has been neglected. A test carried on in the public schools, for instance, may miss a selected segment of one group that normally attends parochial schools(104). Factors like this, so easy to ignore, can readily give us a distorted picture.

In spite of these qualifications and difficulties, however, on the basis of our present tests we cannot expect the average attainment of children in one district to reach the average attainment of a more fortunate community. Accept the present status as a realistic starting point and try to increase that status as much as possible. Feel happy or discouraged as that status changes or fails to change. Do not exult because your select suburban group excels the city norms. Do not despair because your industrial group falls below the standards set by more favored communities. In all this, do not let your generous, democratic impulses prevent you from looking harsh facts in the face. And in a field as complex and unsettled as this, do not become wedded to one single explanation but keep an open mind with regard to the many unproved hypotheses. Above all, remember that these differences hold for group averages only. Never judge the powers or interests of an individual child merely on the basis of the census group to which he happens to belong.

Summary

Many things outside the school can have a close relation to physical and mental growth. At first glance it might seem that physical well-being may be closely related to intelligence and to academic proficiency. Actually, however, this relation does not always appear. Intelligence, for instance, has only a low correlation with size, weight, or even with head size or brain size.

On the average, crippled children and children who have defective vision or hearing tend to have trouble with our tests of intelligence or achievement. This difficulty may be due to handicap in taking the test, to handicap in learning, or to the fact that the conditions responsible for the ailment may also reduce ability to succeed in school. Such children are also, on the average, under some handicap in personal adjustment.

Whatever the explanation for the somewhat poorer showing of children with physical handicaps, we must not be too optimistic about remedial measures. So far the provision of eyeglasses or the removal of tonsils has not always resulted in improved school work, although there seems to be some promise in auditory training.

Hygienic practices within the school are designed, of course, to promote better health. There is some hope, however, that such practices will also have an effect on achievement. Alcohol impairs most psychological functions and certainly ruins judgment. Tobacco has little if any direct effect on ability to learn. Certain drugs, such as benzedrine or caffeine, tend to boost academic performance somewhat but only when taken in doses that would be harmful if used habitually. Little is known about the influence of chronic lack of sleep. Older students may function fairly efficiently even after forty-eight hours of wakefulness, but here, of course, they are on a "dare." Ventilation, especially circulation, affects comfort and the desire to work, but has little effect on actual output. Moderate attention to lighting is necessary for efficient work, but the amount of lighting necessary is much less than is often supposed. Uniformity of light is more important than sheer amount.

Sex differences may play a part in achievement. Girls are ahead in languages and in fine arts. Boys excel in problem solving, mathematics, science, and perhaps in content subjects. Girls have an especial advantage on teacher-marked essay examinations. Perhaps this is due to their superiority in language. For the over-all sex differences we have no clear-cut explanation. Some of these differences are undoubtedly due to training. It is still too soon to say whether all the differences are due to training or whether the genes also play a part.

In many tests of educational development we find superior average performance on the part of white, urban children from professional groups, in better homes, better communities, and living in certain regions of the country. To explain this cluster of differences we could invoke test favoritism, more stimulating environment, selective migration, or heredity. To understand the influence of heredity we must first of all get rid of the idea that we are engaged in a contest between heredity and environment. We are engaged, on the contrary, in an attempt to determine the general effect of each of these forces. The definite influence of heredity is revealed by the fact that identical twins are more similar intellectually than same-sex fraternal twins. This influence is also shown by the fact that there is more resemblance between parent and offspring than between parent and foster child. The influence of environment is shown by the fact that identical twins reared apart are less similar than identical twins reared together, and by the fact that children moved from a poor to a better environment regularly improve in intellect. Thus we see that we can accept the fact that heredity affects attainment and that we can also accept the separate and independent fact that the general environment affects attainment.

The region or community, as one aspect of the environment, is somewhat related to intelligence and achievement. Children from the Northeast and Western states excel children in the Southeast. Children in larger cities excel children in villages and in rural areas. Children in wide-awake communities excel children in backward areas. We must not jump to conclusions in explaining these differences. They could be explained by test favoritism, or by selective migration, or by superior training or environment, or by any combination of these possibilities.

As might be expected, the student's intelligence and achievement are definitely related to family conditions. Of these family factors, the education of the parents has the closest relation, and income has the least relation, although that relation is also positive. At one time children from smaller families excelled children from larger families, but there is some suggestion that this trend may no longer hold. "Class" differences have received a great deal of attention and it is claimed that both schools and tests stress middle class values unfamiliar to lower class children.

Racial differences in intelligence always show wide overlapping between any two groups. North Europeans, Jewish groups, Japanese, and Chinese come close to the average American norms. South Europeans and Negroes, on the average, fall somewhat lower. To account for these differences in the averages, we must examine the familiar hypotheses of test favoritism, unfavorable environment, selective migration. There is also the possibility of some direct genetic factor. None of these possibilities has been settled as yet.

SPECIFIC REFERENCES

1. Klebanoff, S. G., Singer, J. L., and Wilensky, H. Psychological consequences of brain lesions and ablations. *Psychol. Bull.*, 1954, *51*, 1–41.

2. Yates, A. J. The validity of some psychological tests of brain damage. *Psychol. Bull.*, 1954, *51*, 359–379.

3. Scherer, I. W., and others. Psychological changes during the first year following prefrontal lobotomy. *Psychol. Monogr.*, 1953, *67*, No. 7, (357).

4. Hollingworth, Leta S. The comparative beauty of the faces of highly intelligent adolescents. *J. genet. Psychol.*, 1935, *47*, 268–281.

5. Gaskill, H. V., and Fritz, M. F. Basal metabolism and the college freshman psychological test. *J. gen. Psychol.*, 1946, *34*, 29–45.

6. Weber, R. J. Relationship of physical fitness to success in college and to personality. *Res. Quart. Amer. Ass. Hlth. phys. Educ.*, 1953, *24*, 471–474.

7. Pintner, R., Eisenson, J., and Stanton, Mildred. *The psychology of the physically handicapped.* Crofts, 1941.

8. Meyerson, L. The visually handicapped. *Rev. educ. Res.*, 1953, *23*, 476–491.

9. Stedman, Melissa. The influence of health upon intelligence and school grades of high school pupils. *J. appl. Psychol.*, 1934, *18*, 799–809.

10. Conway, Pauline, and Nemzek, C. L. The relationship of school marks to the amount of illness. *J. genet. Psychol.*, 1942, *61*, 315–320.

11. Pintner, R., and Gates, A. I. The value of individual hearing aids for hard-of-hearing children. National Research Council, 1944.

12. Di Carlo, L. M., and Amster, W. W. The auditorily and speech handicapped. *Rev. educ. Res.*, 1953, *23*, 453–475.

13. Lewis, D. K. Rehabilitation of the preschool deaf child. *Laryngoscope,* 1950, *60*, 564–576.

14. Farris, L. P. Visual defects as factors influencing achievement in reading. *J. exp. Educ.*, 1936, *5*, 58–60.

15. Zimmerman, F. T., Burgemeister, Bessie B., and Putnam, T. J. The ceiling effect of glutamic acid upon intelligence in children and in adolescents. *Amer. J. Psychiat.*, 1948, *104*, 593–599.

16. Gadson, E. J. Glutamic acid and mental deficiency—a review. *Amer. J. ment. Defic.*, 1951, *55*, 521–528.

17. Harrell, Ruth F. Further effects of added thiamin on learning and other processes. *Teach. Coll. Contr. Educ.*, No. 928, 1947.

18. Benda, C. E. Empiric risk figures in mongolism. *Amer. J. ment. Defic.*, 1951, *55*, 539–545.

19. Poull, Louise E. The effect of improvement in nutrition on the mental capacity of young children. *Child Develpm.*, 1938, *9*, 123–126.

20. Fritz, M. F. The effect of diet on intelligence and learning. *Psychol. Bull.*, 1935, *32*, 355–363.

21. Carmichael, L., ed. *Manual of child psychology*. Wiley, 1954, Chap. 10, The environment and mental development (Jones, H. E.).

22. Powell, Margaret. An analysis of relationships existent between health practice, adjustment, and physical performance of freshmen women. *Res. Quart. Amer. Ass. Hlth.*, 1947, *18*, 176–186.

23. Jellinek, E. M., and McFarland, R. A. Analysis of psychological experiments on the effects of alcohol. *Quart. J. Stud. Alcohol*, 1940, *1*, 272–371.

24. Marshall, Helen. Alcohol: a critical review of the literature, 1929–1940. *Psychol. Bull.*, 1941, *38*, 193–217.

25. Langfeld, H. S. On the psychophysiology of a prolonged fast. *Psychol. Monogr.*, 1914, *16*, No. 5.

26. Glaze, J. A. Psychological effects of fasting. *Amer. J. Psychol.*, 1928, *40*, 236–253.

27. Edwards, A. S. Effects of the loss of one hundred hours of sleep. *Amer. J. Psychol.*, 1941, *54*, 80–91.

28. Luckiesh, M., and Moss, F. K. Effects of classroom lighting upon educational progress and visual welfare of school-children. *Illum. Engng.*, 1940, *35*, 915–938.

29. Tinker, M. A. Illumination standards for effective and easy seeing. *Psychol. Bull.*, 1947, *44*, 435–450.

30. Hilgard, E. R., Edgren, R. D., and Irvine, R. P. Errors in transfer following learning with understanding: further studies with Katona's card trick experiments. *J. exp. Psychol.*, 1954, *47*, 457–464.

31. Guetzkow, H. An analysis of the operation of set in problem-solving behavior. *J. gen. Psychol.*, 1951, *45*, 219–244.

32. Moraes, A. M. de M. *Récherche psychopédagogique sur la solution des problèmes d'arithmétique*. Louvain: Nauwelaerts, 1954.

33. Fifer, G. Grade placement of secondary school pupils in relation to age and ability. *Calif. J. educ. Res.*, 1952, *3*, 31–36.

34. Pauly, F. R. Sex differences and legal school entrance age. *J. educ. Res.*, 1951, *45*, 1–9.

35. McCarthy, Dorothea. Some possible explanations of sex differences in language development and disorders. *J. Psychol.*, 1953, *35*, 155–160.

36. Brown, S. B. Science information and attitudes possessed by California elementary school pupils. *J. educ. Res.*, 1954, *47*, 551–554.

37. Carter, R. S. Non-intellectual variables involved in teachers' marks. *J. educ. Res.*, 1953, *47*, 81–95.

38. Sobel, Frances S. Teachers' marks and objective tests as indices of school adjustment. *Teach. Coll. Contr. Educ.*, No. 674, 1936.

39. McCandless, B. Environment and intelligence. *Amer. J. ment. Defic.*, 1952, *56*, 674–691.

40. Fischer, Liselotte, K. Psychological appraisal of the "unattached" pre-school child. *Amer. J. Orthopsychiat.*, 1953, *23*, 803–816.

41. Pinneau, S. R. The infantile disorders of hospitalism and anaclitic depression. *Psychol. Bull.*, 1955, *52*, 429–452.

42. Zingg, R. M. Feral man and extreme cases of isolation. *Amer. J. Psychol.*, 1940, *53*, 487–517.

43. Dennis, W. A further analysis of reports of wild children. *Child Develpm.*, 1951, *22*, 153–158.

44. Freeman, F. N., Holzinger, K. J., and Mitchell, B. C. The influence of environment on the intelligence, school achievement, and conduct of foster children. *Yearb. nat. soc. Stud. Educ.*, 27 (I), 1928, 101–217.

45. Burks, Barbara S. The relative influence of nature and nurture upon mental development. *Yearb. nat. soc. Stud. Educ.*, 27 (I), 1928, 219–316.

46. Skeels, H. M. Some Iowa studies of the mental growth of children in relation to differentials of the environment: a summary. *Yearb. nat. soc. Stud. Educ.*, 39 (II), 1940, 281–308.

47. Stroud, J. B. Applications of intelligence tests. *Rev. educ. Res.*, 1941, *11*, 25–41.

48. Skodak, Marie. Mental growth of adopted children in the same family. *J. genet. Psychol.*, 1950, *77*, 3–9.

49. Outhit, M. C. A study of the resemblance of parents and children in general intelligence. *Arch. Psychol.*, N.Y., 1933, No. 149.

50. Bayley, Nancy. Some increasing parent-child similarities during the growth of children. *J. educ. Psychol.*, 1954, *45*, 1–21.

51. Davis, W. A., and Havighurst, R. J. The measurement of mental systems. *Sci. Mon.*, 1948, *66*, 301–316.

52. Shimberg, Myra E. An investigation into validity of norms with special reference to urban and rural groups. *Arch. Psychol.,* 1929, No. 104.

53. Mauldin, W. P. Selective migration from small towns. *Amer. sociol. Rev.,* 1940, *5,* 748–758.

54. Sanford, G. A. Selective migration in a rural Alabama community. *Amer. sociol. Rev.,* 1940, *5,* 759–766.

55. Goodenough, Florence L. New evidence on environmental influence on intelligence. *Yearb. nat. soc. Stud. Educ., 39* (I), 1940, 307–365.

56. Klineberg, O. *Negro intelligence and selective migration.* Columbia University Press, 1935.

57. Klineberg, O. A study of psychological differences between "racial" and "national" groups in Europe. *Arch. Psychol.,* 1931, No. 132.

58. Newman, H. H., Freeman, F. N., and Holzinger, K. J. *Twins: a study of heredity and environment.* University of Chicago Press, 1937.

59. Tyler, Leona E. *Psychology of human differences.* Appleton-Century-Crofts, 1947, Chap. 13.

60. Stephens, J. M. *The influence of the school on the individual.* Edwards Bros., 1933.

61. Leahy, Alice M. Nature-nurture and intelligence. *Genet. Psychol. Monogr.,* 1935, *17,* 235–308.

62. Alexander, H. B. A comparison of the ranks of American states in Army Alpha and in social-economic status. *Sch. & Soc.,* 1922, *16,* 388–392.

63. Stewart, Naomi. A. G. C. T. scores of army personnel grouped by occupation. *Occupations,* 1947, *26,* 5–41.

64. Davenport, K. S., and Remmers, H. H. Educational achievement as compared with money spent on schools. *Sch. & Soc.,* 1945, *61,* 333–335.

65. Bagley, W. C., *Determinism in education.* Warwick & York, 1925.

66. Educational Testing Service. Summary of statistics on Selective Service College Qualification Test of December 13, 1951; April 24, 1952; and May 22, 1952. Princeton, 1953.

67. Forbes, J. K. The distribution of intelligence among elementary school children in Northern Ireland. *Brit. J. educ. Psychol.,* 1945, *15,* 139–145.

68. Thorndike, R. L. Community variables as predictors of intelligence and academic achievement. *J. educ. Psychol.,* 1951, *42,* 321–338.

69. Meredith, H. V. Relation between socioeconomic-status and body

size in boys seven to ten years of age. *Amer. J. Dis. Child.,* 1951, *82,* 702–709.

70. Lund, F. H., Ycomans, E. R., and Geiges, E. A. Health indices in relation to age, sex, race, and socio-economic status. *J. soc. Psychol.,* 1946, *24,* 111–117.

71. Campbell, W. J. The influence of home environment on the educational progress of selective secondary school children. *Brit. J. educ. .Psychol.,* 1952, *22,* 89–100.

72. Davis, Beverly. Eminence and level of social origin. *Amer. J. Sociol.,* 1953, *59,* 11–18.

73. Almy, Millie C. Children's experiences prior to first grade and success in beginning reading. *Teach. Coll. Record,* 1950, *51,* 392–393.

74. Noel, Doris I. A comparative study of the relationship between the quality of the child's language usage and the quality and types of language used in the home. *J. educ. Res.,* 1953, *47,* 161–167.

75. Darcy, Natalie T. Review of the literature on the effects of bilingualism upon the measurement of intelligence. *J. genet. Psychol.,* 1953, *82,* 21–57.

76. Wolfle, D., and Oxtoby, T. Distributions of ability of students specializing in different fields. *Science,* 1952, *116,* 311–314.

77. Lawrence, Evelyn M. An investigation into the relation between intelligence and inheritance. *Brit. J. Psychol. Monogr. Suppl.,* 1931, *16,* 1–80.

78. Davie, J. S. Social class factors and school attendance. *Harv. educ. Rev.,* 1953, *23,* 175–185.

79. Stendler, Celia B., and Young, N. Impact of first grade entrance upon the socialization of the child: changes after eight months of school. *Child Develpm.,* 1951, *22,* 113–122.

80. Eells, K., and others. *Intelligence and cultural differences.* University of Chicago Press, 1951.

81. Eells, K. Some implications for school practice of the Chicago studies of cultural bias in intelligence tests. *Harv. educ. Rev.,* 1953, *23,* 284–297.

82. Tyler, F. T. Comments on the correlational analysis reported in Intelligence and Cultural Differences. *J. educ. Psychol.,* 1953, *44,* 288–295.

83. McGurk, F. C. J. On white and Negro test performance and socio-economic factors. *J. abnorm. soc. Psychol.,* 1953, *48,* 448–450.

84. Tate, Miriam E. The influence of cultural factors on the Leiter International Performance Scale. *J. abnorm. soc. Psychol.,* 1952, *47,* 497–501.

85. Abrahamson, S. School rewards and social-class status. *Educ. Res. Bull.*, 1952, *31*, 8–15.

86. Finch, F. H., and Nemzeck, C. L. Differential fertility. *J. soc. Psychol.*, 1935, *6*, 458–473.

87. Warburton, F. W. Relationship between intelligence and size of family. *Eugenics Rev.*, 1951, *43*, 36–37.

88. Nisbet, J. Family environment and intelligence. *Eugenics Rev.*, 1953, *45*, 31–40.

89. Ferrell, G. V. Comparative study of sex differences in school achievement of white and Negro children. *J. educ. Res.*, 1949, *43*, 116–121.

90. Newland, T. E., and Lawrence, W. C. Chicago nonverbal examination results on an east Tennessee Negro population. *J. clin. Psychol.*, 1953, *9*, 44–47.

91. Fulk, B. E., and Harrell, T. W. Negro-white army test scores and last school grade. *J. appl. Psychol.*, 1952, *36*, 34–35.

92. Jenkins, M. D. The upper limit of ability among American Negroes. *Sci. Mon.*, 1948, *66*, 339–401.

93. Gilliland, A. R. Socio-economic status and race as factors in infant intelligence test scores. *Child Develpm.*, 1951, *22*, 271–273.

94. Williams, Judith R., and Scott, R. B. Growth and development of Negro infants: IV. Motor development and its relationship to child rearing practices in two groups of Negro infants. *Child Develpm.*, 1953, *24*, 103–121.

95. Tanser, H. A. *The settlement of Negroes in Kent County, Ontario, and a study of the mental capacity of their descendants.* Chatham, Ont.: Shepherd Co., 1939.

96. Brill, M. Studies of Jewish and non-Jewish intelligence. *J. educ. Psychol.*, 1936, *27*, 331–352.

97. Portenier, Lillian G. Abilities and interests of Japanese-American high school seniors. *J. soc. Psychol.*, 1947, *25*, 53–61.

98. Carlson, Hilding B., and Henderson, N. The intelligence of American children of Mexican parentage. *J. abnorm. soc. Psychol.*, 1950, *45*, 544–551.

99. Rohrer, J. H. The test intelligence of Osage Indians. *J. soc. Psychol.*, 1942, *16*, 99–105.

100. Cowen, P. A. Testing Indian school pupils in the State of New York. *Ment. Hyg.*, 1943, *27*, 80–82.

101. Leighton, Dorothea, and Kluckhohn, C. *Children of the people; the Navaho individual and his development.* Harvard University Press, 1947.

102. Turner, G. H., and Penfold, D. J. The scholastic aptitude of the

Indian children of the Caradoc Reserve. *Canad. J. Psychol.*, 1952, *6,* 31–44.

103. Lacy, L. D. Relative intelligence of white and colored children. *Elem. Sch. J.,* 1926, *26,* 542–546.

104. Pasamanick, B. The intelligence of American children of Mexican parentage: A discussion of uncontrolled variables. *J. abnorm. soc. Psychol.,* 1951, *46,* 598–602.

SUGGESTIONS FOR FURTHER READING

1. Barker, R. G., and others. *Adjustment to physical handicap and illness: a survey of the social psychology of physique and disability.* Social Science Research Council, Bulletin 55, rev., 1953.

2. Garrett, J. F., ed. *Psychological aspects of physical disability.* Federal Security Agency, Rehabilitation Service Series No. 210, U.S. Gov't. Printing Office, 1952.

   A brief and nontechnical review of the influence of the most frequent handicaps.

3. Pintner, R., Eisenson, J., and Stanton, Mildred. *The psychology of the physically handicapped.* Crofts, 1941.

   This is an excellent account of the early work and is still useful for many aspects of the problem.

4. Tyler, Leona E. *The psychology of human differences.* Appleton-Century-Crofts, 1947.

   See Chapter 4 for an account of sex differences. Chapter 11 is a very readable account of the relation between mental and physical characteristics. Chapter 13 gives a balanced account of the work on heredity and environment.

5. Penrose, L. *The biology of mental defect.* Grune & Stratton, 1949.

   For the influence of prenatal conditions.

6. Di Carlo, L. M., and Amster, W. W. The auditorily and speech handicapped. *Rev. educ. Res.,* 1953, *23,* 453–475.

   Includes brief accounts of some studies on the effect of auditory training on achievement.

7. Travers, R. M. W. Individual differences. *Annu. Rev. Psychol.,* 1955, *6,* 137–160.

   For a brief account of general nonscholastic factors.

8. Beach, F. A., and others. Symposium on heredity and environment. *Psychol. Rev.,* 1947, *54,* 297–352.

   A series of articles on heredity and instinct in animal behavior.

9. Kallmann, F. J. *Heredity in health and mental disorder.* Norton, 1953.

Some impressive evidence of the role of heredity in disease. Also includes material on heredity and personality.

10. Scheinfeld, A. *The new you and heredity.* Lippincott, 1950.

A lively discussion of the mechanisms and influence of heredity. Directed to the layman but accurate and cautious.

11. McCandless, B. Environment and intelligence. *Amer. J. ment. Defic.,* 1952, *56,* 674–691.

A review of the general environmental effects.

12. Carmichael, L., ed. *Manual of child psychology.* Wiley, 1954.

Chap. 10. The environment and mental development (Jones, H. E.)

Chap. 12. Research on primitive children (Mead, Margaret)

Chap. 17. Psychological sex differences (Terman, L. M., and Tyler, Leona E.)

13. Eells, K., and others. *Intelligence and cultural differences.* University of Chicago Press, 1951.

Technical and detailed but an important publication dealing with the question of test bias.

14. Klineberg, O. *Race differences.* Harpers, 1935.

A balanced account of the early work in this complex field.

15. Pinneau, S. R. The infantile disorders of hospitalism and anaclitic depression. *Psychol. Bull.,* 1955, *52,* 429–452.

For a critique of the work on the influence of lack of warm personal relations.

Exercises and Questions for Discussion

1. Which of the physical defects is most closely related to intellectual or academic deficiency? What about cause and effect in these relations? Mention at least three hypotheses to account for the fact that children with certain defects obtain below-average scores on some of our tests.

2. A friend of yours asks you to comment on a speech he plans to make at a parent-teachers' meeting. The following is a brief sketch of the points he intends to make:

For the teacher the health of the child is doubly important. In the first place, health is one of the most important considerations in its own right. In the second place, any improvement in health, hygiene, or physical efficiency will bring rich return in increased academic attainment. By persuading high-school students not to smoke, for instance, the teacher can bring about an increase in attainment. This is shown by the fact that nonsmokers markedly surpass smokers in achievement. Arranging for hearing aids for hard-of-hearing children will increase achievement more than many hours spent in routine teaching. More important, it will make for marked improvement in social adjustment.

Go over the sketch, correcting any errors he may have made and adding any significant facts that belong to his main theme.

3. How do you account for the fact that girls exceed boys in the marks they get on teachers' examinations? List two or three possible reasons and give your opinion of the plausibility of each.

4. Discuss the problem of middle-class bias in intelligence tests. What are some of the problems in eliminating such bias?

5. An investigator is trying out a new test similar to the typical group test but more difficult. He wants to be sure he will have a fair number of children who will make a high score. From which groups should he select the children?

PART three

The Teacher Enters
the Pattern of Forces

It is all very well to observe educational growth and to appreciate the regularities and constancies that characterize so many aspects of growth. It is also most important to see the part played by other agencies in shaping this growth. But the chief question will always be, "What can the school do and how can it do it? Especially, what can I, as classroom teacher, do and what are the tools I can use in the process?"

These are the questions we consider in Part III.

8

Theories of General Behavior

THE THEORIES discussed in this and the next chapter
have played an important part in human thought. At the present, they
are of great concern to those who would like to know the why's and
wherefore's of human behavior. As teachers, we have a ringside seat
for many of the more important phenomena of this human behavior. It
would seem too bad if we did not have some general idea of the broad
questions that have been asked about these phenomena. Among educated
people it will be taken for granted that we know something of the broad
issues to which our work is so closely related.

Over and above this intellectual need to know about the phenomena
in which you are immersed, there are very many practical reasons for
acquiring some notion of psychological theory. The "home-made"
theorizing that you yourself are bound to undertake will be more meaningful if it fits into the broad framework of more systematic theory. The
practical research we shall discuss also takes on more meaning and becomes more reasonable when we are aware of the theoretical issues that
led to the experiments(1). It is often to theory that we turn, moreover,
when we can find no body of experimental data to guide us in our practical work. In the absence of specific data, we try to see if the more
general theories may suggest a course of action. And finally, these general
theories will play a considerable part in the thinking of your superiors
and colleagues. You are bound to encounter theoretical ideas and to be
asked to deal with them.

Many people hold that theory is even more important than our claims would suggest. Some writers hold that one's theory of human nature plays an extremely vital part in the curriculum provided(2) and in the work of the teachers. According to this view, we have the obligation to think through and adopt a defensible theory of human behavior before attempting to teach or to direct educational enterprises. Other psychologists(3), the writer of this text among them, take a less extreme view, holding that much effective teaching is done by people who have little knowledge of theory, and that vast shifts in theory take place with little change in teaching practice. According to these latter views, theory makes teaching more interesting and flexible. It gives the teacher perspective and a feeling of understanding what he is about. But the claims stop with these important values. It is not held that a knowledge of theories of psychology is absolutely essential for success in the classroom.

Much of the "lounge-room" discussion you will encounter, by the way, will remind you of the missionary or the political exhorter. People will try to convert each other to the true doctrine. Often, moreover, in urging the merits of one particular view, the proponents will not stress the truth of that view or its conformity to the observed data. Instead, they may stress the fact that it is democratic, progressive, constructive, or flattering to the human race. In a later section you will be urged not to adopt any theory on the grounds of its emotional appeal and to give serious consideration to the views available. After that consideration you may not find it necessary to form a firm alliance with any one theory. But if you do, you will be in a much better position to make an intelligent decision.

Disagreement in Psychology

The difference between psychologists is not so great as many people believe. The vast majority of psychologists do not spend most of their time in arguing about the merits of this broad theory or that. Most of them are digging up facts which do have a bearing on theory but which are also important in their own right. And with regard to many of these facts there is a substantial amount of agreement.

Disagreement Increased by Lack of Facts. Although the disagreements in psychology are steadily becoming less important, it is still true that such disagreements figure more prominently in psychology than in some other sciences. After all, psychology stretches over a great many areas, and for some of these areas very few concrete facts are available. These relatively empty fields invite speculation; since in those areas speculation is hard to test, one view may be almost as good as another. It is when facts become known that many of the theories are eliminated and that the shape of the acceptable theory becomes more clearly outlined. Some thirty years ago, for instance, there had been published almost a hundred different descriptions of the probable mechanisms underlying color vision. As facts and more facts came in, however, many of these theories were eliminated. Today, although colorists are not sure as to the exact statement of *the* theory of color vision, they are fairly sure of some of the characteristics which it must have. Naturally enough, the more facts there are to explain, the fewer theories there are which can explain all those facts.

Disagreement More Intense in the Field of Human Values. Controversy may also be more pronounced in the field of psychology because of the great human significance of many psychological concepts. When ideas have only academic importance, we are less likely to become violently disturbed about them. Two chemists, for instance, may disagree as to the place of a substance in the benzene ring. But this quarrel seldom reaches the newspapers, because most of us are not greatly concerned. It is when the issue involved has vital significance for our hopes, or fears, or our cherished beliefs that we become very much concerned. A quarrel takes on great importance, for instance, when the question at issue is whether we are free agents or merely elaborate machines. We also become concerned when a theory attempts to decide whether our purposes are as they seem to be, or whether they are merely the perverted expression of frustrated childhood impulses. Such a quarrel concerns things which many people consider important or valuable. To many people, the quarrel over such matters may outrank any data which the rival theories attempt to explain.

The Interrelations and Origins of Current Theories

Three Different Views of Behavior

These are the problems which we face when we try to work out a complete and systematic way of describing or explaining behavior. And considering the complexity of behavior, with its many different phases, it is not surprising that different theorists have come up with different answers. Let us look at a practical example of behavior and see if we too might not be torn between several promising approaches.

A boy of nine or ten is coming down the street. He has a library card in his hand. As he reaches the street corner, he looks to the right where the library is located. Next he turns and looks to the left in a casual way and then continues to gaze in more sustained fashion, directing his attention to the bright letters in the sign of the nearby theater. He hesitates for a time, then turns to the left, goes up to the theater, hesitates again, pays his money, and goes in.

For the description of behavior such as this, there are three main psychological systems in widespread use. The oldest of these three systems goes by the awkward name of *connectionism*. The members of this school will try to divide the whole behavior sequence into two chief parts: (a) those things which were acting on the boy and (b) the things that the boy did. This, they say, will give us a good point of departure. On the one hand, we should visualize a complicated situation, or cluster of situations, acting on the boy. These situations include the sight of the library, the sight of the theater with its lively advertisement, the presence of the library card, and the many ideas and thoughts in the mind of the boy. All these things are acting on the boy. Now, having looked at the things acting on him, let us turn to his behavior. This is made up of a certain amount of vacillation, followed by the act of buying a ticket and going into the theater.

The connectionist holds that we are on safest ground if we merely assume that there are *connections* of one sort or another within the boy, and that these connections account for his behavior. He assumes that this particular boy is so "hooked up" inside that when these circumstances act on him, he will behave in this way. He is also so arranged inside that when different circumstances act upon him he may behave in a different way.

The connectionist, of course, does not stop with this simple process of *translating* observations into situation-response terms. Beginning with this general description, he goes on to explain how these connections come about and how they become stronger or weaker. This, of course, is the problem of learning.

The fundamental approach of the connectionist can be diagramed as follows:

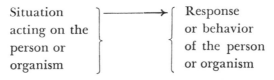

FIGURE 8-1. *The Basic Concept of Connectionism*

The connectionist assumes the existence of some link, or connection, or tendency between the situation and response, and he tries to explain why such tendencies become established and how they acquire different strengths.

A second group of psychologists, the members of the *Gestalt* school, or the proponents of the *Field Theory,* as they are often called, take a different approach. Listening to the connectionist description, for instance, the Gestalt psychologist might object as follows: "This situation you talked about—what goes into it? Is it just the sight of the library plus the sight of the theater? Or is it more complicated? Do these situations ever recur, or is each one something that is absolutely unique? If they do recur, how can you tell whether or not two situations are the same? Must all the physical aspects be the same? or just some of them? Does it make any difference which ones are the same?"

Having thus called the connectionist to task, the Gestalt psychologist will go on to answer his own questions. He points out that the situation which we experience is always organized, or structured, and that this structure may be more permanent than the physical elements on which it is based. He also points out that this organized structure contains some one element that completely dominates the situation. The theater, for instance, may occupy a central focus and the rest of the situation be merely background. Once this is explained, the Gestalt psychologist maintains that the person's actual behavior may be very easy to understand. In Gestalt psychology, therefore, the basic formula is more like this:

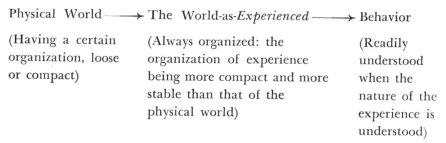

Physical World ⟶ The World-as-*Experienced* ⟶ Behavior

| (Having a certain organization, loose or compact) | (Always organized: the organization of experience being more compact and more stable than that of the physical world) | (Readily understood when the nature of the experience is understood) |

FIGURE 8-2. *The Basic Concept of Gestalt Psychology*

For the Gestalt psychologist the important thing is to understand the relation between the physical world and the world of experience. When that is done, most of the problems of psychology will be solved.

A third group is still to be heard from. Just as the Gestalt psychologist accused the connectionist of using a situation that was poorly defined and oversimplified, so this third group accuses the connectionist of using a response that is poorly defined and oversimplified. These psychologists, whom we shall call *purposivists,* will ask the connectionist what is meant by a response. Does the response refer to the actual movements that the boy makes? If so, the purposivist will point out, the connectionist has told us very little about those movements. We do not know whether the boy ran, or walked, or skipped. We have no idea of the precise muscles involved. We merely know that the boy "went to theater." That is to say, by one means or another, the boy *accomplished a certain result.* Furthermore, the purposivist hastens to point out, it is the accomplishment of this result that really defines the response. When the result is accomplished, we say that the response has taken place.

To the purposivist, the all-important thing about behavior is this business of accomplishing results or reaching goals. The boy's behavior in going to the theater can make sense only if we imagine him, first of all, at a certain stage in the process, wanting or intending to go to the theater. Then we must imagine him going through whatever motions are necessary to get him to the theater. The goal is the determining thing. When that is known, the resulting behavior can be readily understood. This is the general pattern in all behavior. The environmental conditions set up some sort of goal or need. Once this goal is in existence, the person will keep on doing one thing after another until the goal is reached, or until some new goal has replaced it.

For the purposivist, then, the goal dominates behavior. The attainment of the goal defines the response, the search for the goal determines the behavior. The basic formula for the purposivist appears in Figure 8-3.

FIGURE 8-3. *The Basic Concept of Purposive Psychology*

Possibility of Future Synthesis. In the face of all these quarrels, a stubborn but broad-minded connectionist might take over the doctrines of both the Gestalt psychologist and the purposivist. He might work out a theory of connectionism that is something like that in Figure 8-4. Here he agrees with the Gestalt psychologist that a situation is complicated and he accepts the Gestalt psychologist's general method of clarifying the situation. He also agrees with the purposivist that a response can be described only in terms of the results produced. He still insists, however, that the most important part of the story is the complex situation leading to a complex response.

Don't take Figure 8-4 too seriously, by the way. It is not the final answer to our problems by any means. It may help us to see a very general pattern (or Gestalt) into which the three schools fit. But it is necessarily oversimplified. This particular simplification, moreover, shows a connectionist bias, since it suggests that the Gestalt and the purposivist school could be considered as mere amendments to the connectionist school. This, of course, they most assuredly are not. They are schools in their own right. A Gestalt psychologist would not admit that he offers a mere correction to the otherwise adequate doctrine of connectionism. He contends that, in addition to avoiding the errors of the connectionist, he can say everything that needs to be said in his own language without borrowing from connectionism. The purposivist would also claim that his school is self-sufficient and is not a mere amendment to connectionism. Figure 8-4, far from being a final synthesis, merely suggests the possibility that a synthesis might be achieved.

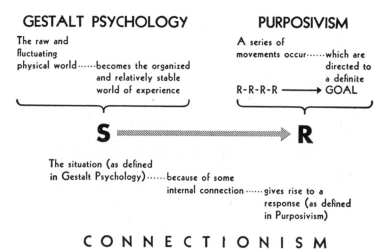

FIGURE 8-4. *Suggested Synthesis of the Three Chief Schools of Psychology*

Prelude to Present-day Controversies

At one time the term *psychology* was chiefly applied to the study of the soul, or of the mind, or to the study of consciousness. Under such circumstances it was most natural that the investigator should turn to the mind or the consciousness most available to him, and that, of course, was his own mind or his own conscious processes. We see now that he was studying a very special kind of mind. The only people who were likely to undertake such a study were people who were curious and intellectually minded to begin with. By the time they began studying their own processes, moreover, they had had much practice in logic and in the manipulation of ideas. Most of them had also developed considerable veneration for ideas and for the intellect and a corresponding aversion, or suspicion, for emotion, or for other nonintellectual aspects of the mind. It is not surprising, then, to find that the early speculations of the mental philosophers led to highly intellectualistic theories, and that the psychology which was propounded consisted largely of ideas, concepts, and other intellectual elements.

Faculty Psychology. Although many of the early theories had a highly intellectualistic slant, it would be too much to expect that all theories should take the same slant. Even within the realm of intellectual theories there is much room for discord and disagreement. Of the rival theories which did result, the two most important were *associationism* and *faculty psychology.* The theory of faculty psychology was set forth by Christian Wolff in 1734. A related version was advanced by Thomas Reid, the Scottish philosopher, in 1785. This doctrine held that the soul or mind was a unit or a single thing. How then can this single mind perform so many functions? Sometimes we find the mind perceiving things. At other times we find it making judgments or making decisions. We even find it experiencing emotions. And, especially if we are professional philosophers, we ofen find it engaged in the many processes that make up logical thinking. Obviously, it was necessary to assume that this single, unitary mind had several separate powers or faculties. The mind had the power or faculty of remembering and also the power or faculty of perceiving relations. As is mentioned in the discussion of transfer of training, by the way, something like this faculty psychology is implied by the people who talk about strengthening the memory, or training the powers of observation. People who talk in this fashion assume that there is some such faculty, and that this whole faculty can be improved by practicing any part of it.

Associationism. In direct contrast to the faculty theories, there flourished between 1750 and 1900 various theories of associationism. The association of ideas, of course, was a very familiar phenomenon and had probably been discussed ever since man was first articulate. The

English philosophers from Hobbes to Hume made much use of this phenomenon to explain the development of ideas. It was David Hartley, however, a country physician writing about the same time as Hume, who first made the extreme suggestion that *all* mental process could be explained by association. This doctrine received much attention, both favorable and unfavorable. Adam Smith made use of it in his famous treatise on economics, and English literature has carried the impact of the idea for some 150 years. The doctrine of associationism received its most extreme statement at the hands of James Mill in the early 1800's. Later writers, including Mill's son, the famous John Stuart Mill, abandoned the extreme position, and the modified doctrine became part of the body of psychology.

According to these theories of associationism, the mind, far from being a single unit, was thought to be merely the aggregate or sum total of a large number of separate, minute ideas, sensations, and feelings. These were all tied together by the process of association. A clap of thunder in the outside world, for instance, causes me to experience a sensation of noise. It happens that in my past experience, moreover, this same kind of noise occurred during a very eventful experience in a sailboat. Because of association, the noise, when it now occurs, does not come alone, but drags along with it the ideas that were present during the sailboat episode and which have become linked to the idea of the thunder clap by virtue of associations. Each of these latter ideas, in turn, is tied to a large number of other ideas, and these also are drawn into my awareness through the bonds of association. And that simple process, according to the associationist, *is* my mind. My mind is nothing more than the aggregate or cluster of ideas, thoughts, feelings, and decisions that I am aware of from time to time.

Dynamic Associationism. Somewhat similar to the theory of classical associationism just discussed, was the view of *dynamic associationism* proposed by Herbart early in the nineteenth century. Herbart agreed that the content of the mind was determined by a large number of simple ideas or small elements. He denied, however, that these ideas or mental elements are passively dragged into our experience through the bonds that tie them to other ideas. He held, on the contrary, that each idea has its own store of energy and that it actually struggles to secure a place in our experience. In this struggle each idea makes use of some other ideas that tend to push it in the same direction, and wrestles with still other ideas that work against it. It is never the mere victim of its connections with other ideas.

These were the great controversies of a past century. The drama of today's battle is written around contestants with different names. In spite of the difference in names, however, much of the essential plot remains the same. The contemporary psychologist who insists on the unity of experience still strives mightily with an opponent who tries to analyze experience into smaller elements. A third psychologist vigorously accuses both contestants of ignoring the role of individual ideas striving for recognition.

Association Theories: Emphasis on Reaction to the Environment

Connectionism or Modern Associationism

The connectionists have had a hard time agreeing on a label. Perhaps it is because most of them are not greatly interested in labels. At any rate, they have been called not only *connectionists*, but *modern associationists, modern functionalists,* and *stimulus-response psychologists,* to mention only the respectable names.

Connectionism developed rather naturally from the traditional associationism of the nineteenth century. About the end of that century, E. L. Thorndike, a young student at Harvard and, later, at Columbia, was engaged in observing the behavior of young chicks. This interest in animal behavior was relatively new for psychologists and was brought about by some earlier quarrels regarding the evolution of mind. In these early quarrels, the critics of evolution had defied Darwin to explain the fact that man reasons but that the animal shows no hint of reason, being governed entirely by instinct. Darwin promptly disputed the alleged fact. He and other evolutionists began to study problem solving on the part of animals, hoping to find some trace of reasoning at these lower levels. The early work of the biologists attracted the attention of some psychologists and it was on this problem, later on, that Thorndike began to work.

In explaining the behavior of young chicks, Thorndike felt that the traditional associationism was a little unwieldy and even slightly grotesque. In describing a chick pecking at a pellet of food, for instance, a typical associationist would proceed along the lines suggested in Figure 8-5. Even this diagram is oversimplified, since a true associationist would talk about the chick's judgment of where the food lay, and whether or not it was within reach, and so forth. Obviously, such an elaborate set of assumptions regarding the chick's mental processes would seem very questionable to a skeptic, and Thorndike was a skeptic of the first water.

The sheer awkwardness of the traditional associationism was not the only factor which suggested a simpler formula. By this time, as it happened, much was known about the science of neurology. The *reflex arc* theory, for example, was well developed and played an important part in physiological thought. This reflex arc explained, or seemed to explain, how some physical stimulus, such as a pin prick, could set in train a neural impulse which would automatically result in a quick jerk of the

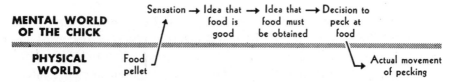

FIGURE 8-5. *A Simple Act Explained in Terms of Classical Associationism*

hand. The famous American psychologist, William James, with whom Thorndike studied, had, just a few years earlier, suggested that such a reflex arc was responsible for all mental events such as ideas or feelings. He suggested that the idea was merely the mental counterpart of "a neural impulse already on its way to instigate a movement."

Under these circumstances, it is not surprising that Thorndike modified the traditional associationism. Instead of the traditional associations between ideas, he talked about a more direct association between the original situation (sight of food) and the response (pecking). He held that we are on fairly safe ground when we say that (S), the situation presented by the food, leads to (R), the response of pecking. When we get beyond this more direct S-R association, however, we become increasingly dependent on inference and surmise, especially when we are describing the behavior of chicks. Thorndike admitted, of course, that there might be an elaborate series of associations in the mental world of the chick. But he preferred not to have to depend on these hypothetical ideas. Actually, when he described the behavior of people, in contrast to the behavior of chicks, he often made use of such mental associations. When he did talk about these traditional mental associations, however, he translated them into his new formula. He considered that each new idea is a *response* to a preceding idea, or a preceding sensation. He held that everything we do, whether in thought or in action, can be described in these situation-response terms.

Connectionism has had a considerable influence on psychology in one way or another. For many years, in the field of educational psychology, connectionism was more or less the accepted doctrine throughout the United States. In other fields, several aspects of connectionism have been taken over and have been worked into the general body of psychology. But it is perhaps as an irritant that connectionism has had its greatest influence. It has acted as the target, or focus of rebellion, for a large number of schools. As a matter of fact, perhaps one of the best ways to get an over-all view of one of the newer schools of psychology would be to ask, "What is *your* objection to connectionism?" That is an exaggeration, of course, but it is in the direction of the truth(4).

The Connectionist's Description of Different Kinds of Behavior. It is easy to see how the connectionist could describe much of the overt behavior that takes place in the school. Each question the teacher asks can be regarded as a situation acting on the student. Each answer the student gives is a response to one of those situations. But the connectionist does not feel restricted to descriptions of this kind of behavior. He holds that his system can be used to describe anything that is known about a person. He believes that such things as abstract qualities can be readily described in connectionistic terms, and, indeed, that the connectionist description is the only safe method to employ. If you say, for instance, that a certain man is honest, the connectionist will feel that you have really told us very little unless we can first imagine some sort of situation confronting the man, and unless, second, we can conjure up some sort of response that an honest man would make and that a dishonest man would not make. If you can say, "He is the kind of man who keeps a supply of personal stationery in the office so that he won't have to use the stationery of his employer," then the connectionist knows what you are talking about and he feels on safe ground. Anything more general than that, he regards with suspicion.

Memory, of course, is readily described in terms of a persisting connection. The connectionist supposes, for instance, that as a result of the history lesson, the youngster becomes so arranged or so "hooked up" that when he hears of the Louisiana Purchase he will respond by thinking of Jefferson. We know this connection exists, because periodically we present him with a phrase such as Louisiana Purchase and see what response he makes. The existence of that connection, moreover, is about all we can be sure of. We do not know that our student has carried the information around with him as part of his daily thoughts. It is conceivable, of course, that he may have. Students have been known at times to seize on a given principle and think of it many times a day. It is more probable, however, that the connection has lain quite dormant until the student, in wild panic, has seen the words Louisiana Purchase staring at him from some surprise quiz.

The Importance of Learning in the Doctrine of Connectionism. In his superficial description of what people are, or what people do, the connectionist is committed to the use of tendencies or connections. But how can he go beyond this superficial description? Can he do anything except translate ordinary descriptions into his new and rather grotesque phraseology? Yes, he claims that he can. He holds that the chief task of psychology is to explain how these tendencies come into being. It is not enough to know that a man stops the car when he sees the red light. The most important thing to know is the process by which such tendencies come to be formed. To understand human nature, we must work out the principles that will tell us which tendencies will come into being. We also need principles that will tell us whether a given tendency will become stronger or weaker, or vanish completely.

There are two general processes by which tendencies may be formed. The first general process, of course, is inheritance. We come into the world with a few tendencies fairly well developed. Upon our arrival, we also have the basic tendencies, or the raw stuff, out of which thousands of other tendencies may be formed. The second general process is that of learning. Through the action of the environment upon us, the primitive tendencies become modified, and new tendencies are produced.

It is to the biologist, of course, that we look for an explanation of the general process of heredity. The general process of learning, however, is well within the field of the psychologist, and it is this process which, according to the connectionist, constitutes the chief problem of psychology. For the connectionist, learning is the central process and all other phenomena are rather incidental.

Connectionism and Neurology. There can be no doubt that connectionism owes its origin, in part, to the neurological notions prevalent in the latter part of the nineteenth century. It is also very true that many of the early writers in this school made definite use of some elementary, but perhaps erroneous, ideas regarding nerves and neural connections. Such early writers made it clear that the tendency or connection which they had in mind was based on a physical connection between two nerves (a synapse) or on several such connections.

In contrast to the early writers, most contemporary connectionists are rather vague about neurology. Most of them, without a doubt, suspect that the connections they talk about are based on some kind of neural process. But, for the most part, they do not specify just what kind of neural process is involved. One or two connectionists(5), it is true, do go into details in their speculations or assumptions regarding the nervous system, but they are the exceptions. Most connectionists leave this problem to the physiologists and anatomists. They know that the man under observation stops the car when he sees the red light, and they talk about some tendency underlying the behavior. They assume that this tendency, in turn, is based on something in the nervous system, but that is about as far as they go or as far as they need to go.

Behaviorism

Behaviorism, when it flourished, represented an extreme form of connectionism. The classical connectionist, it will be remembered, talked about connections, or bonds, between physical situations and physical responses; between mental situations and mental responses; between physical situations and mental responses; and between mental situations and physical responses. He applied his S-R formula indiscriminately to both mental and physical events, although, no doubt, he preferred to emphasize physical situations and physical responses.

In contrast to this naive, but broad-minded attitude of the classical connectionists, J. B. Watson of The Johns Hopkins University proposed, about 1914, that we should use only physical situations and only physical responses. He urged that we should not introduce any mental events into our psychological descriptions. After all, as Watson pointed out, these mental events can be observed only by one person. Each person can observe only his own inner experience. If he tries to study the mental processes of another person, he must rely on what that other person *says,* or *writes,* or on what *signals* that other person makes. And these things, of course, are not the mental processes themselves but are bits of behavior. They are physical responses. How much wiser, Watson held, to admit this fact and to go about the business of studying behavior without deceiving ourselves into thinking we are studying mental life or consciousness.

The new approach, suggested by this special branch of connectionism, caused a great deal of discussion and controversy. In fact, a good bit of psychology between 1915 and 1930 was taken up with the "Battle of Behaviorism." By 1930, however, the quarrel had lost much of its attractiveness. Positions became less extreme. Watson himself had left academic psychology by this time and some of the more ardent early supporters, such as K. S. Lashley, were led by their investigations to take a different view. A younger group of psychologists adopted some be-havioristic ideas, ignored others, and, in general, refused to get excited about the problem. At the present moment, a great many behavioristic ideas are incorporated into general psychology and a fair number of psychologists have very definite behavioristic leanings. But the problem has lost its urgency. The main spotlight has passed away from this issue and has become focused instead upon the major quarrel between con-nectionists, on the one hand, and the various field psychologists, on the other.

Field Theories: Emphasis on the Organized Nature of Experience

Gestalt Psychology

About the same time that the behaviorists tried to limit the then cur-rent descendants of associationism to the study of physical situations and physical responses, a very different group of psychologists began to object most strenuously to the whole concept of associationism. This revolution came largely from the cooperative work of three German psychologists, Max Wertheimer, Kurt Koffka, and Wolfgang Köhler, each of whom voiced somewhat different proposals, but all of whom were in sufficient general agreement to be grouped as Gestalt psychologists. As an early ally of this group, who later developed a novel approach of his own, we should list Kurt Lewin. Although it seems wiser not to include him within the actual fold of the classical school of Gestalt psychology, he does belong among those who adhere to the broader principles of the field theories.

The Prevalence and Dominance of Structure. According to the Gestalt psychologists, experience is always structured. Whenever we are aware of anything, we are aware of it as part of a complex pattern or structure or organization. We never perceive a mere mass of separate details. Some of these details will occupy a prominent place in our experience. Others will play a subordinate role. A painting has a center of interest and a background. A musical composition has a main theme traced against a background of chords or other harmonic devices. In ordinary experience, there is always some aspect which is high-lighted and others which at that moment are chiefly background.

Even when the external environment has little in the way of organiza-tion or structure, the observer will tend to experience some organization.

In Figure 8-6, for instance, the spacing of the dots is perfectly uniform. There is no grouping on the printed page. Yet we may tend to see groups as we look at it. We may see groups of four dots which seem to be a unit. In such a uniform arrangement, of course, the groupings may change or fluctuate. Nevertheless, we will probably be conscious of some grouping, fleeting and transient though it may be.

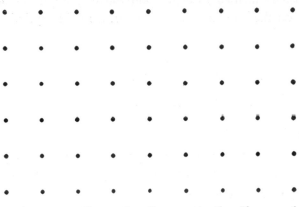

FIGURE 8-6. *Fluctuating Patterns in the Absence of Any Definite Objective Grouping*

If the picture is altered ever so slightly and is made to possess an objective pattern, that pattern will dominate the whole experience. In Figure 8-7, for instance, we are not merely able to see the dots arranged in groups of four, but we are almost compelled to do so.

A pattern such as that in Figure 8-7 is not the result of deliberate effort. We do not first see a group of unorganized dots and then build them into a suitable pattern. The contrary is true. The pattern is there

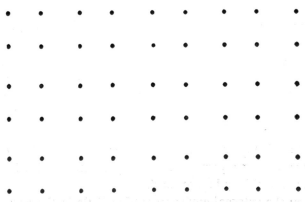

FIGURE 8-7. *Fixed Patterns Resulting from a Very Slight Introduction of Objective Grouping*

first. We see it at once. Indeed, it is only after some effort that we pick out the single dots which make up the pattern.

The pattern or structure of experience completely dominates that experience. It dominates experience to such an extent that, if the pattern calls for a detail, we will see that detail whether or not it is objectively present. Suppose, for instance, we are shown a lantern slide which suggests a wild West holdup. A man stands holding his hands in the air. Confronting him is a masked man whose attitude is decidedly menacing. The picture is left on the screen a few seconds and then flashed off. We are now asked what the masked man had in his hand. Most people will have "seen" a gun, even though the man actually had nothing in his hand. The general "holdup" pattern dominates the picture, and since this pattern called for a gun we "saw" that gun and so filled in the pattern. There are many such incidents. A rough sketch of a triangle in which the corners are imperfectly joined will still be seen as a triangle, and the imperfections may escape our notice. Or a familiar word in print may be seen as normal even though a part of the type is imperfect or even though two of the letters may be transposed. This tendency, incidentally, makes proofreading very difficult for most people who are familiar with the subject matter being read.

Marked Constancy of Patterns of Experience. Some interesting effects arise from our tendency to exaggerate and clarify the pattern to be found in the outside world. For one thing, the patterns of experience may remain fairly constant even in the face of continuous change in the outside world. Let us suppose we are watching a clever sculptor working in clay. He starts with a shapeless ball and begins to mold it. The objective shape of the clay changes continuously, but our awareness *does not* change continuously. We notice nothing out of the way until *suddenly,* as the result of a deft touch, the mass of clay changes into a tiger's head. It stays a tiger's head, becoming merely better and better and more convincing until it seems almost perfect. But even at this point the artist never stops. He changes the clay continuously. Yet, in spite of the distortion he may make, we continue to see a tiger's head, now gradually becoming poorer, perhaps, but still a tiger's head. Then with another sudden flash we see not a tiger's head but an owl. Thus a continuously changing objective situation may act on us by making us see first one relatively unchanging picture followed suddenly by another relatively constant picture.

Constancy of Geometric Forms. One of the most striking illustrations of the constancy of patterns is the constancy of geometrical forms. The window in my room may seldom cast the same image on my retina twice in succession. Whenever I see the window from a different angle, it casts a somewhat different picture on my eye. None of these pictures, moreover, is likely to be of a rectangular window. The actual picture on my retina is some sort of rhomboid figure with some acute angles and some obtuse angles. But I do not see the window as a series of changing rhomboids. I see it as always the same shape and *always as a rectangle*.

Size Constancy. A desk just in front of us acts on us very differently from a desk 15 feet away. The latter casts a much smaller image on our retinas, say about one eighth the size. Yet the more distant desk is seen as the same size as the closer desk. This adjustment is made automatically without any conscious or deliberate action on our part. We do *not* say, "That desk looks smaller, but then it is farther away and therefore if I make allowance for the greater distance, it would probably be the same size." We merely *see* both desks as the same size. This constancy, of course, holds only within certain limits. If the distance is greatly increased, the more distant desk may look smaller and we may find ourselves making such an allowance. This is often brought home when we view a street from an unusually high building. The automobiles and trolleys do look smaller, often to our great amusement.

Perception as the Great Problem in Gestalt Psychology. The problems of perception have proved most interesting to the Gestalt psychologists. They have been greatly concerned with explaining how we become aware of the world. For them, it is most important to explain how it is that our experience of a situation can remain relatively constant when the physical events responsible for that experience fluctuate in such wild fashion. Whereas the connectionist talks about what we will do when we encounter the *same situation* on a subsequent occasion, the Gestalt psychologist tries to work out the laws by which we can tell whether or not there will be a "same situation." How can we have sameness in experience, when the precise physical events will never be quite the same?

Learning as a Problem for Gestalt Psychology. For the Gestalt psychologist, learning or habit formation is not *the* great problem. But when he does turn to the problems of learning, he is likely to use the same ideas that he stresses when he studies the problem of perception. For him, learning is chiefly a matter of coming to see relations. We have to see, within one compact pattern, both the problem-to-be-solved and the means-of-solving-the-problem. When we have learned to use the dictionary, for instance, we have formed a clear pattern. When this has taken place, we cannot be aware of an unfamiliar word without at the same time being aware of the dictionary as a means of solving the problem. Learning consists of acquiring such "means-goal" Gestalts, or patterns. Once the pattern is formed, learning ceases to be a problem. There is needed only a little polishing off, or increased fluency. The bulk of the task has been mastered.

Obviously, the Gestalt psychologist differs from the connectionist in the physical models or analogies which he uses. Whereas the connectionist prefers the rather simple mechanical "being pushed—moving" analogy, the Gestalt psychologist favors the *field* models. In his psychology, for instance, the whirlpool is a better analogy than is the motion of the piston in an automobile. In the whirlpool, there is a very definite pattern which persists in spite of the changing particles of water. The particles of water do not determine the behavior of the whirlpool. On the contrary, the general field of forces determines the behavior of each particle. Each particle, it is true, may contribute to that total field, and so indirectly it may act on another particle. But, notice that it works only through the governing total field. Unless it can influence that total field, it cannot affect the behavior of its neighbors.

Topological Psychology

The special kind of field psychology developed by Kurt Lewin has received the name of *topological psychology*. It is like the classical Gestalt psychology in holding that the over-all pattern or field of events determines experience. It is somewhat different from the classical Gestalt psychology, however, in emphasizing behavior more than experience and in making greater use of motive or drive.

To understand what a person will do (or what he will experience), the Lewinians suggest that we diagram the "life space" of the individual so that we can visualize (and even compute) the forces that are acting on him at the moment. A somewhat simplified diagram appears in Figure 8-8.

In Figure 8-8 the person (P) is rep-

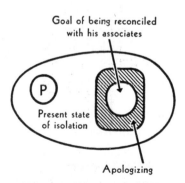

Goal of being reconciled with his associates

P

Present state of isolation

Apologizing

FIGURE 8-8. *Topological Representation of a Simple Conflict Situation.* Redrawn by permission from R. Leeper, *Lewin's Topological and Vector Psychology,* University of Oregon, 1943.

resented as being acted upon by a single force—the desire to regain the esteem of his colleagues. Before he can reach this goal, however, he must first apologize. This necessity of apologizing is represented in the diagram as an unattractive region that he must traverse. It is a barrier which lies between him and his goal. (More about these barriers later.)

The same plan by which we indicate a single goal or force acting on a person can be used to diagram the action of a group or a pattern of forces. The diagram, of course, must include more forces and goals, but the essential relations are the same. The group of forces resolve themselves into a pattern, and it is the total pattern which determines the subsequent behavior.

The forces acting on the person are considered, not as physical forces, but as psychological forces. When a physical force is applied, it will receive a certain place in the diagram, but its position within that diagram will be determined by its psychological nature and not by its physical nature. A given object may be very close to a person in a psychological sense and yet may be thousands of miles away in a physical sense. Similarly, a given route to a goal may be very short physically, but may involve traversing a great many unattractive zones (going past a house where there is a vicious dog). This short route would be diagramed as being psychologically longer, since it means the crossing of more of the difficult or negative zones.

It is this difference between the physical relations and the psychological relations that led Lewin to adopt the ideas of topology. In this branch of mathematics direction and distance are unimportant. If the diagram in Figure 8-8 were drawn on rubber, for instance, it could readily be distorted. The distances between any two points could be made to change and the direction of one point from the other could also be changed. But the number of zones to be traversed in going from one point to the other would not be changed. Neither would there be any change in the sequence in which the zones must be crossed. Hence, in a topological sense, the diagram would be unchanged. In Figure 8-9 we see a wide variety of diagrams, each telling the same topological story. Each one proclaims, if P is to get to G he must move from A through M.

The chief elements of most Lewinian diagrams are goals, barriers, and threats. Goals are said to have *positive valences*. Threats have *negative valences*. Ordinarily, a barrier has no valence. It merely prevents movement toward an object which happens to have positive valence, and prevents movement away from an object which has negative valence. The barrier may be physical, such as a closed door, or the height of a shelf; or it may be entirely psychological, such as a warning from the mother, or a memory of previous difficulty. It is true, of course, that an object which starts out as a neutral barrier may soon acquire negative valence, and may incite in us a desire to attack, as when we kick the closed door or shake the high cupboard which keeps the cookie jar out of our reach. It is also possible that an object which started out as a

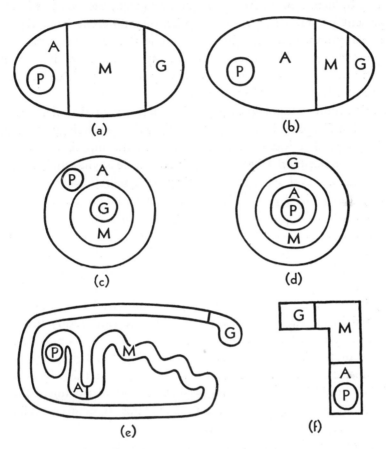

FIGURE 8-9. *A Group of Topologically Equivalent Diagrams.* Redrawn by permission from R. Leeper, *Lewin's Topological and Vector Psychology,* University of Oregon, 1943.

neutral barrier may acquire positive valence, by exerting a challenge. The same fence which once kept the child from visiting his playmate may later become an attractive object to jump.

The statement that the same physical object can change its psychological significance, is another way of saying that the life space is constantly being restructured. The psychological world changes even in the face of a relatively constant physical world, just as, conversely, the psychological world may remain constant in spite of extensive changes in the physical world.

This insistence on the use of psychological forces has led the Lewinians to deny the influence of past experience *per se*. It is only insofar as past experience is reflected in our immediate psychological world that it can have any influence on us. And as we know so well, the event as it acts in our present psychological world may be very different from the event that actually occurred. The childhood home that we now remember so fondly actually may have been a rather squalid place. But if we remember it as attractive, then it will have a very definite positive valence for us no matter how faulty the memory.

The doctrines of topological psychology have labored under two quite different handicaps. When first put forward, this psychology was clothed in a language that was unfamiliar and often incomprehensible. It was difficult to understand what the Lewinians were saying and, more distressing, there was a suspicion that they were merely saying some very ordinary things in an excessively pretentious language. This sort of language, describing one-knew-not-what, gave the new system a marked "negative valence" for those realistic psychologists who feel very unhappy with vague abstractions that cannot be defined in definite, earthy terms. Even in this later day when few psychologists regard the theory as difficult to comprehend, there are still frequent suggestions that the theory is vague. When we know the goals and the barriers as they are structured in the life space of the organism, we can readily understand why he behaves as he does. But how, asks Estes(6), are we to know the structure of the life space except by observing the behavior—the very thing the life space is supposed to explain? Against this objection, the Lewinian would hold that he can predict the sort of treatment that will bring about a given structure, and from this structure-as-defined-by-treatment, he can predict behavior.

Having met and argued with its critics, the Lewinian theory next had to contend with its friends. The very vagueness and seeming pretension which had acted as a barrier for many people proved to have a powerful positive valence for others. There are many people who are not at all repelled by fancy language describing rather vague concepts. Some people, on the contrary, have a vast appetite for impressive terminology that cannot be tied down to anything definite. And many of these people took to the Lewinian concepts as a duck takes to water, with the result that Lewinian ideas have been discussed with more enthusiasm than insight.

In spite of these twin handicaps, the Lewinian concepts have come to occupy an important place in psychology. In this book, for instance, we find ourselves automatically making great use of Lewinian ideas. The whole plan of the book is organized around *patterns of forces* and around the idea that behavior is to be understood in terms of the pattern of forces acting on the individual. Lewin's theories have also led to many interesting speculations, and, more important, to many fruitful experiments. The studies of the memory of incomplete tasks, of the importance of ego involvement, of the democratic environment, and of the group process all come largely from the Lewinian impetus.

Purposive Psychology: Emphasis on Goals as Determiners of Behavior

The Gestalt psychologist is impressed by the constancy of perception, by the fact that a variety of different physical stimuli will give rise to a constant experience. The *purposive psychologist,* on the other hand, is impressed by the *constancy of the result produced,* by the fact that the same result can be attained by a wide variety of movements. The purposivist reminds us that there are a large number of movements, for instance, by which one can sound an automobile horn, close a window, or call a dog. From time to time, moreover, the same person may use different movements to accomplish the same result. At one time he may sound the horn by pressing the button with his left hand, and at another time with his right hand. At still another time he may use his forearm, his thumb, or the back of his hand. Yet with each of these diverse movements he accomplishes the same result and completes the same behavior sequence.

As we point out in more detail in the discussion of transfer of training, it often happens that the result remains constant even when we are forced to abandon earlier, well-established methods of accomplishing that result. Having learned to write with the pen in one position, for instance, we find that we can also write after a radical change in the position of the pen and in the movements that are required.

To explain the dominance of the result to be achieved, the purposivist insists that we must use the concept of goal-striving. How else can we explain the controlling influence of a result which is not yet in existence? Some purposivists, such as the late William McDougall, held that in our explanations we should make use of the same sort of purpose that we notice in our own inner experience. McDougall pointed out that each of us is aware of a definite intention to go to a show, for instance, or to get something to eat, and that we are also aware of setting in motion a train of events by which we hope the result can be obtained. McDougall held that the logical thing to do is to use this very familiar idea of purpose to explain both our own actions and those of others. In opposition to McDougall, Professor E. C. Tolman of the University of California objects to ascribing to rats, or to other organisms, the same kind of purpose which each of us experiences. He insists, however, that whatever the rat may actually experience, we must *invent* or postulate some *intervening variable,* such as purpose, if we are to make sense of the rat's behavior, and if we are to reduce that behavior to some sort of order.

To all purposivists the concept of need, or goal, or purpose is the key for any explanation of behavior. We merely need to imagine (a) that the conditions acting on the organism at the moment will produce in him some goal or need, and (b) that he will proceed to utilize any aspects of the environment that seem to offer some promise of meeting that need. On one occasion when a man feels the need of getting home, for instance, he may board a trolley. At other times, however, he may set out to meet that need by walking via route A. At another time he may walk by route B. At still another time he may hail a taxi. The specific movements are very different and are merely incidental. The constant and significant thing is that he meets his need by making use of whatever means may be convenient at the moment.

Psychoanalytic or Freudian Psychology

Freudian psychology, based on the astounding insights of the Viennese psychiatrist, Sigmund Freud, is really a branch of purposive psychology. For the Freudian the concept of striving or goal-seeking is basic. All Freudian psychology makes much use of the idea of specific *urges* which are struggling to secure various ends or goals. Freudian psychology, however, is different from general purposivism in one important respect. According to the Freudian theory, the person or organism as a whole is not actuated by a single purpose at any one time. On the contrary, he is always the battleground of a whole host of purposes, each struggling to accomplish its own goal and, in so doing, contending with many competing urges. In this respect, Freudian psychology closely resembles the *dynamic associationism* advanced by Herbart early in the nineteenth century. It is also reminiscent of a much earlier, medieval brand of psychology in which each person was supposed to be inhabited by a number of demons—some good and some bad—which urged him this way or that, and which struggled among themselves for the control of his conduct.

Let us suppose that, at this moment, you are being acted upon by two separate urges. One urge wants you to go to the movies. The other urge wants you to study. Both struggle to get control of your behavior. How can either one get its way? According to Freudian psychology, an urge or desire can force you to do its bidding if it can work its way into the focus of your attention and stay there, meanwhile resisting the attempts of the other urges to elbow it out of this favored position. Thus, if the movie-going urge can get complete and uninterrupted possession of your attention for any appreciable time, then to the movies you will go. In the same way, the proponents of this theory would argue that if you are standing on a cliff and you think subconsciously of hurling yourself over the edge, then that is what you will do.

In its struggle to reach the focus of attention, each of these urges is quite aware of the intentions of the other urges. If one of these urges sees its rival gaining ground, it will redouble its own efforts and try to intercept the path of the other. The picture suggests a group of rival courtiers, bringing their petitions to the throne of the monarch, and keeping a watchful eye on the movements of each other. Furthermore, these rival urges may form alliances with similar urges, and "gang up" on some of the antagonistic urges. One of these powerful urges may say to the other, in effect, "You keep so and so out of the way until I get to the focus of attention, and, when I am there, I will do what I can for your petition also."

In the long history of human evolution, according to the Freudians, the many separate urges acting on each of us have become organized into two warring camps. On the one side are all the forces which are concerned with keeping the individual alive and in good prospect of remaining alive. These are the *ego* forces. On the other side are the *id* (Latin for *it*) urges. Most of these *id* urges serve the ultimate goal of keeping the race going. They are the sex urges and similar tendencies involved in procreation and in the care of the young. At least, that is the ultimate biological function which these urges serve. Their immediate goal, of course, is pleasure or gratification. The enmity between these two groups of urges is fundamental and deep-seated. The struggle for mates, the act of bringing forth a child, either of these may endanger the continued existence of the individual. The organized group of ego forces knows this, and looks with a very suspicious eye on any *id* urge which it sees making its way to the throne room or to the focus of attention.

Most surviving organisms have attained their survival only through the aid of a vigilant ego—an ego that is excessively suspicious and touchy. For most of us, this ego can see potential extinction, not only in the more obvious trouble that the *id* urges may bring, but also in the slightest threat to our reputation or to our own good opinion of ourselves. And it is this sense of our self-esteem that the more energetic and less orthodox *id* urges are especially likely to injure.

To make its control of matters doubly, or triply, secure, the ego urges have made use of a number of existing devices and have actually set up still other safeguards. The first feature which they have exploited is the boundary between the conscious and the subconscious. We are all familiar with the importance of the subconscious in Freudian psychology. It is the great submerged nine tenths of the iceberg in which most of our memories and associations and drives or urges reside. A drive or urge that wishes to get across into conduct must, first of all, pierce the barrier to consciousness. It is only after it has accomplished this first step that it can begin to elbow its way into the focus of attention.

This barrier between the conscious and the subconscious provides an excellent vantage point from which the ego can keep a careful check on the various *id* drives. To make the most effective use of this advantage, the ego also uses the mechanism of repression which is enforced by a special part of the ego called the *super-ego*. It is the duty of this super-ego to repress any especially dangerous or unwelcome *id* urge and to prevent it from ever entering consciousness. In this way the ego can prevent the *id* urges from ever taking the first step in an attempt to reach the focus of attention.

This phenomenon of repression is familiar to all of us. We hear, for instance, that some rich uncle is not well. We believe that we are included in his will. We find ourselves, in a dreamy moment, looking forward with some pleasure to the inheritance. Suddenly we come to life saying, "What thoughts are these? What sort of person am I? I mustn't think such things." In true repression, the guilty wish would never quite reach consciousness. In this case of more deliberate *suppression,* the wish was just able to insinuate itself inside the borders of consciousness. But immediately the super-ego came to life, although somewhat belatedly, and began to push the unwelcome intruder back into the unconscious.

What happens to a wish or an idea that is violently expelled from consciousness? Does it quietly sink to the bottom of the unconscious and gradually die out? By no means. It has lost none of its urgency or desire for expression. But obviously it must change its tactics if it is to succeed in gaining entry to consciousness. The simplest thing is to assume some sort of disguise, and this is amazingly easy in the subterranean depths of the unconscious, where there is no supervision and where no logic prevails. In these murky regions anything can happen and the most fantastic associations frequently take place. In the subconscious, for instance, an idea can be easily linked up with its opposite, and the opposite can act as a disguise for the guilty wish. The wish that Uncle Tobias shall die can be linked with the contrary wish that he may prosper. And this direct opposite may act as a disguise for the guilty wish that he may die. Hidden by such virtuous sheep's clothing, the dark wish for our uncle's death may easily rise into consciousness. The super-ego, pleased at such evidence of filial devotion, does nothing to hamper the seemingly virtuous urge. Hence our "front" of interest in Uncle Tobias' health, propelled as it is by the powerful hidden urge, may readily attain the focus of attention and thus cross into conduct. This combination of powerful drive and free passport will make for an unusual expression of our interest. We may find ourselves in daily attendance upon our uncle, urging precaution and medical advice to an unusual extent, and thus, in acting out a kindly interest, really finding a distorted expression of our unconscious wish for his death.

These distortions or complete reversals of unconscious wishes are suggested in general folklore as well as in Freudian circles. One does not need to be a Freudian to feel that our *excessive* concern for our uncle's health must have some hidden motive. And it was many years before Freud that Hamlet's mother suggested that, by protesting too much, the actress queen betrayed almost the very reverse of her protestations.

The wish for the death of a rich uncle by the way, is not a typical Freudian villain. The great threats to the super-ego or to our sense of self-esteem, according to Freud, come not from the wish for rich inheritances but from the sex urges. The greatest threat, moreover, does not come from the urge toward normal heterosexual activity. For people in our culture, the real threat comes from suspected urges toward one of the sexual perversions. For most people, suspicion of an urge toward homosexuality, or incest, for instance, would constitute a terrific shock, so much so, that for those people the protective super-ego would never permit such an urge to approach consciousness in its own right. Freud thinks, however, that in the subconscious of everyone there are some residual urges toward unorthodox sexual acts and that these urges do, in fact, often try to enter consciousness. Being rebuffed, they take on the most diverse kinds of disguises in the manner we have described, and thus effect an entry into consciousness. Once they are in consciousness, driven as they are by such powerful but hidden urges, they lead us to carry out the irrelevant behavior that constitutes the disguise. This disguise may be almost innocent, as, for instance, an urge to rattle keys. It may even be socially productive, as in an urge to collect manuscripts, or it may be incapacitating and disastrous, as in the urge to be sick or in the urge to murder.

Not all psychoanalysts use sex, or sexual perversion, as the arch villain against which the super-ego protects us, sometimes at such disastrous cost. For Alfred Adler and his followers, for instance, the great disturber, against whom the super-ego must protect us at all costs, is the feeling of inferiority. If any idea comes along which suggests that we are seriously inferior, or inferior in any significant respect, then that idea must be suppressed and denied entry into consciousness. If it does come into consciousness it must be disguised or distorted so as to be unrecognizable. The small boy, for instance, will not face the possibility that he cannot hold his own in physical combat. If that idea is to enter his consciousness at all, it must be drastically altered, perhaps completely reversed. It may enter, for instance, in the form of a belief that he can (and must) "lick any kid in the school."

This theory, which has been taken up so widely in popular literature, has relatively little to say about learning. It has had much to say, however, about mental hygiene, about the importance of early childhood experience, about the effects of frustration, and about the genesis of prejudice. Much of the emphasis on motivation in Lewin and in Tolman has a strong Freudian tinge. Much of what is said about personal adjustment comes directly or indirectly from Freudian psychology.

As an over-all metaphysical psychology, Freudianism has much to recommend it. This theory attempts to explain not only mental illness and abnormalities but also forgetting, slips of the tongue, dreams, humor, anti-Semitism, wars, art, science, and religion, or anything else you may care to name. On the scientific or experimental side, however, it has some very definite defects. Its theories are extremely hard to "nail down" so that they can be tested. The basic assumptions are bizarre and too fantastic for many people to accept. Many people rebel, for instance, when asked to believe that the child has a very elaborate sexual life; that each of our separate urges has a drive and intelligence of its own; or that ideas actually reside, as such, in a subconscious.

Summary

Controversy within the field of psychology is not so important as it has been made to seem. Some controversy does exist, however, owing in part to the human importance of some of the doctrines, and the student should be aware of the broad outlines of the main theories.

In describing general behavior, there are three main schools or theories. These are the *connectionists* or *modern associationists,* the *Gestalt* (or *field*) *psychologists,* and the *purposivists* (including *Freudian psychologists*).

Connectionism, descended from the classical associationism of the eighteenth and nineteenth centuries, attempts to explain all behavior as reactions (R) to situations (S). These S–R connections are the units which determine what we are and what we do. These connections can be very broad and inclusive or very narrow. They change continually as the result of maturation and of learning, and this study of the changes which occur in the connections is the chief task of psychology as the connectionist sees it.

To the Gestalt psychologist or the proponents of the field theory, the connectionist has the cart before the horse. The Gestalt psychologist insists that experience or behavior never occurs in small isolated situations, or movements. The situation-as-experienced is always organized or structured into a definite pattern, and this pattern is more pronounced in our experience than the details that make it up. It also comes into our experience before the details do, and it lasts in spite of changes in the component details.

The Lewinian concept of the life space, with its many psychological forces, is one kind of Gestalt psychology or field theory. More than other Gestaltists, however, Lewin emphasizes motive or drive.

The purposivist is impressed by the fact that all behavior is directed toward a goal and that behavior can be understood only in the light of the goal that is sought. In describing actions we do not describe the movements people make, but the results (goals) they pursue.

Freudian psychology is a branch of purposivism, but the Freudians assume that there are many conflicting purposes in each of us, and that these rival purposes or urges contend for the control of our conduct. The Freudians have worked out elaborate procedures which are involved in these struggles and which are assumed to produce many of the ills and much of the interest of life.

SPECIFIC REFERENCES

1. McCandless, B., and Rosenblum, S. Psychological theory as a determiner of experimental pattern in child study. *Rev. educ. Res.,* 1952, *22,* 496–525.

2. Anderson, G. L. Theories of behavior and some curriculum issues. *J. educ. Psychol.*, 1948, *39*, 133–140. Reprinted in Coladarci, A., *Educational psychology: a book of readings.* Dryden, 1955.
3. Hilgard, E. R. The relation of schools of psychology to educational practices. *Calif. J. elem. Educ.*, 1939, *8*, 17–26. Reprinted in Coladarci, A., *Educational psychology: a book of readings.* Dryden, 1955.
4. Tolman, E. C. The determiners of behavior at a choice point. *Psychol. Rev.*, 1938, *45*, 1–41, p. 11.
5. Hull, C. L. *Principles of behavior.* Appleton-Century-Crofts, 1943, Chap. 3.
6. Estes, W. K., and others. *Modern learning theory.* Appleton-Century-Crofts, 1954.

SUGGESTIONS FOR FURTHER READING

For general accounts of the whole field, see

1. Woodworth, R. S. *Contemporary schools of psychology.* Ronald, 1948.
2. Helson, H., ed. *Theoretical foundations in psychology.* Van Nostrand, 1951.

The following books provide interesting general accounts and include some neglected English work:

3. Smith, F. V. *The explanation of behaviour.* London: Constable, 1951.
4. Mace, C. A., and Vernon, P. E. *Current trends in British psychology.* London: Methuen, 1953.

The following sources are for more technical treatments of important questions:

5. Koch, S. Theoretical psychology, 1950: an overview. *Psychol. Rev.*, 1951, *58*, 295–301.
6. Brunswik, E. *The conceptual framework of psychology.* University of Chicago Press, 1952.
7. Hebb, D. O. *The organization of behavior.* Wiley, 1949.
8. Snygg, D., and Combs, A. W. *Individual behavior, a new frame of reference for psychology.* Harper, 1949.

The following books deal with the historical backgrounds of present-day theory:

9. Brett, G. S. *History of psychology.* Abbreviated edition, edited by R. S. Peters, Macmillan, 1953.

10. Flügel, J. C. *A hundred years of psychology 1833–1933: with an additional part on developments 1933–1947*. London: Duckworth, 1951.
    If the 1951 edition is not available, the 1933 edition (Macmillan) will prove useful.
11. Murphy, G. *Historical introduction to modern psychology*. Harcourt Brace, 1949.
12. Boring, E. G. *A history of experimental psychology*. Appleton-Century-Crofts, 1950.
    For condensed treatments of each of the separate schools of psychology, consult the following references:
13. National Society for the Study of Education. *The Psychology of Learning*. Forty-first Yearbook, Part II, 1942.
    Chap. 3. Connectionism: its origin and major features (Sandiford, P.)
    Chap. 4. Connectionism: present concepts and interpretations (Gates, A. I.)
    Chap. 5. The field theory of learning and its educational consequences (Hartmann, G. W.)
14. Hartmann, G. W. *Gestalt psychology*. Ronald, 1935.
15. Leeper, R. *Lewin's topological and vector psychology*. Eugene, Ore., University of Oregon, 1943.
16. Hall, C. S. *A primer of Freudian psychology*. Cleveland: World Publishing, 1954.
17. Monroe, Ruth L. *Schools of psychoanalytic thought*. Dryden, 1955.

For books by the originators of various systems, see:

18. Köhler, W. *Gestalt psychology*. Liveright, 1947.
19. McDougall, W. *The energies of men; a study of the fundamentals of dynamic psychology*. London: Methuen, 1932.
20. Thorndike, E. L. *Selected writings from a connectionist's psychology*. Appleton-Century-Crofts, 1949.
21. Tolman, E. C. *Purposive behavior in animals and men*. Century, 1932. Reprinted, Berkeley: University of California Press, 1949.
22. Carmichael, L., ed. *Manual of child psychology*. Wiley, 1954. Chap. 15. Behavior and development as a function of the total situation. (Lewin, K.), (Supplement by Escalona, Sibylle).

Exercises and Questions for Discussion

1. Thinking of yourself as a teacher, go over each of the theories and list the points of those that appeal to you. List the features of each theory that do not seem to help you as a teacher.

2. Think of yourself as a student of the educational process. You are trying to arrange the many separate facts of education into a neat and organized structure, just as the physicist tries to arrange the many separate facts of the physical world into a meaningful and compact system. Now go over the theories again and list first the features of each which seem promising to you as a student of education and then the features which you consider useless or troublesome.

3. Here is a bit of action that a stenographer happened to observe and record from a classroom scene.[1] A seventh-grade class of 42 pupils is studying about the area of a triangle. T refers to the teacher and P refers to any one of the pupils.

T. Now suppose you had a lot and wanted to sell part of it. (The teacher drew a rectangle on the board, drew a diagonal, and shaded one half of the rectangle.) What do you call this part that I have shaded? The answers were:
P. A three cornered square.
P. It has three corners.
P. Three straight lines. (To this answer the teacher drew 3 lines radiating from one point.)
T. Half of a rectangle is a triangle, but I want you to tell me what a triangle *is*. (With much emphasis on *is*.)
P. A triangle is half of a rectangle.
T. I know it is half a rectangle but what is it? A circle? Certainly not! What is it?
P. An angle.
P. It's a figure.
This answer satisfied the teacher. Everyone gave a sigh of relief. After a brief pause, the teacher began again.
T. What kind of a figure? What are its limitations?
P. The dictionary says . . .
T. I don't want to hear what the dictionary says. Can't you tell yourself by looking at it?
P. Triangle is a figure bounded by 3 lines.
T. That's exactly the word I wanted: *bounded* by 3 lines. What is a rectangle bounded by?
P. Four lines.
T. What is a triangle bounded by?
P. Three lines.

(a) How would the connectionist describe these events? What items that do not appear in the report would he have to add or supply or invent?

(b) How would the Lewinian describe these events? What additional elements would he have to supply?

4. Think of some other science you have studied. Were you conscious of different "schools" in that subject? How do you account for the amount of attention given to different schools of psychology?

[1] From Nyberg, J. A. Verbatim report of a class in arithmetic. *School Science and Mathematics*, 1933, *33*, 303–307. Courtesy of *School Science and Mathematics*.

Theories of Learning

BEHAVIOR is a very inclusive term. It covers everything that people or other organisms do. It includes all their actions and statements and everything from which their thoughts or feelings may be inferred. Learning, on the other hand, is much less inclusive. It makes up one part of behavior, but only one part; there are many aspects of behavior in which there is little need to think of learning. Learning, however, is a most important problem for the teacher and it is wise to consider the general theories that have been suggested to describe this specialized problem.

We have already noticed that learning plays a different part within the several general theories of behavior. For the connectionist, learning is by far the most important topic. For the Gestaltist, on the other hand, it is of much less importance. For some members of the purposivist school, Tolman for example, learning happens to be a crucial problem. Among other purposivists, such as Freudians, learning receives very little attention(1).

Of those theorists who do emphasize the phenomenon of learning, it would be natural to expect that the purposivist and the connectionist would give radically different interpretations. And this is most decidedly the case. These two groups find themselves in continuous and enthusiastic disagreement. But disagreement is by no means confined to these two groups. Even among the connectionists we find several important sub-schools who differ widely in their views of learning. And these "civil wars" within the connectionist camp, although not so continuous or so vigorous as the other discords, have led to much discussion and considerable investigation.

To get a general, over-all idea of the differences between these various views of learning, let us consider a simple example. During the summer a boy has acquired a new bunk bed. Boylike, he customarily sleeps in the upper bunk. He gets into this upper bunk by grasping a nearby pipe and swinging upward. As the summer wears along, he comes to do this naturally and easily with very little thought or effort. Then, one autumn day, the heat is turned on and that night when the boy grasps the pipe he gets burned. Next night he goes to some trouble to avoid the pipe, and gets into bed by a different method. Two or three nights later he touches the pipe but finds himself retracting his hand almost before contact is made. After one or two further near-accidents, he adopts an entirely different method as his regular way of getting into the upper bunk.

Explanations Emphasizing a Change in the Psychological Situation Acting on the Person

The Lewinian Approach

If asked to explain this problem, the Lewinian field psychologist would point out that, in the view of his system, there is really no problem at all. The life space of the individual has changed markedly. Whatever may be the situation in the outside world, there is no question that, in the more relevant psychological world, the pipe has become an entirely different object. Formerly, within that psychological world, the pipe was an important means-to-a-goal. Since the goal had marked positive valence (i.e., since the goal was attractive), the pipe itself may also have acquired some secondary valence. But even if it did not acquire valence in its own right, it was still a means of reaching the goal, and as such it was bound to be used. After the unfortunate experience, however, the pipe comes to play a different role within the life space, or within the psychological world. Now the pipe has become a threat. It has acquired marked negative valence. And, adds the Lewinian, knowing this about the boy's life space, what do you expect? Naturally, the boy will avoid the pipe and will find some other mode of movement toward the goal(2, 3).

For the Lewinian, this problem of learning is in no way unique. To have a clear idea of learning, we merely have to understand how the life space becomes rearranged and how the psychological world becomes restructured. In Figure 9-1, for instance, we see a young child who is trying to reach a goal, but who is hindered by a U-shaped barrier. To solve this problem, of course, the child has merely to "detour" through the open end of the U. The Lewinian will say that he has to see the goal and himself as enclosed in a continuous life space which goes around the barrier. When he experiences the problem in the fashion shown in Figure 9-2, then the problem is solved.

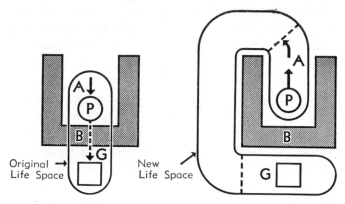

FIGURE 9-1. *Life Space of a Child Kept Away from the Goal by a U-shaped Barrier.* Redrawn from Lewin(2). Courtesy of the National Society for the Study of Education.

FIGURE 9-2. *Life Space of a Child after Solving the Problem of the U-shaped Barrier.* Redrawn from Lewin(2). Courtesy of the National Society for the Study of Education.

From the description just given, we see that learning presents no *new* or different problem for the Lewinian. Like other problems in psychology, it is merely a matter of restructuring the life space. If we can solve the major laws governing the structure or the arrangement of the life space, than we will undertsand all the important problems of psychology—learning among the rest.

In thus showing that the problem of learning should cause us no unique or special bewilderment, the Lewinian would also hasten to warn us not to invoke the boy's past history as a real thing in itself. The boy's recent unfortunate experience with the pipe plays a part in his present behavior only insofar as some aspect of that experience is actually present in his psychological life space.

The Approach of Classical Gestalt Psychology

The classical Gestaltist would agree with the Lewinian to a certain extent. Naturally enough, he would stress the fact that the boy's experience has become radically reorganized or restructured as a result of the experience. The boy's perception of the relations involved has changed. Earlier the pipe, as a means, and getting into bed, as a goal, were inseparably bound together into one single pattern or Gestalt. When he was aware of the goal he was inevitably also aware of the pipe as a means of accomplishing the goal. When he was aware of the pipe he was also aware of its potentialities as a means of reaching the goal. Now all that has changed. The problem will only be solved when he acquires a new Gestalt of means-leading-to-goal. It may be, for instance, that there is some other nearby object, such as a window curtain, which could also serve his purpose and which lacks the unpleasant features of the pipe. The boy may become aware of this fact, perhaps immediately, perhaps after a few trials. At any rate, he may form a new Gestalt in which the window curtain stands out as a good means of reaching the goal, and in which the pipe stands out as an apparent but deceptive means. The closely structured Gestalt would consist of "goal-to-be-reached-by-window-curtain—not-by-pipe." On subsequent occasions it is only necessary that there should be some trace of this neat pattern and that this trace should be linked up with the bedtime situation. In effect, then, as soon as the new Gestalt is formed the problem is solved, no matter how clumsy the boy may be in his first attempt to use the curtain. From now on he merely acquires fluency. Learning as such is accomplished. Later on, of course, mothers being what they are, the window curtain may become a less satisfactory means of reaching the goal, and at that point, a new problem in learning presents itself(4, 5).

Thus we see that both the Lewinians and the classical Gestaltists consider the problem of learning chiefly as one part of the general problem of how we come to experience the world in the way that we do. If we come to experience the world in a different way, then naturally we would be expected to act in a different way. Naturally, the famished prospector in *The Gold Rush* acts differently toward Charlie Chaplin when he perceives Charlie as edible poultry from the way he does when he perceives him as a desiccated human buddy. When he perceives Charlie as poultry he tries to kill him; when he perceives him as a buddy he behaves in less cannibalistic fashion. In each case his behavior follows naturally enough from his perception of the world around him.

Explanations Emphasizing a Change in the Learner

In *The Gold Rush,* through the magic of the movies, we are able to observe the inner psychological world of the famished prospector. As we look through his eyes, it is obvious that, at times, he sees Chaplin as a mountainous fowl and, at other times, he sees him as the frail and pathetic would-be miner that he is. Clearly, Charlie is perceived differently under these different circumstances. In *City Lights,* however, we find another of Charlie's companions who at one moment hugs him to his bosom and at another moment orders him kicked down the stairs. In this latter classic, however, we are granted no magic view into the perceptual world of the fickle companion. We merely know that when the companion is drunk he loves Charlie inordinately and when he is sober he spurns him scornfully. Now there are two ways to diagram this change. We could follow the lead of the Gestaltists and of the producers of *The Gold Rush* and project all the change into the unfortunate person of the tramp. We could imagine that we are looking through the eye of the companion and we could make the camera portray Charlie at times as an attractive and jolly friend and at other times we could arrange to portray him as an inconsequential speck of human debris. If we do this, the action of the companion is explained. On the other hand, the camera could continue to portray Charlie in fairly constant fashion. He could always appear as the pathetic but superbly human little tramp. Obviously, if we choose to present Charlie as a fairly constant situation, we automatically place all the changes within the person of the fickle companion, and we are forced to account for the fact that he comes to react differently to this fairly constant situation.

It is this last approach that most connectionists and some purposivists choose to take. They think it best to assume that Charlie remains the little tramp, and to assume that some change in the internal make-up of the companion causes the latter to react now this way and now that. Or, in the case of the earlier example, they think it best to assume that the pipe in the boy's room has about the same impact on him in winter as in summer, but that the boy has found a new way of responding to it in the course of time.

Principle of Substitution: Conditioned Response Learning

The familiar conditioned response refers to the situation in which a dog sees a flash of light and immediately thereafter is fed and salivates profusely. Later on, after several such experiences, he comes to salivate immediately upon seeing the flash of light, even before he is fed. This humble phenomenon, first extensively studied by the Russian physiologist Pavlov, has become the basis for several theories of learning. In Pavlov's classical concept of conditioning, the food, or other stimulus that is placed in the dog's mouth, plays an important part. It leads the dog to salivate in the first place, and thereby permits the tendency "flash of light—salivate" to be formed. Later on, if ever that tendency should appear to weaken, we have only to arrange to have the food presented again, immediately after the light flashes, and the failing tendency will be *reinforced* or brought up to strength. If we neglect to supply this reinforcement periodically, the tendency will become inhibited and will ultimately disappear. Since Pavlov's time, this concept of reinforcement, which he used in the sense of bringing up to strength, has acquired somewhat different meanings as we shall see shortly.

Of all the modifications of the Pavlovian theory, that of E. R. Guthrie of the University of Washington is basically the most rigorously simple(6, 7, 8). According to Guthrie, the food in the illustration plays only an incidental part. The important thing is that the dog happens to be salivating. We can ignore the circumstances that originally led him to salivate. If any situation, such as the flash of light, should act on the dog while he *happens* to be salivating, then that flash of light will become attached to the response of salivating and whenever, in the future, the dog encounters the flash of light, he will be led to salivate. In the same way, a child in the dark may be terrified by some experience and as a result may tremble or cry out. It is enough that these two events should occur together, namely (a) that he should be in the dark and (b) that he should make the movements involved in trembling or crying out. In the future, this situation of being in the dark will lead to the same muscular contractions. Notice that, in the Guthrie view, the situation is tied up with the actual muscular contraction or glandular secretion. It is not attached to some act or to the result that is accomplished. We do not learn to "open the door" or "sound the horn." A certain group of muscles come to contract in a certain way and this contraction may or may not result in opening the door or in sounding the horn.

This theory holds that, to bring about learning, it is only necessary that we have (a) some response that is occurring, for any reason whatsoever, and that we have (b) one or more situations acting on the organism at the same time. When these conditions are fulfilled, learning will take place. It does not matter in the least what original situation ($S_?$) caused the response in the first place. The dog could be made to salivate by feeding him lemon juice or by feeding him dry meat powder. The boy could have been led to withdraw his hand by a painful burn, by a warning exclamation from a bystander, or by a sudden cramp in his arm. These things simply do not matter. So long as the response occurs, it becomes inevitably (though not permanently) attached to any stimuli that happen to be present at the moment.

The principle of substitution, so very simple in basic principle, is of course much more complicated as it operates in actual life. Responses are continually occurring, and as each occurs, a continuous series of alliances are formed at a fantastic rate and in amazing profusion. When we try to envisage the theory as working in actual life, it is this vast hubbub of thousands of constantly forming bonds that we should keep in mind rather than the tiny example that is neatly dissected out of its setting and that persists as a conveniently stationary diagram while we contemplate it at length.

The Theory of Cue Reduction. This simplified and extreme theory of Guthrie's is only one of several versions of substitution theories. A more moderate version, for instance, regards learning as essentially a process of *cue reduction*(9). Originally, let us suppose, it may take many different stimuli to get the child to pronounce the word *house*. It may take the schoolroom situation, the teacher's urging, a picture of a house, the word on the page, and many other items or cues. Later on, as learning proceeds, the number of necessary cues becomes reduced, until finally the simple word itself will become a sufficient cue. Or, to take another example, a complex situation consisting of many jovial people, good food, excellent service, a certain piece of music, a cocktail or so, and of course, *the* girl, may *combine* to produce in one a pleasant glow, or a feeling of bliss. Later on, in the jungle camp or under very different circumstances, one little part of that complex situation, say, a snatch of the same tune, or the whiff of a certain cigarette, may suddenly reinstate the whole warm feeling originally brought about by the much more complex situation. The snatch of the song or the fleeting odor acts as a substitute or cue for the entire earlier experience.

The substitution theories have many advantages and are also plagued by a number of difficulties. The more important of these advantages and difficulties are discussed after we have considered a rival connectionistic theory.

The Principle of Effect: Trial-and-Error Learning

The *principle of effect,* or the law of effect, was advanced by the late E. L. Thorndike, as a part of the more general doctrine of connectionism. The principle of effect grew up with connectionism. It was described in very general terms at the turn of the century, was systematically stated in

1911, and was radically reformulated in 1931. At present, the original Thorndikean theory is probably no longer the center of controversy. The battle now swirls more violently around other standards. This theory, however, has had an enormous influence on the other theories of learning(10), and we will do well to consider it first in its original form.

Suppose a lively and hungry cat is confined in a puzzle box from which he can escape only by pulling a certain string. To increase his motivation, some odoriferous fish is placed nearby but outside the box. The connectionist will consider this whole cluster of circumstances as an elaborate situation. To this situation, the cat responds by a series of movements. First he bites at the bars. This response brings no distinctive result. Then he claws at the door, again achieving no marked change in the situation. This is followed by still other responses. Finally, he claws at the string, and this time the situation changes. The door opens and he is free to walk out. On later occasions, when he is put in the box, he may still go through some of the movements which proved useless in the earlier trials. As the trials go on, however, these useless movements will gradually drop out, and, after many experiences, the cat will pull at the string as soon as he is put in the box.

Thorndike considered that each of the movements which the cat makes is based on some sort of connection. A connection is made to function, thus leading to a response. If the response is not followed by good results, then the connection is weakened, and some alternative connection takes over. This new connection, of course, leads to some other response. If this latter response also fails to produce good results, its underlying connection also becomes weakened and a third connection takes over. Finally some response does lead to good results and the underlying connection is made stronger by the achievement of those good results. Since only a few responses achieve the good results, it is inevitable that the tendencies responsible for those responses will become stronger and stronger whereas all other tendencies will become weaker.

This concept of *trial and error—law of effect* which arose from the study of animals in a puzzle box was made into a basic theory of learning. The principle of effect, for instance, could easily explain the boy's behavior in getting into the upper bunk. Prior to the evening in question, this theory holds, there was established, within the boy, a well-developed bond or tendency. The cluster of events associated with bedtime act as a situation. This situation has been connected with the response of reaching for the pipe. On this particular evening, the tendency functions and is followed by painful results. Consequently, the original tendency S_1–R_1 is weakened. If the situation S_1 persists, or if it recurs, it will be less likely to elicit R_1. Instead, it will tend to elicit some other response, say, R_n. If this other response leads to bad results, then the tendency S_1–R_n will also be weakened. If R_n leads to good results, the tendency S_1–R_n will be strengthened.

Comparative Advantages and Disadvantages of Substitution and Effect

Each of the principles of substitution and of effect has many definite advantages and many limitations. It happens, moreover, that in one respect, the virtues of one of these principles neatly compensates for the defects of the other and, conversely, the defects of the one are matched in the virtues of the other. This neat arrangement has inevitably led to theories which incorporate the virtues of both and avoid the limitations of either one.

Advantages of Substitution in Explaining Initial Stages of Learning. Let us suppose that a pupil is taking part in an old-fashioned drill on number combinations. At one stage in the proceedings, the following sequence occurs:

S_1	R_1	S_2	R_2
Teacher: "9 + 7?"	Pupil: "18"	Teacher: "No! 16"	Pupil (aside): "Oh! Yes! 16"

Here the bond, S_1–R_1, brings a reprimand or correction S_2. According to the law of effect we would expect that S_1–R_1 would be weakened, or even extinguished, and that the next time S_1 occurs it would elicit some other response. But *which* other response? The principle of effect fails to

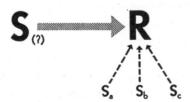

FIGURE 9-3. *Learning According to Simple Substitution*

say. There is nothing in this principle by which we can predict the next response which will follow S_1. In its failure to predict the new response which will become attached to S_1, the principle of effect falls far short of ordinary common sense. Even without the benefit of any elaborate theory, we suspect that the next time the child encounters $9 + 7$ he has a fair chance of thinking *16*, which, by the way, happens to be R_2.

In contrast to the failure of the principle of effect, the principle of substitution provides a very clear description of these common-sense facts. We merely need to consider the sequence just described and to sketch it in a slightly different form.

$$S_1 \ (9 + 7 = ?) – R_1 \ (18)$$
$$S_2 \ (\text{No!} \quad 16) – R_2 \ (\text{Oh! Yes!} \quad 16)$$

Obviously, the sequence is a perfect example of the conditioned response. According to the principle of substitution, S_1 should now come to elicit R_2. And this, as we have seen, is just what happens. This prediction which is beyond the power of the principle of effect, is the natural expectation of the principle of substitution.

Advantages of Effect in Explaining the Final (Adaptive) Stages of Learning. In a modification of the classical conditioned-response experiment, a dog stands on a table with an electrode fastened to his foot. By means of this electrode a shock can be administered. Consider, now, the following sequence:

$$S_1 \ (\text{whistle}) – R_1 \ (\text{turns head})$$
$$S_2 \ (\text{shock to foot}) – R_2 \ (\text{lifts foot})$$

The principle of substitution holds that after several trials, the whistle S_1 should come to elicit the foot lift R_2. And, after a *few trials,* that is precisely what will happen. We notice, however, that this foot lift will accomplish nothing for the dog. Since the electrode is fastened to his foot, the shock will occur in spite of the fact that he has lifted his foot.

This *whistle–foot lift* will continue for the first few trials. After many more trials, however, this tendency S_1–R_2 will be changed. The whistle will cease to elicit the foot lift. Instead of lifting his foot, the dog may actually press harder when he hears the whistle. He seems, as it were, to brace himself for the inevitable and imminent shock.

Now this new tendency, *whistle–bracing,* cannot be predicted by the principle of substitution in its simple form. According to this principle we should expect the early tendency, *whistle–foot lift,* to persist indefinitely. In this illustration, however, the early tendency does not persist and the principle of substitution is to that extent imperfect.

For the principle of effect, this final stage of the learning gives no trouble at all. The principle of effect predicts that, after many trials, the whistle will come to elicit some response which will combine adaptively with the subsequent shock. And in the face of an *inevitable* shock, perhaps the most adaptive response we can make is that of bracing ourselves.

Apparently, then, the principle of substitution tends to be a good description of the early stages of learning but is *not always* a good description of the later stages of learning. The principle of effect, on the other hand, very often fails to predict the early stages of learning, but always provides a very good description of the final stages in which the stronger tendencies are becoming "polished off."

Coincidence of the Principles of Effect and Substitution. To a great extent, the principles of substitution and of effect say the same thing in different words. The principle of substitution states that the dog, in our illustration, will come to respond to the whistle by lifting his foot. The principle of effect states that the dog will come to respond to the whistle by some response which will produce a good result. It happens, however, that the two predictions very often coincide. Very often *lifting the foot* will produce a *good result*. This will occur in the more natural situation in which the electrode is not fastened to the dog's foot. Now, by lifting his foot as soon as he hears the whistle, the dog avoids the painful shock. This is a good state of affairs. Consequently, *both* the principle of effect and the principle of substitution would predict that the dog would continue to lift his foot at the sound of the whistle.

Perhaps more often than not the unconditioned response is the good response to make to the conditioned stimulus. We must remember that the *shock–foot lift* tendency is almost always a well-established tendency and one that is very useful. Lifting the foot is the dog's regular way of taking care of the shock. Now when a new situation, such as the whistle, precedes the shock, he can take this new situation as a signal of the oncoming shock and use his regular way of meeting the shock even before the shock occurs. Over and over again it pays us to "beat the gun" in this way. Suppose, for instance, that the explosion of a bomb in the street makes us duck into any nearby doorway. This is a well-established tendency. Now if this explosion is preceded by a shrill whine, we may find ourselves ducking into a doorway as soon as we hear the whine. Obviously, it is much better to duck into the doorway before the explosion occurs than afterward. Here both principles would agree that we would continue to duck into the doorway as soon as we heard the shrill whine.

Failure of Effect and Substitution to Coincide. The tendency, *conditioned stimulus–unconditioned response*, enables us to beat the gun, and, very often, as we have seen, this is an advantage. But it is not always an advantage. It does not always pay to beat the gun. It does not always pay to respond to an imminent situation in exactly the same way that we would respond to the actual situation. For soldiers in a frontier fort, for instance, the sudden appearance of a superior enemy at the open gates was a situation which normally led to withdrawal into the fort. Suppose, now, there is some signal (sound of approaching footsteps) which fore-shadows the imminent appearance of the enemy. Would it pay the soldiers to respond to this signal as they would to the actual appearance of the foemen, by flight indoors? Perhaps not. Perhaps the most effective way of responding to the signal would be to run *toward* the gates and close them, thus meeting the imminent situation in a much more effec-tive manner. And this latter method of reacting to the signal may readily become adopted *after many experiences with the signal.*

Apparently there are times when effect and substitution tell approxi-mately the same story. There are other times, however, when they dis-agree about the later stages of learning. When they do disagree, the principle of effect seems to provide a more simple explanation of the adaptiveness of these later stages of learning.

Theories which Combine Substitution and Effect

Hull's Reinforcement Theory. Within the group of connectionist psy-chologists the learning theories of the late Clark Hull(11, 12, 13) of Yale University are probably the most prominent at the present time. Hull and his students have formulated the theory in a form which invites experimentation and test, and they themselves have initiated a large number of important and challenging investigations. Naturally, such a theory has become the object of much discussion and controversy.

When Hull first began to formulate his theory, about 1930, he followed a general principle of substitution almost exclusively. Some six years later, however, he assigned an important role to reinforcement or effect, and from that time on his theory has been regarded primarily as a rein-forcement theory, and, indeed, as the *standard* reinforcement theory. In still later revisions(14, 15) the theory has reached a point where, accord-ing to some students(16, 10), it has abandoned its emphasis on reinforce-ment. It is difficult, however, to know just how seriously we should take these revisions that came after 1950. It has been claimed(16) that during this period, and up to his death in 1952, Hull was aiming chiefly at some technical refinements in his theory and that he was "cutting and trying" rather freely in order to reduce his system to more rigorous quantita-tive terms. It has also been held(17) that some of the new features introduced into the revisions were really superfluous. All in all, it will perhaps be better to wait a few years for a more definite statement of the later-day Hullian theory.

Regarding the tremendously important 1943 Hullian statement, there can be no doubt. Here the emphasis was clearly upon reinforcement, although there was some use of the more important features of substitution. Hull's classical attempt to combine the valuable features of both substitution and effect is illustrated in Figure 9-4. In this diagram he asks

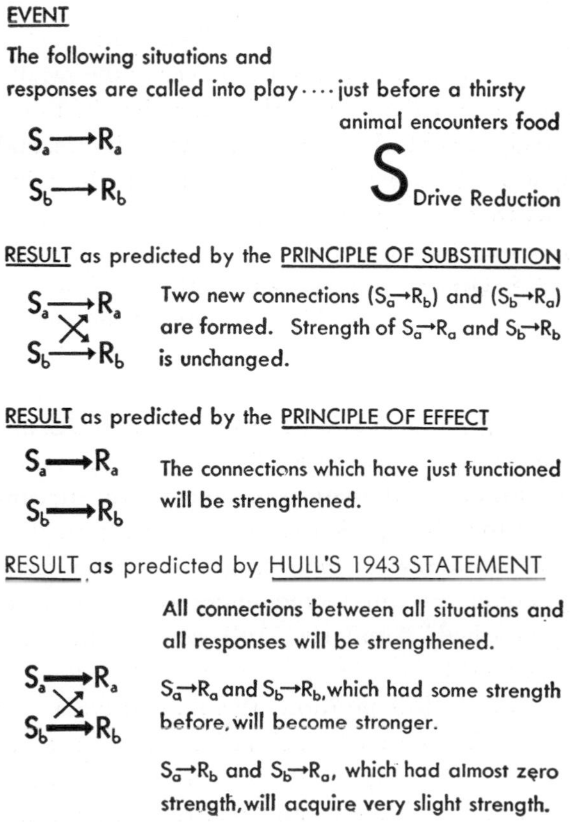

EVENT

The following situations and
responses are called into play····just before a thirsty
animal encounters food

$S_a \longrightarrow R_a$

$S_b \longrightarrow R_b$

S Drive Reduction

RESULT as predicted by the PRINCIPLE OF SUBSTITUTION

$S_a \longrightarrow R_a$
$S_b \longrightarrow R_b$

Two new connections $(S_a \rightarrow R_b)$ and $(S_b \rightarrow R_a)$ are formed. Strength of $S_a \rightarrow R_a$ and $S_b \rightarrow R_b$ is unchanged.

RESULT as predicted by the PRINCIPLE OF EFFECT

$S_a \longrightarrow R_a$
$S_b \longrightarrow R_b$

The connections which have just functioned will be strengthened.

RESULT as predicted by HULL'S 1943 STATEMENT

All connections between all situations and all responses will be strengthened.

$S_a \longrightarrow R_a$
$S_b \longrightarrow R_b$

$S_a \rightarrow R_a$ and $S_b \rightarrow R_b$, which had some strength before, will become stronger.

$S_a \rightarrow R_b$ and $S_b \rightarrow R_a$, which had almost zero strength, will acquire very slight strength.

FIGURE 9-4. *Hull's Integration of the Principles of Substitution and Effect*

us to imagine that a thirsty animal (say a rat) has just encountered water and has started to drink, thus reducing his thirst drive. About the same time that this drive reduction takes place, a great many situations are acting on the animal, and he is also carrying out a great many responses. As examples of the multitude of situations and responses that may have occurred, let us suppose that he has seen the water bottle (S_a) and has responded by sniffing at the bottle (R_a). Let us suppose further that he has also just been stimulated by the bite of a flea (S_b) and that he has responded by scratching (R_b). What will happen to these two tendencies S_a-R_a and S_b-R_b as a result of subsequent reduction of the thirst drive? The principle of substitution, of course, ignoring the fact that a drive has been reduced, would merely predict that two new cross tendencies will be formed. It will predict that, in the future, the sight of the bottle (S_a) will cause the animal to scratch (R_b) and that the bite of the flea (S_b) will cause him to sniff (R_a). The principle of effect, on the other hand, concentrating on the existing tendencies S_a-R_a and S_b-R_b, merely predicts that these tendencies will become stronger as the result of the reduction of the thirst drive. Because of this reduction in thirst, the animal will be more likely to sniff when he sees the water bottle, and he will also be more likely to scratch when bitten by a flea. But the principle of effect does not predict that the sight of the water bottle will affect the scratching response, or that the bite of the flea will come to elicit the sniffing. Hull, in his 1943 statement, agrees with both principles and does so by a rather simple description. In this postulate he merely says that when this drive reduction occurs, every response that is taking place will become more strongly connected with every situation that is acting. S_a will become more strongly attached to its proper response R_a, and S_a will also become more strongly attached to R_b. "More strongly" may sound a trifle queer since we assume that there was almost zero attachment between S_a and R_b prior to this experience. But, upon second thought, this is quite in order. An increase in the strength of the connection from zero to something would certainly come under the heading of "becoming more strongly attached." Similarly, Hull would expect an "increase in the strength" of S_b-R_a.

To simplify Hull's 1943 position, then, we may say that upon the occasion of a reduction in drive, all situations acting at that moment will tend to be linked more firmly to all responses that are being carried out at that moment. If one situation and one response are members of an old pair, their association will be strengthened. If a second situation and a second response "never saw each other before," then their very feeble association will become appreciably stronger.

The preceding statement, of course, is a gross simplification. The 1943 statement itself says much more than this, and this one principle is only one of sixteen important postulates in that extremely elaborate theory. The other postulates, however, may be regarded as supplying the details necessary to make the main postulate work.

As might be expected, the time relations are most important in Hull's general theory. Situations and responses seldom have the neat temporal relations suggested in Figure 9-4. A situation (S_a) may coincide with one response (R_m), may precede another response (R_x) by a few seconds or by many seconds, and may follow another response (R_y) by any length of time. These time relations have a great deal to do in determining which connections shall be most affected by the reduction in drive. Other time relations are also important. In a sense, it is a good thing for a response to occur just before the drive reduction occurs. Looking now at Figure 9-4, suppose, for instance, that R_b had occurred later than R_a, and that R_b was thus closer in time to the reduction of the thirst drive. If this happened, then both the new "cross" tendency S_a–R_b and the old tendency S_b–R_b would be especially favored by the strengthening power of the need reduction. These two tendencies would profit more from the experience than would either of the tendencies "terminating" in R_a.

Skinner's Reinforcement Theory. To understand the position of B. F. Skinner, we should remember that he has a great distrust of over-fine theorizing(18). He likes to stay close to the data. He prefers to keep explanatory concepts such as *connections, life space, cognitions,* to the absolute minimum(16). This close-to-the-data approach is seen in his treatment of the rat in a problem box (known as a Skinner box, by the way). After a while the rat presses a lever and gets some food. What situation leads to this response? Actually, we do not know. Most connectionists, of course, will concoct some sort of general situation such as "being in the box," and they will use this hypothetical situation to account for the response. But Skinner will have none of this. According to him we merely see a response being made. He suggests that we should leave it at that, and that we should talk about that response as an *emitted* response. To explain the learning which involves these emitted responses, Skinner merely suggests that any such response which leads to reinforcement will be strengthened. Notice, it is the *general* tendency to make the response which is strengthened. It is the R which is strengthened, and not a specific S–R tendency. The rat presses the lever and receives food. Because of this, the rat will be more likely to press the lever. Indeed, having received some reinforcement, he may now continue to press it several times even after the food ceases to appear. To explain this fact, Skinner suggests that each reinforcement builds up a *reserve* of responses, just as each gallon of water helps build up the reserve in a reservoir, and these responses stored up in the reserve will continue to pour forth until exhausted, even though no further reinforcement is forthcoming.

These emitted responses play the chief role in Skinner's psychology. In explaining how these responses are affected during learning, Skinner relies heavily on the concept of reinforcement. He also makes some provision, however, for simple conditioning by sheer substitution or contiguity. But this kind of learning is considered as an entirely separate process. In one place, as a matter of fact, he suggests that the two kinds of learning take place in different parts of the body, the simple conditioning being concerned exclusively with autonomic mechanisms, and the modification of the more interesting emitted responses being attributed to the skeletal muscles.[1]

Sign Learning: Learning Through Changes in Cognitions

The principles of substitution and of effect, and the theories based on these principles, are all strongly connectionistic. In these theories, things like purpose, or ideas, or cognitions are phenomena *to be explained.* They are not things to be taken for granted and to be used in explaining other phenomena. These connectionistic theories suggest mechanical models or mechanical illustrations(19, 20). They do not suggest the more mentalistic entities commonly used when nonconnectionists talk about learning.

In marked contrast to the general connectionistic approach, we find E. C. Tolman and his doctrine of sign learning or cognitive learning. It may readily appear, by the way, that Tolman is hard to classify, and, indeed, this is so. In the preceding chapter, for instance, we classed him as a purposivist. Woodworth(27) calls him a behaviorist, whereas Hilgard(28) places him along with the field psychologists. As far as Tolman's theory of learning is concerned, Hilgard is probably right. Tolman does use a field approach in describing learning. Yet he differs somewhat from the classical field psychologists in attaching more importance to learning and in trying to relate learning to important and stable changes that take place within the organism.

According to Tolman, the change which takes place within the learner is the formation of a new realization or expectation. Tolman objects strenuously to the connectionist suggestions that people or animals learn to "do something" in a certain situation. He holds that learning results in something much more fluid and versatile than a rigid S–R. Tolman claims that the boy does not learn *to grasp* the pipe, that he does not

1 For other attempts to integrate the principles of substitution and effect see Mowrer(21), Maier(22), Stephens(23), and important reviews by Shoben(24), Kendler and Underwood(25), and by Osgood(26).

learn *to catch* the window curtain. On the contrary, Tolman contends that what the boy learns is a group of expectations of what will lead to what. Originally, he learned that grasping the pipe leads to an easy way of getting into the bunk. Later he learned that grasping the pipe leads to a burn, and that grasping the window curtain avoids the burn and serves the original function of the pipe.

All behavior is constantly accompanied by the formation of these expectations or realizations or cognitions. A man learns, for instance, that turning up Thornway Road leads to the office, whereas turning up Orpen leads to the railway station. He learns that visiting the Browns leads to an evening of television, whereas visiting the Carters leads to an evening of bridge. He acquires these "cognitive maps," as Tolman calls them, by which he knows where a given route will take him, or what a given kind of behavior will lead to. But these maps do not rigidly determine all conduct. To know what a person will do on any occasion, we would have to know two things. We would have to know where the person *wants* to go or what he wants to accomplish. We would also have to know that person's cognitive map, or his ideas of what leads to what. If our man wants to go to the office, he will turn up Thornway. If he wants to go to the station, he will go up Orpen. If he wants to spend the evening watching television in the shadowy company of some friends, he will visit the Browns.

Differing Positions with Respect to Specific Issues

So far we have taken a brief look at each of a number of theories. Now we change our approach. We pose a series of issues or questions and ask what stand each theory takes with respect to that issue.

Relation to the Nervous System

The theories of both Guthrie and Hull are formulated with the nervous system in mind. Hull makes elaborate assumptions about what the nervous system does and is, and in general his theory makes more sense when we keep before us a clear picture of nerves and neural activity.

Skinner appeals to some well-established facts about neural anatomy —to the division between the central and the autonomic nervous system, for instance. For the most part, however, he is just as reluctant in making "unnecessary" assumptions about neural activities as he is in making assumptions about mental entities.

Tolman makes little reference to the nervous system. He assumes, of course, that the nerves probably play an important part in the behavior that he studies and that he tries to explain. He does not feel the need, however, of supposing one particular kind of neural organization in contrast to another. If he finds a certain kind of behavior going on, and if it seems necessary to imagine some kind of entity, such as cognition, to explain this behavior, then something in the nervous system must be producing what we observe or find necessary to imagine. Other people (29) have suggested neural arrangements that may underlie the Tolman theory, but the theory itself pays little attention to neurology.

The Gestalt psychologists differ rather radically on this point. Köhler's views are geared to very elaborate theories of brain physiology. Köhler thinks that there are some clear-cut physical processes in the brain whereby the relations in nature are translated into the constancies of experience. Lewin, on the other hand, ignores the nervous system. Like Tolman, he assumes that there must be some neural activity responsible for behavior, but the precise nature of that neural activity is not important in his theories.

The Problem of Need or Motive

In educational circles these days we hear a great deal about the importance of motive in learning. Some writers in the field of education claim that a child can never learn anything unless he has a need to learn. True enough, in many of these writings, the concept of need is rather broad(30). It includes not only the things that a child actually wants, ("I *need* a dime") but it also includes what society thinks would be good for him ("What that child *needs* is a good talking to"). Certainly in this sense we could talk of a child's need to learn to read, even though the child himself were blissfully unaware of any such need. In a psychological discussion, of course, a need refers to things like *wants,* and, for the most part, in educational writings also there is a strong implication that we must start with actual wants or the *"felt* needs" of Dewey and Raup.

What about the learning theorists? What part does need or motive play in the views that we have discussed?

For the law of effect and for the 1943 statement of Hull, need, or drive, or motive was central. A satisfying state of affairs is a state of affairs that the organism is "ready" to encounter. It is a good, or pleasant state in that it meets some basic need or motive of the animal. Food for a surfeited animal would not be satisfying. Satisfying or annoying effects make sense only in relation to the needs or drives or motives in operation at the time. In his 1943 statement, Hull was even more clearly committed to the importance of need or drive. Primary reinforcement consisted only of the reduction of some existing need. Consequently, if primary reinforcement is to occur there must be some need present that can be reduced.

It is precisely with this point, by the way, that the recent modification of the Hullian theory deals. Some recent evidence has suggested that in many circumstances, at least, a relevant need is not necessary at the time of learning, and Hull has taken a less drastic stand with respect to the role of need during the actual learning.

For the other theorists, for Guthrie, Tolman, and Skinner, the role of motive or need is purely incidental. An animal that is *completely* devoid of need or motive may not behave at all—indeed he would probably be dead. Hence to get the animal to make a response (Guthrie, Skinner) or to notice what happened (Tolman), we would have to have *some* motive or need acting on him. But one should be as good as another. And all the motive does is to bring the organism into a situation where the more basic forces can do their work. He will not learn unless he makes some kind of movement while a stimulus is acting on him (Guthrie) or unless he does something and perceives what happens (Tolman).

For all theorists, motive clearly comes into play in performance. Tolman and Guthrie would hold, for instance, that a rat does not have to be motivated to *learn* a maze. But he has to be motivated to run a maze. Provided the right experiences come along, a child does not need to be motivated to learn his history, but he has to be motivated before he will exert himself sufficiently to show that he has learned. Of course, as a pratical matter, both theorists would admit that without motivation of some sort, the experiences necessary for learning are not likely to come along.

The Problem of the Permanence or Change in Learning

So far we have been concerned with the way in which learning occurs in the first place. But expectations, connections, or life spaces are seldom permanent. Tendencies and expectations are not only built up but they are also torn down. Any theory, if it is to be complete, must account for both sorts of changes. And most theories try to do so.

For Tolman's theory, the explanation of the abolition of an expectancy is fairly simple. One expectancy vanishes, or is pushed aside when another replaces it. The expectancy that "Calling 'Mama' leads to a solicitous reply, 'What is it, Dear?' " is replaced by the expectancy that "Calling 'Mama' leads to an irritated 'Can't you do anything for yourself?' ", or to the expectancy that "Calling 'Mama' leads to results that are completely unpredictable from time to time." Expectancies may change radically. They shift from a vague and indefinite cognition to one that is precise and closely structured. They may shift quickly from one extreme to the other. But in any situation there is always an expectancy of one kind or another.

Hull thought that each tendency carried in it the seeds of its own extinction. Every time a tendency functioned it was held to build up *reactive inhibition*. This is what we notice when, immediately after making a certain response, we are reluctant to make it again. Having used a distinctive word in one sentence we hesitate to use it in the next. Whenever a tendency functions, it builds up some of this reactive inhibition. If, at that moment, some reinforcement is applied it will probably overcome this reactive inhibition, and the net effect will be one of a building-up or positive nature. If, however, no reinforcement occurs, the only effect will be that of inhibition or weakening. From this it is clear that a tendency that functions several times without any reinforcement will tend to be wiped out.

Pavlov held that the failure to supply reinforcement actually did something of a direct nature. Such a failure was not merely the absence of something that might strengthen. It was providing something that definitely weakened. According to his theory, a tendency could thus not only vanish to zero, but could be pushed to a level below zero. After this treatment, a tendency would require a number of reinforcements before it would appear at all.

Guthrie's theory of the weakening of tendencies is as thoroughgoing and as simple as his theory of the building up of tendencies. Guthrie, it will be remembered, holds that a tendency to cry when the room becomes dark will be formed if ever it should happen (a) the room becomes dark and (b) that the child is crying, for any reason whatever. His explanation of the weakening of that tendency is just as simple. The tendency will vanish completely if by any chance (a) the room should become dark and (b) the child should happen not to be crying. If we wish to have a child get over his tendency to cry when the room becomes dark, we have only to arrange that sometime he should be in the dark room when he is not crying. But how to do this, since we have already assumed that being in the dark will make him cry? There are three main methods: (a) distract him, (b) "sneak up on him," (c) tire him out. To distract him, we could perhaps arrange that he should listen to an engrossing story while being in the dark and thus he would find himself in the dark without crying. This should turn the trick. To "sneak up on him," we merely turn the lights down so gradually that he would fail to notice it is dark, and here, again, he might come to be in the dark without crying and our problem would be solved. To tire him out, we merely let him cry until he is exhausted or tired of crying. (In more barbaric days, stern parents actually used to employ this method.) At this point he would be in the dark and would not be crying, and consequently our essential conditions would be met.

Guthrie points out that the "sneaking up" technique and the "tiring out" technique have long been used in training horses to carry a rider without bucking. In using the "sneaking up" method or the gradual approach, the trainers place very light weights on the horse's back, gradually increasing the weight in "subliminal" amounts until the desired weight is reached. In using the more spectacular tiring out technique, the cowboy mounts the horse and merely stays in the saddle until the horse ceases to buck. At that moment the horse is being acted on by the presence of the rider on his back and he is not bucking, and the tendency to buck has thus been eliminated.

Instrumental Avoidance. There is one interesting phenomenon which has proved awkward for the theories of Hull and Pavlov but which, interestingly enough, gives little trouble to either Tolman or Guthrie. This is the phenomenon of instrumental avoidance. It is the phenomenon in which the dog (a) hears a bell, (b) feels a shock, (c) lifts his paw, and then, later, comes to lift his paw immediately upon hearing the bell and thus avoids the shock. This may become well established so that quite regularly the foot is lifted at the sound of the bell and no shock is ever felt.

As we have said, this final adjustment provides no difficulty for Guthrie or Tolman. Guthrie points out that the bell and the foot lift have been connected together and, according to his theory, they should stay connected unless it should happen that the bell should ring and the dog, for any reason, should not lift his foot. In the Tolman view a fairly elaborate cognition or expectancy has been formed. The bell has become a signal for something like "shock coming on, to be avoided by lifting the foot." And so long as circumstances continue to confirm this expectancy (and they do), there is every reason to expect that it will persist and that the dog will continue to act on it.

But consider the problem from Pavlov's point of view. In his theory, the shock is the unconditioned stimulus for lifting the paw. It is like the meat powder in the salivary-conditioned response. In this case, however, a prompt foot lift means that the shock, the unconditioned stimulus, will never occur, and the tendency will not be reinforced. Theoretically it ought to be inhibited and ultimately wiped out. But in actual fact it shows remarkable persistence. When the shock is very strong, this avoidance response may last indefinitely if no special steps are taken to weaken it(31) and even when elaborate steps are taken to eliminate it, the tendency proves most durable(32).

The persistence of the instrumental avoidance response also poses a problem for Hull. Here, at first glance, we can see very little evidence of need reduction. The dog hears a bell, lifts his foot, and practically nothing happens. He gets no food. He escapes no real pain. No need is reduced and thus there is no reinforcement. Theoretically, reactive inhibition should quickly eliminate the tendency. To meet this difficulty the Hullians have made use of Mowrer's notions about the part played by anxiety or fear. Mowrer points out that the shock brings about fear as well as the foot lift. Through conditioning, the bell also comes to elicit fear along with the foot lift. But fear, unlike the foot lift, is a sustained thing. It continues as long as the bell is ringing. By the same token, the fear vanishes when the bell stops ringing. This reduction in fear or anxiety that comes with the silencing of the bell provides, of course, a considerable need reduction. True enough, the need itself was aroused by the bell, but it is the cessation of the bell and the accompanying reduction of anxiety that coincides most closely with the foot lift. Hence every foot lift that follows the bell will be associated with a reduction in fear through the silencing of the bell. There is considerable evidence, by the way, that a bell, thus associated with pain, will become most annoying in its own right and that rats or other animals will go to some trouble to turn it off. Similarly, a compartment in which a rat has been shocked becomes a place to be avoided even when no shock is present. Escape from this annoying compartment becomes a reward(33).

What to Do about the Controversies

The Problem of a Personal Decision

There are many ways to try to decide the issue between these rival theories, and a vast number of experiments have been undertaken with just that object in mind. Some of these we consider in the chapters on motivation, reinforcement, and transfer. So complex are the issues, however, that we will find few questions clearly settled. There is still room for disagreement and some contestants still dispute the umpire's decision.

The Possibility of an Eclectic Attitude. In the face of this uncertainty, what can we do? We conclude as we began by urging caution, thoughtfulness, intelligent analysis, and, if you are equal to it, suspended judgment in many matters. In your reaction to this problem, you can, if you wish, follow the lead of the majority of working psychologists and refuse to form an exclusive alliance with any one school. You can view each school as a valuable spotlight which helps illuminate one aspect of behavior and which brings into prominence many useful and intriguing ideas. The fact that one school casts more light on one aspect of behavior, whereas a second school illuminates a different area, may make you all the more reluctant to deny yourself the unique benefits of each school.

The Possibility of Preferring One View and Tolerating Others. Such an indecisive, eclectic approach, however, may repel you and may be an impossible position for you to take. In that case, there is nothing to do but adopt one definite view or a combination of such views. In so doing, you would be wise to read much more material than you find in these chapters. Go over some of the suggested readings given at the end of these chapters. Read some of the original treatments. Also, by using the suggestions made in Chapter 3, keep on the lookout for more recent treatments and more recent evidence.

If you do adopt one particular theory, try not to be too contemptuous of the other theories. You can profit much by giving each a sympathetic hearing. You have little to gain by fencing yourself off from all contact with them. Perhaps, in spite of your alliance with one doctrine, you can regard that alliance as being on trial. You may regard it as a compass course you can "fly by" as long as empirical check marks show that you are going in the right direction. In other words, you may accept the theory so long as it continues to explain the data. If new data appear which this theory cannot explain, and if those data appear substantial, then you should be prepared to abandon the theory or, at least, to modify it.

Controversial Theories as a Basis for Educational Reform

Finally, there is the matter of using the controversial theories, discussed in these two chapters, as the basis for far-reaching and uncontrolled changes in the educational system. Not all proposals for educational changes, of course, are based on psychological doctrines. Many suggestions are based on broad philosophical or religious doctrines for which no test or empirical verification is to be expected. Nevertheless, those doctrines may bring complete conviction to many of us, and such doctrines, once accepted, may demand extensive changes in the schools.

Regarding the educational changes which stem from philosophical or religious principles, the psychologist has nothing to say. He has nothing to say, for instance, if you should state, "I insist on these drastic and universal changes because (a) such changes are part of the democratic way of life and because (b) the democratic way of life is the best of all ways." The psychologist, of course, would offer to help you arrange a few experiments if you should care to test the effect of some of your proposals. But for comments on the wisdom of your decision, he would have to turn you over to his friend the philosopher.

Whenever proposed changes are based, not on *a priori* philosophical or religious principles, but on scientific, psychological doctrines, the position of the psychologist becomes very different. Suppose, for instance, you say, "I insist on these extensive and far-reaching changes because (a) they are demanded by the Freudian (or any other) psychology and because (b) the Freudian view has been proved to be correct." In such a case the psychologist should offer three pieces of advice. He should point out, first, that neither the Freudian nor any other of the controversial theories is thoroughly established. He should suggest, second, that, with the theories as they are formulated at present, it is very difficult to be sure just what changes should inevitably follow from any one theory.

The third suggestion made by the psychologist would be more positive. He would urge you to figure out, as rigorously as you can, just what changes would be called for by, say, the (Freudian) view. You should then initiate those changes on an *experimental basis,* being sure that you leave a comparable part of the school system unaffected by those changes to act as a control group. Then you would see whether or not those changes bring about any predictable differences. And, in all this, you would regard these changes, not as procedures that are warranted by some established theory, but, on the contrary, as an empirical means of testing some aspect of the (Freudian) theory itself. If the expected differences should fail to appear, the theory would be questioned. If the differences materialize, however, the theory would pass that test.

After awhile, of course, some one theory may pass a great many of the tests just considered. When that happens, we may feel safe in regarding that theory as a more dependable guide for drastic action. As yet, however, no one theory has passed a sufficient number of these tests. Under the circumstances, then, each theory, as we have said before, should be accepted only tentatively and should be watched most carefully and systematically to see how it works. Any complete acceptance, at this time, must be a matter of faith, hope, intuition, or sheer preference. It cannot be based on unequivocal, scientific evidence.

Summary

Learning is only one aspect of behavior and this narrow aspect receives more attention from some schools of psychology than from others. For the Gestaltist, for instance, and especially for the Lewinian, learning is not a crucial matter. Learning merely comes from a change in the structure of our experience or life space and this restructuring of life space is the basis for all behavior.

To the connectionists and to some purposivists, learning is an important problem, but even among the connectionists there are many diverse ways of explaining learning.

Perhaps the most extreme of the connectionist theories is the principle of substitution as advanced by Guthrie. This principle merely states that if an organism (dog) is doing anything (running) when a certain stimulus (a whistle) acts on him, then in the future that whistle will cause him to run. Once this tendency has been established it can be disrupted in equally simple fashion. If the dog should ever hear the whistle and fail to run, the tendency to run at the sound of the whistle will drop out.

The earlier principle of effect is in some ways the basic rival of the principle of substitution. The principle of effect and its allied concept of trial-and-error learning stress the importance of the events which follow an act. To the situation *8 + 4*, for instance, the child responds by saying *12*. There must have been some sort of tendency in him to reply in this way. Now if he encounters good "effects" after saying *12*, he will be more likely in the future to say *12* when he hears *8 + 4*. If he encounters unpleasant effects after saying *12*, the underlying tendency will be weakened.

The rival principles of substitution and effect supplement each other in very neat fashion. The principle of effect has difficulty in explaining the early stages of learning, and it is in these early stages that substitution is most clearly in its element. Substitution, on the other hand, may have difficulty in explaining the final stages of learning, and here the principle of effect is almost always adequate.

In view of the way these two principles supplement each other, it is not surprising that many people have tried to work the valuable features of each principle into one more inclusive theory. Hull's reinforcement theory is the most ambitious of these. For Hull, reinforcement consists in the alleviation of some need. If we experience some need reduction at a given moment, then all situations, say, smelling smoke and hearing a scream, which were acting on us just prior to that moment will become linked to all responses, say, sniffing the air and trembling, which we were making just prior to that moment. If some situations and responses were already linked, then that linkage will become stronger.

The principle of expectancy, advanced by Tolman, is part of his more general theory of purposivism. Tolman insists that the animal does not merely learn to run when he hears the whistle. What he learns is the knowledge (a) that running will get him to the food in a hurry and (b) that the whistle means that food is ready. Knowing these two things he comes to expect that running will bring him food and he acts accordingly. He does not act automatically. He has some knowledge and he uses this knowledge to accomplish his goal. If he did not *want* the food at that moment, he would not run in spite of the whistle.

The differences between the theories are revealed in the attitudes they take toward some persisting problems. The nervous system, for instance, plays a considerable role in the theories of Hull and Guthrie but is unimportant for Tolman and Lewin. Motive or need is crucial for Hull and for Thorndike but plays only an incidental part in the theories of Tolman and Guthrie. For Tolman, forgetting is largely a matter of one expectancy replacing another. For the other theorists, the weakening of one tendency or cognition and the strengthening of others are quite separate matters. The consistent, successful avoidance of a noxious stimulus poses problems for Hull and Pavlov but gives little trouble to Guthrie or Tolman.

Experiments are continually going on to test these various theories. Until the evidence becomes much clearer than it now is, the teacher should try to take an eclectic and tolerant view of these various theories. If this is impossible, he should read much more widely and, above all, search out facts and face them honestly.

SPECIFIC REFERENCES

1. Misbach, L. Psychoanalysis and theories of learning. *Psychol. Rev.,* 1948, *55,* 143–156.
2. Lewin, K. Field theory and learning. *Yearb. nat. soc. Stud. Educ., 41,* (II), 1942, Chap. 6.

3. Leeper, R. *Lewin's topological and vector psychology.* University of Oregon, 1943.

4. Hilgard, E. R. *Theories of learning.* Appleton-Century-Crofts, 1948, Chap. 7.

5. Koffka, K. *Principles of gestalt psychology.* Harcourt Brace, 1935.

6. Guthrie, E. R. Conditioning: a theory of learning in terms of stimulus, response, and association. *Yearb. nat. soc. Stud. Educ., 41* (II), 1942, Chap. 1.

7. Guthrie, E. R. *The psychology of learning.* Harper, 1952.

8. Voeks, Virginia W. Formalization and clarification of a theory of learning. *J. Psychol.,* 1950, *30,* 341–362.

9. Hollingworth, H. L. *Educational psychology.* Appleton-Century, 1933.

10. Tolman, E. C., and Postman, L. Learning. *Annu. Rev. Psychology,* 1954, *5,* 27–56.

11. Hull, C. L. Conditioning: outline of a systematic theory of learning. *Yearb. nat. soc. Stud. Educ., 41* (II), 1942, Chap. 2.

12. Hull, C. L. *The principles of behavior.* Appleton-Century, 1943.

13. Miller, N. E., and Dollard, J. *Social learning and imitation.* Yale University Press, 1941.

14. Hull, C. L. *Essentials of behavior.* Yale University Press, 1951.

15. Hull, C. L. *A behavior system.* Yale University Press, 1952.

16. Estes, W. K., and others. *Modern learning theory: a critical analysis of five examples.* Appleton-Century-Crofts, 1954, Chap. 1, Clark L. Hull (Koch, S.) Chap. 3, Burrhus F. Skinner. (Verplanck, W. S.)

17. Logan, F. A. A note on stimulus intensity dynamism (V). *Psychol. Rev.,* 1954, *61,* 77–80.

18. Skinner, B. F. Are theories of learning necessary? *Psychol. Rev.,* 1950, *57,* 193–216.

19. Hull, C. L., and Baernstein, H. D. A mechanical parallel to the conditioned reflex. *Science,* 1929, *70,* 14–15.

20. Stephens, J. M. A mechanical explanation of the law of effect. *Amer. J. Psychol.,* 1929, *41,* 422–431.

21. Mowrer, O. H. On the dual nature of learning—a re-interpretation of "conditioning" and "problem-solving." *Harv. educ. Rev.,* 1947, *17,* 102–148.

22. Maier, N. R. F., and Schneirla, T. C. Mechanisms in conditioning. *Psychol. Rev.,* 1942, *49,* 117–134.

23. Stephens, J. M. Expectancy vs. effect-substitution as a general principle of reinforcement. *Psychol. Rev.,* 1942, *49,* 102–116.

24. Shoben, E. J., Jr. Psychotherapy as a problem in learning theory. *Psychol. Bull.,* 1949, *46,* 366–392.

25. Kendler, H. H., and Underwood, B. J. The role of reward in conditioning theory. *Psychol. Rev.,* 1948, *55,* 209–215.

26. Osgood, C. E. *Method and theory in experimental psychology.* Oxford University Press, 1953.

27. Woodworth, R. S. *Contemporary schools of psychology.* Ronald, 1948, pp. 103–108.

28. Hilgard, E. R. *Theories of learning.* Appleton-Century-Crofts, 1948, Chap. 10.

29. Olds, J. A neural model for sign-Gestalt theory. *Psychol. Rev.,* 1954, *61,* 59–72.

30. Low, Camilla M. Determining the nature of the needs of youth. *Yearb. nat. soc. Stud. Educ.,* 52 (I), 1953, 22–43.

31. Solomon, R. L., and Wynne, L. C. Traumatic avoidance learning: acquisition in normal dogs. *Psychol. Monogr.,* 1953, *67* (4), (No. 354).

32. Solomon, R. L., and others. Traumatic avoidance learning: the outcome of several extinction procedures with dogs. *J. abnorm. soc. Psychol.,* 1953, *48,* 291–302.

33. Miller, N. E. Studies of fear as an acquirable drive: I. Fear as motivation and fear-reduction as reinforcement in the learning of new responses. *J. exp. Psychol.,* 1948, *38,* 89–101.

SUGGESTIONS FOR FURTHER READING

1. Hilgard, E. R. *Theories of learning.* Appleton-Century-Crofts, 1948.
   This is the most complete treatment of the different theories of learning. Some people detect a field bias, but even so there is a very thorough summary. Difficult in spots.

2. The National Society for the Study of Education. *The psychology of learning.* Forty-first Yearbook, Part II, 1942.
   This is an earlier summary written by a number of authors, including some of the theorists themselves (Guthrie, Hull, Lewin). Perhaps much of it is easier to read than Hilgard, but the coverage is not so complete. There is no chapter on Tolman, for instance.

3. Stolurow, L. M. *Readings in learning.* Prentice-Hall, 1953.

4. Osgood, C. F. *Method and theory in experimental psychology.* Oxford University Press, 1953.

5. Stevens, S. S. *Handbook of experimental psychology.* Wiley, 1951, Chap. 18, Theoretical interpretations of learning (Spence, K. W.).

6. Estes, W. K. Toward a statistical theory of learning. *Psychol. Rev.*, 1951, *58*, 94–107.

7. McCorquodale, K. Learning. *Annu. Rev. Psychol.*, 1955, *6*, 29–62.

8. Spence, K. W. Mathematical theories of learning. *J. gen. Psychol.*, 1953, *49*, 283–291.

9. Estes, W. K., and others. *Contributions to Learning Theory.* Appleton-Century-Crofts, 1954.

10. Deese, J. E. *The psychology of learning.* McGraw-Hill, 1952, Chap. 2 and 17.

11. Miller, N. E., and Dollard, J. *Social learning and imitation.* Yale University Press, 1941.

12. Various. Symposium on learning. *Psychol. Rev.*, 1951, *58*, 350–386.

13. Mowrer, O. H. *Learning theory and personality dynamics.* Ronald, 1950.

14. Mowrer, O. H. Learning theory. *Rev. educ. Res.*, 1952, *22*, 475–495.

15. English, H. B. *The historical roots of learning theory.* Doubleday, 1954.

16. Skinner, B. F. Science of learning and the art of teaching. *Harvard educ. Rev.*, 1954, *24*, 86–97.

Exercises and Questions for Discussion

1. Go back to Exercise 3 at the end of Chapter 8.
   (a) What kind of learning seems to predominate here? Trial and error? Substitution? Need reduction? Expectancy?
   (b) Consider the following sequence:

   P. Triangle is a figure bounded by 3 lines.
   T. That's exactly the word I wanted: *bounded* by 3 lines.

Let us assume that, in the future, this particular pupil would give the same definition more quickly. Show in detail how this change or improvement would be explained by each of the following theorists: Hull, Thorndike, Guthrie, Tolman.

2. A young child is ordinarily brought to school by his mother and cries as soon as she leaves. How would you go about helping him get over this if you held to the Guthrie theory? If you held to the principle of effect? If you were a follower of Tolman?

10

Utilizing Motivation and Experience

Throughout his work the teacher is concerned with helping the student find better ways of doing things. The things which the student must do are of many kinds. At times the things he does are set off by some external problem. The car won't start. He is failing in English. His parents refuse to welcome his friend into the home. Now, of course, these external problems never stand in clear-cut isolation, neatly removed from all other problems. Such external problems are always intimately related to the student's inner needs and wishes and fears. Indeed the external problems only become problems and acquire significance when they are closely related to the fundamental needs. But, even so, there are times when the appearance of the external problem is the immediate occasion calling for action. It is true that the balky car becomes a problem only because the student wants to get somewhere. But that need to get somewhere was present all the time, and it is the balky car which calls for action.

At times the necessity for doing something arises, not so much from any immediate happening in the external world, as from the clear emergence of an inner need. The student, for instance, may be overwhelmed by a need to be more popular. This need may not be set off by any immediate slight or rebuff but may have emerged from a vague cluster of events, none of which stands out clearly. Here the inner need is the impetus which calls for action. The student must try to find some way of satisfying it or adjusting to it.

There are times when the things to be done are rather simple. A light

294

is to be switched on. A word is to be spelled. A sum is to be computed. An equation is to be solved. True, these more simple tasks always occur within the framework of larger needs and larger problems. If it were not for the need of succeeding in a profession or of doing well in school or of avoiding the teacher's disapproval, the algebraic equation would be no problem. But when those more basic needs are present, the smaller and simpler tasks do set off behavior and become things to do.

Educational growth means acquiring better ways of doing these many things. Such growth means that the student is solving his problems in better ways. It means that he is adjusting to his needs in a more satisfactory manner. It means, too, that he is reacting to the more simple tasks in more adequate fashion. He spells more words correctly. He solves more equations correctly and solves more difficult equations. He makes more adequate reactions to the ideas he encounters in history and literature.

In the next few chapters we consider the many things which a teacher can do to bring about better ways of behaving.

It is only through experience that the student can acquire better ways of doing things. If he is to acquire a better way of dealing with the balky automobile, he should have experience with this problem or with similar problems. If he is to find better ways of solving equations, he must have experience with equations or with similar problems.

We must not suggest, of course, that any experience will do. Some kinds of experience are much more helpful than others. Certain kinds may actually be harmful. It is never enough just to be sure that the student gets experience with the problem. But, although this is never enough, it is the first step. The first thing the teacher must do is to make sure that the student will go on encountering the problem and that he will continue to try to do something about it.

It is often very easy to make sure that the objective problem will continue to exist. The car may remain balky, the student may still lack popularity, the equation may remain unsolved. But it is not always so easy to make sure that the student will continue to face the problem or that he will continue to do something about it. It is possible to ignore objective problems. It is possible to try to ignore internal needs. It is easy to ignore algebraic equations.

To make sure that the student continues to face the necessary problems and that he continues to do something about these problems, the teacher employs the mechanism of motivation.

The Role and Importance of Motivation

At the outset let us face the uncomfortable fact that we are not sure just how any motive operates. From much of our evidence, in fact, it is impossible to tell whether the motive helped the students acquire any additional skill at all, or whether the motive merely led them to make more vigorous use of the skill they had. Most of us, for instance, would run faster under a strong motive than under a weak one. But does the motive give us additional competence in running? Or does it merely make us utilize the competence we had all along? Some theorists (Chapter 9) hold that motive plays little direct part in learning but merely leads to greater utilization of learning that is acquired by other means.

Even when we can show that motivation has had an effect on learning as well as on performance, we cannot be sure just what the motive did to facilitate learning(1). As we note in Chapter 9, the motive may merely have led the student into situations that produced learning. In addition to this general role, the motive may have contributed directly to reinforcement, as Hull would expect. Finally, the motive may have elicited useful responses (correcting an answer, hitting a different key) that the student learns to make to some new stimulus (Guthrie).

When all these uncertainties are ironed out, our use of motivation may become much more deft and precise and perhaps more economical. Meanwhile, however, we can accept the very comforting fact that, by *some means* or *other,* motivation does have a powerful influence. Of all the devices available to us, motivation is, perhaps, the most important. If we do nothing more than make it important for a child to learn a given thing, there is a fair chance that he will learn it. It is true, of course, that there are additional mechanisms necessary for learning and that motivation can never produce learning without the aid of these other mechanisms. But the application of motivation very often will automatically invoke those other necessary mechanisms. Hence by making it important for a child to learn, we may set in motion all the forces necessary for learning.

No one, of course, would recommend that we merely apply motivation and stop there. The resulting learning would be precarious, and even when it did take place, it might be very inefficient and might readily have many undesirable concomitants. Motivation is stressed to this extent, not to suggest that we rely on it exclusively, but to suggest the great importance of this primary mechanism.

Motivation Used by the Teacher

In discussing the general problem of adjustment (Chapter 16) we pay considerable attention to the basic physiological and physical needs that lead to action. Within the schoolroom, however, the more primitive motives are seldom involved in direct fashion. The teacher seldom relies on the direct need for food as a motive. The need to avoid pain, at one time a very prevalent motive within the school, is now rarely used. The need for sexual stimulation, again, is almost never used as a direct motive within the school. True enough, there may be times when the teacher makes indirect use of these primitive motives. At times the teacher may appeal to the student's need to avoid drowning in the future or to his need to secure a mate in the future. This, however, merely represents indirect use of the basic motives.

In general, the teacher makes only indirect use of the physical and physiological motives, although these latter are always in the background and cannot be disregarded by the teacher. It is the social and intellectual motives to which the teacher appeals in most direct fashion and which he applies most freely. The teacher is free to utilize the child's need to be with people, his need to secure the attention of other people, his need to influence people and to help them, his need to have people think well of him, his need to move things around, to manipulate, to rearrange ideas, to create and to express himself, and his overpowering need to think well of himself.

The Effectiveness of Different Motives

Fortunately, the very motives which come most readily to the teacher's hand are those which have been investigated most frequently. Let us look at the results of these investigations.

Intention to Learn

The very least we can do by way of motivation is to let the student know that he is expected to learn. Remember, of course, that this will never be the only motive working on him. But, taking the other motives as we find them, we can manipulate this one. We can find out if the student will learn more when he is clearly aware that he is expected to learn than when he has no such awareness.

Intention Not Absolutely Necessary: Incidental Learning. People frequently do learn material even when they make no effort to do so and when they have no idea that they are intended to do so. In your own experience you may have observed that you remembered telephone numbers, automobile licenses, snatches of poetry, names of people, even when you made no deliberate effort to do so and when you had no clear intention of doing so. This common experience is born out by systematic experiments. Suppose, for instance, that young students are set to learn a list of symbols such as the alphabet. As far as they know their only task is to learn to say the alphabet forward. Yet after they have completed the task, they will also have some skill in saying the alphabet backward. They will have learned some things which they never set out to learn. This phenomenon is known as *backward association*.

The phenomenon of incidental learning appears even when students are guided away from learning, so to speak. In one experiment(2) students were shown a list of words and were deliberately assigned a misleading task. They were told that the object of the experiment was to find out if any of the words evoked associations in their minds. Their task was merely to raise their hands whenever the word being presented made them think of other words. The investigator then noted the number of hands and presented the next word. The list was presented several times in the same order. Then, and only then, the students were asked to recite as many of the words as possible. Even though they had no idea they were supposed to learn the list, many of the students could recall considerable portions of it.

Apparently, much learning(3, 4) can take place when the student merely attends to material that he is not told to learn. It is possible, of course, that students may suspect that learning is in order and may "play it safe," although one would not expect this when the students are actually given a different task to perform.

There is a great deal of interest at the present time regarding the possibility of learning while one is asleep. A number of rather careful studies have seemed to find such learning, but other investigations have come up with negative results. The problem has been to be sure that the students really were asleep when the material was being presented(5). In the near future there may be some more definite information on this interesting subject.

Acquisition of Attitudes. Although there is less experimental work on the acquisition of attitudes, it is more than probable that many attitudes are learned without any intention whatever. Children learn to like dogs or hate them, to loathe spinach or to love carrots(6) without any intention on their part. It is also most probable that they learn to suspect foreigners, to hate people of other religions, or to love their own locality without ever intending that this should come about.

Deliberate Intention a Great Aid to Learning. Although some learning can take place without any deliberate intention to learn, there is no question that such deliberate intention is a great aid to learning. It is true that the students who were misled did learn some of the words in the list that was presented to them. They did not learn nearly so many words, however, as a comparable group of students who knew from the outset that they were supposed to memorize the list. It is also true that intentional learning is less subject to interference from other learning(7).

In the field of academic learning, most experiments bear out the common-sense expectation that intending to learn will greatly expedite learning. In most school situations something will be gained by the mere announcement that this task is important(8), that this learning is expected of the students. Truly this is motivation at its lowest level. A teacher would have to be stupid, if not altogether perverse, not to use a motive as simple as this.

Unfortunately the experiments do not extend to the field of attitude formation. As yet we do not know whether students will be more likely to appreciate Bach if we tell them in advance that we want them to come to appreciate Bach. We cannot say that students will come to be more tolerant of foreigners if we tell them in advance that the object of our lesson is to make them more tolerant of foreigners. It may be possible that for some highly emotional attitudes such an announcement might interfere with the desired change. But this is conjecture.

Ego-involvement

Ego-involvement means that the student feels and accepts a certain challenge. By saying that the student's ego is involved, we mean that, in his mind, failure in the assigned task will lead to some impairment of the ego, to some loss of self-respect, or to a reduction in his sense of worth. The ego is involved whenever the student feels that an important part of him is wrapped up in the outcome of the task.

The amount of ego-involvement, of course, varies greatly from task to task. In many of the tasks we undertake, we can face the prospect of failure with little or no concern. In many party games, for instance, one is expected to fail. The game would lose its point otherwise. At other times the task may be clearly beyond our powers, and in such a case we may go through the motions of trying and yet feel little concern as to possible failure. In still other cases we may feel that the job to be done is not a relevant test of the "real" us. The successful man-of-affairs, for instance, may experience no crushing sense of failure over his clumsiness in tying a hair ribbon on his child's doll, or he may only be mildly amused at his lack of prowess in throwing a ring around a carnival kewpie.

There is no question that a moderate amount of ego-involvement is a powerful aid to learning(9). Students will perform better and acquire more skill when they are made to feel that success in the assigned task is important to them, that in some way it is a measure of their real worth as persons. In some experiments this ego-involvement has been induced by the mere announcement that the assigned exercise was a test of intelligence. Apparently for college students this is a "sure-fire" means of appealing to the ego. Failure on a test which measures intelligence is something which no student can contemplate with indifference.

There are numerous ways in which the teacher may enhance the amount of ego-involvement experienced by the students. One method is to encourage the feeling of initiative. If the student feels that he thought of a project or an idea(10), he will feel more responsibility for it and will accept it as a part of himself. This philosophy of student initiative is so thoroughly accepted by modern theorists that it needs no further development here.

As you might expect, the use of ego-involvement can be overdone, especially for people who are tense or anxious to begin with(11). Such people may do worse when "put on the spot." Even if it did not occasionally work in reverse, there is the danger of undue strain or tension on the students. At its worst it may lead to a crushing sense of failure, worthlessness, or guilt. The judicious teacher must encourage the student to distinguish between those tasks which call for everything he has and those needing only casual interest.

Frequent Tests

Tests are often intended as motives. Many teachers believe that if a student knows he is going to be tested on a certain lesson he will study harder and learn more about it. Teachers may also believe that a test in the near future is more likely to act as a motive than a test in the remote future.

At the college level the results of the different investigations show considerable disagreement(12, 13, 14). If anything the trend suggests that there is no definite advantage for frequent tests over tests given once or twice a term. From his review of the early literature, Noll suggested that after a weekly or biweekly quiz, students tend to say, "Well, that's that," and proceed to forget about the material on the test. For the dull student, on the other hand, there may be a definite value in frequent as opposed to infrequent tests.

Our statement about the limited value of frequent tests holds, of course, only for their value as *motivation* when they are given merely to encourage the students to study harder. When, on the other hand, the tests are made the basis of remedial work, there may be much more improvement.

At the high-school level, the story seems to be somewhat different. At this level there is probably an advantage for *fairly* frequent tests. Even here, however, there are some important cautions. First, the tests should not be too frequent. In one study(15), for instance, tests given every day were not so effective as tests given every two weeks. Indeed, in a second study(16) in this same series, it appeared that daily tests were worse than no tests at all.

As a second caution, we should not put our faith in surprise tests as opposed to tests that are announced ahead of time. The results so far suggest that at the end of the term the students working under a system of surprise tests learned less than those who knew in advance when the test was to occur.

Objective Knowledge of Results

There is no doubt that a clear knowledge of how well one is doing has a definite effect on performance or output. A student squeezing a dynamometer will squeeze harder if he can see the needle move. A student who sees a graphical record of his progress in arithmetic or typing will, in most cases, perform at a higher level.

Although it is clear that this motive makes for much more vigorous practice, we cannot yet be sure that it also brings about greater learning. The necessary controls (to be discussed later) have not yet been applied. At present we can be sure that the use of motives of this type will bring about more effort and more zestful practice, and we have reasonable grounds for hope that it may also bring about an improvement in learning(17).

If this motive does prove to be beneficial for learning, it should be a highly desirable motive to use. It is desirable partly because it is a safe motive. When we try to excel our own past performance we compete against ourselves. And for most of us this is a contest in which we can hope for considerable success. We are not asked to match the record of the best student in the class or some unattainable ideal. We are merely asked to beat our own previous score.

In addition to being safe, this motive is often readily available. Indeed it may be hard to avoid. When a student answers a question in class the teacher's facial expression or the reactions of the other students may clearly tell him whether he is right or wrong. In mechanical work, in penmanship, or art, he can often tell whether his performance is satisfactory or not.

When knowledge of results is not available automatically, the teacher can often take pains to make the results available as definitely and quickly as possible. *Examinations can be returned promptly.* Often students can correct their own papers from a model paper as soon as they finish their exercises. Many drill tests provide special features to permit easy self-scoring.

The teacher of special subjects may be able to work out other devices which will provide students with more immediate and more definite knowledge of their progress. These devices should stimulate immediate performance and may have a beneficial ultimate effect on learning.

Failure (and Blame) versus Success (and Praise)

In the investigations just discussed there was no attempt to manipulate the kind of information that comes to the student. Under ordinary circumstances he will receive some information that means he has hit the target and some information to indicate he has missed. In any case there is no attempt to make him feel a sense of failure or unworthiness.

In contrast to these experiments, there have been many attempts to select or manipulate the information that comes to the student. Some students are told that they are doing well (success, praise). Others are told that they are doing poorly (failure, blame). Under other circumstances the students are told what is normal achievement. Some of these are given false and inflated standards, so that, if they believe what they are told, they are almost bound to think they have failed. Others are given false but easy norms, so that almost any performance on their part will appear to be good. In most of these circumstances there is an attempt at ego-involvement. The instructions are not set up so that the student will merely think, "Hm! Missed it that time," but, on the contrary, he is likely to think, "How could anyone do so poorly?"

The results of these investigations are quite conflicting. This appears in Schmidt's(18) summary of the work before 1940 and in the work that has come out since then(19, 20, 21). If anything the results from school situations suggest that blame may be more likely to induce greater effort. But the advantage, if any, is slight and in no way dependable. Either praise or blame is typically more effective than nothing. The results remain in conflict when we try to determine the effects on children with different personalities(22). Some studies suggest that failure or blame will boost the performance of extraverts but not of introverts. Other studies produce results in the opposite direction. Some work on anxiety may be promising in this respect. It suggests that failure or blame may be especially bad for people who are very tense to begin with, but may help people who show little anxiety(23).

All in all, it would seem wise to consider the whole question of praise versus blame as completely unsettled. We might suspect, but we do not know, that the personality of the teacher might have much to do with it(18). We might also suspect that a steady diet of either success or failure, praise or blame, would be bad. From the point of view of personal adjustment (Chapter 21) we shall see that an uninterrupted sequence of serious failure can be harmful. For many students, moreover, a steady diet of success is boring and stultifying. If such students are to remain "on their toes," this success must at least be hazardous. If not actual failure, there must at least be a definite threat of failure(24). We also know that an uninterrupted series of successes followed by a serious failure can be damaging. Taking everything into account it would seem that we may as well let nature take its course, avoiding undue reliance on either praise or blame. In the long run we might aim at a balanced diet with success predominating. On any specific occasion, however, we might very well act in a way that seems natural under the circumstances.

Social Factors

By social factors(25) we refer, in general, to the influence of classmates on each other. Classmates, of course, may act on each other in various ways and it will be best to consider these various ways separately.

Being in a Group, but Working Privately. This is the typical study-hall situation. There is some evidence that the *output* of younger children is increased when they are studying with a group. If, on the other hand, both the children studying alone and those studying in a group are urged to do their best, or motivated in other ways, the superiority of studying in a group vanishes.

Observing the Work of Others, but Working Privately. This is the situation which prevails when one or two good students are working at the board and the other children working at their desks. When this pace-setter arrangement is in effect there is some increase in speed of output but no increase in the quality of the output. The presence of the pace-setter induces the children at the desks to do more exercises but does not prevent them from making errors.

Being Observed by Others. If the child is working at the board where all the class may see (and perhaps comment) will he perform better than he would working at his desk? The answer is twofold. Under such obtrusive observation the quantity of work done will increase tremendously. The quality, however, will decrease. These remarks refer to output. We do not know what happens to learning when the student works in the limelight. An unseen radio or television audience can cause more tension or disturbance than an audience that is visible to the student(26), although these effects tend to wear off.

Competition. Several investigations have shown that competition can be depended on to increase output. When grade six children were urged to see who could make the greatest gain in adding number couplets, the class gained some thirty-two examples, a gain that exceeds the difference between the performance of students in grades eight and five(27). Of course, their skill did not increase that much. They merely made better use of skill they already had.

In the experiment just mentioned, it was found that individual competition was much better than group competition. The children performed at a higher level when each child was trying to excel all other children. When, on the other hand, one class as a whole was trying to excel another class, the influence of competition was less marked. Group competition was fairly effective when a group of boys tried to excel a group of girls.

So far we have discussed competition in which the competitors cannot watch the progress of each other. This is like a foot race against time rather than a foot race against other runners on the same track. In activities, such as button sorting, there is a further increase in the amount of work done when each competitor can see how well the others are doing. Under these conditions, however, there is no increase in quality or accuracy of performance.

It is obvious that individual competition can interfere with a complex "team" task(28). So far, however, we do not know whether people who compete vigorously against each other in one activity (tennis singles) are in any way handicapped when they are later paired as a team as in tennis doubles.

A Standard to Be Attained

Most of us will exert ourselves to attain a standard which has been set. This motive can be used to affect output. To an enormous extent we do what we think is expected of us. We often go so far as to ask for a goal, and we feel happy when one is set for us, if it is within reasonable reach. Teachers may readily utilize this urge by setting short-time goals. If a student is adding twenty-seven couplets a minute, the teacher may assign thirty as his standard for next day. The standards, of course, should be set individually and should be based on the student's previous performance. Older students can use this motive by setting standards for themselves. For instance, a student may set himself the task of attaining a speed of reading standard of sixty-five by next week, and once that is attained he may set a new short-time goal.

When a material reward is attached to these standards the output is further increased. Leuba(29) had students take a test in addition, and on the basis of the first test he assigned goals to be attained. He continued this, sometimes promising a chocolate bar to each child who attained the standard, sometimes not promising a reward. There is no question that the reward acted as an incentive. This feature is not very feasible in the regular classroom, and it may have undesirable aspects from the point of view of character.

Intrinsic versus Extrinsic Motives

In Lewinian psychology (Chapter 8) there is a great emphasis on the distinction between intrinsic and extrinsic motives(30). In connection with the washing of hands, for instance, a child's need to get rid of that grimy feeling would be an intrinsic motive. His need to avoid a scolding from his mother would be an extrinsic need. Or, to take an academic example, his wish to be able to read would be an intrinsic motive, whereas his hope to gain the teacher's approval would be extrinsic.

There is, of course, a very important practical difference between the two kinds of needs. An intrinsic need can be met only by the behavior in question, only by washing the hands or by learning to read. The extrinsic needs can be met by various roundabout devices. Or, more accurately, a person may *try* to meet these needs by roundabout devices.

Without washing his hands, the small boy may *try* to avoid trouble with his mother by staying out of her way, by pretending illness, or by keeping his hands well up into his sleeves. Without learning to read, the child may *try* to curry favor with the teacher by lavish use of apples, babyish behavior, or by acting as teacher's little helper.

Obviously, whenever we have a clear choice, the intrinsic motive is to be preferred. It leads more directly to the behavior that we desire. When we use this motive, moreover, there is less need for supplementary restraints to prevent roundabout behavior. We must realize, however, that in some cases there may not be an intrinsic motive on which we can readily lay our hands in the hurly-burly of teaching. In that event, temporarily at least, we will have to use some less intrinsic form of motivation.

Utilizing Existing Interests and Activity Already in Progress

It is not always necessary for the teacher to anchor his motivating devices directly to the basic motivations. Often, on the contrary, the teacher will find that the basic urges have developed into very strong interests in some activity or other. Because of the basic motives, for instance, the student may have developed a strong interest in collecting trolley transfers, in airplanes, in basketball, or in fishing. When these strong interests are already developed, it is foolish not to use them. In so doing we do not need to inquire into the detailed basis of the existing interest. We need only to tie on to it and utilize it. Knowing the student's great interest in flying, we can seek to relate the work in geography to that interest. Knowing his interest in fishing, we can seek to utilize that interest in motivating his study of biology and fluid dynamics. Knowing his interest in photography, we can bring in the relevant portion of chemistry and optics.

Existing interests are always useful as motives. Some of these existing interests, moreover, will already have begun to express themselves in actual conduct, and such interests, naturally enough, are even more useful than those that are merely latent. Interests that arouse activity must be strong to begin with. Over and beyond this fact, moreover, the activity, once under way, acts as an additional motive in its own right. Suppose, for instance, that the students have begun to make a detailed map of the neighborhood. The very fact that they are engaged in this activity will in itself act as a motive for doing the necessary intermediate tasks. This activity already begun can be used as the motive for moderate study of scales and measurements, for the acquisition of moderate skill in mechanical drawing, and even, perhaps, for a study of the rudiments of surveying. Notice that we have hedged a bit here. We must not kill the goose that lays the golden eggs. By tying too many uninteresting tasks to the activity in progress, we might do just that. We might drain the large project of its inherent interest.

The Urge for Achievement

Many students, by the time they reach college at least, have already developed a powerful drive to do well, to succeed, to excel, or to become a leader in college or in life(24). This achievement drive is, of course, much more powerful in some college students than in others. It is thought to be brought about by almost any family pattern—laudable or unfortunate—that makes for independence or individuality on the part of the child. Students highly driven by this urge will achieve more in typical academic tasks than those only moderately affected by this need(31). This need can be manipulated. Students taken off a task when success was just within their grasp, for instance, will show more of this need than students who have been allowed to finish the task or those who have never been allowed to start.

The business of achieving, or of making a success out of life, is one activity that is almost always going on. It is a motive that we very often use and, within limits, it is proper that we should. If we can show in a convincing manner that a certain school subject has a bearing on the student's life work or on his social success, we can use the drive behind the main activity to supply motivation for the new subject. Obviously, we would be very foolish to ignore this rich reservoir of motivation which is almost always at hand. Good teachers will never miss the opportunity to show whatever utilitarian value there may be in the task about to be undertaken.

Interest in life success, of course, can be overworked. The fact that it is always present may lead us to use it when much simpler and more immediate motives would do just as well. At times, moreover, we may stretch this motive too far as when, for instance, we try to develop an interest in Virgil on the grounds that the student will need Latin if he is to become a successful doctor.

Manipulation, Curiosity, and Play

One of the intrinsic motives that lies ready to hand is that of sheer physical or ideational manipulation. In rats, monkeys, children, and adults there is a powerful need to move things around and to see things happen(32). Monkeys will solve puzzles for no other reward than the pleasure of moving bolts and levers(33). Rats are "rewarded" by entering an alley that is merely complex and "interesting." Children will pile blocks or make marks on paper with no extrinsic reward in evidence. For some students it is *fun* to do experiments in physics. It is fun to reduce a complicated algebraic statement to a simple expression. It is fun to complete the paradigm of the Latin verb. People do not need to be led by the obvious goal of success in life to do crossword puzzles, to play chess, or to read stories. They do so for the sheer enjoyment of the intellectual manipulation.

Reducing Distraction

Motives are devices by which we encourage students to keep on facing problems and to continue applying themselves to the tasks we consider to be important. Distractors, on the other hand, are active influences which tend to make the student less likely to continue at his task. Distraction, then, may be considered as a sort of negative or inverse motivation. How is our task affected by this negative motivation?

The harmful effects of distraction have probably been overemphasized. It is true, of course, that, under some circumstances, distractors may cause a severe loss in efficiency. Under ordinary circumstances, however, their influence is very slight, and, in some cases, a mild distraction may actually result in a slight increase in achievement(34, 35). Of course, we should avoid serious distractions whenever possible. Even when they fail to reduce efficiency they often add to the feeling of difficulty and bring about more effort and tension. A student working under conditions of distraction may apply more force to the keys of the typewriter, grasp a pencil more tightly, or take a tighter grip on the chair legs with his ankles.

Although distraction has less effect than we might ordinarily suppose, there may be some harmful effects when the distracting stimulus is highly unusual, or when it competes with the same sense avenue (a light flashing in our eyes while we are reading), or when it is annoying. At one time it was thought that meaningful distraction (listening to a talk on the radio) was more serious than meaningless distraction. It seems, however, that this is not always so(36). Some early work had also suggested that distraction will interfere if the student expects it to interfere. This suggestion, like the other, has not been confirmed by recent work(36).

Motivating Students: The General Problem

After all this detailed consideration of individual motives, can we reach any general conclusion? Are there any important cautions to keep in mind?

Dependable Conclusions. Most of the motives that we have discussed can be depended upon to get students into action, to bring about behavior or performance of some kind. This rather modest conclusion, moreover, is not to be despised. If a student is to learn, we must arouse him to action of some sort. We must get him to come to school, to open his book, to sit at the typewriter, to get into the swimming pool. Over and above this obvious fact, we can assume that, within limits, the more the performance, the greater the opportunity for learning. The child who spends more time with his book has more opportunity to master its contents than the child who spends less time. It seems clear then, that these motives can certainly be used to place a student in the situation in which learning can occur.

Areas of Doubt. Once we have motivated the student to study his lesson, to practice his typing, or to work on his swimming, we cannot be sure whether or not the continuation of the motive adds to the efficiency of learning. Although we can be sure that the highly motivated student will perform more exercises and attempt more tasks, we cannot be sure that the eager, zestful practicer will acquire more skill than his more indolent, lackadaisical twin brother. There are many instances in which indolent and dilatory practice has resulted in a very considerable increase in skill.

Notice that we say we cannot be *sure*. It is still quite possible that vigorous, zestful practice will be more effective than the indifferent, heel-dragging performance we so often deplore. Certainly the highly motivated behavior is more pleasant to observe. It is possible, moreover, that grudging indifferent practice may lead to a habit of lack of effort. In view of all this, there is much to suggest that we should encourage a reasonable degree of effort on the part of our students. The additional effort may do some good. Within limits, it should do no harm. But let us not be too disturbed when an exceedingly indolent performer proves to have learned as much as his more conscientious classmate.

Can we overmotivate? Is it possible to overdo this business of getting the students stirred up, eager, and on their toes? Apparently this can happen. When students are at the point where no mistake is likely—

when they are taking part in a drill on well-learned material—then the more anxious and eager they are the better. When, however, they are just as likely to make an erroneous response as a correct response, then the highly motivated, anxious people will do worse than their more relaxed, indifferent classmates(1). The interpretation of this evidence, by the way, is still far from settled. Tentatively, however, we might suggest that in the early stages of learning, when errors are very likely, we might do well to keep motivation at a fairly low level and avoid a tense, eager, stirred-up state. In these early stages, as we have seen, a certain amount of learning can take place from sheer passive exposure when the students have no intention of learning. Later in the learning, when mistakes are less likely, an intense eagerness should do less harm and may readily be of great value.

Finally, in our confession of doubts, we must admit that we do not know the precise mechanisms by which motivation accomplishes whatever it does accomplish. For all we know, the stirred-up state, the strong need, may be an essential ingredient in the process of learning. Some theorists (Hull, Thorndike) have held this to be true. It is quite possible, however, that this zestful, motivated state may fail to do anything in its own right. It may merely act as a rough all-purpose device that brings more specific devices into action. It may be like the rough shaking of a stopped watch. In an indirect and clumsy way it may bring about adjustments that a more knowing craftsman can achieve more directly and with less over-all disturbance.

But these are speculations. Lacking a dependable knowledge of these more precise influences, we can, for practical purposes, fall back on a rule of thumb. Some motivation is necessary to bring students into the situation in which learning can occur. Motivation may also play a part in the actual process of learning. Although motivation can be overdone, especially in the early and confused stages of learning, on the whole we will find it our most valuable single instrument, crude and inefficient though it may be(37).

Types of Practice or Activity

Let us suppose we have arranged the general conditions so that the student will practice; that is to say, we have taken care of the problem of motivation. Our next step is to direct his practice along the most efficient channels. Let us see what is known about the influence of various types of practice.

Reading or Listening

Some people have assumed that it is only physical activity which will produce learning. To their minds there can be no learning unless children are moving around, building cardboard stores, painting murals, or constructing stone monuments. Actually nothing could be farther from the truth. To a great extent the activity necessary for learning can take place while pupils are quietly reading or even listening to a lecture. In the art of reading there is usually continuous activity. Let us suppose, for instance, that a student reads the following account of a minor incident:

> It was dark outside. Inside the office of the village constable, it was quiet and pleasant. Suddenly the phone rang. It was Perkins from the garage. Someone had parked a car across his driveway. Well the regulations were clear. Cars parked illegally were to be towed to the police yard and impounded. Might as well get it done.
>
> Back again in the comfortable office and again the phone. This time it was his son Arthur. The family car had been stolen from downtown. A growing suspicion! Taking his flashlight he went out to the police yard and examined the impounded car. Sure enough - - - - -.

The quoted words are not merely taken in or absorbed by the act of reading. In addition, they are almost bound to evoke some kind of response. Most people will respond to the statement by finishing the story for themselves. Some people will respond by a feeling of irritation and by asking, "Why don't they finish the story?" But some response is almost bound to occur.

Reading or listening to a lecture is a continual series of such "responding-to-ideas" episodes. Each statement in the book or lecture acts on us in some way and typically makes us respond by thinking of something else. Very often upon hearing the first part of a sentence we respond by guessing what the rest of the sentence is going to be or by completing the sentence by ourselves. When listening to a very slow or deliberate speaker, we often find ourselves running ahead of him. We may even be tempted to complete the sentence for him. Perhaps, by the way, we could utilize this tendency of the reader to get ahead of the text. We could merely write the first part of a sentence and leave the student to

---------------------.

We do not, of course, always respond to a statement by guessing the next statement. Perhaps, in fact, this is only a very elementary, unimportant way of responding. Other types of responses or associations are perhaps much more important. When we read of Napoleon's invasion of Russia, for instance, we may respond by thinking of Hitler's invasion of Russia. Or upon reading of a serious flood, we may think of the conditions which brought it on or means of avoiding it in the future. When we hear of a new invention we may respond by thinking of the changes it will bring about. When Milton has us read about music which

> Drew iron tears down Pluto's cheek
> And made Hell grant what Love did seek

he intends us to respond by thinking of the Orpheus legend. We may fail, of course, to respond in this very appropriate way. We may merely respond by wondering what Pluto has to do with it or by wondering what the author is driving at. But the latter response is clearly not the intention of the author.

An enormous part of the school's work consists of establishing appropriate responses to situations such as that taken from Milton. To a great extent, the school tries to establish connections between ideas. The school hopes that as a result of its work the student will come to respond to a given idea by thinking of a cluster of other ideas or by feeling all over again an emotion he has experienced before. We hope that when the youngster encounters the word Thermopylae he will think of a small band holding back a huge army, of Sparta, of Leonidas, of heroism, perhaps of the general idea of sacrifice for one's country. When the little child hears someone say, " 'I won't,' said the pig," we hope some remnants of a whole story will race through his mind and that perhaps he may smile in the warmth of his recognition. We hope that when the older student hears of a Machiavellian principle he will respond by thinking of a cluster of ideas or attitudes attributed to that theorist. We try to arrange connections so that when our older student sees $ax^2 + bx + c = 0$ he will respond by thinking of $x = \dfrac{-b \pm \sqrt{b^2 - 4\,ac}}{2a}$, or that $y = a + k \log x$ will make him visualize a series of curves all having some common properties. We may try to ensure that when he hears of size constancy he will think of an object receding in space and yet retaining its apparent size. Nor should we neglect those magic words like Pickwick, Quixote, Sidney Carton, or John Silver which we hope will elicit a smile, a warm feeling of amusement, a mild shudder, or the quiet hush of remembered fear.

Since so much of our work consists of connecting idea to idea, we should not hesitate to make sure that much of the student's activity is of this ideational sort. We should not be afraid of giving him a great deal of experience with ideas in the form of written or spoken symbols and words.

Whenever we do arrange that students will have experience with written or spoken words, we should try to be sure they are really responding to the essential ideas in the material and not merely responding to incidental and irrelevant items in the room or in their own heads.

Responsibility of Lecturer. In securing responses to spoken material, the teacher quite frequently has almost the entire responsibility. If he is doing the talking he must arrange and present his material so as to secure a series of definite and relevant silent responses from as many students as possible. If his is a discussion class he must try to direct discussion so that it elicits a maximum of relevant responses, oral and silent, from as many students as possible.

To understand the problems facing the lecturer, we must remember that lecturing does not consist of telling people things which they are to remember. Lecturing consists of holding an idea in front of people so that it acts on them and elicits a series of reactions. By thus holding an idea before people and getting them to react to it, the lecturer may be able to get them to react in the right way. With this aim in view, he keeps the idea working on them. They keep on reacting. Ultimately they may come to react in a way which makes sense, or which lines up with their previous ideas.

The good lecturer must allow for the many silent responses which are being made to his remarks. When he introduces a novel idea (and surely many of the ideas he introduces will be somewhat novel) he should not pass over this idea too quickly. He should linger over it, repeat it in slightly different words, state it this way and state it that way, and dwell on it for some time. By thus holding the idea before the students for a considerable length of time, and holding it before them in a stimulating way, he not only gives them time to make several reactions to the idea but, when he is good, he actually impels them to make these reactions. One of these responses has a chance of being the right one.

It is most important that the speaker should have the knack of thus lingering over ideas. If he merely announces an idea which to him seems elementary and axiomatic and then rushes on to some new point, his listeners may be still stumbling around reacting to the first idea while he is talking about something else.

Responsibility in Leading a Discussion. Offhand one might suspect that the leader of a discussion group had little need to worry about a student blundering around with silent reactions. If a student makes his responses out loud, the teacher can tell immediately if he is wrong and can proceed to straighten him out, rather than let him struggle along by himself. Although this fact brings some advantages, it is not an unmixed blessing. The student's oral remark is not merely a private communication between this student and the teacher. The student's overt announcement of his erroneous idea will also act on the other students and in so doing may induce a wide variety of silent reactions on their part. A student who is completely off the track may, by his oral response, lead other students still further astray and may confuse them so much that it is beyond the power of the ordinary instructor to bring them back. When we recollect the inevitable irrelevant reactions set up by many "contributors" to discussions, the possibility of distraction is truly alarming. And these irrelevant and distracting comments are exceedingly hard to control. The typical instructor may find it easier to control the many silent reactions of his listeners when he is doing most of the talking. In other words, the typical instructor may be better at lecturing than at directing discussion.

Comparison of Lecture and Discussion Method. The suggestions just advanced should make us think twice before we automatically assume that all lecturing is bad teaching and all class discussions are good. Even more important than our casual suggestion are the experimental investigations(38) in this field. These investigations show no clear superiority for the discussion method. Some studies find no general difference between the two methods but suggest a superiority of the lecture method for bright students and a corresponding superiority for the discussion method for dull students(39). Other studies find straight lectures or a combination of two-lectures-one-quiz-period to be better than straight discussion(40). In general there is no apparent difference between straight lectures and the lecture-quiz arrangement(40, 41).

At this point we are merely concerned with the presentation of academic material and are interested in the academic mastery that comes from the two types of presentation. In Chapter 18 we turn to the influence of the democratic or student-centered approach, as opposed to the autocratic or subject-centered approach. At that point we are also interested in these approaches as they affect the group process or the students' satisfaction in group work.

From this viewpoint of straight academic mastery, it appears that the discussion method is not demonstrably better than the lecture method. It is, of course, not markedly inferior. Consequently, if a teacher *prefers* to use the discussion method he should feel free to do so. He should not, however, feel especially virtuous in so doing.

If the teacher does use the discussion method he should lead each student to participate in the discussion. Granted that the discussion method is to be used, it has been shown(42) that the participating students will profit more than the students who merely listen to the discussion. This, of course, does not contradict the results which show that absence of student discussion may be better than, or equal to, any student discussion. The combined results suggest that (a) listening to the instructor is good for the student, (b) talking is good for him, (c) listening to other students is less effective.

Drill

The term *drill* has an old-fashioned sound, and there is an entirely proper reluctance to use it in place of *understanding* or *insight*. After a degree of understanding has been attained, however, and when mistakes are unlikely, there is no reason why a certain amount of drill should not be in order. As we have seen, motivation may be made fairly intense at this stage. If the student can know his successes and his failures, the practice should work. Short, lively drills can be interesting and even pleasant. If use of drill is coupled with use of other devices, it seems an excellent vehicle for developing skill in many subjects(43).

Factors Affecting the Efficiency of Practice

Sensory Avenue

Many people have marked preferences for one sensory mode over the other. Some people believe that they can learn better if they listen to the material that is to be learned. Other people feel uncomfortable while listening to oral presentations and feel the need of seeing the material.

Preferences such as these probably arise from the fact that auditory presentation has social aspects which are pleasant and reassuring to some people but disturbing to others. Other incidental aspects of the methods may influence preference.

Preferences must not be taken as a gauge of efficiency, since experiments show no great superiority of any one sensory avenue over the other. The differences are very slight and are not always consistent from one experiment to another.

When adults are learning nonsense syllables, or other rote material, each student studying by himself, the following rules seem to hold:

1. Visual learning is perhaps more efficient than any other single sense avenue.
2. It is about a tossup whether combined visual-auditory presentations are better than visual alone.
3. When the learner recites the material aloud, the results are usually better than when he merely reads it or listens to it.

When adults are learning short prose selections and several people are studying in the same room, either visual presentations or a combination of visual and auditory presentation is most efficient. The auditory sense avenue alone is slightly less efficient.

When adults are studying extended lecture material it makes no difference whether they read the material or hear it delivered in lecture form(44).

When children study extended material, they learn more effectively through listening. The results are slightly less favorable when they read the material(40).

From all this the most important conclusion would seem to be that, since the differences are so slight and so undependable, the teacher should feel free to use either auditory or visual presentation, choosing the method which is more convenient.

Amount of Material

In rote learning the difficulty of the task increases much more rapidly than the length of the task. If we can learn twelve nonsense syllables in $1\frac{1}{2}$ minutes, we cannot expect to learn twenty-four nonsense syllables in 3 minutes. It is more likely that we shall need 5 minutes for this longer task. This tendency of the longer task to require disproportionately more time also holds in learning difficult mazes and in the solution of certain kinds of puzzles.

The learning of meaningful material, on the other hand, does not follow the same simple rule. It is true that doubling the amount of material usually more than doubles the length of time required to learn the material. But it does not always double the *number of trials* required. After a certain point has been passed, an increase in length may bring about less than a proportional increase in difficulty. Lyon(45) found that whereas the memorization of 10,000 words of prose required 4200 minutes, the memorization of 15,000 required only 5500 minutes. If the increased difficulty had been in strict proportion, the longer task would have required 6300 minutes.

The Course of Practice

Practice is necessary for learning. But is practice uniformly effective? Will practice show its effect from the very first, or will some time elapse before its influence is felt? Will practice continue to be effective for an indefinite time, or will we reach a point when no amount of practice will produce further improvement? These are questions which occur to us when we try to work out any program of practice for ourselves or for our students.

The story of Helen Keller's mastery of language provides an interesting account of the course of practice. For a long period Helen's teacher worked hard but secured no appreciable results. Helen's understanding of language remained practically nil. Then one day she gained an understanding of one word, the word "water" spelled into her hand by her teacher. This represented a measurable increase in skill. This word also acted as a terrific stimulus. Still more important, it pointed the way to an extremely valuable guiding principle. The pressures put into her hand by the patient teacher took on a tremendous new significance. *These were names.*

The learning of this one word helped in the learning of other words. Hence the rate of progress quickened. Originally many hours of practice had produced mastery of only one word. Now a few hours resulted in the mastery of many words. Many of these words in turn acted as tools which aided the learning of still other words. This results in a certain snowballing effect in which each dose of practice makes the succeeding dose more effective.

The first diagram in Figure 10-1 shows what would happen if we followed the learning through this stage of *increasing returns* and stopped there.

It is unlikely, however, that this snowballing effect could continue indefinitely. After a time most of the tool words would be learned and when that happens each word will merely be added to the total. While this is going on we might very well encounter a period of *equal returns* in which each additional period of practice would add the same amount to the score. This is shown in the section *BC* on the graph.

If the learning proceeds for a long time, we should expect that this period of equal returns will often give way to a period of decreasing returns. We cannot go on increasing our skill indefinitely. There must come a time when we shall reach our peak. When this time is reached we can expect little if any return from further hours of practice. Helen Keller, for instance, must have reached a point when, in spite of all her practice, her mastery of the language merely remained constant. This period of decreasing returns is shown by the portion *CD* in the graph.

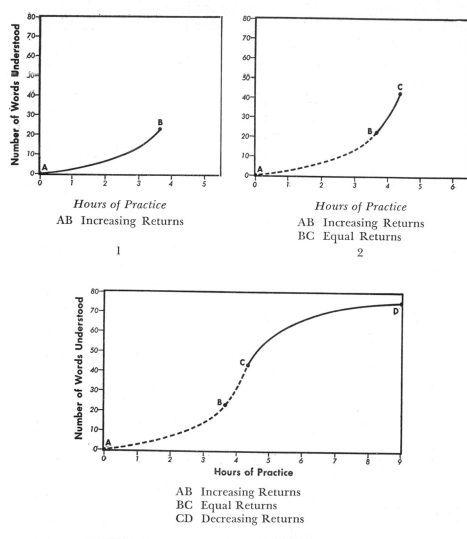

Hours of Practice
AB Increasing Returns

1

Hours of Practice
AB Increasing Returns
BC Equal Returns

2

AB Increasing Returns
BC Equal Returns
CD Decreasing Returns

FIGURE 10-1. *Theoretical Graph of Improvement with Practice*

Observed Graphs of Learning

This theoretical graph that we have plotted in Figure 10-1 may some times actually appear. It has been observed in some conditioned-response experiments, and, occasionally when animals or people are learning to make difficult discriminations(46). These are exceptions, however. For the most part this complete curve is the exception rather than the rule. It is likely to appear only when we start from the very first and continue the practice for an extended period.

Conditions Making for Special Types of Graphs

If a student started some task that was quite new and stopped after a very short time, we might readily get a graph corresponding to the *AB* section in our general graph. This would show increasing returns (positive acceleration) throughout. This sort of curve is likely to appear when the whole task is limited. In learning the names of the people in a small class, for instance, there is such a limit. When you have learned the (say) fifteen names, that particular task is over. In this case, moreover, after you have learned most of the names, there are fewer names left to guess at, and the last few names and faces are more quickly matched. Here we might readily get a graph consisting of increasing returns throughout. If we were to extend the task, however, so that you now had several hundred names to learn, you could not expect the phenomenon of increasing returns to continue indefinitely.

A graph showing sudden or increasing returns is likely to appear when the task consists chiefly in "catching on" to a single idea. Here we may go suddenly from complete bafflement to almost complete understanding. It has been suggested(47), by the way, that the fairly smooth graphs that we frequently observe could really be made up of a great many smaller graphs of the all-or-none sort.

Suppose, for some reason, we were not able to get a record of the learning until much practice had taken place. If we began to keep our record, for instance, after the learner had reached point *C* in the graphs, we would get a graph showing *decreasing returns throughout*. Starting at *C* we would find a fairly rapid rise, followed by increases that became more and more gradual from then on.

Very often we do, in effect, start to observe the learning after much prior "practice" has taken place. The student may not have had any actual experience in typing, but he has had much experience in looking at words or letters and in using his fingers. These things may *transfer* to the new task and he can use these previously learned things in the early trials.

We are also likely to get a graph showing decreasing returns throughout, the *CD* portion in Figure 10-1, if the student is able to learn the easy parts of the task first. Sometimes he may try this deliberately, actually looking around for verses that are easy to remember, or for letter-key combinations that come easy. Even without trying, however, the easy items are likely to be mastered in the early trials, leaving the more difficult items for the later trials. Under these conditions it is natural that the student will learn more items in the early trials.

Plateaus and Their Causes

If learning extends over any considerable portion of time, there are likely to be periods where no progress can be noted. Practice may continue in the regular manner, but the achievement stays at the previous level. This level stretch in the graph of learning is called a *plateau.* These plateaus are by no means inevitable, but they occur with some frequency and deserve the attention of the prospective teacher. They may arise from any one of a number of causes.

Lack of Maturity. In some tasks sheer physical maturity is necessary for a high degree of skill. In typing, for instance, a certain hand span and degree of finger strength is necessary for the highest attainment. For this reason, a young child in practicing typing may reach a level beyond which he cannot proceed until he grows older.

Use of an Inefficient Method. A plateau may come from the fact that the method employed has reached the limit of its usefulness. Further progress will depend on acquiring a more efficient method of work. Children in learning to add, for instance, often count on their fingers. This is a fairly useful device in the early stages of learning, but it permits only a limited degree of progress. The student will not be able to go beyond a certain point as long as he retains this cumbersome device. The period during which he is learning to abandon this device would be represented as a plateau.

There are many other illustrations of methods of attack which work very well for moderate degrees of skill but which are of little use beyond a certain point. The two-finger system of typing is one such illustration. In learning to read, progress may be held up while the student is acquiring the knack of seeing whole phrases instead of isolated words. In studying a foreign language, the improvement may stop until the student ceases to translate into English and learns to think directly in the foreign language.

Failure to Master a Vital Point. Upon first taking up a game such as tennis or badminton, a certain degree of improvement is inevitable. Later on, however, a dead level of achievement may be reached. Often any advance beyond this level depends on mastering some new crucial technique, such as learning the importance of regaining position after each play.

This problem may be even more marked in intellectual activities. In learning statistics we can make a certain amount of progress by slavishly following a few simple rules. Further reaches of attainment may be beyond us until we have mastered a few, perhaps only one or two, difficult concepts. While wrestling with those concepts, our graph of achievement would represent a plateau. As soon as we master the crucial concepts our achievement may suddenly shoot up to new heights.

Concentrating on Only One Aspect of a Complicated Task. According to some experimental work(48), plateaus may result from the tendency to neglect many features of a complicated task while concentrating on one troublesome feature. In playing a violin we may, for a time, concentrate entirely on the bowing and give little attention to the problems of fingering or of holding the violin or of keeping time. During this period, a plateau may appear in the record of achievement.

Boredom or Fatigue. Boredom is the first factor which most people think of as a probable cause of a plateau. Actually, however, the importance of boredom has been overrated. Any marked boredom must, of course, interfere with progress. But plateaus appear even when interest is intense. Actually the popular impression probably has the cart before the horse. Boredom is much more likely to be the result of a plateau than a cause of its occurrence. There is perhaps no surer guarantee of loss of interest than a long period of faithful practice which brings nothing in the way of returns. Anyone who persists on a dead level of attainment for a long period of time is almost bound to become discouraged.

Discouragement or loss of interest which arises from a plateau may be counteracted by calling attention to the long-term improvement. This is especially helpful if we have a record of improvement over a period of time. The student, reacting to the immediate past, is prone to say, "I am making no progress at all." If we have a record available we may be able to show him that although there has been little improvement during the very recent past, he is much farther ahead than he was several weeks or months ago.

Cessation of Growth

There is almost always an end to improvement if practice continues long enough. For some time the graph of learning will rise, but in almost any activity this cannot keep up forever. After a time the graph will reach a level which is not changed by a subsequent spurt.

What causes this cessation of improvement? There could be two reasons. It could be that after a great many practices and a great deal of effort, the student may reach his *physiological* limit. His fingers or limbs may move as fast as his nerves and muscles can function. If this happens, no amount of practice or effort can bring about further improvement.

The physiological limit just mentioned is very seldom reached. A few athletes may reach the stage where they run the 100-yard dash as rapidly as their nerves and muscles will let them. There may also be other activities which have been going on for a long time in which a few people attain the physiological limit. But this is very rare. Certainly most of us never even approach the physiological limit in our performance of any task.

For most of us the limit of attainment is a practical or a psychological limit. We reach a stage of efficiency which is acceptable to ourselves or to our superiors or our associates, and then we quit improving. Every one of us could greatly improve our ability to read, our speed of walking or bathing, the quality of our penmanship, or the purity of our diction. We could do these things, and we would do them if we had to. If some one, including ourselves, were to put "the heat on," we would reach new heights of attainment in any of these activities.

Practical Uses of Graphs of Learning

Graphs of learning may be used with great effectiveness as motives. A student who keeps a graph of his progress in typing should find much encouragement from the indication of growth which it provides. Such a graph also provides a mark to shoot at. It acts as a very effective form of objective knowledge of results. The student is constantly reminded of the score he has to beat. By using a graph as a motive, the student is encouraged to compete with his previous attainment. And as we mentioned before, any one of us has a fair chance of winning in a competition of this sort.

For the teacher there is a very important moral in any graph of learning like that in the *C-D* portion of Figure 10-1. These graphs tend to "level off" after a good deal of practice. In this stage of the curve, improvement is very costly. It takes a great deal of practice to produce a slight increase in skill or knowledge. In view of this fact, the teacher should ask himself just how much achievement is necessary or desirable. Exceptional skill in penmanship or in adding can be attained. But the last increments of skill are extremely costly. Perhaps, in these tasks, a reasonable modicum of skill would suffice for most students.

Cautions in Interpreting the Role of Practice

Practice is an important aspect of the learning process. It is also one aspect that comes readily to the teacher's hand. Of all the tools of learning that we are to discuss, in fact, practice is probably the first device that anyone would think of. It is certainly a device that has been honored in the observance for thousands of years.

When considering a device that is so useful, so readily available, and so thoroughly supported by age-old tradition, we must be careful not to read too much into it. We must be on our guard lest a device with so much to recommend it should oversell itself. Actually, practice is only one of a number of instruments which play a part in the learning process. Some of these additional instruments are absolutely necessary if learning is to take place. There are others which may not be completely essential but which are so helpful that we would be most foolish to ignore them. All in all, practice is likely to be ineffective unless other devices, either through good luck or through deliberate arrangement, are also brought into operation.

It is easy to make the mistake of thinking that, since *some* practice is necessary, more practice should be correspondingly better. Very frequently this has proved not to be the case. Over and over we come across evidence that there is little relation between the *amount* of practice and the proficiency of students in reading, spelling, writing, or in English composition(49). This does not mean that all practice is wasted. It merely means that there may be no value in additional doses beyond a certain minimum.

Negative Practice. Very often people deliberately arrange to have an individual "practice" a tendency for the sole purpose of weakening the tendency. In more barbaric times, for instance, brutal fathers were known to encourage their sons to practice smoking (preferably on an ancient pipe) for the sole purpose of weakening the tendency to smoke. Teachers have also forced students to "practice" throwing spit balls or to "practice" running up and down stairs or to "practice" chewing gum, again in the hope that the practice would lead to the elimination of the habit.

The late Professor Knight Dunlap suggested that negative practice might be valuable not only in discouraging small boys from smoking but in many other ways. He states that he eliminated the tendency to type "hte" for "the" by systematically practicing the error, realizing all the while that it was an error. We can imagine Professor Dunlap saying to himself in disgust, "All right! If you want to write 'hte,' go to it. Go ahead and write it over and over!" Professor Dunlap also advocated negative learning as a cure for thumb sucking, stammering, and other inconvenient habits.

There is as yet no clear-cut evidence on the relative value of negative practice(50). For correcting spelling errors, negative practice is just as valuable as positive practice. It has also proved useful in eliminating errors in piano playing, but it is impossible to say it is more useful or less useful than positive practice in this field.

These, then, are some of the cautions which must be kept in mind when considering practice as a tool in learning. It is a most valuable tool, but it is in no way self-sufficient. If it is to be effective, it must be used in conjunction with other tools. It is also a two-edged tool. It can be used to strengthen habits or to demolish them, again depending on the other instruments that operate along with it.

Summary

In helping the student to find better ways to solve problems or to perform other activities, the teacher must make sure that the student has consistent experience or practice with the problems. To make sure that the student continues to apply himself to the problems, the teacher uses various kinds of motivations. The motive is applied to increase the student's immediate output, performance, or effort. It is also applied in the hope that more vigorous performance will lead to better learning. Intention to learn, while not absolutely essential to learning, greatly boosts performance and is the simplest motive to use. A program of frequent testing may boost output in the high school but has not proved so effective in college. Even in the high school the test should not come too often. Once a week is better than once a day. When students can observe the objective results of their performance, their output will be increased. The value of praise and blame is still in doubt, although blame may be of more value for immediate output. Social facilitation, scrutiny by others, and competition will increase speed but may not improve quality of performance.

Intrinsic motives are less precarious than extrinsic motives. Among the intrinsic motives we can list the need to manipulate, the need to achieve, and the need to make a success out of life. There is a vigorous dispute regarding the precise part played by motivation. By one means or another, however, it will contribute to efficiency in learning.

Distraction, especially mild distraction, is not always harmful. It may merely elicit greater effort. Unaccustomed distraction and meaningful distraction are more disturbing than mere noise, especially if the noise is not a new experience.

Practice may take many forms. Even imaginary practice may help at times. Certainly practice need not always involve violent physical activity. Much of the activity necessary for learning takes place while the student is reading or listening. To secure adequate practice in these activities, the teacher requires special skill. The old-fashioned drill is still a useful device for many types of practice. The efficiency of practice is perhaps not greatly dependent on the sense avenue used. As the length of the task is doubled the amount of practice must be more than doubled.

In any extended learning, improvement will occur slowly at first. It should occur at an increasingly rapid rate after a few successes and then should taper off as later practices lose effectiveness. Very often this theoretical graph does not appear. It is replaced by a graph which is negatively accelerated throughout. This is likely to occur if a great deal of learning has taken place before observation begins or if the student has had practice in similar problems before or if he is permitted to learn the easy items first. Graphs which are positively accelerated throughout may occur if the task to be learned is quite novel and if an arbitrary perfect score may be achieved in a few trials.

SPECIFIC REFERENCES

1. Farber, I. E. The role of motivation in verbal learning and performance. *Psychol. Bull.*, 1955, *52*, 311–327.
2. Porter, E. H., Jr. The influence of delayed instructions to learn upon human performance. *J. exp. Psychol.*, 1938, *23*, 633–640.

3. Stevenson, H. W. Latent learning in children. *J. exp. Psychol.*, 1954, *47*, 17–21.

4. Saltzman, I. J. The orienting task in incidental and intentional learning. *Amer. J. Psychol.*, 1953, *66*, 593–597.

5. Simon, C. W., and Emmons, W. H. Learning during sleep? *Psychol. Bull.*, 1955, *52*, 328–342.

6. McGeoch, J. A. *The psychology of human learning.* Longmans, 1942, Chap. 7.

7. Aborn, M. The influence of experimentally induced failure on the retention of material acquired through set and incidental learning. *J. exp. Psychol.*, 1953, *45*, 225–231.

8. Pepitone, Emmy A. B. Responsibility to the group and its effects on the performance of its members. *Dissertation Abstracts*, 1952, *12*, 223.

9. Alper, Thelma G. Task-orientation vs. ego-orientation in learning and retention. *Amer. J. Psychol.* 1946, *59*, 236–248.

10. Sutton, Rachel S. Improvement of reading skills through the preparation of materials. *J. educ. Res.*, 1954, *47*, 467–472.

11. Sarason, S. B., and others. The effect of differential instructions on anxiety and learning. *J. abnorm. soc. Psychol.*, 1952, *47*, 561–565.

12. Noll, V. H. The effect of written tests upon achievement in college classes: An experiment and a summary of evidence. *J. educ. Res.*, 1939, *32*, 335–358.

13. Fitch, Mildred L., and others. Frequent testing as a motivating factor in large lecture classes. *J. educ. Psychol.*, 1951, *42*, 1–20.

14. Mason, J. M., and Angell, G. W. An experiment in evaluation in biological science. *J. educ. Psychol.*, 1953, *44*, 296–304.

15. Gable, Sister Felicita. The effect of two contrasting forms of testing upon learning. *Johns Hopk. Univ. Stud. Educ.*, No. 25, 1936.

16. Weiden, Sister Robertine. The effect of checked directed study upon achievement in ninth grade algebra. *Johns Hopk. Univ. Stud. Educ.*, No. 34, 1945.

17. Angell, G. W. Effect of immediate knowledge of quiz results on final examination scores in freshman chemistry. *J. educ., Res.*, 1949, *42*, 391–394.

18. Schmidt, H. O. The effects of praise and blame as incentives to learning. *Psychol. Monogr.*, 1941, *53*, No. 240.

19. Grace, Gloria L. The relation of personality characteristics and response to verbal approval in a learning task. *Genet. Psychol. Monogr.*, 1948, *37*, 73–103.

20. Thompson, G. G., and Hunnicutt, C. W. The effect of repeated

praise or blame on the work achievement of "introverts" and "extroverts." *J. educ. Psychol.*, 1944, *35*, 257–266.

21. Potter, E. H. The effect of reproof in relation to age in school children. *J. genet. Psychol.*, 1943, *63*, 247–258.

22. Lazarus, R. S., and others. The effects of psychological stress upon performance. *Psychol. Bull.*, 1952, *49*, 293–317.

23. Mandler, G., and Sarason, S. B. A study of anxiety and learning. *J. abnorm. soc. Psychol.*, 1952, *47*, 166–173.

24. McClelland, D. C., and others. *The achievement motive.* Appleton-Century-Crofts, 1953.

25. Murchison, C., ed. *Handbook of social psychology.* Clark University Press, 1935, Chap. 23. Experimental studies of the influence of social situations on the behavior of individual human adults (Dashiell, J. F.).

26. Wapner, S., and Alper, Thelma G. The effect of an audience on behavior in a choice situation. *J. abnorm. soc. Psychol.*, 1952, *47*, 222–229.

27. Maller, J. B. Coöperation and competition. *Teach. Coll. Contr. Educ.*, No. 384, 1929.

28. Mintz, A. Non-adaptive group behavior. *J. abnorm. soc. Psychol.*, 1951, *46*, 150–159.

29. Leuba, C. J. A preliminary experiment to quantify an incentive and its effects. *J. abnorm. soc. Psychol.*, 1930, *25*, 275–288.

30. Hilgard, E. R., and Russell, D. H. Motivation in school learning. *Yearb. nat. soc. Stud. Educ.*, 49 (I), 1950, 36–68.

31. Lowell, E. L. The effect of need for achievement on learning and speed of performance. *J. Psychol.*, 1952, *33*, 31–40.

32. Harlow, H. F. Mice, monkeys, men, and motives. *Psychol. Rev.*, 1953, *60*, 23–32.

33. Harlow, H. F., and McClearn, G. E. Object discrimination learned by monkeys on the basis of manipulation motives. *J. comp. physiol. Psychol.*, 1954, *47*, 73–76.

34. Cason, H. The influence of attitude and distraction. *J. exp. Psychol.*, 1938, *22*, 532–546.

35. Poffenberger, A. T. *Principles of applied psychology.* Appleton-Century, 1942, Chap. 7.

36. Mech, E. V., and others. The effects of "set" on group performance under strong auditory stimuli. *J. Psychol.*, 1953, *36*, 187–194.

37. Coleman, J. C. Results of a "total-push" approach to remedial education. *Elem. Sch. J.*, 1953, *53*, 454–458.

38. Ruja. H. Experimenting with discussion in college teaching. *Educ. Admin. Sup.,* 1953, *39,* 321–342.

39. Gerberich, J. R., and Warner, K. O. Relative instructional efficiencies of the lecture and discussion methods in a university course in American National Government. *J. educ. Res.,* 1936, *29,* 574–579.

40. Stroud, J. B. Experiments on learning in school situations. *Psychol. Bull.,* 1940, *37,* 777–807.

41. Longstaff, H. P. Analysis of some factors conditioning learning and general psychology. *J. appl. Psychol.,* 1932, *16,* 9–48 and 131–166.

42. Walther, E. C. A study of participation in discussion as a factor in the learning of factual materials in social subjects. Unpublished dissertation, Johns Hopkins University, 1941.

43. Stroud, J. B. The role of practice in learning. *Yearb. nat. soc. Stud. Educ., 41* (11), 1942, 353–376.

44. Elliott, F. R. Memory for visual, auditory and visual-auditory material. *Arch. Psychol.,* N.Y., 1936, No. 199.

45. Lyon, D. O. *Memory and the learning process.* Warwick & York, 1917.

46. Adams, D. K., and others. Learning theory, personality theory, and clinical research (The Kentucky Symposium). Wiley, 1954, Chap. 1. Current interpretations of learning data and some recent developments in stimulus-response theory (Spence, K. W.).

47. Voeks, Virginia W. Acquisition of S-R connections: a test of Hull's and Guthrie's theories. *J. exp. Psychol.,* 1954, *47,* 137–147.

48. Kao, Dji-Lih. Plateaus and the curve of learning in motor skill. *Psychol. Monogr.,* 1937, *49,* No. 219.

49. Dressel, P., and others. The effect of writing frequency upon essay-type writing proficiency at the college level. *J. educ. Res.,* 1952, *46,* 285–293.

50. Peak, Helen. Negative practice and theories of learning. *Psychol. Rev.,* 1941, *48,* 316–336.

SUGGESTIONS FOR FURTHER READING

1. McClelland, D. C., ed. *Studies in motivation.* Appleton-Century-Crofts, 1955.

2. McGeogh, J. A., and Irion, A. L. *The psychology of human learning.* Longmans, 1952, Chap. 6.

3. Seward, J. P. Introduction to a theory of motivation in learning. *Psychol. Rev.,* 1952, *59,* 405–413.

4. Farber, I. E. The role of motivation in verbal learning and performance. *Psychol. Bull.,* 1955, *52,* 311–327.

5. Lazarus, R. S., Deese, J., and Osler, Sonia F. The effects of psychological stress upon performance. *Psychol. Bull.*, 1952, *49*, 293–317.

6. Hilgard, E. R., and Russell, D. H. Motivation in school learning. *Yearb. nat. soc. Stud. Educ.*, 49, (I), 1950, 36–68.

7. Adams, D. K., and others. Learning theory, personality theory, and clinical research (Kentucky Symposium). Wiley, 1954, Chap. 3. Motivational forces underlying learning (Harlow, H. F.).

8. Woodruff, A. D. Motivation theory and educational practice. *J. educ. Psychol.*, 1949, *40*, 33–40.

9. Deese, J. E. *Psychology of learning.* McGraw-Hill, 1952, Chap. 5.

Exercises and Questions for Discussion

1. Recall some class in which the teacher tried to get you interested in a subject. To what needs or interests did the teacher appeal? Was the appeal reasonably effective? Can you think of some other need that might have provided more effective motivation in your case?

2. Make a list of some of the important abilities, opinions, tendencies, and attitudes that you have *acquired* in the past few years. For each of these, ask yourself whether or not you intended to acquire this ability or opinion or attitude at the outset. If you had felt a clearer intention or determination, would your learning have been more effective? On what do you base your answer?

3. Outline a talk on "Motivating the Student by an Appeal to His Need for Vocational Success: Possibilities and Limitations."

4. What is your reaction to the results of the experiments on the lecture versus the discussion method? Suggest some hypotheses to account for these results. How could you test the truth of some of these hypotheses? Do you think that the type of examination has anything to do with the results? Describe a type of examination on which you would expect superior results from the students taught by the discussion method.

5. List some of the more frequent causes of plateaus: What are some of the probable consequences of an extended plateau? How can these consequences be avoided?

6. What are some of the advantages of having students keep a graphical record of their progress? Under what circumstances would you expect such a graph to show decreasing returns from the outset? Under what conditions would you expect the record to show no further improvement?

7. What is the physiological limit? How important is it in the work of the teacher?

8. Discuss the advantages and disadvantages of competition as a motive in producing immediate performance; in the development of long-term attitudes; in preparing for life as the student will face it.

11

Providing Guidance and Reinforcement

<hr>

$\mathbf{M}$OTIVATION AND EXPERIENCE, to be effective, must be supplemented by other important tools or mechanisms. Whenever motivation and experience seem self-sufficient, it is because, in the act of motivating, we may automatically supply these additional tools. The additional mechanisms that we stress are reinforcement, guidance, and insight. Guidance and reinforcement are discussed here and the mechanism of insight is treated in the next chapter.

The theoretical position of both reinforcement and guidance is considered at length in Chapter 9. Positive reinforcement occurs when a thirsty animal makes a response, encounters water, and reduces his thirst; or when a child in chronic need for affection pronounces a word correctly and is rewarded with a smile. Negative reinforcement occurs when there is no reward after the action, or when the action is followed by a painful experience or by an expression of disapproval. Guidance, in its most mechanical sense, is supplied when, through the principle of substitution, an animal is led to respond to a signal (the bell) in the same way that he usually responds to the main event (the meat powder); or when, through the same principle, a child is led to respond to the arrival of the family car in the same way that he used to respond to his father's call.

Interrelation between Reinforcement and Guidance

Reinforcement and *substitution* or *guidance,* it will be remembered, are closely linked together. Under natural circumstances, anything that provides reinforcement can very often provide some guidance as well. Consider, for instance, a very primitive kind of learning in which a child, walking across a field, hears a novel buzzing noise (S_1). He keeps on going but looks in the direction of the noise (R_1). In an instant he sees a snake coiled and threatening (S_2). Instantly he jumps back (R_2). In this illustration, the snake can readily provide negative reinforcement. The tendency S_1–R_1 might well be weakened and, in the future, the child might be less likely to keep on going when he hears the peculiar buzz. But the sight of the snake does not only provide negative reinforcement. It also forces the child to jump back. According to the theory of substitution, moreover, from this combination of events we should expect that in the future the child will jump back as soon as he hears the buzzing sound. The sight of the snake, that is to say, not only acts as reinforcement, but also forces or guides the child into a fairly adequate way of responding to the original signal.

In the schoolroom, as in raw nature, reinforcement and guidance or substitution often go hand in hand. A student, for instance, sees *ami* and hesitantly asks, "Friend?" The teacher replies, "That's right, friend." This comment may readily help by virtue of sheer reinforcement. Over and above this, however, the teacher's comment also forcibly points the way to the correct response and may lead the student to repeat, with more confidence, the word friend. Or, to take another case, suppose that a younger student has come across $3 \times 4 =$ and has replied "7." The teacher says, "No. It's 12." Here again we have negative reinforcement that may weaken the student's tendency to say "7," but we also have a definite cue from the teacher that, by virtue of substitution, guides the student into the correct response.

Although reinforcement and guidance or substitution tend to go hand in hand, things can be arranged so that either one of these comes to the fore and the other becomes less important. Upon hearing the student say "7," for instance, the teacher could merely say, "No." This would provide considerable negative reinforcement, but very little guidance. Or, conversely, the teacher of French could present a new word, *bijou* and, before the student had a chance to make any response whatever, could immediately say "jewel" and thus lead the student to echo "jewel." This sequence, by virtue of the substitution principle, should guide the student toward the correct reply. In this, however, there is little if any reinforcement since the student did not have time to make a response that could be reinforced.

To summarize, we can say that when we let nature take its course we shall find that anything that is done to provide reinforcement will very often provide some guidance as well; and that any guidance we offer will contain some element of reinforcement. By making special effort, however, we can invoke one of these forces and at the same time play down or minimize the role of the other.

Arranging for Reinforcement

Even when guidance or conditioned-response learning is kept to a minimum, reinforcement coupled with motivation and practice can bring about some learning. Suppose, for instance, I ask you to sketch an angle of 35 degrees, and for some reason you make the attempt. I merely say, "Right (or wrong). Try again." We keep this up. My comments are restricted to "Right" or "Wrong." I do not say, "Make it a little larger" or "Too small." But even without this guidance some learning would probably result. After many trials you would be closer to the standard.

There are many instances of learning in which guidance is kept to a minimum and in which learning proceeds chiefly from motivation, practice, and reinforcement. In one experiment(1), for instance, a little girl is told to find some candy which has been hidden behind a book in a library. The child proceeds to pick up one book after another. She picks up book A and finds no candy (bad results). She goes on, book B and no candy, book C and no candy, and finally she picks up book N and finds the candy (good results). The next time she does not go directly to book N but she goes in that general direction and makes only a few false moves before picking the right book. Ultimately, of course, she learns to go to the right book without any false moves.

Both of the examples just cited are illustrations of what is frequently called *trial-and-error* learning. The learning proceeds essentially from a series of trials, many of which lead to error (negative reinforcement) but some of which lead to success (positive reinforcement). Learning which depends exclusively on motivation, practice, and reinforcement is likely to result in such trial-and-error learning. In such learning there is no guidance toward the correct way of doing things. The learner is merely left to thrash around until he hits upon a way of behaving which brings fairly good results. Neither is there any attempt on the part of the observer to help the student formulate or organize his ideas as he goes along. No one points out, "It is the fifth book from the dictionary."

Automatic Reinforcement. Fortunately there are many kinds of practice in which the necessary reinforcement is bound to occur, whether the teacher does anything about the situation or not. Such automatic or inevitable reinforcement is often found in the schoolroom. A student in learning to type, for instance, usually knows when he strikes the wrong key or when he strikes a second key before the first has returned. The student learning to drive an automobile can easily distinguish between a correct and an incorrect release of the clutch. He is also reminded very forcibly of his error when he shifts gears from first to reverse instead of from first to second. A student of music who has any ear at all can tell when he has played the wrong note. Similarly, in an endless number of activities the correct and incorrect reactions will bring about striking differences in reinforcement.

It is not only in acts of bodily skill that effects may be automatic and striking. In solving a mathematical problem, for instance, it is often obvious that we are on the wrong track. In translating from a foreign language, a mistake may reveal itself by the failure of the subsequent context to make sense. We can tell that we must have made a mistake somewhere. This is also true in ordinary reading. An erroneous interpretation of a word or phrase will produce the effect of confusion or nonsense or the feeling that something is amiss.

Casual Reinforcement. Very often the teacher will apply the appropriate effect with no effort whatever. If the pupil makes an incorrect response the teacher's eyebrows may rise, or an expression of surprise or annoyance may cross his face. In addition to these subtle expressions of concern, he is often impelled to make some comment. Conversely, the teacher's facial expression often shows a child that the answer is correct.

The teacher, of course, is not the only one who reacts unconsciously or spontaneously to the responses which occur in the classroom. The other students inevitably indicate their attitude by a variety of expressions. These may include the guffaws or snickers which greet a real boner or the violent shaking of hands offering to supply the right answer or a quiet acceptance of a proper response.

The More Deliberate Application of Reinforcement. The teacher should welcome the automatic or casual effects which supply the necessary reinforcement for many tendencies. He should not, however, rely entirely on such casual reinforcement. An important part of his work is to see that, as far as possible, fruitful effects are applied whenever necessary. It is not difficult, for instance, to use verbal commendation or correction whenever it is in order. We do this spontaneously for many kinds of behavior. We can do so deliberately after any behavior sequence which should be encouraged or discouraged. As a further means of securing adequate reinforcement, the teacher can arrange for the use of self-correction devices. The "answers" in the back of textbooks represent such self-corrective devices. Standards of handwriting may be employed in a similar manner.

In addition to the familiar self-checks, many teachers use mechanical devices to enable the student to learn how well he is getting along. Teachers of speech or of foreign language record the student's oral efforts and play them back to him. Teachers of physically handicapped children often employ mirrors or moving pictures to enable a student to see how well he is getting along. The self-marking tests described in earlier sections also enable a student to know immediately whether his response is right or wrong(2).

Immediate Reinforcement Is Best. Experiments have shown that reinforcement which follows immediately after a behavior sequence is more effective than reinforcement which is delayed for a few seconds(3, 4, 5). This does not prove, of course, that effects which are delayed forty-eight hours are less effective than effects which are applied within twenty-four hours(6). In general, however, it is wise to make sure that corrections or other reinforcements are applied as soon as possible. Practice work done under the eye of the teacher should be advantageous from this point of view.

It happens that the automatic or casual effects tend to be applied with very little delay. The teacher's smile or frown or look of bewilderment is almost immediate. So too are the snickers of the fellow pupils or the frantic rush of hands to offer a correct answer for the error just committed. It is most fortunate that these minute-by-minute reinforcements are applied so promptly, for they make up a very large part of the school's instructional contribution.

Partial versus Regular Reinforcement. Under laboratory conditions, we can if we wish make sure that every single response is reinforced. In the schoolroom and in the home, however, this is often quite impossible. Many of the activities may take place when we are not around to apply any reinforcement. In many kinds of learning, some of the responses may be silent or not observable.

What happens when only some of the responses are reinforced? In general, the rate of learning will be somewhat slower(7) under this partial reinforcement. Students will not learn quite so rapidly as they would if every act were reinforced. Under these circumstances, however, forgetting or extinction is reduced. Let us suppose, for instance, that every time Ralph turns on the starter of his car he hears the motor start (100-percent reinforcement). Pete, on the other hand, has tried to start his car about the same number of times but has been reinforced by hearing it start only about half the time (50 percent reinforcement). Now, in our experiment, we arrange things so that neither car will start. How long will each boy continue to try to start the car before he gives up? The experiments show that we can expect more attempts from Pete, who has experienced partial reinforcement, than from Ralph. A habit acquired under partial reinforcement resists extinction more effectively, or extinguishes more slowly. If we wish a habit to persist through a period of discouragement, or no reinforcement, we should see that the habit is acquired under conditions of partial reinforcement(8).

As you might expect, learning theorists have been quite concerned about the fact that partial reinforcement makes for more resistance to extinction. Offhand, it would seem that Hullian theory would expect a stronger habit from 100-percent reinforcement. Each additional reinforcement should add something to the strength of the habit, and the stronger habit should be able to resist extinction. There have been many attempts to reconcile these facts with Hullian theory but as yet the results have not produced much agreement.

Tolman, of course, should expect more permanent results from partial reinforcement. According to his theory, Pete comes to "expect" that the car will start some of the time but not all the time. A long series of failures would not greatly disturb this expectation and Pete would be expected to continue to act on it. Ralph, on the other hand, has come to expect results every time. The first few failures would violently upset his expectation and might readily lead to the expectation that the car will not start at all without some repair.

Skinner pays little attention to theory under any circumstances. He has been greatly interested in partial reinforcement, however, and has worked out *reinforcement schedules* that will keep an animal responding at a high rate with very little reinforcement.

Arranging for Guidance or Conditioned-response Learning

In the field of learning, guidance refers to any arrangement whereby the learner is led, or directed, or forced into correct behavior. Guided learning is distinguished from *trial-and-error: reinforcement* learning in which the learner flounders around until he stumbles upon the correct way of doing things. The conditioned response represents the most primitive and mechanical form of this kind of guidance. It is not the sort of guidance by which we seek to make the learner understand or comprehend. We merely force him to make the correct response. If we want the dog to salivate when he hears a whistle, we merely find something that is sure to make him salivate and then apply that unconditioned stimulus after he has heard the whistle.

To use the elementary form of guidance which is found in the conditioned response, we need merely to follow a rather simple rule. If you want to make sure that a student will make a certain response, R, whenever he encounters a situation, S_1, you must first find some other situation, S_2, which will force him to make the response, R, or which will guide him toward making this response. Then you must present S_1 and follow it with S_2.

Such is the simple rule stated in abstract terms. Now, consider a few actual examples. You want the child to say "cat" when he sees the symbols $c\ a\ t$. First, find something which is already adequate to make him say "cat." Perhaps the sight of a real cat will do. Perhaps a picture of a cat. Perhaps, if you are tired or if your ingenuity is at a low ebb, a simple request, "Say 'cat,'" will do. Now you must first of all present the symbols $c\ a\ t$ and then present the stimulus which you have chosen to force him or lead him to say "cat." Present the symbols $c\ a\ t$, then a picture of a cat. This is teaching according to the principles of the twentieth-century conditioned reflex. Such is progress.

You want the student to think *now* when he sees the French word *maintenant*. Formula: find some situation which is already capable of making him think *now*. Perhaps, if you do not mind being obvious or hackneyed, the English word *now* will do. Present the word *maintenant* and an instant later present the word *now*. Do this several times and he will think *now* whenever he sees *maintenant*.

You want the student to smile rather than sulk when he has been defeated in a game. Find something which you know will lead him to smile (perhaps a jolly approach on your part) and apply this as soon as he has experienced defeat.

The political candidate wants the voter to feel well disposed whenever he hears the name *Senator Fearing*. He must find something that is already capable of making the voter feel good and arrange that this magic something will act on the voter after he hears the name *Fearing*.

The form of guidance just discussed is very mechanical and arbitrary. The guidance is very positive. We almost force the student to make the correct response. We try to find some situation which will leave him no alternative. This rather rigid guidance, of course, is only one kind of guidance and the most primitive kind at that. No teacher would limit himself to guidance as mechanical as this.

But do not disdain this simple form of guidance just because it is primitive and rather arbitrary and trite. In many simple activities, such as learning a new vocabulary or in a number drill or in learning to spell, this rather simple method of guidance will prove very effective.

Classroom Adaptions of Conditioned-response Guidance

The teacher is by no means restricted to the arbitrary form of guidance provided by the simple conditioned-reflex formula. There are many additional procedures which are much more elaborate and which are less rigid. These more elaborate and more flexible devices, however, incorporate the basic principle of conditioned-response guidance. They point the way to the correct behavior, or they lead the student toward a better way of doing things. By means of these devices, we take some steps to prevent the student from merely floundering along on his own.

Manual Guidance or Tuition. When a student is learning to write or to draw or to use an instrument of any kind, the teacher may provide ordinary physical guidance. The teacher may place the pencil in the student's hand so that he holds it properly. Or he may move the student's hand so as to form the letter correctly. He may help guide the saw. In teaching physical education, he may move the student's body to a position which gives a more adequate posture. When students in a laboratory are learning a pencil maze, the experimenter may take the learner's hand and guide it around the correct path. These are merely illustrations of what is meant by manual guidance. These procedures do not always bring about good results(9). Sometimes this mechanical guidance is extremely irksome to the subject. There are other times, as we shall see, when guidance of any sort is of little use.

Rereading of Material To Be Memorized. When material has finally been memorized a whole host of tendencies or habit units have been formed. When, for instance, we hear, "Mary had a little lamb," we are led to think, "Its fleece was white as snow." One idea suggests the other. The question is, how to use guidance in forming these associations or tendencies. It happens that the simple process of rereading the material provides perfect guidance. If, after reading the first line, we immediately proceed to read the second line, we are getting a maximum of guidance. We are being led to make the correct response to the first line. On the other hand, if we covered up the second line, we would be deprived of that guidance. Theoretically our next response could be anything in the way of a guess. With the line uncovered there is no guess but almost perfect guidance.

Learning Vocabulary by Looking Rather than Guessing. In learning a vocabulary list, a student will get the maximum amount of guidance if, after looking at the foreign word, he looks immediately at the English word. In this way he will be prevented from making the wrong response. He will be guided into correct association for that particular foreign word.

Use of Rhetorical Questions. Teachers very frequently answer their own questions. This practice, of course, can be overdone and may even reach the stage of becoming an automatic mannerism. Nevertheless it is a form of guidance. The teacher asks the question. Before the student has a chance to give a wrong answer, the teacher provides the right answer, thus guiding the student inescapably toward the correct behavior. An instructor of aerial navigation, for instance, may ask, "What is that town off toward four o'clock?" Then, when the students are still frantically trying to identify the town from their maps, he may add, "It is obvious that this town must be Centerville. See how the railway comes in from the northwest, crossing a loop of the river on the two bridges."

Recitation in Unison. The ancient practice of having the whole class recite in unison provides a type of guidance. When any member of the class begins to falter he is bound to be guided back to the right path by the statements of the rest of the class. Each student is thus guided or forced to respond in conformity with the majority. Of course, if the majority should be wrong, this would provide guidance in the wrong direction.

The Overlapping of Guidance and Reinforcement

In an earlier section, we pointed out that it is difficult to apply reinforcement without also providing some guidance. True enough, it can be done, but one must go to some trouble to arrange it. By the same token it is difficult to provide guidance without at the same time providing reinforcement. Let us think of the dog learning to salivate when he hears the sound of the whistle. In this illustration the meat powder was considered as guidance. It forced the dog to salivate which is, of course, what we want him to do when he hears the whistle. But, later on, this same meat powder will act as reinforcement. The dog will salivate as soon as he hears the whistle. At that stage the meat powder will come into the picture after the dog has salivated. Now, coming upon the heels of the response, the meat powder has become a type of reinforcement. If the dog has already salivated and the meat powder is then put into his mouth, we have a good result and the tendency to salivate will be strengthened. If, on the other hand, the salivation occurs but no meat powder follows, we would have a bad or useless condition, and the tendency to salivate would be weakened.

For the dog learning to salivate at the sound of the whistle, the meat powder can act either as guidance or as reinforcement. It can either point the way to a new kind of response, or it can confirm (or discourage) a response that has just been made. Which of these roles the meat powder assumes depends, of course, on the timing. If it is presented before the dog makes any response, it will act as guidance. If it is presented after the dog has made a definite response, it will act as reinforcement.

Just as the meat powder may act either as a guide or as reinforcement, so may the teacher's comment act in either capacity. When the students are learning a list of French words, for instance, the teacher can supply the new word immediately or he can wait for a short interval. If the teacher says, *"Maintenant,"* and immediately thereafter says, "Now," the English word can only act as guidance. If, however, the teacher says, *"Maintenant,"* hesitates a few seconds, and then says, "Now," the English word may act as reinforcement. Presumably during these few seconds, the students have silently guessed an English word, and the teacher's statement then merely confirms, or corrects, a response already made.

As in the vocabulary lesson, so also in many other activities, the teacher can switch from guided learning to reinforced learning merely by altering the timing of his comments. After posing a question in any subject, the teacher may rush in to give the answer before the students have a chance to make an incorrect answer. Here he is using a primitive form of guidance. Instead of rushing in with the answer, however, he may hesitate after he gives a question and may wait until the students have made silent reactions on their own. Here he is using a form of reinforcement. Often he may use this latter form of reinforcement in a straight lecture. He merely begins a statement, hesitates a few seconds (in which time the students may silently complete the sentence), and then finishes the statement. If the students have been stimulated to finish the statement for themselves, this would constitute a form of reinforcement.

Limitations of Guidance

Learning which is deprived of guidance, and which is reduced to sheer trial and error, appears to be a stupid, cruel, and perverse form of learning. And, in truth, one of the teacher's main tasks is to provide guidance and thus eliminate much of the unnecessary floundering around which characterizes trial-and-error learning. All in all, guided learning seems intelligent, humane, and civilized.

In considering these things, however, we must not be misled by the claims of gentility or niceness. The fact that guidance seems less brutal and more intelligent should not blind us to the harsh fact that guidance has limitations. It is very seldom that the student can be guided into perfection or even into acceptable proficiency. In almost all learning, there comes a stage when the student can improve only by a certain amount of trial and error on his own. We can guide his hand while he forms the letters, but we can help in this way only up to a point. After awhile he must try out different movements on his own, and, after a certain amount of blundering, he will come to produce letters which have a more acceptable appearance. Similarly, we can do much to guide the movements of the student swimmer. We can tap him when it is time to breathe. We can place his arms in this position or that. But before he becomes a skilled swimmer, he must flounder around a bit, trying this device and that, until he finally hits on a cue for breathing at the right time. For the student learning to speak in public, we can provide much guidance. We can signal him to use more gestures or to cut down on his gestures or to tell a joke or to launch into his final statement. But ultimately he must experiment on his own and try this method and that, getting different kinds of reinforcement from different approaches.

Guidance is a most valuable tool. But, like other valuable tools, there are times when it should be used and times when it should be laid aside.

The Different Treatment of Weak and of Strong Tendencies

As learning progresses, we find that tendencies change in strength. Some tendencies or ways of behaving become more strongly established. A large part of our task, of course, is to ensure just that. We want the student to be sure to think of *cat* when he sees *c a t*. Every time he sees

(x^2) (x^3), to take another example, we want him to think of x^5. As this goes on, of course, other tendencies are becoming weaker. The tendency to think of (x^2) (x^3) as x^6 should drop out. His tendency to say "Please help Billy and I" should change to a more grammatical request. This weakening process, however, will be largely ignored. We shall concentrate on the tendencies that are gradually getting stronger.

As tendencies become stronger and as ways of behaving become more definitely established, the task of the teacher changes markedly in character, and the methods to be used must change correspondingly. For weak tendencies, guidance is the rule. The teacher must point the way to the correct mode of behavior and must provide encouragement, confirmation, and reward. At this stage, it is unwise to force the student to guess. It is unwise to make him commit himself in flat-footed fashion. At this stage, almost any effective means of guidance or reassurance is permissible. At this stage, it is permissible to help the student cover his naked awkwardness by having the class recite in unison or supply the correct answer if the student is about to make a mistake.

In the final stages of learning, on the contrary, the teacher must give up this close guidance and must rely on reinforcement and trial-and-error learning. Now he must force the student to make some response. He must encourage the student to commit himself as to the answer, and he must stand ready to apply correction if that answer is in error.

Dealing with Weak Tendencies

Use Guidance. As the student begins to learn any given task, lavish guidance is the rule(10). Use the primitive guidance to be found in conditioned-response learning. When the student is about to encounter a *new* problem or a *new* situation, think up some way of guiding him into the correct way of responding to that problem and apply this guidance as soon as he encounters that new problem. In this stage, manual guidance(11) may help. In this stage, have him learn the French vocabulary by looking at both the French and the English words. Do not have him guess(12). At this stage, do not hesitate to use the rhetorical question. Ask the question and, before the students have a chance to "make a boner," answer the question yourself. When memorizing a poem, have the student reread the passage a few times before he tries to recite(13).

Whenever possible try to present the material so that only one reaction is likely or possible. In these early stages, there should be no room for doubt. In one experiment(14) students viewed lantern slides that were ambiguous enough to permit any one of several interpretations. Later

they saw the slides when they were so clear as to permit only one interpretation. But the initial chance for error continued to show its harmful
effects even after the ambiguity had been cleared up. It is especially important to avoid opportunity for error when we are dealing with students
who are tense, anxious, or highly motivated(15). Such students are very
likely to be handicapped when confronted with material in which errors
are apt to occur.

Reward rather than Punishment for Weak Tendencies. In the early
stages of learning, reward should be provided in liberal doses. This
injunction applies especially to the teaching of such arts as penmanship,
sketching, singing, acting, or the pronunication of foreign words. In
teaching of this kind, the teacher may provide stimulus and some very
general guidance. Specific guidance, however, is very difficult. It is hard
to find a dependable way to force an English-speaking student to pronounce *Töchter*. Because of the difficulty of providing precise guidance,
the teacher must merely wait patiently for the correct response to be
made. When this first timid, tentative, correct response does appear, the
teacher must make sure that it receives every encouragement. The more
weak or tenuous the underlying tendency, the more lavish should be the
praise or enthusiasm.

While waiting for the perfect response to appear, the teacher should
still be generous in his use of reward and encouragement. An early response which merely shows good intentions should receive definite commendation. By such commendation we are, at least, strengthening the
tendency to try or to make an effort.

It may be objected that such a profuse application of reward may
encourage a few undesired tendencies. This is true, but it should not give
us a great deal of concern. In the first place, the formation of such undesired tendencies is an almost inevitable aspect of learning. Such tendencies will be formed whether we apply lavish encouragement or not. In
the second place, we are not trying to develop perfection at this time.
We are merely trying to make sure that the learning is proceeding in the
desired general direction. Later on, we shall have opportunities to put the
student on a more precise course. A certain amount of refinement or
polishing off is always necessary in the later stages of learning, and at
that time we shall easily remove any errors we may have inadvertently
encouraged.

Punishment, unlike reward, is utterly useless in the early stages of learning. A punished response at this stage of the game, in fact, is just as likely
to reappear as a response which is ignored. Suppose, for instance, that

we have observed two very weak tendencies which happen to be incorrect. We discourage one of these and ignore the other. Now if we make a test tomorrow or the next day, we will probably find no difference in the strengths of these tendencies. The one we discouraged will be no weaker than the one we ignored. Both of them, of course, were almost as weak as they could be before the discouragement was applied. Consequently, it is not surprising that no further weakening occurs(16).

Although theoretically it is always desirable to ignore a weak, incorrect response, it may happen that it is impractical to do so. The practical situation may compel us to comment. The other students in a class, for example, may be surprised or bewildered if we accept an incorrect reply. A visiting supervisor might also be led to wonder. For our own satisfaction, however, we can remember that there is no real need to be over-zealous in stamping out errors, provided those errors are the result of weak and transitory tendencies.

Dealing with Strong Tendencies

As learning progresses and as tendencies acquire some degree of strength, the role of the teacher gradually changes. He ceases to act as the reassuring guide who practically forces the student into making the desired response. He must gradually assume the role of the quiz master who presents a situation or problem, who then demands an unaided reaction, and who finally approves or rejects the reaction which takes place.

In the later stages of learning, our instructor of aerial navigation will no longer come to the rescue of his students. He will no longer hasten to supply the answer and thus prevent the students from committing themselves to an error. Rather he will point out the town to be identified and will require each student to commit himself definitely to some decision. Preferably he will insist that the decision be in writing or in a form from which there is no later escape or compromise. He will do this in spite of the frenzied reluctance of the students to commit themselves definitely. When they have committed themselves, and only then, he will indicate whether or not the decision is correct.

The instructor in the illustration is using the trial-and-error plus reinforcement procedure. He insists on a clear-cut response to the question or the problem, and then he applies one kind of reinforcement to a correct response and another kind of reinforcement to a response which is wrong. In dealing with these stronger tendencies, there is little place for guidance. We find, for instance, that guidance provided for maze learning does little or no good in the later series of practices(17).

Employing Recitation in Memorizing. When a student first begins to memorize a selection of prose or poetry or a list of words, he employs the method of rereading. As soon as he has made any progress at all, however, he should abandon this method and force himself to try to recite. Perhaps as much as 80 percent of the total time available should be spent in attempted recitation(13). At first, much of this testing time will be spent in sheer effort to recall material which the student is sure he does not know. This effort, even if unfruitful, is valuable. Consequently, as soon as he has completed one or two readings of the material, the student should adopt some means of trying himself out. He can, for instance, close the book and force himself to try to recall as much of the material as possible. If a portion is a complete blank, he should go on to a part which he can recall and then go back to the vague portion. When he has recalled everything he can, he should check with the original material and then study the parts he has wrong or which he does not know. After a further short period of study, he should repeat the test.

The student will find this method of recitation extremely irksome. He will prefer to remain in the rereading phase for a long time. He would much rather go over and over the material than take a test or commit himself by guessing at the answer. By this reticence he shields himself from the unpleasant consequences which so often follow wrong guesses. This reticence is very natural for all of us. It is natural largely because the reinforcement which is necessary to weaken a tendency is unpleasant reinforcement. Consequently, whenever we are in doubt and thus face the possibility of making a wrong response, we tend to avoid committing ourselves. If the needed response is a written word, we tend to scribble it so that the crucial parts are illegible. If the response is to be spoken, we mumble it so that the listener can give us the benefit of the doubt. If we are called on to move a pawn or to play a card, we do so lingeringly or reluctantly, ready to retract hurriedly if some fleeting clue should suggest that we are wrong. If we must respond by an extended statement, we begin with meaningless generalities, frantically searching the listener's face the while for some hint of pleasure or displeasure.

These devices keep us from the unpleasant consequences which would follow outright erroneous responses. In this way they are undoubtedly valuable in actual life. It is obvious, however, that they interfere with the trial-and-error phase of learning. In the classroom, during the later stages of learning, the student should be encouraged to make his answer boldly and definitely and take the consequences. (The consequences in the classroom, unlike the consequences of real life, are seldom disastrous. They are merely unpleasant.) The unpleasant consequences from which these devices shield him constitute reinforcement, and this is the only medicine which will cure his erroneous tendencies. If his response is correct, the consequences will be pleasant and will strengthen the underlying tendency. If the response is wrong, the consequences will be unpleasant, and the tendency to make that response will be weakened.

The method of recitation or of making bold, overt statements can also be used in learning the names of people. The easy, and natural, method of learning the names of one's students in a class, for instance, is to call out the name and see who answers. This method, besides being congenial, is also efficient during the early trials. After a few such trials, however, we should use the method of recitation or trial and error. If we have the weakest hunch that this man's name is Smith we should look him boldly in the eye and say, "Smith." If we are right, we may feel a mildly pleasant effect and the hunch will be strengthened. If we are wrong, we will feel somewhat discomfited, and this erroneous hunch will be weakened.

Punishment or Verbal Correction for Strong but Erroneous Tendencies. As has already been stated, punishment is useless for tendencies which are very weak. And, indeed, at one time it was thought that punishment was ineffective in any learning. There is some evidence, however, that a tendency which is very well established can be weakened by symbolic punishment or simple verbal correction(18). Suppose, for instance, I ask a beginning student of psychology whether the removal of diseased tonsils will improve school performance. The student answers, "Yes," and is quite sure of his answer (a strong tendency). If I say, "Correct," I will not add significantly to the strength of the connection, since it is about as strong as it can be already. If, on the other hand, I point out that this is wrong, I may readily weaken the tendency, so that the next time I ask that question the student will be less likely to answer, "Yes."

As in so many things, there is considerable disagreement regarding the precise mechanisms by which punishment functions, whenever it does function(19, 20, 21).

At the risk of oversimplifying, this writer would suggest the following rules:

If the teacher observes a tendency which is well established and undesirable, he should punish or discourage it. If he observes a tendency which is clearly very weak or transitory (e.g., a grammatical slip which is not habitual with the child) and which is undesirable, he should ignore it. Since it *is* weak it will probably drop out of its own accord. If this same tendency should reappear, thereby showing that it is fairly strong, it should be punished or discouraged. A tendency which is weak and desirable (Jimmy having his homework done for once) should be rewarded. A tendency which is strong and desirable (Jimmy playing with the fellows) may be ignored. In the latter illustration, reward would not hurt, but it would probably be superfluous.

Identifying Weak and Strong Tendencies

It is all very well to call for one kind of treatment of weak tendencies and another kind for strong tendencies. But how can we tell whether a tendency is weak or strong?

Transition is Gradual. As we might expect, tendencies do not suddenly stop being weak and start being strong. The change is gradual. In spite of this, however, we can suggest some things that might help us in deciding when to switch from guided learning to a trial-and-error-reinforcement approach.

Novel Material. When the student first begins his study of reading, long division, algebra, or Spanish we can adopt the working assumption that all the tendencies we are interested in are weak and tentative. For our purposes we can assume that almost no Spanish word is strongly attached to its correct English counterpart. No algebraic axiom is clearly understood. True enough, we will find that this assumption does not hold. Some students may have a fair Spanish vocabulary. Some may have half learned much of algebra from their work in arithmetic. But these exceptions need not disturb us. It will be safer to assume little strength in the tendencies we are trying to develop. As soon as we find we are wrong, of course, we can reclassify that tendency or that student.

Frequency of Error. If a student frequently mistranslates a Spanish word, or frequently makes mistakes in removing the parentheses in algebra, it is obvious that the correct tendency is not well established in his case. Here, then, no matter how long the subject has been studied, we are dealing with a weak tendency.

Confidence of Manner. Very often we can get some hint of the strength of a tendency by a student's manner as he translates, answers a question, or corrects and recorrects the spelling of a word. This is not a sure test, of course, but in the hurly-burly of teaching it is one that we can sometimes use.

General Suggestions. Ordinarily it would seem wise to start any new material on the assumption that all tendencies are weak. After a very few trials, however (after two readings of the poem, after two or three trips through the vocabulary list), we might try out the trial-and-error procedures. If we find that a student is making many mistakes, or is unduly uncertain, we can then revert, or have him revert, to guided learning. After another practice or so, we can again try out the trial-and-error approach. In general, after being careful to start people off with guided learning, we should push them into the trial-and-error phase just a little faster than they want to go but should be prepared to fall back on guidance whenever we find many errors or a severe lack of confidence.

Summary

Guidance and reinforcement are important devices in learning. Unless one of these devices is present, either through good luck or through deliberate arrangement, no learning will take place. Unless both are used, learning will fall far short of its real potentialities. As it happens, these two mechanisms tend to go together and whenever we arrange for one we are likely to bring the other into play as well. By taking deliberate steps, however, we can accentuate the role of one and minimize the part played by the other. Reinforcement refers to the events which follow an act. These events may encourage the student to act the same way in the future (positive reinforcement) or may discourage him from behaving in the same way (negative reinforcement).

Reinforcement may be automatic, as when a music student strikes a wrong note, or casual, as when the teacher unconsciously looks disturbed on hearing a wrong answer, or deliberate, as when a teacher says, "Right" or "Good." Reinforcement should be applied with as little delay as possible. It is not necessary that reinforcement be applied after every single act. For purposes of retention, as a matter of fact, we may find sporadic reinforcement superior to regular reinforcement. This fact has had great significance in theoretical discussions of learning.

If learning is to get beyond blind trial and error, guidance must be used in addition to reinforcement. Guidance of a very simple sort occurs even in raw nature and is exemplified in the classical conditioned response. Guidance at this automatic level can be used in many school tasks. The basic conditioned-response formula can be used in teaching a child his first words in reading or in teaching a foreign vocabulary. An almost equally primitive form of guidance is used when the teacher guides the student's hand.

At a more intellectual level, guidance is used when students reread material to be memorized rather than attempt to guess. A similar sort of guidance is provided when the teacher answers his own question or when the class recites in unison.

The food powder which the dog receives in the conditioned-response experiment will act as guidance if it comes before the dog salivates. It will act as reinforcement if it comes after the salivation has occurred. The same event can be either guidance or reinforcement depending on the timing. Similarly, the teacher, by his timing, can change gradually from guidance to reinforcement. A question followed immediately by the answer constitutes guidance. A question followed by a pause, followed by an answer, constitutes reinforcement.

Guidance should be the rule at the outset of learning. At this stage the student should not be permitted to flounder but should be guided into the correct way of behaving. As learning progresses, the guidance feature should be withdrawn and reinforcement introduced. In this later stage, the student is forced to answer the question himself before the teacher confirms it by supplying the correct answer.

Other changes are also in order as the learning progresses from awkwardness to proficiency. At the outset, reward should be used in plentiful doses, punishment never. For well-established, undesirable tendencies, however, verbal reprimand may be in order. At the outset, the students memorize the poem by rereading. Later they attempt to recite the poem with books closed. At the outset, the students look at the French word and then immediately look at the English equivalent. Later they look at the French word, first try to guess the English equivalent, and then look at the book.

SPECIFIC REFERENCES

1. Miller, N. E., and Dollard, J. *Social learning and imitation.* Yale University Press, 1941.
2. Stephens, A. L. Certain special factors involved in the law of effect. Ohio State University, *Abstracts of Doctoral Dissertations,* 1950–51, 1953, *64,* 505–511.
3. Stephens, J. M. The influence of different stimuli upon preceding bonds. *Teach. Coll. Contr. Educ.,* No. 493, 1931.
4. Forlano, G. School learning with various methods of practice and rewards. *Teach. Coll. Contr. Educ.,* No. 688, 1936, pp. 61–62.
5. Hull, C. L. *Principles of behavior.* Appleton-Century-Crofts, 1943, Chap. 10.

6. Auble, D., and Mech, E. V. Response strength in a classroom task related to a "forward" delay in reinforcement. *J. educ. Psychol.*, 1954, *45*, 175–181.

7. Jenkins, W. O., and Stanley, J. C., Jr. Partial reinforcement: a review and critique. *Psychol. Bull.*, 1950, *47*, 193–234.

8. Mech, E. V. "Resistance to extinction" of two patterns of verbal reinforcement. *J. exp. Educ.*, 1953, *22*, 155–163.

9. Bilodeau, E. A. Transfer of training between tasks differing in degree of physical restriction of imprecise responses. USAF *Hum. Resour. Res. Cent., Res. Bull.*, 1952, No. 52–40.

10. Craig, R. C. *The transfer value of guided learning.* Teachers College, Columbia University, 1953.

11. McGeoch, J. A. *The psychology of human learning.* Longmans, 1942, pp. 555–559.

12. Forlano, G., and Hoffman, M. N. H. Guessing and telling methods in learning words of a foreign language. *J. educ. Psychol.*, 1937, *28*, 632–636.

13. Forlano, G. School learning with various methods of practice and rewards. *Teach. Coll. Contr. Educ.*, No. 688, 1936.

14. Wyatt, D. F., and Campbell, D. T. On the liability of stereotype or hypothesis. *J. abnorm. soc. Psychol.*, 1951, *46*, 496–500.

15. Farber, I. E., and Spence, K. W. Complex learning and conditioning as a function of anxiety. *J. exp. Psychol.*, 1953, *45*, 120–125.

16. Thorndike, E. L. *Human learning.* Appleton-Century-Crofts, 1931.

17. McGeoch, J. A. *The psychology of human learning.* Longmans, 1942, p. 557.

18. Stephens, J. M. The influence of symbolic punishment and reward upon strong and upon weak associations. *J. gen. Psychol.*, 1941, *25*, 177–185.

19. Deese, J. E. *The psychology of learning.* McGraw-Hill, 1952, Chap. 6.

20. Dinsmoor, J. A. Punishment: II. An interpretation of empirical findings. *Psychol. Rev.*, 1955, *62*, 96–105.

21. Stone, G. R. The effect of negative incentives in serial learning. VII. Theory of punishment. *J. gen. Psychol.* 1953, *48*, 133–161.

SUGGESTIONS FOR FURTHER READING

1. Deese, J. E. *Psychology of learning.* McGraw-Hill, 1952, Chap. 6.
   A most complete account of punishment and reward.

2. Miller, N. F., and Dollard, J. *Social learning and imitation.* Yale University Press, 1941.

Although this book is devoted primarily to the problem of imitation the first few chapters provide a very clear statement of the role of reinforcement in learning.

3. Forlano, G. School learning with various methods of practice and rewards. *Teach. Coll. Contr. Educ.,* No. 688, 1936.

Prior to the account of his own experiments, Forlano gives a summary of the earlier studies on recitation versus rereading and on various methods of reinforcement.

4. Postman, L. The history and present status of the law of effect. *Psychol. Bull.,* 1947, *44,* 489–563.

This is a most extensive and somewhat technical review of the problem of symbolic punishment and reward.

Exercises and Questions for Discussion

1. A group of students is receiving instruction in golf. One student has just swung at the ball and has missed. List some probable events that may act as automatic reinforcement; as casual reinforcement; as a deliberate reinforcement.

2. Show how and at what stages you would use the two mechanisms of guidance and reinforcement in memorizing a poem: in teaching a student to appreciate a concerto; to pronounce *pleurer;* to saw a board in a straight line.

3. List several instances in which a verbal correction might be useless or even harmful; in which it might be permissible or valuable. What is the key to such decisions?

4. In general, do you expect that your students will be more likely to want to remain too long in the guided, conditioned-response stage of learning; or to be too eager to plunge into the trial-and-error, reinforcement stage?

5. Can you think of any recent experiences in which you had to learn by trial and error, even though you felt the need of guidance? Can you think of any experiences in which someone insisted on "showing you how" when you would have preferred to puzzle it out on your own?

6. A person says, "Don't tell me. I'll think of it in a moment." What is he trying to avoid? Why?

7. List five teaching tasks in which conditioned-response techniques could be used with very little modification.

12

Meaningful Relations in Learning and in Problem Solving

LEARNING of a certain kind may often take place when there is nothing more than motivation, practice, and reinforcement. To these three mechanisms add the fourth mechanism of guidance, and we can now arrange for a great deal of learning at the associative level. But even with the benefit of guidance, we are still far from making the most of our teaching opportunities. If we are to begin to make the most of these opportunities, we must make consistent use of the meaningful relations in the material we are teaching. Very often, by making full use of these meaningful relations, we can almost transform the teaching task. At the very least, the judicious utilization of meaning will always expedite the scholastic growth of the students.

Failure to make use of the meaningful relations in the work undertaken by the students would not be merely a failure to avail ourselves of a useful tool. Such a failure would actually be a perversion of teaching. Typically, we do not have to supply meaning in the same way that we supply guidance and reinforcement. Typically, meaning is there, actually in the experience of the students, and needs only to be used, or to be permitted to play its natural role.

The fact that experience is always structured or organized or meaningful is stressed in our discussion of Gestalt psychology. In that discussion, we point out that the organization or meaning is not something which we have to add to an otherwise meaningless experience. The meaning or structure is there first. The many details that make up our experience are perceived only after we are aware of the pattern. Those details are always perceived, moreover, in such a way as to fit in with the requirements of the pattern. If the pattern demands that we perceive a certain detail, then we tend to perceive that detail whether it is actually present or not. Finally, this dominating pattern not only precedes the details in time but outlasts them as well. It may persist in spite of substantial changes in the details of which it is formed.

The Value of Structure in Experience

The structure or pattern or organization which dominates all our experience is extremely useful. We find it much easier to deal with a general pattern than with the individual details which make up that pattern. We can grasp the general idea of a melody even though we do not have the slightest idea of the individual notes on which it is based. We take in the general appearance of a new acquaintance but may be completely at a loss if someone should ask about that person's complexion or eyes or other features. We remember the general shape of a certain graph of learning, but we may have no idea of the detailed points through which that graph passes.

The General Structure Easier to Learn. The general structure of an experience is more readily grasped than the details when we first encounter that experience. The general structure is also easier to learn. To satisfy yourself on this point, memorize the lists of syllables which are given below. Start with the first list. First read the list through. Count that as one trial. Then cover the list with a sheet of paper. Try to think of the first word in the list. If you cannot think of anything, uncover the first word and try to think of the next. In this second trial, do not force yourself to guess but take advantage of any guesses you feel like making.

List Number One	List Number Two	List Number Three
jex	cat	long
tib	pink	sentences
yuz	ball	are
var	street	easier
zad	man	to
sov	car	learn
gax	noise	than
mup	jump	shorter
yil	curb	meaningless
zim	cry	lists

On the third trial, force yourself to guess at the word before you uncover it. Make a check mark under "Trial 3" for each error. Keep this up until you can go through without a mistake. Count up the number of trials and total number of errors. Then do the same for the next two lists.

The third list should be much easier to learn. Really it is not a list of ten words. It is a single sentence. You do not have to learn ten separate words. You merely have to learn *one* thought. As soon as you understand that one thought, the separate details will almost take care of themselves. We say *almost* because you might be able to give the same thought in slightly different words. Consequently, in memorizing these words, you might have to spend a little time in making sure that you get the actual words right as well as the general idea.

The second list should also be easier to learn than the first list. It has no over-all, ready-made structure. The words in it do not make up a single thought or unit. But it has some advantages over the nonsense syllables. It has latent structure. Each of the meaningful words is taken out of a vague general structure or cluster of associations. The word *cat* brings with it a definite meaning and a host of associated ideas. The same is true for each of the other words(1). The patterns or contexts which belong to each word have a chance to form an over-all pattern. Some of the associations with *cat,* for instance, may link up to some of the associations with *ball* and these, in turn, may link up with *pink.* Thus the general structure or context, in which each word is embedded, aids greatly in giving a new structure to these separate words. Incidentally, you probably found yourself making up a little story about the cat and the ball. This device has been greatly used by professional "memory experts" and others who give rapid courses on methods of improving the memory. Although it is no magic tool, it often proves useful. It is discussed in detail later on.

There is no question that meaningful, highly structured material is easier to grasp, easier to learn, and easier to remember. Experiment after experiment shows that structured material may be learned in one fourth or even one eighth of the time required to learn the same quantity of meaningless material(2). The memory is also more lasting. Katona(3) presents an excellent illustration of this fact. He asked students to memorize the number 581215192226. This seemed quite a task until he pointed out that the number was made up of a sequence: "Starting with five keep on adding three, then four." The task then became very easy. The students had no need to remember twelve numbers. They had only to remember three numbers (five, three, and four) and a simple rule.

Once the principle is known, the large number is easily "remembered" or reproduced.

The Use of Meaning and Structure in Presenting New Material

In Teaching Meaningful Material

Since experience is always structured and since a good structure is much more easily learned and remembered, the teacher's responsibility is obvious. Make use of the fact that the general pattern is easier to grasp than the details. Try to bring out the kind of structure which will be most useful in the task that confronts the student.

Present General Pattern First. If the material to be presented is almost completely new, make a point of presenting the general pattern first(4). Keep the following facts in mind: (a) even if you start off with details, the student will grasp the details as part of some structure, and perhaps the structure he supplies on his own will be an awkward or misleading structure; (b) ordinarily, the general structure or pattern is more readily grasped than any of the details; (c) a fair grasp of the general pattern will be of tremendous aid in mastering the details. If the student is to learn a new musical selection, let him grasp the entire melody before he works on the detailed passages. If he is to learn a play, let him understand the plot before he begins to memorize separate lines. If he is to learn to swim or to play badminton, be sure that he knows the *main* points to be kept in mind before he concentrates on the details. If he is to study the history of a certain culture, let him see something on the broad general outline. If he is to learn to read, let him master the sentence or some other structural unit before he has to master the individual letters.

For the rules just laid down, there is, as so often happens, an important exception or qualification. The structure which the teacher presents at the outset of the new material must be such as can be readily grasped by the student at his particular stage of development. The structure is presented early in the hope that the student will take it in his stride and that his mastery of the structure will facilitate the subsequent steps. The sructure should not be a formidable task in and of itself. It must be something readily within the student's grasp.

There are times, of course, when the essential structure of the new material may be very difficult for the students to grasp. If the new material is a symphony, for instance, it may be possible that the over-all "architecture" is beyond the grasp of younger students. Yet there may be individual passages which such students can readily master and appreciate. In such a case, it would be a perverse use of structure to try to force the students to grasp the subtle relations between, say, the first and the fourth movements before we let them study the passages they can comprehend. *The structure presented at the outset should be the structure which can be readily or immediately appreciated by the students.*

From common sense it would seem that the structure or meaning that is clearly comprehended by the student can provide a most useful introduction or approach. A complex structure, however, that is beyond the grasp of the students may get in their way at the outset. Under these circumstances it would be much better to treat this large structure or understanding as a goal or outcome of the teaching. It should be the final insight that summarizes and gives meaning to what has gone before. Meanwhile, you may have to use a less inclusive structure or occasionally you may have to resort to sheer rote learning. There is an elaborate and beautiful structure underlying the processes of addition, for instance. It is entirely possible, however, that this may not be comprehensible to a child in grade two or three. Some of those underlying processes, of course, may be readily apparent to children of very tender years(5) and, if so, they should be presented at the outset. Other underlying processes may be understood after some experience, and this understanding may be taken as a goal of the teacher but not as an introduction to the teaching.

An insistence on a structure which intrigues the teacher but which eludes the child, far from aiding the student, may merely place an additional burden on his shoulders. One teacher, for instance, in using the *development lesson* as a device for bringing more meaning into teaching, attempted to derive the whole history of Minnesota from three things, namely (a) the western grain fields, (b) the northern lumber industry, and (c) the falls on the Mississippi River at the site of Minneapolis. As the lesson went on, it was apparent that the children were learning the facts of the history, but they were making scant use of the elaborate device. At intervals, of course, they would "drag in" the deductions to make the teacher happy, but these deductions, instead of being an aid, were merely additional things to be learned. In many other subjects, children also solve the problem as best they can and then obligingly give the approved reasons for doing it as they did.

As we have suggested, the more complex elusive structure which makes for a poor introduction may well constitute the final goal of teaching. It is possible, however, that many activities which really have a definite structure and meaning may persist indefinitely as rote or mechanical processes. There is a complete and rigorous set of reasons underlying the process of finding the square root of a number. It is quite possible, however, that many a child may be able to perform the operations and yet may never be able to understand the reasons. There is likewise a definite and intriguing reason for every move made in starting a car, yet many a person prefers to deal with this as a rote problem or arbitrary task.

In view of these exceptions we must not be surprised to learn that, occasionally, some tasks are more rapidly mastered by the rote-learning approach(6). Even here, however, the students who worked on achieving a basic understanding were better able to attack a new and similar problem.

So much for the cautions and exceptions. Whenever there is meaning or structure that can be readily grasped by the student, use it at the outset and build the rest of your teaching around it.

Present Additional Material as Part of the Established Pattern. It is seldom that the material to be presented is completely new. More often it is a continuation of something already considered. In this situation some sort of structure already exists, since the material already dealt with is organized in some manner, whether that organization be complete or crude. Here, of course, the additional material is presented as a part of the existing structure. It is presented as one of the details which help to round out or complete or enrich the patterns which the students already have in mind. After having learned how to solve the quadratic equation by factoring, for instance, the student can be encouraged to see the method of completing the square as an alternative method of achieving the same result. Or, having discussed the Industrial Revolution and its general effects, the teacher can present event X as one special example of those general effects.

Additional material will be much more readily digested if there is a structure already waiting for it. Often, as it happens, such additional material will come, not as an extra task to be mastered, but as a welcome completion or refinement of a structure that is incomplete. It may come as the final note to an incomplete musical chord or as the denouement of an exciting story.

Bring Out the Meaningful Relations within the Material. It is important to make use of the external relations of the material to be taught and to exploit the surrounding framework into which the new material must fit. But it is also important to utilize the relations within the new material. It is important to help the students see the internal structure. It is not only important, for instance, to see the new unit on Brazil in relation to the larger unit of world relations, but it is also important to see the material about Brazil itself in clearly organized form.

At every turn, the teacher should try to bring out the meaningful relations within the material. Any relation which can readily be apprehended by the student should be used for all that it is worth to help provide the structure and organization which will make the material so much easier to deal with. Cause-and-effect relations that are within the grasp of the student should be stressed. Helpful analogies should be used. The analysis of material into main topics and subtopics can always be invoked when no more dramatic structure is available. Any meaning or organization that is latent in the material should be brought out and stressed.

In Teaching Arbitrary Material

It should not prove difficult for the teacher to persuade himself to make his lessons as meaningful as possible. Most people are happier when dealing with subject matter that is meaningful and organized. Neither student nor teacher relishes a subject which consists largely of a host of isolated, unrelated facts. The common aversion to such arbitrary, mechanical learning should constantly remind the teacher to organize his teaching and to bring out meaningful relations at every opportunity.

Our aversion to rote teaching, however, must not blind us to the fact that a certain amount of it may be necessary. We must remember that some things are almost completely arbitrary. The alphabet, for instance, has little inherent structure. Yet it should be learned. Counting and spelling are largely arbitrary. It is true, of course, that there are recurrent patterns in counting, and the wise teacher will certainly bring them out. It is also true that certain general (and treacherous) principles of spelling may be worked out, but for the young child many of these skills are largely arbitrary. Often the names of streets, capitals, or oceans are arbitrary.

Supplying Artificial Structure. When the material to be learned has no usable, inherent structure, good teachers often provide an artificial structure into which the arbitrary material may be organized. This artificial structure, of course, should never be used instead of the genuine or essential structure if that is available to the student. On the other hand, it should not be spurned. Do not hesitate to use jingles or diagrams or other *mnemonic aids* to help the student with rote material. Do not be afraid to let the student learn, "Thirty days hath September," "In 1492 Columbus crossed the ocean blue," "*i* before *e* except after *c*," and countless other jingles which have helped students to master material which is purely arbitrary. The alphabet has often served as the system or organization into which isolated material has been fitted. A student who could not remember whether or not Madison preceded Monroe as President was reminded that *Ma* precedes *Mo*. Another student knew that the rods and cones of the eye had specialized functions, one serving in daylight and the other in twilight. He could not, however, remember which was which until it was pointed out that the *c* of cones and the *d* of daylight belonged together in the alphabet while the *r* of rods and the *t* of twilight had a somewhat similar proximity.

In these latter illustrations, it will be observed, there are also meaningful and inherent cues which could have been used. After all, an adequate view of the whole structure of early nineteenth-century American history would have provided a framework into which Madison and Monroe would have fitted with no room for doubt. Similarly, there are reasons why the cones are especially responsive to certain ranges of light intensity. For the final outcome this more meaningful grasp is infinitely to be preferred. But for a quick mastery of an individual fact, the complete structure is sometimes an expensive aid.

Although the standard devices listed above are not to be scorned, they are perhaps less useful than devices which the student works out for himself. In the first place, the devices which help one person may actually get in the way of another person. The stunts used by our friends to remember telephone or license numbers are weird and mystifying to us, but they do help our friends. In the second place, there is always the possibility that the very act of working the material into a device will help the student learn the material itself.

Learning by Wholes

When faced with the task of memorizing a poem or other material of moderate length, we can adopt either one of two different procedures. We can learn it as a whole, or we can learn it by parts. The terms are largely self-explanatory. Learning the poem as a whole means trying to memorize it as a unit, going over it in its entirety until it is completely learned. In learning by parts, on the other hand, we choose a verse or other convenient unit and memorize it. We then drop that unit for the time being and proceed to another unit. We must, of course, put the units together by some means or other, perhaps by stringing them together as we go along.

If we are to utilize any structure which a selection may possess, it would seem wise to learn that selection by the whole method. It is only in this way that we can see the parts in relation to each other or that we can see the broad outline or general pattern of the material. It is by the whole method that we should master the crucial idea around which the rest of the material is organized.

As we have said, learning by wholes should enable the student to take advantage of any structure which the material may possess. Conversely, there should be no marked advantage from learning by wholes unless the material has a structure which is readily apparent to the student. When the cashier at the grocery store is faced with the task of memorizing the prices for a wide variety of articles, she should lose nothing by learning a few items at a time. The same would hold true for the teacher learning the names of his class, or perhaps for a student learning a portion of a foreign vocabulary.

So much for expectations. The experimental results are much more complicated. A great many other factors enter the picture, and very few rules hold equally for all people. Here are the more important results.

1. Even when learning the same type of material, the results vary from person to person. Some people learn more efficiently by the whole method; others by the part method.

2. The method *preferred* by the student is not necessarily his best method(7).

3. Those students who secure better results with the whole method are likely to be somewhat brighter and more mature.

4. The relative advantage of the whole method increases as a result of increased familiarity with both methods.

5. In general, we may say that results favoring the whole method are more likely to come from learning which employs distributed practices, a topic to be discussed later.

6. Our general expectation does not always hold. In some experiments, card sorting, which has no unity, has been learned more effectively by the whole method. Conversely, there are occasional studies in which poetry has been more readily learned by the part method.

It is obvious that this problem presents many unanswered questions. Until more of these questions do receive an answer, the student would do well not to go to much trouble to revolutionize his own study habits or those of others. In his general thinking on the problem, he might be guided by the following judicious summary by Woodworth(8):

> The net result of all the studies of part and whole learning seems to be something like this: the parts are easier to learn than the whole and the learner is often happier and better adjusted to the problem when beginning with the parts. He carries over some of the skill and knowledge gained in learning the parts into the subsequent learning of the whole performance. But he finds that putting together the parts is a serious problem requiring much further work. In the end he may have saved time and energy by commencing with the parts—or he may not—much depending on the size and difficulty of the total task and on the learner's poise and technique. If he can adjust himself to the whole method and handle it properly, he can learn quite complex performances effectively by the whole method. In a practical situation it is probably best to start with the whole method while feeling free to concentrate at any time on a part where something special is to be learned.

Meaning and Insight in the Application of Reinforcement

So far we have discussed the role of meaning in presenting material to the student. It is easier to motivate students to study meaningful material. After they are motivated and have begun to practice or study, the meaningful material is much easier to learn and to remember. But meaning and structure not only facilitate motivation and practice; meaning also enhances reinforcement.

The word insight as used here will refer to meaningful reinforcement. It refers to the fact that after some kinds of reinforcement the student gets a clear picture or idea of "what leads to what." After some kinds of reinforcement the student is able to say, "Immersing your head well into the water (behavior) gives you increased buoyancy (reinforcement)," or "Keeping the violin bow parallel to the bridge reduces the danger of a horrible screech," or "Starting the detective story before doing homework leads to disaster." Each of these represents an *insight*. Each of these illustrations suggests a compact idea in which a certain kind of behavior is tightly linked with a certain result or reinforcement. These two form an integral pattern. When we think of one, we think of the other. When we think of the behavior, we think of the corresponding result. When we think of the result, we think of the behavior which will produce it.

The General Role of Insight

To Tolman and his students (Chapter 9) this matter of insight is the central point of all learning. According to these psychologists, the problem is solved as soon as the learner acquires the appropriate insight. The learning is accomplished, for instance, when the cat in the puzzle box realizes that pressing the button will open the door, or as soon as the rat realizes that turning to the left will lead to water, or as soon as the badminton player realizes that using the wrist brings a snappier return.

Learning with Little Verbalized Insight. We should note in passing that there may be some learning in which insight plays relatively little part. Some learning can take place even though the learner is unable to state in clear language just what sort of behavior achieves the result(9). Suppose, for instance, that you try a key in a new lock and find that it does not work. Very probably, you will resort to typical trial-and-error learning. You will twist this way and that, pull on the door, lift on the handle, and so forth. Finally the key may work. Now it is possible that on later trials you may be able to work the key the very first time, and yet you may be unable to tell exactly what little trick is responsible for the better result. It is true that in such instances there may be a great deal of insight. You may be able to say, "The trick is—." But very often there is no insight that can be verbalized. Yet learning has taken place.

Prevalence of Insight. Although a certain amount of learning can take place with little *verbalized* insight, such learning is not the rule. Typically the student who acts in a certain way and encounters reinforcement also forms some insight. Typically he is able to verbalize. The student of swimming, for instance, can not only swim farther under water, but he can put his finger on the key to this desired outcome. He knows that taking a few deep breaths before submerging helps to get greater distance. The student of marksmanship knows that pulling the trigger will bring one result, whereas squeezing it will bring another. The student trying to increase his rate of reading comes to realize that looking for the topic sentence proves to be a great help.

Insights are very likely to develop even when there is no intention that they should develop. Even in undirected, haphazard, trial-and-error learning, the student is very likely to acquire some idea of the relation between his behavior and the outcome. If he spills the ink, he knows what to expect. If he wants to make the teacher smile, he knows what to do.

The Importance of Insight. Whenever it does occur, insight should prove most helpful(10). In some learning, indeed, the whole problem hinges on some crucial insight. In some forms of parlor games, for instance, the whole problem is to select a key code or to "catch on" to some double meaning in the directions given to one. As soon as this relation is understood, the problem is solved and often solved at the 100 percent level. In such an instance the successful insight is the determining thing. Lacking it, our score is zero. Attaining it, our score is 100. In a great many athletic or gymnastic activities, a certain kind of insight may be noticed. We suddenly "get the hang of it" or "catch on," and from that point on our improvement is very rapid.

Enhancing Insight

As we have said, a certain amount of insight will come about from the student's unaided efforts. It is natural, however, that the teacher can help out in this phase of learning. For one thing, the teacher can often call attention to potential reinforcement which may escape the child's attention. The mother may say, "See, the dog doesn't growl when you pat him on the head." The swimming coach may call attention to the fact that by keeping his head well immersed the student has been able to float for two minutes. The teacher of English may be able to show that by using an outline the student has produced a much clearer theme. Any one of these results may have escaped the student's attention. The teacher brings these results into the foreground and at the same time links them up with the act or behavior which brought them about.

Supplying Ready-made Insights

In addition to helping the student verbalize and sharpen his own vague insights, the teacher often supplies insights that have been handed down from generation to generation. These ready-made insights often take the form of maxims or catchy slogans. Such rules as *More haste, less speed; Out of sight, out of mind; God helps those who help themselves* are intended to serve as insights. They point to a way of acting. They suggest that if we want to achieve a certain goal, we should act in this particular way. They serve to remind us that this way of behaving will lead to a given reinforcement.

Such highly verbalized, cultural insights may often be useful. We should not overrate them, however, and should not consider them as adequate substitutes for the insights which the student acquires as the result of his own experience. The mere fact that a student can recite one of these maxims in glib fashion does not mean that it is a convincing insight for him. His ability to verbalize does not mean that the insight is actually absorbed into the structure of his own experience.

Ready-made maxims or rules may serve some purpose when presented prior to the student's own experience. They are likely to be most useful, however, when they are used to organize and enhance the vague insights which he has already come to feel in a nebulous sort of way as a result of his own experience. When a student, for instance, has already behaved in a certain way and has encountered a given kind of reinforcement, he is likely to experience some vague feeling of "what leads to what." As this feeling struggles, so to speak, for a more compact structure, the neat, catchy phrasing of a standard maxim or rule may prove exceedingly valuable. It may crystallize and clarify the general insight which the student has already begun to experience. It is possible that many of the delights of great literature spring from this process. The great writers put into precise and glorious language the vague and confused thoughts toward which the rest of us have groped. As a result of our own experience, each of us has formed vague and fuzzy insights regarding the pangs of remorse or the tragedy of indecision. It remains for Shakespeare, however, to thrill us by picking up these vaguely felt presentiments and returning them to us as insights that are neat, compact and magnificently ordered.

Meaning as a Prime Goal of Teaching

Meaning, insight, and organization are important devices to be exploited. By making the most of meaning and structure, for instance, we can be more effective in teaching the students about the exports of Brazil. Meaning is thus an intermediate step leading to whatever goal we may have in mind at the moment.

It is obvious, however, that meaning is not only a device for the attainment of minor goals. The attainment of rich meaning and comprehension and understanding is itself one of the major goals of education. It is not merely a means to more fundamental pedagogical goals.

A rich store of meanings, of comprehensive understandings, and of functioning insights is one of the greatest gifts that the school can bestow on the student. True enough, the facts which he learns in the school are important too. But if those facts can be contained within a few highly structured, general principles, they are infinitely more valuable. A relatively few scientific principles, for instance, clearly comprehended, can give meaning and direction to a whole host of practical problems in engineering, in homemaking, in agriculture, and healthful living. Other principles actually understood enable the banker or businessman to think about his problems in more intelligent fashion. Similarly, a somewhat larger number of less structured principles from psychology may help in teaching and in the more complicated business of getting along with people.

A rich store of meaningful principles, in addition to pointing the way to the solution of practical problems, also contributes directly to sheer intellectual satisfaction. The need for understanding is a real need. It functions at different levels in different people and is much stronger in some people than in others. But it is present at some level, and in some degree, in all of us. We are bound to work out some principle to help us organize the haphazard world around us. That "principle" may be crude and childish ("People never understand me") or elaborate and sound ("Don't expect that people will always act in strictly logical fashion"). But some principle will prevail. Since that need is present and since it must be partially filled in one way or another, the teacher should make sure that the principles attained are as comprehensive and as valid as possible. Some students may be able to comprehend and absorb principles that are exceedingly complex and inclusive. Others may have to be content with rather simple principles. But for each student, the teacher can do much to help him attain a more adequate set of principles, insights, and understandings.

Use of Standard Mechanisms of Learning

To bring about growth in the student's understanding and in his comprehension of meanings, the teacher, naturally enough, can use the rules already stressed for teaching in general. Motivation, practice, reinforcement, guidance, and insight will serve just as well in teaching students to grasp a general principle as in teaching them to spell *anxious*, to draw a book, or to sing a song.

To motivate the tendency to seek out meanings and general principles, the teacher should exploit the student's existing need to see relations. With very little encouragement, students will seek out similarities, analogies, and general relations. In studying the history of Brazil, they may comment spontaneously on parallels to the history of the United States. In studying the rhythm in poetry, they may be reminded of some of the properties of rhythm in music. It will be the unusual class in which some child is not reminded of some other matter which must be adjusted to the structure of his present experience.

Encourage this general tendency. Even when the actual principle announced by the student is farfetched and invalid, the *tendency* itself can be encouraged. Be enthusiastic about the fact that the principle was stated, but ask him to regard it as tentative until more cases have been examined.

It is not enough merely to take advantage of the spontaneous expression of the student's need for broader principles. Stimulate that need. By your actions show that you too are interested in these generalities. Let the search for generalities pervade even the most ordinary teaching. The teacher of French can ask, "Does that remind you of anything in Latin (or English)?" The teacher of geography can ask for analogies or contrasts between the pampas and the plains of the United States. The teacher of music can stimulate the amateur tune detective who can spot passages from Handel or Scarlatti in the current popular hit.

These illustrations, of course, represent the incidental uses of motivation that accompany the daily teaching. At the more overt and intellectual level, students can also be motivated to master general principles. The teacher can show how a mastery of these principles aids in earning a living, in contributing to human welfare, in attaining the esteem of one's fellows, and in experiencing a very real intellectual satisfaction.

In using the mechanism of practice to help develop meaningful relations, we should rely more on emphasis and less on formal practice sessions. In teaching most material, there are numerous occasions when general principles can be stressed and when meaningful relations can be brought out. It is much more important to seize upon these natural opportunities and to develop them than it is to arrange for more formal practice sessions devoted exclusively to the study of general principles. Otherwise we may disrupt the natural intricate relation between fact and principle.

The mechanism of reinforcement is easy to use in the development of meaningful relations. Commend with enthusiasm the student who sees the material being discussed as part of a larger structure or who can see the analogy between this usage in French and a related usage in Latin. Be especially zealous to commend the student who can summarize the main point of a lesson in a pithy and precise insight.

The mechanism of guidance can be used with great effect, especially in pointing out the many minor principles or generalizations that we hope our students may attain. Much can be done by the mere arrangement of the material. Simply by placing rainfall maps of North America and

South America side by side, for instance, we may have automatically arranged things so that the general principle is almost staring the student in the face. Similarly, in biology, there are many parallel sketches of the skeleton of man and horse, or parallel diagrams of frog and man, and these can be depended upon to point the way to the mastery of some of the general principles of anatomy or physiology.

This problem, by the way, is also discussed in the chapter on transfer of training. Part of the problem of securing effective transfer is this task of arranging for a group of generalizations or principles that will actually function in as many situations as possible.

Special Problems in the Development of Meanings and Understanding

Although the teaching of meanings is essentially the same as any other kind of teaching, there are a few details which become especially important when we turn to the more complex area of meanings and abstractions and general principles.

Meanings Arise from Experience. Meanings can never far outrun direct concrete experience. At least, they can never do so safely. A meaning that is not closely anchored to some clear experience is likely to be wide of the mark. In one of her novels, for instance, Gene Stratton Porter made interesting use of the kind of misconception that is likely to arise when a word or meaning or concept is not tied up with actual experience. In this story a neglected waif was rescued from her squalid surroundings and moved to a better home. Here she became inordinately fond of milk and extended her affection to cows. She had never seen a cow but learned of them as the givers of the delectable food. She heard a great deal about the function, the utility, and the disposition of the cow, but nothing of its size. Her first encounter with an actual cow was traumatic. She had visualized something like the later "Shmoo" immortalized by Al Capp. She expected something small and round and cuddly, perhaps like a rabbit. She was in no way prepared for the behemoth which welcomed her with an uncouth and monstrous noise.

Similar misconceptions are encountered by every teacher. The pedagogical literature is filled with amusing examples of such incidents. A grade four youngster, for instance, reads about the army officer who provided his men with "quarters for the night." We can easily understand his visual picture of the officer handing each soldier a 25-cent piece to pay for his lodging. A second student is said to have stated that *furlough* meant *mule*. To support his unorthodox definition he produced a picture of a soldier riding a mule, underneath which was the unmistakable caption, *Civil War soldier going home on a furlough*. The writer once asked his grade six class to write out the story of Lochinvar. In one place Lochinvar declaims,

> I long woo'd your daughter, my suit you denied.
> Love swells like the Solway but ebbs like its tide.

One student paraphrased the first line thus: "I long woo'd your daughter, but you wouldn't give me back my clothes." One wonders at the background structure of the student's impression within which this misconception was formulated. But it is a reasonable interpretation of the denial of a suit.

In each of these illustrations, the student was called upon to deal with a word or a concept before he possessed the general background or structure into which the word would fit. In each case, we asked the student to attain a meaning which at that time was too far in advance of his concrete experience.

It would be ridiculous, of course, to imply that meaningful ideas must always be anchored *directly* to concrete experience. One can often proceed a few steps from concrete experience and still avoid serious misconceptions. The tutors of the little girl could have given her an adequate idea of the cow's size if they had made use of her concrete experience with horses or ponies or other large objects. The teacher of history could have found a chain of concepts from "quarters" to tourist camps or to some idea of lodgment which came within the child's actual experience. By the use of analogy or of similarities within our own experience, clever writers are often able to give us a very accurate concept of things we have never experienced. Intensive reading, for instance, is alleged to have given Rex Stout such a vivid picture of Manhattan that the city held no surprises for him when he visited it. Similarly, on the basis of sheer verbal description, he was prepared for everything he actually encountered when he heard his first symphony(11). Few psychologists will be completely convinced that unaided verbal description can do so much. It is possible, however, that a large number of parallel descriptions, each giving somewhat different illustrations, can give a fairly accurate picture of an unfamiliar scene.

Rather than depend too much on intermediate links to anchor the new meaning to concrete experience, the teacher should use photographs, moving pictures, and other visual aids when the actual concrete experience is lacking. Records and sound films can also bring the song of the skylark (a bit insipid after reading Shelley) or the roar of Niagara. As yet there are no artificial or substitute devices which will simulate the taste of champagne or the odor of Naples. It is quite possible, moreover, that the student who has encountered these things only in literary descriptions may be in for a bit of a shock when he experiences the real thing.

Although our discussion has centered around the meanings of individual words, we must remember that we are seldom called upon to deal with words in isolation. Words are usually encountered in a sentence or in a phrase or in another context. And, typically, the broader structure determines the meaning which we attach to the word. The *"tear* in her eye" is a very different thing than the *"tear* in her dress," but ordinarily the difference would cause us no trouble. It is the entire phrase that determines the meaning, and the same words really mean different things in different contexts.

These contextual clues are to be utilized. It is a great help when the new word is encountered in its proper context. The context provides important guidance and almost forces the student to interpret it more or less adequately. He is able to react to the passage as a whole and is not held up while he stumbles around trying to deal with an individual word. When he reads, for instance, that "The cruel bombing left Warsaw a reeking shambles," he can readily surmise that *reeking* and *shambles* describe the destruction wrought by the bombing. These new words will not prevent him from grasping the main idea. So long as these words remain in their present context, they will cause no difficulty. It is only when the student wishes to use either one in a new context that he may encounter trouble. At that time he will need to know whether shambles means litter or blood and whether reeking means smoking or odoriferous.

Attaching Meaning to Abstract Concepts. Mastering the meaning of such concepts as justice or squareness or democracy is much more difficult than mastering the meanings of such terms as money, cow, or trireme. In teaching the abstract concept we cannot find a single object in the child's experience—we cannot show him a picture of justice or present a sound recording of democracy.

And yet if students are to acquire any understanding at all of abstract concepts, they must acquire that understanding largely from experience with concrete objects. To a limited extent, of course, we can use a group of abstract concepts, such as the three normal dimensions, as a basis for speculating about a fourth dimension which we have never experienced. But our grasp of those concepts which go beyond our experience is very uncertain and vague. Typically we cannot go many steps beyond concrete experience if we are to understand an idea in a dependable manner.

A grasp of abstract concepts, of course, must come from experience with many objects. To understand *squareness,* for instance, the student must see square papers and square boards and a square drawn on the blackboard. He must see red squares and white squares. In other words, he must see a variety of concrete objects, all having the common property of squareness. He must also see a large number of concrete objects somewhat similar to the above but which lack the property of squareness. To understand the concept of rhythm as an abstract idea, the student must encounter rhythm in one selection after another. He must also encounter somewhat similar selections in which the element of rhythm is lacking. To understand the term *justice* in any precise fashion, the student must encounter a large number of situations, real or hypothetical, each of which exemplifies justice. He must also encounter similar situations in which justice does not appear but in which are to be found such things as kindness, sympathy, or unselfishness with which justice may be confused.

In teaching abstract concepts, choose those concrete materials in which the abstract idea is fairly prominent. The squareness of a piece of paper may be more prominent, for instance, than the squareness of a room. The paper would therefore be preferable for beginning the teaching of squareness. Similarly, the rhythm in a waltz may be more prominent than the rhythm in a tone poem. Choose the waltz at the beginning of the instruction. The concept of justice versus mercy may stand out more clearly in *The Merchant of Venice* than in *The Brothers Karamazov.* Choose the former to begin with.

Although we wish that the quality to be taught shall stand out, we should never try to isolate that quality, even if we could. Never try to present pure rhythm. Let it always appear in a fairly natural context. Do not seek for a literary situation from which all extraneous details have been removed and in which the concept of justice is presented with almost no irrelevant background. The natural context should be there, but at the outset it should be in the background, and the abstract quality should be quite prominent.

Use many concrete examples chosen from a wide variety of settings. Justice as portrayed in one play could easily be confused with incidental qualities which appear in the same play. Use many literary selections or other examples. If you have to teach the concept of individual differences, for instance, use examples of individual differences in height, weight, hair density, and wealth. Never let the students feel or infer that individual differences refer only to differences in intelligence or any other single trait.

Use a multitude of practical examples in testing as well as in teaching. And provide much opportunity for testing. The mastery of abstract concepts depends, after all, on the student's own activity. You cannot do everything for him. After an initial guided approach, let him try himself out frequently with many different kinds of examples. Let him pick out the square face of the pyramid, the square pane of glass, the square in the pattern of some cloth. Let him beat out the rhythm in a song, in a poem, in rhythmic prose, or perhaps in a graphic pattern. Let him point out the rival claims of justice, mercy, and expediency in newspaper reports of trials, in fables, and in the problems before the United Nations. His *final* mastery of these concepts will come largely from his own trial-and-error efforts and from the reinforcement and insight which follow these efforts.

Developing Skill in the Use of Abstract Concepts. We have laid down certain rules for teaching new words and for teaching the *meaning* of abstract concepts. These rules also hold when we are helping the students to develop skill in the manipulation of abstract concepts. They hold, for instance, when we are teaching students how to manipulate the abstract x's and y's of algebra. At first, make sure that the problems deal with concrete materials well within the student's experience. The student is less likely to make a mistake in manipulating these familiar materials. The materials themselves provide the guidance so necessary in the early stages of the acquisition of skill. If by some chance he should begin to go astray in using familiar concepts, his error is likely to become immediately and glaringly apparent, thus providing the automatic reinforcement which is so helpful to learning at all stages.

To illustrate the difference between reasoning in the abstract and in the concrete, consider two syllogisms. Here is one that is highly abstract:

$$\text{All } S\text{'s are } M$$
$$\text{All } P\text{'s are } M$$
$$\therefore \text{ All } S\text{'s } \textit{are } P\text{'s}$$

True or false? How sure do you feel? Now try it in concrete form:

$$\text{All } (S)\text{cotchmen are } (M)\text{en}$$
$$\text{All } (P)\text{ortuguese are } (M)\text{en}$$
$$\therefore \text{ All } (S)\text{cotchmen are } (P)\text{ortuguese.}$$

What is your reaction? And how sure do you feel? Actually, there is probably no comparison in your reaction to the two problems. Any child who knows the meaning of the three terms can see that the last conclusion is fallacious. Many a college student, on the other hand, may fail to see that the first conclusion is invalid. To render a fallacy glaring and apparent, merely translate it into familiar and common-sense content. When this is done, a child of seven can detect the most complex logical fallacies(12).

So much for the beginning stages of teaching the manipulation of abstract concepts. But we cannot keep on using familiar material forever. To do so would negate our goal. Gradually we must withdraw the guidance supplied by the familiar material. As some skill develops, we try to get the students to feel more at home with the abstract symbols, so that now they need only refer occasionally to familiar material to see if their conclusions check with common sense. Ultimately, a very few students may acquire such competence in dealing with abstract symbols that they can proceed accurately, even when the material has no relation to common sense or when the assumptions are in direct contradiction to common sense. The physicist, for instance, who reasons about the characteristics of the fifth dimension can receive little confirmation from the dictates of common sense. But this quality is rare. Few people are able (or willing) to work with bizarre assumptions that fail to accord with common sense.

The Dangers of Unanchored Abstractions. Abstractions have proved of stupendous value in our lives. We are greatly attached to them, and properly so. Sometimes, too, we regard them as pretty things in their own right, and this attitude is laudable and harmless. Sometimes, however, we regard them as *actual* things in their own right, and this is often dangerous. An abstraction should never be used for any length of time without frequently coming back to earth and firmly anchoring that abstraction to something concrete and objective.

Many students, for instance, have a great deal of difficulty with the word intelligence. It is an abstraction. It is a quality which pervades a great many acts. It also, unfortunately, has value connotations. It is a "good" word or a nice sounding word. No one likes the sound of being called "unintelligent," no matter what the user *meant* by the term. Very frequently students will use the term *intelligence* over a period of time without ever asking themselves for a concrete example of what is meant by intelligence. When they do realize that the concrete process most often implied is merely getting a score on an intelligence test, they feel a bit of a jolt.

There are many abstractions which cause us endless trouble if we fail to bring them back to earth at frequent intervals. We hear, for instance, that a man is dishonest. Honesty or dishonesty is an abstraction. They are words describing aspects of many ways of behaving. To get any *clear* idea of what is meant, we should ask our informant for a concrete illustration. In commenting on his wife's new hat, for instance, the man may merely have expressed an enthusiasm which he did not genuinely feel. He may have used some of the office stationery for his own personal correspondence. He may have defrauded a trusting widow. Each of these concrete acts could be classified as dishonest. Until the abstract word is clearly anchored to some such concrete act, it has little clear meaning. Unanchored, it is also a dangerous word. It could lead to serious misconception.

Try to get students to probe behind the sound of ever-present abstractions. Get them to give concrete illustrations of what they mean by *undemocratic, liberal, progressive,* or *sophisticated.* Get them to demand such concrete illustrations from those who would seek to sway them by words that have a pretty sound but which may fail to convey any precise meaning.

Meaningful Relations in Thinking and Problem Solving

If meaning and meaningful relations are so important in ordinary learning, they should be even more important in problem solving, creative thinking, and in the higher mental processes generally. By and large, the very heart of these latter activities is the fruitful use of relations and of meaningful concepts. In these activities, meanings, insights, and relations are the materials with which we work.

We should point out, in passing, that there is nothing absolutely new and distinctive about meaning and problem solving. These higher order processes have much in common with the learning that we have been discussing all along. Rather than visualizing two or three distinct kinds of learning, we would do better to visualize a continuous line. At one end of this line we should place such automatic learning as learning to salivate at the sight of a juicy lemon. At the other end of the line we place the creative thinking of the poet or scientist. In between, we have the whole range of learning, extending from the very simple to the exceedingly complex. But the differences are differences of degree and not of kind. Underlying all activities on this continuous line, we find many similar or identical processes and mechanisms.

We cannot, and should not, confine the treatment of thinking to one small section of one chapter. Actually, this whole text is concerned with the problem of thinking. One of our chief concerns has been to learn how to think correctly about educational problems. Not only have we been anxious to know *what* to think, but we have been equally concerned to find out *how* to think and how to reach valid conclusions in a field such as this.

In your study of the pitfalls which surround educational thought, you have come face to face with problem solving in its clearest form. Throughout the text, moreover, you are continually required to face a problem, to suggest several hypotheses for the solution of the problem, and to work out some means of testing those hypotheses. This is the general field of problem solving, and these are the main steps by which problems are mastered.

Having had much practice in problem solving on our own, let us now look at the process more intently from the viewpoint of teachers. Let us see what we can find out about the process which will help us teach students how to solve problems.

General Processes in Problem Solving

Problem solving comes into play whenever the free movement of the organism is impeded, or whenever the first spontaneous response fails to bring him discernibly closer to his goal. So long as our habitual modes of action carry us along smoothly, there is no problem to be solved. Even when we encounter a new situation, such as the need of finding the railway station in a strange city, we would feel no problem if our first natural move brought us some evidence that we were headed in the direction of the station. It is when we are blocked and when our simple spontaneous behavior receives no confirmation that there is a problem to solve.

Orientation. To solve a problem, it is necessary to keep oriented to the problem, and this is not so simple as it may sound. If the problem appears very difficult or if we have faced it for some time with no evidence of progress, we tend to leave it, to think of something else, to "leave the psychological field" as the Lewinian would say.

In keeping ourselves oriented toward the problem, we may get some help from sheer physical orientation. We can keep our eyes focused on the jigsaw puzzle, or at least on the table where it lies. If it is a problem that is highly verbal in character, we may get some help from vocalization, in which we repeat the problem to ourselves at frequent intervals.

Along with these devices at the physical level, of course, we ordinarily take steps to attend mentally to the problem.

As we begin to make progress in the solution of the problem, the orientation becomes more specific. We feel the need of concentrating on a particular phase of the problem. We feel that the crucial point lies in one section of the jigsaw puzzle, for instance, or in one baffling set of circumstances in the detective story, or in one disturbing group of experiments on the comparison between the lecture method and the discussion method. Under these circumstances it is necessary not only to keep ourselves oriented to the problem as a whole, but also to keep ourselves working at the important phase of the problem. This is especially true when some irrelevant detail of the problem tends to distract us from what we consider to be the crucial point.

Search for Solution. Search and orientation are two aspects of problem solving. They are by no means clearly separate and successive steps. We must not think that there is a clear-cut period of orientation followed by a later clear-cut period of search. The two activities are interspersed. Shortly after we encounter the problem, for instance, we may search for the key point in the problem. We may ask ourselves, "What is the crucial aspect on which I must concentrate? Which section of the jigsaw puzzle should I try to block in first? Which minor detail in this detective story must I keep in mind?"

As we have suggested, there is, or should be, much search of the problem itself to see just what is required or to pick out the feature that should receive the bulk of our attention. In this preliminary search, we often have to overcome our tendency to concentrate on the immediate cause of our frustration. A large tree, for instance, has fallen across the road and blocks the path of your car. At first you will tend merely to glare at the tree itself. For a time it seems that the tree *is* the whole problem. Then comes the realization that, so long as you keep your thoughts focused on nothing but the tree, you will never solve the problem. You look away from the tree to see if there are any aspects of the total situation which present more promising leads. This search of the problem may be intelligent and analytic or merely a vague feeling that "This won't get me anywhere."

As the problem is being searched, we are unconsciously setting up a *model* which can be used in our later search for a solution. Looking at the vacant space in the jigsaw puzzle, for instance, you may say to yourself, "I need a piece that looks like a sheep and has some yellow on the nose," or you may form a visual image of the missing piece. These things act as *search models* as you look for an answer to your problem. You keep this model in mind as you search the jigsaw pieces that are available. The search model for the solution of the blocked road is more obvious and less clearly defined. You need a way around the tree, safe and passable for the car, and not too far out of your way. In some instances, the search model that you keep in mind may be much more abstract. Suppose, for instance, that you feel baffled, and perhaps irritated, by the apparent fact that the lecture system in college works as well as the discussion method. Here your search model is made up of some sort of hypothesis which must fit in with general principles of psychology and which must solve the paradox.

The model which you keep in mind while you are searching the available material is partly determined by what you see in the problem itself. It is largely determined by your idea of the shape of the vacant space in the jigsaw or by your idea of the kind of hypothesis necessary to explain the good showing of the lecture method. Unfortunately, however, the search model is not determined exclusively by the requirements of the problem. The model used in the search is also affected by many nonlogical characteristics of the searcher. Some children, for instance, will give preference to a jigsaw part that is pretty, even though there is nothing in the problem which requires a pretty part. Some people, in searching for hypotheses to explain the data on the lecture method, will lean toward hypotheses that are original, or ingenious, or perhaps cynical. One doctrinaire Communist student in the writer's acquaintance could always be depended upon to come up with an hypothesis which was derogatory to the capitalist system. This was part of his search model. Any hypothesis which failed to indict the capitalist system would not be considered. Unfortunately, moreover, this factor of bias in search models is not restricted to Communists(13).

This search may be highly systematic or largely random. We may line up all the unused pieces in the jigsaw puzzle and run over each according to some system, or we may merely let our gaze wander over the board, being attracted unconsciously now to this piece, now to that. The search, however, is never completely random. It is always limited by our orientation to the main problem. It is limited, for instance, to jigsaw pieces.

The solution to the search may come gradually as the result of prolonged analysis, or it may spring suddenly and unaccountably from the "unconscious." This latter experience is probably the more frequent. We form an image of the needed jigsaw piece. We let our gaze wander over the board, and suddenly one particular piece seems to stand out. Just why, we may not be able to say. Similar results may occur in our attempt to explain the baffling results regarding the lecture method. We have an idea of the problem to be solved. With this in mind, we go over all the circumstances we can think of and all the psychological principles that we can remember at the moment. Then, suddenly, we find ourselves saying, "Of course. The instructor makes the tests and the instructor does the talking. . . ." or "Certainly. It's all a matter of silent practice and casual reinforcement." Somehow the model when "held near" one or more of the many possible jigsaw pieces or circumstances or psychological principles will cause one of them to come to life. It is almost as if we had a tuning fork and wished to select a matching fork from a vast number placed helter-skelter on a shelf. Here we could set our standard fork (search model) in vibration and rapidly pass it close to the forks in the cupboard. Any fork that began to vibrate would be the tentative answer to our problem.

Trying Out the Tentative Solution. Our search produces only a *tentative* solution. It produces only the first plausible guess that must always be tested before any reliance can be placed upon it. Typically, moreover, it actually is tested, in a kind of way at least. The promising piece of jigsaw puzzle may be actually tried and rejected. The first idea of how to get around the fallen tree receives further thought. The first explanation of the results of the lecture method is considered critically, for a time at least.

The test of the tentative solution involves some manipulation, either symbolic or overt. We may actually pick up the jigsaw piece that springs into focus, or we may merely take a mental image of it back to the vacant place. The testing of the apparent solution may be almost random or it may be highly planned. Feeling that route A is the best way around the road block, we may merely proceed along route A for a space and then, for no particular reason, switch over to route B. At the other extreme, we may go to a lot of trouble to figure out a test of our solution. When testing a hypothesis to account for the results on the lecture system, for instance, we may institute an elaborate program of research lasting over many months. These are the theoretical extremes. Any actual test is likely to involve both features. It is never completely the one or the other. In even the most systematic attempt to test a solution, by the way, some sort of random behavior is almost bound to occur if the problem becomes sufficiently frustrating. People facing very difficult problems and making no discernible headway often resort to aimless fiddling and manipulation with only the vaguest notion of a guiding plan. This is true not only of young children but even for advanced students working under close scrutiny.

The Problem of "Set"

Running through this whole matter of problem solving is the question of "set." Any experience we have in the solution of one problem will bring about a set or attitude that will affect our approach to a similar problem. Ask a friend, for instance, how to pronounce m-a-c-m-a-h-o-n (you spell the word orally). He may hesitate at first but will pronounce the word "MacMahon." Now try m-a-c-i-n-n-e-s. He should pronounce MacInnes more readily and with more confidence. Try m-a-c-e-w-e-n. Now try m-a-c-h-i-n-e-r-y. You may get MacHinery instead of machinery. The "set" built up by the first few experiences may readily carry over to tasks where it gives improper or erroneous results.

Obviously set can be a help or a hindrance. So long as the problem remains fairly constant, the factor of set can be very useful. When the problem changes, it may get in our way. Ideally, to be good at problem solving, we should be able to acquire a set fairly easily and should also be able to get rid of it, or to rise above it when it no longer serves any purpose, or when it is a nuisance.

Unfortunately these two abilities do not always go together. People who are good at acquiring a set may or may not be good in surmounting it when circumstances demand it(14). Men and women are equally susceptible to set, but men, on the average, are better able to overcome the set when it no longer helps.

Acquiring a Set. A set can be established by direct experience in problem solving, as indicated in our illustration. It can also be established by incidental prior experience. A student who happens to have seen a clamp and a string lying close together is more likely to use these together later in solving a problem than a student who has not seen this combination. By the same token such incidental experience can steer a student away from a useful set. Suppose a student has recently had considerable experience in using a specialized tool, say a socket wrench, for its proper purpose. Now he faces a problem that he could solve by using the wrench as a pendulum bob, or as a lever. He is less likely to use it in this way than another student who has not had the earlier experience(15).

As might be expected, students who are highly motivated or tense or anxious are somewhat more likely to acquire a set than those who are indifferent or less anxious(16).

Overcoming the Influence of Set. The persistence of set when it is no longer useful is often decribed as *rigidity*. Notice that we apply this term to the person who holds on to a set when it is no longer appropriate. The term does not refer, as some people have mistakenly suggested, to any person who acquires a set(17). Rigidity as measured by the persistence of set has played a considerable part in the discussion of personality, especially in discussions of prejudice (Chapter 17). There is much controversy on this matter, however, and in spite of some evidence(18) it is probably too soon to say whether or not the rigidity that appears in one kind of problem solving is the same thing as the rigidity that is observed in other ways(17).

It is important to remember, by the way, that even when the persistence of a set interferes with maximum theoretical efficiency it does not always lead to results that are harmful in the long run, or in the practical sense. The route that you have found best for getting to work in the morning rush hour may not be best when you have to go back in the evening or on a holiday. A continued use of that method might be evidence of a rigid set. But taking everything into account, it may sometimes be better to continue the method that is reasonably efficient than to worry unduly over the necessity of gaining the last ounce of efficiency.

Although rigidity is not always a serious handicap, it can be very harmful in some situations. Those scientists who are judged to be most creative tend to be extremely flexible and varied in their approach to problems(19). In some experiments it has been found that set will be less rigid if students are shown a variety of approaches in their original experience with problems(20). There is also some evidence that formal, direct sessions on the techniques of problem solving will increase the competence of students in this matter(21) and also in the general processes of logical reasoning and critical thinking(22).

Providing Guidance in Problem Solving

There are a few definite steps you can take to help students solve their problems in more effective fashion. These rules arise partly from our understanding of the general process and partly from the results of specific experiments.

Encourage Persistence. Problem solving is often very unrewarding in its early stages. The student makes movement after movement and tries one solution after another and yet receives no reinforcement. As far as he can see he is not even gradually approaching the distant goal. He is getting nowhere. In a situation like this, anyone is likely to give up, to leave the field, to resort to daydreaming, or to become angry. At this stage, judicious encouragement is in order. Remind the student that lack of success is typical in the early stages and that attainment of success often comes suddenly and unexpectedly.

Concentrate on Problem, Forget About Self. Students get along better if they can orient themselves more to the problem and less to themselves. This is very difficult to do. Ego-involvement, discussed in Chapter 10, is likely to be at a high level. The student is likely to feel a glaring spotlight shining on him and to think that he is being judged for all time to come. He may assume that there is an obvious answer and that you are just standing there, impatiently waiting for his stupidity to pass.

Try to encourage him to concentrate on the problem. He may be more at ease if you also regard it as a problem and make it clear that you and he are engaged in a joint search for a solution. Mere assurance that everyone has to go to some trouble to solve these problems may also help. The "speed" set may be troublesome. Sometimes, of course, the problem actually calls for a speedy solution. At other times, speed may not be important. Even when speed plays no real part in the solution, however, the student may assume that it does. Perhaps it is merely that the unsolved problem imposes a strain that becomes less and less tolerable the longer it remains unsolved. Perhaps some extraneous circumstances, such as the instructor's restlessness, may add to this feeling of urgency. Whenever speed is not actually important, you should not only avoid all evidence of impatience but you should go to some trouble to keep the student away from a speed set. Tell him to take his time, that this is not a matter of a few seconds.

This speed set, by the way, is a very serious handicap for young pilots when they first face the problems of identifying landscape features or check points from the air. A terrific sense of urgency and ego-involvement is set up by the very speed with which the airplane passes over the check point and by the presence of an instructor who presumably knows the answer. To offset this sense of urgency, many instructors tell the student to make up his mind that he is going to fly over the check point at least twice no matter how soon he identifies it.

Delaying the Decision. As we have pointed out so often, there is a great tendency to accept the first reasonable solution of a problem that comes to mind. For most efficient problem solving, we must not let our great need for a solution drive us to accept the first reasonable suggestion. Young students especially must be encouraged to keep trying to think of other good solutions as well.

Giving up Apparent Solutions that Prove Unfruitful. It is always difficult to know when to keep going along a certain route and when to turn back. To get around the road block, for instance, you decide to try a certain trail. You keep on for a time and nothing of promise comes into sight. How long should you continue before turning back and trying a different route? Of course, there is no certain rule. If it should be the right road, it would pay you to keep on in spite of discouragement. If it is the wrong road, the sooner you try a different path the better.

In general, children are inclined to pursue an unfruitful plan too long. They are not so likely to make the mistake of trying another plan before giving the first plan a fair test. Children, of course, may readily give up the *whole* problem if they are unsuccessful in a given attempt. But whereas adults will give up an unprofitable attempt fairly soon, with the idea of trying a different route, children are less adaptive. They tend to continue the first route indefinitely or to quit altogether. They are less likely to give up the first route in favor of a new approach.

In the experiments on problem solving, both adults and children do better when they are urged in the direction of giving up a particular route sooner than they normally would. Even before the student confronts the problem, it helps to warn him that he should be ready to abandon his first attempt and to consider other possible means of solution. After the student is actually working on the problem, moreover, and is balked for the time being, it also helps to ask, "Do you suppose another approach might prove valuable?" or, "Have you considered all the other possibilities?"

Tolerate Efforts that Are Nonlogical. Do not expect the student to proceed to the solution of his problem by a series of neat, logical steps. Problems are seldom solved that way, even by competent logicians. The apparent solution, the trial hypothesis, is attained by any one of a number of methods, some of which may be very unsystematic.

Logic, of course, has its place. That place is in the testing and demonstration of solutions. It is after the student has hit upon his tentative solution that you should encourage him to test that solution by the use of the best logic that he can command. Show him, too, how a logical development will help him to present his solution to others, now that he has hit upon it. When engaged in these tasks of testing apparent solutions and explaining them to others, logic is of inestimable value.

Rest Periods after Intensive Application. Later, when we study about interference and about the salutary effects of spaced practices, we shall not be surprised to learn that a rest period may turn out to be valuable in problem solving. At all events, this is true. After the student has applied himself for some time and has still reached no solution, he may well be encouraged to put the problem aside for a short time and to take it up again after a rest. Many scientists, inventors, and creative artists report that, after they have reached a certain stage, they regularly lay a problem aside and let the matter "incubate" for a time. Most creative thinkers who have written on this subject, or who have been questioned, claim that they are more likely to achieve the necessary insight if they come at the problem somewhat refreshed.

In advising the student to set the problem aside, however, we must remember that this is profitable only if he has reached a certain stage of preparation. The scientists and artists who have achieved such brilliant insights state that the rest or incubation is likely to be useless unless they have already done much work on the problem. Before they permit themselves to set the problem aside, they make sure that they have the nature of the problem clearly in mind. If it is a complex problem they make sure they know the over-all structure. If it is a simpler problem they may even memorize the details. But one thing is certain: *they do not rest just because they are discouraged or tired.* They lay the problem aside only when they have a clear idea of the nature of the problem itself.

Summary

Experience always comes to us in organized or structured form. When the external world is largely structured, we react to general patterns. When the outside world is only partially patterned, we enhance and add to the pattern that is there. The pattern dominates our experience. If some detail is necessary to complete the pattern, we will experience the detail whether it is in the external world or not. The general pattern often is experienced as constant, even though the details may be altered.

One of the great tasks of the teacher is to make use of this tendency to see things in patterned form. It is easier to learn the general meaningful pattern than to learn the details. When the pattern is learned, many of the details are mastered with little effort. The general pattern is also remembered long after many of the details are lost. The general pattern or over-all meaning should be presented first whenever that pattern can be apprehended by the students. Details should be presented in relation to the over-all pattern. Hidden or elusive patterns should be brought out. If the material is arbitrary and completely devoid of an inherent pattern, an arbitrary pattern in the form of mnemonic devices may be used.

Because general patterns are more easily learned, there has been some suggestion that selections should be memorized as "wholes." This suggestion must not be overworked, however, since other factors, such as discouragement, may make "whole" learning less efficient.

Meaningful relations should be stressed, not only when presenting materials, but also when arranging for reinforcement. It is most important that, whenever possible, the student realize that "this way of acting leads to that kind of reinforcement." When such a relation is clearly apprehended, learning will be greatly facilitated. Some such insight, of course, will appear even without the aid of the teacher, but the teacher can do much to enhance insight and to bring out relations that the student otherwise would miss.

Meaning is a device that can be used to expedite general learning. More important, however, meaning is a prime goal of teaching. A rich store of broad, meaningful principles is the greatest gift the school can confer, not only as an aid in solving the practical problems which the student faces, but also to help the student satisfy his natural need to see the world in meaningful and ordered form.

To develop meanings, the teacher uses the standard devices of motivation, practice, reinforcement, and guidance. In teaching, it is important to remember that an understanding of abstract principles arises from experience and can never far outrun concrete experience. Abstract words for which there is no experiential background can be grossly misunderstood. Abstract concepts can be developed from the use of a large number of concrete experiences in each of which the abstract principle is involved.

Thinking and problem solving, so important in the work of the teacher, are not new and completely different processes. They overlap processes discussed throughout the book. Problem solving calls for *orientation,* first to the problem itself and then to one or more narrow aspects of the problem. It is also necessary to *search* the problem to see what is called for and to search the available material, looking for a solution. In searching the available material, we usually employ a *search model* which we keep in mind as we inspect possible solutions. The search model is determined not only by the problem but also by our biases. The first tentative solution, when it does appear, often comes as a surprise and without deliberation. It may be evoked by some sort of resonance with the search model. Following the appearance of a tentative solution, some sort of *trial* is necessary and usually appears. This can be symbolic or overt, highly systematic or almost random. Some random trials are inevitable when the student is completely baffled.

The "set" or approach adopted in solving one problem will help in solving similar problems but may be a hindrance when different problems are faced. Ideally, students should quickly acquire a set, but readily abandon it when the set no longer applies.

To help the student solve his immediate problem, it is important to urge persistence even when there is no evidence of progress; to encourage him to concentrate on the problem and not on his own performance; to be skeptical of the first solution which presents itself; and to be prepared to consider a radically different approach if the first attempt does not succeed. After much systematic preparatory work has been done, it may be wise to set the problem aside for a time. Logic is not to be expected in the task of evoking or reaching the tentative solution or hypothesis. Logic is to be invoked, of course, in testing the solution and in explaining it to other people.

SPECIFIC REFERENCES

1. Noble, C. E. The role of stimulus meaning (m) in serial verbal learning. *J. exp. Psychol.*, 1952, *43*, 437–446.
2. McGeoch, J. A. *The psychology of human learning.* Longmans, 1942, pp. 157–160.
3. Katona, G. *Organizing and memorizing.* Columbia University Press, 1940.
4. Reed, H. B. Factors influencing the learning and retention of concepts. I. The influence of set. *J. exp. Psychol.*, 1946, *36*, 71–87.
5. Brownell, W. A., and Moser, H. E. *Meaningful vs. mechanical learning.* Duke University Press, 1949.
6. Hilgard, E. R., and others. Rote memorization, understanding, and transfer: an extension of Katona's card-trick experiments. *J. exp. Psychol.*, 1953, *46*, 288–292.
7. Jensen, M. B., and Lemaire, Agnes. Ten experiments on whole and part learning. *J. educ. Psychol.*, 1937, *28*, 37–54.
8. Woodworth, R. S. *Experimental psychology.* Holt, 1938, p. 223.
9. Walk, R. D. Effect of discrimination reversal on human discrimination learning. *J. exp. Psychol.*, 1952, *44*, 410–419.
10. Postman, L., and Jarrett, R. F. An experimental analysis of learning without awareness. *Amer. J. Psychol.*, 1952, *65*, 244–255.

11. Johnston, A. Profiles, Alias Nero Wolfe—II. *The New Yorker,* 1949, *25,* No. 22 (July 23, p. 30).
12. Woodworth, R. S. *Experimental psychology.* Holt, 1938, p. 813.
13. Thistlethwaite, D. Attitude and structure as factors in the distortion of reasoning. *J. abnorm. soc. Psychol.,* 1950, *45,* 442–458.
14. Guetzkow, H. An analysis of the operation of set in problem-solving behavior. *J. gen. Psychol.,* 1951, *45,* 219–244.
15. Birch, H. G., and Rabinowitz, H. S. The negative effect of previous experience on productive thinking. *J. exp. Psychol.,* 1951, *41,* 121–125.
16. Maltzman, I., Fox, J., and Morrisett, L., Jr. Some effects of manifest anxiety on mental set. *J. exp. Psychol.,* 1953, *46,* 50–54.
17. Taylor, D. W., and McNemar, Olga. Problem solving and thinking. *Annu. Rev. Psychol.,* 1955, *6,* 455–482.
18. Cowen, E. L., and others. Generalization of problem-solving rigidity. *J. consult. Psychol.,* 1953, *17,* 100–103.
19. Stein, M., and Meer, B. Perceptual organization in a study of creativity. *J. Psychol.,* 1954, *37,* 39–43.
20. Schroder, H. M., and Rotter, J. B. Rigidity as learned behavior. *J. exp. Psychol.,* 1952, *44,* 141–150.
21. Bloom, B. S., and Broder, L. J. *Problem-solving processes of college students.* University of Chicago Press, 1950.
22. Morgan, W. J., and Morgan, Antonia B. Logical reasoning: with and without training. *J. appl. Psychol.,* 1953, *37,* 399–401.

SUGGESTIONS FOR FURTHER READING

For advanced treatments of the whole problem of thinking, see any one of the following sources:

1. Humphrey, G. *Thinking: an introduction to its experimental psychology.* Wiley, 1951.

   This book covers the whole field, but gives special emphasis to the early laboratory studies.
2. Vinacke, W. E. *The psychology of thinking.* McGraw-Hill, 1952.
3. Johnson, D. M. *The psychology of thought and judgment.* Harper, 1955.

For a more concise treatment, see any of the following:

4. Stevens, S. S. *Handbook of experimental psychology.* Wiley, 1951, Chap. 19. Cognitive processes (Leeper, R.).

5. Woodworth, R. S., and Schlosberg, H. *Experimental psychology*. Holt, 1954, Chap. 26.

6. Munn, N. L. *The evolution and growth of human behavior*. Houghton Mifflin, 1955, Chap. 11. Symbolic processes in children.

Emphasis on the development of ability to deal with symbolic processes.

The following reference discusses problem solving in relation to the classroom:

7. Thorndike, R. L. How children learn the principles and techniques of problem solving. *Yearb. nat. soc. Stud. Educ., 49*, (I), 1950, Chap. 8.

For specific references dealing with detailed aspects of problem solving, see the following bibliographical sources:

8. Russell, D. H. The development of thinking processes. *Rev. educ. Res.*, 1953, *23*, 137–145.

9. Taylor, D. W., and McNemar, Olga. Problem solving and thinking. *Annu. Rev. Psychol.*, 1955, *6*, 455–482.

Exercises and Questions for Discussion

1. You are teaching a student in the first grade the word *mother*. What aspects of the "structure" of the word would you emphasize?

2. You are teaching a high-school student, who has already studied Latin, the meaning of *madre*. What aspects of the structure would you emphasize?

3. To what extent and under what conditions will you encourage your students to employ the whole method in memorizing selections of poetry?

4. Can the teacher do anything to sharpen insightful reinforcement at the outset of learning; in the early stages of learning; after some progress has been made? Illustrate the appropriate steps that might be taken at each stage.

5. Outline a lesson for teaching young children the meaning of *above*.

6. When teaching students to use a new and complex process, be sure that they use it at first in connection with familiar material. This familiar material acts as a form of guidance which keeps the student on the right path.

Illustrate this point as applied to the teaching of algebra; as applied to the teaching of syllogistic reasoning.

7. Two wordings are suggested for the title of a debate:

    (a) Resolved that the nation's interest would be best served by encouraging at least 50 percent of the general population to continue formal education until the age of twenty-two. (b) Resolved that higher education should be democratic rather than aristocratic.

Discuss the advantages and disadvantages of the two wordings. Prepare a third statement which is an improvement on either.

8. Here are two problems:

   (a) The ages of a man and his wife are together 98. He is twice as old as she was when he was the age she is today. What are their ages?

   (b) A physician wishes to subject an internal tumor to an intense X-ray treatment. He wishes to apply a total dosage which is so strong that it would also injure the tissues through which it would pass. Can you suggest any solution to his problem?

After solving these problems, go over the steps you took. How did you go about getting a clearer view of the essential problem to be solved? Did you employ any specific devices such as setting up an equation, or making a diagram? Did you talk to yourself about the conditions that had to be met? Were you conscious of a deliberate attempt to *test* your tentative solutions?

9. Recall some recent experiences in which you were puzzled and felt the need of figuring the problem out. (For instance: A friend of yours has suddenly begun to act "distant" or cool. You are curious about some new gadget on a television set.) Try to recall the different steps that occurred.

13

Reducing Interference and Confusion

THE TOPICS CONSIDERED so far in Part Three are the chief devices and tools that the teacher uses in his daily classroom work. In directing the learning process, the teacher must make continual use of motivation, practice, guidance, reinforcement, and insight. He must also make use of the meaningful relations within and around the materials of instruction. In using these valuable tools, however, the teacher must be prepared to encounter results which he did not anticipate and which, perhaps, he did not desire. For these powerful tools, like so many other devices, can work in more ways than one. Even with the greatest skill, many undesirable results are bound to occur. Because of this inevitable fact, we must now consider means of reducing these undesirable features and of eliminating or correcting them when they do occur.

Learning Is Seldom Neatly Channeled

Most of us, in our haphazard thoughts, are inclined to regard teaching as an arduous but relatively straightforward task. In describing teaching, we are inclined to use such metaphors as "molding" character or "building" desirable attitudes. By such metaphors we imply that the teacher has a very definite control over the ideas, the skills, and the attitudes that he develops in his students. We suggest that he can act on one idea or attitude without affecting other ideas or attitudes to any appreciable extent, just as the sculptor can modify one portion of the statue and still leave the other portions intact if he so chooses.

Actually, of course, the teacher's control over his "material" is nowhere near so precise as that of the sculptor or carpenter. The teacher cannot act directly on the ideas and skills of his students. He must work in indirect fashion and can never be sure that any one move of his will have the precise effect intended. And he most certainly cannot be sure that the effects of his acts will be limited to those intended. On the contrary, he must accept the inevitable fact that, in bringing about one change in the student, he is bound to produce other changes as well, some of which he may desire and some of which he may wish to avoid.

A much safer analogy or metaphor for the description of the teacher's task is that of guidance, and guidance of a very fluid and elusive substance. In guiding the ideas, tendencies, or behavior of a child, it is as if we were trying to herd a group of lively animals along a prescribed path. We can apply stimulation to start the animals moving, hoping that they will move in the right direction. If they do not, we can apply supplementary stimuli to discourage them from going in certain directions. But our control is far from definite. We do not transport them. We depend on their activity. We stimulate and we guide. We know full well, however, that in spite of our guidance the herd may seek a roundabout route whenever they encounter some slight obstacle in the path we have set. We know that even if we succeed in keeping them more or less along the desired route, we will have minor difficulties to contend with. Even while going in the right direction, they may spill over onto territory we should like them to avoid. Moreover, in getting a certain number of animals to follow the path, we may inadvertently include a few stragglers. At times the presence of these uninvited guests may not disturb us. At other times it may be necessary to interrupt our main activity to get rid of the intruders. Our efforts to drive them back, however, may also chase away some of the animals we wish to retain.

Such is a fair analogy of the task which the teacher undertakes in directing the development of behavior and of the separate tendencies and insights of children. As in managing the herd, the direction of development involves guidance of a very general sort, with effects which cannot always be confined to the behavior we are interested in. Certainly it is a type of guidance which, at the best, is likely to be very imperfect.

Because of this loose and unprecise form of guidance we face two kinds of difficulties. Our most serious worry is that these extraneous doings will actually prevent us from ever accomplishing our primary task. As a secondary worry we must face the fact that when we do accomplish our primary task we may also produce many additional extraneous results. Some of these may be all to the good, but some may be harmful.

Primary Task Circumvented by Extraneous Learning

Suppose a child in school is asked a question and replies by awkward floundering. On this account he experiences some unpleasant results or some negative reinforcement. The teacher, for instance, may let out a roar of disapproval or may look hurt or surprised. The other pupils may give evidence of amusement or mild disdain. Such annoying social results constitute most powerful negative reinforcement, and ordinarily something will be done to avoid them. Naturally, the most straightforward way of avoiding such results in the future is through the direct learning intended by the teacher. The most straightforward arrangement, that is to say, is that the next time the student encounters that question or a similar question he will respond in a more adequate way. If he comes to respond in this more adequate way, he will secure better social results.

Teaching would be much easier than it is if all learning were of the straightforward variety just discussed. Unfortunately, however, learning is seldom completely straightforward. The student does not always avoid the annoyance of negative reinforcement by coming to make a more appropriate response to future questions. There are many other ways of avoiding the annoyance of an effect. These other ways, since they defeat the teacher's purpose, are considered as types of roundabout learning.

Extraneous Methods of Reducing Negative Reinforcement

Avoiding the Situation. A student who has been embarrassed by his answer to a certain question may try to avoid that embarrassment in the future by trying to escape being questioned. The most drastic way of avoiding such question is to stay away from school. Because of truancy laws and parental authority, this extreme device is seldom available to young children. It is available to adults, however, and to older high-school students and is sometimes used by them. As a less drastic step, the student can try to change teachers or to drop that particular subject. At a still less drastic level the student may merely try to avoid the teacher's eye, or to make himself inconspicuous by one of the many devices that children use.

Dodging the Annoyance of the Results. Dodging the situation is not the only indirect means of making life more tolerable. A student can continue to attend class, continue to face questioning, continue to answer by awkward floundering, and yet, by one means or another, he may be able to reduce some of the original annoyance. Theoretically, he might induce the teacher to become less critical, or the guffawing classmates to be more indulgent. Such developments, however, are not especially likely. And they are not the chief devices at our disposal. Even if other people continue to poke fun at our ineptitudes or heap scorn on our replies, we may find internal devices which alleviate the annoyance. We may pretend, to ourselves or to others, that no genuine scorn is intended. When the brutal husband, for instance, makes some withering comment on one of his wife's ideas, she may be able to pretend that he really does not mean it that way. Many a helpless person, when subjected to abuse, concocts a pathetic smile which seems to say, "I know you don't really mean it."

We can also lessen the annoyance of social disparagement by affecting, or feeling, a lofty disdain for the source of the disparagement. If anyone has bested us in an argument, for instance, and has thus made us feel small or cheap, we may try to wipe away some of the annoyance by a remark, often completely irrelevant, intended to make our opponent seem less worthy. We may comment on his immediate or remote ancestry or on his stature or his lack of hair. Anything which makes him seem less important may, illogically enough, lessen our chagrin at the annoyance he has caused us.

A further mechanism at our disposal is that of merely refusing to be aware of the contempt of other people. As we point out in other sections, most people are able to forget or ignore incidents which hurt their self-esteem. And there is every reason to suppose that many of us try to suppress our worries about the contempt other people may feel for us.

Many of these mechanisms or devices for indirect learning are available to school children and are undoubtedly used by them. A youngster who has responded in such a way as to bring down ridicule on himself may secure some solace by persuading himself that the subject is unimportant or the teacher unreasonable, the question is vague and impossible, and the guffawing students are beneath contempt. Insofar as he is successful in using any or all of these devices, the annoyance is partially removed, or at least palliated. When much of this annoyance or negative reinforcement is thus dissipated through indirect channels, there is less likelihood that the reinforcement will act directly to induce the student to respond in a more adequate way.

Significance for Personal Adjustment

It will be realized, of course, that in the broad view the chief significance of the various evasive devices for indirect learning does not lie in the fact that they hinder academic growth but in the fact that, carried to an extreme, they may warp and twist the personality of the child. It will be seen that most of these devices for getting rid of annoyance by blaming others, by pretending to be indifferent, or by refusing to attend to unpleasant things, when used too freely can lead to more drastic methods of escaping reality. Indeed, any interference with academic growth would be of slight moment compared to the general harmful influences that these devices exert on the general personal and social growth of the child. This important problem occupies a considerable portion of Part Four which is concerned with the promotion of personal adjustment. Meanwhile we consider these extraneous devices as they plague us in the development of academic growth.

The Use of Properly Graded Tasks

We are not bound to be foiled in attaining our primary objectives by the student's use of one of these extraneous, roundabout paths. Roundabout learning is typically a device of desperation. To most people, straightforward learning would be more acceptable if the choice were open. But when denied success by a legitimate or regular approach, people will adopt some other indirect route if it will lead to a more bearable state of affairs. Because of this fact, we can often prevent roundabout learning by making legitimate success more readily attainable.

The teacher easily has it within his power to enable pupils to attain legitimate success. The simplest method, of course, is to arrange the material in easy gradations. This, clearly enough, is a very large order. To accomplish this arrangement, no single rule can be given for all subjects or for all pupils, since steps which are exceedingly easy for one student may be too difficult for another. It is possible, however, to consider a few general suggestions.

In these, as in many other matters, the teacher should be guided by his day-to-day experience. In beginning any new subject, he might do well to err on the side of making each new step too easy. He should follow this procedure until all pupils have experienced a measure of success and have realized the pleasure that comes from legitimate mastery of subject matter. As the work progresses and as he finds more and more pupils taking the work in their stride, he might properly increase the difficulty of the steps. A moderate amount of difficulty or frustration is less likely to cause trouble once the pupil knows from previous experience that a legitimate solution is possible. A certain amount of difficulty, moreover, adds zest and challenge to the learning task and provides a valuable experience. While gradually making the steps more difficult, the teacher should keep a watchful eye on all pupils and should maintain an especially careful watch on the slower pupils. As soon as he finds pupils adopting any of the various roundabout devices and persisting in these in spite of increased motivation, he should consider the advisability of presenting the material in more gradual steps.

Primary Task Accomplished, but with Extraneous Side Effects

So far the discussion has covered extraneous learning which circumvents or negates the learning which we intend. This is not, however, the only way in which extraneous learning may work. Very often the extraneous learning does not prevent or circumvent the intended learning. The learning may proceed more or less along the channels just as we intend, but, in so doing, it may also "spill over" and include more territory than we intend. We may, to forsake the metaphor, succeed in establishing the behavior we have in mind, but in so doing we may also bring about other results which we did not foresee. And these results may or may not suit our purposes.

The Dual Action of All Stimulation and Reinforcement

In the discussion of reinforcement and guidance (Chapter 11) we make much of the close relation between reinforcement and stimulation. A student reading a selection aloud sees the new word indecorous (S_1) which he pronounces "indeCORous" (R_1). To guide him into a correct response you provide an additional stimulus (S_2) by saying "inDECKorous." To this new stimulus he responds (R_2) by a hasty correction "inDECKorous." This guidance (S_2) that you provided led to a new and correct response (R_2). But this is not its entire effect. It also acted as negative reinforcement for the tendency $S_1 - R_1$. This additional effect is all to the good. It may also, however, have provided negative reinforcement for his tendency to read aloud. And this additional effect may not be one of your wishes or purposes.

Anything we do to a student to elicit new behavior is bound to have reinforcing side effects. Anything we do to produce reinforcement is bound to elicit some new behavior. Let us consider these complexities in more detail.

Unintentional Reinforcement from a Simple Request. A student comes into my office just as I am about to leave for a class. I say, "Could you make it this afternoon? I have to rush off to a class." Now these words are designed merely to bring about a specific piece of behavior. They are designed to bring the student back to my office at a later time. But is this all the influence which those words will have? By no means. Those words did not fall into the student's life in a complete void. He encountered those words just after he had acted in a certain way. Those words must be regarded in the light of the broader picture. To understand their effect we must go back at least one stage.

Let us suppose the student happened to be going by the office and, seeing me not engaged, he just dropped in to pass the time of day. Here, then, is vague motivation, stimulation, and behavior. My comment suggesting a future conference follows his behavior. Will it act as negative reinforcement or discouragement? Will my remarks make him any less likely to drop into my office in casual fashion when he sees me unoccupied? Very probably. It is quite possible that those remarks, directed solely to a future conference, may still discourage his tendency to drop into the office in this way. It may act on that tendency whether I want it to or not.

The Stimulating Effects of Reinforcement Applied to Past Behavior. I dictate a letter to President Copeland. The letter comes back addressed to President Kaplan. It is an understandable mistake on the part of my new stenographer. But it is one that should be avoided in the future. It would be better in the future, when she hears the same slurring sounds issuing from my mouth, that she should respond by typing Copeland. So I apply mild discouragement or negative reinforcement. Anxious to weaken her present way of doing things, I call attention to the mistake. Now I have no desire that my admonition should elicit any definite immediate behavior. I do not wish the stenographer to break into tears, to apologize abjectly, or to make a huffy remark about my sloppy enunciation. I merely want to weaken the tendency to spell "Copeland" with the letters K-a-p-l-a-n. But in spite of my intentions, it is quite possible that my comment will elicit some undesirable reaction.

Dealing with the Dual Action of Stimulation and Reinforcement

The inevitable dual action of stimulation and reinforcement at times may be quite in accord with our intentions. Let us suppose that a young child, stimulated by the white handle of the valve on the gas stove, responds by reaching out and moving the valve. Immediately following the behavior sequence, the alarmed mother applies a sharp slap to the child's hand. Now this slap does at least two things. It initiates immediate behavior in that it leads the child to withdraw his hand, and perhaps to whimper. It also acts as discouragement or negative reinforcement on the child's tendency to play with the gas valves. In this illustration, as it happens, the dual action may be all to the good and may fit in with the mother's intentions. She probably wants the child to get his hand away from the stove, and she also probably wants him to leave the stove alone in the future.

Another illustration: Encouraged by the green light, the automobile driver continues across the intersection. A pedestrian wanders absent-mindedly into the street. The driver sounds the horn. Like the slap on the hand, this horn may act on the unwary pedestrian in two ways. It may make him jump back, right now. It may also cause him to be more cautious in the future. In this instance, both of these results may fit in with the driver's intentions. It is certainly a good thing for the pedestrian to jump back now. It would be a good thing if he were more careful in the future.

Although there are times when this dual action is intended and is all to the good, there are other times when such dual action runs counter to our wishes. There are times when we wish to elicit new behavior from a person, and yet at the same time we do not wish to cast any reflection on his previous conduct. There are other times when we wish to correct an unfortunate tendency in our friends or in our charges, but in doing so we would like to prevent them from feeling crushed or angry.

Eliciting New Behavior without Reflecting on Past Behavior. This problem occurs over and over again in daily living. You ask your neighbor at the dinner table to pass the salt. Your sole intention is to elicit a simple response. You have absolutely no wish to reprimand him or to call attention to his negligence. Yet your request will probably act as a mild reprimand. You will probably get the salt but will also get an apology. Try to work out a way of phrasing your request so that it will not seem to reflect on what he has done (or not done). It is hard to do!

Another illustration: A student leaving my office sees the open door and starts to close it. I say (in my most casual way), "Just leave the door open, please." The student responds to this simple request by hurriedly jerking his hand from the door and saying, "I'm sorry." Now I did not intend this request as negative reinforcement of his previous behavior. My sole object was to have the door remain open. Yet whether I wished it or not, my remark acted as a mild scolding. It said, in effect, "You were wrong to close that door." In spite of my intention that the remark should act only in a forward direction, it inevitably reflected on the conduct just finished.

The teacher often faces this problem of inducing a response without acting in an undesired manner on previous behavior. For instance, let us suppose the teacher has asked Sam a question, and he has replied satisfactorily. The teacher now merely wants to draw Mary into the discussion. Immediately after Sam has replied the teacher says, "What do you think, Mary?" Now this question, while not *intended* to act as a mild reprimand for Sam, *may* act this way. It may make Sam think he was wrong. The same danger may arise when a student has answered satisfactorily as far as he has gone, but the teacher wants a more complete statement. The teacher, in attempting to draw the pupil out, may unintentionally give him the idea that his first answer was on the wrong track.

Present Appropriate Reinforcement First. Such undesired back action may often be avoided by presenting the "reinforcement" aspect of the new request before presenting the rest of it. We can say, "That's fine, Sam," (reinforcement). "Have you anything to add, Mary?" (new stimulus). Or we can say, "You're on the right track. Tell us a little more about it." Observe any good teacher and notice how often he will take care of this problem. He will be sure to provide any necessary comment on preceding conduct before he goes on to make a new request or suggestion. These prefatory comments are often very unostentatious and fit smoothly into the flow of the lesson. Yet they prevent many a pupil from suspecting that he has been wrong.

It is true that good teachers seem to honor the rule just discussed, even without thinking about it. It is surprising, however, how often some teachers and parents not only fail to observe this rule but go out of their way to violate it. A mother, for instance, wishes her daughter to help with the dishes. At the moment she does not contemplate any radical reform of her daughter's character. She just wants to elicit a simple behavior series, namely, helping with the dishes. If she were to follow our injunction she would say, "Mary, you have been very good about helping me lately, but would you mind doing one more thing?" Instead of using this approach, however, mothers often say, "Mary, it wouldn't hurt you to do the dishes *for a change*." This additional sting which the mother throws in for good measure accomplishes no purpose whatsoever. It makes Mary feel very angry or guilty. It does not make her any more inclined to do the dishes. It may, perhaps, help the mother get some annoyance out of her system, or may justify her in her own mind for making the request. Apart from that, however, it could much better have been left out and a more tactful remark inserted in its place.

Preventing Necessary Reinforcement from Eliciting Undesired Responses. There are many times when we wish to weaken an undesired tendency but do not wish to elicit an abject apology or tears. A subordinate, for instance, appears to have the tendency to broadcast confidential matters too freely. You feel sure that this is not just a weak transitory tendency which will drop off anyhow. You decide that it is necessary to weaken this tendency. Yet you do not wish to make him feel bad, flare up in anger, or resign. You merely want him to be more discreet in the future. In such a situation you face a problem. It will be difficult to apply any discouragement which will weaken the tendency and which will not at the same time elicit an undesired immediate reaction.

The problem just outlined has an obvious converse. You may wish to strengthen a weak but commendable tendency, and yet at the same time you do not wish your praise to elicit blushing embarrassment on the one hand or a strutting cock-o'-the-walk attitude on the other. This latter problem, of course, is less serious than that in the original illustration.

In the schoolroom we often need to discourage a tendency but wish to avoid the logical reaction to any statement we may make. Any correction or reprimand that we apply is not likely to stop just where we want it to. It may make the pupil feel cheap, ashamed, or angry. It may make him sulk, bluster, or induce prolonged worry. We wish to weaken the tendency, but we do not wish to elicit any of these responses. What shall we do? Good teachers have found many devices to take care of this problem. These devices come under two headings: (a) Do not make too much of the mistake or dereliction. (b) By explicit statement, or by general manner, or by some other means, indicate that the reprimand is directed to the sin and not to the sinner.

Necessary Criticism or Punishment Should Not Be Too Discouraging.
In the later stages of learning, some correction, criticism, or punishment
will inevitably be needed. No teacher can bring about genuine mastery
of a subject without a fair amount of correction or even a modicum
of downright censure. There are, however, all degrees and types of correction and censure. Keeping this in mind, the teacher should be sure that
his criticisms are within reasonable bounds. His disparagement, if used,
should not be more severe than is necessary. He should distinguish between the amount of criticism necessary to weaken the tendency which
has just functioned and the amount of criticism necessary to relieve his
own outraged feelings. The former is often much less than the latter.

Reprimands May Be Casual, Short, and Snappy. It is very often the
unduly prolonged reprimand which induces sulkiness, anger, or humiliation. The hurt of the reprimand may come, not from the actual statements made, but from the mere fact of being singled out for prolonged
derogatory attention. The longer this unflattering attention persists, the
greater the hurt. This is probably true no matter whether the scolding
is violent and abusive or sweet and reasonable. Indeed many people
believe that to reason with a youngster in a sweet, pained, understanding
tone is a more fiendish form of torture than verbally "pinning his ears
back."

With a short, casual reprimand, then, we run less risk of making the
youngster feel the discomfort of an unflattering spotlight. A snap of the
fingers, a lift of the eyebrow, a meaningful glance, or a simple "Break it
up!"—any of these should prove effective as a reprimand and yet should
be unlikely to produce any intense resentment or other undesirable
attitude. Certainly it seems wise whenever possible to make the reprimands short, casual, and relatively impersonal. Do not make too much
of the incident. Get the reprimand over with and do it with the least
possible interruption to the normal flow of events. Save the heart-to-heart
talks for cases that refuse to yield to a grimace or a snap of the finger.

*Reprimands Should Be Accompanied by Some Evidence of Acceptance
of the Student.* There are many ways by which we can say in effect
"You are a swell kid, but if you do *that* again I'll——." The easiest way
(and perhaps the worst way) is to make some such statement explicitly.
This is better than nothing, though it does verge on the maudlin. Very
often, however, we can achieve the same effect by the use of humor. By
this means we may convey the idea that something has gone wrong, but
we still find the world relatively habitable. Sometimes good teachers, by

the very exaggerated and semihumorous violence of their assault, make it very clear that the mistake or misdemeanor is something less than fatal.

The Role of Extraneous Stimuli

In the conditioned-response experiments, we ordinarily focus our attention on two or three stimuli. We observe the sound of the tuning fork and the meat powder as they act on the dog. But we know that many other stimuli may be acting on him. Each of these, moreover, even though uninvited, may take an enthusiastic part in the transaction. After a few experiences the squeak of the door or the sight of the experimenter might readily elicit the salivary reflex. To reduce these extraneous effects as much as possible, Pavlov and his students conducted their experiments in soundproof, lightproof rooms.

These same effects operate in the schoolroom. Using the conditioned-response technique, for instance, we present a child with the symbols d-o-g and immediately thereafter show him a picture of a dog, eliciting the word "dog." Later the symbols themselves should be enough to elicit the word "dog." While he was learning these new things, however, other aspects of the environment were acting on him. A patch of sunlight warmed his shoulder. The smell of geraniums stimulated his nostrils. The pattern on the dress of the girl ahead of him engaged his attention. Now any one of these things which was present while he was learning to respond to d-o-g may, in the future, make him think of "dog." This kind of stimulus spread happens continually in all our learning. Sometimes, by the way, this process causes us great bewilderment as when we are suddenly reminded of some old idea and cannot put our finger on the fleeting odor or pattern or squeak that brought the forgotten memory back to mind.

Trace Conditioned Response. Our worry is not limited to things that are actually present at the time that the main stimuli become connected with the response. A stimulus that was present a few seconds ago may also become involved in this process. The symbols d-o-g that he saw just before he saw the picture of the dog will acquire the power to make him think of "dog." But the symbols that he saw a few seconds, or even minutes, earlier may also acquire this power, though fortunately not to the same degree of strength. These trace conditioned responses and the trouble they make for us are discussed in detail later on.

Stimulus Generalization. It is bad enough to have our young child coming to think of "dog" when he encounters stimuli that just happened to be present at the time of the original learning, or that were present a few seconds earlier. But this is not our only worry. Our student may also be led to think of "dog" when he encounters some stimuli that he has never experienced before. This is seen quite clearly in the conditioned salivary response. Here, let us suppose, a dog has learned to salivate whenever the tuning fork sounds at middle C (256 vibrations per second). During this learning, and during his entire life, let us suppose, he has never heard any other note. Through stimulus generalization, however, he will also be led to salivate when he hears the notes C# or D# or even F. True, he will not salivate quite so much when he hears these adjacent notes, but he will salivate to some extent. Thus in establishing one tendency, we automatically established other tendencies, although of somewhat lesser strength. This phenomenon is called *stimulus generalization,* for the simple reason that the dog, in learning to respond to one stimulus, has also learned to respond to the whole general class of stimuli.

The phenomenon of stimulus generalization is most pronounced when, as in the illustration just used, the generalization spreads to other stimuli in the same sense avenue(1). For instance, in learning to respond to one tone, the dog automatically learns to respond to other tones. Or in learning to salivate when he sees a light of a given brightness, he also learns to salivate when he sees lights of similar but not identical brightness. But stimulus generalization is not restricted to such simple kinds of generalization. Young children, for instance, who learn to think of "dog" when they see the symbols d-o-g, will also think of "dog" when they see similar symbols(2). They may think of "dog" when they see the symbols d-a-y or d-i-g. They learned to think this way at the same time that they learned to think of "dog" when they saw d-o-g. In the same way, the infant who has learned to say "da da" at the sight of his father may also have learned, embarrassingly enough, to respond similarly to any other man.

Extraneous Learning May or May Not Be Desired

If a child has learned to respond to one dog by affectionate approach, he is very likely to respond to any similar dog in the same way. If we wish him to adopt this trusting attitude toward dogs, all and sundry, then the secondary learning has been a distinct advantage. If, however, we wish him to be somewhat less effusive in his reactions toward strange dogs, the secondary learning will be a hindrance. Or, to take another example, in teaching him to respond to his own family situation by speaking frankly on very personal biological matters, we have also probably taught him to respond to other family situations in the same way. If this second type of behavior is desirable in our eyes, the secondary results of our teaching are all to the good. If the second type of behavior may lead to near disaster, the incidental results have, to this extent, been a nuisance.

It is apparent that sometimes these secondary or additional results are desired and at other times they are not. It may be that in teaching a child to keep away from candle flames we definitely hope that we shall also induce him to respect gas flames, bonfires, and father's pipe. It may be that having taught his elder brother to like Rimsky-Korsakov, we shall be overjoyed to find him also appreciating Wagner, Johann Strauss, and Carrie Jacobs Bond. We may, on the other hand, wish the student to discriminate between somewhat similar situations. We may wish him to pet our dog but to keep away from the neighbor's "Mutt." We may wish him to kiss Aunt Hattie but not her cook. We may wish him to like the blood and thunder of *Treasure Island* but to eschew Dead-eye Dick. In these instances, of course, the added learning is a nuisance.

Practice as a Means of Reducing Extraneous Learning. Fortunately, sheer practice will often reduce the influence of sensory generalization. This convenient arrangement is due to the fact that the tendency which we actually work on is usually stronger than any of the incidental tendencies which happen to be formed at the same time. The dog salivates more profusely to the sound of middle C than to the adjacent sounds he never heard. The pupil is much *more* likely to think of "dog" when he sees the letters d-o-g than when he smells geraniums or when he feels a warm patch of sunlight on his shoulder. The same is true for a whole host of incidental tendencies initiated by stimuli which just happened to be present when the main learning took place.

All during the learning period, the practiced tendency will maintain its lead over the incidental tendencies. In each practice session the main tendency will gain more in strength than any incidental tendencies which happen to be reinforced during that time. The main tendency, moreover, will be practiced each time, whereas many of the incidental tendencies will not be practiced each time. The smell of geraniums may not be present every time the child is learning to read the word dog.

As a net result of practice, then, the main tendency will gain in strength at a more rapid rate than the tendencies produced by sensory generalization.

Specific Discouragement as a Means of Reducing Stimulus Generalization. It will be noted that practice will cause the secondary tendencies to lose out in relation to the main tendency. General practice cannot be depended on, however, to reduce the absolute strength of any single bothersome tendency. To bring about such a reduction in strength, we should resort to direct correction or discouragement. Suppose, for instance, stimulus generalization has led the child to be too free with strange dogs. Practice in being friendly with his own dog will not reduce this tendency. He must be corrected when he is too free with the strange dog. It will be remembered that this correction should not be applied until we are sure that the undesired tendencies will not drop off of their own weight. It is foolish and unnecessary to discourage tendencies which are about to die out anyway. We should also delay the application of punishment or correction until the practiced or desired tendency has considerable strength. We should wait until the child feels quite at ease in the presence of his own dog before we discourage him from playing with strange dogs. These warnings, of course, are in line with the general advice on the application of punishment and reward.

The Problem of Extraneous Learning in Teaching Abstract Concepts

Extraneous learning can be very troublesome in teaching concepts(3). Many of the difficulties mentioned in this connection in Chapter 12 arise from the sort of extraneous learning just discussed. To teach such abstract ideas as *nineteen* or *square* or *red* or *just,* we must use some concrete materials. We must have nineteen objects or marks, we must have a square paper or diagram, we must have a red paper or cloth or block, and we must have characters to exemplify the concept of justice. When the child is confronted with nineteen marbles and learns that this is nineteen, he may of course come to respond correctly to the idea of nineteen. He may also, however, respond to a group of marbles by thinking nineteen. Similarly, a figure in medieval costume may come to suggest the idea of justice if the character chosen to exemplify this trait were so garbed. Most of us carry around a host of such illogical associations built up in this way.

Naturally we wish to prevent these incidental stimuli from eliciting the essential reaction. To do this, we must present the essential idea in many contexts. The child must encounter nineteen in connection with things other than marbles. He must react to squareness in tables, papers, diagrams, and garden plots. The concept of justice must appear in many different contexts. By such means, the essential idea will be practiced over and over again, while the incidental stimuli of any one example will be practiced only a few times.

The Spread of Reinforcement or Effects [1]

I find my five-year-old child at my workbench playing with a sharp chisel. Considerably agitated, I exclaim, "Put the chisel down." The child quickly drops the chisel, and I see that I have frightened him. This correction or negative reinforcement may well discourage the child from playing with the chisel in the future. This is quite in line with my wishes. The negative reinforcement may not stop here, however. It may also discourage the child from ever going near my workbench. This may or may not be in line with my wishes. The correction, moreover, could have even more far-reaching consequences, discouraging him from having anything to do with harmless tools or with the whole area of the workbench or with me.

To guard against the undesirable spread of reinforcement of this type, it is merely necessary to keep the reinforcement within moderate dosages. Be sure that the reinforcement is no more powerful than is necessary. It is much better to apply reinforcement that is too weak and to have to supplement it, than to apply reinforcement which may have a marked and undesirable effect on more inclusive behavior.

Should we expect "trace effects" as well as trace-conditioned responses? Suppose, for instance, a student hears "6 + 8" and says "14" but the teacher fails to comment. Right away the teacher asks "9 + 2?" The student says, "11" and the teacher says, "Right." We will expect the announcement of "Right" to strengthen the tendency to give "11" as the sum of 9 and 2. But is it possible that hearing "Right" for this question may also carry back to the previous experience and strengthen the tendency between "6 + 8" and "14"?

According to both Hull and Thorndike we should expect effects to spread or work back in this way. At one time, moreover, there was considerable evidence to indicate that such a spread may take place. From more recent investigations(4), however, it appears more likely that this apparent spread may be due to some incidental condition in the early experiments.

[1] The terms *spread of reinforcement* and *spread of effects* are used interchangeably. In the literature the latter phrase will be found most frequently.

Special Problems in Teaching a Fixed Series of Tendencies

Suppose the student is memorizing a list of names such as the sequence of presidents of the United States. Let us suppose this list is being learned by the aid of a "memory" drum—a device by which a strip of paper is made to move past a small window, exposing one name at a time. Let us suppose the name of Washington has appeared in the small window and has been followed a few seconds later by "Adams," and now the name of Jefferson has appeared.

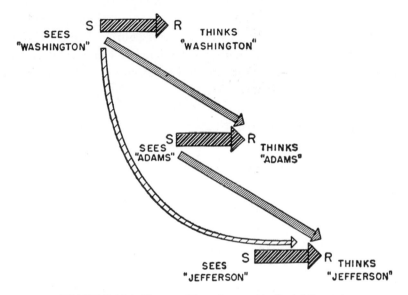

FIGURE 13-1. *Types of Interference in Serial Learning*

In Figure 13-1 the events in the memory-drum illustration are translated into conditioned-response terms. As indicated by the three heavy arrows, it is assumed that seeing the name of each President will automatically lead the student to think of the name, or perhaps even to say it to himself. A lighter arrow shows how "Washington" should become the conditioned stimulus for thinking "Adams," and how "Adams" should become the conditioned stimulus for thinking "Jefferson." So far everything is working very well. Unfortunately, however, we still have to reckon with trace-conditioned responses. At the time that "Adams" is being linked to "Jefferson," for instance, the name of "Washington" is still leaving a trace of itself in the experience of the learner. And so long as this trace is present, it is almost bound to get linked up to "Jefferson." This is shown by the lightest arrow.

Fortunately the link between "Washington" and "Jefferson" is weaker than the link between "Washington" and "Adams" or the link between "Adams" and "Jefferson." It has some strength, however, and what with the natural fluctuation of these strengths, it is most likely that once in awhile it will come to the fore. It is not infrequent that people listing the Presidents go right from Washington to Jefferson. In the same way a young child, learning to count, will occasionally say, "1, 2, 4" or "1, 2, 3, 5." One of these incidental connections has momentarily gained the upper hand.

When a fairly long series is to be memorized, the number of these incidental and interfering tendencies becomes enormous. Figure 13-2 diagrams these for a list of seven items. In this figure, there is no attempt to show the different strengths of the tendencies. From what has been said, however, it is clear that the links become weaker as they are stretched to span more items.

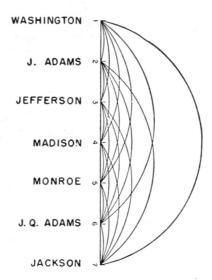

FIGURE 13-2. *Possibilities of Interference During the Learning of a Longer Series*

Fortunately the interfering remote connections are seldom as strong as the more direct connections. With continued practice, this advantage for the direct connections will gradually increase. We must not feel too much surprise or irritation, however, when one of these remote connections occasionally rises to the surface and wins out over the desired direct connections. This mistake does not come from perversity or indifference. The mistake is something that we have produced in the student, by the very same process that served to produce the direct learning we desire.

To get rid of these intruders we need, not scolding or censure, but patient practice and, as we shall see later on, a program of rest periods between practices.

Current Learning as Affected by Earlier or Later Learning

Suppose that at 2.00 P.M. one student, Bert, has had some practice with $3 \times 4 = 12$, and that at 2.30 P.M. he has some experience with $2 \times 6 = 12$. How will these two experiences affect each other? Will one get in the way of the other, or will they help each other, or will one have no influence whatever on the other? In Chart 13-1 we give the answers to this and to similar questions and try to work out a general rule.

Notice that, for Ann, there is no difference between the activities prac· ticed at two and at two-thirty. The stimuli for the two activities were identical. So were the responses. Here we would expect that the two-thirty practice would increase the skill that was developed at two. In the same way we would expect that the total result of the two-thirty practice will be all the greater for the previous experience at two.

Bert's problem is a little different. For him the tasks practiced at two and at two-thirty are somewhat similar but not completely similar. Specifically, we see that the questions (stimuli) for the two tasks are quite different but the answers (responses) happen to be the same. In a situation like this there is some evidence that the two activities will help each other to a slight extent. The two-thirty practice on $2 \times 6 = 12$ will slightly augment the skill acquired at two in mastering 3×4. The two-thirty learning, in turn, will be all the more effective for having had the two o'clock practice on the somewhat different task.

For Carol the two tasks are different both in stimuli and in responses. Here the evidence suggests that the activities will have no effect on each other. Carol's two-thirty experience with $8 + 6$ will not work back to weaken or support what was learned at two. And her mastery of $8 + 6$ at two-thirty will not receive any advantage or handicap from the fact that she has dealt with 3×4 at two.

David's review of "baby" arithmetic is harmful. His study of algebra at two-thirty will actually be handicapped by his two o'clock review. He would have less trouble with the two-thirty task if he had not had the two o'clock review of 3×4. By the same token, if his mastery of 3×4

CHART 13-1

Student	Items Practiced at 2.00 P.M.		Items Practiced at 2.30 P.M.		Relation of the Two Activities		Effect of One Activity on the Other
	Question (Stimulus)	Answer (Response)	Question (Stimulus)	Answer (Response)	Stimuli of the Two Activities	Responses of the Two Activities	
Ann	3×4	12	3×4	12	Same	Same	Helps $(+ + +)$
Bert	3×4	12	2×6	12	Different	Same	Helps $(+)$
Carol	3×4	12	$8 + 6$	14	Different	Different	None (0)
David	3×4	12	$a^3 \times a^4$	a^7	Similar	Different	Hurts $(-)$
Eva	Capital of France	Paris	Largest city in France	Paris	Some similarity	Same	Helps $(+ +)$
Frank	Capital of India	New Delhi	Largest city in India	Bombay	Some similarity	Different	Hurts $(-)$
Gloria	Capital of India	New Delhi	Largest city in France	Paris	Different	Different	None (0)
Harry	Meeting another car (U.S. rules)	Keep right	Meeting another car (English rules)	Keep left	Very similar	Different	Hurts $(- -)$

was none too good, it will become even more shaky from having had to work with the $a^3 \times a^4$ at two-thirty.

Follow the chart through and try to work out a general rule to tell when the two experiences facilitate each other and when they interfere. Whenever the same stimulus (car approaching) calls for different responses (pass on right or pass on left) at different times, we find interference. The fact that two different stimuli (3×4) and (2×6) call for the same response (12), however, produces no interference and may make for facilitation. When both the stimuli and responses of the two tasks are similar, we have, of course, merely a continuation of the same task. When the stimuli of the two tasks are different and the responses are also different, one task will have little or no effect on the other(5).

The illustrations from the chart are shown graphically in Figure 13-3. Whenever the two stimuli are the same (the part of the diagram

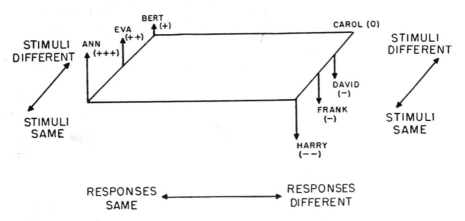

FIGURE 13-3. *Facilitation (+) and inhibition (−) in relation to the similarity of stimuli and the similarity of responses*

closest to you), response similarity plays a vital part. By arranging for similar responses we can produce marked facilitation. By arranging for different responses, we produce marked interference or inhibition. If the stimuli are different, however, (the line at the back of the diagram), similarity of the responses does not matter so much. As we move from the front to the back of the diagram, the marked influences of response similarity are ironed out. With different stimuli the effects may be zero or slightly positive, but never very extensive.

From all this it appears that there are several possible relations between two activities. One activity (2.00 P.M.) can facilitate some learning that is about to occur (*proactive facilitation*). The two o'clock activity, on the other hand, can interfere with some learning that is about to occur (*proactive inhibition*). The two o'clock activity may have no effect whatever on the learning that is about to occur. Conversely, the two-thirty activity can work back to facilitate the learning that took place at two o'clock (*retroactive facilitation*), or the two-thirty activity can work back to interfere with the two o'clock learning (*retroactive inhibition*). Proactive facilitation and proactive inhibition represent the same phenomena as positive and negative transfer and these important topics are discussed at length in the next chapter.

Retroactive Inhibition. The sort of interference offered by retroactive inhibition is likely to be most serious when motivation is low and when rote memorization predominates. It will play little part when students are working with material that is meaningful or highly structured, and if motivation is at a reasonable level. By the same token, the facilitation we have discussed can be increased by the use of meaning or insight. In general, it will be remembered, we can expect some facilitation whenever the two activities are similar in the responses involved. This facilitation can be increased if we are careful to point out the similarity in the responses or to bring out a subtle similarity that is really there but may escape the student(6).

General setting also plays a part in retroactive inhibition. Merely by moving our students to a different classroom when they are about to study interfering material, we can reduce the amount of retroactive interference to some extent(7). This change in room, of course, cannot be expected to rule out all interference.

As we might expect, retroactive inhibition is more likely to occur when both the original and the new materials are imperfectly learned. Your understanding of English, for instance, is not likely to be greatly harmed by a study of some new language even when that new language calls for different responses to the same stimuli. It is when both activities are in about the same stage of development(8) and in a fairly early stage at that, that we can expect them to get in the way of each other.

In general then, tasks that are well mastered are less susceptible to retroactive inhibition than tasks which are only partly learned. To this rule, however, Prentice(9) has discovered an apparent exception. He found less retroactive inhibition on the part of students who were forced to leave off learning the original material while some of the tasks were still incomplete. Prentice thinks, however, that this reduction of retroactive inhibition is not due to interruption in and of itself, but due to the fact that the interruption rouses or challenges the student and gives him new determination or intention. Thus, interruption may be just another aspect of intention to learn.

The whole problem of the influence of interrupting a task is rather complex(10). At times this interruption leads the student to remember the task better and to wish to return to the interrupted task. At other times this is not so. It is possible that whenever interruption of a task does affect memory for the task, it does so by changing the student's attitude toward the task. If the interruption acts as a challenge or sets up tensions, we may find greater interest and better memory. And typically, it is the student with a strong need for achievement(11) who most clearly shows better memory for incomplete tasks. It is possible, of course, that this could be carried too far. Under some circumstances, the interruption might give a student a crushing sense of failure. If this happens, the proud or sensitive student, or the student who is highly ego-involved, might actually suppress his memory(12).

Reducing the Effect of Interference

In studying the conditions under which interference is likely to occur we have inescapably pointed the way to the reduction of interference. Insofar as we can avoid these conditions, we can reduce the influence of interference.

Avoiding the Conditions that Produce Interference

Interference is most likely to occur in rote memorization under conditions of moderate motivation. It is obvious, therefore, that we can do much to reduce it by arranging for greater motivation and for more meaning and structure in the materials being studied. It would be easy, of course, to say that all learning should be meaningful and well motivated. No teacher, however, is likely to attain this difficult objective, and there may be some question whether all rote learning should be abolished even if it were possible. Consequently, we suggest the more realistic aspiration of pushing our teaching more and more in the direction of meaningful and motivated learning, although entertaining no illusions of complete success in this enterprise.

To some extent we can be guided by the more detailed conditions that affect interference. There may be times when we can arrange the schedule so that succeeding lessons do not call for conflicting responses to the same stimuli. The lazy or safe way to do this is to avoid using the same stimuli in successive lessons. The deft and elegant way is to make sure that successive activities call for the same responses. But this latter procedure is delicate and treacherous and may call for more effort than the results will justify. We can do something to make sure that new and interfering material is not introduced until the older material has reached a reasonable strength.

Use of Distributed Practices

By paying continuous attention to the conditions that make for interference, we can, as we have seen, do something to combat the process. It is obvious, however, that this is an intricate and exacting job and that it is easy to make a false step. Fortunately there is one rather general, over-all device that will do a great deal to reduce the amount of interference. This is the device of distributed practices. It calls for practice periods that are fairly short and that are separated either by rest or by some activity that is quite different.

Let us suppose that a student is about to memorize the lines for his part in a short play. There are a great many ways in which he could arrange his practice sessions. Theoretically he could try to master it all in one session. This would be about the worst thing he could do as far as efficiency is concerned. As soon as he decides on a reasonable length for a practice period, he can think about the intervals between practices. If he decides on a twenty-minute practice period, for instance, he could arrange to study this length of time once every hour, once every two hours, once every four hours (time for sleep would be a problem in all of these), once every eight hours, once a day, once every two days, and so forth. The longer he rests between practices, of course, the greater the time that will elapse before he finishes.

Fortunately, in this matter it will not pay us to strive for the very best arrangement of practices. We can be fairly sure that almost any reasonable way of spacing the practices will give some advantage. But we cannot be so sure that one particular schedule of spaced practices is markedly superior to another particular system of spacing, provided, of course, that they both employ spacing. This is the important thing.

Insofar as one system of distributing practices does seem to be better than another, we can suggest a few tentative rules. The chief advantage seems to lie in using brief practice periods. The interval between the practices does not matter so much(13, 14, 15) or at least we cannot be so sure about the part played by the rest interval. Certainly there is no advantage from extremely long rest periods. In many activities, a rest of a few seconds or minutes may do as much good as a rest of several hours.

We might tell our student, then, that almost any system of spreading out his practices will prove useful. If he wants to go even further in his search for efficiency, he should perhaps cut his practice periods down to the minimum consistent with the practical circumstances. A one-minute practice, for instance, might be quite efficient under some circumstances. It might be impractical, however, if it took him five or ten minutes to get his desk cleared of other material, to get the light and papers arranged, and to develop a set for memorizing. If he is to spend five or ten minutes in the incidentals, he might spend almost an equal amount of time in practice. When our student has worked out a practice period that is reasonable and short, he can adopt almost any convenient schedule of intervals between practices.

In general teaching, by the way, there are many times when we can use exceedingly short practice periods to great advantage. A lively one-minute drill, for instance, could accomplish a good deal. By the same token, we can be grateful for the many brief rest periods that circumstances provide. In some kinds of learning, a rest period of a few seconds may prove very valuable. Students seem to have some built-in intuition of this fact and are very often able to work out brief rests, or brief periods of inattention, with little help from us.

In straining for further efficiency, we might ask about the best sort of activity for these rest periods. As far as the material being memorized is concerned, sleep would represent the ideal way of spending the rest periods. If this is impractical, some less extreme relaxation is helpful. If other responsibilities prevent complete relaxation, then the rest period should at least be free from activity that involves stimuli similar to the stimuli of the material being memorized.

Values and Limitations of Spaced Practices

The distribution of practices is recommended as a means of reducing interference. When other conditions are such as to make interference likely, distribution of practices will make learning more efficient. If there is little likelihood of interference(16) anyhow, distribution of practices may have little or no advantage. Spaced or distributed practices, for instance, are more important in memorization of arbitrary material than in understanding connected or meaningful material. Distributed practices are more important in learning a long series (a, b, c, d; Washington, Adams, Jefferson), where interference is very likely, than in memorizing isolated pairs (*amicus-friend, spes-hope*)(17). They will be more effective when learning a group of items that could readily be confused with each other than when learning a group of items that are readily distinguished from each other. They are more useful for a long list with much chance of interference, than for a short list in which interference is less likely. Distributed practices do more to eliminate mistakes in the middle of a long list (See Figure 13-2), where many mistakes occur, and do less to eliminate errors at the beginning or the end of the list being memorized.

Reasons for the Superiority of Spaced Practices

Whenever we do get some advantage from spaced practices, that advantage may come from any one of several factors.

Reducing Reactive Inhibition. According to Hull, the very performance of an act, or the mere making of a response, will make us less likely to perform that act or to make that response in the next few seconds. This inhibition reduces our likelihood of making the correct response. This inhibition or reluctance fades away with time, however, and if we wait for a short period, as we do with distributed practices, we should suffer less handicap.

Differential Forgetting. With the passage of time all tendencies are likely to become somewhat weaker. This holds for the main tendencies that we have developed and also for the interfering tendencies that have inevitably been developed at the same time. Fortunately, however, the interfering or incidental tendencies are seldom as strong as the tendency that receives the bulk of the practice. If we rest for a period, all tendencies will become weaker, but those tendencies that were very weak to begin with may fade to the point of extinction, or may, at least, become so weak that they cannot be elicited by a normal stimulus. This gives the practiced tendency a differential advantage.

The Possibility of Review During Practice Periods. Students may spend a portion of the interval or rest periods in some sort of practice. Thus the total amount of practice would be increased by spaced practices. This suggestion, of course, cannot account for the entire superiority of spaced practices. It would not account for the fact that some methods of distributing practices are better than others, since in both methods there is an opportunity for review. Spaced practices, moreover, improve maze learning in rats, and here sporadic review is out of the question.

The Possibility of a Decrease in Fatigue. A very long practice period would undoubtedly induce fatigue, and this could reduce the effectiveness of learning. Fatigue is not, of course, sufficient to account for all the superiority of spaced practices. In many of the experiments the practices have been too short (on the order of a minute or so) to induce fatigue. Moreover, Jost, many years ago, showed that when the "rest" interval is filled with strenuous mental work, different from memorizing, the spaced practices still were better than massed practices.

The Possibility of Increased Zest. Boredom, like fatigue, could quite easily reduce learning if the practice periods were very long. Boredom, however, cannot account for all the superiority of distributed practices. In some tasks, practices of half a minute have been found superior to practices of one minute. The difference in boredom in such periods would be negligible.

Summary

Dealing with the complexities and interactions of the learning process presents one of the most baffling but challenging aspects of teaching. To prevent roundabout learning, the teacher should make sure that some success can be attained by straightforward learning. He should also make sure that the necessary corrections are not too hard to endure. When students make marked use of such roundabout devices as truancy or negativism, the teacher should make sure that these do not yield too much satisfaction.

The teacher often faces the necessity of eliciting a response without reflecting on the past conduct of pupils. Often this can be done by a preliminary remark approving the past conduct. The converse problem occurs when the teacher must administer a reprimand but does not want to induce a violent reaction of shame or anger. To accomplish this double aim he should use short casual reprimands, being careful to show his acceptance of the student. Often the use of humor or even of mock violence may help establish this acceptance.

Learning is made complicated by stimulus generalization, trace conditioned responses, and the presence of incidental stimuli. At times these complications are valuable. When they are harmful, their influence can be reduced by ordinary practice and by specific discouragement of each undesired tendency. The spread of reinforcement may also interfere with the teaching goals.

Retroactive and proactive inhibition are serious forms of interference. Things which we do now may reduce our mastery of things learned just recently (retroactive inhibition). Our present activities may also reduce our potential mastery of things we are about to study (proactive inhibition). Rote learning is especially likely to be interfered with by any subsequent activity with new material. Retroactive inhibition is especially likely when a new response must be attached to an old stimulus. Retroactive inhibition will be greater if the original learning is very incomplete, and if there is a great amount of activity with new material following close on the heels of the original learning.

Some retroactive inhibition is inevitable. It has less effect on learning that is intentional than on incidental learning. Under ideal conditions, retroactive inhibition can be reduced by resting after study. Otherwise the device of spacing practices may be used to advantage.

Spacing practices is an important aid in offsetting most kinds of interference. According to the rules for correct spacing of practices, some spacing is better than none. Short practices are best. The length of the rest period is less important. Spacing is especially important at the beginning of a series and for a long series. For some learning which demands insight, on the other hand, massed practices may prove advantageous.

Besides reducing retroactive inhibition, spaced practices may provide for incidental review between trials. Spacing may also reduce fatigue, may cater to our reluctance to repeat acts in too close succession, and may permit interfering tendencies to "evaporate."

SPECIFIC REFERENCES

1. Hovland, C. I. The generalization of conditioned responses: I. The sensory generalization of conditioned responses with varying frequencies of tone. *J. gen. Psychol.,* 1937, *17,* 125–148.

2. Gibson, Eleanor J. Retroactive inhibition as a function of degree of generalization between tasks. *J. exp. Psychol.,* 1941, *28,* 93–115.

3. Smoke, K. L. An objective study of concept formation. *Psychol. Monogr.,* 1932, *42,* No. 191.

4. Sheffield, F. D., and Jenkins, W. O. Level of repetition in the "spread of effect." *J. exp. Psychol.,* 1952, *44,* 101–107.

5. Osgood, C. E. The similarity paradox in human learning: a resolution. *Psychol. Rev.*, 1949, *56*, 132–143.

6. McFann, H. H. Effects of response alteration and different instructions on proactive and retroactive facilitation and interference. *J. exp. Psychol.*, 1953, *46*, 405–410.

7. Bilodeau, Ina M., and Schlosberg, H. Similarity in stimulating conditions as a variable in retroactive inhibition. *J. exp. Psychol.*, 1951, *41*, 199–204.

8. Underwood, B. J. Learning. *Annu. Rev. Psychol.*, 1953, *4*, 31–58.

9. Prentice, W. C. H. Retroactive inhibition and the motivation of learning. *Amer. J. Psychol.*, 1943, *56*, 283–292.

10. Prentice, W. C. H. The interruption of tasks. *Psychol. Rev.*, 1944, *51*, 329–340.

11. Atkinson, J. W. The achievement motive and recall of interrupted and completed tasks. *J. exp. Psychol.*, 1953, *46*, 381–390.

12. Eriksen, C. W. Defense against ego-threat in memory and perception. *J. abnorm. soc. Psychol.*, 1952, *47*, 230–235.

13. Norris, Eugenia B. Performance of a motor task as a function of interpolation of varying lengths of rest at different points in acquisition. *J. exp. Psychol.*, 1953, *45*, 260–264.

14. Deese, J. E. *The psychology of learning*. McGraw-Hill, 1952, Chap. 8.

15. McGeoch, J. A., and Irion, A. L. *The psychology of human learning*. Longmans, 1952, Chap. 5.

16. Underwood, B. J., and Richardson, J. Studies of distributed practice: XIII. Interlist interference and the retention of serial nonsense lists. *J. exp. Psychol.*, 1955, *50*, 39–46.

17. Tolman, E. C., and Postman, L. Learning. *Annu. Rev. Psychol.*, 1954, *5*, 27–56.

SUGGESTIONS FOR FURTHER READING

1. Deese, J. E. *The psychology of learning*. McGraw-Hill, 1952, Chaps. 4, 8, 9, 10.

   A very complete account of the major facts of interference and the underlying theory.

2. McGeoch, J. A., and Irion, A. *The psychology of human learning*. Longmans, 1952, Chaps. 4, 5.

   Covers many of the phenomena treated by Deese.

3. Stevens, S. S. *Handbook of experimental psychology*. Wiley, 1951, Chap. 17. Human learning and retention (Hovland, C. I.).

   A concise account of the more important studies.

4. Woodworth, R. S., and Schlosberg, H. *Experimental psychology.* Holt, 1954, Chap. 24.

A clear account of the many side effects in any act of learning. Includes transfer of training as one of these.

Exercises and Questions for Discussion

1. A student in a classroom situation sees the word *été* and immediately thereafter hears the teacher say *summer.* As a result of this experience, a great many associations or tendencies or ways of behaving may be acquired. List a number of new associations which you consider probable or possible. Distinguish between the *main* association or associations, and those that you consider incidental. Of the incidental associations, indicate those which are helpful, those which are neutral, and those which are harmful.

2. A student in a class in creative English is describing a proposed play dealing with a Christmas scene in an army camp in Australia. He talks about the falling snow and the instructor comments, "Now you should know better than that."

This comment should affect the student in many different ways. Describe as many of these probable effects as you can. Indicate those effects which are to be desired and those which should be avoided. What could have been done to eliminate some of the undesired results?

3. Your students have become interested in some aspects of life in Brazil. One of the students suggests that they get in touch with a school in Brazil and start a correspondence. In the midst of his proposal he mentions the possibility that some members of the class may be able to write in Spanish. You are worried about the fact that he thinks that Spanish is the language of Brazil.

Describe the problem that faces you and suggest a feasible way of handling it.

4. Go over your own schedule of study and see how it may be affected by retroactive inhibition. Which of the subjects in your program are especially likely to be affected by retroactive inhibition? Where should these be located? Could your schedule be improved with respect to the spacing of practices? Which of your subjects should have short, frequent practices? Which might profit more from fairly prolonged periods of study? What is the basis for your decision?

14

Teaching for Permanence and Transfer

So far we have discussed learning as if it were a day-by-day or a minute-by-minute process. We have assumed that our task is to develop immediate skill that will function at the moment. We have visualized the teacher trying to make sure that in this lesson the student will master this principle in algebra, or this problem in French grammar, or that skill in multiplication.

But no one would be interested in the mastery of these tasks unless this mastery would also be useful under some other circumstances. We hope that it will also be useful at a later date. We hope, too, that it will be useful outside the classroom. It is to this problem that we now turn. We ask how we can teach so that the results of learning will persist for a reasonable time, and so that those results will be applicable in a wide variety of situations. First let us consider the problem of persistence or permanence of learning.

The Permanence of Learning

It is too much to expect, of course, that the results of learning shall be completely permanent. We may as well reconcile ourselves at the outset to the fact that there will be a considerable degree of forgetting, especially in some kinds of material. Indeed, we may go further and welcome the inevitable prospect of forgetting, since much of what we learn has merely transitory importance and should make way for newer and more important truth or, as is so often the case, for "true-er" truth.

Although we must accept, and perhaps may welcome, a substantial amount of forgetting, we may still hope to keep the amount or degree of forgetting within bounds. We hope that the present achievement of our students, although bound to change, will not prove too transitory. And certainly we will devote our efforts to an increase in the permanence of the learning. Although we admit that complete permanence is neither feasible nor desirable, still we believe that we could do with more permanence rather than less, and we further believe that increased permanence is likely to be attained only by deliberate efforts to that end.

The Relation between Interference and Forgetting

Much of the loss in learning is clearly the result of interference. As we have seen in our study of retroactive inhibition, the learning of some new thing is very likely to interfere with our mastery of something just learned. Here then is one very direct source of forgetting. Interference and forgetting go hand in hand, and since interference is a very familiar phenomenon, forgetting is likely to be equally prevalent.

Many psychologists hold that interference is by far the most important source of forgetting. According to these psychologists, when learning is followed by a very deep sleep it will undergo very little forgetting. Most of what had been learned should be present upon waking from the sleep.

In addition to interference, there may be other causes of forgetting. At one time, for instance, there was much talk about disuse as a cause of forgetting. According to this view, forgetting is something like decay, or evaporation. The theory of disuse assumes that our learning is based on some highly unstable, organic structure and that this physical base loses its precise structure much as any other organic substance, such as a piece of wood, may decay or disintegrate. The theory of disuse has been under severe attack for a good many years(1), and it does not receive the emphasis that it once did. It still plays a minor part, however, in several present-day psychological theories(2).

Whatever may be the effects of normal structural changes, there is some evidence that retention is hurt by the brain disturbance that comes from an electroconvulsive shock. Material learned just before the shock is more seriously affected than material known for some time. For ordinary shock, the memory recovers fairly rapidly.

It is possible that some forgetting may be due to the actual repression of unacceptable ideas. According to the Freudian theory (discussed in

Chapter 8), we are equipped with a *censor* who protects us from ideas or thoughts or wishes that are too disturbing. If any experience has been painful to us, this censor will push the idea of that experience out of consciousness and into the subconscious. This ejection of the idea of the painful experience constitutes forgetting. According to the Freudians, all forgetting takes place for this reason. We forget only what we wish to forget, or, more properly, what the censor or superego thinks we would dislike to experience.

As yet the evidence for the Freudian theory of forgetting is not clear cut. In the succeeding discussion it is assumed that interference is the chief cause of forgetting, although mere disuse and active repression may also play subordinate roles.

Methods of Measuring Retention

The Method of Recall. Let us suppose that a student has learned to count up to twelve in German, and that it has taken him ten repetitions to do so. A few days later we wish to know how much of this he has retained. How shall we test his memory? We could use the method of *recall.* In doing this, we would merely ask him to recite the first twelve numbers in German and give him credit for all he got right. If he could give us nine, we would say he had retained 75 percent of the original learning. This method is very often used in schools. Its chief handicap is its severity. By using this method we tend to mark the student much too low. After several days, for instance, the student may not be able to recall a single German number, and yet his score may not really be zero. He may have a very substantial latent memory which merely fails to rise to the surface. How could we measure this latent retention?

The Method of Relearning (or Saving Method). In the pioneer investigation of memory, Ebbinghaus conceived the brilliant idea of using relearning as a measure of latent retention or hidden memory. If we wished to use this device we would merely set our student at relearning the twelve numbers and find out if he can relearn these numbers in fewer than the ten trials it took him at first. If he again requires ten trials, he would, of course, have zero retention. If he requires only three trials he shows a saving of seven trials or 70 percent. This 70 percent would be our measure of retention.

This saving method was designed for use with short selections used over a span of a few days. When used over a considerable period of time, it has some dangers as both Cruze(3) and Bunch(4) point out. The saving in trials to relearn may come not only from retention but perhaps also from increased maturity which the student acquires between the two trials. It is also possible that during the interval the student may have some other experience which he can transfer to the original task and thus do better on the second trial. This danger was apparently recognized by Ebbinghaus, but because he used such a short span of time, he took no account of it in his actual experiments.

In view of the possible error in the saving method when used to measure long periods of retention, it is wise to introduce a modification. Rather than compare the relearning with the original learning, it is better to compare the trials needed to relearn with the trials needed to learn some new but comparable material. Rather than have the student relearn to count to twelve in German, for instance, we could have him learn to count to twelve in Italian, provided, of course, that we could be sure that this latter task is equally difficult. If the student required eight trials to learn the Italian and only two to learn the German, his saving score would be six out of eight or 75 percent. In this method, we must take some steps to be sure that the two tasks are of comparable difficulty.

The use of this modified version of the saving method has other advantages. Notice that we did not need to refer to the trials required to learn the original material. Thus, if we had neglected to keep a record of the trials required for the original learning, or if it had been impossible to secure such a record, we could still obtain a measure of retention. Burtt(5) took advantage of this feature of the modified saving method in an interesting experiment on memories of early childhood. He began his long-range experiment by reading selections (twenty lines each) of Greek drama to, or at, his fifteen-month-old son. He read each selection some ninety times, presenting several such selections in this way between the ages of fifteen months and three years. When the son reached the age of eight and a half years, Burtt had him learn (relearn?) some of these selections. He found that the boy required 30 percent fewer trials to learn (or relearn) these selections than were needed to learn *other new selections of comparable difficulty*. Obviously the saving method was out of the question, since in using that method we compare the trials required for the original learning with the trials required for relearning. And obviously there could be no record of the trials needed by the fifteen-month-old infant to learn the material in the first place. But, even though he was unable to use the saving method, Burtt was still able, by using comparable new material, to get a measure of the influence of the early experience.

The Method of Reconstruction. If we were content to measure only one phase of the student's retention of the German numbers, we could give him the first twelve numbers but in a "scrambled" order (say, *drei, fünf, zwei,* etc.) and then have him rearrange the numbers in their proper order. This is called the *method of reconstruction.* Obviously it is useful only when the items have a definite serial order. It could be used, for instance, to see if a young student could arrange the days of the week in the right order, or to see whether or not a streetcar conductor could arrange the names of the streets in their correct order.

The Method of Recognition. One further method of testing one limited phase of our student's retention of German numbers would be to see if he could merely recognize those numbers when he saw them. We could present him with those numbers mixed in with a large number of other words, (*sept, fünf, octavo, très, zwei, ein, uno,* etc.) and ask him to underline the words he had previously studied. Obviously this method would give us no indication whatever of his ability to recite these words in their proper order. The method of recognition would be useful when it is important to remember that a certain group of French verbs, for instance, follow a given rule. Here it would be sufficient if, whenever he encountered any of these verbs, he could identify them as members of this group.

It will be seen that the methods of reconstruction and recognition act so as to supplement one another. The method of reconstruction is excellent when we are interested only in the student's ability to arrange the items in the correct order and when we have no concern about his ability to recognize the items as belonging to a group. The method of recognition, on the other hand, is excellent when we are merely interested in the student's ability to identify items, but it is useless to test his ability to place the items in a correct order.

Obviously, some of the methods just described are rather lenient whereas some are rather severe or strict. It is not surprising, then, that different methods of measurement give different results. In the graphs in Figure 14-1, for instance, the method of recognition shows as much as 70 percent retention at the end of two days. The method of recall, on the other hand, shows only 10 percent or 20 percent retention at the end of the same period. These differences merely mean that the student can recognize more than he can recall.

Figure 14-1 points to the very obvious moral that we should test for the kind of retention we are trying to achieve. In some of our teaching, sheer recognition may be enough. We may be quite happy if the student can recognize a story he has read or a character he has studied. In such a case, the method of recognition would be an excellent test of retention whereas the method of recall would be much too severe. There may be other times, however, when we wish the student to be able to recite a poem or to speak the lines of a play. In this instance, the method of

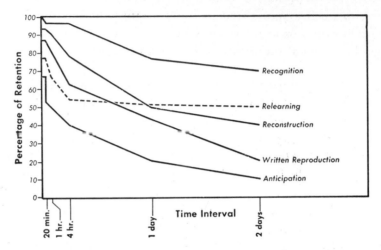

FIGURE 14-1. *Forgetting as Related to the Method of Measurement.* Redrawn from C. W. Luh, "The Conditions of Retention," *Psychol. Monogr.* 1922, *31,* No. 142. Courtesy of the American Psychological Association.

recall, severe as it is, would be the only satisfactory measure of the mastery we have in mind. If the method of recall showed almost zero retention, we could, of course, use the more sensitive measures to determine how much latent retention was present.

Speed of Learning and Degree of Retention

In the world at large there is a belief that the rapid learner is sort of a "flash in the pan," that he learns quickly and forgets quickly. This same belief holds that the slow learner has superior retention. People often remark, "It takes me a long time to learn anything, but once I do get it, I never forget."

For the most part this Hare-and-Tortoise philosophy, or the belief in "easy come, easy go," does not hold up under investigation. We must hasten to admit that we cannot be too sure of the scientific answer since the problem is beset by an unusual number of difficulties. Moreover, the answers are somewhat complex, giving partial support to both sides of the controversy. At one time it appeared that when all factors were taken into account, the fast learner remembered somewhat more(6). From a more recent analysis(7), however, it appears that there is no difference in the amount retained by slow and by fast learners.

The Course of Retention

A student has finished studying a section of French vocabulary or a part for the high-school play or a unit in biology. He puts the material away and goes on about something else. Suppose now we could obtain a continuous record of his mastery of the material from the very moment he ceases to study. What would this record look like?

Reminiscence or Increased Mastery after Study. Under certain conditions, our student may have a higher degree of mastery some time after his study than he had immediately upon the completion of his study. The curve of mastery, instead of showing a decline, may actually show a rise. This phenomenon goes by the technical name of *reminiscence*.

There are probably two definite types of reminiscence. At least there are two very distinct circumstances under which it is observed. Reminiscence is very likely to occur when meaningful material is learned incompletely. Grade-school students, for instance, may study a poem that is well within their comprehension. They study to the point where they know most of it but are far from a complete mastery, as shown by a test at the conclusion of the studying. Different groups of these students are given subsequent tests at different intervals. Very often we shall find that the students tested one day, or two or three days, later may know more about the poem than they did immediately after the practice(8, 9, 10). This is especially true for young students.

For certain kinds of material, the gains to be had from reminiscence may last indefinitely. Suppose the students were working on biology and had just mastered an idea such as the principle of evolution. It is quite possible that this impressive idea would intrigue them and recur to their minds after the lesson. It would not be surprising if through this reworking and through other mechanisms their mastery would be even more complete a few days later. Furthermore, it is very probable that such a neat and rewarding principle would never be forgotten but would continue to be understood at a level noticeably higher than it was at the end of the lesson. Experiments show(11) that some very meaningful ideas persist for years in undiminished degree or even gain in strength as the years pass(12).

Under other circumstances, reminiscence will be followed by a period of forgetting. Although an important, insight-giving principle may be remembered forever, we cannot expect mere meaningful content to share the same success. Poems or knowledge of history may be completely meaningful at the moment of learning, and may profit from later reminiscence, but it is unlikely that mastery will remain at a high level if there is no further practice. Here then we may get reminiscence at first, followed later by a decline which brings the level of mastery well below what it was at the conclusion of the learning.

A second kind of reminiscence occurs under quite different circumstances. Suppose we have students memorizing a list of nonsense syllables —material that is almost completely devoid of meaning. Instead of letting the students rest a few seconds between trials, we have them learn the lists under the adverse condition of massed practices. We test them immediately upon the conclusion of the last trial and again after a few seconds' rest. Upon this latter trial, we will notice a definite improvement(13).

This latter kind of reminiscence, often labeled the *Ward-Hovland effect,* is linked up with the interference that occurs during learning. Reminiscence of this kind is most likely to occur when the material was learned under conditions that invite interference. It is more likely to occur after learning a series of items, for instance, (one, two, three, four) than after learning a number of pairs (*ein*-one, *zwei*-two, *fünf*-five). It is more likely to occur after learning nonsense materials than after learning lists of meaningful items(14). It is more likely to occur when the material has been presented at a rapid rate and with no rests between practices. It is especially likely to occur if something is done to disentangle the inhibition or interference that has been developed during the learning(15).

This relation between interference and reminiscence suggests that reminiscence is largely the process of recovering from the effects of interference. If there is little interference to recover from, there will be little reminiscence. Any interference that has developed, however, will begin to "evaporate" or dissipate as soon as the learning stops. It will dissipate more rapidly than the main tendencies that have been practiced regularly. Thus for a few minutes after learning there is a period of consolidation during which the original learning becomes even better established. If this consolidating process is interrupted by subsequent activity or by anything as severe as an electroconvulsive shock(16), there will be no reminiscence and there may be a decline.

The Ward-Hovland type of reminiscence, of course, has little practical significance for the teacher. It is concerned with rote learning of the most arbitrary sort. The reminiscence that does occur, furthermore, is so rapid and fleeting that it can only be observed under laboratory conditions. This latter type of reminiscence, however, does have much significance for basic theories of learning. It also reminds us of the inevitable inter-ference which accompanies all learning, and with which all learning must contend.

Forgetting: Its Nature and Extent. As we have said, the gains from highly meaningful learning may last indefinitely and show little, if any, forgetting. For most learning, however, some forgetting is inevitable, and for rote learning very rapid forgetting is the rule. Most school subjects, of course, involve both meaningful and rote material, and in these sub-jects we must expect that students will forget a good bit of the material, especially over a long period of time. We must not be unduly surprised if the students we test today do not know so much history or algebra as they knew a few years ago.

It may be hard for us to get much consolation from the sheer fact that a certain amount of forgetting is inevitable. Some part of our grief may vanish, however, when we realize that the forgotten material may be quickly relearned. As further consolation, we should remember that students may still profit from things which they have once learned but have now largely forgotten. Even if a student cannot recall an idea, he may recognize it. Even if he fails to recognize it in any convincing way, he may have acquired a better attitude toward it. The present writer, for instance, can recall very little of the specific laws in the code of Draco. Yet he feels better when he hears the expression "Draconian Code" than he would if he had never studied that topic. If he had never studied the topic, he would probably feel worried and inferior if he should encounter the term. As it is, he is able to wave it aside by saying, "Oh, yes! That's what old Pettigrew tried to teach us!" or something equally casual.

Forgetting, however inevitable, is seldom complete. Even with very little intervening practice, memorized material may persist some thirty or forty years(17). The experiment by Burtt shows that meaningless mate-rial (for surely Greek drama would be meaningless to a child under three) may be retained to a discernible extent for four or five years and to a smaller but still perceptible extent for eleven to thirteen years. Some trace of lists of nonsense syllables may remain for four months after the last practice. In acts of skill, there is seldom complete forgetting.

When forgetting does occur, the loss is exceedingly rapid at first and then continues at a more moderate rate. This is shown in the lower graph in Figure 14-1 and also in the graphs of Figure 14-2. For the arbitrary material in this experiment, the mastery takes an abrupt nose dive and then gradually levels off to a certain extent, but the decline continues. For more meaningful material, as opposed to arbitrary, rote material, the initial drop is seldom so abrupt but is still present in some degree.

Forgetting during the Summer Vacation. The facts revealed by the many investigations(18) of summer forgetting are such as we would expect from our knowledge of the general principles of retention. When the skill acquired during the school year is consistently employed during the vacation, as in the case of reading, there is very little forgetting and there may even be marked gains(19). Naturally enough this is especially true for older children and for brighter children, who do more reading anyhow. The summer vacation does less harm to meaningful material than to material that is learned by rote. Ability to solve arithmetical problems, for instance, suffers only a slight loss, although some loss does occur. Arithmetical computation, on the other hand, often undergoes a severe decrement. In one investigation, the summer loss was not made up until December of the following term. There is some evidence(20), by the way, that specific training at the close of the school year may reduce the summer loss in arithmetic. Spelling ability, like ability to compute, also decreases during the vacation. The loss is especially severe for the younger students who presumably make less use of spelling in their vacation activities.

For history and science, the experimental results are somewhat conflicting. There is some suggestion of a summer gain in nature study and in narrative history as studied in the elementary grades, and of a loss in the more formal aspects of history and science as studied in the high school and college. These conclusions, of course, fit neatly into our expectations—perhaps too neatly, in view of the small number of experiments.

Nature of the Errors in Forgetting. So far we have been concerned with the number of correct items which a person can remember. We have merely asked, "What *percent* of his erstwhile knowledge does the student retain?" We have asked how many more mistakes he makes now than he made before, but so far we have not asked, "What kind of erroneous answers does he give?"

A faulty memory for a given item may show itself in several ways(21). In searching for the elusive name of a person, for instance, we may, on occasion, find ourselves unable to recall anything. Our minds may be a complete blank as far as that topic is concerned. More usually, however, we can give *some* reaction to the problem. We say, "It's a very ordinary, simple name," or, "It begins with an *M*," or, "It is something like Zeigarnik," or we may give a whole series of names which come to mind when we think of the person in question. Often we know these names are incorrect. At other times we may give an incorrect name with a fair degree of confidence.

There has been a growing interest in the nature of the incorrect responses which become substituted for the once-remembered ideas or associations. Many investigators have studied the changes which take place in our memory for forms or diagrams. Early studies showed that a person reproducing a design from memory is more apt to give a general outline than to give all the details. If the original design was thought to resemble a familiar object, the reproduction would be even more like the familiar object. This suggests that the person did not remember the form itself but really remembered the name of the object and then tried to draw the object. Minor irregularities, such as slight departures from the vertical, tend to be corrected in the reproductions, and there is some tendency toward increased symmetry. It is possible, of course, that these changes are not entirely due to memory. When children keep on drawing a design which is continuously before them(22), they also tend to make the later drawings more structured, even though there can be no memory factor at work.

Factors Affecting Retention

As we have seen, retention varies considerably from material to material and from one condition to another. Let us look at those conditions which affect retention and, in so doing, try to determine what the teacher can do to obtain a reasonable degree of retention on the part of his students.

Meaning or Structure. Of all the factors which affect memory, meaningful structure is perhaps the most important for the teacher to keep in mind. If the material is sufficiently meaningful, there may be no forgetting whatever. An important governing principle, like the idea of the conservation of energy, may so help us organize the rest of our ideas that it stays with us for life. Content that is not so brilliantly structured, but which still has much meaning, will be remembered in proportion to its meaning. Nonsense material is headed for extinction before the last syllable is uttered.

The more the student can be made to see the material as an organized group of large governing principles, the better he will remember. The moral is obvious; the practical application is difficult. Large (and true) governing relationships are sometimes hard for young students to see. And, remember, it is the student who must see or experience these relations and not merely the teacher. Sometimes the teacher may labor at relations or principles which are beyond the grasp of the students at their particular level of maturity. All in all, however, the gains from clear understanding and from a sure grasp of principles are so great that the teacher may well lean over backward to try to secure them. The steps discussed in the chapter on meaning and insight are the surest guarantee of more permanent learning.

Motivation. Motivation, like meaning, is one of the surest guides to effective learning. Like meaning, motivation is also one of the most effective means of ensuring a greater degree of retention. Students who learn material under a high degree of ego-involvement, for instance, show more initial reminiscence and a higher level of retention throughout than students who learn under more prosaic motivation(23). In general, we may expect that any motive which increases the efficiency of learning will also work toward a greater degree of permanence.

Overlearning. Retention is clearly affected by the amount of practice during learning. If we have spent much time practicing one set of material and little time on another comparable set, we shall find that our retention at a later date will be in almost direct proportion to the amount of practice.

For both teacher and student, it is important to realize that practice carried on *after* we have first reached mastery of the material is of great value to retention. This additional practice is called *overlearning*. Overlearning, by the way, takes a bit of "selling." Students who have achieved mastery are reluctant to go on practicing. When a student has studied a number of foreign words until he has gone through the list once without a mistake, for instance, it is most natural for him to assume that the job is done. He will not be happy about any suggestion of further practice. In spite of his feeling, however, he should not stop here. If he will go over the list many more times—even spending as much time after learning as he did before (100 percent overlearning) he will have a much better chance of remembering the list in the future. This is shown very forcibly in Figure 14-2. The graphs show the retention of lists of nouns during twenty-eight days. The top line shows the results after 100 percent overlearning. The second line shows the retention for 50 percent overlearning, whereas the lower line shows the retention for those who ceased practice as soon as they reached mastery. A comparison of these lines shows that overlearning by at least 50 percent has a great advantage. Whether the additional 50 percent overlearning "pays" or not depends on the cost of that additional overlearning and the value of the additional retention.

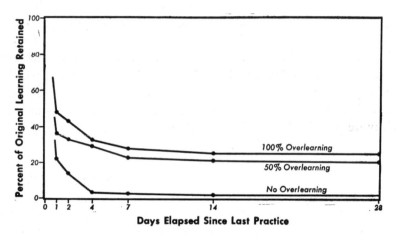

FIGURE 14-2. *Forgetting after Different Degrees of Overlearning.* Data from W. C. F. Krueger, "The Effect of Overlearning on Retention," *J. Exper. Psychol.,* 1929, *12,* 71-78.

Review. It is to be expected that review of material learned will aid in retention. Review may be of two general types. It may consist of a test in which the student is required to recall what he has studied. On the other hand, it may be a restudy of the material. We repeat here what we have previously said about the most efficient use of these two types of review. Both types of review will help retention. Each method, however, has its own special value. Immediately after learning there should be a recall test in which the student is required to reproduce the material or to answer questions about it(24). At this stage, such a test will be more valuable than a mere rereading or restudy of the material, although the latter will be of some use. Later on, the test becomes less useful as an aid to retention. When as much as two weeks have gone by, it will be better to use the method of rereading or restudying in order to secure maximum retention.

The teacher can do a great deal toward making effective use of motivation, meaning, overlearning, and review. There are some other conditions, however, which the teacher can do less about, but which also play a part.

Mental versus Motor Learning. There is a prevalent impression that skill in motor activities is inherently easier to retain than proficiency in verbal or mental activities. This may be true. It is undoubtedly true, however, that the motor skill which stays with us so faithfully is a skill which has received an enormous amount of practice. The specific acts of balancing while cycling, or of leg movements while skating, ordinarily receive many hundreds or thousands of repetitions, far in excess of the repetitions ordinarily given to the specific items of verbal material.

When students are required to learn a verbal sequence of letters such as *L R R L L R L R*, etc., and a motor task in a stylus maze requiring a similar pattern of right and left turns, they are able to retain the verbal pattern about as well as the motor pattern. If, however, they are given much more practice in learning one than the other, the more practiced pattern will be better retained.

Pleasant versus Unpleasant Materials. According to the Freudian theory, all forgetting is due to the actual repression of unpleasant or threatening ideas. From a series of episodes, therefore, we should remember the pleasant or neutral items but forget those that were disturbing. As we pointed out earlier, it would be difficult to explain all learning in this way. It is possible, however, that there is some tendency to retain pleasant or favorable material. In the recall of the experiences that have occurred in ordinary living, we find a slight preponderance of pleasant memories. We cannot be sure, however, that this is entirely the work of memory. There is always the comforting possibility that, in the lives of most people, pleasant experiences actually do predominate. Hence our subjects may remember an equal proportion of both types but may have had more pleasant experiences to draw from. It is also possible that the subject may actually remember as many unpleasant episodes but that he may hesitate to report them to other people. This is especially plausible if part of the original unpleasantness came from shame or embarrassment.

In some experiments there is an attempt to control the experiences. Students are required to memorize pleasant and unpleasant words and are later tested. Here again the pleasant items are more likely to be recalled. But apparently this method also has its pitfalls. There is a disturbing possibility, in some of the experiments at least, that the more pleasant and interesting items were better learned in the first place(25). The superior performance after a rest could merely reflect this superior learning.

As we have long suspected, a person is more likely to remember things that are flattering or that boost his ego, than things that are derogatory. In one experiment, Negro and white boys studied material that included statements about Negroes. Immediately after the learning, the Negro boys were more likely than the white boys to remember any statement whatever, favorable or unfavorable, that dealt with Negroes. With the passage of time, however, this better memory was observed only in the case of the favorable items(26). This change in the recall of the different kinds of material would seem to be the work of memory.

Amount of Material. We have stated earlier that a long selection is disproportionately harder to learn than a short selection. The long selections are, however, no more difficult to remember. We are, in fact, likely to remember a larger proportion of the longer selection. Part of this is due to the fact that in learning a longer selection we repeat the easy parts very often while we are still learning the difficult parts. Even when this factor is taken into account, we still find a greater proportional retention of longer selections, especially over a length of time. Perhaps we are more successful in grouping or arranging longer selections in a meaningful way.

Amount of Interference during Learning. Distribution of practices will reduce interference during learning and will often ensure the efficiency of that learning. We cannot be sure, however, that the distribution of practices will make for better retention. Many investigations, in fact, report better retention after massed practices. All in all, it would be best to conclude that the issue is very uncertain. We cannot be sure whether distributed or massed practices make for better retention(27). As a tentative guide we might suggest that retention will be better whenever the potential interference has already been overcome during the course of the learning. Material mastered in spite of the interference might be better retained than material learned under more favorable circumstances.

Teaching for Transfer

The things that we do at two-thirty this afternoon can work back in the form of retroactive inhibition to produce forgetting. As we have seen, moreover, these two-thirty activities can also work ahead to produce proactive inhibition or proactive facilitation. By proactive inhibition we mean that the things we do at two-thirty may interfere with the learning we are about to undertake this evening, tomorrow, or next week. By proactive facilitation we mean that these two-thirty activities may help us when we undertake a new task at some future time.

Proactive inhibition is the same thing as negative transfer. Proactive facilitation is the same thing as positive transfer. It is possible, by the way, that you may feel some annoyance at this business of jumping around from one high-sounding label to another when all the time we are talking about the same thing. Perhaps someday we will settle on one label and let the other go. As things stand at present, however, one label, proactive facilitation, is used when we are emphasizing the mecha nisms or basic processes. The other label, positive transfer, is used when we are emphasizing the process as seen in the schoolroom or in practical situations. In somewhat the same way, when you are talking about the basic principles of television you might use such terms as cathode ray tube, stream of electrons, and so forth. In actually using the television, on the other hand, you are more likely to talk about the "picture tube."

Positive transfer, then, refers to proactive-facilitation-as-it-appears-in-actual-practice. Negative transfer corresponds to proactive-inhibition-as-seen-in-actual-practice. In considering the matter of transfer, we no longer keep the spotlight on the tiny bits of experience. In this section, on the contrary, we will be interested in how the study of one formal school subject, such as geometry, may affect our performance in a different subject, such as sociology. Here we will be interested in transfer as it operates in large blocks of behavior. And here we shall be especially interested in the problem of how to teach so as to ensure the greatest amount of useful transfer to other areas of life.

General Ideas Regarding Transfer

The idea of transfer is probably basic to the whole notion of schooling. It is probably true that few people would be willing to conduct school or to support the schools unless they believed that some of the things learned in the schools would function outside of the school. Those who support the schools and those who devote themselves to teaching agree in assuming that the arithmetic learned in the school lesson can be used in the more practical world as well, and that the character traits developed in the school environment will stand the student in good stead as he moves in a nonscholastic world.

In the past, certainly, and to some extent in the present, people have expected a great deal of this transfer of training. They have believed that a person who has learned to be neat in manual training will also be neat in the arrangement of his clothes, his papers, and even of his ideas. They have believed that a man who has acquired skill in teaching has also acquired proficiency in administering a school system. They pretend to be surprised when a man who has acquired enough ability to write a book shows pathetic incapacity as he contemplates a refractory door latch.

To some extent, our expectations of a great deal of transfer may come from the sheer words we use. The word *jump,* for instance, refers to an ability that is fairly general. A man who can jump a table should also be able to jump a log or a fence, with equal, or almost equal, proficiency. Now at one time it was assumed that we had mental abilities or faculties comparable to such physical abilities as the ability to jump or to squeeze or to push. Just as a man had a certain ability to jump, so he had a certain ability to *think.* And if he were good at thinking about one thing he should be almost equally good in thinking about all things. Any man who had "learned to think" at all should be able to think about Latin grammar, politics, industrial management, and military tactics with equal skill. The belief that there is general thinking ability and that this may be trained is still fairly prevalent. Over and over again we hear speakers claim that what we need are people who are trained to think. They seldom feel any need to say what they should be trained to think about. In their opinion, thinking is thinking.

Whether or not "thinking is thinking" constitutes a very complex question. It is a question to which the method of factor analysis has just begun to be applied. Definite answers are not yet in. Meanwhile, we may guess that those answers will be various. It may later appear that thinking really is thinking. The man who is a marvel at thinking about physics may be equally good in thinking about religion, although Newton's experience leaves one suspicious. Even though thinking may turn out to be a general trait, we should be surprised if all other activities were equally general. Take "driving" for instance. Is a man who has acquired proficiency in driving a car equally able to drive a tank or airplane? What about the activity of "judging"? A man who has become an expert judge of tea may be an indifferent judge of bathing beauties, or even of whisky. Whatever may be the truth in a particular instance, it seems dangerous to assume that all activities described by the same word are one and the same thing.

To some extent, the great expectations associated with transfer may have come from confusion between cause and index. This fallacy, which we have mentioned so many times, has had its share in persuading people that there is a vast amount of transfer. Suppose, for instance, that a great many students master such difficult subjects as Latin and mathematics and that, later on, these same students become more proficient in letters, art, or statesmanship than their unschooled fellows. What could be clearer than that the Latin and mathematics disciplined their minds and thus brought about exceptional ability in these other matters? This question, of course, will not mislead the readers of this text. The astute student, we hope, will immediately see another and equally plausible hypothesis. He will ask, "Why did some of these people study such hard subjects while others did not?" And he will answer, "Precisely because the scholars were more able before they ever started the hard subjects." And he will go on to point out that this original superior ability itself would have caused the students to stand out above the crowd, whether they had studied Latin and mathematics, or whether they had studied music and horsemanship.

Illustration of Positive Transfer

The amount of positive transfer is, at times, very large. In learning to drive the family Chevrolet, for instance, I would acquire much skill that would help me in driving another Chevrolet of the same year. Since these tasks are very similar, we would expect, in fact, that the mastery of my car would have brought with it an almost equal mastery of the other car. This would represent almost 100 percent transfer, meaning that I have learned just as much in the unpracticed task as in the practiced task.

Transfer of training is, of course, not always at the 100 percent level. Less than 100 percent of transfer would be expected when I come to apply my experience in learning to drive my Chevrolet to the new problem of driving a Chrysler or Ford. Undoubtedly, the early experience would help to a considerable extent, but I would probably still require a little additional training or adjustment to this particular task. Thus my mastery of the Chrysler is not quite equal to my mastery of the Chevrolet. If I turn from the Chevrolet to the management of a truck or a bulldozer or an airplane, I should find that I needed a great deal of additional training for these specific tasks. In this case, the transfer from learning to drive the Chevrolet would fall far short of 100 percent.

The actual experiments show a wide variety of results. Some show marked positive transfer. Some show almost zero transfer and others may show negative transfer.

Marked positive transfer is to be expected, and is actually found, when there is a mere shift in sense organs. If you practice judging the area of coins, for instance, while your left eye is closed, you would still be able to judge the areas almost as well when you now close your right eye and open the left. Similarly, if you gain some skill in reading Braille with one finger, you will find that you have almost as much skill when you shift to an unpracticed finger(28).

Positive transfer is also found when you shift to a different responding member. By learning to trace a maze with one hand, you will also have acquired some skill in tracing with the other hand. This phenomenon, known as *cross education,* has been the subject of a great deal of study. A similar kind of transfer is called *response generalization*(29). Under these circumstances, a student learns to respond to a signal by pushing a lever and acquires considerable skill. Later he is required to pull the lever instead of pushing it. Very often it appears that the early experience, instead of hindering, as one might expect, actually helps. Apparently, the student does not learn to make a certain movement. On the contrary, he learns to achieve a certain result. If he learns to achieve a certain result by one movement he may also have increased his ability to produce that same result by a very different movement. Someone, for instance, who has learned to drive a car with one gearshift may be able, with very little difficulty, to drive a car which has a somewhat different gearshift. Or a student who has learned to write while holding his pen in a certain way may find that, with very little trouble, he can also write when holding his pen in an altogether different manner.

Learning to Learn. Marked positive transfer will occur whenever the learner works on a series of complex but similar problems. Monkeys faced with the problem of discriminating between two stimuli rapidly acquire a *learning set*. After solving a few discrimination problems, they approach the next problems in a more systematic and businesslike manner and with a definite improvement in performance(30). There may be some danger of expecting too much from this very primitive form of transfer, but there seems no question that a certain amount of gain will occur(31). Human learners demonstrate the same phenomenon in memorizing nonsense syllables. Learning the first list helps us to learn the second. In one classical experiment, Ward(32) found that it took some thirty-eight trials to learn the first list of twelve nonsense syllables. After learning eleven similar lists, however, the twelfth list was learned in sixteen trials. The same trend holds true for mazes. Learning one maze helps us to learn a second maze of the same general type but having a different pattern.

Test constructors, by the way, often find it necessary to take account of the fact that mastering one task helps us in mastering a similar task. Students who have had previous practice on similar tests would have an unfair advantage. To reduce this unfair advantage, test constructors very often provide preliminary practice exercises which are performed before the student encounters the test proper. This preliminary practice should provide help for each student when he undertakes the main task.

General Prevalence of Transfer

To get an over-all picture of the prevalence of transfer, Orata(33) tabulated 211 studies of transfer published between 1890 and 1941. These studies have been lumped together in order to show whether or not transfer *in general* takes place. The results of Orata's summary appear in Table 14-1.

TABLE 14–1

The Percent of Studies in Different Periods Showing Various Amounts of Transfer

	Prior to 1927	1927 to 1935	1935 to 1941	All Years Combined
Considerable transfer	32%	22%	14%	25%
Appreciable transfer	49	45	35	45
Depends on conditions		7	28	8
Very little transfer	8	10	12	9
No transfer	2	8	5	4
Other conclusions	9	8	6	9
Total number of studies	100	68	43	211

The table reveals that during any period transfer is more likely to appear than not to appear. Most of the studies carried on showed that learning of one thing is likely to influence some other type of behavior.

The third row of figures in Table 14-1 reveals an interesting trend. An increasing number of studies show that the amount (or occurrence) of transfer depends on the conditions. The increase in such conclusions is undoubtedly due in part to the greater number of studies deliberately designed to find out which conditions actually do influence transfer. These conditions which seem to affect transfer are discussed in a later section of this chapter.

Transfer to General Reasoning. Experiments on the transfer of training in reasoning have shown conflicting results. This is not surprising since there is no sure agreement as to what is meant by reasoning. Exercises in reasoning and tests of reasoning ability, moreover, must vary exceedingly. It is encouraging to note that such a subject as geometry, *when deliberately taught to bring about transfer,* will bring about a definite improvement in reasoning ability in other subjects(34). The devices used to expedite transfer are discussed later.

Transfer in School Situations

Arithmetic. Practice in some phases of arithmetic will undoubtedly bring about increased skill in some other phases. Olander(35) found that children who practiced only 110 addition couplets were just as able to add the remaining 90 couplets as the children who had practiced all 200 couplets. Thus pupils who practiced on such couplets as 6 + 6 and 6 + 8 were also able to deal with 6 + 7 and 6 + 9, and to deal with them as well as comparable students who had actually studied these latter couplets. Similarly, students who practice adding numbers in one order, viz, 8 + 3, also learn to add those numbers in the other order(36) as in 3 + 8.

Even with no special effort to attain transfer, we can expect practice with some material to increase our skill with other material. This transfer can be greatly increased, however, by some deliberate efforts to secure transfer. There will be much greater transfer to unpracticed tasks if the drill or practice is accompanied by deliberate generalization. Transfer in one instance was greatly increased, even at the second-grade level, by having the students generalize or work out simple rules to describe what they were doing with the practiced material. Thus pupils concluded that in adding 1 "you count up 1," or "the answer is the next number." Apparently they were able to use those rules when they encountered novel material(37).

Spelling. In view of the unsystematic nature of English spelling, it is not surprising that transfer in spelling may be either positive or negative. Learning to spell one word may help us to spell some unstudied words and make it harder for us to spell others. Learning to spell *search,* for instance, may handicap a child when he comes to spell *journey,* since the *ear* and *our* in these words have very similar sounds. Likewise, learning to spell *excelling* (the derived form) may interfere with the correct spelling of *excel* (the base form). Learning to spell *create* (the base form) may interfere with the spelling of *creating* (the derived form). More often, however, our experience with the base word may help us in spelling the derived form.

There is some evidence that study of spelling rules brings about some improvement in actual spelling(38). In a subject as unsystematic as spelling, however, we should be foolish to rely wholly on rules. Indeed, some students of spelling have gone so far as to contend that each form of each word should be taught as a separate problem(39). More recent research, however, suggests that this is an unduly pessimistic view and that rules can be of considerable value. The teaching of rules may be especially valuable if we concentrate on a very few rules which (a) cover a great many words, (b) which do not have too many exceptions, and (c) which are not too difficult to learn(40).

The study of rules is especially likely to be valuable if those rules are developed inductively from the student's own experience with groups of words selected to bring out the rule. From experience with a group of similar words, the student reaches certain conclusions and forms his own rules. These are, of course, scrutinized and corrected by the teacher. This procedure seems to have a definite value(41). Breed suggests that rules which the student helps to work out are more likely to induce transfer than ready-made rules taught to the students.

Latin. Great interest has been attached to Latin as a possible source of transfer. At one time it was expected to bring about almost all the intellectual virtues. Although these great hopes have not been justified, it seems safe to say that Latin can be made to increase ability to read and spell English words and to help in the mastery of some other languages(42). In these, as in other investigations, it is apparent that transfer is more likely to occur if it is deliberately taught and if students are deliberately encouraged to apply their new knowledge to aspects of other languages.

Science. Mudge(43) attempted to see if a year's training in high-school chemistry would increase a student's ability (a) to answer questions on a "functional" chemistry test and (b) to read popular scientific literature in more intelligent fashion. The functional test included items such as the following: "A piece of material is advertised as all wool. Which of the following would test the purity of a small sample of it? Which would not? (a) household ammonia, (b) vinegar, (c) alcohol, (d) lye, (e) carbolic acid."

These tests, and a test in the subject matter of chemistry, were given to fifty-two students in grades ten to twelve who were about to study chemistry, and to forty-one comparable students in the same grades who were not to study chemistry that year. All tests were repeated for both groups at the end of the academic year. It was found that the group not studying chemistry made slight but negligible gains on both the regular and on the functional test, whereas the students actually taking chemistry boosted their scores from 11 to 63 points on the regular test and from 36 to 63 points on the functional test. When these numbers were converted to standard scores, so as to make them comparable, it was found that a gain of 2.2 standard score units on the regular test was accompanied by a gain of 1.6 standard score units on the functional test. This suggests that about 75 percent of the gain on the regular course applied to the unpracticed functional test.

In Dr. Mudge's study, there was no special attempt to teach for transfer. An experiment by Babitz and Keyes(44) suggests that by constantly encouraging pupils to make practical applications of principles, the teacher may definitely increase the amount of transfer.

High-school Subjects and College Success

There is considerable evidence that students who take Latin in high school, especially those who take several years of Latin, get along better in college than students who have no Latin, or very little. The more recent investigators have realized, of course, that intelligence must be controlled, otherwise we may merely find that bright students take Latin and also do well in college. Hence they have been careful to secure groups of comparable intelligence but varying in the amount of high-school Latin. When intelligence is thus held constant, we still find that the students who take Latin are significantly ahead of their intellectual peers who do not take Latin(45, 46). They are especially apt to be ahead in languages but are also ahead in nonlinguistic subjects.

The reason for this superiority is not readily apparent. Even though intelligence has been controlled it is still possible that the other things which induced the students to take Latin in high school (academic-mindedness, parental pressure, docility, and so forth) also enabled them to secure higher marks in college. It may be, on the other hand, that taking Latin, especially for three or four years, induced habits of working and thinking, or attitudes or interests which aided in college work.

There have been many attempts to see if a course in high-school science is of value to a student taking a similar course in college(47). One unpublished summary of sixteen separate studies on this problem showed almost an equal division between those who report a noticeable advantage from the high-school course and those who report little if any difference. In only five of these studies is there any report of an attempt to hold intelligence constant. Of these five studies, three report no special advantage in college from high-school science, and two report that they do find such an advantage.

As we see, there has been considerable work on the possible advantages of high-school Latin and science. The role of other subjects, however, has not been as well explored. Two studies(48, 49) report that high-school history is of no special advantage in college history. From the few studies(50) made, it appears, on the other hand, that students who take mathematics in high school tend to get along better in college mathematics. In these studies intelligence has been held constant, but other things, such as interest in mathematics, academic-mindedness, academic or professional drive, have not. Hence we cannot, as yet, decide whether mathematics in high school actually does something to students which enables them to do well in college mathematics, or whether the high-school course merely selects students who will do well in college anyway.

Factors Affecting Amount of Transfer

We have seen that although some spread of learning is inevitable, such spread may not proceed in the direction or in the manner we wish. If that spread fails to help us in a given task, we say that there is zero transfer. If the effect of the spread is to handicap us in that second task, we say that there is negative transfer. It is not surprising, then, that transfer does not always occur, and certainly not surprising that it does not always occur in the direction we wish.

There seems no question that transfer may be increased by deliberate teaching to that end. The methods to be used must depend on the subject matter being taught and the aspects of the subject matter which may be of use in other fields. There are at least two procedures, however, which may be advocated as general rules.

Emphasizing the Feature of the Lesson Which May Be Applied to Other Fields. A teacher who hopes to induce transfer should first of all decide which aspect of the lesson or course of study he thinks may be of use in other fields. In teaching geometry, for instance, he may wish to develop a more logical approach to certain other problems. He should then be sure that this logical approach is brought to the fore in his teaching of geometry. (This is by no means always done in the teaching of geometry.) Or, to use another example, the teacher may hope that, through the study of educational psychology, the student will be in a better position to evaluate other data in sociology, such as newspaper reports on delinquency or on the relation of disease to food shortage. If such is his hope, he should take pains to see that this method of inspecting data is brought into focus and emphasized. If the teacher hopes to improve general literary taste by teaching a given selection of literature, he must be sure that any widely applicable principles appearing in this selection are brought out and noticed. If methods of work, neatness, or accuracy are to be transferred, these must be clearly highlighted.

Very often the thing to be transferred can be stated as a rule or principle or formula or insight. If so, it seems only wise to be sure that the students attain such a formula, that they become consciously aware of the thing to be used(51). Indeed some psychologists(52) believe that transfer depends on insight or on the student's acceptance and realization of the thing to be transferred, whether that "thing" should be a principle or a method of work, an attitude or an ideal. As we have already shown, there is some suggestion(37, 41) that it is better for the students themselves to work out this principle or formulate the rule or describe the essential method or approach. Let the students work it out for themselves, and let them do so fairly leisurely. According to one study(53), too precipitous a verbalization of the rule or principle may actually reduce the amount of transfer. In any case, of course, it is important for the teacher to examine the generalizations suggested by the students and to suggest further exercises if those generalizations are not acceptable.

Practice in Application to Other Fields. Not only should the element to be transferred be brought into clear focus and, if possible, formulated and clearly structured, but it should also be applied to fields outside the subject matter of the lesson. If the teacher of geometry hopes to induce a logical approach to mystery stories or military strategy or ethics, he should give his students practice in applying the rules to these or other fields. If the teacher of educational psychology wishes his students to be more cautious in their interpretation of general sociological data, he should be sure to apply this critical approach to other data. Where clearcut applications are not feasible, the teacher should at least call attention to the fact that the aspect in question has other applications.

Although it is clear that we should give much practice in making applications to other fields, we must not conclude that the subject matter itself should be a conglomerate of many fields. There is nothing to suggest, for instance, that the geometry course should consist of equal parts of Euclid, of exercises in syllogisms, and of logical analysis of ethical problems. One laboratory study(54), at least, suggests that intensive practice in a single task (such as tracing a design in a mirror) brought about more transfer to new tasks than did an equal amount of practice spread over four different but related activities. Such a conglomerate of diverse activities, in fact, may retard the appearance of the crucial insight on which the transfer depends.

Identifying and Naming Basic Elements. A young child is having difficulty in distinguishing *bay* from *day*. Under these circumstances, he will clearly profit from some practice in locating the crucial difference (*b* versus *d*) and in learning to distinguish between *b* and *d*. This supplementary activity, in other words, will transfer to the more intrinsic skill of distinguishing between the two words. There is no question about the fact that this supplementary activity frequently transfers(55, 56). There is some question, however, about the help we may get from naming or labeling the things that have to be discriminated. Consider the matter in the case of a more difficult problem. You are to watch for spots of light on a radar screen and are required to sound a signal if the spot attains a certain brightness. Would your task be any easier if, previously, you had practiced attaching distinctive names to spots of different brightness (cigarette glow, firefly, electric spark)? At the present stage we cannot be sure whether the advantage from this preliminary experience comes from the naming or merely from the increased attention and analysis given to the spots(57, 58).

Amount of Experience with the Original Task. Up to a point, at least, we are more likely to get transfer if we provide a reasonable amount of experience with the original task(59). Animals are more likely to learn "how to learn" when their first tasks are definitely learned to completion(60). The more completely we memorize one list of nonsense syllables, the more likely we are to use that mastery in learning a similar list of nonsense syllables.

This does not mean, of course, that it will always pay us to spend more time on the task from which we expect to get transfer. Rather than spending more time on helping the child distinguish between *b* and *d,* it might be better to go directly to actual reading practice involving *bay* and *day*. There are times, however, when we do not have this choice. Sometimes actual practice is out of the question (escaping from the enemy, rescuing a drowning man) and we must rely entirely on make-believe practice in the hope that it will transfer. Under such circumstances, it is well to remember that the more practice, the more the likelihood of transfer.

Intelligence and Other Characteristics of the Student. There is some suggestion that transfer is more likely to occur in extroverted than in introverted students, and in younger than in older students. Not enough work has been done on these topics to make us very confident about the answer.

Intelligence has long been assumed to be an important factor in transfer. It would be amazing if the intelligent student were not more successful in perceiving and formulating the general principle, and if, as we have suggested, this formulation of the general principle is an aid in transfer, the bright student should have an advantage. Conversely, we might expect that negative transfer when it occurred would be a more serious problem for the brighter students. To support this latter expectation, there is some evidence. Whenever the retention of previous habits or the utilization of a previously learned rule tends to act as a handicap, then bright students are more affected by that handicap(61).

Theories of Transfer

Ever since the turn of the century there has been a vigorous controversy over the mechanisms by which transfer takes place. A large part of the controversy has been between the proponents of the identical elements theory of Thorndike and the generalization theory of Judd. This argument, however, is rapidly coming to have merely historical importance, since it becomes more and more evident that the contrast between the two theories is not very clearly drawn.

The theory of identical elements states that transfer is due to the number of tendencies or behavior units that are common to the practiced and the unpracticed activity. If in practicing the adding machine, for instance, we have learned to respond to *three* by hitting a certain key marked 3, and to *five* by hitting a different key marked 5, then those same tendencies may be expected to function when we begin to practice typing. More general tendencies developed in one activity may also be used in any other activity. The generalization theory, on the contrary, holds that transfer is due to generalizations or to general principles built up in one activity and utilized in the other.

As Sandiford(62) has pointed out, the two theories may be saying one and the same thing. The generalization developed in one activity may be regarded as a bond or group of bonds which is involved in the mastery of the other activity.

Even if we could see clearly drawn differences between these two theories, it would be surprising if either one could be shown to be exclusively true. It would be hard for the proponents of generalization to show that small isolated habits learned in one activity could not be utilized in other activities. Such small isolated habits may be automatic and utterly unconscious. For instance, the many intricate bonds built up while the child is learning to stand in an upright position may quite probably be used when he tries to skate. Yet these bonds are hardly explicit generalizations. The proponents of the theory of identical elements, on the other hand, must admit, as we have shown repeatedly, that emphasis on conscious generalization will often expedite transfer.

What to Expect from Transfer

From the preceding discussion, it is apparent that transfer may readily be brought about by direct teaching to that end, and that it may occur spontaneously. It has been equally apparent, however, that the gain in an unpracticed art or task is rarely if ever as great as the gain in the practiced art. If we gain 100 points in the knowledge of academic chemistry, we will do well to gain 75 points in unstressed functional chemistry.

Each of these principles points to an obvious moral. The first principle tells us that it is foolish to rely on transfer if direct practice is readily available. Never, for instance, try to give your students skill in typing by having them practice on an adding machine if you can just as readily have them practice on the typewriter itself. The second principle reassures us that when direct practice is not possible or feasible it is quite proper to use transfer as a "next best," especially if you arrange your teaching in such a way that you secure a maximum of transfer.

This second moral, by the way, is in no way a mere afterthought put in for the sake of logical completeness. On the contrary, it covers a large number of practical situations. It happens, very often, that direct practice may not be feasible or possible or wise. Direct practice may be expensive and wasteful in materials, as any director of vocational education realizes most acutely. Direct practice may be dangerous to the student, as it would if he were to practice fire-drill or parachute jumping under the conditions in which he is expected to use his skill. Direct practice may also be dangerous to others, as when young surgeons first begin to get experience. Because of this, such early practice is usually restricted to work on animals or cadavers. We sincerely hope, moreover, that this early experience will have contributed a great transfer effect by the time the young surgeon approaches the live human being.

In addition to those activities in which direct practice would be dangerous, expensive, or impolitic, there may be activities in which direct practice is essentially impossible. In the field of character education, for instance, we want people to be kind, considerate, and thoughtful, and not too arrogant. But do we want children to think, "Now I am being kind, or modest or humble?" In the view of the writer, any activities too deliberately directed to such desirable goals suggest the prig. To many other people, an essential aspect of many virtues is their unconscious spontaneity. Who wants to be treated kindly by a person who knows (and shows) that he is being kind?

Note on Methods for Efficient Study

The discussion of the management of learning has been written with the teacher in mind. It elaborates principles which the teacher should know when he contemplates teaching others. It is natural, however, that many of these principles also apply to the student studying by himself. Here are the more important rules which might be used by the individual to facilitate his own study.

1. Secure Motivation. Whenever possible, set a definite goal for the period of study. "Tonight I must prepare pages——— to ———, or I must write so many words." Describe the goal so that you can tell when you have reached it.

2. Seek Out Meaning. Look over the task quickly at first to see the general arrangement and to see if there are any large general principles. Then study with the general plan in mind. Later on, make an intensive study, being careful to relate the details to the general plan whenever possible.

3. Or Create Meaning. If the material to be learned has no apparent pattern or organization, it may pay you to give it an arbitrary pattern or structure by the use of some simple mnemonic device.

4. Arrange for Activity. After some initial acquaintance with the material, try to study it actively. Do something with it. Reorganize it. Relate it to similar material. Invent questions about it. Explain it to someone else. Test yourself by trying to recall what you have studied.

Have someone else quiz you. Anything is better than nothing. The things you "do about" the material should fit in with your purpose for study. Use it to answer imaginary examination questions if that is your immediate need, or to quote at a party if that is what you have in mind, or to incorporate into a paper.

5. *Make Use of Guidance.* In the early stages of practice, be sure to make use of anything that will point the way to the correct method of dealing with the problem. During the *first two or three practices,* in learning foreign vocabulary, do not guess. Look at the right answer. For the *first two or three exercises* in algebra, do not hesitate to look at the answer in the back of the book even before you finish the problem. In memorizing, read the material over once or twice before trying to recite it from memory.

6. *Proceed Promptly to the Trial-and-Error Stage.* Guidance is permissible and valuable at the outset but must be abandoned for the less pleasant method of trial-and-error learning. After one or two readings, test yourself by attempting to recite. After one or two careful readings of the foreign vocabulary, force yourself to guess. After the first few exercises in algebra, force yourself to complete the problem, and to write down the answer before you peek at the answer in the book.

7. *Practice Even Where Understanding Is Incomplete.* By all means seek out the meaning in your new material. Try to see the general process and the rationale underlying the task you are about to attempt. Get a general picture of the dancing steps you are to learn, of the words you are about to pronounce, of the problems you are to solve. But do not insist on perfect understanding before you begin to practice. Get a reasonable amount of familiarization. Then plunge in. If you are learning dancing, get up on the floor and try to dance. If you are learning mathematics, start doing the exercises even though you do not understand everything the text says. Understanding often follows manipulation. In writing an English exercise, do not wait for the muse to visit you with a perfect theme. Start to write. At first you will write rubbish, but it may get you into the swing of writing, and anyway you may be able to salvage something from it when you correct it later on, as, of course, you must. People who insist on a perfectly complete understanding of the underlying reason before they make a single move often fail to make that first move.

8. *Handle Distractions Systematically.* Do not use up too much time or energy in trying to rule out distractions by sheer will power. Physical distractions may often be avoided altogether. Try to find a place where you do not hear other conversations, speeches, or plays from the radio. Casual music probably will not bother you a great deal. Neither should meaningless noise unless it is too intense or unpleasant.

It is not only with physical distractions that you will have to deal. Many people lose more time, perhaps, through the intrusion of their own irrelevant ideas than from outside physical distractions. There is no single method for handling these internal distractions. One psychologist used this system: whenever he found an irrelevant idea cropping up with bothersome frequency, he used to jot it down in a "commonplace book" he left on his desk. If, while marking papers, for instance, he found his mind occupied with ideas for constructing a new piece of apparatus, he would make a brief sketch in the notebook. Even more frivolous persistent ideas would be dealt with in this same way. He might write down, "Tell Bill story about———," or, "Dean———had no business making me take over that extra section," or, "Try to make up to Mary for the dirty crack I made about her hair-do." His theory, of course, followed something of a Freudian trend. He believed that any idea which kept bobbing up must have had some powerful drive behind it. Suppressing a powerful drive will, of course, be difficult. By writing it down, he promises, in a sense, to give it due attention later on.

Summary

To a large extent forgetting may be caused by interference from subsequent activity. The amount of forgetting (or retention, the converse of forgetting) may be measured by recall, by noting the amount saved upon relearning, by having the student reconstruct a scrambled list, or by testing his ability to recognize studied material. Different methods give different results, the method of recall being the least sensitive.

The more rapid learner usually retains more of what he learns than does the slow learner.

Upon cessation of practice, mastery of a subject may increase slightly for a short time (reminiscence), or it may begin to decline immediately. Reminiscence may occur in the space of a few days with meaningful material that is incompletely learned. The gain achieved in reminiscence of meaningful material may persist indefinitely. More often, however, this gain is followed by a definite decline. With rote material, the decline sets in very early and proceeds at a very rapid rate. Forgetting is seldom complete with either meaningful or rote material.

During the summer vacation, there is definite forgetting of arithmetic and spelling and other subjects seldom used during this period. In reading and literature, on the other hand, there may be an actual increase in mastery.

As forgetting proceeds, the concept of the material studied is likely to become more structured or conventional.

Not all materials are equally susceptible to forgetting. Meaningful material is more readily retained than rote material. There may be a slight tendency to remember pleasant material more easily than unpleasant material. There is also a tendency to remember things that flatter us. Acts of motor skill are no easier to retain than verbal materials. Motor skill, however, often receives much more practice. Longer selections are forgotten at about the same rate as shorter selections.

Forgetting may be reduced by introducing more meaning and motivation into the learning and by carrying the practice far beyond the amount needed for one perfect performance. Forgetting is also reduced by frequent review. We are not sure as yet whether distribution of practices aids retention.

In the past, people have expected a great deal from the transfer of training. This expectation was due in part to a belief that things which were called by the same name were psychologically alike. This belief may be valid for some traits and not for others. The method of factor analysis (used in studies of intelligence) tries to find which traits are psychologically alike. The belief in extensive transfer came also in part from failure to consider the various cause-effect hypotheses. Students who took large amounts of Latin in high school were observed to do much better in college than students who took little or no Latin. It was assumed that the Latin caused the superior work in college. Actually, when intelligence is held constant, the students who have taken Latin are only slightly ahead in college, although they are still ahead.

Investigations during the past forty years have shown that transfer may be great or may be zero or even negative. Of 211 investigations, 70 percent showed definite transfer, 13 percent showed little or no transfer, while 10 percent showed negative transfer in one form or another.

Transfer has been observed in the laboratory in very similar tasks or in continuations of the same task. There is evidence that we "learn how to learn." It has frequently been noticed in school subjects, especially when teachers have deliberately tried to achieve it. Transfer can be increased if during the learning of task A the teacher helps the student isolate and attend to the elements, principles, or techniques which can be used in task B. It can also be increased by giving practice in applying those things to other tasks. In some cases there is a gain from studying the separate elements in a problem before studying the problem itself.

Either the theory of generalization or the theory of identical elements would account for a great deal of transfer. If there is any clear distinction between the two theories, it has chiefly historical significance.

Ordinarily it would be foolish to study subject *A solely* for its transfer to subject *B*. It would be better to study subject *B* directly. There may be some subjects, however, which cannot be studied directly, and here, of course, we must rely on whatever gains may be exacted from transfer of training.

To increase the efficiency of study, the student should utilize and create motivation. He should seek out the meaning of the material or create artificial meaning. He should arrange for some activity and after a few trials should force himself to adopt trial-and-error techniques. Distractions, mental and physical, should be met by some systematic method. The student should not try to overcome them by sheer will power alone.

SPECIFIC REFERENCES

1. McGeoch, J. A. *The psychology of human learning*. Longmans, 1942, pp. 453–457.
2. Melton, A. W. Learning. *Annu. Rev. Psychol.*, 1950, *1*, 9–30 (See page 26).
3. Cruze, W. W. *Educational Psychology*. Ronald Press, 1942, p. 224.
4. Bunch, M. E. The measurement of retention by the relearning method. *Psychol. Rev.*, 1941, *48*, 450–456.
5. Burtt, H. E. A further study of early childhood memory. *J. genet. Psychol.*, 1937, *50*, 187–192.
6. Gillette, Annette L. Learning and retention: a comparison of three experimental procedures. *Arch. Psychol.*, N.Y., 1936, No. 198.
7. Underwood, B. J. Speed of learning and amount retained: a consideration of methodology. *Psychol. Bull.*, 1954, *51*, 276–282.
8. McGeoch, J. A. *The psychology of human learning*. Longmans, 1942, pp. 343–353.
9. Buxton, C. E. "Reminiscence" in the studies of Professor English and his associates. *Psychol. Rev.*, 1942, *49*, 494–504.
10. English, H. B. Reminiscence—Reply to Dr. Buxton's critique. *Psychol. Rev.*, 1942, *49*, 505–512.
11. Tyler, R. W. Permanence of learning. *J. higher Educ.*, 1933, *4*, 203–205.
12. Lahey, Sister M. F. Louise. Permanence of retention of first-year algebra. *J. educ. Psychol.*, 1941, *32*, 401–413.

13. McGeoch, J. A. *The psychology of human learning*. Longmans, 1942, pp. 325–327.

14. Noble, C. E. The role of stimulus meaning (m) in serial verbal learning. *J. exp. Psychol.*, 1952, *43*, 437–446.

15. Riley, D. A. Reminiscence effects in paired-associate learning. *J. exp. Psychol.*, 1953, *45*, 232–238.

16. Melton, A. W. Learning. *Annu. Rev. Psychol.*, 1950, *1*, 9–30. (See page 26).

17. Smith, Madorah E. Delayed recall of previously memorized material after forty years. *J. genet. Psychol.*, 1951, *79*, 337–338.

18. Stroud, J. B. Experiments on learning in school situations. *Psychol. Bull.*, 1940, *37*, 777–807.

19. Keys, N., and Lawson, J. V. Summer versus winter gains in school achievement. *Sch. & Soc.*, 1936, *46*, 541–544.

20. Morgan, L. D. How effective is specific training in preventing loss due to the summer vacation? *J. educ. Psychol.*, 1929, *20*, 466–471.

21. Bartlett, F. C. *Remembering: a study in experimental and social psychology*. Macmillan, 1932.

22. Burton, A., and Tueller, R. Successive reproduction of visually perceived forms. *J. genet. Psychol.*, 1941, *58*, 71–82.

23. Alper, Thelma G. Task-orientation and ego-orientation as factors in reminiscence. *J. exp. Psychol.*, 1948, *38*, 224–238.

24. Sones, A. M., and Stroud, J. B. Review, with special reference to temporal position. *J. educ. Psychol.*, 1940, *31*, 665–676.

25. Underwood, B. J. Learning. *Annu. Rev. Psychol.*, 1953, *4*, pp. 52.

26. Taft, R. Selective recall and memory distortion of favorable and unfavorable material. *J. abnorm. soc. Psychol.*, 1954, *49*, 23–28.

27. Underwood, B. J., and Richardson, J. Studies of distributed practice: XIII. Interlist interference and the retention of serial nonsense lists. *J. exp. Psychol.*, 1955, *50*, 39–46.

28. McGeoch, J. A. *The psychology of human learning*. Longmans, 1942, pp. 405–406.

29. Wickens, D. D. Stimulus identity as related to response specificity and response generalization. *J. exp. Psychol.*, 1948, *38*, 389–394.

30. Harlow, H. F. The formation of learning sets. *Psychol. Rev.*, 1949, *56*, 51–65.

31. Harlow, H. F., and Warren, J. M. Formation and transfer of discrimination learning sets. *J. comp. physiol. Psychol.*, 1952, *45*, 482–489.

32. Ward, L. B. Reminiscence and rote learning. *Psychol. Monogr.*, 1937, *49*, No. 220.

33. Orata, P. T. Recent research studies on transfer of training, with implications for curriculum, guidance, and personnel work. *Harv. educ. Rev.,* 1941, *11,* 359–378.

34. Hartung, M. L. Teaching of mathematics in senior high school and junior college. *Rev. educ. Res.,* 1942, *12,* 425–434.

35. Olander, H. T. Transfer of learning in simple addition and subtraction. *Elem. Sch. J.,* 1931, *31,* 358–369.

36. Beito, E. A., and Brueckner, L. J. A measurement of transfer in the learning of number combinations. *Yearb. nat. soc. Stud. Educ. 29,* 1930, 569–587.

37. Thiele, C. L. The contribution of generalization to the learning of the addition facts. *Teach. Coll. Contr. Educ.,* No. 763, 1938.

38. Watson, Alice E. Experimental studies in the psychology and pedagogy of spelling. *Teach. Coll. Contr. Educ.,* No. 638, 1935.

39. Horn, E. The influence of past experiences upon spelling. *J. educ. Res.,* 1929, *19,* 283–288.

40. Breed, F. S. Generalization in spelling. *Elem. Sch. J.,* 1937, *37,* 733–741.

41. Gates, A. I. Generalization and transfer in spelling. Teachers College, Columbia University, 1935.

42. Jordan, A. M. *Educational Psychology.* Holt, 1942, 278–291.

43. Mudge, Evelyn L. Transfer of training in chemistry. *Johns Hopk. Univ. Stud. Educ.* No. 26, 1939.

44. Babitz, M., and Keys, N. An experiment in teaching pupils to apply scientific principles. *Sci. Educ.,* 1939, *23,* 367–370.

45. Sorenson, H. High-school subjects as conditioners of college success. *J. educ. Res.,* 1929, *19,* 237–254.

46. Smith, Mary E., and Douglass, H. R. The relation of high-school Latin to marks in the first year of Arts College. *Sch. Rev.,* 1937, *45,* 695–701.

47. Hoff, A. G. The effect of the study of high school chemistry upon success in college chemistry. *J. educ. Res.,* 1947, *40,* 539–542.

48. Douglass, H. R., and Friedman, K. C. The relation of certain factors to achievement in college social studies and history. *Sch. Rev.,* 1937, *45,* 196–199.

49. Smith, C. A. High school training and college freshman grades. *J. educ. Res.,* 1939, *32,* 401–409.

50. Byrns, Ruth, and Henmon, V. A. C. Entrance requirements and college success. *Sch. & Soc.,* 1935, *41,* 101–104.

51. Meredith, G. P. The transfer of training. *Occup. Psychol.,* 1941, *15,* 61–76.

52. Hamley, H. R. Formal training: A critical survey of experimental work. *Brit. J. educ. Psychol.*, 1936, *6*, 233–249.

53. Hendrix, Gertrude. A new clue to transfer of training. *Elem. Sch. J.*, 1947, *48*, 197–208.

54. Ryan, T. A., and Schehr, Frances. General practice in mirror tracing. *Amer. J. Psychol.*, 1940, *53*, 593–599.

55. Gagné, R. M., and Baker, Katherine E. Stimulus pre-differentiation as a factor in transfer of training. *J. exp. Psychol.*, 1950, *40*, 439–451.

56. McAllister, Dorothy E. The effects of various kinds of relevant verbal pretraining on subsequent motor performance. *J. exp. Psychol.*, 1953, *46*, 329–336.

57. Gass, A. E. Transfer as a function of type and amount of preliminary experience with task stimuli. *J. exp. Psychol.*, 1953, *46*, 419–428.

58. Arnoult, M. D. Transfer of predifferentiation training in simple and multiple shape discrimination. *J. exp. Psychol.*, 1953, *45*, 401–409.

59. Duncan, C. P. Transfer in motor learning as a function of degree of first-task learning and inter-task similarity. *J. exp. Psychol.*, 1953, *45*, 1–11.

60. Hayes, K. J., Thompson, R., and Hayes, Catherine. Discrimination learning set in chimpanzees. *J. comp. physiol. Psychol.*, 1953, *46*, 99–104.

61. Ryans, D. G. An experimental study of the transfer of training with special attention to the relation of intelligence test performance. *J. educ. Psychol.*, 1936, *27*, 492–500.

62. Sandiford, P. *Educational Psychology.* Longmans, 1928, p. 298.

SUGGESTIONS FOR FURTHER READING

1. Deese, J. E. *The psychology of learning.* McGraw-Hill, 1952, Chaps. 9, 10, 11.

2. McGeoch, J. A., and Irion, A. *The psychology of human learning.* Longmans, 1952, Chaps. 9, 10.

3. Stevens, S. S. *Handbook of experimental psychology.* Wiley, 1951, Chap. 17. Human learning and retention (Hovland, C. I.).

    Each of these three references covers the ground quite completely. All are rather technical. Deese goes to more trouble to bring out the interrelations.

4. Monroe, W. S. *Encyclopaedia of educational research.* Macmillan, 1950. Article on transfer of training, 1483–1489 (Andrews, T. G., Cronbach, L. J., and Sandiford, P.).

A more general account of the whole problem. Includes the historical significance for teaching.

5. Tolman, E. C., and Postman, L. Learning. *Annu. Rev. Psychol.,* 1954, 5, 27–56.

   For some references on a general factor in interference and inhibition.

6. Woodworth, R. S., and Schlosberg, H. *Experimental psychology.* Holt, 1954, Chaps. 23, 24, 25.

   These three chapters cover the general field of learning. Chapter 24 shows the relation between interference and transfer.

Exercises and Questions for Discussion

1. A student is memorizing his part for a high-school play. Which method would you use to test his retention?

   You are teaching a class some of the classical myths and fables. As one of your objectives, you hope that these fables will add to the student's enjoyment of the literary works that allude to these myths. As far as this objective is concerned, which measure of retention would prove most valuable?

2. What is meant by reminiscence? Under what conditions is it likely to occur?

3. List, in order of importance, several things a teacher can do to ensure greater retention.

4. Summarize in four or five sentences the main points that a teacher should keep in mind with respect to transfer.

5. Think over several of the recent general articles or editorials on education that you have read. Did these articles make any assumptions regarding the amount of transfer that we can expect?

6. There is a popular impression that motor skill such as skating is better retained than verbal skill such as speaking a foreign language. If this should be true, how could you account for it?

7. A great many experiments in the field of transfer of training have dealt with Latin. How do you account for this fact?

8. A student, who has been ill for some weeks, finds that he must quickly learn the English meanings of some 120 French words if he is to go along with the class in regular fashion. He is anxious to make the best use of his study time and comes to you for advice.

   First of all, for your own guidance, list the factors in the situation which are favorable to his objective. List the factors which will handicap him.

   Work out with him a list of detailed, concrete rules that should help him in his task. Use everything that you have learned that will apply to his particular problem.

15

Administrative Influences: Their Powers and Limitations

THUS FAR we have had a good look at the direct forces which act on the student and which thereby induce academic development. We have examined the powerful forces of heredity, maturation, and family stimulation. We have seen the many influences which the teacher brings to bear through the use of the various devices and tools under his control. Now we ask, "What can be done by the principal, the superintendent, or the state legislature to facilitate academic development? How important are these administrative features when added to the forces which are already at work in the interests of scholastic growth?"

Academic growth, it will be remembered, comes partly from the operation of a group of nonscholastic factors such as heredity, maturation, the influence of the home and the community, and partly from the teacher's application of the psychological mechanisms of motivation, practice, reinforcement, guidance, and insight, and especially from their operation on a maturing organism. The administrator has no direct access to these psychological mechanisms. It is only the classroom teacher who actually manipulates them. These mechanisms will be used more effectively only when those of us in the classroom use them that way. The administrator can encourage us and guide us, but he cannot by-pass us, or take over the controls himself. The actual instruction, in the last analysis, can be no better than that provided by the classroom teacher.

To get a down-to-earth view of the question that we face, let us suppose that the administrator has hired us and arranged for some sort of salary, that he has put us in a classroom with maturing students, and that he has arranged for basic facilities, perhaps at the subsistence level. Starting from this primitive condition, he could now arrange for improvements. He could get rid of us and engage "better" teachers with more training. He could secure better salaries and tenure. He could provide much more in the way of facilities. He could arrange for a program of supervision and in-service training. Our question is, "What can we expect of these improvements that may be added to the primitive, basic situation?"

First of all, we must realize that, psychologically speaking, the improvements enter the picture rather late in the game. The improvements do not start at the very outset but are applied to some very considerable forces already in operation even in the primitive, basic arrangements.

Let us consider what it means to enter the picture late in the game, so to speak. Let us suppose that an average teacher working under average conditions is already engaged in his task. Because of his ordinary interest in academic matters, he is bound to apply some motivation. He is bound to make academic matters acquire some importance in the eyes of the students. He is also bound to instigate some practice or experience, be it ever so humdrum, with academic matters. Automatic reinforcement will occur even without his efforts. Unless he is extremely perverse, moreover, he cannot fail to make some use of casual reinforcement. Even the average teacher will go beyond these inevitabilities and make some use of deliberate reinforcement. Even the mediocre teacher, indeed, will make use of guidance and will help sharpen the student's understanding of what leads to what. And the spacing of practices—that marvelous means of reducing interference—is bound to be employed to some extent(1).

Now all these forces, even though they may be operating in disgustingly mediocre fashion, will have pushed the attainment of the students to some level. Mediocre though the teacher may be, his efforts, applied day after day, may even have pushed the students to that part of the learning curve where decreasing returns have set in.

It is at this point that any new contribution on the part of the administrator must enter the picture. By some means or other, let us suppose that the administrative change leads the teacher to a more effective use of the various mechanisms of learning. But this change cannot accelerate the student's maturation. Even if the student is well below his maturational capabilities, the additional force unleashed by the administrator must often operate in the realm of decreasing returns, where much more energy is required to produce an observable gain.

In thus focusing our attention on the difficulties which confront the administrator, we run the risk of suggesting that he can do nothing at all. This, of course, would be going too far. Even though his contributions may operate within the area of decreasing returns, they are still positive returns. His efforts have some yield, even though they lack the richer yield of efforts applied at an earlier stage. His contributions should facilitate the efforts of most teachers, even though there is no precise or rigid control by which that contribution will be channeled directly into the classroom. And, at the very least, he can be of inestimable help in improving the lot of the teachers, a value that is not to be scorned.

Statistical Evidence on Administrative Factors

Common sense suggests that we should not pin our faith exclusively on administrative innovations or devices. And even if common sense did not point in this direction, there is much statistical evidence that would call for serious thought. Consider the child in some distant country engaged in a home-study course. He has the materials of instructions. He gets some help by way of correspondence from a distant "teacher." He has the direct help of a sincere and conscientious layman in the person of his mother or father. But the administrative facilities are far from lavish. The immediate teacher is almost completely untrained and has no help from a visiting supervisor or principal. Library, laboratory, and other teaching devices must be very ordinary.

In spite of this dearth of administrative facilities, we find that typically students in correspondence courses equal, *or may even surpass,* comparable students attending regular schools(2). The key, of course, may lie in the considerable individual attention received by correspondence students, or perhaps in the high motivation. In any case, we cannot regard such studies as conclusive. Until the results are more carefully analyzed, however, we must at least consider the possibility that we should not expect radical gains from administrative innovations.

Size of School

In studying the influence of school size we are plagued by the pitfall of the common cause. Naturally, the larger schools are found in the larger communities. Large consolidated schools, until recently, were more likely in wealthy and progressive communities. Children from larger, wealthier and more progressive communities tend to be above average in intelligence. Consequently the superior intelligence to be found in the larger schools could produce superior achievement.

In the elementary school, when the IQ and the socioeconomic status of students are matched(3), we find little consistent difference between the achievement in schools ranging from the one-teacher schools to the larger seventeen-teacher schools. For the dull children there is a suggestion of superior performance in the larger schools. This is not clearly established, however, and for other groups there is no clear trend.

At the high-school level, the children from very small schools (three teachers or less) do suffer a slight handicap. Students from schools of four or five teachers, however, get along about as well as students from much larger schools(4), in most subjects at least(5).

Cost and Quality of the Schools

If we fail to rule out factors of intelligence and of socioeconomic status, we will find a very definite relation between the attainment of students and the amount spent on the schools(6). But here we do not know whether it is the money or the superior intelligence that is responsible. When intelligence is held constant, we find a certain amount of conflict between different studies. The early investigators found little difference in achievement between first-class schools and those rated as less satisfactory. Two investigations by Orr(7, 8), however, leave the issue in doubt. The first study by Orr suggests no relation. The second, employing some modified procedures, suggests superior attainment from the better schools.

Recently there has been some encouraging evidence that sheer improvement in the lighting and painting of the classroom will bring about an increase in attainment(9).

Selection and Training of Teachers

What are the characteristics of a successful teacher? To this question there have been many answers based on general observation, common sense, and analysis. There are many opinions available and some of these have become firmly entrenched in the literature and in educational practices.

Views derived in this way may well be true. Unfortunately, however, they have so far eluded almost all statistical or empirical tests. In spite of score upon score of empirical investigations(10, 11, 12, 13, 14) we still do not know, with even moderate certainty, just how much intelligence counts in teaching, or which personal qualities help and which hinder us in our task. We are equally ignorant about the role of knowledge of subject matter and professional training.

Teacher's Intelligence and Knowledge. In some investigations, the more intelligent teacher has also turned out to be the better teacher. In other investigations, there is little if any difference between the dull and the bright teacher. Turning to the teacher's knowledge of his own subject, we find a similar conflict in results. Sometimes knowledge of subject matter seems closely related to teaching success and at other times it seems to play little or no part.

There have been many attempts to explain this baffling confusion of results. It is possible that intelligence and knowledge of the subject are more important at one level than the other. Detailed mastery of subject matter, for instance, may be more important in college than in the elementary school. Similarly, a high IQ may be more necessary in dealing with more advanced students.

As another hypothesis, some people hold that the confusion in our results merely reflects the fact that neither intelligence nor knowledge of subject has a one-to-one relation with teaching success. At any given level, there may be an optimum range of either knowledge or intelligence. Below this, too little knowledge can make for a poor teacher. Above this, as any college students can attest, too much knowledge may also be a handicap. The specialist who knows the subject too well may be reluctant to spend the necessary time in developing the elementary stages. He may be unwilling to linger over simple ideas. He may also be unduly impatient with the seemingly inexcusable floundering of his charges.

The same complex relation may hold for intelligence. The moron would be a poor risk for many teaching tasks. For many kinds of teaching, however, the genius might also be a failure. An Einstein or Goethe might have only limited success in teaching grade-two arithmetic or reading.

According to this latter hypothesis, we would get different results according to the range of talent studied. If we concentrated on the range from low to average, we would find that the talent helped. If we concentrated on the range from average to superior, we might find that with increasing talent there comes a decline in ability.

Personality of the Teacher. It would be surprising if some aspects of the teacher's personality were not of great importance in producing academic achievement in pupils. It is one thing, however, to feel sure that something must be at work, and quite a different thing to be able to put one's finger on a precise, identifiable trait and say, "This is the key to good teaching." Personality, moreover, as we show in a later chapter, is a very inclusive and vague term. No single investigation has been able to examine the relation between the whole of personality and ability to induce growth in children. Those personality tests which have been used have yielded disappointing results. In their early work at the University of Wisconsin, Barr and his associates found correlations ranging from −.15 to .30 between the teacher's score on a personality test and the growth of his pupils. In the later series under Barr's guidance, there was no significant correlation between pupil gain and the teacher's score on a standard personality test(15).

The results just discussed must not be considered as final. New personality tests may be devised which may change the picture. More important, perhaps, the tool of factor analysis is being applied to teacher characteristics. By means of this device it may be possible to tell the basic dimensions in which teachers differ. Already there is some suggestion that many of the differences among the ratings given teachers can be linked with three general factors: (a) the friendly-aloof dimension; (b) the systematic-disorganized dimension; and (c) the stimulating-dull dimension(16, 17). When we know how a teacher stands on each of these dimensions, we know a good deal of all that is said about him on a typical rating.

One interesting study(18) deals with the characteristics of those college teachers who were able to develop (and inspire) a large number of their students for careers in science. To an exceptional extent, these college teachers were active in professional affairs. They were unusually demanding in that they refused to be satisfied with poor work. They were also zestful in their teaching. They were above average but less outstanding in personal warmth, and only moderately proficient in lecturing or in administrative ability.

Attitude of the Teacher. Are there any attitudes which may help to distinguish the good teacher from the poor teacher? Investigations suggest that such attitudes or cluster of attitudes may be found. Already there is some evidence that good teachers are more apt to be well informed on the principles of mental hygiene, and that they can better detect symptoms of pupil maladjustment. There is also some evidence that specific courses of training for teachers in these matters will bring about an increase in the achievement of pupils(19).

The influence of other attitudes is hard to determine, since there is considerable confusion in the results. Some studies(20) have found a liberal philosophy of education and sensitivity to social problems to be correlated with pupil gain. The Wisconsin studies, on the other hand, found no such relation. In one instance, in fact, it was found that a liberal attitude toward methodology was typical of the less successful teachers. The matter is further confused by the fact that, in one study(21), the teachers rated highly by principals and supervisors showed more than average ethnocentrism or antiminority prejudice. According to some theorists, this is supposed to be an index of the rigid, authoritarian, conforming person.

These comments refer to the influence of the teacher's personality on the academic attainment of students. The influence on the personality or character of the students is discussed in Chapter 20.

Experience. Sheer practice or experience, as we learned earlier, does not always guarantee an increase in proficiency. Very often, however, the other necessary ingredients may be expected to come along with experience so that improvement is likely to occur. Certainly the statistical evidence supports this hope(20). During the first few years of teaching, there is a definite increase in the ability of the teacher to induce growth in his students. From what we know of the frequency of decreasing returns, however, we would not expect this happy improvement to continue at the same rate for an indefinite period of time. For most teachers in the field, the improvement begins to taper off after four or five years(22, 23). It may still be possible, of course, for the zealous and conscientious teacher to continue to improve throughout his career. These statistical results refer to the general actual practice and not to ideal conditions.

It seems certain that there is no absolute need for an *exceptional* amount of experience. In one study after another(24), it has been shown that classes taught largely by student teachers gain as much as comparable classes taught by experienced teachers. In this case, of course, any handicap produced by the inexperienced cadet teachers may be made up by the superior ability of the regular teacher with whom the cadet teacher ordinarily works.

Professional Training of the Teacher. As we learned in the introductory chapter of this book, there is every reason to expect that an increased understanding of the educational process will help the teacher to practice his craft. Knowledge obtained from professional courses should enable the teacher to see his task in its larger perspective. Such knowledge should help immeasurably in understanding the nature of educational development and in dealing with the many responsibilities to be encountered outside the classroom. Some knowledge of the drives, needs, and conflicts of children should also enable the teacher to accept his students in more understanding fashion. And the sober, statistical record, as a matter of fact, does show that a course in mental hygiene definitely adds to a teacher's effectiveness.

Clearly we should expect a reasonable mastery of professional subjects to show itself in increased efficiency of the teacher. From what we know about decreasing returns, however, we would not expect course piled on course in an endless series to continue to show comparable increases in efficiency. There must come a time when mere increase in knowledge of techniques will lose its magic. A shrewd Yankee farmer, upon being urged to buy a set of books on farming, once replied, "Shucks! I ain't farming half as well as I know how to, now." Similarly, after a certain point, the teacher may readily come to know more than he can actually use. At any rate, there is little evidence that sheer cumulation of a large number of professional courses will greatly boost the teacher's efficiency. Sometimes, as a matter of fact, we find that the champion "course takers" have a poorer classroom record than those with only moderate professional training(22, 23). In considering this factual evidence, however, we must be on guard against reversed causality. It is possible that an incompetent teacher, either through his own suspicions or through the direct advice of his supervisor, may be led to take more than an average number of courses. Thus it may be that we should consider incompetence as the cause of course-taking rather than course-taking as the cause of incompetence.

Let us sum up this way: a moderate amount of professional training should be a wonderful boon in actual classroom practice. Beyond that, moreover, you will want additional training or reading to enable you to satisfy your professional curiosity and to help you take part in the many outside activities that will play a part in your professional life. But as far as classroom effectiveness is concerned, be prepared to meet decreasing returns. Do not expect the same classroom returns from the third or fourth course that you got from the first.

Reducing the Teacher's Working Load

At first glance it would seem almost inevitable that the teacher would be able to accomplish more for each pupil if classes were smaller or if each teacher were responsible for a smaller number of subjects. First glances, however, may be deceptive. After further thought, and after considering what we know about the learning process, we may wonder whether the matter is as simple as it seems on the surface. We remember, for instance, the tremendous influence of maturation, and we realize that in many classes students may be working fairly close to their maturational limits. This means, of course, that further improvement must wait on further maturation, no matter whether the teacher's efforts increase in intensity or whether they remain at the earlier level. We remember, too, the many opportunities for silent practice and for automatic or casual reinforcement even in a large class. Keeping in mind the lesson of spaced practice, we also remember how important it is for the student to effect a psychological "escape" from the teacher at frequent intervals. With a class made up of one teacher and one pupil this would be next to impossible. When there are many pupils, however, each one has more chance to acquire brief informal rest periods.

Whatever our expectations, the evidence clearly warns us against expecting marked improvements from sheer reduction in class size. This problem has received a vast amount of study in the past forty years. Stephens(25) in 1933 summarized some thirty-four studies, some of them very extensive. Since then many other investigations have been carried out. In all these studies, the overwhelming consensus is that reduction of class size does not lead to increased academic achievement(26). In one study previously mentioned, for instance, Rolfe(22) found a correlation of .10 between size of class and growth of pupils in grades seven and eight. This correlation suggests almost complete lack or relation between size of class and pupil growth. Any slight relation that may exist seems to favor the large class. Indeed, it seems fairly generally true, especially at the college level, that if there is any difference at all, that difference favors the large class. It is, of course, still possible that in some conditions the small class is more efficient. But as a general policy, it seems very unlikely that a general reduction of class size will lead to increased achievement. Indeed, the investigations suggest that children are not even handicapped by being placed in a room in which children of a different grade are being taught(27).

The Student's Time in School and in Study

In considering the matter of attendance and the length of the school year, we must once more draw on what we have already learned if we are to escape a severe jolt. It seems almost self-evident that attendance and achievement must go hand in hand. Surely if we can accomplish a certain amount in 180 days, we must be able to accomplish more in 200 days. Certainly if we were building a brick wall, we could only expect to accomplish something when we were actually at work. Certainly, too, we should accomplish more for each additional day we are at work.

But we are not building a brick wall, or anything like it. A better analogy for our task would be the cultivation of a hedge. And, here, there is no guarantee that the more we work, the more we accomplish. We must wait on the growth processes. More important, perhaps, we can *rely* on the growth processes. If we must neglect the cultivation of the hedge for a couple of weeks, we do not necessarily face the prospect of a two-week setback in our task.

In view of all this, we would be most unwise to expect a neat one-to-one correlation between attendance and achievement in all subjects. Some attendance, of course, is absolutely necessary. Without some attention the hedge cannot be expected to assume the shape we desire. Without some action on the part of the school, the student cannot be expected to develop acceptable modes of academic behavior. But in stating that some attendance is essential, we are not necessarily stating that the more attendance the better.

In general, the investigations point to a positive but moderate correlation. In the early investigations, as a matter of fact, there appeared to be a rather high correlation between attendance and achievement. It is obvious, however, that this simple relation is liable to two important pitfalls. In the first place, the common cause may be at work. Dull children and children from unfavorable homes may be less likely to attend school in the first place. They are also less likely to achieve when they do attend. Consequently, the dullness or poor home background may be the cause of both the poor attendance and the poor achievement. In the second place, we encounter the pitfall of reversed causality. Even when intelligence is held constant, the child who is doing poorly in school may be more anxious to avoid school than the child who is doing well. Hence the poor achievement may be the cause of the poor attendance.

Unfortunately, in a statistical investigation it is difficult to protect ourselves against the pitfall of reversed causality. As far as we can tell, this may still account for the apparent relation between attendance and achievement. Several investigations(28, 29), however, have ruled out the influence of intelligence as a common cause. These investigations report a low correlation in the neighborhood of .20 or .30. As we have indicated, it is impossible to say for sure whether this reveals the influence of attendance on achievement, or the influence of achievement on attendance, or both. At any rate, the relation is very low.

So far we have spoken of the sporadic variations in attendance from child to child. In these studies, all children have had an opportunity to attend but some have made more use of their opportunity than others have. But what happens when the school itself is kept open for more days during the year, or when an eleven-year school system is changed to a twelve-year school system? Here again, the increased schooling shows surprisingly little in the way of academic results. For the high schools, there may be a slight advantage for the systems which are open more than nine months per year(4, 30). Again we must remember, however, that it is the schools in the better communities which are open for the longer school year. For the elementary schools, even ignoring the boost from the better community, we find no advantage for the ten-month school over the nine-month school(31). With regard to twelve-year systems versus eleven-year systems, it is hard to detect any marked difference, in spite of the fact that the graduates of the twelve-year systems have the additional advantage of being a year older when they finish school. Certainly by the time the graduates of the two systems reach college, the advantage of the twelve-year system has been lost(32, 33, 34).

Acceleration. Children who receive a double promotion or skip a grade, or part of a grade, almost automatically reduce their school attendance. We find that such accelerated children in later school work suffer no academic handicap when compared to their intellectual peers who for some reason did not skip a grade(35, 36).

Time Spent with Radio or Television. As we point out in other sections, the radio and television have proved most attractive to children of school age, especially to children in the elementary school. When television first came into the homes, many children spent as much as twenty-five hours per week in watching the new medium. After a year or so of ownership there is a drop to about twenty hours, but this still represents about as much time as the child spends in school.

Is school work affected by the vast amount of time spent in this form of recreation? Apparently not. Children who spend much time with television(37) or radio(38, 39) do about as well in school as comparable children who spend little or no time with these forms of entertainment.

Time Spent in Extracurricular Activities. It has long been known that on the average students who participate extensively in extracurricular activities obtain better marks than students who do not participate(40). This has been clearly shown for such activities as dramatics and journalism, although it is less certainly true of athletics. Perhaps it would be fair to say that there is no clear difference between the academic performance of athletes and students who participate in no activities. Students who participate in debating, journalism, and scientific clubs, however, are clearly ahead of both nonparticipants and athletes.

Having in mind the pitfall of the common cause, we realize that these data cannot be taken at their face value. They do not necessarily mean that participation in debating or journalism, for example, will improve the grades of a given student. They may mean, instead, that clever students, who would get good grades anyhow, are attracted to certain activities and can afford to spend the time on them. The less able, less alert student, who will get poor grades anyhow, may shun activities partly through lack of inclination, partly through fear of doing even more poorly. In some schools, it is also possible that a certain academic standing is required before extensive participation is permitted.

When the common influence of intelligence is removed, by making sure that each participating student is matched in intelligence with a nonparticipating student, we still find the participating student ahead in college marks(41). Other studies have avoided the pitfall of the common cause by comparing the performance of the same student when he is participating to a less extent. When such a comparison is made we find little difference in grades(42). In general, it seems that the amount of extracurricular activity has little relation to the academic progress of the student.

Time Spent in Earning while Studying. This problem has received a good deal of attention. Different educators have taken different attitudes toward it. Some people have assumed that time spent in earning money must inevitably reduce the time spent on study. Other people have felt that the added motive of self-reliance will more than offset any reduction in hours of preparation.

In this problem, as in so many others, we are plagued by the role of the common cause. Earning and nonearning students necessarily differ in many other respects. The earning students obviously tend to come from less wealthy homes, and since socioeconomic status is related to intelligence we should expect a lower *average* intelligence on the part of the students who are partially self-supporting. Although there are many brilliant students who earn part or all of their expenses and many very dull students who are completely provided for, still it is true that on the average the earning students are somewhat less intelligent than their more wealthy classmates(43).

A second complication enters the picture in the case of those students who worked in a special federal program. Such students had to attain a certain academic status to keep their jobs. Hence, all these earning students were automatically working at an acceptable grade, whereas there was no necessity for other students to attain this standard. The presence of this minimum standard also probably acted as a motive which was lacking in the case of other students.

In view of these difficulties, a comprehensive review by Newman and Mooney(44) excluded studies of the special program. The authors also treated separately those studies in which the intelligence of the earning groups was comparable to that of the nonearning groups. They found that the investigations which failed to take intelligence into account disagreed widely. Five of such studies showed the earning students to be ahead in scholarship, four showed them to be behind, whereas seven found no difference between earning and nonearning students. The studies which did take care of intelligence show the same even balance between positive and negative results. Apparently self-help is not a significant factor as far as student grades are concerned.

Encouraging Students to Spend More Time on Study. If we cannot help the student by eliminating the things which compete for his time, can we do anything by merely persuading him to devote more of his time to study? Here again it is most important to take care of the matter of intelligence. Otherwise we may find that the clever student spends less time on study and also gets better grades. This would give us a spurious relation suggesting that the more time a student puts in study the poorer his grades.

Several investigations have been able to take care of the factor of intelligence. They have done this merely by finding one student who studies only a moderate amount of time and finding another student of comparable intelligence who spends much time on study. When students are thus matched in intelligence, there is almost zero relation between hours of study and the extent of the achievement. The student who spends only a little time on his homework gets almost exactly the same grades as his equally intelligent classmate who spends a great deal of time in studying(45).

Teaching the Student How to Use His Time in More Effective Study. From all this, it appears that we cannot greatly boost the achievement of students by finding more study time for them or by encouraging them to spend more time in study. Could we, however, help them by teaching them to make more efficient use of whatever time they do use for study?

In the past, such a hope seemed justified not only from common sense but also from the frequently reported fact that good students have more systematic habits of study than poor students. The good students are more likely to make outlines of material, to carry out a preliminary overview of the material, to follow this overview with a more detailed study, and to review this work at frequent intervals. Poor students are more likely to read the material over and over in aimless fashion, hoping that some of it will stick. They also have more difficulty in reading at a rapid rate.

Although such differences between good and poor students were not always found, they appeared often enough to suggest that if poor students were taught adequate techniques they, too, might become good students. Such reasoning, of course, fails to consider intelligence as a possible common cause. It is possible that sheer intelligence produces both good study habits and also more successful school work.

Bennett(46) reviewed some six studies which attempted to hold the influence of intelligence constant. Of the six studies, one brought about a negligible improvement, two were followed by a slight improvement, and three by a definite gain. Several studies not reported by Bennett show the same trend(47). It is more than likely that some how-to-study courses are effective in improving grades while others are not.

The Philosophy or Organization of the School

So far we have been speaking almost exclusively of academic development. The larger area of personal and social development is treated in a subsequent section. We may anticipate, however, and show how the philosophy or the organization of the school does have a very definite influence on the *personal* growth of the students. This, by the way, is a welcome change from our depressing account of the slight academic gains to be had from administrative steps in the area of academic growth. There is much evidence to suggest that schools classed as activity schools, or progressive or experimental schools, are able to develop more initiative, self-reliance, and cooperation in their students(48, 49, 50). To some extent, there is also less cheating in such schools. So far, however, we cannot be sure that the newer schools develop the freedom from tension or strain that many mental hygienists desire. The investigations suggest that there is as much worry among students of activity schools as among students of the more traditional schools(51).

The philosophy of the school is probably not intended to have a profound effect on the academic attainment of students. Indeed, one of the important postulates of many of the newer schools is the need to get away from the exclusive emphasis on academic concerns and to pay attention to more vital aspects of growth. At any rate, it is comforting to note that the increase in personal adjustment can be brought about with no loss in academic status. In the famous eight-year experiment(48, 52) undertaken by a group of progressive schools, there was practically no difference between the academic performance of the students from the progressive high schools and that of the students from the traditional high schools. In another comprehensive experiment, students in "activity" schools in New York City showed little if any differences in achievement from children in those New York schools which have not adopted the activity program. Of the thirty-three comparisons, the activity schools were significantly ahead in fourteen, the traditional schools were significantly ahead in seven, while in one comparison, the difference was a neat zero(53). When two small groups were matched in intelligence (but not in initial score), the traditional schools excelled in the Modern School Achievement tests with a difference bordering on significance, whereas the activity schools were ahead on the Comprehensive Achievement Tests by a clearly insignificant amount.

Reacting to Unpalatable Evidence

So far we have made out a rather poor case for the administrator. True enough, he is an important feature of our work. We could do nothing unless he provided us with the buildings, with salaries, with materials, and with rules of operation. He can do much to make us happy and to provide working conditions that are tolerable, attractive, or inspiring. But we seem forced to the conclusion—not so surprising on second thought—that the academic development of the student rests primarily in the hands of the teachers and only incidentally in the hands of the administrator.

To those who have put great reliance on the gains to be had from more liberal financial support for education, the record of uncertainties and negative results so far available must make dismal reading. It is possible that there are catches or jokers somewhere in the studies and that better studies may bring a brighter picture. Perhaps you can advance some optimistic alternative hypotheses. Perhaps these failures in the area of academic attainment may later be countered by a story of success when investigators finally turn more of their attention to the effect of administrative factors on personal adjustment and social effectiveness. These are reasonable hopes and are frequently advocated by many students of education.

Along with our reasonable hopes for a more rosy picture in the future, we must contemplate the possibility that this vast area of information has really been pointing in the true direction. We cannot reject this possibility merely because it is unpleasant. It is quite possible that, after all, the buildings, the money, or the teacher's working load do have little actual influence on educational attainment. Perhaps that attainment can not be greatly affected by legislative action or by more bountiful support. Perhaps, on the contrary, educational growth will come almost exclusively from the hour-by-hour, or minute-by-minute activities of the classroom teacher.

While waiting for further evidence, suppose that you feel driven to accept the view just expressed as the most plausible *tentative* hypothesis. Does that necessarily commit you to a gloomy and pessimistic view of education? By no means. Actually there is something very reassuring in the apparent immutability of the essential processes of educational growth. It is reassuring to learn afresh that children are sturdy and resilient organisms. It has always been reassuring to see children continue to grow and to thrive physically on a wide variety of fairly good diets. It is now reassuring to see that they also develop educationally in fairly regular fashion under widely varying programs. This sturdy, adaptive power of the student makes it safe for us to innovate and to try now this device and now that without fearing some grave and irremediable harm. It makes it safe for us, as we shall stress in a later chapter, to let ourselves go and to be ourselves in the classroom. True enough, this view of education prevents us from expecting the administrator to wave some golden wand and thereby to solve most of our problems for us. But by the same token, it gives us the confidence that so long as we are in the classroom with the powerful tools of learning at our disposal, then with good administration or with bad, and in spite of administrative negligence or excess, a vast amount of scholastic growth will continue to take place.

Summary

The efforts of the administrator can do much to improve the working conditions of the teacher and to make his labors more satisfying. These efforts, however, coming as they do on the top of powerful forces already in operation, cannot be expected to work magic or to make the chief difference between success and failure. Certainly many administrative improvements have had surprisingly little influence on academic attainment. Children working on "home study" courses do as well as children working in the schools. The size of the school is only slightly related to the attainment of the students. When intelligence and SES are held constant, there is little difference between the gains of students in small, cheap schools and the gains of comparable students in the larger, more costly schools.

Although teachers vary widely in their effectiveness, it has so far been impossible to secure one sure-fire external index of teaching effectiveness or to determine the characteristics necessary for teaching success. Experience helps a little, especially for the first few years, but may be partially offset later on by the tolls of age. Some knowledge of subject matter must be necessary, but experiments have failed to reveal any *consistent* advantage beyond the minimum found in all teachers. The same holds true for intelligence and for the amount of professional education. Perhaps in these matters, we can have both too little and too much. The quest for significant personal traits has also been disappointing as far as academic growth is concerned. There is some evidence, however, that the personality or attitude of the teacher will affect the personality of the student.

In spite of much agitation, a large number of experiments agree that class size has little if anything to do with academic gain. The presence of two grades in the same room, likewise, has little influence on academic achievement. The effect of these factors on personality or social adjustment is, as yet, undetermined.

Attendance has a slight, but only a slight, relation to achievement. Accelerated children learn about as much as their intellectual equals who elect not to skip a grade. Little or nothing is gained by protecting a student from the distractions of TV, radio, extracurricular activities, or from the necessity of earning moderate amounts of money. Courses designed to enable the student to use his time more effectively have reported a number of successes and a few failures.

The organization or the philosophy of the school is perhaps not expected to have a marked effect on academic development. The more progressive or experimental schools, however, are able to induce more growth in such personal traits as leadership, initiative, and resourcefulness with no loss in academic growth.

In this array of depressing statistical results, there is still to be found a silver lining. These results suggest a certain ruggedness and resilience in the process of academic growth. With good administration or with bad, and in spite of administrative neglect or interference, the teacher, by his own resources, can still produce substantial academic growth.

SPECIFIC REFERENCES

1. Stephens, J. M. Spontaneous schooling: a neglected feature in theories of education. *Sch. & Soc.,* 1951, *73,* 337–341.
2. Childs, G. B. A comparison of supervised correspondence study pupils and classroom pupils in achievement in school subjects. *J. educ. Res.,* 1954, *47,* 537–543.
3. Sprol, S. J. The influence of school size on academic achievement. Unpublished dissertation, Johns Hopkins University, 1940.
4. Smith, H. L., and Eaton, M. T. Analysis of the proficiency in silent reading of 11,424 sophomore pupils in 243 high schools in Indiana. *Bull. Sch. Educ. Ind. Univ.,* 1946, *22,* No. 1.
5. Boles, R. C. Some relationships between size of school and academic achievement of high school seniors in Florida. Abstracts of Doctoral Studies in Education. College of Education, University of Florida, 1953.
6. Davenport, K. S., and Remmers, H. H. Educational achievement as compared with money spent on schools. *Sch. & Soc.,* 1945, *61,* 333–335.
7. Orr, Harriet K. A comparison of the records made in college by students from fully accredited high schools with those students having equivalent ability from second and third class high schools. *J. educ. Res.,* 1949, *42,* 353–364.
8. Orr, Harriet K. Measuring the output of high schools. *J. educ. Res.,* 1952, *46,* 305–312.
9. Kephart, N. C., and Floyd, W. Classroom environment and pupil welfare. *J. educ. Psychol.,* 1954, *45,* 52–59.
10. McCall, W. A. Measurement of teacher merit. Raleigh, N. C., State Department of Public Instruction, 1952.
11. Domas, S. J., and Tiedeman, D. V. Teacher competence: an annotated bibliography. *J. exp. Educ.,* 1950, *19,* 101–218.
12. Fulkerson, G. Resumé of current teacher personnel research. *J. educ. Res.,* 1954, *47,* 669–681.
13. Watters, W. A. Annotated bibliography of publications related to teacher evaluation. *J. exp. Educ.,* 1954, *22,* 351–367.
14. Barr, A. S., Eustice, D. E., and Noe, E. J. The measurement and prediction of teaching efficiency. *Rev. educ. Res.,* 1955, *25,* 261–269.

15. Rostker, L. E. The measurement of teaching ability: Study Number One. *J. exp. Educ.*, 1945, *14*, 6–51.

16. Ryans, D. G. The investigation of teacher characteristics. *Educ. Record*, 1953, *34*, 371–396.

17. Bendig, A. W. An inverted factor analysis study of student-rated introductory psychology instructors. *J. exp. Educ.*, 1953, *21*, 333–336.

18. Knapp, R. H., and Gooderich, H. B. Origins of American scientists. University of Chicago Press, 1952.

19. Ojemann, R. H., and Wilkinson, F. R. The effect on pupil growth of an increase in teacher's understanding of pupil behavior. *J. exp. Educ.*, 1939, *8*, 143–147.

20. Desing, Minerva F. The relation of pupil achievement gain to certain personal and environmental elements. University of Pennsylvania, 1940.

21. Fink, M. Ethnocentrism as it relates to teaching success. *Calif. J. educ. Res.*, 1953, *4*, 111–114.

22. Rolfe, J. F. The measurement of teaching ability: Study Number Two. *J. exp. Educ.*, 1945, *14*, 52–74.

23. Stephens, J. M., and Lichtenstein, A. Factors associated with success in teaching grade five arithmetic. *J. educ. Res.*, 1947, *40*, 683–694.

24. Walker, Helen M., ed. *The measurement of teaching efficiency*. Macmillan, 1935. Part III., pp. 143-237, Pupil achievement and the N S trait in teachers (Betts, G. L.).

25. Stephens, J. M. *The influence of the school on the individual*. Edwards Brothers, 1933.

26. Spitzer, H. F. Class size and pupil achievement in elementary schools. *Elem. Sch. J.*, 1954, *55*, 82–86.

27. Adams, J. J. Achievement and social adjustment of pupils in combination classes enrolling pupils of more than one grade level. *J. educ. Res.*, 1953, *47*, 151–155.

28. Finch, F. H., and Nemzek, C. L. Attendance and achievement in secondary school. *J. educ. Res.*, 1940, *34*, 119–126.

29. Nemzek, C. L. The value of amount of tardiness and absence for direct and differential prediction of academic success. *J. exp. Educ.*, 1938, *7*, 4–10.

30. Remmers, H. H. The achievement of our high schools—Results of the state high school testing program, 1930–1931. *Purdue Univ. Stud. higher Educ.*, 1931, No. 18.

31. Smith, H. L., and Eaton, M. T. Analysis of the proficiency in silent reading of 15,206 sixth grade pupils in 648 schools in Indiana. *Bull. Sch. Educ., Ind. Univ.*, 1945, *21*, No. 6.

32. Judd, C. H., and others. Report of the commission on length of elementary education. *Supp. Educ. Monogr.*, 1927, No. 34.
33. Edwards, A. S. Comparison of university students having eleven with students having twelve years of preparation. *Educ. Adm. Superv.*, 1939, *25*, 229–232.
34. England, O. C. Comparative university achievement of students having 11-year and 12-year elementary-secondary school preparation. *Stanford Univ. Bull.*, 1948, Eighth Series, No. 19, Abstracts of Dissertations, *23*, 246–253.
35. Herr, W. A. Junior high school accelerants and their peers in senior high school. *Sch. Rev.*, 1937, *45*, 186–195 and 289–299.
36. Engle, T. L. A study of the effects of school acceleration upon the personality and social adjustments of high-school and university students. *J. educ. Psychol.*, 1938, *29*, 523–539.
37. Clarke, W. J. *Of children and television.* Xavier University, 1951 (pamphlet).
38. Ricciuti, E. A. Children and radio: a study of listeners and non-listeners to various types of radio programs in terms of selected ability, attitude and behavior measures. *Genet. Psychol. Monogr.*, 1951, *44*, 69–143.
39. Heisler, Florence. A comparison between those elementary school children who attend moving pictures, read comic books and listen to serial radio programs to an excess with those who indulge in these activities seldom or not at all. *J. educ. Res.*, 1948, *42*, 182–190.
40. Strang, Ruth M. *Group activities in college and secondary school.* Harper, 1941, Chap. 9.
41. Dunkelberger, G. F. Do extracurricular activities make for poor scholarships? *J. educ. Sociol.*, 1935, *9*, 215–218.
42. Remmers, H. H., ed. Studies in extracurricular activities. *Purdue Univ. Stud. higher Educ.*, 1940, No. 39, pp. 16–30, The effect of participation in extracurricular dramatics upon scholastic achievement (Dietrich, J. E.).
43. Reeder, C. W., and Newman, S. C. The relation of employment to scholarship. *Educ. Res. Bull.*, 1939, *18*, 203–214.
44. Newman, S. C., and Mooney, R. L. Effects of student self-help. *J. higher Educ.*, 1940, *11*, 435–442.
45. Strang, Ruth M. *Behavior and background of students in college and secondary school.* Harper, 1937 (See especially page 488.).
46. Bennett, Margaret E. Techniques of guidance: group guidance. *Rev. educ., Res.*, 1939, *9*, 217 220.
47. Fahey, G. L., and Waller, C. H. An experimental investigation of the

effectiveness of certain diagnostic and guidance procedures when applied in cases of low school achievement. *J. educ. Res.*, 1941, *34*, 335–345.

48. Aikin, W. M. *The story of the eight year study.* Harper, 1942.
49. Gardner, D. E. M. *Testing results in the infant school.* London: Methuen, 1942.
50. Jersild, A. T., and others. A further comparison of pupils in "activity" and "nonactivity" schools. *J. exp. Educ.*, 1941, *9*, 303–309.
51. Jersild, A. T., Goldman, B., and Loftus, J. J. A comparative study of the worries of children in two school situations. *J. exp. Educ.*, 1941, *9*, 323–326.
52. Baker, G. D. ed. *New methods vs. old in American education.* Teachers College, Columbia University, 1941.
53. Sells, S. B., Loftus, J. J., and Herbert L. Evaluative studies of the activity program in the New York City public schools: A preliminary report. *J. exp. Educ.*, 1941, *9*, 310–322.

Exercises and Questions for Discussion

1. Summarize your convictions on the contribution of administrative forces. Are your convictions in any way at odds with the evidence? If so, how do you propose to resolve the conflict?

2. Suggest two or three hypotheses to account for the apparent trend of the investigations of administrative forces. If possible, suggest means of testing these hypotheses.

3. Outline a talk on "The Little Red Schoolhouse: Its Advantages and Limitations."

PART four

Personal and Social Growth

The areas of physical and mental growth considered in Parts Two and Three are exceedingly important for the student and for the group to which he belongs. They are areas, moreover, in which the school has a unique responsibility, since no other agency stands ready to take over if the school should falter in these fields.

Important as physical and mental development may be, however, they are still only one aspect of the complete person. Compared to the personal and social development of the student, the more academic aspects of mental development may seem of minor importance. Certainly, to the student and to his associates, this development of personality and of competence in dealing with other people is a most important goal.

Fortunately in this most important enterprise of furthering social and personal development, the school and the teacher have many powerful and interested allies. The home and the church and many youth organizations take a keen and continuous interest in this phase of the student's life. The interest of these allies, moreover, does not stop with blessing and good wishes, as it often does in the case of academic or scholastic development. On the contrary, this interest expresses itself, day in and day out, both by way of spontaneous stimulation and advice and by way of elaborate programs deliberately designed for the inculcation of personal and social virtues.

Just as the teacher may expect powerful aids from some non-scholastic sources, so he must be prepared for disturbing interferences from other agencies that operate from outside the school. When it comes to the development of worthy character and wholesome social attitudes, the teacher may readily find himself in serious conflict with many haphazard or organized forces, ranging from those that are merely tawdry and cheap to those that are almost vicious in intent.

16

Personal and Social Adjustment: Basic Needs and Processes

IN STUDYING THE GROWTH of students in the more academic subjects, we take brief notice of the basic drives which lead people to action. We also take some account of the conflict and interaction of those drives. These matters, which have considerable importance for the understanding of physical, intellectual, and academic growth, will be seen to have overwhelming importance for the study of personal and social growth. For in this new area, our chief task is not to apply motives for the sake of inducing the student to act this way or that. Our task now, on the contrary, is to understand the student (and to help him) as he deals with one or another of the powerful motives that are already in action. These motives or drives are no longer handy devices by which we can expedite the task of the school. Instead, these motives and the interrelation between them actually constitute our task.

Needs and Drives

In the study of personal and social relations, it is helpful to describe behavior in terms of the result that is produced or accomplished. The behavior that we shall be interested in will seldom consist of a single isolated movement, such as underlining the *true* or the *false* on an examination, or giving the correct sum to $8 + 7$. Instead, this behavior will consist of a complex series of movements, often extending over a considerable period of time. This series of movements, moreover, cannot ordinarily be described in terms of the movements themselves. The series can only be described in terms of the results accomplished.

Any act such as eating dinner, writing an essay, or making a grand slam is exceedingly hard to describe in terms of muscle behavior. It is much easier to describe in terms of the environmental changes which those movements bring about, in the fact that the food is transferred from plate to stomach, that a certain number of words are written, or that all the cards are collected in neat piles in front of one of the players.

This result-producing aspect of behavior has received great emphasis in discussions of personality and in descriptions of general behavior. In this wider field, even more than in the schoolroom, it has become important to realize that, very often, human action or behavior can be described in terms of the end product of the behavior.

In the descriptions of general behavior, this varied activity leading to a fairly definite goal is often called *drive*. The word drive implies some force which tends to keep the organism responding until a certain end result is attained. Just as a strong flood moves its flotsam by an erratic and unpredictable swirling path to a fairly predictable destination, so the hypothetical drive is considered to impel a complex and unpredictable series of acts toward a predictable end point. Any one piece of material caught in the flood may at times hesitate, deviate, or even reverse its direction. But by and large, most of those bits of debris will reach the lake or certainly will land some distance downstream. Similarly, in animal life, the rat may approach the food in a series of movements which from moment to moment may be quite unpredictable. He may turn and explore a new corner, or stop and clean his whiskers. Sooner or later, however, most rats in this situation will reach the food. The behavior of any other animal is almost equally unpredictable if we regard it from one minute to the next. It is seldom that we can predict what any individual will do in the next instant. But, typically, we can predict what he will accomplish in the near future. And to describe this erratic and unpredictable progress by which a predictable goal is reached, we have invented the concept of *drive*.

Just as it is convenient to assume that some force or drive is giving direction and continuity to a series of individual acts, so it is also convenient to assume that the drive is operating in the service of some *need*. A need is the thing which sets a drive in motion. A need, of course, always calls for some object or condition. A hunger need, for instance, calls for food. The food or other object is to be attained ordinarily only by a series of movements. And the drive is the force which keeps the organism doing one thing after another until the goal is attained. Need is a condition which calls for action toward a certain goal. Drive is the force which keeps the action continuously directed toward that goal.

Typical Needs and Their Associated Drives

Physiological Needs

Physiological needs are closely associated with definite bodily conditions. The need for oxygen(1), for instance, is governed by the condition of the blood or, more precisely, of the hemoglobin in the blood. The associated drive will call for breathing. This behavior, of course, is relatively simple but by no means uniform. Under some conditions, however, the behavior may become very complex, as when the smothering organism thrashes around and claws at the air in furious fashion.

A complete list of physiological needs would be very long indeed. There is a need to escape a pain-producing situation. With this is associated a very powerful drive which commands a wide variety of actions and directs them with considerable persistence. Other harmful conditions, such as undue heat or cold and various itches, also constitute needs and call into play a variety of drives. Hunger, of course, is such a physiological need, although it has many nonphysiological components. Thirst is in much the same category. The physiological condition of the sex organs may set up needs, colored again by conditions not completely physiological. Various visceral tensions or irritations may set up eliminatory needs with drives to urination or defecation. Another group of needs is concerned with readiness for activity. At times, there is great need for rest. At other times, there may be an urgent need for activity, and at these times, the resting state tends to be avoided.

Social Needs

Not all needs can be neatly tied in with some known physiological condition. There are many needs which refer to the relations between people. Among these, we can list the need to be with people, the need for love, the need for the good opinion of others, the need to dominate, the need to manipulate or influence people, the need to help those in trouble, the need for revenge(2).

These social needs are of vast importance to anyone who seeks to deal with people. It is chiefly by invoking social needs that we exert our control or influence over people. (Few of the motives discussed in Chapter

10, for instance, were of a physiological nature. Even the punishment and reward discussed in that section were social punishment and social reward.) True enough, there are times when individuals or governments, in attempting to achieve their program, feel forced to rely on physiological needs such as hunger, thirst, or the need to avoid pain. It is also true that even in less grim circumstances we may trade on the need for activity, the need for rest, or the need for some specially desired food. But these uses are the exception, and ordinarily indicate that an appeal to other needs has failed or would be expected to fail. In our dealings with people, in selling them soap or in encouraging them to study, we entice them with the promise of social popularity and prestige, or frighten them with the fear of disdain or ostracism. We seldom promise them more abundant food or threaten them with physical pain.

The Need to Manipulate or Explore

In monkeys, apes, and people there are strong needs to move things around, especially if such manipulation will bring about interesting results. This need can be used as a motive to induce people, or monkeys, to solve puzzles or to work out problems and it has been discussed as one of the methods of motivating classroom work. Here we are interested in this need as an important part of our personality. For most people it is a fairly powerful need, and the drive that serves it must be taken into account. We do not know, of course, whether the tendency to manipulate is always a fundamental drive, or whether it is derived from some other more basic process. But in students and in ourselves we can expect to see it in evidence. As children, we bang on tables, rumple or tear paper, or push over piles of blocks. Later we may drag a stick along a paling fence, skip stones on water, make marks on inviting stretches of white wall, or dash milk bottles on the pavement. When still older and more inhibited, our manipulations tend to become either more subdued and restricted or more elaborate. We may beat a tattoo on the table with our fingers or jingle coins or play with an ear or a mustache or demolish daisies with a swish of a stick or "doodle" on notebooks or make sketches on the walls of telephone booths. For more elaborate manipulation, we knock balls around with various instruments, fire guns which smash clay pigeons, or bring animals crashing to the earth.

Ego Needs

Most of us have a fairly clear idea of the kind of person we really are or might be when circumstances are favorable. This picture of our real self is seldom a composite picture of the self that we actually see from moment to moment. It is rather an ideal or purified self that is seldom perfectly shown but is really there underlying the more awkward and human self that we so often present to the world.

There is a strong drive to preserve our idea of this ideal self. We will strenuously resist any consideration which suggests that we must scale this ideal down a few notches or replace it with a less worthy concept of ourselves. This same drive, indeed, may work on us to enhance our idea of ourselves and to work out a believable model or ideal that is better than the one we use now(3).

Need for Achievement

Closely related to this ego drive, among older students at least, is the need for achievement. According to McClelland and his colleagues(4), this is a powerful drive that not only expresses itself in the overt statements of students but also reveals itself in fantasies and in the way they interpret the things around them. Among older students in our culture there is a strong need to have behind one a worthy accomplishment. By experimental manipulation this need can be gratified or starved and, as a consequence, it will appear in reduced or increased intensity. For this need to be satisfied, the achievement must be genuine and call for real effort. A task that is too easy or that carries no risk of failure will not do. Real satisfaction calls for the mastery of a task that is close enough to the limit of our ability to involve a clear risk of failure.

The Need for Security

Along with these needs clustering around fear or danger are those associated with security. The need for security, of course, is closely related to the need to avoid danger or to escape from danger. But even though this need is undoubtedly derived from more primitive needs, still it may readily function when no specific physiological or social factors are invoked. This need for security is not restricted to danger that is actually present. It involves not only the drive to get away from the painful or dangerous object but, to avoid the *fear* of the object, the idea of danger. Insecurity, in fact, is felt typically, not when we confront the menace face to face, but when we face the *idea* of the menace. Thus the drive to avoid the vague but sometimes terrifying feeling of insecurity is not precisely the same as the more primitive physiological drive to avoid pain, nor the more definite drive to escape danger.

The need for security has impressive significance for us in our attempt to direct students into a wholesome personal and emotional development. Under present-day conditions, the urge toward security may be more important than the drive to avoid danger or pain. The fear of poverty may induce more tortuous and destructive behavior than does actual poverty itself. Similarly, the fear of social disapproval or scorn may lead to extremes of behavior that would rarely be elicited by any scorn actually encountered. A great many of the deviations from wholesome personal development, in fact, stem from this powerful need to avoid the insecurity to which we are all liable.

Catalogues of Needs Are Merely Illustrative

It is important to remember that any list of needs given at this time must be very incomplete. Unlike the chemist, we have as yet no periodic table of basic needs, and it will probably be some years before we even begin to get one. Before we can begin to achieve such a table it will be necessary to go over each proposed list with several questions in mind. We must ask: (a) Is the list complete? Or is there some behavior which cannot be described in terms of any of the needs on our list? (b) Are all the items necessary? Could we eliminate some of the needs and still not greatly impair our description of behavior? (c) Are all the items on our list independent? Or is there a great deal of overlapping? Perhaps, for instance, two needs listed separately are made up largely of the same element. (d) To what extent is each of these needs a direct result of inheritance and to what extent is each an outcome of experience?

So far the questions just raised are largely unanswered. Until we are much closer to an answer than we are at present, it will be wise to consider any list of needs as merely illustrative. This list, in other words, shows what we mean by needs. It also shows the general type of needs which we think will be used to describe behavior. But we cannot say these are *the* needs by which human activity is to be understood in all situations.

Possible Relation between Needs

In spite of the fact that our list of needs is by no means complete or final, it is still possible to consider some broad groupings into which those needs fall and the possible relations between the groups. Classifying needs as physiological, social, and "other" needs is one such system of classification. This classification, however, is merely at the descriptive level and gives us little insight into basic differences between needs. Other systems try to go beyond mere description. Some writers have divided needs into those which call for approach (hunger, thirst, sex) and those which call for avoidance (pain, cold, danger). Others (notably the early Freudians) put into one group all the needs which keep the organism alive (the ego needs) and put into another group all the needs which serve to perpetuate the race or species (the libido needs). Thus the needs concerning hunger, danger, and so forth, would be in the ego group, while sex, protection of young, and the like would belong to the libido group.

In addition to this attempt to classify needs into a few consistent groups, there has also been some effort to arrange the groups of needs into some sort of hierarchy or priority list. Maslow(5, 6), for instance, holds that there are five levels of needs. Those having an A-1 priority are the physiological needs. Next on the list are the needs involved in avoiding danger or securing safety. Then there is the need to secure love from other people. One step beyond this is the need for esteem. For Maslow, esteem includes both the good opinion of other people and self-approval. Finally there is the need for manipulation, or mastery or achievement or self-expression. By thus arranging needs in a hierarchy, Maslow seeks to emphasize the fact that a second-order need will be at a disadvantage in competing with a first-order need. A fairly strong urge toward artistic creation, for instance, might be ruled out by a weaker but more primitive need to avoid the contempt of others. Or, at the other end of the scale, when one is torn between the need for safety and the need for love, the former need may win out. We know, of course, that this does not always happen. The need for love may win out on occasion. This is so unexpected, so out of the ordinary, however, that it justifies a story or drama.

Types of Frustration

It is the fate of drives to meet resistance in their efforts to satisfy a need. It is only in the Edens and the fabled Golden Ages that a need can be met simply by reaching out for the food, or by commanding a jinni to provide us with shelter. In our world, a drive can be opposed by some simple physical barrier such as the automobile that will not start or the knot that refuses to come untied. A drive can also be opposed by some other drive as when our need to eat contends with our need to finish the story we are reading or the task upon which we are engaged. An especially serious form of frustration is likely to arise when one of our needs, such as the need to strike out or our need to run, comes into conflict with our need to think well of ourselves.

Most frustration does involve this conflict between needs. The frustration imposed by a simple physical barrier is likely to bring about other drives or needs and these in turn will often come into conflict with other needs. The frustration aroused even by the knot that will not untie may well evoke anger and an urge to attack the inanimate source of our frustration. Since this urge toward aggression may well conflict with our sense of self-esteem, we may readily find ourselves with a new and more serious frustration between the need to lash out and the need to consider ourselves as a reasonable person.

When another person is the source of our frustration, the urge toward aggression is even more likely to be aroused(7) A young child may readily resort to kicking or biting when he is thwarted by some other person. Older children and adults also feel such aggression, especially if they believe that the person who stands in their way is acting in some arbitrary fashion. If the behavior of the obstructing person appears to us as being justified we are less likely to feel strong aggression.

Conflicts Not Involving the Need for Esteem

Occasionally we encounter a fairly simple type of conflict in which the need for esteem plays little part. This occurs, for instance, when we are torn between two shows, two choices on the bill of fare, two companions, or two vacations, and when both shows are on the same intellectual plane, or when both companions are equally worthy. At this time we shall forget the type of conflict in which one show is essentially low-brow and the other elevating, or where we are torn between the corned beef and cabbage which we really like and the frogs' legs which we think we are expected to like. For the time being, we are merely confronted with the choice between roast beef and roast pork, between Victor Herbert and Johann Strauss, or between a vacation at the seashore and a stay in the mountains.

In the simple type of conflict, there are very few serious pitfalls to plague us. It is not from conflict such as this that serious personal trouble is likely to develop. Such conflicts tend to settle themselves. Typically, moreover, they are on the surface and the problems are fairly visible both to the individual and his advisors. Above all, effective methods of handling conflict of this sort can be acquired from overt instruction.

What are some of the dangers or difficulties, mild though they be, which may follow from the more simple type of conflict? The chief danger is that of an inefficient solution. We may decide too hurriedly and with insufficient consideration. In so doing we may select the alternative which, after further consideration, we would have rejected. More serious, perhaps, we may fail to see a possible compromise by which we could achieve both goals and so remove the conflict. Although there can be no assurance that such acceptable compromises always exist, the possibility should usually be considered, especially if both conflicting needs are important. More to be feared, perhaps, than the precipitous decision is vacillation or sheer absence of decision. Like the donkey in the fable, we may starve to death because of the neatly balanced pull of the two adjacent haystacks. In our indecision between the two shows, we may miss both. We may hold up our choice of beef or pork until both have been taken off the menu. Meanwhile, in addition to failing to satisfy either need, we have suffered the sheer discomfort of useless indecision.

In addition to the type of vacillation or indecision which avoids an overt choice, there is the type which fails to make a clean-cut and final decision. We refuse, so to speak, to "write off" the discarded alternative. We make our choice but still try to feel as if the rejected choice were still available. Maud Muller may choose the rustic suitor and may back up her decision by marriage and by loyal wifehood. Emotionally, however, she may still cling to the "might-have-been" but now wholly unavailable rival. At every turn we find ourselves in this unrealistic situation of eating our cake and still dreaming that we have it. We buy the new car and still half-believe that we are going to take the trip abroad. We give up college for the well-paid job and still imagine ourselves pushing on to a scientific career.

The undesirable features just discussed, although not catastrophic in their results, should be cut down wherever possible. There are a few rules which, if passed along to students, may help them overcome some of the worst features of this conflict.

1. Make a genuine effort to find out if the conflict as you see it is really the basic conflict. Try to be honest with yourself and ask if there is some furtive fear or longing involved which has not yet been brought out into the open. Even with all the effort and honesty in the world, you may still be fooled in this matter. But there may be times when you suspect that the conflict is between something you secretly want but are ashamed to admit and something that you feel you ought to want but which has little appeal to you. In that case the rules which follow do not apply. The rules stated here belong only if you believe that the conflict is between two external drives both of which are fairly easily discerned.

2. Once you decide that the conflict is what it appears to be on the surface, give it a reasonable amount of thought. Do not just sit around feeling worried or uncomfortable. Work it out fairly systematically. You may find it wise to write down the advantages and disadvantages of each alternative. At any rate try to be thorough. There is a chance that by considering the alternatives from every angle you may be able to see possible solutions that you did not see at first. At the very worst, you will feel better in the future if you can clear yourself of a charge of a hasty decision.

3. Very often you may get help from discussing the problem with some understanding person. Do not expect that person to solve your problem for you. He may be able, however, to suggest angles which have escaped you. Anyway, the very act of describing your problem to someone else should help you enormously by bringing the true nature of the conflict into clearer focus in your own mind.

4. Set a deadline for the decision. Allow enough time for reasonable consideration, but set a point beyond which you will not delay.

5. Once having made the decision, burn your bridges as far as fantasy is concerned. Force yourself to realize that the choice is made and forbid yourself the luxury of the lingering fantasy which permits you to dream that you have not quite given up the discarded alternative.

So much for the problem of surface frustration or surface conflict between two external recognizable drives. So long as such frustrations or conflicts remain on the surface, they are unlikely to cause serious damage. At most, they are likely to lead to an inefficient solution or to a prolonged stalemate. The important thing to remember, however, is that such frustrations or conflicts cannot be depended on to remain on the surface. Even at the outset, thwarting or conflict which is apparently external and on the surface may really have strong hidden components. And certainly genuine, clear-cut surface frustration or conflict, when prolonged for a period of time, is likely to generate deeper components even if such deeper components were not present at the outset.

Conflict Which Involves the Need for Esteem

The conflicts which we have just been considering are fairly forthright and ordinarily call for a fairly clean-cut decision. One need can lose, the other can lose, or both can lose. But it is very seldom that both can win. We may marry Joan or Ada or neither. Ordinarily we do not marry both. We can choose medicine, engineering, or neither, but seldom both. This simple picture becomes markedly changed, however, whenever our need for esteem, especially for self-esteem, enters the conflict. The need for esteem has devious and roundabout methods by which it may attempt to win in the face of a formidable adversary. When our need for an extra afternoon of golfing threatens to deprive us of the esteem we need from our colleagues, we may be tempted to salvage the latter by deceitfully claiming a business appointment or a headache. If the same need for the golf game should menace our good opinion of ourselves, we can plead the necessity of keeping fit, or the increase in productivity that follows recreation.

It must be noted at once that the two kinds of stratagems are seldom equally effective. It is extremely difficult to deceive our colleagues into crediting us with motives more worthy than we possess. They frequently see through us. Our attempts to deceive ourselves, however, ordinarily meet with better success. The limp by which we try to excuse our failure to go to work may bring only formal condolences from those to whom it is exhibited. As far as we ourselves are concerned, however, that limp may appear as very convincing evidence that we really would be foolish to go to work. The stratagem, in other words, may fail to secure the esteem of others but may enable us to retain our own approval. These examples are far from rare. Attempts at a greater or less degree of self-deception are perhaps the rule. At random moments during any day, if we were to stop and analyze the nature of our conflicts, we would often find ourselves trying to extract more self-esteem from the solution to the conflict than the objective circumstances warranted. And very often an outside observer would find us succeeding in this attempt.

The need for esteem, which we are so often tempted to attain by indirect means, is a most powerful urge. True, it comes rather late in the Maslow hierarchy. True, again, we might expect it to come off second best if it conflicted with any *serious* need for food, safety, or other more primary needs. But it happens that in our present society those more primary needs seldom attain serious proportions. We seldom deal with children who are in the throes of powerful, primitive needs. And when those earlier needs are relatively quiescent, the later needs have the stage more or less to themselves. The power of these secondary needs is accentuated, perhaps, by the fact that they are socially acceptable and may operate in the open. One hesitates to announce his sexual needs too openly. His need for the esteem of other people, however, is under no such ban. A decent respect for the opinion of others is a highly commendable trait. The need for self-esteem or self-respect is in even better standing. At any rate, whether or not their strength derives partly from their freedom from secrecy, there can be no denying that in the typical person in our civilization these needs for the good opinion of others and for the esteem of oneself are very powerful forces and are the determining factors in much human behavior.

Roundabout Enhancement of Self-esteem

In the need for esteem, to recapitulate, we have an urge which is very powerful, which is not always easy to attain by direct means but which, because of the ease of self-deception, can often be attained by indirect means. The significance of this combination is obvious. From such a combination we would expect a great deal of indirect activity toward the surreptitious satisfaction of these needs. And that, of course, is precisely what we get. A great deal of the literature in mental hygiene, in fact, is concerned with an elaboration of the various devices or mechanisms by which we can secure more self-esteem than the objective circumstances would provide.

Before listing these mechanisms, we should point out that this discussion is oversimplified. Many students would not concede that all the mechanisms about to be considered consist simply of clandestine paths to the fulfillment of the powerful need for self-esteem. Some people(8, p. 163) hold, for instance, that these mechanisms cannot be understood without the concept of *anxiety,* and that anxiety in turn must be understood in the light of fear or punishment. In neglecting these more involved or complicated mechanisms, however, we shall not do great violence to the main picture.

Sublimation. In sublimation we have a minimum of distortion of a primitive drive. The drive which threatens our sense of self-esteem may be more or less recognized. The behavior which acts as a substitute for the original drive, moreover, is somewhat similar to the original rejected behavior.

Consider the case of a man with a strong sense of honor who finds himself in love with the wife of a friend. He does not try to keep from himself the real nature of his feelings but regards those feelings as impossible of complete expression. In this situation he may find some partial expression of his desires by friendly or helpful acts toward the family as a whole. Many romantic poems or songs achieve a similar partial expression for urges which are clearly acknowledged but which cannot be granted complete expression. Aggressive urges that are acknowledged but impossible of execution may also be sublimated by letters that are not sent, or by imagined revenge feelingly described to a friend.

Repression. In sublimation the person may be more or less aware of the drive toward unacceptable behavior. Repression, on the other hand, refers to the refusal to admit the existence of the troublesome drive. The drive which threatens our sense of self-respect may be driven from consciousness. This hurried rejection of an idea is a phenomenon each of us may have experienced. In the discussion of the general Freudian theory, this mechanism of repression is explained in some detail. In that section we also show how repressed wishes, like the desire for the death of an aged relative, do not always remain quietly repressed but often take on fantastic disguises and reenter consciousness under the guise of an innocent or virtuous desire.

The wish for the death of parents or other adults is not uncommon. Most children, after unjust treatment, must have wished occasionally that the parent would die or would suffer some injury. With increasing maturity, this urge may threaten the sense of self-respect to the point of panic and may result in the denial and dismissal of the unflattering wish. There are many other drives which would throw us into wild unreasoning fear if we suspected them in ourselves. The wish for the death of a parent or friend, in fact, is probably very mild compared to some of the other wishes or drives which have terrified us. The many sexual perversions constitute drives of this type for many people. Most people, perhaps, would feel unspeakably guilty if they suspected that they had an urge toward homosexual behavior or to incestuous relations. Several convincing dramas have been woven around the shattering tragedy experienced by people when they come to suspect themselves of such reprehensible tendencies. The overwhelming sense of guilt expressed by some mental patients who speak of the unpardonable sin often arises from the suspicion of desires for forbidden sexual activities.

Wishes for harm to relatives or urges toward reprehensible sex acts by no means complete the list of ideas which may prove unbearable to our conscious minds. Any idea which implies incompetence or which suggests that we are insignificant may cause us intolerable distress and may be ejected from our awareness. Any idea or urge which does serious violence to our conception of ourselves can evoke this mechanism of repression.

It will be seen that from an immediate or superficial point of view, repression has considerable value to the individual. For the time being, this mechanism removes a source of pain and distress. By refusing to admit the existence of the forbidden drive, we eliminate the conscious conflict between that drive and the need for self-esteem. The need for self-esteem is left in control of the field.

In spite of its immediate palliative value, the mechanism of repression opens the way for all kinds of problems. The difficulty with repression comes from the unfortunate fact that a drive expelled from consciousness is not necessarily a drive extinguished or written off(9). As we point out at some length in the discussion of Freudian psychology, a powerful drive, even after it is expelled from consciousness, may find some indirect method of expression. It may express itself in some roundabout activity, an activity which the person himself will not regard as related to the forbidden urge. By this roundabout activity, we are able to give some distorted expression to the forbidden urge and yet shield our sense of self-respect from the injury which ordinarily would follow.

The expelled drive, in seeking some disguised or roundabout expression, may lead to all sorts of fantastic behavior. It may result in some relatively harmless tic or compulsion. It may result in boasting or in an overbearing manner. We may cut ourselves off from normal emotional life. We may develop a powerful suspicion of our associates or acquire an inconvenient ailment. All in all, repression is a dangerous mechanism. The behavior it produces may be quite harmful and may more than offset the questionable relief to be had from the repression itself. Some repression, of course, is bound to occur. Ideally, however, it should be discouraged as much as possible. Ideally, we should not try to solve the conflict between two drives by refusing to admit that one of these drives exists.

Compensation. In general, compensation refers to the tendency to make up for a deficiency in one trait by excelling in some other activity. A child with poor vision may work hard to listen to and remember slight auditory cues. A boy who lacks athletic ability may concentrate on succeeding as the manager of the team. A girl who has little success in attracting boys may be motivated to work even harder at her studies.

From the illustrations, it is apparent that compensation could include any drive toward success which arises from a sense of deficiency. At times this compensation may be quite conscious. The person may realize his handicap and may deliberately set out to make up for it. The direction of such compensation may be logical and sensible. The individual may aim at success in a field which actually yields real promise of satisfaction.

Unfortunately, compensation is not always, perhaps not typically, rational. Even when the person realizes the true nature of his handicap, he may not select his substitute activity wisely. He may try to excel in the very field of his deficiency, using sheer will power and unusual ap plication to overcome his handicap. This is seen when a physical weakling sets out to be an athlete. Although there are times when such a venture has met with success, it usually represents a terrific struggle which many people would find far too demanding. Most important here, perhaps, is the attitude with which the task is undertaken. It is far better for the handicapped to participate with moderate eagerness than to retire from any activity in which his handicap would embarrass him. It is bad, however, when he enters the competitions with tight-lipped frenzy, refusing to admit the handicap and prepared to lash out at anyone who dares to make any allowance for him.

Compensation always becomes dangerous when the student refuses to admit his handicap or his feeling of inferiority to himself. And compensation may be used for just this purpose. It may be used, that is to say, to keep oneself from realizing the true nature of one's worry. Plagued by glimpses of an unbearable suspicion of inferiority, the child may resort to boasting, braggadocio, bullying, or other forms of aggression to deceive, not others, but himself. This objective evidence of competence may keep him from facing his basic feeling of inferiority.

Solution by Fantasy. This is perhaps the most familiar device by which we maintain our self-esteem in the face of unflattering reality. In fantasy, the need for affection or for sex becomes satisfied. In fantasy, the vast need for recognition and approval reaches its measure of fulfillment. That fulfillment may be shown by the reception given a returning conquering hero, or it may be the more belated recognition evoked from contrite friends by the sight of our mangled remains.

Fantasy is inevitable. A certain amount of it is probably harmless or beneficial. Without it, the harsh edges of an unyielding reality might press too hard. Obviously, however, it can be overdone. It is too readily available. We may come to turn too easily to this effortless solution of problems and thus forgo the more substantial satisfaction to be had in the outside world. It is especially dangerous if we come to confuse the dream world with the world of reality.

Rationalization. By the use of rationalization we are able to find good and worthy reasons for doing things we are going to do anyway. By rationalization, we can justify the new car we are about to buy but cannot quite afford. We can work up good reasons for our decision although the reasons had little to do with the decision. The fact that the decision did not stem from the reason is probably apparent to everyone but ourselves. These pseudo-reasons, however, protect our sense of self-esteem. Because of these good reasons, we do not feel like an irresponsible person who squanders his funds and mortgages his future to satisfy the whim of the moment.

Rationalization, like fantasy, is inevitable to a certain extent. Unlike fantasy, however, it has little to recommend it. This mechanism undoubtedly must take some of the blame for much of the loose thinking and tortured logic which plagues the world. One of the great services of the school would be to reduce the prevalence of this means of retaining self-esteem.

Projection. When our sense of self-respect is assailed by some unacceptable drive, we may readily project that drive onto someone else. We may accuse that other person of the sin which tempts us(10). The reformer who sees evil in the simplest act of others may really be fighting a similar tendency in himself. Projection in its many forms guards our sense of self-respect in two ways. It may actually transfer the guilt to someone else. We may be completely convinced that all the hostility resides in our colleague. And thus we are completely relieved from the feeling of guilt. Or it may fail to achieve a complete transfer of guilt. We may be vaguely aware of our hostility, but because of our "belief" in the hostility of the other one, we may feel better about our own half-conscious aggression. It may also make us feel better about our half-conscious guilt.

Like rationalization, projection has little to recommend it as a method of resolving conflict. It provides an unsatisfactory solution and can itself cause considerable harm.

Identification. Through identification we are able to take unto ourselves some of the esteem which really comes to the hero of the story or to our favorite athlete or politician. In his successes, we take on additional stature. We feel a little of the same glow or exaltation that we would feel if we had achieved that success ourselves. The hero in the movies carries us with him in his exploits and permits us to share the adulation and the romantic reward. At a more personal level, we swell with pride at the success of an associate or at the praise bestowed on our organization. Like fantasy, a certain amount of this is harmless, but it could easily be overdone.

Solution through Ailments. Ailments are especially convenient solutions to conflict between the need for withdrawal and the need for self-esteem. This use of ailments is very prevalent. It is seen in little children who acquire all sorts of convenient disabilities when unpleasant duties are imminent. It is also seen in mothers who experience an aggravation of a mild heart weakness whenever they fail to persuade their children by ordinary reasoning. It is seen too in fathers who develop back pains when house cleaning threatens.

Ailments are not confined to simple and easily-seen-through devices. They sometimes assume major proportions and reduce the subject to a life of invalidism or to a very restricted range of activity. They may take the form of general weakness, headache, lack of energy, heart trouble, or weak back. They may come as paralysis of the hand, as writer's cramp, or as the inability to detect sensations in some part of the body.

In addition to giving us a good excuse to withdraw from frightening or unpleasant tasks, ailments may provide us with some much relished attention. The sick child secures mothering. The sick man, likewise. An unusual ailment may bring notoriety which may be moderately pleasing.

Personal Adjustment as Actually Observed

The items that we have considered so far may be regarded as the basic elements that go into personal adjustment. It is from needs, conflicts, frustrations, and mechanisms for dealing with the same that personal adjustment is made up. But a knowledge of these elements, however helpful, is not enough. We must also look at the resulting personal adjustment as it is actually observed, charted, and measured.

Common-sense Definitions of Personality

To enable each of us to know what the other fellow means by the terms *personality* or *personal adjustment* or *social adjustment,* it is necessary to have some fairly definite description by which we can distinguish between the area of personality on the one hand and, say, the area of intellectual development on the other hand.

Like the common-sense definitions of intelligence, the common-sense definitions of personality have had rather heavy going. So many different definitions have been offered that the whole enterprise has almost bogged down by its own weight. Allport(11), for instance, lists some fifty definitions of personality that have been used at one time or another. Many of these definitions, of course, are concerned with the legal or the theological aspects of personality and not with the psychological aspect. Those definitions of personality which are psychological in nature tend to stress one or more of three different features, namely: (a) the over-all or inclusive nature of personality; (b) the social-stimulus aspect of personality; (c) the role of personality in making us unique or individual persons.

Personality as the Whole Person. For some psychologists, personality is the whole of life. They tend to define personality as the entire organization of the individual at each stage of his life. Such a description, of course, is valuable in warning us about the complexity of personality. It is not very helpful, however, in determining or setting definite boundaries for the subject under discussion. On the contrary, it tells us that there are no boundaries to our subject. And for working purposes, such a definition is not very satisfactory, since, temporarily at least, we must parcel out the whole area of psychology into manageable portions or areas.

Personality as Integration or Organization. Other psychologists who stress the inclusiveness of personality see that inclusiveness in the organized nature of personality. For such psychologists, personality could never be the mere sum total of all the traits that are to be found in an individual. The individual's personality would lie not so much in the list of such traits as in the integration or organization of the traits. According to this view, the essential aspect of personality is the way in which the various traits are related to each other. We gain insight into an individual's personality, not from a consideration of his status in each of several traits, but from a consideration of his relative status in different traits. Taken by themselves, for instance, needs or desires do not give us a valuable picture. Similarly, abilities when taken by themselves also fail to tell a very complete story. It is when needs or desires are considered *in relation to* abilities that important personality pictures begin to emerge. Thus an individual who greatly feels a need for outward success, and who also has great ability, might have a personality very similar to another person who felt less need for success and who had less ability. This essential similarity in personality might persist even though the two people differ both in need and ability. Fertility of imagination, to take another example, may mean much or little depending on the presence or absence of other traits. Lack of imagination may have very little effect on a person who lives a gregarious, social life, whereas it may have a marked effect on a more retiring person. The latter individual, cut off from internal resources, would be less happy than the more gregarious person who relies less on internal resources anyhow.

Personality as Social Impact. Many of the definitions of personality strongly emphasize the idea of social impact. In these definitions, personality refers to the way we affect other people. If a person stands out, or if he cannot be overlooked, he is said to "have" personality. Usually, of course, this use of the term implies that the person stands out in some acceptable way, but this is not always essential. We may resent him but may still grudgingly admit that he has personality.

The psychologist, of course, is not likely to talk about anyone as "having a lot of personality." Still, he is interested, among other things, in the total quantity of social impact, and especially in the type of impact made by the person in question. Although social impact is not the beginning and the end of personality, it is one important feature of most definitions or views of personality.

Personality as the Basis for Individuality. Many of the definitions of personality stress the feature of uniqueness or distinctiveness. In these definitions, personality is that quality or combination of qualities which sets us off from other people. Personality consists of those qualities by which one person can be distinguished from another. This approach, of course, is merely an aspect of the definitions. Although most laymen and some psychologists undoubtedly have this feature in mind when they speak of personality, very few serious students would be willing to define personality entirely in terms of uniqueness.

Operational or Working Definitions

The common-sense definitions of personality represent what we would like to know about this subject, or what we set out to know. These definitions probably describe the general concept we have in our minds when we begin to read a book or a chapter which professes to tell us about personality. It is most probable, too, that these were the general ideas in the minds of the early investigators who first set out to study the facts of personality. They undoubtedly hoped to get some information about the integrated, unique person in his relations to other people.

It is helpful to keep the hopes and intentions of the investigator in the back of our minds. It would be a great mistake, however, to assume that the investigator has always observed exactly what he set out to observe. With the very best of intentions, he may design tests which he hopes will reveal aspects of "personality" as it is commonly understood, only to find out later on that his tests are really picking up something very different.

If we can bring ourselves to accept this hard and unpleasant fact, we will realize that here, just as in the case of intelligence, the phenomenon studied is really "defined" by the nature of the tests or by the techniques of observation. Our knowledge is limited to the things that will come through these measuring instruments. If our tests can reveal the "integration of traits which make a person unique," then that is what we are actually studying. If the tests or observational techniques, on the contrary, reveal only the ability to distinguish pretty adjectives from those which are reprehensible, then that is the trait we are studying.

Adopting this hard-boiled, operational approach, we should be prepared to find personality-as-investigated to be somewhat different from personality-as-envisaged-on-the-mountain-top. To a great extent, the investigations do not stress integration or uniqueness. They stress, on the contrary, a large number of separate traits. For the most part, the investigations have used measures of such narrow traits as honesty, soci ability, introversion, neuroticism, and the like. And it is this aspect of personality that we shall learn about from the investigations. The personality which we will study will very frequently turn out to be a cluster of traits in which people vary, with special emphasis on nonintellectual traits and on traits that emphasize mental health and social adjustment.

The Measurement of Personal Adjustment

The Interview

The clinician who depends on the interview may also use many supplementary devices. On the other hand, he may rely largely on rather simple discussion, basing his estimate on the answers to his questions and on the information volunteered by the person being interviewed. This is one of the oldest and most direct methods of determining adjustment or lack of adjustment. Used by a trained and judicious inquirer, it can bring to light information which could be obtained in no other way. Typically, in fact, some sort of interview is used as a court of last resort when we seek to determine the validity of any other measuring device. After we give these other tests to a number of people, we try to see whether or not the test results agree with the impressions reached by a trained clinician who interviews people who have taken the tests.

All this is not to say, of course, that the interview is infallible. At its best, it is limited by the skill of the individual investigator using it. And even under ordinary circumstances interviewers have been accused of too much zeal in the detection of problems. In one investigation(12), for instance, a group of twenty-four children, all apparently normal, were sent through a child-study clinic. Many problems were found, some of them serious. If these were a random selection of children it would suggest either that the concept of problem child has lost much of its meaning or that in some cases problems may be detected too readily.

The informal interview, of course, is no device for the amateur. The untrained person may miss much that is significant and may misinterpret a good deal of what he does observe. Even worse, his clumsy probing may frighten the person off and make him less ready to reveal worrisome matters to a more qualified interviewer.

Typically, the informal interview does not yield a quantitative score. Instead it provides a judgment of whether or not the person needs help. It may also provide suggestions for the type of help that should be obtained. Typically, the interview is directed less toward the obtaining of precise scores and more toward the immediate problem of helping the person to improve his adjustment.

Not all interviews are of the informal type. Interviews conducted for research purposes, for instance, are very likely to use elaborate check lists of questions to be asked. Some interviews in the field of personality evaluation are as highly standardized as the Binet test "interview" in the field of intellectual evaluation. The interviews in the Kinsey investigations of sexual behavior(13) follow a schedule and procedure that is highly standardized and very elaborate indeed.

The Questionnaire or Inventory

Most of the data on personal adjustment have been gathered through some form of personal data sheet, personality schedule, or personal inventory. Typically these questionnaires contain a long list of symptoms or complaints often reported by people who have been classified as neurotic. The person taking the test then merely indicates whether or not he has ever experienced this symptom. He is asked, for instance, if people often talk about him behind his back, or if he is usually tired upon awakening in the morning, and so forth. A person who checked a large number of the complaints typical of neurotics would obtain a low score on personal adjustment.

There are, of course, many objections to the questionnaire. The person taking the test may "see through" the questions and check the answer which he thinks will give him a "good" score rather than the answer which he regards as true. Against this theoretical possibility, however, there is considerable evidence that people will often report some very unflattering things about themselves. The empirical validity of these questionnaires has also been the subject of much discussion(14). This, of course, has been a difficult problem, since it is hard to get a good criterion of adjustment against which the questionnaires can be checked. At present

we had better regard the question as unsettled. The various questionnaires most probably measure some aspect of adjustment, but it is unlikely that they measure precisely the same thing that the psychiatrist has in mind when he announces that a given person is poorly adjusted.

Along with these more elaborate questionnaires, aimed at revealing subtle or hidden matters, there are a number of more direct inventories, such as the

FIGURE 16-1. *Type of Inkblot used in the Rorschach Test.* Reproduced from Stagner, *Psychology of Personality*. Courtesy of the McGraw-Hill Book Company, Inc.

Mooney Problem Check List and the SRA Inventory which do not probe beneath the surface but which merely ask students to list worries or problems as they see them.

Projective Techniques

In the earlier discussion, it was pointed out that the actual investigations of personality do not show that emphasis on integration which appears so often in the definitions of personality. Most of the measuring devices discussed so far, for instance, are designed to cast light not on the integrated personality but on various isolated traits of personality. This emphasis on isolated traits, however, is by no means universal. Several attempts have been made to devise tests which will reveal an integrated pattern of personality. Prominent among these are the so-called projective techniques, and of these techniques the best known is the Rorschach Ink Blot Technique. In this technique, the subject is shown a standardized series of ink blots which are made by dropping some ink in the fold of a paper and squeezing the paper together. Figure 16-1 shows the general type of blot that results. These blots suggest various pictures to different people, and since one is free to see almost anything in them, the reaction is supposed to indicate tendencies in the person.

Very elaborate methods of scoring and interpreting the Rorschach test(15) have been worked out. From reaction to ink blots, Rorschachers believe they can determine productiveness of the imagination, spontaneity, impulsiveness (or susceptibility to emotions), degree of control of emotions, and so forth. More important, perhaps, they believe that they can see these traits in relation to each other. They see, for instance, emotionality in relation to emotional control.

A method somewhat similar to the Rorschach is the Thematic Apperception Technique(16). In this method, the subject is shown a picture, for instance, of an older man taking hold of the arm of a startled young woman. The subject is told that this is a test of fertility of the imagination. He is asked to give a story into which the picture would fit. The resulting story is supposed to give some insight into the hopes and fears and needs of the subject. A special group of such designs have been provided for adolescents(17), and still other forms have been devised for young children. One of these, the Children's Apperception Test, makes considerable use of animals on the assumption that children might more readily project their needs and fears into animals. So far the evidence suggests that the use of animals adds very little and that elementary-school children give no different response to these than to the standard tests(18, 19).

The Blacky Tests(20) also rely on children's reactions to animals to bring out some aspects of development with special emphasis on psychosexual development as interpreted by the Freudians.

Along with these standardized published tests there has been much use of the child's expressive movements as revealed in painting, drawing, or writing to reveal characteristics of his personality. The Machover Draw-a-person Test, for instance, relies on this procedure. So does the H-T-P test in which a student is asked to draw a house, a tree, and a person. These tests have been given to many children and the various features of the drawings have been studied and have been correlated with facts already known about the children.

Many people have been misled by the apparent simplicity of these tests. On the surface, it seems that one merely looks at the child's drawing and uses one's common sense. If there is a double padlock on the gate of the house he has drawn it is symbolic of fear. If there are large splotches of red under the trees he has painted, it shows a need for aggression, or certainly a preoccupation with violence. Actually these glib, spur-of-the moment intuitions are most undependable. We must test many, many children and compare the various "signs" with other diagnoses before we can tell what it means when a child draws children that are bigger than the house, or dogs that are bigger than either. Resist the temptation to jump to free and easy conclusions in these complicated and tricky matters.

Unlike the amateur who merely looks at a work of art and proceeds to hold forth on the personality of the one who created it, there have been several serious attempts to work out dependable rules for the interpretation of expressive movements(21). These more systematic efforts are now under critical study, and it is still too early to say how valuable they may prove to be(22).

Rating Scales

Rating scales are exceedingly familiar devices. Few of us have escaped the obligation of rating our friends and acquaintances on such matters as loyalty, honesty, ability, industry, and on a host of similar traits. Each of us in our turn, we can be sure, has been rated by teachers, colleagues, friends, and employers.

These rating scales take many forms. They may consist of a group of adjectives from which the rater selects the most appropriate. More often, however, they take a graphic form in which the descriptive phrases are located along a straight line, as in the following illustrations:

Punctuality:

1	2	3	4	5
Very unpunctual	Late at times	About average	Seldom late	Never late

Attends to Important Details:

1	2	3	4	5
Un-dependable	Most of the time	About average	Seldom neglects	Never neglects

Limitations of Rating Scales. Obviously these scales have many imperfections and anyone using them must make allowance for the many weaknesses. In the first place, the rater is asked to compare this one person with the average as far as punctuality or attention to detail is concerned. But what is "average punctuality?" Clearly different raters may have different opinions on this matter, and consequently they may rate the student differently because of these different standards. Even more important, unless great care is taken in the wording of the scales, the rater may not be sure what sort of punctuality he is supposed to have in mind.

Does it refer to punctuality in reaching class, in keeping general appointments, or in getting work in on time?

In addition to these uncertainties in the interpretation of the questions and of the standards to be used, the rater is undoubtedly influenced by the *halo* effect. A rater, that is to say, who thinks well of a student in one trait will tend to rate him highly in most other traits as well. If you think Bob is a good student in general, you will be inclined to rate him favorably in many separate traits. You will do this even though upon closer consideration you would admit that in this one trait he is no better than a poor student to whom you tended to give a lower rating.

The bias of the rater is more apparent some times than others. In rating a painting, for instance, I am clearly aware that my judgment is partly a reflection of my tastes or idiosyncrasies. I should not be at all surprised if other people rate it differently. In rating a friend, on the other hand, I may be less aware that my judgment may arise partly from my own taste and prejudices. I may think that the judgment comes entirely from the man, and that I am merely observing what is actually there. As a matter of fact, of course, this judgment is no more free from bias than my judgment of the picture.

To some extent, these defects may be overcome by pooling the ratings of different people. If these people do not all have the same kinds of ignorance and defects, the composite may cancel out the idiosyncrasies of the individual raters. We notice that when ratings are pooled there is a tendency for the composite to rate most people above average. This is due, perhaps, to a streak of kindness or generosity which impels us to give a high rating, especially when in doubt.

Man-to-man Scales

The man-to-man scale has proved useful both in rating people on a single trait and in rating a group of people on several traits at once. It was developed in the First World War in rating men for potential officer material. To use this scale, all the raters must know a number of people who can be lined up in an order, such as the following:

Individual	*Agreed Judgment of the Raters*
Aronson	Best man to go through this school
Baumgarten	Superior
Caldwell	Average. Good man
Dupree	Barely passable
Ewart	Not acceptable

Once the raters have agreed on such a scale, they may rate new men in terms of these known men.

Social Distance

Attitude scales often use the concept of social distance. The student indicates how close a relationship he is willing to contemplate with a member of certain groups. Such scales of social distance may ask, "Would it bother you to think of a (Hindu) as a husband or wife, as a relative by marriage, as a member of your club, as a neighbor on your street, etc.?" By comparing answers to the same question regarding other national or cultural groups, one can obtain a scale of tolerance for the respective groups.

Performance Tests

To measure many aspects of personal or social adjustment, it is possible to put a student in a test situation and to see how he actually performs. It is possible, for instance, to give him a test in which he has an opportunity to cheat and to determine whether or not he succumbs to the temptation. In the Maller Self-Marking Test, for instance, the student takes a test which includes items of moderate difficulty and also some items that no one could be expected to answer. These latter ask for the weight of the moon, the population of Java, the number of diesel locomotives in use, and for other information equally esoteric. The student is given the answer sheet and scores his own paper. If he claims more than one or two hard items he is cheating.

Other performance tests are also used. In a test situation, a student making a purchase is given too much change. What does he do? In a test of altruism, a student is given a set of toys or tools and then told that there are not enough to go around. Will he give up any of his kit?

Using the Different Tests of Personality

The tests discussed in this section are extremely useful in showing us something of the nature of "measured" or "investigated" personality. It is obvious, however, that some of these tests are not especially useful to the classroom teacher. Some tests, in fact, should be used only by the highly trained specialist. Others are not hard to give but are tricky to interpret and are likely to mislead the amateur. Along with these tests which are of questionable use, there are, of course, many others which will prove most valuable to the average teacher in guidance and in measuring the results of instructional programs.

In general, the projective tests should not be used by the amateur. They must be administered with great care. Scoring is difficult and exacting, and interpretation is exceedingly complex. Many of the tests of personal adjustment are easy to give and can be returned to the testing agency for scoring. The interpretation of these tests, however, is very uncertain. Ordinarily these should be used by the classroom teacher with great caution. Ideally, a program which involves extensive use of these tests should be under the direction of someone trained in clinical psychology or in guidance procedures.

In contrast to the more technical projective tests or the tests designed to reveal definite personal disorders, the teacher will find many of the other tests extremely useful. He could hardly avoid using direct observation, and he would be almost perverse not to inspect the student's cumulative record card and to note the outstanding achievements and the difficulties. Although the teacher will do well to avoid the prolonged, probing interview, he will naturally make use of the shorter, casual interview to ascertain the student's interests or superficial problems. Interest inventories or questionnaires and problem check lists will also prove useful to the teacher who has had some guidance training. Rating scales, of course, will be used with considerable frequency in keeping a record of the student's status in a wide variety of traits.

Differences and Patterns in Personal Traits

Individual Differences

It is well known, of course, that there are vast differences in the personality and in the social adjustment of children. Different children have different methods of reacting to the same problems or to the same type of frustration. Whereas one child will react by a sustained effort toward a solution, another will react by an emotional physical attack or by childish weeping. Whereas one child may rush to the front in almost any social situation, another child may respond to such an opportunity only upon rare occasions. In one investigation it was found that some children exploited 65 percent of the opportunities to exert leadership, whereas other children took advantage of only 5 percent of the opportunities. It has also been shown that popularity, as indicated by the sociogram, is very unevenly distributed(23). A few children are likely to be very popular indeed, whereas a large number are chosen as friends with moderate frequency, and a smaller number are selected very seldom or not at all.

At one time there was a great tendency to classify people into clear-cut types. Faced with the task of describing a person, we would try to decide whether he was an introvert *or* an extrovert, whether he was determined *or* vacillating, and so forth. As test results began to come in, however, it soon became apparent that people could not be grouped in this way. From our tests, it is no more possible to say whether a person is honest or dishonest than it is to say whether he is intelligent or dull, or whether he is tall or short. The test results showed a continuous distribution in almost all the measured traits.

The distributions in Figure 16-2 are merely samples of the sort of individual differences we often find. Notice that there are no gaps in the distributions. Notice, too, that there is only one mode and that this occurs somewhere between the extremes. In these particular examples the distributions are skewed, in that the people tend to pile up toward one end of the scale. We must not assume that this skewness is universal for tests of personality. It is fairly frequent, however, and should cause us no surprise.

It is too soon, of course, to say that there are no personality types or that all traits are distributed in the continuous fashion shown in Figure 16-2. It is quite possible that this apparent continuity may come from the mechanical nature of the tests that are used. These tests are so constructed that they might tend to hide clear personality types even if such existed.

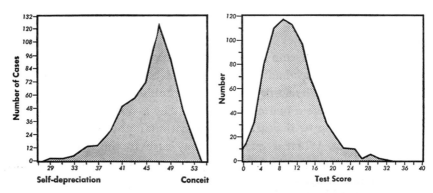

FIGURE 16-2. *Sample Distributions of Personal Traits.*

(Left) Scores on self-esteem from Stagner, *Psychology of Personality.* Courtesy of the McGraw-Hill Book Company, Inc.

(Right) Scores on personal adjustment from OSRD report No. 4870, "An Evaluation of the Personal Inventory for Predicting Success in Parachute Schools," 1945. Authorization from Research and Development Board.

Basic Patterns of Personality

Although formal statistical factor analysis of personality has been undertaken only recently(24, 25, 26, 27), the basic enterprise itself is by no means new. We are all factor analysts at heart. We all make such statements as, "Show me a man who is vigorous and effective, and I will show you a man who is somewhat conceited," or, "Examine a person who is cold or aloof, and you will find that he is also a stickler for habit or routine." And it is toward conclusions such as these, stated in more precise terms, of course, that the work of the factor analyst is directed.

The amateur and the factor analyst, alike, are appalled by the vast number of separate descriptions that we may collect for a given person. That person may be described by some three or four hundred separate statements. These statements may indicate his liking for parlor games, his hopes for salvation, his taste in neckties, his attitude toward his mother, his liking for responsibility, for company, for important people, for security in his work, and so on endlessly and forever. Anyone looking at this stupendous list is almost compelled to ask: Are these things actually separate and distinct traits, or on the contrary, may we not merely have a small number of basic underlying traits of which these are but separate samples or indexes? If we knew how a man stood on one of these traits, would we not also have a hint as to where he stands on some of the others? Could we not break this vast list down into some six or twenty groups of traits, taking care that all the traits in one group will have something in common, but also being sure that the groups do not overlap one with the other?

Suggested Factors or Dimensions in Personality

The factors that we shall talk about come from two chief sources. On the one hand we have the brilliant insights or intuitions of a few thoughtful men and on the other hand we have the painstaking work of the factor analysts whose approach we consider at length in the discussion of intelligence-test results. To some extent these two approaches have reached the same conclusions and to some extent they have come up with quite different results.

Extroversion-Introversion. One famous result of the intuitional approach is the Extroversion-Introversion dimension suggested by Carl Jung. The phrases, of course, are well known to everyone. The original concepts, however, were not as simple as those we hear used so frequently at the cocktail party or in the newspapers. Perhaps the clearest idea of the original Jungian concept is to be had by considering how people try to resolve their serious frustrations or tensions. Roughly speaking, the introvert when faced with a problem will make his most satisfactory adjustment by some rearrangement of his own ideas or by thinking it out. The extrovert, on the other hand, reacts to the problem whenever possible by rearranging the environment or the outside world. Let us suppose, for instance, that your partner has absconded with your money. This produces severe tension or frustration. How can you release those tensions? If you are an extreme extrovert, you will get most satisfaction from vigorous outward action. You may try to apprehend the thief. In some cases you may resort to fist fighting. After doing so you may feel some release. If you are an extreme introvert, on the other hand, you may get your greatest relief from rearranging your ideas to make such conduct understandable. After you have thus reorganized your philosophy of life, you may feel better about the problem.

In the original Jungian concept there was nothing to demand that the introvert should be shy, seclusive, frightened, timid, or neurotic. The concept merely demanded that most of his satisfactions came from within, from ideas and feelings. There is no reason why an introvert in the Jungian sense should not be very sociable and very fond of company(28). Of course solitude might be more acceptable or tolerable to one who obtained many of his satisfactions from within. And no matter what was in the mind of the Swiss scholar, it is perhaps inevitable that a society as practical and outgoing as our own should regard the lover of ideas as a bit queer or neurotic.

Basic Values or Needs. In addition to classifying people according to whether they are orientated to the inward or to the outward world, we could classify them according to the values which predominate in their lives. We would ask, for instance, which of the many areas of life have most attraction for this person and which areas are relatively less important. According to one well-known theory, we should get a fairly good picture of any one man by seeing how much importance he attaches to each of six areas. The six areas are the theoretical (in which scientists and scholars usually rank high), the economic, the esthetic, the social, the political, and the religious. Most people, of course, will have some interest in several of the areas, but typically the interest in one or two areas will outweigh the attraction of the others.

In this case, intuition and the more prosaic method of factor analysis do not agree completely. In one investigation(29), at least, the scale of values measures some ten factors rather than six, and some theoretical values seem to involve at least two of these factors.

Factor Analysis

The general procedures of factor analysis are discussed in Chapters 4 and 5. There it is pointed out how one attempts, by the study of the relations between test items, to see which items belong together in a single cluster and which others belong in a separate cluster. These clusters make up the factors. Whenever we find such a factor that will "stand up" after repeated investigation, we hope that we may have come across a basic trait of which each specific item is a partial expression or an index. French(30) has attempted to bring together the results of some 68 separate investigations of this topic. Starting with the enormous number of detailed statements that tests may include, these 68 investigations had, all told, cut the list down to 450 factors. But even this is grotesquely unwieldy. By eliminating overlapping and by grouping whenever possible, French has tried to reduce this list to a manageable size. He comes out with 36 factors dealing with general personality, and 12 more dealing with specific interests.

The essential thing about these 36 factors, of course, is that they are separate. One is not related to the other. Knowing where a person stands on one factor, we still cannot tell where he stands on the other. Any grouping we may do, therefore, is purely arbitrary and has value only for convenience. It is like grouping people alphabetically or by date of birth.

Factors that Refer to Relations to Other People. The following factors, all separate from each other in spite of their somewhat similar names, seem to refer to relations to other people: gregarious, sociable, lonely, self-sufficient, self-conscious, agreeable, dependable, honest, conventional, dominant, sensitive to the emotions of others, impervious to social demands.

Factors that Refer to Mood or Temperament. The following separate factors have been suggested: anxious, fearful, given to day-dreaming, given to "nervous" illness, emotional, excitable, free-and-easy expression of emotions, amount of energy or drive, oscillation of mood, oscillation of attention, persistence, self-confidence, emotional conflict over will, meticulous attention to detail, delusions, psychotic tendency.

Factors Referring to Intellectual Aspects. The following separate traits seem to have a relation to intelligence or culture: Sophistication, fondness for culture, alertness to surroundings.

Clusters of Interests. The following factors refer to the things one likes to do or to read about: Interest in athletics, in business, in clerical tasks, in science, in sex, in family, in social welfare, in religion, in linguistic matters, in artistic things, in philosophizing, or in solving problems.

Remember that each of the phrases we have listed above is merely the name that someone (Dr. French, in this case) has given to a cluster of traits that seem to go together. Perhaps you, in looking at each cluster, would give it a different name. We find, for instance, that the following traits go together: liking to be with people, liking for parties or dances, preferring to work in a group, dislike of being alone. For this cluster, French offers the label *gregarious*. Taking another example, we find the following traits forming a different cluster: quick to make friends, readily starts conversation with others, enjoys making acquaintances, does not try to stay in background on social occasions, takes prominent part in social activities, active in organizing clubs, talkative, not shy or certainly not bothered by shyness. These things tend to go together. Knowing a person's status in some of these traits we can predict his status on the others. To this cluster French gives the label *sociable*. Notice that in spite of the similarity in the words *gregarious* and *sociable* the traits that make up the two clusters are quite different. A person could get a high score in the things that make for gregariousness (as used here) and still get a low score on the things that make for sociability.

This extensive summary is by no means complete. Almost every little specialized aspect of personality has had its own factor analysis(31, 32). One study, for instance, has been devoted to a search for basic Freudian concepts in character in an attempt to see if the factors do not relate to the oral, anal, and phallic aspects of personality emphasized by the Freudians(33).

Differences within the Individual

When the factors described above have been substantiated and have settled down, they should permit us to get a much clearer and more accurate idea of the differences that exist within an individual. If it turns out to be true that we must employ some forty-eight concepts to get an accurate picture of the various facets of personality, then we can construct an elaborate *profile* in which the student's status in each factor is indicated. The information on such a profile should help us in deciding which characteristics need attention. We say "help us decide" because we could not, of course, assume that every child who was below average in gregariousness, to take one example, should be brought up to average. Neither should we assume that a child who is well above average in his "sensitivity to the emotions of others" should be allowed to rest on his oars in this respect. In his particular case, the reverse may well be true. In a different chapter we discuss at length this worrisome question of deciding on the proper goals for the various facets of personality.

Meanwhile, even though we probably do not have the final answer regarding the basic factors of personality, we can still do something toward constructing useful profiles of the students in our care, based on the traits or factors that we do know about.

The Constancy of Personality

Do personalities or social attitudes tend to remain with us relatively unchanged or do they fluctuate with the passing years? This is, of course, a fundamental question. If personality fluctuates wildly from day to day, from situation to situation, then there is no great point in studying it. Instead of studying personality we should merely study the situation on which personal reactions depend.

From our general impressions, most of us assume that personalities do not fluctuate wildly. From our ordinary observations, we feel we can depend on people to keep their present personalities for some time. Within limits, we can predict the future reactions of different people in different situations. We say, "Bill would appreciate that story," or, "I wish Harriet could see this scene." Similarly, we can imagine how another person would be shocked, or baffled, or bewildered by another situation. True enough, we are prepared to see our predictions go unfulfilled upon occasion. The shy, bashful lad may react to the "gorgeous gal" in a more adequate manner than one anticipated. The hearty, easygoing man may inexplicably take offense. But these exceptions we regard as unusual and transitory. A marked change in personality, like the conversion of Scrooge or of Silas Marner, is unusual enough to justify a novel.

A few published studies tend to confirm our general impression(34). An interesting study of this type at the nursery-school level is reported by McKinnon(35). In this study sixteen nursery-school children were observed and the predominant characteristic of each child determined. Four main characteristics were used, namely, conformity, caution, aggression (invasiveness), and withdrawal. Some five or six years later the same group was reclassified. Ten of the sixteen children were still in their original group. The six who did change moved from other classifications into the conformity group. These results suggest a fair degree of consistency, even at the nursery-school level.

Constancy over a wide span of years is also reported on occasion. In one investigation(36), babies were observed during the first two years of life and the outstanding personal characteristics of each were noted. When these infants had reached the age of sixteen or seventeen their acquaintances were able to select from the group of anonymous infant-personality sketches the one that belonged to the adolescent they knew. Proceeding to an even greater span of years, we note another investigation(37) in which six elderly adults of the same family could be matched with the personality estimates derived from a diary kept by the mother when they were young children.

So much for general, over-all personality. In the matter of personal adjustment versus neuroticism, we also find a good deal of constancy. Inventory tests given some six years apart(38) yield correlations of about .50. This correlation, although less than that for intelligence, is fairly substantial when we consider the probable unreliability of tests of neuroticism in the first place. When retests are given after only a short time, we find, as we might expect, even greater constancy or less change. When tests are retaken after only two weeks(39) we find correlations between .70 and .80.

In the discussion of the more specific aspects of personal adjustment it will be seen that there is also a definite, but by no means perfect, constancy over a period of years. In most of its aspects, apparently, personality is a quality of the individual and is not merely the result of the momentary situation in which he finds himself.

Age Changes in General Personality

The constancy that we have been discussing is, of course, a relative constancy. It means that children to some extent keep the same relative positions in most traits as they grow older. It does not mean that they stay still. In the discussions of the more detailed aspects of personality, we shall see numerous systematic changes as students move toward maturity. In the more general matter of personal adjustment versus the disturbed personality we can also note some clear trends. The sort of nervousness that is indicated by nail biting, for instance, increases fairly steadily during the early school years, reaching its peak at about eight years of age(40). From there it declines fairly steadily, especially for girls, throughout the remainder of the school period. In one investigation in Chicago(41), however, some 28 percent of eighteen-year-olds still bit their nails.

One very simple index of personal adjustment, or its lack, is being referred to a clinic. This may not hold for young infants, since no high degree of adjustment is expected at this stage. From one to six years of age, however, there is a marked increase in the number of children who are reported to child guidance clinics. Most frequently such children have been referred for such complaints as nail biting, daydreaming, or acting depressed. As the graphs in Figure 16-3 suggest, however, there is little change in these "referrals" during the school years. For other disturbances, such as restlessness or acting spoiled, there is a fairly steady decline throughout the school years.

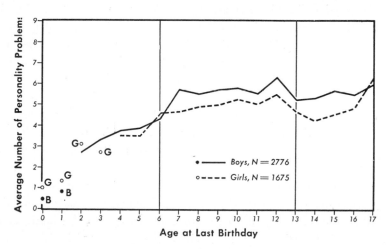

FIGURE 16-3. *Increase in Personality Problems with Age.* Redrawn by permission from Figure 330 in Shuttleworth (See Fig. 7-4 for reference).

Children referred to clinics, of course, may have troubles that range from the transitory or trivial to those of more serious proportions. In young children we are unlikely to find disturbances serious enough to call for commitment to a mental hospital. Between the ages of ten and fourteen, however, very few children (4 out of 100,000) are committed to institutions for the mentally ill. And during the later teens the number increases tenfold so that 40 out of every 100,000 children between the ages of fifteen and nineteen are committed to an institution. Although the proportion of children actually affected is still small, the astounding relative increase during this period is most disquieting.

The students just discussed are those who have come to the attention of parent or teacher or doctor. When we leave these people who are definitely in trouble and turn to the general population, we find a somewhat different story. For the most part, the questionnaires and neurotic inventories show some improvement as the student grows older. In most studies, older students and younger adults make a somewhat more favorable showing. With the approach of old age, of course, the number of mental ailments increases sharply(42).

Summary

Social and personal growth, of course, might properly be considered to include the whole of educational growth. Here, however, we shall not include the physical, intellectual, and academic development treated earlier. Personal and social behavior are best understood in terms of goals and goal-seeking behavior. To describe this sort of behavior, we make much use of the concepts of *need* and *drive*. The need represents a condition to be achieved (or avoided). The drive is the name given to that force which keeps the organism active until the need is satisfied.

People are affected by sheer physiological needs, such as the needs for oxygen and food. They are also driven by the social needs, such as the need for the esteem of others, and the need to dominate. Along with these, there is the powerful need to think well of ourselves. One further group of needs might be termed the creative or manipulative needs. These needs are concerned with securing interesting results, sometimes frivolous, sometimes of a serious nature, as in the need for achievement.

In human beings the needs and drives are complicated by ideas and by subtle associations. We are driven to avoid not only the fearsome object but also the feeling of fear. Often our struggle to avoid the feeling of fear is more strenuous than our struggle to avoid the actual evil itself if it were present. Poverty may be less disastrous than the fear of poverty. This urge to avoid the feeling of fear is part of the need for security.

Needs never act separately but always in a complex pattern. Two needs may reinforce each other or may conflict. Some needs (the need for esteem) may be completely free to operate only when more basic needs (the need for water) are partially satisfied.

It is the fate of drives to be thwarted. They may be thwarted by the physical world or by some other drive. Thwarting by the physical environment may give rise to other needs, such as the need for aggression or the need to give up, and these new needs may conflict with our need for self-esteem. Thwarting by a person is even more likely to arouse aggression.

Conflict between two external needs is uncomfortable but seldom dangerous. At the worst such conflict may result in a precipitous decision or in a stalemate. Such conflict can be aided by a few simple rules. Conflict is likely to become serious when our need for self-esteem is one of the antagonists. There are many devious or artificial ways in which we can protect our need for self-esteem from the demands of some need which would make us feel cheap or unworthy. These familiar mechanisms for escaping reality can lead to behavior that is trivial and harmless, or to behavior that is seriously incapacitating.

Needs, conflicts, and reactions to conflict perhaps make up the dynamics of personality. These elements, however, are seldom seen directly. Personality adjustment as observed starts with the totality of the person, or with his unique traits, or with his impact on other people. Many investigations study only one trait or one aspect of personality.

Personality has been observed by direct inspection, by simple or elaborate interviews, by the use of questionnaires or inventories answered by the subject himself, by various techniques in which the subject *projects* his own wishes and fears into an ambiguous design or sketch, by rating scales, and by tests of actual performance. Each of these reveals clear distributions of individual differences in personality.

There have been many attempts to work out the basic structure of personality. The intuitional approach has suggested the introversion-extroversion dimension and dimensions based on values. Factor analysis has suggested a large number of elements (from 36 to 450) referring to relations with people, to mood, to the dominance of intellect, and to clusters of interests. As the basic factors become better identified we should be able to construct fairly complete profiles of an individual. Even now such profiles are useful.

Various aspects of personality remain surprisingly constant throughout the life span. A child who is unusually timid for a four-year-old may have more than average timidity as an adult.

For the general population there is an increase in the overt signs of nervousness and maladjustment during the early school years, followed by an improvement at the approach of adulthood.

SPECIFIC REFERENCES

1. Morgan, C. T., and Stellar, E. *Physiological psychology.* McGraw-Hill, 1950. Chap. 18. The bodily needs.
2. Taba, Hilda, and others. *Diagnosing human relations needs.* Amer. Council on Education, 1951.
3. Carmichael, L., ed. *Manual of child psychology.* Wiley, 1954, Chap. 14. Emotional development (Jersild, A. T.).
4. McClelland, D. C., and others. *The achievement motive.* Appleton-Century-Crofts, 1953.
5. Maslow, A. H. A theory of human motivation. *Psychol. Rev.,* 1943, *50,* 370–396.
6. Maslow, A. H. "Higher" and "lower" needs. *J. Psychol.,* 1948, *25,* 433–436.
7. Pastore, N. The role of arbitrariness in the frustration-aggression hypothesis. *J. abnorm. soc. Psychol.,* 1952, *47,* 728–731.
8. Symonds, P. M. *The dynamics of human adjustment.* Appleton-Century-Crofts, 1946.
9. Hendrick, I. *Facts and theories of psychoanalysis.* Knopf, 1947.
10. Sears, R. R. Experimental studies of projection, I. Attribution of traits. *J. soc. Psychol.,* 1936, *7,* 151–163.
11. Allport, G. W. *Personality, a psychological interpretation.* Holt, 1937.
12. Harris, A. J. What is a "normal" child? *J. Teach. Educ.,* 1952, *3,* 58–61.
13. Kinsey, A. C., Pomeroy, W. B., and Martin, C. E. *Sexual behavior in the human male.* Philadelphia, Saunders, 1948.
14. Ellis, A., and Conrad, H. S. The validity of personality inventories in military practice. *Psychol. Bull.,* 1948, *45,* 385–426.
15. Klopfer, B., and Kelley, D. M. *The Rorschach technique.* World, 1942.
16. Murray, H. A., et al. *Explorations in personality.* Oxford, 1938.
17. Symonds, P. M. *The Symonds picture-story test.* Teachers College, Columbia University, 1948.
18. Biersdorf, Kathryn R., and Marcuse, F. L. Responses of children to human and to animal pictures. *J. projective Techniques,* 1953, *17,* 455–459.
19. Light, B. H. Comparative study of a series of TAT and CAT cards. *J. clin. Psychol.,* 1954, *10,* 179–181.
20. *The Blacky Pictures: a technique for the exploration of personality dynamics.* Psychological Corporation.

21. Alschuler, R. H., and Hattwick, L. B. W. *Painting and personality.* University of Chicago Press, 1947.

22. Thomas, R. M. Effects of frustration on children's paintings. *Child Develpm.*, 1951, *22,* 123–132.

23. Bonney, M. E. A study of social status on the second grade level. *J. genet. Psychol.,* 1942, *60,* 271–305.

24. Wolfle, D. Factor analysis to 1940. *Psychometric Monogr.,* 1940, No. 3.

25. Cattell, R. B. *Description and measurement of personality.* World, 1946.

26. Eysenck, H. J. *Dimensions of personality.* London: Paul, Trench, Trubner, 1947.

27. Guilford, J. P., and Guilford, Ruth B. Personality factors D, R, T, and A. *J. abnorm. soc. Psychol.,* 1939, *34,* 21–36.

28. Gray, H., and Wheelwright, J. B. Jung's psychological types, their frequency of occurrence. *J. gen. Psychol.,* 1946, *34,* 3–17.

29. Brogden, H. E. The primary personal values measured by the Allport-Vernon test, "A Study of Values." *Psychol. Monogr.,* 1952, *66* (*16*).

30. French, J. W. *The description of personality measurements in terms of rotated factors.* Educational Testing Service, 1953.

31. Tyler, F. T. A factorial analysis of fifteen MMPI scales. *J. consult. Psychol.,* 1951, *15,* 451–456.

32. Barron, F. Complexity-simplicity as a personality dimension. *J. abnorm. soc. Psychol.,* 1953, *48,* 163–172.

33. Barnes, C. A. A statistical study of the Freudian theory of levels of psychosexual development. *Genet. Psychol. Monogr.,* 1952, *45,* 105–174.

34. Roberts, Katherine E., and Fleming, Virginia V. Persistence and change in personality patterns. National Research Council, 1943, Vol. 8, No. 3.

35. McKinnon, Kathern M. Consistency and change in behavior manifestations. *Child Developm. Monogr.,* 1942, No. 30.

36. Neilon, Patricia. Shirley's babies after fifteen years: A personality study. *J. genet. Psychol.,* 1948, *73,* 175–186.

37. Smith, Madorah E. A comparison of certain personality traits as rated in the same individuals in childhood and fifty years later. *Child. Develpm.,* 1952, *23,* 159–180.

38. Crook, M. N. Retest correlations in neuroticism. *J. gen. Psychol.,* 1941, *24,* 173–182.

39. Pintner, R., and Forlano, G. Consistency of response to personality tests at different age levels. *J. genet. Psychol.,* 1943, *62,* 77–83.

40. Birch, L. B. The incidence of nail biting among school children. *Brit. J. educ. Psychol.,* 1955, *25,* 123–128.
41. Malone, A. J., and Massler, M. Index of nail-biting in children. *J. abnorm. soc. Psychol.,* 1952, *47,* 193–202.
42. Various authors. *Mental disorders in later life.* Stanford University Press, 1945. Chap. 4. Psychological aspects of mental disorders in later life (Jones, H. E., and Kaplan, O. J.).

SUGGESTIONS FOR FURTHER READING

1. Carmichael, L., ed. *Manual of child psychology.* Wiley, 1954, Chap. 14. Emotional development (Jersild, A. T.).

   A comprehensive summary of the important investigations. Detailed, but easily read.
2. Segal, D. *Frustration in adolescent youth.* U. S. Govt. Printing Office, 1951.

   A general survey addressed to the classroom teacher.
3. Vernon, P. E. *Personality tests and assessments.* Holt, 1954.

   A discussion of the more important tests. Factual and businesslike, but easily understood.
4. Freeman, F. S. *Theory and practice of psychological testing.* Holt, 1955.
5. Anastasi, Anne. *Psychological testing.* Macmillan, 1954.
6. Cronbach, L. J. *Essentials of psychological testing.* Harper, 1949.

   These three books provide excellent accounts of personality tests along with other types of tests.
7. Taba, Hilda, and others. *Diagnosing human relations needs.* American Council on Education, 1951.

   A specialized treatment but useful to the classroom teacher.
8. Cattell, R. B. *Personality: a systematic, theoretical and factual study.* McGraw-Hill, 1952.
9. Eysenck, H. J. *Scientific study of personality.* Macmillan, 1952.

   These two books provide an intensive study of personality, with emphasis on the results of factor analysis.
10. Mid-century White House Conference on Children and Youth. *Personality in the making.* Harper, 1952.

    This book, directed to workers in the field, contains many practical suggestions.
11. McClelland, D. C., ed. *Studies in motivation.* Appleton-Century-Crofts, 1955.

A collection of original contributions dealing with many phases of motivation.

12. Maslow, A. H. *Motivation and personality*. Harper, 1954.
See for details on Maslow's views.

Exercises and Questions for Discussion

1. Visualize a child in grade three taking part in a lesson on reading. Construct an imaginary list of the detailed needs that may be acting on him during the course of the lesson. Which of these needs will be satisfied with very little trouble? Which must be deferred for later satisfaction? Which may conflict with other powerful needs? Which may threaten the child's sense of self-esteem?

2. In teaching a unit on "Knowing Our Community" to grade-five students, which needs would you deliberately try to invoke? Which needs would you welcome, but would do little about? Which needs might you have to combat? Which could you ignore?

3. List a series of practical conflicts in which either decision would be better than none. List another series in which this would not be true.

4. Why is there so much trouble from conflicts which invoke the need for self-esteem?

5. In the section on "Utilizing Motivation" much was said about knowledge of results. Which needs are satisfied by such knowledge?

6. Make a list of the things you can remember doing in the last few hours. Include some minor acts (rubbing your nose) as well as some major acts (reporting in class). For each act try to estimate the underlying drives or combination of drives.

7. List the methods of measuring personality which appear to be most useful to the teacher in his regular work. List those for which the teacher will have little direct use. Is there any reason why the teacher should know anything about the latter group of tests?

8. You probably find it easy to realize that people differ by imperceptible gradations all the way from very short to very tall. Perhaps you can think the same way about differences in intelligence. But what about neuroticism? Do you find it easy to think of people having all shades of adequate adjustment? Or do you think of them as being either normal or neurotic? sane or insane?

17

Adjustment in Major Aspects of Personality

H OWEVER MUCH we may feel that personality is a unitary thing, not to be broken into parts, we seldom study it in that way. If we are to learn about personality, therefore, we must get much of our information from studies of various separate aspects of personality, from studies of anger and affection, of delinquency and deceit.

Emotional Development

It is, of course, impossible to say whether or not the subjective aspect of an emotion changes with age. Quite possibly some emotions may remain fairly constant from one age to another whereas other emotions may change in character. The rage felt by the frustrated infant, for instance, is probably very similar to the rage felt by adults when frustrated. The devastating fear which overcomes the child may be very much like the wild, unreasoning panic which takes possession of his elders. It is possible, however, that the emotions which cluster around sex constitute a very different experience for the child than for the adult.

Whatever may be true for internal emotional experience, there can be no doubt that there are marked changes in the manner of emotional expression. The young infant, for instance, shows almost no differentiation in his emotions. Looking at him, we can tell that he is excited. But when the child is very young, it is difficult to tell whether that excitement should be described as pleasant or unpleasant. Later on we can readily distinguish pleasant from unpleasant emotions, but we cannot so easily distinguish between anger and fear, on the one hand, or between affection and joy, on the other. As the child grows older, however, he expresses finer and finer shades of emotion. Unpleasant emotion is no longer merely unpleasant emotion. It can be fear or disgust, or anger or jealousy, or a mixture of several of these. Pleasant excitement is also differentiated into joy or elation or affection, and this affection in turn is still further differentiated. The affection expressed for the mother, for instance, may be different from that shown to an older brother or a friend of the same age. Finally, when still more mature, the student may experience and express that vast range of emotions indicated by the hundreds of words used to describe subtle emotional distinctions.

Along with finer differentiation of emotions, we find increasing restraint in the expression of emotions. The complete, uninhibited expressions of joy or fear or rage become less and less frequent. Joy comes to be expressed by a chuckle and not by a convulsive laughter. Anger is shown by a frown or a hardening of one's expression and not by enthusiastic screaming, kicking, or biting. The expression of fear may be markedly suppressed until it can be detected only by such "give-away" reactions as perspiration, blanching, or tremor.

It has been suggested that, in our culture at least, there is a continual contest in the matter of emotional expression. As we get older, we acquire more and more effective defenses to hide our emotions from other people. At the same time, we acquire greater and greater skill in penetrating each other's defenses. We become more skillful in interpreting the unconscious indicators of dislike or fear. We pay more attention to the hardening of the mouth line, to the flushing of the skin, or to excessive swallowing.

Anger and Aggression

Anger is the most frequently reported of the powerful emotions with which we have to deal. It may be, of course, that people are more ready to admit anger than fear or sexual impulses. Or it may be that, with us, anger is a very prevalent emotion.

As the child matures, there is a marked change in the situations which will set off his anger. There is also, as we have suggested, a change in his manner of expressing his annoyance. The young child is thrown into a fit of rage by anything which impedes his free physical movement. He becomes angry if his arms are held to his sides, or if they are forcibly moved while he is being dressed. He expresses his anger by crying, stiffening his body, getting red in the face, and threshing around with arms and legs. These outbursts rarely outlast the immediate cause of the annoyance.

The preschool child is more tolerant of brief physical restraint but may become intensely annoyed by anything which interferes with larger units of activity. He resents having to interrupt his activities to have his face washed or to be taken to the toilet. This anger is expressed by vehement protest, screaming, jerking away from the offending adult, and by the well-known temper tantrum. These reach their peak about the age of two. At this stage anger becomes highly socialized and the child frequently indulges in quarreling. From the point of pure frequency, as a matter of fact, quarreling reaches its peak around three or four years of age. Close companions are especially likely to quarrel. These quarrels are often set off by struggles over toys or possessions.

The quarrels of early childhood are likely to be brief and transitory unless they are given formal recognition by the attention of adults. When this happens, there is more at stake, and the quarrel may be prolonged. These quarrels are carried on with enthusiastic screaming, kicking, pommeling, and with occasional resort to biting or spitting. There is also some use of epithet and verbal abuse.

In addition to the anger induced by some specific situation, there is, in preschool children, a certain amount of stored-up aggression that reveals itself in many ways. It has been most carefully studied in standard doll-play situations in which the child plays with furniture, utensils, and with dolls, representing the father, the mother, the baby, the older brother, and other members of the family. This aggression is more marked in boys than in girls(1) especially with respect to the father doll. It is also reported that a boy will show more aggression toward the father doll when his father is away from home. The aggression shown by girls is not affected by the father's absence. We must be careful, of course, not to jump to conclusions as to what causes what in this case. For boys, this doll-play aggression reaches its peak about the age of three(2).

During the elementary-school period, anger becomes more and more a social matter. True enough, tempers can be lost over obstreperous mechanisms or over knots that refuse to become untied. It is the social annoyance, however, which predominates. During this stage there is more quarreling among boys than among girls, and the boys go about their conflicts in more direct fashion. These quarrels may result in pitched battles, scheming for revenge, and in a considerable exchange of insult and epithet.

For the adolescent, physical frustrations continue to be hard to take. Mechanical failure is also a serious source of annoyance. A broken shoelace, a lost earring, a car that refuses to start, any one of these may be the occasion for a wild display of temper. As might be expected, however, these physical matters become less and less important. It is the social slight that rankles. Anger is also set off by being treated unfairly or by being lied to. Sarcasm, bossiness, nagging, being reminded of the virtues of brothers or sisters—all these contribute to the annoyance of the young adolescent. At this stage also anger can come from annoying mannerisms or characteristics of parents even when those mannerisms do not interfere with the activities of the adolescent.

Nothing is more likely to provoke fierce resentment than to be left out of a party, to be snubbed, or to be considered unimportant. At this stage, girls are more frequently involved than boys. And, as folklore has maintained, girls go about their quarrels in less direct fashion. Whereas boys may "have it out," girls are more likely to complain to a third party or to try to gain sympathy, supporters, or allies for their cause. For both sexes, of course, verbal expression comes more and more to dominate. Except in the heat of a game which involves close physical contact, verbal aggression is the chief means of expressing anger among students, both boys and girls, of the high-school level. About this age, many students gain some skill in "keeping their temper," or in refraining from any overt expression of anger. With increasing experience, a few individuals become able to inhibit the more important semiautomatic indicators of rage. They learn to avoid any distortion of the features, to keep from trembling, and to speak in a quiet, controlled manner.

It may be surprising to note the amount of suppressed hostility or aggression on the part of adolescents. In studies of adolescent fantasy or projection, hostility is by long odds the dominating theme. In one study(3) one fourth of all the fantasies dealt with hostility, with "getting even," or with "putting someone in his place." Surprising as it may seem, hostility was far ahead of romance or sex. Aggressive themes exceeded the more tender fantasies by a ratio of four to one.

A fair share of this extensive hostility of the adolescent is directed against his parents. This is especially true in later adolescence. The source of this hostility seems to be the age-old problem of too much control and direction on the part of the parents as expressed either by direct orders or by excessive advice, questioning, or "nagging."

At first glance, it seems appalling and sad that so much of the adolescent's inner life should be taken up with fantasies of hostility. It would seem that this inner life ought to be richer and directed to more important things, or at least to more pleasant and constructive things. It is much too soon, of course, to say just what can be done about this situation, or even what should be done. Certainly, however, the teacher should be sympathetically aware of this problem as he faces his classes. Certainly, too, as we point out in the next chapter, he will work to keep this suppressed hostility from reaching the danger point.

Fears and Worries

The infant is likely to be afraid of any intense or unexpected stimulus. A loud noise, a sudden flash of light, a sudden movement of the body, a rough push for which there has been no preparation, any of these will elicit fear reactions in the young infant. Later on he acquires new fears. He is frightened of high places, of the dark, and of strange people. Still later he may be frightened of some imaginary creatures, of being alone, or even of some free-floating, generalized danger.

As new fears develop, older menaces may drop off. Fear of a loud noise may come to have little emotional effect. Strange people may fail to frighten the preschool child, and a certain amount of tolerance for high places may develop.

In the changes just sketched, learning and experience undoubtedly play a large part. Through experience, new fears are acquired, and through experience, we become habituated to dangers. We cannot be sure, however, that all changes are due to learning or experience. Fear of strange people, for instance, appears so often that some students believe it to be largely the result of maturation. Certainly changes in fears are not always caused by the direct personal experience of the child. Fear of wild animals plays a large part in the lives of many children, yet only an inconsequential proportion of children have ever been attacked or bothered by wild animals.

Perhaps age and maturation act chiefly by increasing the powers of perceiving and understanding, and these increased powers, in turn, lead to fear of the newly perceived or appreciated danger. Fear of disease, for instance, may be impossible without some knowledge of the disease, and, conversely, knowledge or understanding of the disease may lead to fear, or perhaps to outright acquisition of symptoms. It is often held that the illnesses of medical students follow the course of instruction in pathology.

What has been said about changes in fears is reflected also in changes in worries. When asked to make a list of things that worry them, boys and girls in the first grades frequently mention accidents, kidnapping, or other examples of physical violence or injury. By the age of nine, fear of the dark is still a problem and the fear that parents may die is becoming important. By the end of the elementary-school period, however, these latter fears have decreased sharply. Many children express worries about habits they seem powerless to break. Almost one third of children say they worry about nail biting(4) and this worry is more pronounced among the older children.

By grade four we find worries about school subjects, arithmetic and geography being mentioned frequently. Even at this stage there is also some concern about a career. These matters assume even greater importance later on and form a considerable share of the worries of high-school students and college students. School failure, especially, is mentioned frequently by both high-school and college students. Loss of social standing, social awkwardness, or bad manners begin to worry the high-school student and continue as problems into college. Financial matters are also frequently mentioned in late adolescence(5). Among college students, fear of scholastic failure still looms large while financial concerns are even more important. During the high-school or college period there is also some worry about possible moral unworthiness, about religion, and about a satisfactory philosophy of life. Concern about this matter may become increasingly important beyond the period of adolescence. Disturbance about love, courtship, or romantic problems increases during adolescence and into the late twenties. For people beyond the twenties this problem causes less concern.

Joy or Happiness

When a child is asked to describe one of the happiest days in his life he may recall a variety of events. For children under the age of twelve, the outstanding occasion for happy memories is a holiday(6) or some festive event. After the age of twelve this feature loses its outstanding attraction but continues to play some part. Girls over twelve refer most frequently to occasions involving close companionship of relatives or friends. This source of happiness, by the way, ranks high with younger girls also but is of only moderate importance for boys. Trips, camping or otherwise, are also mentioned frequently by both sexes and at all ages, becoming the outstanding incident for boys over fifteen. Sports are also mentioned frequently by boys, becoming slightly more important as the boy gets older. The receipt of gifts ranks close to trips for younger boys and girls, but drops in importance, especially for girls, after the age of twelve. Two sources of happiness seldom mentioned before the age of fifteen come to play an important part thereafter. These are memories of success or achievement in or out of school, and occasions such as the end of the war or some other event where the benefits were general and not chiefly personal.

Affection

As the child comes to know more and more people, it is natural that the group for whom he feels some affection should become somewhat larger. To be sure, there is some dropping out and replacement. The new friend or sweetheart displaces the old. To a large extent, however, these new friends are added with few casualties among the old. Affection for parents persists as affection also becomes focused on playmates and on other adults. Fondness for the chums back home does not necessarily interfere with affection for the college friend. Devotion to a sweetheart does not necessarily lessen love for one's home or affection for friends at the fraternity or office.

Although new friends do not inevitably replace old, it is still true that affectionate relations are subject to a well-known cycle that may lead finally to coolness or estrangement. Very often there is excessive and unrealistic affection at first. The child's love for his parents makes them appear perfect. His fondness for his new friend clothes that friend in raiment that no mortal can wear for very long. The inevitable disillusionment may bring with it such revulsion and anger that the affection may never return. Fortunately, however, this pendulum swing is usually followed by a more realistic affection based on a more complete and more tolerant understanding. Parents have faults but also many virtues and vast attractiveness. The friend may irritate us in many ways, but considering the fact that he is human, he is a very wonderful person.

Insofar as these forces operate, we should find that the child, in growing older, acquires a wider circle of friends, dropping some friends, of course, but fitting his new friendships into the old patterns. With each new friendship, there may be the pendulum swing from excess to disillusion, and from disillusionment to a more balanced position. Within the over-all cluster of friends, however, there should be an increasingly realistic evaluation and an affection that can persist in spite of acknowledged defects. As the student grows older, moreover, there will be an increasing number of criteria in the way of manners, character, social standing, or appearance that any new candidate for friendship must have before he is to be considered seriously.

Interests, Attitudes, Ideals

These things included under the term *interests* cover a very wide range. By the use of factor analysis, Guilford(7) and his associates have tried to bring some order into the picture. Starting with 1000 statements of various kinds of interests, they have isolated some 28 separate factors, which still leaves the matter highly complicated. They suggest that 6 of these factors have to do with vocational or career interests. Most of the remainder, however, refer to the major ways in which a person searches for basic satisfaction.

As in the field of general personality, it is apparently too early to seek a usable description of the basic patterns of interests. Lacking such an organized picture, we can merely describe the various kinds of interests that have been investigated, being careful to remember that the groupings and labels we use must not be taken too seriously.

Recreational Interests

Play. Prior to the school years, there is a steady increase in the number of play activities. The six-year-old plays a larger number of games than the two-year-old and spends more of his time in play. Early in the school period, however, the number of play activities reaches its peak, and from the early grades on the trend is reversed. From grades four through eight, the most popular activities as reported by questionnaires are not play but television or radio(8), movies, and reading, although there may be such unorganized play as roller skating or playing catch. In general, in the latter half of the elementary school the student plays fewer games and spends less of his time in play.

As children grow older, there are changes not only in the amount of play but also in the nature and complexity of the games. For the young child, the play consists of sheer manipulation, moving objects from one place to another, putting sticks in bottles, or piling up sand. Later the play involves a definite pattern and even a complex set of rules.

Toward the end of the elementary school, more extensive recreational activities are undertaken. About this time, camping and hiking become very attractive activities. Team games involving extended schedules also become popular. Interest in sports also becomes more specialized. One or two popular games or activities may absorb a considerable share of the energy, to the exclusion of all other recreational activities.

As the student proceeds through adolescence, actual participation in sports falls off rapidly, especially for girls. Very few girls, and only a minority of the boys, continue to play active games. This is not to say, of course, that there is no interest in sports. On the contrary, the older adolescent, both boy and girl, becomes an enthusiastic spectator and follower of the current sports. Students of this age divide into a few performers, on the one hand, and a much larger group of "rooters" or supporters, on the other hand. In the United States football has been the most popular organized sport with adolescents. In most sections of the country, swimming is the most popular unorganized sport.

Conversation. "Talk" or conversation is an entrancing activity from the very early years. The young child maintains a running commentary on his own doings; asks questions, not necessarily waiting for an answer; and chatters endlessly. Later on, the conversation becomes more functional and fits in more closely with larger activities. At all times, talking serves several functions. Ordinarily, it is a sign of friendly recognition of the other person. For human beings, "talk" serves the same function that back-scratching or grooming serves in other animals. It is a gesture by which we acknowledge and accept the presence of the other person. Silence or lack of conversation may be interpreted as hostility or coolness.

In addition to serving as a loose social binder or as a dignified substitute for back-scratching, conversation can be highly functional. It enables the young child to get a drink of water, as well as attention. It enables the older child to cooperate with his playmates or to assault his enemies. At all ages, conversation is used to have one's wishes carried out, to formulate ideas, and to express and perhaps relieve tensions, fears, and uncertainties.

By the time the student reaches high school, conversations have become fairly elaborate and have come to play an enormous role in social relations. During the later high-school years, there is a steady increase in conversation about "dates," about general social events, and about sex. The younger high-school student spends much time in discussing the movies, but this topic loses out toward the end of high school. Sports, too, show a rise and fall as a topic of conversation, the peak occurring about the second year of high school.

The trends observed in high school continue into college. "Dates" are perhaps the most frequent subjects of discussion among both men and women. Social activities are typically very popular and fraternity matters are important on some campuses. Sports and dancing are farther down the list. On most campuses, between 1930 and 1950 at least, politics, world affairs, or even grades or studies, played only a minor part.

Adult conversations overheard on city streets or in restaurants show sharp divergences between the sexes. Men talk mostly about money and business and somewhat less about women, surprising as this may be to those who have participated in extensive male discussions. Women talk chiefly about people, especially other women, about men, about clothes, and about home matters. The conversations observed, of course, cover very narrow samples and are confined chiefly to brief, casual conversations in city surroundings.

Reading Interests. Before he can read, and just as he enters school, the young child prefers to hear short, improbable stories about animals, fairies, and young children. Humanized stories of animals and their young are especially attractive. These early interests persist after the child has begun to read on his own. Interest in comics also develops early and this interest persists into the late teens. During the first three grades, *Bambi, Little Black Sambo, Cinderella, Pinocchio,* and *Billy and Blaze* are the great favorites. At the time of this investigation(9), both *Bambi* and *Pinocchio* had profited from the attentions of Mr. Disney, but *Cinderella,* at that time, made the grade on her own merit.

In grades four to six, animals and animal adventures are still important. During 1945, *Lassie* was a great favorite in these grades. *Black Beauty* and *Mr. Popper's Penguins* were also popular. In these grades, *Tom Sawyer* has a number of devotees, and the occasional child votes for *Alice in Wonderland.*

For many students, the period in grades seven and eight sees the peak of reading for entertainment. Girls read more than boys. Comic books and fiction form the most important items for both sexes, with the girls having a slight preference for fiction. Interest in fiction ranges from juvenile stories (*Sue Barton*) to books intended for adults (*A Tree Grows in Brooklyn*). Even at this age, animal stories still retain their appeal. *Lassie* and *Silver Chief: Dog of the North* have large followings. Adventure and Westerns are also popular, and Robin Hood, Robinson Crusoe, and Buffalo Bill receive many votes. At this age there is also some interest in sports, such books as *All American* and *World Series* being fairly popular.

In grades seven and eight there is considerable magazine and newspaper reading—or at least magazine "looking." One group of 700 students listed 67 favorite magazines(10). Of these, *Life* led the field. When reading newspapers, both sexes of these grades turn to the comics first and then to the general news. A few years later, the boys may turn to the sports section as soon as they finish the comics, and then to the general news.

Radio, Television, and Movie Interests. For young children of either sex, the favorite programs in radio, television, and in the movies are the Westerns and the stories of fantastic adventure(11, 12, 13, 14). In TV and in the movies, cartoon stories are also popular. At the high-school level there are clear sex differences in preferences. On all three media, boys prefer sports, comedy, and adventure. On television and radio, the typical variety show is also popular with high-school girls. Regular plays are popular, however, and in the movies, musical shows and plays of romance receive the first votes of most girls.

In the case of television there may be a new factor at work. At both elementary-school and high-school level many students give as their top favorite the program that is most popular among adults. At one time both elementary-school students and high-school students gave first place to *I Love Lucy.* A few years later it was *Dragnet.* It was only in the second-place choices that the youthful preference for *Roy Rogers* or *Superman* became distinguished from the high-school preference for sports, *Arthur Godfrey,* or *Toast of the Town.*

Television is most popular with young children, where it is a three-to-one choice over radio(12). In urban areas many elementary-school children spend twenty hours per week watching TV. High-school students spend somewhat less time with this medium.

Hobbies and Collecting. It is difficult to see a clear pattern of changes in hobbies or collecting as children grow older. As is suggested by Figure

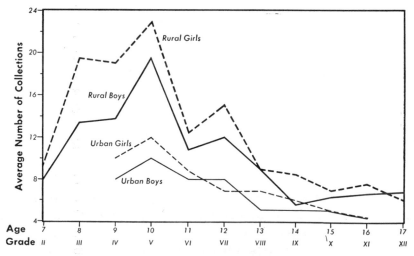

FIGURE 17-1. *Amount of Collecting by Rural and Urban Children of Different Ages.* Redrawn by permission from Figure 293 in Shuttleworth (See Fig. 5-2 for reference).

17-1, collecting reaches its peak by the age of ten or eleven. This is especially true for collections of such miscellaneous items as matchbook covers, streetcar transfers, or playing cards. More serious collecting of autographs or letters, on the other hand, may continue for a longer time, and stamp collecting, of course, may become a lifelong hobby. At most ages, girls are more given to collecting than boys, and girls are more likely to collect things that have some esthetic value in themselves.

Other hobbies also reach their peak about the beginning of high school. During high school, there is a steady decline in such things as constructing model airplanes, working with electrical equipment, or making doll clothes.

Interests as an Index of Maturity

Clearly there are rather definite changes in interest as the child grows older. This fact has led to the development of age scales or measures of maturity of interests. In the Furfey scale(15), for instance, a boy is asked whether he would rather "be a cowboy or a newspaper reporter, dance or play 'Puss in the Corner,' see a beautiful sunset or a fairy prince, think about college life or think about pirates."

In these illustrations, it is not hard even for the layman to pick out the choices of the more mature students. Other choices in the same scale are not so sharply differentiated. In these latter items, the more mature choice has been determined by referring to the actual preferences of older children.

The Furfey scale, by the way, is especially designed for boys. A companion scale more suitable for girls has been constructed by Sullivan(16).

Vocational Interests

As might be expected, the vocational aspirations of the young child are based almost entirely on such things as glamor or excitement. Among children in the early grades, a few occupations, such as fireman, soldier, pilot, cowboy, or movie actress, will take care of most of the choices. Toward the end of the elementary school, however, the choices become more widespread and include some of the less obvious avenues for excitement, but those choices are still very unrealistic and are not such as to be taken seriously.

It is in the early high-school years that vocational choices settle down, so to speak, and begin to exert a serious influence on the student's actual work. Ideas in effect at this time should be given earnest consideration.

The most striking feature of vocational interests at this period is the disparity between the choices, on the one hand, and the actual opportunities, on the other. In the 1930's and 1940's, for instance, 90 percent of boys wished for white-collar jobs, in spite of the fact that only 3 percent of adult men at that time were engaged in white-collar occupations. As time goes on, of course, it is possible that the proportion of these professional jobs may increase, or the attractiveness of such jobs may diminish. Insofar as the discrepancy persists, however, it will make for a great deal of disappointment and possibly for a very sour social situation. It would seem important that the teacher should be careful not to oversell the white-collar vocations and should make sure that the student is aware of the very real dignity and substantial rewards of many of the skilled manual occupations. To bring out the advantages of various occupations, many teachers use such devices as pamphlets, motion pictures, talks by people in various jobs, visits to work that is going on, or actual work experience.

Along with the tendency to ignore job opportunities, the teacher will find a companion tendency on the part of high-school students to ignore special abilities or the lack of them. High-school students are not likely to consider whether or not they have the ability required to become a doctor or lawyer or business executive. Without some careful advice or instruction, students are apt to assume that anyone can succeed in any occupation provided he has the interest, the courage, the determination, and, of course, his fair share of good luck.

Like so many other things, vocational interests have been subjected to factor analysis. One study(17) suggests that preferences cluster along the lines of varied versus routine work, indoor versus outdoor, hazardous versus safe, sedentary versus physically active, working in isolation as opposed to working in a crowd, and work that is meticulous and exacting as opposed to that which is rough-and-ready.

Persistence of Vocational Interests. Within the high-school years there is a considerable permanence in vocational interests(18). As students grow older many of them show a greater interest in selling and other occupations in which persuasion is involved. Apart from this, however, the interests indicated in grade nine tend to hold at the end of high school. For older students, the constancy of vocational interests is even more pronounced. Strong(19) found that the interests indicated during the college period showed a correlation of about .75 with the interests of the same men when tested twenty-two years later. This is about the same correlation as we observe between grades nine and twelve.

Attitudes

As students become older, they acquire more and more elements from which a strongly socialized character may be built. Typically in our culture, for instance, high-school boys acquire more sympathy for the weak or helpless. They acquire more feeling for social causes or crusades, and they develop stronger feelings of loyalty toward people they know or admire(20). The mere availability of these elements, however, will not guarantee that they will be used for improved social attitudes. During college years there is usually a general increase in understanding and tolerance for other cultures and other political views(21, 22).

In general it appears that many of the specific attitudes of students closely reflect the prevailing attitudes in the home and community(23, 24). With respect to feelings toward specific national groups we also note that children of one decade seem to reflect the views of their predecessors in the decade before(25).

Religious Attitudes. Most investigations show a decrease in religious practices and in formal doctrinal beliefs on the part of older students. Older students, certainly, profess less belief in such specific doctrines as the virgin birth of Christ, a literal heaven or hell, or in a God that has human form or attributes. There is less change, however, in the abstract beliefs regarding some eternal governing principle, the fellowship of man, or the immortality of the spirit. There is also, among college students, a growing tolerance for divergent beliefs. Some, but not all, of these changes are attributed to specific college courses.

Ideals. As children grow older, the change in their ideals follows an irregular but definite pattern. Young girls tend to admire people who are quick and "funny." As they enter adolescence, girls reserve their admiration for people who approach adult standards and who do more or less what adults expect of them. Still later, the emphasis is on the glamorous, lively, entertaining person. For boys, there is a fairly steady change from admiration for the rebel against adult authority to admiration for courage that operates more in conformity to adult standards(26).

After the early years of adolescence, both sexes increasingly stress reliability, broad-mindedness, and willingness to cooperate as the qualities they admire. Among the college group there is a steady decrease in admiration for sheer liveliness or clowning.

In addition to the changes in the qualities admired, there is a fairly definite sequence in the kind of people likely to be idealized. Very young children are likely to build their ideals around a somewhat older friend, or around one of the parents. Still later they may idealize a teacher. In the late elementary-school period, the ideals may shift to some adult in the community, to a scoutmaster, to a lifeguard, or to a local athlete. During high school, the idealized person may be a public figure, such as a baseball star, movie actor, or a military or aviation hero. At this stage, historical personages may also become the ideal(27).

Prejudice

One of the most important attitudes that we might consider is that of a bitter and distorted dislike for members of another group. Prejudice such as this not only makes for an unhealthy society and for unhappy minorities, but may also have a corrosive effect on the person who nurtures the attitude.

To decry these distorted and malicious views is not, of course, to say that everyone must love everyone else and that all enmities must be resolved. A vigorous, open, and enthusiastic antagonism between equals is something that many people would regard as fairly wholesome. Certainly the world would lose some of its sparkle if we were to wipe out all the antipathy between Republican and Democrat, between capital and labor, or between Florida and California.

The Structure of Prejudice. Is it proper to say that a person is prejudiced or not prejudiced in general? Or is it possible that a person may be extremely prejudiced toward one group and may still feel no prejudice whatever toward another group? There has been a great deal of argument on this point. Frenkel-Brunswik(28) and her associates, in the elaborate California study, claim that prejudice is a fairly general factor, that it is an integral part of one's personality and intimately associated with the kind of home life during early childhood. These workers(29) hold that the gentile, Anglo-Californian child who shows prejudice toward Negroes is also the child who shows prejudice toward Jews, Mexicans, and Chinese. The child who is tolerant toward one of these minority groups, on the other hand, is tolerant toward all. Other investigators(30), however, have not always found this neat correlation. The familiar technique of factor analysis also suggests that prejudice against Jews may be different from prejudice against Negroes. This same technique suggests that some aspects of prejudice are related to nationalism, others to puritanism, and still others to a fear of socialism.

Apparently it is too soon to decide whether or not prejudice is a single thing and typical of a certain kind of personality. But whether it is one thing or many separate things, it is probable that marked prejudice, in one form or another, goes along with other personality traits. The California investigators, working from a Freudian base, suggest that prejudice—a single thing in their eyes—is the mark of a sick personality. In their view the prejudiced person abhors any departure from the approved way of doing things, is somewhat puritanical, has a great respect for strength, and has contempt for the intellectual, whom he regards as a weakling. This pattern of personality is related in turn to the early home life. It is said that the parents of the prejudiced were greatly concerned about social status and were also unduly restrictive, punishing the child for any hostility shown to the parents. It is suggested, of course, that this program of child rearing brings about a sick personality and that it is the suppressed hostility and related traits that later lead to prejudice and to other undesirable traits. Other investigators, however, do not believe that this elaborate train of causation is established. They suggest that children may take over their parents' attitudes directly, even if no hostility or other stress were induced. Adolescents' attitudes toward Russia, for instance, are more closely linked to the direct attitude of their parents than to any basic hostility the children may feel(24).

Prejudice, whether one thing or many, seems to be typical of people who are suspicious, worried, apprehensive, lacking in self-control, and a little bewildered at the raw deal life has given them(31, 32). The highly prejudiced may also be more "rigid." To get at this trait of rigidity, a group of people are given problems to solve and are shown one method or approach that works very well for these problems. They are then given other problems, some of which can be solved by much simpler methods. The highly prejudiced are held to be less likely to see the simpler solution or to break away from the method they have already mastered. Like so many other aspects of this important area, however, this suggestion has also been challenged(33), and it has been held that it is all a matter of being too quick to generalize. The man who generalizes too readily may condemn a whole group because of the behavior of one member of the group and thus become prejudiced. The same man may too readily conclude that the way to solve one problem is the way to solve all problems. Although leading to the same result in this case, this poor reasoning ability, or hasty inference, is probably different from the concept of the sick personality who rigidly and fearfully refuses to look at other possibilities.

The Development of Prejudice. To be aware of racial or group differences is not the same thing, of course, as being prejudiced. Prejudice must be based on some such awareness, however, and the two things have often been studied together. In some communities this race awareness develops very early(34). By the age of three, for instance, many children are aware of differences in skin color and will react differently to pictures that are identical except for the fact that one includes Negroes and the other does not. At this age there is no clear preference, but the remarks and other actions show that the difference in color is noticed. Although these differences in color are perceived at an early age, few children before the age of three or four refer to such differences in describing themselves or the people they know. After the age of four, however, such distinctions are fairly frequent, and most Negro children especially frequently refer to race in describing themselves and others(35). This early awareness of membership in a minority group, by the way, has also been observed in Jewish children. By the age of four some 75 percent of the Negro children would prefer to be white. They also tend to choose white dolls in preference to Negro dolls. This preference, of course, may be due to the greater prevalence of white dolls and to the fact that until recently Negro dolls were often unnatural if not actual caricatures.

Racial preferences are often tested by pictures of groups of children engaged in various activities. For each activity there is one picture of white children only, one picture of Negro, and one picture of a mixed group. A given child is shown these pictures, one at a time in a random order, and asked if he would like to play this game. By the age of five the game is more attractive to white children if the picture does not contain Negroes. This preference increases with age. By the age of eight or nine children tend to acquire the prejudices typical of the adults around them.

Instead of depending on picture tests and on interviews, we might observe the behavior of children at play when both white and Negro children are present. Prior to the age of nine or ten the age-old boy-girl antipathies govern, and race makes less difference. Beyond this point, however, race cleavages appear, begun, apparently, by Negro children if they happen to be in the majority.

Correlates of Prejudice. Apparently age plays a part in prejudice. What other factors seem to go hand-in-hand with these attitudes? As we have already mentioned, one group of investigators stresses the child-rearing practices of the home. It is also possible that parents in more direct fashion instill attitudes of various kinds. In one community(36), for instance, about one third of the Protestant and Catholic parents spoke of other racial or religious groups in hostile terms or in terms that included all members of the out-group under one unflattering phrase. As many as one quarter of the parents deliberately sought to make their children think poorly of one group or another. Many younger students and some older students say that their attitudes come from parents. Many of the older students, however, also mention other influences. In general, there is some correlation between the prejudice of children and the behavior or attitudes of the parents, but the correlation is far from perfect(29, 37).

In many cases it has been found that students and adults from the lower socioeconomic groups are somewhat more prejudiced toward minority groups. It is impossible to say just which forces are at work here. Education may play a part. So may competition for jobs. In one investigation(38) the lower class school showing the least favorable attitude toward Negroes was also the only school in which Negro students were found. In general, prejudice is higher when there are many members of the minority group in the general vicinity(39). Prejudice is often lower, however, among those who live in closer contact with the minority group, as in the same housing project.

The role of education in this matter is not so clear as we would like to see. There is some suggestion that people with more education are less prejudiced than those with less. But many college students still accept the stereotypes prevalent in their community no matter how ill-founded those stereotypes may be. In one study, anti-Semitism was actually more intense among those with more education.

Knowledge of other groups is no sure antidote for prejudice. There is some relation, of course, but many people who are accurately informed about minority groups still feel some prejudice. Close contact with minority groups, in contrast to living in the same neighborhood, may reduce prejudice. White women living in housing projects that include Negroes express more favorable attitudes than white women in segregated housing projects. Here, of course, we must reckon with reversed causality, since those more favorably inclined to begin with may have been more easily persuaded to live in the integrated housing units. More convincing than the housing evidence, perhaps, is the fact that white soldiers who have served in companies containing Negroes tend to approve of the arrangement much more than soldiers who have never had the experience. In the case of young people attending mixed camps, however, things can work either way. For some children, pencil-paper tests showed a better attitude, but overt behavior changed little. For one group of boys, thought to be rather aggressive, dislike for Negroes increased during camp.

Ethical Behavior and Conduct

Simple Conformity

The young child is very apt to show strong evidence of *negativism*. When asked to do something he may take a very stubborn attitude. We get the feeling that he would have been very glad to wear his sweater, for instance, if only we had not suggested it to him, but now he will not wear it. This negativism is a very real phenomenon. It reaches its peak around two or three years of age and steadily diminishes from then on. It is less frequently observed in elementary school, and becomes very rare by the age of nine or ten.

Suggestibility is the opposite extreme of negativism. It refers to the unthinking execution of almost any suggestion. At the suggestion of an older child or an associate, the young child may jump in the puddle, throw stones at the dog, or perform numerous other acts that bring no satisfaction and much annoyance. This unhesitating acceptance of suggestions is very marked in children of six or seven but is less prevalent from those years on.

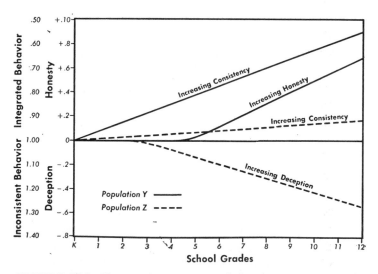

FIGURE 17-2. *Changes in Honesty and Consistency for a High Socioeconomic Group (Y) and for an Underprivileged Group (Z).* Redrawn by permission from Figure 291 in Shuttleworth (See Fig. 5-2 for reference).

It has been suggested(40) that both negativism and suggestibility come from a limited repertoire of social responses. Unable to express slight shades of disagreement, the child merely expresses absolute disagreement. Unable to say effectively, "In a little while," or "Glad to this time, but can't keep doing it forever," the child reacts by an unequivocal "No," and makes up for his lack of explicitness by sheer vehemence and persistence. Similarly, he cannot express qualified agreement. To a positive invitation he is not yet ready to say, "Some other time," or "You go ahead, but I don't like the stuff." If he does not refuse by an absolute and stubborn "No," he must comply with an all-out "Yes." Later, as these subtle shades of agreement and disagreement become available to him, he has less necessity for the protection afforded by the unreasoning but emphatic "No," or for the equally unreasoning and enthusiastic "Yes."

Ideas of Right and Wrong

As might be expected, knowledge of right and wrong increases fairly steadily as the child grows older. This, undoubtedly, is partly due to increased understanding. It takes a certain amount of perspicacity to grasp some of the more intricate ethical problems, and this increased understanding should boost the score on a test of ethical knowledge.

Children of different ages differ in the things that they hold wrong. In the classical investigations, for instance, six-year-olds are chiefly perturbed by smoking, card playing, and divorce, whereas these problems are of little concern to older adolescents. Such things as bribery or being conceited, on the other hand, leave the young children undisturbed but are serious matters for the college student. Along with this shift in the emphasis given various infractions, there is also an increase in minor distinctions. Older children are more reconciled to "white" or "social" lies, whereas for the young child, "lying is lying."

This increase in ethical knowledge and in subtle ethical distinctions, of course, is by no means the same thing as increased morality. Juvenile delinquents, as a matter of fact, often equal other children in scores on these tests(41).

Performance on Objective Tests

On tests of honesty, cooperation, or altruism, there is little clear-cut relation to the age of the child. In tests of honesty or cheating, however, the child does come to reflect his home background more and more as he becomes older. In Figure 17-2, for instance, we see a much clearer relation between socioeconomic status and cheating in the case of older children.

Persistence, like self-control, does increase fairly steadily with age. The older child will spend more time in trying to solve difficult problems and shows more power to resist tempting distractions(42).

Delinquency

A great deal of attention is being given to delinquency and it is commonly assumed that this problem is reaching more serious proportions. This may well be true. Certainly it seems that youthful offenders are much more closely organized, more defiant, and occasionally go in for more atrocious crimes. It is difficult to say, however, whether or not the common run of delinquency is increasing. Only a small fraction of delinquencies, perhaps less than 2 percent, ever become matter of record or play a part in our statistics. In one study(43), for instance, some 114 boys were known to have committed over 6000 violations of the law during a five-year period. Of these 6000 violations, however, only 95 were ever matters of official complaint or came in for public attention. Yet it is upon this small fraction of the cases that we get our impression that delinquency is rising or falling. A moderate increase in the proportion of reported cases would give the impression that the amount of delinquency had doubled or trebled.

The amount and kind of delinquency reported to clinics and police authorities naturally changes with age. The little child has small powers for criminality or delinquency. The older child is not so handicapped. A very typical trend is shown in Figure 17-3. Even by the tender age of six, there is a sharp increase in the number of children reported to clinics for serious conduct problems(44). During the elementary-school period, these problems are running away, being unmanageable, and destructiveness. As they grow older, more and more children are reported to the clinics, to the truant officers, or to the police. For boys, serious delinquency reaches its peak during the late teens, and for girls, a little earlier. At all ages, however, girls form only a fraction of the reported delinquents. Young delinquents continue the destructiveness shown by the younger problem children. In addition to this early form of trouble-making, the delinquents are also accused of incorrigibility, habitual truancy, and theft. Among older delinquents, there are also reports of assault and sexual offenses. These statements hold chiefly for boys. For girls, sex offenses predominate.

Beyond the twenties, there is a fairly steady decline in delinquency. Fewer older people are brought to trial. Of the people who have been convicted, the older parolees have a better record for reforming and "going straight" than the younger(45).

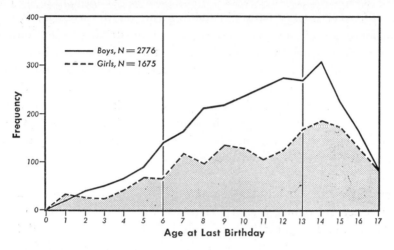

FIGURE 17-3. *Number of Problem Children Reported from Different Age Groups.* Redrawn by permission from Figure 328 in Shuttleworth (See Fig. 5-2 for reference).

The Nature of the Delinquent and His Background

Inevitably, a great deal of attention has been given to the factors associated with delinquency. Certainly there are wide individual differences and one can find exceptions to any general statement that can be made. With these conditions in mind, however, we can trace a sort of composite picture for the youthful delinquent boy.

Home Background. The delinquent comes from an exceptionally unfortunate background. His home is likely to be in the slums where his family moves frequently from one address to another. In poorer times the meager family income came only partly from legitimate earnings and was supplemented by relief or criminal enterprises. Frequently he did not live with either parent but was handed around from unmarried mother to grandmother or to some other relative. Other delinquents live with the mother, the father being absent from the home. In any case, the home he lives in is likely to be characterized by criminality, immorality, and mental retardation. There is little supervision of the boy and less than ordinary understanding of his interests and concerns(46). The attitude of the adults in the home is likely to be one of indifference or outright hostility. We must keep reminding ourselves, of course, that these statements hold for the average, and that many delinquents come from much less sordid surroundings.

Intelligence. Intellectually the delinquent, on the average, is somewhat below normal, but again there are many striking exceptions. His school work is especially poor, being more deficient than his intelligence would suggest(47). One of the most characteristic traits of the delinquent, indeed, is his dislike for school, his rebellion against it, and his poor scholastic performance. His recreational interests include excessive movie attendance, a tendency to play in distant neighborhoods, to go in for irregular activities such as stealing rides, smoking at an early age, and an aversion to supervised playgrounds.

Personality. On the adjustment side, the delinquent has more than his share of nervous habits, is short on realism, and has less insight into his own make-up. He is particularly blind to his limitations and has an unwarranted self-confidence. He readily blames others for his failures. On the other hand, he does not lack vigor. Of an athletic build, he is adventurous, assertive, self-confident, feels that he counts in this world, and is regarded as lively or vivacious(48, 49).

Can these different descriptions be organized into a few meaningful factors? Lorr and Jenkins(50) suggest that we can separate the traits which characterize the delinquent and truant (socialized aggression) from those which are typical of the withdrawn or overinhibited child. They also distinguish between the more organized and deliberate socialized delinquency on the one hand and the unplanned, unorganized, unsocialized aggression on the other.

From studies such as these it may be possible in the future to select with some accuracy those children who are delinquent prone(51, 52).

Reducing Delinquency

This description of the home life and the general environment of the delinquent presents a grim picture. To a large extent these are the children who never had a chance. A drastic improvement in the environment is called for in any case, and it would seem natural to assume that such an improvement would reduce the amount of delinquency. We must remember, of course, that these statistical relations may be complex and that it is dangerous to jump to a conclusion as to what is causing what.

In this case, moreover, we must remember that some factor is at work to lead parents to neglect or hate their children or to go in for a life of drunkenness and crime. And this same factor or deficiency might affect the child even though the superficial home condition were improved. It is also possible that the delinquency of the child may contribute to the disruption of home life and may lead to hostility or rejection on the part of the parents.

These complexities which, in all honesty, we are compelled to face, should caution us against promising too much for any remedial program until that program has been tried out. The experimental studies show a variety of results(53). Certain programs that have aimed at arousing community concern and at providing better recreation and supervision have reported favorable results. Favorable results have also been reported by individual workers who gradually attached themselves to gangs and gained their confidence(54), but failures(55) in this respect must also be noted.

Many of the reports just described have come from projects which, understandably enough, were designed primarily to help the boys, and only incidentally designed to get unambiguous evidence regarding the effectiveness of the plan. It is not surprising, then, that some of these investigations leave something to be desired from the scientific point of view. It is most discouraging to report that the more carefully designed investigations report results that are not nearly so promising. The most ambitious investigation of all(56) found almost no difference in the delinquency of a group of predelinquents counseled over a period of years and a matched control group of boys left to their own devices. Careful as this experiment was, however, it is not without its critics, and some of the latter suggest that the elimination of the defects might give us more hopeful results.

Summary

Whether or not the actual content of an emotion changes with the passing years, there can be no doubt that the emotions come to be expressed in different fashion, and that they are set off by different situations. For very young infants, it is difficult to tell whether the emotion expressed is pleasant or unpleasant. But this rudimentary distinction soon appears and is followed by finer and finer distinctions until the older student becomes capable of expressing a large repertoire of finely shaded emotions. During all this time, the expression of the emotions becomes more restrained and comes to depend chiefly on verbal expression.

In the young child, anger is set off by physical restraint or by interference with play or by the aggression of another person. With older students, social slights are important causes of anger. Hostility or aggressive urges play a large part in the fantasies of adolescents. The worries of students change from fear of obvious physical harm to fear of school failure, fear of social inelegance, and worry about personal unworthiness. The student's feeling of affection comes to include more and more people selected on a more discriminating basis.

Play activities reach their peak in the elementary school. During this period the student spends much time in play and goes in for a wide variety of activities. From then on, he plays fewer games and spends less time in play. From mid-adolescence on, spectator roles predominate, especially for girls. The spontaneous conversations that have been observed in high school and college are given over to "dates" and to social activities. Young children, when they read or listen to stories, prefer short, improbable tales of animals or fairies. By grade six, more elaborate animal stories are popular and some interest in general adventure appears. Reading for fun may reach its peak shortly after grade six. The reading interests of young children are reflected in their TV, radio, and movie preferences. During the teens, dance programs and the variety programs become more popular radio fare.

Television interests are not unlike the radio interests, although a new factor may be at work in that the top favorites of children are apt to be the most popular general programs.

The vocational interests of young children run monotonously to fireman, cowboy, soldier. By early high school, there appears some evidence of serious thought and of a degree of persistence. Vocational choices at this age, however, are rarely based on job opportunities or on the student's own special talents.

With increasing age, there develops more sympathy for the underdog, less faith in the detailed points in religious doctrines, but there is little change in the basic general attitude toward spiritual values. Older students are likely to take religious or historical figures as ideals, whereas younger children, of course, are more likely to build their ideals around parents, teachers, or other community persons.

The part that prejudice plays in our make-up may be due to our basic personality and this in turn may stem from our early upbringing. This matter is in great dispute, however. There is even some disagreement whether or not prejudice is a single thing or whether the same person may dislike one minority group and admire another. There is much to suggest that highly prejudiced people are also fearful and bewildered, with a craving for order.

By the age of three, many children are clearly aware of group differences, especially Negro-white differences. At four or five, this distinction plays a big part and is associated with definite preferences for one group. Many Negro children at this age would prefer to be white. The violent expression of prejudice is more frequent in low SES groups. No sure antidote has been found. Education helps at times but not always. Some kinds of close association (housing projects, army life) seem to help, other kinds may hurt.

The moral demands of the home and the community give the child considerable trouble. To the intricacies of these demands he may early react by an irrational "No" or by an unthinking "Yes." Later he makes more subtle distinctions. Moral problems change. The young child worries about smoking; the college student about political graft or the callousness of nations.

Detected delinquency represents only about 2 percent of actual delinquency. Using the former as an index, however, we see a steady increase into the late teens on the part of boys. Girls are less frequently delinquent. The delinquent typically comes from a most squalid environment and from extremely unpromising stock. Normal family life is the exception. He is nervous and has little self-insight. He is slightly below average in intelligence and detests school. He is confident, adventurous, lively and of an athletic build. It is difficult to know what causes what in this cluster of relations. In view of this uncertainty, it is not surprising that as yet there has been no sure preventative of juvenile delinquency.

SPECIFIC REFERENCES

1. Sears, Pauline S. Doll play aggression in normal young children: influence of sex, age, sibling status, father's absence. *Psychol. Monogr.,* 1951, *65* (6).
2. Ammons, Carol H., and Ammons, R. B. Aggression in doll play: Interviews of two- to six-year old white males. *J. genet. Psychol.,* 1953, *82,* 205–213.
3. Symonds, P. M. Inventory of themes in adolescent fantasy. *Amer. J. Orthopsychiat.,* 1945, *15,* 318–328.
4. Remmers, H. H., and Bauernfeind, R. H. *The SRA junior inventory* (Manual). Science Research Associates, 1951.

5. Thorpe, L. P. Mental-health practices at the college level. *Yearb. nat. soc. Stud. Educ.,* 54 (II), 1955, Chap. 11, 236–270.

6. Carmichael, L., ed. *Manual of child psychology.* Wiley, 1954, Chap. 14. Emotional development (Jersild, A. T.).

7. Guilford, J. P., and others. A factor analysis study of human interests. *USAF Hum. Resour. Res. Cent. Res. Bull.,* 1953, No. 53-11, iv.

8. Sullenger, T. E., Parke, Libbie H., and Wallin, Willma K. The leisure time activities of elementary school children. *J. educ. Res.,* 1953, *46,* 551–554.

9. Witty, P., Coomer, Ann, and McBean, Dilla. Children's choices of favorite books: a study conducted in ten elementary schools. *J. educ. Psychol.,* 1946, *37,* 266–278.

10. Andersen, Esther M. A study of leisure-time reading of pupils in junior high school. *Elem. Sch. J.,* 1948, *48,* 258–267.

11. Witty, P. Children's interests in comics, radio, motion pictures and TV. *Educ. Adm. Superv.,* 1952, *38,* 138–147.

12. Witty, P. Comparative studies of interest in TV. *Educ. Adm. Superv.,* 1954, *40,* 321–335.

13. Lyness, P. I. Patterns in the mass communications tastes of the young audience. *J. educ. Psychol.,* 1951, *42,* 449–467.

14. Ricciuti, E. A. Children and radio: a study of listeners and non-listeners to various types of radio programs in terms of selected ability, attitude, and behavior measures. *Genet. Psychol. Monogr..* 1951, *44,* 69–143.

15. Furfey, P. H. A revised scale for measuring developmental age in boys. *Child Develpm.,* 1931, *2,* 102–114.

16. Sullivan, Sister C. A scale for measuring developmental age in girls. *Stud. Psychol. Psychiat. Cathol. Univ. Amer.,* 1934, *3,* No. 4.

17. Long, W. F. A job preference survey for industrial applicants. *J. appl. Psychol.,* 1952, *36,* 333–337.

18. Rosenberg, N. Stability and maturation of Kuder interest patterns during high school. *Educ. psychol. Measmt.,* 1953, *13,* 449–458.

19. Strong, E. K., Jr. Permanence of interest scores over 22 years. *J. appl. Psychol.,* 1951, *35,* 89–91.

20. Leal, Mary A. Personality traits and maturing in children of normal IQ. *J. educ. Res.,* 1931, *23,* 198–209.

21. Davidson, Helen H., and Kruglov, Lorraine P. Some background correlates of personality and social attitudes. *J. soc. Psychol.,* 1953, *38,* 233–240.

22. Mull, Helen K., and Sheldon, Ann. A comparison of students of

1941 and 1951 in a liberal arts college in respect to their understanding of social issues. *J. soc. Psychol.*, 1953, *38*, 283–285.

23. Young, N., Mayans, F., Jr. and Corman, B. R. The political preferences of adolescents. *Teach. Coll. Rec.*, 1953, *54*, 340–344.

24. Helfant, K. Parents' attitudes vs. adolescent hostility in the determination of adolescents' sociopolitical attitudes. *Psychol. Monogr.*, 1952, *66*, (13), 1–23.

25. Zeligs, Rose. Children's concepts and stereotypes of Turk, Portuguese, Roumanian, Arab, Chinese, French-Canadian, mulatto, South American, Hawaiian, and Australian. *J. genet. Psychol.*, 1953, *83*, 171–178.

26. Tryon, Caroline M. Evaluations of adolescent personality by adolescents. *Monogr. Soc. Res. Child Developm.*, 1939, *4*, No. 4.

27. Stoughton, M. Louise, and Ray, Alice M. A study of children's heroes and ideals. *J. exp. Educ.*, 1946, *15*, 156–160.

28. Adorno, T. W., and others. *The authoritarian personality*. Harper, 1950.

29. Frenkel-Brunswik, Else, and Havel, Joan. Prejudice in the interviews of children: Attitudes toward minority groups. *J. genet. Psychol.*, 1953, *82*, 91–136.

30. Campbell, D. T., and McCandless, B. R. Ethnocentrism, xenophobia and personality. *Hum. Relat.*, 1951, *4*, 185–192.

31. Gough, H. C. Studies of social intolerance. (Parts I–IV). *J. soc. Psychol.*, 1951, *33*, 237–246; 247–255; 257–262; 263–269.

32. Vosk, M. Correlates of prejudice. *Rev. educ. Res.*, 1953, *23*, 353–361.

33. Levitt, E. E., and Zelen, S. L. The validity of the Einstellung test as a measure of rigidity. *J. abnorm. soc. Psychol.*, 1953, *48*, 573–580.

34. Landreth, Catherine, and Johnson, Barbara C. Young children's responses to a picture and inset test designed to reveal reactions to persons of different skin color. *Child Developm.*, 1953, *24*, 63–80.

35. Goodman, M. E. *Race awareness in young children*. Addison-Wesley Press, 1952.

36. Radke-Yarrow, Marian, Trager, Helen, and Miller, Jean. The role of parents in the development of children's ethnic attitudes. *Child Developm.*, 1952, *23*, 13–53.

37. Bird, C., Monachesi, E. D., and Burdick, H. Studies of group tensions: III. The effect of parental discouragement of play activities upon the attitudes of white children toward Negroes. *Child Developm.*, 1952, *23*, 295–306.

38. Hayes, Margaret L. Attitudes of high school students toward Negro problems. *J. educ. Res.*, 1953, *46*, 615–619.

39. Hofstaetter, P. R. A factorial study of cultural patterns in the U.S. *J. Psychol.*, 1951, *32*, 99–113.

40. Anderson, J. E. *The psychology of development and personal adjustment.* Holt, 1949, p. 276.

41. Bartlett, E. R., and Harris, D. B. Personality factors in delinquency. *Sch. & Soc.*, 1936, *43*, 653–656.

42. Kremer, A. H. The nature of persistence. *Stud. Psychol. Psychiat. Cathol. Univ. Amer.*, 1942, *5*, No. 8.

43. Murphy, F. J., Shirley, Mary M., and Witmer, Helen L. The incidence of hidden delinquency. *Amer. J. Orthopsychiat.*, 1946, *16*, 686–696.

44. Ackerson, L. *Children's behavior problems.* Vol. II. Relative importance and interrelations among traits. University of Chicago Press, 1931.

45. Metfessel, M., and Lovell, Constance. Recent literature on individual correlates of crime. *Psychol. Bull.*, 1942, *39*, 133–164.

46. Cass, Loretta K. Parent-child relationships and delinquency. *J. abnorm. soc. Psychol.*, 1952, *47*, 101–104.

47. Eckenrode, C. J. Their achievement is delinquency. *J. educ. Res.*, 1950, *43*, 554–558.

48. Glueck, S., and Glueck, Eleanor. *Unravelling juvenile delinquency.* Commonwealth Fund, 1950.

49. Gough, H. G., and Peterson, D. R. The identification and measurement of predispositional factors in crime and delinquency. *J. consult. Psychol.*, 1952, *16*, 207–212.

50. Lorr, M., and Jenkins, R. L. Patterns of maladjustment in children. *J. clin. Psychol.*, 1953, *9*, 16–19.

51. Hathaway, S. R., and Monachesi, E. D., eds. *Analyzing and predicting juvenile delinquency with the MMPI.* University of Minnesota Press, 1953.

52. Axelrad, S., and Glick, Selma J. Application of the Glueck Social Prediction Tables to 100 Jewish delinquent boys. *Jewish soc. Service Quart.*, 1953, *30*, (2), 127–136.

53. Witmer, Helen L., and Tufts, Edith. *The effectiveness of delinquency prevention programs.* U.S. Dept. Hlth. Educ. & Welf. U.S. Govt. Printing Office, 1954.

54. Crawford, P. L., Malamud, D., and Dumpson, J. R. *Working with teen age groups.* Welfare Council of New York City, 1950.

55. Mitchell, R. Capturing boys' gangs. *Human Organization,* 1951 (Summer), *10*, 26–31.

56. Powers, E., and Witmer, Helen. *An experiment in the prevention of delinquency.* The Cambridge-Somerville Youth Study. Columbia University Press, 1951.

SUGGESTIONS FOR FURTHER READING

1. Carmichael, L., ed. *Manual of child psychology.* Wiley, 1954.

    Chap. 11. The adolescent (Horrocks, J. E.).

    Chap. 13. Character development in children—an objective approach (Jones, V.).

    Chap. 14. Emotional development (Jersild, A. T.).

    These three chapters provide a great deal of information on many of the specialized aspects of personality.

2. Lindzey, G., ed. *Handbook of social psychology.* Addison-Wesley, 1954, Vol. II, Chap. 27. Prejudice and ethnic relations (Harding, J., Kutner, B., Proshansky, H., and Chein, I.).

    An inclusive summary of the investigations in this complex field.

3. Allport, G. W. *The nature of prejudice.* Addison-Wesley, 1954.

    A more extended and more general treatment than that given in the *Handbook.*

4. Adorno, T. W., Frenkel-Brunswik, Else, Levinson, D. J., and Sanford, R. N. *The authoritarian personality.* Harper, 1950.

5. Christie, R., and Jahoda, Marie, eds. *Studies in scope and method of "the authoritarian personality."* Free Press, 1954.

    The book by Adorno and others is an important landmark in the study of prejudice. The second is a critique of the original study. Together they show the complexity of this important problem.

6. Wrenn, C. G. *Student personnel work in college.* Ronald, 1951.

7. Pressey, S. L., and Jones, A. W. 1923–1953 and 20–60 age changes in moral codes, anxieties, and interests, as shown by the "X–O Tests." *J. Psychol.,* 1955, *39,* 485–502.

    These two references deal with the worries of students of different ages.

8. Witmer, Helen L., and Tufts, Edith. *The effectiveness of delinquency prevention programs.* U.S. Dept. of Hlth. Educ. & Welf., U.S. Govt. Printing Office, 1954.

    A balanced and readable account. Directed to the general reader.

9. Brickman, W. W. Causes and cures of juvenile delinquency. *Sch. & Soc.,* 1952, *75,* 405–411.

    A collection of important references with brief comments on each.

10. Ullman, C. A. The socially maladjusted. *Rev. educ. Res.*, 1953, *23*, 432–452.

An analysis of the problems and a source for further references.

11. Norvell, G. W. *The reading interests of young people.* Heath, 1950.

Useful as a means of determining the interest shown in many specific materials. Not for general reading.

Exercises and Questions for Discussion

1. Prepare an outline for a talk on juvenile delinquency.

2. From your local library secure a list of recently published books that are recommended for children of each age from eight to twelve. How do these new books compare with the reading interests of children as reported in the investigations?

3. How do you feel about the change from participant to spectator that takes place in adolescents with respect to games and athletics? Should participation be encouraged? for both boys and girls? Can you suggest means of securing this participation?

4. What kind of incidents would you mention if you were writing about "The Happiest Day in My Life"? Which of these might also be mentioned by a person of the same sex but six years younger? Which would not be likely to be mentioned?

5. You are thinking of writing a small book which you hope will be popular in grade three. What sort of story should you plan? What about a book for grade six?

6. How do you account for the fact that in television programs children's preferences often coincide with adult favorites, whereas in radio this is less likely to be true?

7. List some of the points that should be covered in a discussion of "The Roots of Prejudice."

18

Social Patterns: Individual Reaction and Group Processes

_____

The Development of Social Behavior

        SOCIAL ACTIVITY has its vague beginnings when the infant shows a pleasurable reaction to the presence of older people. This reaction becomes more marked and more elaborate as the child continues to enjoy the attention of adults. At an early age, however, he also shows a special kind of response to the presence of other children. He watches them intently, vocalizing occasionally, and perhaps reaching toward them.

By the time the child is two years of age, we may observe the phenomenon of parallel play. Several children in the same play yard or sandbox will do similar things. They will watch one another and will imitate each other. They will contend vigorously for the same toys or implements. But the play itself is largely individual. The talk is a collection of monologues, each child describing his own doings. One monologue may be influenced by the babblings of a playmate, but this is merely to incorporate a new theme. It is in no way a directed response to the neighbor's prattling.

By the age of three or so, the parallel play begins to give way to a rudimentary sort of cooperation. There is some rough and tumble. There is talk about what to do or who can do it best. There is some agreement and much disagreement. But certainly there is much social interaction. The other child is not merely "here too." He is someone to be taken into account. He is someone to be exploited, to be reckoned with, to be helped, or to provide aid. Whereas the parallel play could take place in separate cubicles, much of the later play would be impossible without the participation of other children.

In early elementary school the social play becomes more formal and more highly organized. There is much "turn about" or rotating play. In such games as hopscotch or skipping, each child is given his turn at a fairly complicated routine, the others acting as spectators or incidental aids the while. Toward the end of the elementary-school period, these rotating games give way to the still more highly organized team games, such as baseball, basketball, or football, in which each player has a rather definite and specialized function and in which there is need for a very definite team spirit.

Along with these changes in the types of social activity we may note changes in the number of people involved. As the child grows older, he comes in contact with more people, at least in a casual sort of way. It is more and more necessary that he take account of other people, and that he meet them in larger and larger numbers. The home and the immediate friends and neighbors no longer constitute his social world. He comes to reach out to the street, to the school, and to the community, and he must learn to get along in these larger groups. The statistics in Table 18-1 reveal this two-way increase in the size of the social group and in the amount of time spent in group contacts.

TABLE 18–1

Changes in the Frequency and Extent of Social Contacts

	Age in Years			
	2	3	4	5
Casual Social Contacts				
Percent of time spent in social contacts	41	64	77	
Percent of contacts of more than two children	36	55	70	
Size of Play Groups				
Percent of two-child groups	30			9
Percent of five-child groups	8			23

Adapted from Anderson (1), p. 347

Social Sensitivity and Responsibility

Test results show that as the child grows older he is better able to comprehend both social situations and complicated social problems. When shown a group of pictures, for instance, older children are more likely to comment on the social relations involved. Part of this superiority, of course, may come from growth in intelligence and from increased general discernment. This is not the whole explanation, however, since even among children of identical intelligence there is more social sensitivity among the older than among the younger.

At the outset of his life, the infant, far from exhibiting social responsibility, is completely dependent on the social activities of others. His first

FIGURE 18-1. *Illustrations of Responsibilities that May be Expected from Children at Different Ages.* Reproduced from Doll, *Your Child Grows Up.* Courtesy of the John Hancock Mutual Life Insurance Company.

step toward social responsibility is to take over more and more responsibility for himself. At a very primitive level, he gradually ceases to depend on other people to move him from place to place and comes to take over this responsibility himself. He also takes on some of the responsibility for eating, for dressing, and even for keeping himself clean. Later he takes on more responsibility for his own elementary affairs and also takes a minor share of responsibility for a younger child or for domestic animals and pets.

Some of the more typical landmarks of social responsibility have been incorporated into the *Vineland Scale of Social Maturity*. A few representative items from this scale are illustrated in Figure 18-1.

Being Accepted by Others

Social adjustment, of course, is a two-way affair. One must not only become aware of others and take part in their doings, but it is also essential that one be accepted and liked, to a greater or lesser degree, by others. Some people have a vast desire to be liked by everyone. Others have more modest aspirations. But everyone feels the need for some acceptance.

The typical method of measuring the degree of acceptance is the sociogram(2). Each student in a class or other group is asked to name the two or three members of the group that he would most like for his friends. The results are then plotted as in Figure 18-2. The number of arrows pointing to a child indicates the number of times he was selected. The whole cluster also shows the general pattern of friendships, some of which are reciprocated and some of which are not. It also reveals a small clique where there are reciprocated friendships within the clique but few friendships experienced, or desired, outside its boundaries.

This has proved to be a very valuable instrument and is fairly easy to use. Ordinarily it will provide us with important information that corrects and supplements the teacher's offhand estimate(3).

As we might expect, this instrument has its limitations. In the first place, the pencil-and-paper choices do not always correspond(4) with the actual choices made later on when opportunities present themselves, although the pencil-and-paper choices are a fairly good indication of real choices that have already been made. In the second place, we must remember that children wisely vary their choices with the situation. A student may give one classmate first preference in selecting the chairman of a committee but might readily choose someone else if selecting a companion for some social activity(5).

The sociogram can be used to indicate two rather different things. The number of times a child is chosen, no matter by whom, can be used to indicate his general popularity or degree of acceptance. A mutual choice, on the other hand, is an indication of reciprocal friendship. Let us look, first of all, at the factors related to general acceptance or popularity.

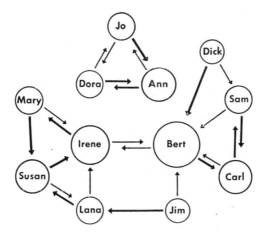

FIGURE 18-2. *Sociogram for a Small Group of Children.* The heavy arrow leaving each child goes to the friend he chooses first. The light arrow indicates his second choice. The size of the circle indicates the number of times that the child has been chosen.

Popularity. The student who is much sought after or whose friendship would be welcomed by a large number of other students tends to be somewhat similar to the people who hold him in esteem. His intelligence is likely to be a little above average. He comes from about the same socioeconomic group and is more likely to be popular with coreligionists. Typically he lives fairly close to those who like him. Often he is blessed with parents who welcome his friends into their home. He is above average in appearance and certainly tends to be free from marked physical handicap. He is genial, outgoing, has some sense of humor, is a good sport, and is cooperative. He has moderate aptitude for leadership (6). He also has considerable self-confidence and sets high expectations in discussing his future achievement. The classmates who choose him also expect higher than average achievement from him (7). Most studies suggest that he has better than average mental health(8). He is also likely to be slightly ahead in his schoolwork, although not markedly advanced.

Certainly he is not likely to be chosen from the pupils too old for their grade(9), or from those destined to drop out of school prior to completion(10).

Apparently some aspects of popularity can rest on very superficial matters. College seniors, after a few seconds interview, can judge with considerable accuracy whether or not a given freshman will be pledged to a fraternity(11).

There has been some suggestion that the person often selected has better than average ability to detect the feelings of others (12). He has also been held to be especially apt in knowing who is likely to select him. This point has been challenged (13), however, and it has been suggested that the frequently selected person, because of his many contacts, merely happens to find out his standing in the eyes of other people(14).

When nothing is done to alter the situation, popularity turns out to be almost as constant as intelligence or achievement(15, 16, 17, 18). This refers, of course, to general popularity and general friendliness. Specific friendships between any two children show nothing like this degree of constancy.

Social Participation

So far we have concentrated on the student who is frequently selected by his fellows. What about the student who seeks many contacts with other students and who participates widely in extracurricular activities? To a certain extent, of course, participation and acceptance may go together, but the two things are by no means identical. We find that the participating(19) student is self-confident and has a feeling that he is accepted. He has a strong feeling of identity with the various campus groups. He has many friends and is tolerant of other people. He shows more general restraint, though he is also considered to be more straightforward or candid in his dealings with others. His academic achievement is above average(20).

Friendships

As we have suggested, friendship differs from acceptance or popularity in that friendship is a two-way affair and calls for a personal involvement that is not necessary in popularity. The friendship that one person feels for another obviously can range from intense comradeship to mere recognition. At the one extreme, we have the buddies, the confidants, who spend much time together and who feel a great deal of freedom and trust in the presence of each other. Each feels he can express himself fairly freely. In any one situation, each person is likely to have only one "buddy." But the college student may have one buddy on the campus and another in the home town. Beyond the more intense comradeship, there are various stages of friendship, the intimate with whom we can talk and joke freely on a more superficial level, the acquaintance whom we like but with some reserve, the person with whom we work and whom we know chiefly in relation to the office or factory or committee, and finally the person whom we know by sight, and partially by reputation, and with whom we pass the time of day as the occasion permits.

Close friends of the same sex tend to come from the same district and very often from similar socioeconomic groups. Friendships are most frequent within the same race and age groups. Mental age may be even more important than chronological age. Friends tend also to be comparable in physical vigor. The qualities desired in friends change as the child grows older. Children in the second grade stress physical appearance and home conditions (21). By the sixth grade, however, these factors become less important and the chief stress is on cheerfulness, enthusiasm, friendliness, and popularity. At the high-school level, friendliness and popularity are still important in choosing a friend of the same sex. High-school students planning on college ask that their friends be good talkers, talented, and serious, whereas those not planning on college stress the good listener, the athlete, the lively practical joker who is also neat and personable (22).

In choosing friends of the opposite sex, older students profess to be affected by a number of standards. Good manners stand high in the list for both sexes. Ability to converse and to dance are also listed frequently by both boys and girls. Boys want their girl friends to be considerate and, especially, to keep their tastes in entertainment within moderate financial limits. Girls are anxious that their escorts shall make a good impression with other people. Personality also comes high in both lists and, like all the rest of the traits mentioned, is more important than good looks or physique. Humor is mentioned favorably but far down the list. Reprehensible traits are also listed, and for both sexes these include untidiness (or at least unorthodox untidiness), conceit, and vulgarity. Boys also worry about the giggler and the girl who must always be entertained. Girls mention drinking and "sponging" as traits they abhor in their "dates."

Boys, by the way, distinguish rather clearly between friends on the one hand and romantic attachments on the other. When asked to describe an ideal *friend,* older boys, like younger boys, tend to describe another boy of about the same age. The older girl, however, unlike her younger sister, will picture her ideal friend as a boy somewhat older than herself. For older boys, it appears, there are friends and there is also a sweetheart. For older girls, on the other hand, there is a sweetheart and whatever else is necessary to fill in the details of life.

The duration of a given friendship increases as the child grows older. Young children form attachments early in the school year(23) and may keep them throughout the year. For older students we can expect friendships to last much longer(22).

As the student becomes older he desires a larger number of friends. Typically he also acquires more. Both desire and attainment reach their peak about puberty. This is the age when the child wants many, many friends and has quite a few. From this period on, he has less frantic need for a large number of friends and tends to concentrate on a smaller number of intimates.

Groups and Group Processes

So far we have been concerned with the child or the student and his general relation to other people and to society. We have watched his reaction to parents and to other children and we have been interested in the extent to which he is liked and accepted by other people. The spotlight has been on him. The other people in the picture have significance only because of our interest in him.

At this point we change our emphasis and direct our attention to the groups to which an individual may belong. Our spotlight no longer selects a single person and asks about his relations to the others. Now we focus on the group itself and consider it as an entity, made up of individuals, of course, but constituting something more than a mere collection of individuals.

In many groups, the individual may merge himself to the point that he can remember more readily what the group has done than what he himself has contributed. When the group goal is unattained he worries and feels unhappy even though his own personal task may be quite completed. He also feels marked relief when the group or team has come through even though he himself played no part in this particular success(24, 14).

This urge to complete a task, by the way, is often quite powerful. Very often each of us feels a need that a certain task be completed, that an unpainted square on a wall be filled in, that the two parts of the road should be joined. Most of us feel some satisfaction when this gap

is filled or the pattern completed, no matter by whom. We feel even better, however, when the task is completed by someone we regard as a partner or as a member of our group. If we have been led to believe that the group feels a strong need to complete the task, the memory of that uncompleted task will stay with us for a long time. If, however, we are made to think that the group is indifferent we will be less likely to remember the unfinished job.

It is well known, of course, that the group sets standards to which the individual must conform. A group of docile children, formed into a group, will readily set such standards and will impose them on a new-comer who is much more aggressive than any single member of the group(25).

Spontaneous Groups

Many of the groups to which people belong have no formal structure or no membership rolls. No one may be able to remember how the group was formed. These groups, however, are very real entities and may have strong claims on their members.

The Childhood Group. The childhood play groups(26), observed in preschool days and during the first school grades, are largely based on propinquity and have little continuity or solidarity. The children who are thrown together merely play together in one way or another. After the early school grades, however, these childhood groups take on more form and structure. Boys play with boys and girls with girls. The group seems a more universal phenomenon for boys, and the groups of boys are larger than the corresponding groups of girls. In these later childhood groups, there is very little selection. For the most part, any child who is on the spot becomes a member of the group. When the group has become more or less established there is often a definite pattern by which a new child is admitted(27). The new child typically makes the advances. Often he imitates the most conspicuous member of the group. At first he is admitted provisionally and may pass through several stages before attaining full-fledged membership. In these groups there need be little mutual affection, and when one member moves out of the community the ranks close, so to speak, and he is missed only slightly unless he leaves the group undermanned or lacking a strategic player on the baseball team. These childhood groups often lack both leadership and sense of function. They go in for vigorous activity and are likely to exploit any interesting situation. It is not surprising, therefore, that the group or gang is often responsible for considerable mischief.

During the elementary-school period the groups may become better organized into more clear-cut gangs. These are very prevalent. Three quarters of one group of student teachers(28) in Australia, for instance, reported that they had been members of childhood gangs. In some cultures(29) these gangs may have a very authoritative leader who maintains strict discipline. Impressive names may be used. Gangs of boys, especially, may become very destructive.

The Adolescent Crowd. During the early teens the childhood gang is less prevalent. Some members drop out and the gang shrinks in size. The brighter and more studious members tend to drop out first. By the age of fourteen the childhood gang contains chiefly the retarded students and those for whom the gang life has a strong attraction.

The adolescent crowd which replaces the childhood gang or group has its own characteristics. In this group both sexes, of course, are represented, often in equal numbers. Here sheer geography or propinquity is less important. The members may live in different blocks or districts. There is a great degree of solidarity, each member feeling considerable affection for some if not all the other members. Newcomers are definitely, if not formally, passed upon before being admitted.

The activities of the adolescent crowd are less vigorous than those of the younger group. It seems enough just to be together, to talk, listen to the radio or the juke box, to dance, to utter strange sophisticated exclamations over and over again, and above all, to consume food and beverages. Unorganized amusements such as swimming, skating, and driving are popular at times. There is relatively little mischief. The meeting place may be selected deliberately or may be adopted or appropriated almost unconsciously. A porch, a club basement, a drugstore with a juke box—any of these may become the rendezvous. Like a swarm of bees, once these adolescents have settled, they may be difficult to dislodge, no matter how seemingly superior the proffered alternatives may be.

The Clique. Very often an adolescent crowd upon analysis will turn out to be a cluster of cliques. Within the smaller cliques, loyalties are more intense, confidences are more intimate, and associations are more continuous. The grouping of cliques becomes evident when the major group must be sorted into automobiles, restaurant booths, or theater seats. The primary loyalties to the clique are accepted by the group without undue resentment provided they are not carried to extremes. In most studies, the cliques are more important to the girls than to the boys.

Cliques often appear prior to the emergence of the adolescent crowd. In childhood, a clique may consist of a pair of children who are close chums plus the less favored friends of each member of the pair. Such a clique may also be made up of a less-structured group in which there are no marked "chum" or "buddy" relations.

Cliques such as these are often thought to bring considerable distress to those left out. In one study(30), however, no marked antagonism was reported by a group of girls who did not belong to the clique in question. The outsiders did believe that the clique members were more socially acceptable than themselves but held no apparent resentment.

Leadership in Spontaneous or Accidental Groups

Here we consider the *emergent* leader, the one who gets to be a leader through the action, or lack of action, of the group itself. The term *leader* in the emergent sense covers quite a range of meanings. Obviously it includes the one who comes to be formally elected as president of a class or club. It also includes those who hold no formal office but come to be imitated a great deal, or whose suggestions are frequently adopted by others. In some discussions, the leader is anyone who has an influence on the group. In this case, the extent of his leadership is the difference between the influence he gives and the influence he accepts(31). A few discussions stretch the concept of leadership to include anyone who does anything to keep the group going, or whose presence helps to keep the group intact even though his part may be that of a clown or a scapegoat.

In a summer boys' camp one or two boys in each cabin will come to exert an unusual amount of influence(32). These are the boys who are frequently imitated by others and whose suggestions are frequently accepted. The other boys are aware of the status of these boys. There are no clear physical differences that set these influential boys off from the others. Those studied in the camp setting, however, happened to be good at fighting. Most significant perhaps, such "leaders" tend to feel fairly secure and tend to act freely and spontaneously. This matter of unhesitating and spontaneous action, by the way, may be important in other situations. If a minor emergency occurs, when the boys first meet each other, for instance, any boy who acts spontaneously toward a generally accepted solution will find himself imitated. For the moment, at least, his behavior will determine the actions of the others.

The qualities that enable a person to exert exceptional influence on a group may not serve to get him elected to some office. To exert considerable influence on a group it is not necessary that a man be talkative, genial, enthusiastic, or original. But these qualities do help him get elected to some office. Getting elected, in fact, is much more a matter of being conspicuous, vigorous, and friendly and much less a matter of providing helpful direction. Sheer friendliness or sociability, with prominence or vigor lacking, will not lead to election. In view of the role of prominence, it is not surprising to find that sheer physical bulk may also help a little. Elected leaders are, on the average, a little taller and heavier than the nonleaders. For social leadership, general appearance plays a part. The leader is also somewhat ahead in intelligence and in scholastic or other achievement. He is more self-assured, more adventurous, and more capable of warm, human responses. He is persistent, industrious, tends to dominate, and has objectives that excel those of his fellows. He is likely to be aware of his own powers and limitations. Where such things are valued, he has often superior family background. In all this, the leader cannot depart too much from the norms of the group. He is only slightly more intelligent, slightly more dominant, slightly more adventurous. The one who is markedly out of line in anyway is not likely to be elected.

Unfortunately there is a good deal of uncertainty in our information about leadership and a good deal of inconsistency from study to study(33). It is obvious that leadership is never completely general. A person who readily becomes a leader in one situation may never emerge as a leader under different circumstances. Among college women, for instance, Dunkerly(34) thought she could detect three types of leaders, the intellectual, the social, and the religious. Between the intellectual and the social there were rather clear differences. For one thing, contrary to most studies, the purely social leaders were not more extroverted than the nonleaders. On the contrary, they were more introverted and also more neurotic. The intellectual leaders, in conformity with the general trend, were more extroverted and less neurotic than the nonleaders.

There are also differences in the leaders, formal and informal, chosen at different ages. The young child will follow the aggressive, bossy companion who makes his wishes known in no uncertain terms. As an adolescent, however, he demands more subtlety in his leaders. To become a leader, the adolescent cannot merely dominate. He must influence and persuade. True enough he must be decisive and must take responsibility, but he cannot be too heavy-handed in the matter.

These differences do not contradict the fact that leadership tendencies may persist to a remarkable extent. In one investigation of leadership in women, the high-school leader turned out to be the college leader, and to a certain extent the college leaders also became club women and influential citizens in the community(35).

The Working Group and Its Tasks

The groups we have described so far are formed by accident, as in a dormitory, or by mutual attraction, or in some other incidental manner. The people in these groups are not brought together to accomplish any definite goal nor do they assemble primarily for that purpose. After they are formed, of course, these spontaneous or accidental groups may often decide on some goal or course of action, and thus, for the time being, become a working group. But that is not the basis for their organization.

As yet we do not know whether or not a working group is more effective when it happens also to be a natural or spontaneous group. In the case of factory workers(36), the most productive teams are often those with the smallest amount of purely social interaction. On the other hand, two-man working teams formed on the basis of mutual choice proved to be more stable and showed less wastage of material. Teams of seventh-grade girls(37) were more productive when made up of mutual friends. And as far as mutual influence is concerned, it is clear that people strongly attracted to each other because of friendship, admiration, or dependence have a marked effect on each other. The mutual influencing is less when the attraction is lacking. A group at work faces a variety of tasks and these in turn vary widely from one situation to another. In each case, however, there are some general problems that arise very frequently whenever group activity is in progress.

Reaching a Decision

At the very least, most working groups face the problem of reaching a decision. They must decide whether to put on the play or not, whether or not to admit the new member, or which magazine subscriptions should be ordered for the library.

Although reaching a decision is a task that the group can seldom escape, it is by no means the only problem to be faced. No group can congratulate itself merely because it has reached a decision. For most groups, it is also important that, as far as possible, the decision should reflect the views of all members. Often, of course, it is quite impossible to attain 100 percent agreement. But it is an ideal that can be approached. This urge toward as much agreement or consensus as possible comes partly from the democratic belief that this is right, and partly from the fact that decisions supported by the group as a whole are more likely to be carried out with enthusiasm and effectiveness.

Collecting Suggestions and Ideas of Members. One task of the group is to gather together the ideas of its members. This is important not only due to the fact that many of the ideas will turn out to have intrinsic merit, but also because each member is more likely to accept the decision if he feels that he has participated. In the minds of some students, one of the chief functions of a discussion leader is to elicit as much participation as possible and especially to bring out the divergent minority views that otherwise might be suppressed by the majority.

Influencing the Members of the Group. Not all decisions call for a great deal of unanimity. In deciding on the color scheme for the auditorium, for instance, a substantial minority might remain unconvinced but willing to bow to the will of the majority. In other cases, however, a high degree of consensus is important, and the project decided upon can succeed only when backed by the genuine conviction of most members. In such cases there is genuine need that one faction will persuade the other or the other the one. Even when there is no external necessity for agreement, we find, in most groups, a powerful urge to bring about such conformity or agreement. This drive to induce conformity is so strong on the part of group members that any extreme divergence causes acute distress. Even a powerful leader who has brought about the norms that the other members now espouse may find himself powerless to escape from the standards he himself established. Some divergence is tolerated, of course, on the part of popular members of long standing, especially if their over-all allegiance cannot be questioned. For the person less firmly established, however, tolerance may be lacking.

This drive to induce conformity or agreement on the part of members of the group will be especially strong when there is no objective means of testing the correctness of the proposed decision. Divergent views may not cause too much distress, for instance, in deciding whether or not Exeter High School will probably accept our basketball challenge. A hold-out group may arouse much more agitation, however, in considering the ethics of racial segregation, or the merits of appeasement versus strength. Naturally there will be more urge to put pressure on the nonconformist when the success of the venture calls for a united front and especially if there should be a great deal at stake. Under these circumstances, much of the total energy of the group will be used in hammering the deviant or "hold-out" into line. We will argue with him, plead with him, threaten him, often making no attempt to disguise our displeasure and antagonism.

Conformity in Individuals. Most of us need very little outside pressure to bring us into line. Most people, even with no overt pressure whatever, feel keenly uncomfortable if they find themselves in a minority position. We feel uncomfortable when we are told that "most people" feel differently. We hasten to conform to the opinions of an impressive stranger (probably planted in the group by some investigator). But we are especially likely to be influenced by the views of a group for which we have a great liking. If we are very fond of a group or an organization, we are much more easily swayed from the claims of logic or the evidence of our senses if that is necessary for conformity. Sometimes, of course, we do find ourselves voting officially against the majority of a group that is important to us. In that case we often persuade ourselves that most of the other members would really be on our side if they were only free to express themselves(38).

We feel discomfort at being in the minority not only with respect to important issues but also with respect to trivial issues. Suppose, for instance, that you are comparing the length of two lines x and y, and it appears that x is longer than y. You find out (or are led to believe) that most of the people looking at the lines claim that y is the longer. Many of us in that situation will straightway change our opinion to go along with the majority(39). The influence of a majority will increase with its size up to a preponderance of 75-25. Beyond this, there is little increase in influence. The influence of the majority is more marked when there is some room for doubt or when the material is unfamiliar. Depending on the situation, some 30 to 80 percent of adults will reverse their judgments to coincide with the majority. Those who resist the opinion of the majority and stand by the evidence of their own senses are somewhat more intelligent, have more rated "ego" strength, and have more propensity for leadership. They are less authoritarian or puritanical on the California scale and are less conventional in their religious attitudes(40).

Exploiting Group Pressure in Changing Attitudes. This urge to conform to the standards of a group that we like has long been used by youth workers and reformers who try to work with groups and their leaders. This knowledge has been greatly systematized by a vast new movement in group dynamics and social engineering. Suppose, for instance, that we are attempting to induce a student to enlarge his tastes in reading to include something in addition to comic books. We could, of course, work on each member simultaneously, hoping to change the attitude of the entire group. In each case, however, we would be contending against the pull of the as yet unchanged group. Following the pioneer work of Lewin, there has been much emphasis on working with the group as a unit. In this case, any change that does take place in the attitude of the group is readily sensed and the individual is pulled to that new position. In getting people to adopt different working arrangements, or changing their buying habits during the war, it was found(41) that group discussions were more effective than equally informative lectures. Theoretically, in the discussion, the members could more readily detect group changes or changes in the attitudes of others.

Keeping Conformity within Bounds

Conformity, in and of itself, is neither good nor bad. Sometimes conformity of action, as in keeping to the right in traffic, is absolutely necessary. Conformity of belief, however, is seldom that vital and the pressure toward conformity can be a downright evil when it leads to beliefs that go against all observation and logic. Even less extreme conformity may be harmful in suppressing the variety and divergence of views from which the truth or the correct solution may arise. How can we guard against undue conformity? As we have seen, some people are less susceptible than others. In general, the weight of the group has less effect on people who have had more experience with the issue at hand. It is the less experienced person who makes unreasonable concession to group opinion(42). We are also less likely to conform if we see someone else refusing to go along. This is especially true if the resister is a trusted friend or partner. It is suggested that a skillful leader can encourage those who hold minority views to speak out. One honest person who points out that the "emperor really has no clothes" can start a chain reaction and encourage a whole group to discard the grotesque illusions engendered by the fear of being different.

Maintaining Satisfactory Group Relations

Ordinarily it is not only necessary that the group reach some decision but that in so doing the group should remain intact and that the members should feel the experience has been satisfactory. Indeed we might go back one step and suggest that it is sometimes necessary that during the discussion the assemblage of people should *achieve* real group status.

The students of group dynamics have held that there is a fairly definite transition starting with an aggregation of people, each one occupied by his own concerns and desire for status, and ending with a genuine concern for the problems of the group(37). Whether or not this transition is a regular thing, it is clear that the people taking part may either gain or lose a sense of group membership and that the general experience can be satisfactory or the reverse. Some of the conditions under which the group is working may facilitate this group feeling and other external conditions may make for difficulty. When people are working for an individual prize, for instance, there are many more negative, divisive reactions within the group than when the objective is a group prize or group trophy(43).

Achieving an Effective Solution

A group may reach a decision and have a satisfactory experience in the process and still come out with a decision that turns out to be wrong. In some cases, of course, it is impossible to tell whether or not the decision is correct. In other cases the adequacy can be estimated with more or less accuracy. The likelihood of a good decision or a correct decision is greater when the goal adopted by the group is really accepted by the members, when the members are not completely naive in group work, when the leader in charge is accepted by the group, and when the leader is not changed too often. In technical problems a satisfactory solution is unlikely unless some member possesses the necessary knowledge or skill or unless this technical proficiency can be brought in. Groups vary, of course, in their ability to utilize such skill either from their members or from the outside(44).

Size of Groups. A large group working on a complex problem will very often set up one or more smaller committees to bring in a recommendation or other suggestion. This practice is soundly based. Not only does it save the time of some of the members of the larger group, but for many tasks the small group is much more efficient. A group of five, for instance, will reach a consensus more quickly than a group of twelve, especially if discussion time is limited. In a group of twelve, or even in a group of seven, there may be several people who do not contribute at all and whose ideas never come before the group. In groups of three, four, or five this is less likely. Here the shy person is less inhibited, and since his silence is more obvious in the small group, there is more pressure on him to take part. In the small group, moreover, there is less need for a clearly defined issue. Quite often a small group can be assigned a rather vague problem and still get somewhere. This is not so likely in the larger group. The small group lends itself to a different kind of atmosphere and a different kind of leadership. As the group gets larger and larger we find more and more that one prolific contributor almost takes over. There is a "runner up," quite a distance behind, and then a very few who make some scattered contributions. The contributor in this case is likely to be a fairly positive fellow with a good deal of initiative and a liking for authority. The leadership that emerges in this larger group tends to be formal and authoritative. Added to all this is the fact that, at the high-school level at least, most students report more satisfaction in their work and feel more confidence in the decisions reached when working with small groups. Finally, groups of twelve, or larger, tend to break up into small groups no matter how they are formed originally(45).

Obviously there are many advantages for the small group. The picture, however, is not completely one-sided. In the first place, there are fewer ideas or suggestions to be had from a small group. Although it will frighten many people into silence, the large group, by sheer virtue of numbers, will put out a larger number of suggestions. This trend holds for groups up to ninety or one hundred. The sense of ease and congeniality in the small group, moreover, is not always an unmixed blessing. Sometimes contention and opposition may prove useful, partly by bringing out genuine weakness in proposals and partly by stimulating some people to more adequate suggestions. In the small group we may not find the range of views and temperaments necessary for this salutary clash. In some cases, the larger group is less at the mercy of a really troublesome member. An obstreperous person who might wreck a small group has more chance of being kept in line within a larger group. For one thing, sheer size may inhibit him as it does others. Even if it does not, however, there is more chance that the larger group may include someone who can deal with him(46).

All in all, it would seem that the student of average or less than average dominance should have much experience in working with groups of three or four or five. He should also have occasional experience in somewhat larger groups, hoping that, when he really has something to say, he will gradually acquire the confidence to speak up in more formidable gatherings. Larger groups should be used freely when it is important to get as many different suggestions as possible, as, for instance, when a complex and costly project should be examined for flaws before it is finally set in motion.

Groups of the same size may well vary in cohesiveness. This factor is especially important when one of the group goals is to hold production down. Here the group discourages those who try too hard or who turn in too much work. Under these conditions the more cohesive group will be more successful in enforcing the low standards. There is less evidence that greater cohesion will help a group enforce high standards.

Effectiveness of the Group Process in Problem Solving

As we have already pointed out, it is obvious that the working group should accomplish something. Are groups fairly efficient in solving problems? Or would it be better to depend on individuals working by themselves? Naturally we shall not expect an all-or-none answer. There are problems in which the group excels and other problems that do not lend themselves to the group approach.

The group has an obvious advantage when (a) there is one single result to be accomplished, when (b) a successful performance of one person will solve the problem for the whole group, when (c) the success or failure is readily apparent, and when (d) the efficiency of any one person does not depend on the efficiency of another. This process is easily seen in the nonintellectual problem of sinking a floating mine by rifle fire. There is one rather clear-cut job to be done. One successful shot will solve the problem for the whole team. It is easy to decide whether or not the mine has blown up. No man is greatly dependent on the cooperation of any other. Suppose that, under the condition of firing, each man on the team has a .2 (or 20 percent) chance of missing the target. By sheer probability, then, the chance of two men both missing the target would be $.2^2$ or .04. In other words, a two-man team would have only four chances out of 100 of missing or 96 chances out of 100 of succeeding. In the case of a three-man team, the chance of all three missing would be $.2^3$ or .008. This leaves 992 chances out of 1000 of succeeding. Clearly, the likelihood of success increases with the size of the team(47, 48). The larger the group, the better. This obvious superiority of the group would hold if the problem consisted of a number of such tasks to be accomplished in a given order. We would expect the group to surpass an individual, for instance, even if there were a series of mines to be destroyed and mine A had to be destroyed before we could get close enough to mine B to shoot at it.

In solving a jigsaw puzzle, as in shooting at a mine, it is fairly easy to see whether or not the piece you have selected will fit (i.e. whether your proposal is valid). If there are only one or two pieces left (alternatives), of course, the group will not be much better than the individual. But if there are a great many alternatives, a group should complete the solution more quickly than the individual can. In this sort of task, the more alternatives to choose from, the greater the superiority of the group over the individual. This rule does not hold, however, when it is difficult to tell whether a proposed solution is correct. In *constructing* a crossword puzzle, for instance, there are many possible words one could use. But it is not until the puzzle has taken some form that we can tell whether or not our early choices were wise. Here, in spite of the vast number of alternatives, the group has no advantage over the individual.

The advantage of group problem solving also falls off to some extent, or perhaps completely, when there is a great deal of interdependence or chain effect. Suppose, for instance, that the job of firing at the target is parceled out among several men, one man loading, a second aiming in the vertical dimension, a third aiming in the horizontal direction, and a fourth pulling the trigger. In that case there would be no guarantee that our four-man group would excel the individual(49).

So far, we have only considered the advantages that come to groups from the shotgun effect—from the fact that the gaps left by the accidental shortcomings of one person will not be the same as those left by the accidental deficiencies of another. Does the group contribute to problem solving in any other way? Probably so. The group may also motivate people to come up with suggestions that otherwise might never occur to them. This could come from the ordinary desire to appear well in the eyes of others. It may also happen that one person may contribute "half an idea" so to speak, and this half an idea, perhaps by its very incompleteness, may stimulate someone else to think of the other "half." Thus we might have a complete idea whereas without the group we would only have the first half. Because of the pressure it exerts toward conformity, the group quickly squelches erroneous suggestions which might otherwise distract a single individual for some time. This same process, of course, can suppress some original and highly important truths. On the average, however, the gain from suppressing error may more than make up for the occasional harm in suppressing truth. In the group, there is greater likelihood of an error being brought to the surface and rejected. All this will be hastened if it should happen that the more knowing people should also be the more confident and thus be led to speak first. This should establish a "set" in the right direction and put the forces of conformity at work in suppressing real error instead of fancied error(25).

From this analysis we would expect that the group would excel in many tasks but that it would be at a disadvantage in others. Statistically, most studies do report an advantage for group problem solving, but, as we should expect, this is not always so(50). We must also remember that in much of this we have ignored the matter of efficiency. In playing the guessing game of twenty questions, for instance, teams of four can come up with the answer very quickly and with few questions, surpassing both individuals and smaller teams. In terms of man-minutes, however, the team of four was more costly than the team of two or the individuals(51). Often, of course, the question of man-minutes is not especially vital. The important thing may be to get the problem solved in the shortest possible time.

Some Problems of the Leader. Earlier, we considered the characteristics of the person who emerges as the leader during the activities of the group. From now on, however, we include leaders who are appointed from above, as well as leaders who are chosen, formally or informally, by their associates. For the most part, by the way, the leaders who came to be appointed from above are not greatly different from those who emerge, except that the latter turn out to be somewhat more authoritarian and less permissive(52). This is not surprising when we remember that, in large groups, it takes a bit of authoritarianism to contribute to the group and thus become conspicuous enough to be selected. In any case it is a mistake to think that the appointed official is always the "big bully" and that the man from the ranks is always more understanding and considerate. On some occasions(53), enlisted men suggest much harsher punishment for infractions of army rules than the officers do. And many a hard-boiled teacher has been astounded at the severity of the punishment meted out by student councils.

Anyone functioning as a leader is often torn between the need to make unpleasant decisions and the need to be liked. In some experimental situations with college students this conflict has been made very severe as when he, the leader, is called upon to decide who is to get a high rate of pay and who is not. In such situations, most young men prefer to give up their role as leader. Even when the conflict is less drastic, and when a man merely feels that he is risking antagonism by his contributions to the group, he tends to cut down on the number of contributions. The emergent leader who becomes fairly well established as such has faced these conflicts. He must have had something in him which made him accept leadership with all its risks. The appointed leader is not similarly tested while he is in the process of attaining his leadership. And because his role does not depend on remaining conspicuous, he may never resolve the conflict in clear-cut fashion.

Training Leaders. There is some suggestion that trained leaders may be more effective than untrained leaders. As we have seen, they are better able to bring out and utilize minority opinion. There is also some evidence that groups under trained leaders are more successful in attaining a new or creative solution. Suppose, for instance, that a group of teachers is faced with a proposal. This project is attractive in most respects but it involves giving up the teachers' lounge. With untrained leadership there is likely to be outright rejection or, less frequently, outright acceptance. With a trained leader, however, there is less likely to be outright rejection and more likely to be some compromise or "creative" plan that permits the general acceptance but avoids the complete loss of the lounge(54).

The training to be effective must not only bring about new kinds of skill. For most people it must also bring about a change in attitude. The leader, after all, will be asked to give up a considerable measure of control and this may be a very frightening thing. To the untrained leader, for instance, the suggestions that will come from the group can be regarded as a criticism directed to him as a person, and the sensitive leader may feel a severe threat to his status or his ego.

In view of the complex demands, many people have suggested that the prospective leader should be trained by taking part in several group projects in which he is required to plan group activities, to help carry them out, and to work with the group in analyzing group experiences. There is some evidence that these activities change ideas and attitudes(55). But we still do not know whether or not they also lead to actual increase in leadership skill in another situation.

The Group-centered Classroom

The group-centered approach is usually contrasted with the autocratic, teacher dominated classroom. As we might expect, however, the group approach itself can vary within wide limits. At one extreme it could refer to the class in which the lecturer permits an occasional interruption. At the other extreme, it could mean that the teacher offers no direction whatever but merely acts as another member of the group. Somewhere between these extremes we find the democratic approach in which the teacher takes due account of the goals that the group may have. He takes the initiative, however, in helping the students to formulate the goals and to decide upon ways of achieving them. He may set limits to the sort of goals they may adopt, and he probably supplies a fair amount of technical information. To a greater extent than the students, he also passes judgment on what is said. For the most part, however, he is chiefly a member of the group, making suggestions, offering corrections much as the students themselves might do.

Most of those who stress the group-centered approach suggest that the leader or teacher must often define the general task. He should also make sure that the group knows the external conditions under which it works— number of hours available, examinations to be taken, papers to be submitted. Over and above such mechanical matters, he often helps formulate an issue that he thinks is present but not clearly defined. He may ask a question to help a student bring out a point that is not quite clear. At times he may try to keep the group oriented toward the problem at hand. At other times he may permit a new problem to replace the old. On still other occasions, suspecting that the issue under discussion is gradually changing, he may get the group to consider whether it would be better to return to the old issue or to formulate the issue that appears to be taking over. Often he feels obligated to get the group to bring to the surface some troublesome but important question that they seem reluctant to face. Many leaders make it a point to bring out minority views. Often this means calling on people who would not otherwise speak, and encouraging the objective consideration of unorthodox views. When trained leaders excel their untrained counterparts, it is most often due to the fact that they do bring out and develop divergent views that might otherwise be submerged(56).

Advantages and Disadvantages of the Group-centered Approach

The group-centered approach should be distinguished from the discussion method that was treated in Chapter 10. The discussion method may or may not be group centered. The instructor permits or encourages the students to talk, but he is not bound to be guided by their interests. He may be chiefly concerned with their ability to grasp the materials of the course. The group-centered or democratic approach suggests a more flexible attitude on the part of the instructor.

The more extreme student-centered approach, by the way, has received much discussion(57) but very little investigation. Most of the investigations have dealt with the more moderate democratic approach as described in the preceding section. As in so many areas, the results of the investigations are by no means clear-cut. The early experiments based on shop-work projects gave excellent results for the democratic approach. From this early work we would judge that students working under democratic leadership come to adopt a much more wholesome attitude toward their work. Their minds are focused on the job to be done and not on how they stand with the teacher. There is also less general aggression and meanness. In the more autocratic classrooms one or two students were likely to become scapegoats and to receive a good deal of persecution. In the more democratic atmosphere, however, this scapegoat phenomenon did not appear(25).

From these early studies it also appeared that the more group-centered or student-centered approach also brings about better liking for the group and a better feeling for the particular group with which the student has worked. This greater zest for group experience is held to be one of the great merits of the more democratic procedure.

But there are exceptions. Even in the shop-work situations, some more recent studies(58, 59) report that, under certain circumstances, the democratic approach does not go over very well. These may represent exceptional cases, however. In the more regular classroom situation, especially at the college level, the results fail to give a clear advantage to either system. As far as achievement is concerned, the more directive approach has a very slight advantage in the majority of the studies. As far as liking for the particular group or for group work is concerned, the honors are about evenly divided. From his summary of the work prior to 1953, Ruja(60) concluded that the group approach generally brought about a better feeling in this respect. More recent studies(61, 62, 63) show that this advantage is not always found. With respect to fondness for the subject taught, again we get conflicting results. In the teaching of general psychology, one experiment(64) found that the section taught by the student-centered approach had a more favorable attitude toward the subject. A more recent study(65) involving a total of twenty-six different sections and eight different instructors found that, to an insignificant extent, student-centered sections showed a higher rating for psychology. More students from the directive sections, however, planned to take more work in psychology. In this latter extensive study, by the way, the directive sections got a higher score on the final examination. There were no differences between the sections in critical thinking, attitude toward psychology, or in the presence of frequent misconceptions.

Obviously this is not the time to be dogmatic on the proved virtues or drawbacks of the group-centered approach. This seems to be one question that we should regard as unsettled. But in any case the differences are very slight. In such a situation you have every reason to follow the method that you prefer. And many people will find the democratic, group-centered approach more to their liking than the more autocratic teacher-centered approach.

If you should adopt the student-centered approach you will have the satisfaction that it is probably just as good as any other and it may possibly have a slight advantage in some respects. But do not expect miracles. And be prepared for a few disappointments. In the first place, you may find it difficult to use with some classes. Teachers who readily use democratic, permissive procedures in teaching a bright class may find themselves resorting to a more authoritarian technique when they face a dull class(66). In the second place, you may be disappointed to discover that this permissive approach will not always bring out the student who has most to contribute or who has the keenest interest in the subject. Among older students it is true that the degree of participation may reflect the student's interest in the activity(67). This does not hold for younger students, however, and it is not the governing force in students of any age. The prolific contributor is distinguished from his quieter classmate by his general intelligence, his talkativeness, and his dominance, but not by his superior knowledge or his interest(68, 69). Often the one who has most to say is more poorly adjusted than the others. He may even have a chip on his shoulder and a belligerent compulsion to set other people right(70). In this situation, moreover, when participation is not controlled by the teacher the heavy participator does not learn any more than an equally intelligent student who remains quiet. Nor does the participating student gain in adjustment during the course.

And finally, we must be prepared to find that not all students, especially at first, will like the group approach. Adults studying under the democratic procedure may actually resent the lack of positive leadership(25). Some college students, probably those who will do the best work academically, will simply ignore the democratic features or the group approach and go blithely about the business of getting good grades(61). From one elaborate experiment(62) we must conclude that it is extremely difficult to decide just who will get the most out of group work. In this case it was the student unusually concerned about fears and anxieties who seemed to profit from the group approach. It was not the student who had a prior interest in groups or the student who resented authoritarianism. Actually the students who rejected authoritarianism placed a low value on group work. Those who objected to group work stressed the lack of intellectual stimulation in this type of activity.

These difficulties should not prevent you from adopting the group-centered approach if you desire to use it. Any approach you adopt will have many difficulties. And difficulties are only difficulties. They are not necessarily insurmountable obstacles. By becoming aware of these difficulties, however, you should avoid the danger of feeling that it is all very simple, and that, by adopting this new, attractive, and much talked-of approach, you will solve all your problems.

Summary

As the child grows older, he spends more time in the company of children his own age, and he comes to be associated with larger groups. From the point of view of sheer numbers, puberty is the "friendliest" period of all. Among young children, friends are valued for liveliness, but the great determiner is propinquity or convenience. Sex has little influence at this stage, but later it becomes the basis for antagonism and still later for romantic pairings. Adolescent boys distinguish between ideal friendships and ideal romantic associations. For girls, there is less differentiation.

The child who is very popular, as shown by sociogram choices, has slightly better than average health and achievement and is considerably ahead in self-confidence. The qualities making for popularity are often apparent at a first meeting.

The social group is important in the life of the individual child. Groups are also interesting in their own right and many groups have characteristics they can impose on the group members. Individuals, for instance, often accept group goals. Group standards may keep an aggressive individual in check. The spontaneous groups of early childhood are based on propinquity and age. The group as such has little pull. Later these groups may become highly organized gangs of boys or girls. The adolescent crowd has great significance for its members but is seldom highly organized. Both sexes are represented. Members are drawn from wider geographic areas. Within the crowd there may be several cliques.

A boy is more likely to become influential in a group if he acts spontaneously and confidently. Physical size is not always important but skill of some sort often is. These qualities which make for spontaneous leadership may not be enough to get one elected to formal office. To attain this latter form of leadership, a person should be talkative, genial, and conspicuous. It is not necessary to contribute helpful ideas. In general, the elected leader is somewhat ahead of the group in his objectives, in industry, persistence, and intelligence, but must not be too far ahead. Young children will accept leadership from the noisy, bossy companion. Older children and adults accept dominance but often insist that it be expressed in genial and human terms.

A working group at times may also happen to be a social group. The evidence is conflicting as to whether such working groups are any more productive. Typically the working group is faced with the problem of making a decision. There should be some means of collecting ideas from the members. There should also be some machinery whereby members can try to influence each other. Usually there will be great pressure exerted to make dissident members conform. Typically most people feel uncomfortable when they find they are markedly out of line in their judgments or opinions. This urge to conform to the judgments of a valued group has been used to alter group opinion and group tastes. Conformity, of course, can be overdone, and the skillful leader tries to keep the pressure within bounds and to encourage the expression of minority opinion.

It is not enough to reach a decision. Ordinarily, in the process the group must maintain satisfactory group relations and should also reach an effective solution. The leader can keep the group needs to the fore and thus promote group solidarity. An adequate solution is more likely when the leader is accepted by the group and when there is agreement on the broad goals of the group. For exploratory work, groups of four or five are more efficient than larger groups. For revealing weaknesses in an elaborate proposal, larger groups may be more effective. The larger group is also better able to deal with a troublemaker.

Group problem solving is likely to be efficient when a single successful step will suffice and when this step can be taken, independently, by any member of the group. The group is also at an advantage when there are many possible solutions to be considered and when the correct one will be obvious as soon as it is proposed. The group has little advantage when there are fewer alternatives or when there is difficulty in deciding whether or not a proposed solution will work. Over and above these mechanics of group work, there is a possibility that the group may provide added motivation in problem solving. The group leader can expedite problem solving but to do so he may have to do things that are distasteful, disturbing, and difficult. Training of leaders has proved to be a problem.

Should the group-centered approach be adopted by teachers in the classroom? There is conflicting evidence on this point. Academic achievement is little affected by such an approach. The expected increases in group appreciation have not always appeared.

SPECIFIC REFERENCES

1. Anderson, J. E. *The psychology of development and personal adjustment.* Holt, 1949, p. 276.
2. Northway, Mary L. *A primer of sociometry.* University of Toronto Press, 1952.
3. Gronlund, N. E. The accuracy of teachers' judgments concerning the sociometric status of sixth-grade pupils. *Sociometry,* 1950, *13,* 197–225; 329–357.
4. Byrd, E. A study of validity and constancy of scores in a sociometric test. *Sociometry,* 1951, *14,* 175–181.
5. Horrocks, J. E., and Wear, Betty A. An analysis of interpersonal choice relationships of college students. *J. soc. Psychol.,* 1953, *38,* 87–98.
6. Bonney, M. E., and Powell, Johnny. Differences in social behavior between sociometrically high and sociometrically low children. *J. educ. Res.,* 1953, *46,* 481–495.
7. Harvey, O. J. An experimental approach to the study of status relations in informal groups. *Amer. sociol. Rev.,* 1953, *18,* 357–367.
8. Bedoian, V. H. Mental health analysis of socially over-accepted, socially under-accepted, overage, and underage pupils in the sixth grade. *J. educ. Psychol.,* 1953, *44,* 366–371.
9. Bedoian, V. H. Social acceptability and social rejection of the underage, at-age, and overage pupils in the sixth-grade. *J. educ. Res.,* 1954, *47,* 513–518.
10. Kuhlen, R. G., and Collister, E. G. Sociometric status of sixth- and ninth graders who fail to finish high school. *Educ. psychol. Measmt.,* 1952, *12,* 632–637.
11. Roff, M., and Brody, D. S. Appearance and choice status during adolescence. *J. Psychol.,* 1953, *36,* 347–356.
12. Ausubel D. P., Schiff, H. M., and Gasser, E. B. A preliminary study of developmental trends in sociempathy: Accuracy of perception of own and others' sociometric status. *Child Develpm.,* 1952, *23,* 111–128.
13. Gage, N. L., and Exline, R. V. Social perception and effectiveness in discussion groups. *Hum. Relat.,* 1953, *6,* 381–396.
14. Horwitz, M. Conceptual status of group dynamics. *Rev. educ. Res.,* 1953, *23,* 309–328.
15. Bonney, M. E. The relative stability of social, intellectual, and academic status in grades II to IV, and the inter-relationships between these various forms of growth. *J. educ. Psychol.,* 1943, *34,* 88–102.

16. Hartley, Ruth E. Sociality in preadolescent boys. *Teach. Coll. Contr. Educ.*, No. 918, 1946.

17. Horrocks, J. E., and Thompson, G. G. A study of the friendship fluctuations of rural boys and girls. *J. genet. Psychol.*, 1946, *69*, 189–198.

18. McGuire, C., Lanmon, M., and White, G. D. Adolescent peer acceptance and valuations of role behaviors. *Amer. Psychologist*, 1953, *8*, 397.

19. Gough, H. G. Predicting social participation. *J. soc. Psychol.*, 1952, *35*, 227–243.

20. Willerman, B. The relation of motivation and skill to active and passive participation in the group. *J. appl. Psychol.*, 1953, *37*, 387–390.

21. Dymond, Rosalind F., Hughes, Anne S., and Raabe, Virginia L. Measurable changes in empathy with age. *J. consult. Psychol.*, 1952, *16*, 202–206.

22. Carmichael, L., ed. *Manual of child psychology*. Wiley, 1954, Chap. 11. The adolescent (Horrocks, J. E.).

23. McGuire, C. Family and age-mates in personality formation. *Marriage and Family Living*, 1953, *15*, 17–23.

24. Festinger, L., Pepitone, A., and Newcomb, T. Some consequences of deindividuation in a group. *J. abnorm. soc. Psychol.*, 1952, *47*, 382–389.

25. Lindzey, G., ed. *Handbook of social psychology*. Addison-Wesley, 1954, Chap. 21. Experimental studies of group problem solving and process (Kelley, H. H., and Thibaut, J. W.).

26. Guilford, J. P., and Guilford, Ruth B. Personality factors D, R, T, and A. *J. abnorm. soc. Psychol.*, 1939, *34*, 21–36.

27. Phillips, E. L., Shenker, Shirley, and Revitz, Paula. The assimilation of the new child into the group. *Psychiatry*, 1951, *14*, 319–325.

28. Crane, A. R. Pre-adolescent gangs: A topological interpretation. *J. genet. Psychol.*, 1952, *81*, 113–123.

29. Wolman, B. Spontaneous groups of children and adolescents in Israel. *J. soc. Psychol.*, 1951, *34*, 171–182.

30. Keislar, E. R. Girls' social groups rate each other. *Calif. J. educ. Res.*, 1953, *4*, 227–232.

31. Lindzey, G., ed. *Handbook of social psychology*. Addison-Wesley, 1954, Chap. 24. Leadership (Gibb, C. A.).

32. Lippitt, R., Polansky, N., and Rosen, S. The dynamics of power. *Hum. Relat.*, 1952, *5*, 37–64.

33. Stogdill, R. M. Personal factors associated with leadership. *J. Psychol.*, 1948, *25, 35–71.*

34. Dunkerly, Mother Mary D. A statistical study of leadership among college women. *Stud. Psychol. Psychiat. Cathol. Univ. Amer.*, 1940, *4,* No. 7.

35. Courtenay, Mary E. The persistence of leadership. *Sch. Rev.*, 1938, *40,* 97–107.

36. Lindzey, G., ed. *Handbook of social psychology.* Addison-Wesley, 1954, Chap. 22. Psychological aspects of social structure (Riecken, H. W., and Homans, G. C.).

37. Benne, K. D., and Levit, Grace. The nature of groups and helping groups improve their operation. *Rev. educ. Res.*, 1953, *23,* 289–308.

38. Belknap, G., and Campbell, A. Political party identification and attitudes toward foreign policy. *Publ. Opin. Quart.*, 1951–52, *15,* 601–623.

39. Crutchfield, R. S. Conformity and character. *Amer. Psychologist,* 1955, *10,* 191–198.

40. Hoffman, M. L. Some psychodynamic factors in compulsive conformity. *J. abnorm. soc. Psychol.*, 1953, *48,* 383–393.

41. Coch, L., and French, J. R. P., Jr. Overcoming resistance to change. *Hum. Relat.*, 1948, *1,* 512–532.

42. Swanson, G. E. A preliminary laboratory study of the acting crowd. *Amer. sociol. Rev.*, 1953, *18,* 522–533.

43. Stendler, Celia, Damrin, Dora, and Haines, Aleyne C. Studies in cooperation and competition: I. The effects of working for group and individual rewards on the social climate of children's groups. *J. genet. Psychol.*, 1951, *79,* 173–197.

44. Darley, J. G., Gross, N., and Martin, W. C. Studies of group behavior: Factors associated with the productivity of groups. *J. appl. Psychol.*, 1952, *36,* 396–403.

45. Hare, A. P. A study of interaction and consensus in different sized groups. *Amer. sociol. Rev.*, 1952, *17,* 261–267.

46. Thelen, H. A. Group dynamics in instruction: Principle of least group size. *Sch. Rev.*, 1949, *57,* 139–148.

47. Taylor, D. W., and McNemar, Olga. Problem solving and thinking. *Annu. Rev. Psychol.*, 1955, *6,* 455–482.

48. Lorge, I., and Solomon, H. Two models of group behavior in the solution of Eureka type problems. Rept. No. 7 (Contract Nonr. 226–21). Teachers College, Columbia University, 1954.

49. McCurdy, H. G., and Lambert, W. E. The efficiency of small human

groups in the solution of problems requiring genuine cooperation. *J. Pers.*, 1952, *20*, 478–494.

50. Perlmutter, H. V., and de Montmollin, Germaine. Group learning of nonsense syllables. *J. abnorm. soc. Psychol.*, 1952, *47*, 762–769.

51. Taylor, D. W., and Faust, W. L. Twenty questions: Efficiency in problem solving as a function of size of group. *J. exp. Psychol.*, 1952, *44*, 360–368.

52. Carter, L., and others. The behavior of leaders and other group members. *J. abnorm. soc. Psychol.*, 1951, *46*, 589–595.

53. Henry, A. F., and Borgatta, E. F. A comparison of attitudes of enlisted and commissioned Air Force personnel. *Amer. sociol. Rev.*, 1953, *18*, 669–671.

54. Maier, N. R. F. An experimental test of the effect of training on discussion leadership. *Hum. Relat.*, 1953, *6*, 161–173.

55. Gordon, T. What is gained by group participation? *Educ. Leadership*, 1950, *7*, 220–226.

56. Maier, N. R. F., and Solem, A. R. The contribution of a discussion leader to the quality of group thinking: the effective use of minority opinions. *Hum. Relat.*, 1952, *5*, 277–288.

57. Cantor, N. *The teaching-learning process.* Dryden, 1954.

58. Tizard, J. The effects of different types of supervision on the behavior of mental defectives in a sheltered workshop. *Amer. J. Ment. Defic.*, 1953, *58*, 143–161.

59. McCurdy, H. G., and Eber, H. W. Democratic vs. authoritarian: A further investigation of group problem-solving. *J. Pers.*, 1953, *22*, 258–269.

60. Ruja, H. Experimenting with discussion in college teaching: A survey of recent research. *Educ. Adm. Superv.*, 1953, *39*, 321-342.

61. Johnson, D. M., and Smith, H. C. Democratic leadership in the college classroom. *Psychol. Monogr.*, 1953, *67*, No. 11 (361).

62. Watson, G. An evaluation of small group work in a large class. *J. educ. Psychol.*, 1953, *44*, 385–408.

63. Eglash, A. A group-discussion method of teaching psychology. *J. educ. Psychol.*, 1954, *45*, 257–267.

64. Bills, R. E. An investigation of student centered teaching. *J. educ. Res.*, 1952, *46*, 313–319.

65. Guetzkow, H., Kelly, E. L., and McKeachie, W. J. An experimental comparison of recitation, discussion and tutorial methods in college training. *J. educ. Psychol.*, 1954, *45*, 193–207.

66. Wandt, E., and Ostreicher, L. M. *Variability in observed classroom*

behaviors of junior high school teachers and classes. N.Y. Office of Research and Evaluation, 1953.

67. Shears, L. W. The dynamics of leadership in adolescent school groups. *Brit. J. Psychol.*, 1953, *44*, 232–242.

68. Bass, B. M., and others. Situational and personality factors in leadership among sorority women. *Psychol. Monogr.*, 1953, *67*, 1–23.

69. Klubeck, S., and Bass, B. M. Differential effects of training on persons of different leadership status. *Hum. Relat.*, 1954, *7*, 59–72.

70. Smith, H. C., and Dunbar, D. S. The personality and achievement of the classroom participant. *J. educ. Psychol.*, 1951, *42*, 65–84.

SUGGESTIONS FOR FURTHER READING

1. Lindzey, G., ed. *Handbook of social psychology.* Addison-Wesley, 1954, Vol. II.

    Chap. 21. Experimental studies of group problem solving and process (Kelley, H. H., and Thibaut, J. W.).

    Chap. 22. Psychological aspects of social structure (Riecken, H. W., and Homans, G. C.).

    Chap. 24. Leadership (Gibb, C. A.).

    These chapters from the *Handbook* are the most useful sources for the "next step" in obtaining more complete materials.

For further references and for some helpful analysis of this rapidly growing field, consult any of the following bibliographical sources:

2. Benne, K. D., and Levit, Grace. The nature of groups and helping groups improve their operation. *Rev. educ. Res.*, 1953, *23*, 289–308.

3. Horowitz, M. The conceptual status of group dynamics. *Rev. educ. Res.*, 1953, *23*, 309–329.

4. Roseborough, Mary E. Experimental studies of small groups. *Psychol. Bull.*, 1953, *50*, 275–303.

5. Crutchfield, R. S. Social psychology and group processes. *Annu. Rev. Psychol.*, 1954, *5*, 171–202.

6. Festinger, L. Social psychology and the group processes. *Annu. Rev. Psychol.*, 1955, *6*, 187–216.

7. Taylor, D. W., and McNemar, Olga. Problem solving and thinking. *Annu. Rev. Psychol.*, 1955, *6*, 455–482.

8. Ruja, H. Experimenting with discussion in college teaching: a survey of recent research. *Educ. Adm. Superv.*, 1953, *39*, 321-342.

The following books provide helpful advice on some of the more practical problems:

9. Cunningham, Ruth, and others. *Understanding group behavior of boys and girls.* Teachers College, Columbia University, 1951.

10. Thelen, H. A. *Dynamics of groups at work.* University of Chicago Press, 1954.

11. Northway, Mary L. *A primer of sociometry.* University of Toronto Press, 1952.

Exercises and Questions for Discussion

1. Discuss the role of sex in friendship patterns or social groupings from the preschool through high school. Is there any connection between these changes and the question of co-education?

2. Is there any difference in the qualities that go with popularity and those that go with leadership?

3. By what means could you decide whether or not a person had "identified" with a given group?

4. What part does spontaneity play in friendship at different ages? In leadership?

5. Prepare an outline for a paper on the need for conformity in groups and in individuals.

6. What sort of a group might prove best for each of the following tasks:
   (a) Looking for flaws in a plan that has been carefully worked out, but is up for a last-minute revision?
   (b) Providing a chance for a timid student to learn to express himself in public?
   (c) Keeping a noisy, aggressive student within bounds?
   (d) Writing a sketch for the school variety hour?

19

Personal and Social Adjustment: Major Forces and Interrelations

---

Pᴇʀsᴏɴᴀʟ ᴀɴᴅ sᴏᴄɪᴀʟ ᴀᴅᴊᴜsᴛᴍᴇɴᴛ cannot be isolated from the rest of the person, or from the world in which that person lives. It is only natural to suppose, for instance, that a student's adjustment may be closely related to his health, to his intelligence, and to his performance in school. It is also natural to assume that his personal and social adjustment will be closely related to the community he lives in, to the position of his family in the community, to his general home life, and, perhaps, to his genetic background. When we were studying the development of intelligence and achievement, it will be remembered, we found it necessary to explore the role of these nonscholastic factors. In the same way we must examine the part these forces play in the social and personal growth of the child.

Physique, Health, and Personality

In much of folklore one often finds suggestions that physique and personality are closely connected. The fat, jolly Falstaff and the lean and envious Cassius are familiar and easy to accept. Scientific investigators of this problem have frequently claimed to have substantiated and extended the general beliefs. Sheldon, for instance, claims that somatotype and temperament definitely go hand in hand. If endomorphy predominates we will find sociability and a liking for comfort and for

582

ceremony. For the mesomorph the important thing is action and chal-lenge. The ectomorph, with so much surface in relation to his bulk feels the necessity of keeping the environment from pressing too closely and is led to the search for privacy and a concentration on the inner life. The ectomorph is conspicuously lacking among delinquents of both sexes. Among male delinquents, the mesomorph predominates(1). Among female delinquents we also find a preponderance of mesomorphs but some endomorphs(2).

Although the relation between somatotype and delinquency has been supported by a number of investigations(3), it would be best to regard the more general relations within the normal population as suggestive and tentative(4, 5).

Whether or not physique and temperament are tied together in some inherent way, it is clear that there are some ways in which body build or bodily condition is likely to affect happiness and the amount of worry. Worry over body build, or pimples, or other physical conditions is very frequent(6). In one study(7) some 30 percent of boys and 40 per-cent of girls were definitely disturbed by some physical feature, and height and weight figured prominently among them. Boys were most likely to be worried about being short or fat. Girls, on the other hand, were worried about being tall, fat, or short, or about any combination which marked them as extreme. In general, as one might expect, the worry was due to the *general* physical appearance and not to any one clearly identifiable characteristic. Boys especially were worried about any part of their appearance which made them appear feminine(8).

Physical Disability

Apart from specific worries, we find very little relation between ordinary physical fitness and general personal adjustment(9). With respect to severe physical handicap, however, the results may be differ-ent. Here, of course, we must be extremely cautious. The many studies on this subject present a wide variety of results and the teacher who would stick reasonably close to the facts must avoid sweeping generalities in his discussions of the subject. With these dangers clearly in mind, let us see if we can achieve a general picture that does not do too much violence to the detailed results.

If you are about to work in a school for the physically handicapped, you could assume fairly safely that, *on the average,* you will find a lower degree of maturity, personal adjustment, social competence, social ac-ceptance, and self-acceptance than you would find in other schools(10,

11, 12, 13, 14). Here we are lumping together different kinds of disability and are also grouping together all the children in each kind of ailment. *On the average,* again, this exceedingly general statement will hold for blind children, (but not for children with less serious visual defects), for deaf and hard-of-hearing children, for most types of orthopedic handicaps (but apparently not for poliomyelitis), and for children suffering from cerebral palsy and cardiac conditions. Most emphatically, our statement will not hold for every child in each group. We are speaking only of average differences.

Very often the differences that we report will be found to vanish when other factors are held constant. They are somewhat less when the handicapped and the nonhandicapped are matched(15) for age and sex. They are reduced even further when the groups are matched for socioeconomic status(16). But even here, we must not be lulled into thinking that the issue is all settled and that any differences reported must arise from failure to control other factors. For one thing the various studies have not always used the same kind of tests.

If, clearly aware of all this uncertainty, we go on to the more detailed matters reported, we find many things that seem to make sense (but are not, thereby, to be regarded as true). In many people with a physical handicap there may be a disturbing feeling of being different, of belonging to a minority group. There may be an image of the self as a rather pathetic person, although, in amputees at least, this may change when the person honestly faces the fact of loss. Many handicapped people feel hurt by the help offered to them and are also hurt by seeming neglect. Similarly, many of the handicapped resent undue curiosity about their defect and also resent a conspicuous effort to ignore it. The handicapped person may have more difficulty in attaining a fair measure of genuine social acceptance. Most nonhandicapped college students claim to see their handicapped classmates as no different from anyone else except for lower self-confidence and for the fact that other people (not the person answering the question) are less likely to accept them.

Many writers stress the attitude of the home in discussing the emotional adjustment of the handicapped(17). When parents feel a sense of shame or guilt over the defect, or even when they go too far in providing protection or help, some emotional problem may readily arise.

One study of a hundred women afflicted with lameness, heart disease, or epilepsy suggested a concomitant delay in the development of sexual interests and activities. These handicapped women, when compared with normal women, reported less autoerotic activity, fewer adolescent crushes, and later emancipation from parental control. For the most part the retardation did not seem to come from active repression, but rather from reduced interest in sexual matters(18).

There is a tradition that some diseases, notably tuberculosis, may generate a considerable degree of cheerfulness or optimism. There is little justification for this belief. Fear is the rule among tuberculous patients. Such patients are also more irritable and neurotic than people who have escaped the disease(19).

It is not surprising that extensive loss or destruction of brain tissue, whatever its effect on intelligence (Chapter 7), has a fairly definite effect on personality. Extremely subdued patients who have had part of the frontal lobes of the brain removed(20) become more active and, for some time at least, seem to be in better contact with the environment. The changes revealed by test scores do not always agree with the general impressions of those who have observed the patients. The latter frequently report greater talkativeness, less restraint or inhibition(21), and perhaps less social sensitivity, loss of anxiety, and often a mild euphoria.

Intelligence in Relation to Personality Adjustment

There is some suggestion(22) that intelligence is related to the basic needs or concerns of the student. It is not surprising to learn that the very bright children (IQ 120-200) when compared to dull children (IQ 70-100) show more concern about achievement and recognition, that they express more curiosity, and have a more creative urge. They are also more independent and more likely to dominate than to follow or to accept leadership. They have more zest for games and fun. Socially, they are more likely to be helpful and less likely to reject others or to seek seclusion. In each of these traits it is easy to see how intelligence might play a part.

There is still a moderate correlation between intelligence and personality when the latter is considered as general all-round adjustment(23). Whenever we turn to the more detailed aspects of personal adjustment, however, we are less likely to find any dependable relation. Over a number of studies the correlations range from −.40 to .20 with an average close to zero(24). When we attempt to correlate detailed aspects of personal adjustment, we are extremely unlikely to find any relation that will hold from one group to another(25).

As we might expect, popularity or social acceptance, especially in the classroom, has some relation to intelligence. Children with definite mental deficiency are not so likely to be accepted by their classmates. This is true both in the traditional and in the more progressive schools(26). Even in special institutions for the mentally defective, the more the defect the more likely it is that the student will be rejected(27).

Intelligence and Delinquency. At one time it was assumed that delinquency and mental defect were almost one and the same thing. After some dozens of investigations throughout the years, however, it has become clear that, although there is some relation, it is much less than was previously thought. A fair number of delinquents are recruited from those below 70 IQ. The majority, however, tend to fall in the range between 85 and 90 with the average close to 90. There are also quite a few delinquents with superior intelligence(28, 29). Among delinquents, girls and very young boys are especially likely to have a low IQ, although here, too, we find a wide range of intelligence.

Before making too much of this relationship, we should note that the delinquent probably reflects his family and sociological background. As we have seen, he tends to come from an extremely tawdry environment, and in some investigations(30) he has been found to have about the same intelligence as his nondelinquent brother.

Ethical Behavior as Measured by Tests. Delinquency, of course, is an extreme form of immorality. In studying delinquency we limit ourselves to those who have been officially convicted of some breach of our laws. Obviously there are many less extreme deviations from accepted stand-

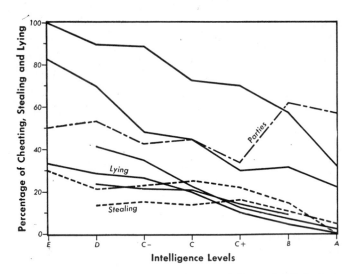

FIGURE 19-1. *Cheating, Stealing, and Lying in Relation to Intelligence.* Redrawn by permission from Figure 289 in Shuttleworth (See Fig. 5-2 for reference).

ards, such as those measured by the many tests of altruism, of honesty, and of ethical knowledge. To what extent does intellect correlate with the ethical behavior revealed by these tests? To answer this question, Miss Chassel(31) examined the results of some three hundred separate investigations. The 300 coefficients of correlation reported in these investigations ranged from .10 to .40. Many of the tests of ethical behavior, of course, are very unreliable. If corrected for this unreliability, the coefficients would be considerably higher. It appears, therefore, that there is an appreciable correlation between intelligence and the kind of goodness that is measured by our tests, although clearly this correlation is low enough to permit a great many marked exceptions to the rule.

The graphs in Figure 19-1 show many of these trends. In almost all measures of cheating or lying or stealing we find more offenders as we move from the higher to the lower intelligence levels. There is one noticeable exception to this rule, however. One test of cheating involved performance on "stunts" in a party situation. Here a student could improperly boost his score by "peeking" or by similar infractions of the rules. In this situation, we find somewhat more cheating on the part of the brightest children.

Achievement in Relation to Personal Adjustment

Several aspects of personal and social behavior have a fairly close relation to scholastic achievement. Interests, for instance, are indicative of achievement in that students with marked interest in academic subjects achieve somewhat more than students whose interests are in the vocational subjects(32, 33). At the junior-high-school level we sometimes find better achievement on the part of students who like school(34), but in one investigation this did not hold at the college level(35). Strong interest in a future career, at this level, however, does seem to be related to achievement(36).

In an attempt to bring some order into this confusing field Carter(37) selected those items of a questionnaire that seemed to distinguish between successful and unsuccessful students. He then subjected these items to factor analysis. Four chief factors emerged. Carter suggests that these are: (1) Morale (self-confidence, rather than a feeling of hopelessness). (2) Accepting the things for which the school stands. Some students understand these values but scorn them. Other students seem never to have had their eyes opened to the things that count academically. Both groups have trouble in school. (3) Sheer mechanics of study; taking notes, intelligent review, and so forth. (4) Long-term planning or deliberation (arranging a schedule for review, trying to get a picture of the things to be done, and planning what to do).

These are the chief factors that seem to go along with achievement. It would be a mistake, of course, to jump to conclusions regarding the causal pattern. High morale could lead to success; success may boost morale; some fortunate facet of one's make-up may account for both.

So far we have been considering general academic success. What about the relation between interest in a special field or a special subject and achievement in that field or subject? For any individual student, there is a moderate relation. He does better in the subjects of high interest than in the subjects for which he has little interest(38). Here again we do not know which is cause and which effect. Paradoxically, even this moderate relation may vanish when we lump together in one group all the students who are interested, say, in science and in another group all those who have little interest in science. We do not always find that the first group excels in science grades(39).

Whatever may be the relation between interest and the amount or degree of achievement in a subject, it seems clear that our interests or attitudes have some influence on the particular ideas that we absorb or remember. We will more readily comprehend a message that means success than one that means failure or humiliation. A Negro child and a white child, for instance, reading an identical passage on race relations might come away with quite different impressions of what the passage contained(40).

Teachers' Ratings. In many schools teachers are asked to rate their students on a variety of personal traits. In these ratings, the teachers give their opinion of the student's ambition, stability, reliability, co-operation, initiative, attentiveness, persistence, trustworthiness, and accuracy. When these ratings are correlated with the student's academic standing, we find very substantial relations. In some of the investigations these correlations range from .40 to .80. Correlations of this size are as high as the correlations between intelligence and achievement or indeed a little higher. When we take into account the probable unreliability of the teachers' ratings, the close relationship becomes even more significant, since the reported correlations have already been reduced by the unreliability(41, 42, 43).

Some of the correlation between achievement and teachers' ratings of personal traits may well be due to the halo effect. This is especially probable if the teacher already knows something of the student's academic performance before the personality ratings take place. Under such circumstances, it would be almost inevitable that the teacher should be inclined to rate the good student somewhat higher in desirable personal traits.

Although the halo effect undoubtedly plays some part in producing the high correlations between achievement and teachers' ratings, it would be a mistake to assume that the entire relation is due directly to this effect. For one thing, there is some correlation between personality ratings given by high-school teachers and the academic performance of students after they reach college(44). Here, of course, the high-school teachers could not be directly influenced by the nonexisting college performance.

Correlations between high-school rating and college performance do not reach the same size as those between high-school ratings and high-school marks. College grades correlate about .30 or .35 with the high-school teacher's estimate of independence in getting work done and about .20 or .30 with the teacher's estimate of emotional control. Such grades have zero correlation with the high-school teacher's estimate of personal appearance.

There is a danger, of course, in reading too much into these general over-all relations. There are many intricate possible relations which must be examined before we can say definitely just what is causing what. For the time being at least, we should accept the possibility of the direct halo effect and of an indirect halo effect in which the high-school work affects the high-school teacher's rating and in which the high-school work *also* affects the college success. We should also accept the possibility that the traits which the teachers rate highly actually help the student to obtain good grades. It will be noted, by the way, that the traits which have the clearest relation are those of earnestness, industry, attentiveness, independence of work habits, persistence, and the like. It would be surprising if such traits did not contribute something toward academic grades.

Adjustment as Measured by Tests and Inventories. If the informal, unreliable ratings of teachers have a substantial relation to academic performance, we might expect the more carefully developed standard inventories to be even more productive. Unfortunately, however, this is not the case. For the most part, the relation between such questionnaires or inventories and achievement is quite low. The correlations seldom exceed .20 or .25. This holds true especially for the high-school and college levels(15, 16, 47). Whenever relationships do appear, they are somewhat similar to those we considered under intelligence. Like his dull classmate, the child of average intelligence who is behind in his schoolwork will show lack of confidence, will be unwilling to take blame for his difficulties, and may be self-centered, aggressive, or "cocky" in his attitude(48). Tentatively we could consider the matter about as follows: with respect to adjustment, the differences between the good student and the poor student are not at all marked. On the average, however, any maladjustment shown by the poor student is likely to be of the assertive, noisy type. Maladjustment of the good student, when it is found, is more likely to be of the subdued, overinhibited type(49, 50).

Major Forces in Personal and Social Adjustment

In discussing various aspects of personal and social adjustments we have necessarily had much to say about the factors that may have played a part. In these discussions, however, the comments on any single force or agency were necessarily scattered. In this section, therefore, we attempt to scrutinize each major force in its own right, trying to assess the part it may play in the various aspects of development.

Sex Differences in Personal Traits

It is clear that boys are more obstreperous than girls and contribute far more than their quota to the misdemeanors of home, school, and community. (For every girl or woman arrested there are from two to nineteen men arrested.) Boys are also rougher, more assertive, more aggressive, more quarrelsome and unruly, perhaps more persistent(51), and more fond of vigorous active games and of games involving teamwork. Later they show more interest in machinery and in the materials of natural science. They continue their greater interest in more active recreations and show more fondness for the outdoors. In their reading, movie, or radio habits they show a preference for excitement and adventure. The conversations of mature American men often center on money and business, as well as on women.

Girls are unquestionably quieter, more docile(52), and less likely to get into trouble. In their play, they are inclined to games involving less vigorous activity, often being content to sit still for a period of time which would be unbearable for many boys. Along with sedentary activity goes a preference for playing with scissors, colors, and dolls, as opposed to the boys' preference for building blocks or structural materials. In spite of their willingness to sit still for longer periods of time, young girls change their play activities more frequently than boys.

Science supports popular impression in the belief that women are more interested in attire and personal appearance. It also partially confirms the belief that women have a greater predilection for the fine arts. In contrast to the male interest in things mechanical, women are more intrigued by personal and social relations. Some of this interest, at least, may be related to a greater feminine concern over social welfare and more solicitude for human relationships in general. Adult women, when conversing, find other women one of the most intriguing topics of discussion.

Women are often considered more intuitive and emotional(53) and, indeed, they seem to be more given to emotional expression, especially to the expression of emotions involving pity, disgust, or moral disapproval. Women also have a more favorable attitude toward church and religion(54). There is some evidence(55) also that women are more subject to fluctuations in mood. On the more stable side, however, we find that women are more inclined to reflective thinking and are also more willing to admit fears and feelings of personal inadequacy.

In our culture the typical adolescent girl has an intense desire to please, although she is not always sure what she must do to accomplish that objective(56). When girls are reminded of the importance of being liked or accepted by others, their need for achievement and accomplishment is brought to the fore, whereas boys show no such response to this type of urging(57). Girls, on the other hand, do not respond in this way to a reminder of the importance of leadership and initiative—a most effective argument for boys.

There have been several attempts to introduce some order into this haphazard cluster of facts. Naturally factor analysis has been called in to see what it can do in the field of masculine and feminine interests. One study(58) suggests that in addition to the matter of sheer interest we can find a factor of "tough-mindedness" working in the case of boys and two other factors, sensitivity and social role, at work in the case of girls. And it seems that many specific items could be related to these factors or dimensions. In line with this dimension of tough-mindedness, for instance, we find that boys are more in favor of universal military training, are more convinced of the likelihood of a depression in the future, do not like the idea of awarding letters to honor students, do not favor close cooperation between teachers and parents, and would more readily permit teachers to strike. More boys would also insist on work experience as a requirement for graduation(59).

Many people have suggested that, to make sense out of these sex differences, we have only to remember that girls and women can accept fairly easily the role that the culture imposes. When the culture stresses the homemaker, many women can comply. Many of them can also comply when the culture and the situation demand independent achievement(60). We have no clear evidence of the adequacy of this view. With respect to the purely social roles, conformity seems to be more important for girls than for boys(61). With respect to the more differentiated sexual roles, however, this is probably not true. A boy might well be less disturbed than a girl at the thought of failing to meet the conventions demanded of both boys and girls. He would probably be greatly disturbed, however, to be considered a sissy, or to fail to live up to the masculine ideal.

Differences in the roles of the sexes are rather clearly set forth in our culture. Middle-class fathers(62), in setting forth ideals for their sons, tend to list such virtues as initiative, responsibility, and a reasonable amount of aggressiveness. They hope for scholastic success and perhaps a successful business career. In listing the traits they would like to see in their daughters, they mention affection and docility, and, of course, a career of marriage.

Between the ages of three and four, if not earlier, most children have a pretty clear idea that some things are expected of males and other things of females. Young boys have clearer ideas on this score than girls, and the distinction is clearer in lower class homes. In one study of homes in which the father was absent on military service, boys were later in becoming aware of the sex role.

In the elementary school, these sex roles are constantly emphasized. Adherence to them is often one of the conditions of popularity(63), especially for children in the intermediate grades. A boy must be energetic and venturesome and a girl quiet and modest.

It would be amazing if this consistent and powerful pressure did not have much to do in producing sex differences. It could well force a tomboy girl to repress her more active tendencies. It could also force her quieter brother to affect a devilishness for which he had no real appetite. Powerful as these forces are, however, we must not assume that they are the only influences at work. It is still too soon to say that the genes responsible for physical differences in the sexes may not also contribute to the differences in personality that we have noted(64, 65, 66).

Family Background

No discussion of personality development proceeds very far without some mention of family life and early upbringing. Let us look at several aspects of family background as possible forces in personal and social adjustment.

Heredity. Uncongenial as the idea is to many people, we should try to see whether or not personality may be affected in any way by sheer genetic constitution. There have been a number of attempts to investigate this problem, chiefly through the comparison of identical twins with same-sex fraternal twins. This method has been used a good many times to determine the influence of heredity on delinquency. The overwhelming conclusion of these studies is the fact that heredity does play a part in many kinds of delinquency. This is not to say, of course, that heredity is the only factor involved. The results indicate, however, that with environment held constant, certain hereditary conditions are likely to play a part in delinquent behavior. In the most extensive investigation of this type(67), it was found that 68 percent of identical twin pairs had similar criminal histories. If one member of the twin pair was delinquent, the other member was also likely to be delinquent. For fraternal, same-sex twin pairs, however, the story was very different. Here only 18 percent of the pairs had similar criminal histories.

It is also apparent that identical twins are much more similar than same-sex fraternal twins in such things as incidence and type of insanity(68) and in homosexuality. If one identical twin is homosexual the other is almost always homosexual. In same-sex fraternal twins this is true in only 40 percent of the cases(69). With respect to the sort of adjustment measured by inventories and tests, we also find much more correspondence on the part of identical twins (69 percent agreement, correlation of .85) than on the part of fraternal twins (33 percent agreement, correlation of .21)(70, 71).

One interesting investigation attempted to determine the extent to which the alcoholic personality could be inherited(72). This study compared two groups of foster children. One of these groups was descended from alcoholic parents, the other from nonalcoholic parents. The children of both groups had been reared in foster homes. In this study, the differences were very slight, suggesting that the traits making for alcoholism are probably not inherited.

We must again stress the fact that our information on this important topic is by no means complete or final. In this situation, the thing to do, of course, is to accept the inevitable uncertainty. We must not let our need to know the answer force us to see an answer where none exists. Meanwhile we can accept the sketchy information as a slight guide. The evidence strongly suggests that heredity plays a part in one or two aspects of personality, but there are also some negative data. All in all, it is most likely that heredity is important in some traits but that it is not equally effective in all aspects of personality.

Social Class of the Family. In another section we point out that social class is a complex thing including income, education, and occupation, but not made up exclusively of these things. Family background and source of income also play a big part. Most important perhaps are the social groups for which one is eligible. We all realize, of course, that there are vast differences between the homes in different classes(73). If we are chiefly familiar with the average socioeconomic status group, however, we may be astounded to find the cultural differences in many homes. In the investigation of one SES group, for instance, it was found that 30 percent of the homes had absolutely no books of any kind. Other cultural gaps were almost equally impressive.

These differences in SES and in cultural level are reflected in the reading interests and play interests of the children. The children from the higher SES groups play more varied games and are more likely to play adult-type intellectual games in which their parents take part(74). As we have already seen, among older children especially, the children from the better homes are less likely to cheat. They are also less likely to become delinquent(75). Although children from the better SES groups exhibit the same sort of fears and worries as their less fortunate class-mates, we find a better, or at least a more enlightened, program for meeting those fears on the part of the more educated parents. In general we also find somewhat better personal adjustment in the middle and upper SES groups(76, 77). One quite analytical study(78), however, reports that lower-class adolescent girls are generally more mature and have certainly fitted into their sex role in a more mature way. The middle-class girls are ambitious, but anxious and dependent.

Davis(79) has called attention to the great variation in ethical standards to be found between different SES groups. Physical aggression with fist or with knife is encouraged in some homes. In these same homes, there is nothing unchivalrous in hitting a woman, but it is unsporting to cut her in the face. Attacking a teacher or a supervising adult is merely a matter of expediency. It is permissible if you can get away with it. Ordinary heterosexual activity is also more a matter of discretion than of ethics. In these homes, however, we must not suppose that there are no codes or systems of ethics. Aggression must be fairly direct. Poison, for instance, is frowned on. So is rape. Stealing is restricted to certain groups who are "fair game."

The value system of the so-called middle class has received a good deal of attention. The middle class is supposed to venerate education(80) and to stress the importance of hard work and self-denial in the present in the hope of future gratification(81). Middle-class children do adopt this attitude and also come to value conformity to adult standards, whereas their classmates from the other side of the track will stress self-assertion and aggression(82).

Not only are middle-class parents considered to have different standards, but they are more "standard" conscious, so to speak, and are greatly concerned that their children attain those standards. Certainly in the middle-class homes there is a wider gulf between the standards set and the behavior of the children(83). To many theorists, this severity and the rigid insistence on conformity to rather conventional standards is a typical feature of middle-class child rearing. In contrast we often hear of the more indulgent, relaxed, and permissive attitude typical of the lower-class parent. This view has been strenuously challenged, however, and several writers claim that the lower-class home is by no means as permissive(84, 85, 86) as we have been led to believe. In these homes there may be less severity with regard to manners or cleanliness, but there may be even more severity over the interruption of father's Sunday nap or the destruction of a prized parental possession.

Many sociologists attach great significance to this seemingly vast gulf between the values held by the two classes. Many of the children in the schools live in homes with lower-class values. Many of the teachers, on the other hand, come from the middle class. And those who come from the upper-lower class, it is claimed, are even more frantic than the rest in their devotion to middle-class values. Obsessed with their own values, teachers cannot conceive that some people really do not care much about education, about manners, or respecting the conventions. Seeing parents or children lacking in these things, they assume that this lack is due merely to indolence or worthlessness.

There is some suggestion, by the way, that teachers entering the profession now come from a somewhat lower socioeconomic background than those who started teaching twenty or thirty years ago. At present the family background of beginning teachers is likely to be that of farmer or clerk. Few teachers of our day come from the professional class or from the homes of proprietors or business owners(87). This change in the class background of teachers, however, does not necessarily mean that teachers are less likely to impose middle-class values.

In describing this problem we must not seem to suggest that the remedy is obvious or easy. In the first place, the question is not wholly a psychological issue. In the second place, the question is quite complex. The middle-class values nurtured by the school may have genuine social importance. There may be no way to preserve these without making things somewhat awkward for people who do not take to them naturally. In that case we would have to balance whatever harm may come from the inevitable tension against the importance of propagating the values in question.

The Environment within the Family

The social group within which the family finds itself clearly has some relation to the personality and the adjustment of the child. We would expect, however, that the immediate family situation would be even more closely related. Families which contain an unusual number of adults seem to exert a strain on the young child. At any rate, we find more temper tantrums from children who come from such homes. The influence of a large number of children is harder to assess. There is some evidence that children from large families are less likely to turn up in child guidance clinics(88). On the other hand, the only child, so frequently an object of pity, seems to do very well(89). He is just as friendly and popular and just as well adjusted as the child from a larger family.

In the discussion of delinquency we stressed the frequency of the broken home. Delinquents are much more likely to come from homes from which the father or mother has deserted, or where there has been divorce or the death of one of the parents. We will do well to remember, however, that very frequently children adjust quite satisfactorily to tragedies such as these, and that prior to divorce or desertion there is usually some abnormal strain(90).

Parental behavior, like so many other things, has received the benefits of factor analysis(91). Apparently, to get a complete account of the differences in child-rearing practices we should have to tell, first, the extent to which the parents encourage or permit the child to retain an attitude of dependence; second, the extent to which practices are democratic rather than arbitrary or authoritarian; and third, the extent to which orderliness and neatness are stressed. If we know these things we can do much toward inferring the more detailed practices.

Over and above the specific practices to be found in the home, there is the less tangible general emotional climate. In contrast to the practices, this climate is seldom a deliberate affair. Some people are naturally lively, affectionate, easygoing, and indulgent. Others are more withdrawn, cautious, and exacting. These are not things that are readily turned on or off at will, nor are they necessarily the result of insight or good intentions. Some of the warmest, most accepting homes, in fact, are to be found among people who have had precious little benefit from parent education or child study. Some of the most worrisome parents, harassed by overconcern, are to be found among people who consume books on child psychology in large and uncritical fashion.

It would be interesting to single out the aspect of home life which has the closest bearing on wholesome personality development. There is, as yet, no clear-cut answer to this question. Recent writers have stressed the importance of affection and cheerfulness in the home and have criticized the aloof, rigid parent as well as the unbalanced, overemotional, over-solicitous parent. Shirley(92), for instance, blames the rejecting and the oversolicitous mother for the lack of adjustment shown by some children. Lack of affection from parents, or a feeling of being discriminated against, may also be a factor in delinquency.

It is possible that some combinations of these aspects may be especially significant. A combination of a cruel, rejecting father with an over-protecting mother who encouraged dependency, for instance, turned out to be a frequent home condition in the lives of boys who later became schizophrenic(93).

The philosophy of the home, or its intellectual attitude, or its policy of childhood education, in contrast to the emotional climate, can be based on an intellectual decision and can be turned on or off at will. It would be most important to see how these controllable forces affect the child's personality. One study(94) along this line suggests that children brought up under the democratic philosophy are more lively, more aggressive, more likely to lead, more likely to plan their own doings, but are also more likely to show a cruel streak. Children from homes in which there is more control are likely to be quieter and better be-haved but they also tend to be more restricted in interest and curiosity.

More specific practices, such as the amount of punishment employed by the mother, are also related to the child's personality but in a com-plex way. Young children who are frequently punished show marked aggression when playing with dolls representing members of the family(95). But they do not always show more of the sort of aggression that is observed on the playground(96). Boys who have received much punishment are more dependent than those receiving little punishment. But the reverse is true for girls!

Identification and Understanding between Parent and Child

Frequently a child is asked to fill out an interest inventory in the normal way. He is then asked to fill it out the way he thinks his father (or mother) would fill it out and finally to answer it as he thinks most people would. From comparisons of these inventories we can see whether the child visualizes himself as having more in common with the parent than with most people. To the extent that he does, we speak of a sense of identification with the parent.

As might be expected, boys who identify strongly with the father tend to be better adjusted and have less difficulty in adjusting to the demands of the masculine sex role(61, 97). It may be more surprising, however, to find better adjustment also on the part of girls who identify with the father(98).

By a modification of the technique just described we can get some idea of an adult's awareness of a child's needs or problems. To do this we ask the child to fill out an inventory of worries, or needs, or interests, and then ask either parent to fill out the same blank as he thinks the child would. In mother-daughter relations, at least, lack of such awareness goes hand in hand with contention and with poor adjustment on the part of the daughter, especially if there is rather strict control. When this lack of awareness is associated with a disturbed home life, we find more than average juvenile delinquency(99).

There is a close resemblance between the general social attitudes of parents and those of the children. On politics, attitude toward labor, or toward minority groups, children reflect the attitudes of parents much more closely than the attitudes of their teachers(100). Young children even acquire the specific fears and worries of their mothers.

Irreversibility. It has long been suspected that quirks or peculiarities established in early life may be difficult to eradicate. To a certain extent this belief has been supported by more elaborate studies(101). Problem children who have been rejected or neglected in early years often find it impossible to respond to patient and genuine attempts to gain their friendship. The suspicion, bitterness, and hardness seems almost impossible to overcome. Even less drastic disturbances may persist in spite of efforts at correction. It was found in one study(92), for instance, that young children were less disturbed on their first appearance at nursery school if they were accompanied by their mothers. Later it was arranged that the frightened children should be accompanied by the mothers and that the well-adjusted children should attend alone. When this change was made, the previously adjusted group began to show signs of insecurity, but unfortunately, the poorly adjusted children were little improved by the presence of the mother.

Need for Caution in Interpreting the Role of the Family

So what can we conclude? On the surface, it seems that science now confirms what people of intelligence and good will have been saying for some time. The results seem to stress the importance of love and affection warmly and consistently expressed, of much lively and good-natured give and take, of taking the child into one's confidence and giving him as much voice as possible in the things that affect his interests, of understanding the needs and urges that drive him whether those needs be pretty or unpretty, and of curtailing the use of punishment. No ordinary mortal, of course, could hope to maintain a program of child rearing that would meet all these requirements. For the time being, however, it seems wise to accept this as an ideal toward which we might move. Clearly it is a program in which we would like to believe. It is a program in which kindness, intelligence, and understanding predominate and in which harshness and arbitrary dictation play little part. It is fortunate that this program, so clearly in line with enlightened opinion and having such an appeal to our most worthy sentiments, is also supported by the bulk of the evidence available so far. All in all, when we have occasion to talk to parents, we might properly say, "In spite of its exacting standards, this is a course that seems the most promising at the moment. It is also a course that you will enjoy insofar as you are able to keep to it."

But there are some cautions to be kept in mind. We must not be lulled into complacency by the fact that the most efficient course also happens to be the one that accords with our preferences and our preconceptions. Although giving the parents a course they may follow, we must check again and again to see if by some chance this course may be in error.

There are some areas of doubt. We have few long-range studies that have followed the children from cradle to adulthood. The studies that we do have are not all unambiguous. The more carefully controlled investigations(102) report results that are exceedingly varied. Trends that hold for girls do not hold for boys. Factors associated with one kind of aggression seem to have little to do with another kind of aggression. It could be that these matters are really as complex as they seem to be. Or it could be that we have not got at the main forces and are focusing our attentions on some capricious by-products.

Apart from the inconsistencies and the limited time span, we face the ever-present question of what causes what. The trends that we have observed could mean, as so many people assume, that the broken home actually leads to delinquency; that parental rejection actually leads to maladjustment; that frequent punishment creates or enhances aggressive impulses; that lack of understanding or identification creates stress. But these possibilities represent only one type of hypothesis. The trends may not mean these things at all. They may mean, on the contrary, that it is the child's behavior that determines the treatment he receives. The data may merely mean that aggressive children are more likely to be punished; that children who get into trouble may incur parental displeasure or rejection; that the presence of a delinquent in the family could lead to parental discord or to the disruption of a home; that well-adjusted children can identify themselves with the traits in the father, whereas poorly adjusted children shrink from tough-minded masculinity. Finally it is possible that both these hypotheses are false and that the trends merely reflect some common cause. Something is at work to lead mothers to punish excessively, to lead parents to reject their children, or to lead to divorce or desertion. The same things that produce these conditions could, in and of themselves, produce the quirks in the children. Poverty or resentment against discrimination could lead to excessive punishment of children. But these same factors could induce aggression in the children even if the mother restrained herself. Some defect in gene or make-up, some lack of responsibility must lie behind desertion. And these deficiencies, if transmitted to the child, could lead to delinquency even if the father were induced to remain at home.

General Community Differences

By looking at cultures somewhat different from our own it has been possible to see, in better perspective, wide differences in personality, attitudes, and values on the part of peoples and cultures. It would be ridiculous to suppose, of course, that everyone within a given culture has the same personality. Even in the face of wide individual differences, however, anthropologists have been able to delineate rather definite contrasts between gentle self-effacing Indian groups on the one hand and fiercely assertive competitive tribes on the other. The contrasts on this continent are duplicated in East Indian societies where we find a wide range from some tribes where vigorous aggression is the virtue most prized to others where genial relaxation is the norm or certainly the ideal.

As yet it has been impossible to select the feature or features of the child-rearing program of the culture which is responsible for the predominating character. In one comprehensive survey(103) it has been suggested that extreme frustration of activities, such as aggressive behavior, during childhood is associated with an unusual concern over that activity throughout life. There is less evidence that unusual indulgence of an activity might also imprint it firmly in the child's habit system.

Several anthropological studies have called attention to the fact that in many cultures child rearing calls for great restriction (being swaddled or strapped to a tree board) and for complete submission to the patriarchal father without any observable disaster(104, 105).

There are several communal religious colonies in this country which represent cultures of their own. Among the Hutterites, for instance, all property is owned in common and is administered by a firm group of leaders. There is an other-worldly atmosphere and a strong emphasis on social support, kindness, nonviolence, and duty. There is little fear of want or of severe social rejection. At one time it was thought that mental illness was almost nonexistent among this group. A more careful study(106), however, shows an average amount of mental disorder but of a type that could be managed without hospitalization. The children of another religious sect, the Amish, feel different and at a disadvantage when they come in contact with the outside world(107).

Rural-Urban. Studies of rural-urban differences in this country produce few surprises. Rural children have stricter and more consistent discipline at home. They are less aggressive, less prone to the "gang" type of delinquency, and are also less liberal in their social attitudes. They are not inferior in general personal adjustment.

City Neighborhood. There is much indirect evidence that the community has a great influence on personality and on social development. Some of this evidence is as forceful (and as uncontrolled) as the melodramas of the "Dead-End Kids." Some of the evidence, on the other hand, has come from carefully arranged studies. In general, it is true that the more densely populated parts of cities have more than their share of delinquency (Figure 19-2). It is also true that certain notorious communities spew forth a disproportionate share of delinquency and crime, no matter which national or ethnic group inhabits that particular region(108). Such evidence, of course, must be considered indirect until we can show that the region does not attract or select potentially antisocial elements.

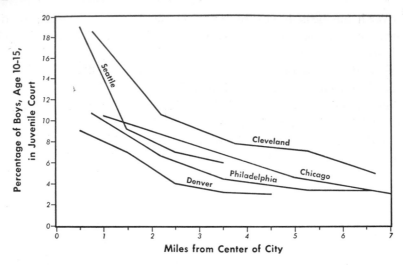

FIGURE 19-2. *Delinquency in Relation to Distance from Center of City*. Redrawn by permission from Figure 353 in Shuttleworth (See Fig. 5-2 for reference).

Carroll(109) has shown that the announced ideals of students also vary with the type of environment. For Negro children living in a low-class neighborhood friendship and social standards are based entirely on a very pathetic utility. Friends are to be desired because, in a pinch, they may loan you money. Stealing is wrong because you might get caught. In describing the ideal adult, these children frequently mention traits of beauty and glamor, but the concept of kindness does not occur to them. In all these reactions, the children just described were markedly different from other Negro children living in middle-class neighborhoods.

National and Racial Groups

Literature and folklore are filled with many definite views regarding the personal characteristics of different national or racial groups. The imperturbable American Indian, the gay Negro, the volatile Italian, the restrained Englishman are clearly fixed in our minds and have become literary stereotypes. Actually, of course, the truth is much more complicated. The Indian is imperturbable only in certain situations. At other times he may show his anguish in wholehearted fashion. The Negro can be somber enough on occasion.

Although these impressions are quite clear-cut, the actual research on the subject is very spotty indeed(110). In setting goals for himself and his children, the Englishman stresses a rich inner life and avoidance of antisocial behavior. His American cousin emphasizes the challenge of the environment and the perils of a personality at cross-purposes with itself(111).

Negro children, on the average, fall somewhat behind white children in self-adjustment and social adjustment. Negro boys, understandably enough, are less likely to regard the world as friendly(112). On projective tests they also show more than their share of aggression but worry less than white boys about rejection by their families(113). Along with this greater aggression, perhaps as one aspect of it, we note that Negro college students show somewhat more prejudice against the people of foreign countries(114). Many theorists, of course, would expect greater prejudice on the part of a group subjected to discrimination. In overt statements made to interviewers, Negro boys naturally show great distress over the ridicule and discrimination to which they are subjected(115).

Some test results suggest that Jewish groups(116) score above average in dominance. In one study(117), using both test scores and ratings by the faculty, there was a tendency for the Jewish students to score higher on aggressiveness. The instructors also rated the Jewish students higher in alertness and enthusiasm, but lower in reliability and in personal attractiveness. On the formal tests, the Jewish students had higher scores for liberality, radicalism, and gregariousness, but lower scores for religion, timidity, and emotional stability.

Delinquency. We must be extremely careful in drawing conclusions about the relation of racial or national factors to delinquency. Racial groups who differ in criminal tendency also tend to vary in type of environment and in cultural advantages. And it is difficult to say whether the racial factor or the community factor determines the relationship.

Immigrants have a lower crime rate than adult descendants of native parents. The status of the children of immigrant parents, however, is less clear. In some industrial communities, at least, the children of immigrant parents have a markedly higher rate than that of children of native parents. There is evidence, however, that this higher rate for children of immigrants may not hold over the country at large(118).

In industrial areas, certain racial or national groups (Negroes, Russians, Italians) exceed their quota of delinquency(75, 119). Again, we do not know if this trait comes from some genetic or inherent culture factor, or whether it is a result of the social conditions in which the more delinquent groups live.

Motion Pictures, Radio, Television, and Comics

In considering the nonscholastic forces which may affect personal development, we should not neglect the moving pictures, the radio, television, the magazines, and the much-discussed comics. Unfortunately, however, regarding many of these agencies we have very little evidence(120). Among normal children there is little relation between adjustment and the number of comics read(121). Delinquents, of course, spend an unusal amount of time with the comics and tend to choose the more unwholesome of these(122). In this case, however, it is impossible to know whether the comics contribute to the delinquency or whether they merely appeal to someone who is maladjusted for some other reason.

As far as personal adjustment is concerned we can find no marked influence of ordinary exposure to the radio(123, 124) or television(125, 126, 127). It is true that there is more nervousness among children who have a strong addiction to horror stories, but here, of course, we cannot tell whether the addiction is the cause or the result of the nervousness. It is perhaps too soon to say much about the long-range effects of television. When television first came into the home many children spent an appalling amount of time watching it. Some school children reported as much as thirty hours per week. There is some evidence that this excessive viewing decreases with age and as the novelty wears off. Even so, however, a very moderate effect could reach considerable proportions when viewing is so extensive.

The one agency which has been repeatedly investigated is the motion picture. The results show clearly that the motion picture can definitely affect attitudes toward social groups. In a series of careful experiments, Thurstone(128) has shown that a gangster film made students more critical of gambling, and conversely, that a picture presenting a German family in a sympathetic light definitely increased the student's liking for Germans.

During World War II a group of films were shown to soldiers with the intention of developing more favorable attitudes toward our allies. These were quite effective in changing opinions about specific items (to whom do we owe the development of radar?) but did little to change general liking or preference(129). Apparently adults are less susceptible to this approach than students. Certainly in the case of young children it would be surprising if the moving pictures were not effective in developing many attitudes. With their verisimilitude and devastating authority, they carry a conviction which the typical teacher can seldom hope to approach.

Facts observed in movies tend to be remembered, often for periods of months. Certainly, too, children are moved or affected during the show and for some time after. There is much more nocturnal squirming and disturbance of sleep after movie attendance. This same disturbance has been observed, by the way, after radio listening.

The School as a General Force

There are some features of the school which are beyond the control of the individual teacher and which may affect the personal development of the student. Several of these influences were mentioned in the discussion of the school as an involuntary force in the academic development of the student. The general philosophy of the school, for instance, goes far beyond the control of the individual teacher, and yet this general philosophy will leave its imprint on the student. The students who attend the progressive or new-type schools tend to show more initiative, resourcefulness, and leadership than students from the more traditional schools(130, 131, 132, 133, 134). As yet, however, there is little to suggest that such children are any more secure or that they show superior emotional adjustment. There is some evidence of more shifting around of sociometric choices in the more progressive schools(135). This "shaking-up" process does not guarantee greater general acceptance, of course, but it does permit such a general increase. It has also been suggested that social acceptance will increase when students in one class are frequently regrouped for various projects(136). Apparently this increase in acceptability is in no way hampered by having more than one grade level in the same room(137).

One investigator(138) reports a comparison of students at coeducational versus single-sex high schools. Apparently the coeducational schools attract the better adjusted students, especially the better adjusted girls. During the high-school period coeducational students lose a little in adjustment but are still ahead of the seniors in the single-sex schools. Although the latter students start out behind the coeducational students, they do not lose during the school period and so are not quite so far behind as seniors.

Summary

Personal and social adjustment is closely related to other aspects of growth and to a great many factors outside the schoolroom. The age-old ideas of body build and temperament are still under study and little has been settled. Physical defects, mild or severe, are associated *on the average* with lack of maturity and less adequate adjustment. Marked sensitivity is also present. The causes for the relation are unknown. Parental attitude may play a part. One physical change, removal of brain tissue, seems to make for free expression of impulses, but this issue is most controversial.

There is some relation between intelligence and personality, especially in the realm of interests, drive, and confidence. This relation holds for all-round adjustment. It is harder to find a relationship between intelligence and any specific facet of personality as revealed by inventories. On the average, delinquents fall below the norm in intelligence, but not below the norm of nondelinquents from the same neighborhood.

Successful students excel in morale, adjustment to the school's demands, and in systematic planning. They are also more interested in academic activities and receive higher ratings from teachers in industry, dependability, and similar virtues. When they do have personal troubles, they are more likely to become subdued and overinhibited. The poor student, when maladjusted, is more likely to become noisy, "cocky," and self-centered.

There are marked sex differences in personality. Boys are much more likely to get into trouble. In general, science supports our common knowledge in this area. Boys are more assertive, more vigorous, more tough-minded and have stronger need to succeed. Girls are more anxious to please and have a stronger social orientation. We cannot be sure whether heredity or social expectation is responsible.

The family has much to do with personal and social adjustment. Sheer heredity seems to play a part in delinquency, insanity, and neuroticism. There are marked class differences in child-rearing practices and these may affect adjustment. The warmth, acceptance and mutual understanding (identification) within the family is closely related to adequate adjustment, but we still do not know what causes what.

Personality differences between cultures, natives, or ethnic groups have received intensive study. There have been many attempts to link these differences to the marked differences in child rearing.

Such outside influences as the movies, TV, radio, or comics have received some attention. For young children, the movies can be used to change attitudes. The influence of the other media is less clearly established. For adults, the influence of the movies is more questionable.

Children from progressive schools show more initiative and resourcefulness. Their status with respect to adjustment or freedom from tension is less sure.

SPECIFIC REFERENCES

1. Glueck, S., and Glueck, Eleanor. *Unravelling juvenile delinquency.* Commonwealth Fund, 1950.
2. Epps, Phyllis and Parnell, R. W. Physique and temperament of women delinquents compared with women undergraduates. *Brit. J. med. Psychol.,* 1952, *25,* 249–255.
3. Sheldon, W. H. *Varieties of delinquent youth.* Harper, 1949.
4. Alt, P. M. Relationship of physique and temperament. *Sch. Rev.,* 1953, *61,* 267–276.
5. Garn, S. M., and Gertler, M. M. An association between type of work and physique in an industrial group. *Amer. J. phys. Anthrop.,* 1950, *8,* 387–397.
6. Frazier, A., and Lisonbee, L. K. Adolescent concerns with physique. *Sch. Rev.,* 1950, *58,* 397–405.
7. Stolz, H. R., and Stolz, Lois M. Adolescent problems related to somatic variations, *Yearb. nat. soc. Stud. Educ., 43* (I), 1944, 80–99.
8. Schonfeld, W. A. Inadequate masculine physique as a factor in personality development of adolescent boys. *Psychosom. Med.,* 1950, *12,* 49–54.
9. Weber, R. J. Relationship of physical fitness to success in college and to personality. *Res. Quart. Amer. Ass. Hlth. phys. Educ.,* 1953, *24,* 471–474.
10. Barker, R. G., and others. *Adjustment to physical handicap and illness.* Bull. 55, revised, Social Science Research Council, 1953.
11. Garrett, J. F., ed. *Psychological aspects of physical disability.* Fed. Sec. Agency, Rehabilitation Series No. 210, U.S. Govt. Printing Office, 1952.
12. DiCarlo, L. M., and Amster, W. W. The auditorily and speech handicapped. *Rev. educ. Res.,* 1953, *23,* 453–475.
13. Meyerson, L. The visually handicapped. *Rev. educ. Res.,* 1953, *23,* 476–491.
14. Hollinshead, M. T. The orthopedically handicapped. *Rev. educ. Res.,* 1953, *23,* 492–507.
15. Gates, Mary F. A comparative study of some problems of social and emotional adjustment of crippled and non-crippled girls and boys. *J. genet. Psychol.,* 1946, *68,* 219–244.
16. Cruickshank, W. M., and Dolphin, Jane E. Emotional needs of crippled and noncrippled children. *J. except. Child.,* 1949, *16,* 33–40.
17. Sommers, Vita S. *The influence of parental attitudes and social*

environment on the personality development of the adolescent blind. American Foundation for the Blind, 1944.

18. Landis, C., and Bolles, M. Marjorie. *Personality and sexuality of the physically handicapped woman.* Hoeber, 1942.

19. Shultz, I. T. Psychological factors in tuberculous patients. *Amer. Rev. Tuberculosis,* 1941, *43,* 557–565.

20. Scherer, I. W., and others. Psychological changes during the first year following prefrontal lobotomy. *Psychol. Monogr.,* 1953, *67,* No. 7 (357).

21. Allison, H. W., and Allison, Sarah G. Personality changes following transorbital lobotomy. *J. abnorm. soc. Psychol.,* 1954, *49,* 219–223.

22. Lightfoot, Georgia F. Personality characteristics of bright and dull children. *Teach. Coll. Contr. Educ.,* No. 969, 1951

23. Hinkleman, E. A. Intellectual level and personality adjustment. *Elem. Sch. J.,* 1951, *52,* 31–35.

24. Lorge, I. Intelligence and personality as revealed in questionnaires and inventories. *Yearb. nat. soc. Stud. Educ.,* *39* (I), 1940, 275–281.

25. Trumbull, R. A study in relationships between factors of personality and intelligence. *J. soc. Psychol.,* 1953, *38,* 161–173.

26. Kirk, S. A., and Kolstoe, O. P. The mentally retarded. *Rev. educ. Res.,* 1953, *23,* 400–416.

27. Hays, W. Mental level and friend selection among institutionalized defective girls. *Amer. J. ment. Defic.,* 1951, *56,* 198–203.

28. Williams, H. M. Intelligence and delinquency. *Yearb. nat. soc. Stud. Educ.,* *39* (I), 1940, 291–297.

29. Clark, J. H. Intelligence test results obtained from a specific type of army A.W.O.L. *Educ. psychol. Measmt.,* 1948, *8,* 677–682.

30. Healy, W., and Bronner, A. F. *New light on delinquency and its treatment.* Yale Univeristy Press, 1936.

31. Chassel, Clara F. The relation between morality and intellect. *Teach. Coll. Contr. Educ.,* No. 607, 1935.

32. Johnson, G. R. Bright pupils who fail in high school. *Amer. Sch. Bd. J.,* 1939, *98,* 25–26.

33. Klein, A. Failure and subjects liked and disliked. *High Points,* 1939, *21,* 22–25.

34. Malpass, L. F. Some relations between students' perceptions of school and their achievement. *J. educ. Psychol.,* 1953, *44,* 475–482.

35. Schultz, D. G., and Green, B. F., Jr. Predicting academic achievement with a new attitude-interest questionnaire II. *Educ. psychol. Measmt.,* 1953, *13,* 54–64.

36. Weignad, G. Goal aspiration and academic success. *Personnel Guid. J.*, 1953, *31*, 458–461.

37. Carter, H. D. What are some of the basic problems in analysis of study techniques? *Calif. J. educ. Res.*, 1951, *2*, 170–174.

38. Fransden, Arden N., and Sessions, Alwyn D. Interests and school achievement. *Educ. psychol. Measmt.*, 1953, *13*, 94–101.

39. Givens, P. R. Kuder patterns of interest as related to achievement in college science courses. *J. educ. Res.*, 1953, *46*, 627–630.

40. McKillop, Anne S. *The relation between the reader's attitude and certain types of reading response.* Teachers College, Columbia University, 1952.

41. Leipold, L. E. Who are our good students? *J. educ. Res.*, 1945, *38*, 529–533.

42. Stagner, R. The relation of personality to academic aptitude and achievement. *J. educ. Res.*, 1933, *26*, 648–660.

43. Wolf, S. Jean. Historic background of the study of personality as it relates to success or failure in academic achievement. *J. gen. Psychol.*, 1938, *19*, 417–436.

44. Wrenn, C. G., and Crandall, Elizabeth B. Behavior ratings and scholarship among college freshmen. *J. educ. Res.*, 1940, *34*, 259–264.

45. Darley, J. G. Scholastic achievement and measured maladjustment. *J. appl. Psychol.*, 1937, *21*, 485–493.

46. Drought, N. E. An analysis of eight measures of personality and adjustment in relation to relative scholastic achievement. *J. appl. Psychol.*, 1938, *22*, 597–606.

47. Spinelle, L., and Nemzek, C. L. The relationship of personality test scores to school marks and intelligence quotients. *J. soc. Psychol.*, 1944, *20*, 289–294.

48. Spache, G. D. Personality characteristics of retarded readers as measured by the Picture-Frustration Study. *Educ. psychol. Measmt.*, 1954, *14*, 186–192.

49. Shaffer, R. H. English deficiency and social adjustment. *J. higher Educ.*, 1949, *20*, 373–376.

50. Clark, J. H. Grade achievement of female college students in relation to non-intellective factors: MMPI items. *J. soc. Psychol.*, 1953, *37*, 275–281.

51. Schofield, W., Jr. An attempt to measure "persistence" in its relationship to scholastic achievement. *J. exp. Psychol.*, 1943, *33*, 440–445.

52. Sears, Pauline S. Doll play aggression in normal young chil-

dren: influence of sex, age, sibling status, father's absence. *Psychol. Monogr.*, 1951, *65*, (42).

53. Gray, H. Jung's psychological types in men and women. *Stanf. med. Bull.*, 1948, *6*, 29–36.

54. Diggory, J. C. Sex differences in the organization of attitudes. *J. Pers.*, 1953, *22*, 89–100.

55. Guilford, J. P., and Martin, H. Age differences and sex differences in some introvertive and emotional traits. *J. gen. Psychol.*, 1944, *31*, 219–229.

56. Frank, L. K., and others. Personality development in adolescent girls. *Monogr. Soc. Res. Child Developm.*, 1951, *16*, No. 53.

57. McLelland, D. C., and others. *The achievement motive.* Appleton-Century-Crofts, 1953, pp. 178–181 (For an unpublished study by W. F. Field).

58. Ford, C. F., Jr., and Tyler, Leona E. A factor analysis of Terman and Miles' M–F test. *J. appl. Psychol.*, 1952, *36*, 251–253.

59. Remmers, H. H., and others. Introduction to educational psychology. Harper, 1954, p. 235.

60. Veroff, J., Wilcox, S., and Atkinson, J. W. The achievement motive in high school and college age women. *J. abnorm. soc. Psychol.*, 1953, *48*, 108–119.

61. Schoeppe, A., Haggard, E. A., and Havighurst, R. J. Some factors affecting sixteen-year-olds' success in five developmental tasks. *J. abnorm. soc. Psychol.*, 1953, *48*, 42–52.

62. Aberle, D. F., and Naegel, K. D. Middle class fathers' occupational role and attitudes toward children. *Amer. J. Orthopsychiat.*, 1952, *22*, 366–378.

63. Tuddenham, R. D. Studies in reputation: I. Sex and grade differences in school children's evaluation of their peers. *Psychol. Monogr.*, 1951, *66*, (I).

64. Carmichael, L., ed. *Manual of child psychology.* Wiley, 1954, Chap. 17. Psychological sex differences (Terman, L. M., and Tyler, Leona E.).

65. Scheinfeld, A. *Women and men.* Harcourt Brace, 1944.

66. Klein, Viola. *The feminine character; history of an ideology.* London, Paul, Trench, Trubner & Co., 1946.

67. Rosanoff, A. J., Handy, L. M., and Plesset, I. R. The etiology of child behavior. *Psychiat. Monogr.*, 1941, No. 1.

68. Kallmann, F. J. *Heredity in health and mental disorder.* Norton, 1953.

69. Kallmann, F. J. Twin and sibship study of overt male homosexuality. *Amer. J. hum. Genet.*, 1952, *4*, 136–146.

70. Eysenck, H. J., and Prell, D. B. The inheritance of neuroticism: an experimental study. *J. ment. Sci.*, 1951, *97*, 441–465.

71. Shields, J. Personality differences and neurotic traits in normal twin school children: a study in psychiatric genetics. *Eugen. Rev.*, 1954, *45*, 213–246.

72. Roe, Anne, and Burks, Barbara. Adult adjustment of foster children of alcoholic and psychotic parentage and the influence of the foster home. Memoirs of the Section on Alcohol Studies Yale Univ., No. 3, 1945, Pub. by *Quart. J. Stud. on Alcoh.*

73. Bossard, J. H. S. *The sociology of child development.* Harper, 1954.

74. Woody, Grace. Similarities and differences in the play activities of children in two public schools with contrasting environment. *J. exp. Educ.*, 1938, *7*, 145–157.

75. Blue, J. T., Jr. The relationship of juvenile delinquency, race, and economic status. *J. Negro Educ.*, 1948, *17*, 469–477.

76. Drucker, A. J., and Remmers, H. H. Environmental determinants of basic difficulty problems. *J. abnorm. soc. Psychol.*, 1952, *47*, 379–381.

77. Pattie, F. A., and Cornett, S. Unpleasantness of early memories and maladjustment of children. *J. Pers.*, 1952, *20*, 315–321.

78. Frank, L. R., and others. Personality development in adolescent girls. *Monogr. Soc. Res. Child Developm.*, 1951, *16*, No. 53.

79. Davis, A. Socialization and adolescent personality. *Yearb. nat. soc. Stud. Educ.*, *43* (I), 1944, 198–216.

80. Hieronymus, A. N. A study of social class motivation: Relationships between anxiety for education and certain socio-economic and intellectual variables. *J. educ. Psychol.*, 1951, *42*, 193–205.

81. Schneider, L., and Lysgaard, S. The deferred gratification pattern: a preliminary study. *Amer. sociol. Rev.*, 1953, *18*, 142–149.

82. Pope, B. Socio-economic contrasts in children's peer culture prestige values. *Genet. Psychol. Monogr.*, 1953, *48*, 157–220.

83. Ort, R. S. A study of role-conflicts as related to class level. *J. abnorm. soc. Psychol.*, 1952, *47*, 425–432.

84. Maas, H. S. Some social class differences in the family systems and group relations of pre- and early adolescents. *Child Develpm.*, 1951, *22*, 145–152.

85. Maccoby, Eleanor E., and Gibbs, Patricia K. Social class differences in child-rearing. *Amer. Psychologist*, 1953, *8*, 395.

86. Coladarci, A. P. *Educational psychology: a book of readings.* Dry-

den, 1955, Chap. 8. Methods of child rearing in two social classes (Maccoby, Eleanor, and others).

87. Clark, D. L., and Burke, A. J. Economic, legal, and social status of teachers. *Rev. educ. Res.*, 1955, *25*, 239–251.

88. Ellis, A., and Beechley, R. M. A comparison of child guidance clinic patients coming from large, medium, and small families. *J. genet. Psychol.*, 1951, *79*, 131–144.

89. Bonney, M. E. A study of the relation of intelligence, family size, and sex differences with mutual friendships in the primary grades. *Child Develpm.*, 1942, *13*, 79–100.

90. Haffter, C. *Kinder aus geschiedenen Ehen* (Children from broken homes). Bern: Huber, 1948.

91. Lorr, M., and Jenkins, R. L. Three factors in parent behavior. *J. consult. Psychol.*, 1953, *17*, 306–308.

92. Shirley, Mary M. Children's adjustments to a strange situation. *J. abnorm. soc. Psychol.*, 1942, *37*, 201–217.

93. Frazee, Helen E. Children who later became schizophrenic. *Smith Coll. Stud. in Social Work*, 1953, *23* (2), 125–129.

94. Baldwin, A. L. Socialization and the parent-child relationship. *Child Develpm.*, 1948, *19*, 127–136.

95. Hollenberg, Eleanor, and Sperry, Margaret. Some antecedents of aggression and effects of frustration in doll play. *Personality*, 1951, *1*, 32–43.

96. Sears, R. R., and others. Some child-rearing antecedents of aggression and dependency in young children. *Genet. Psychol. Monogr.*, 1953, *47*, 135–236.

97. Cava, E. L., and Raush, H. L. Identification and the adolescent boy's perception of his father. *J. abnorm. soc. Psychol.*, 1952, *47*, 855–856.

98. Sopchak, A. L. Parental "identification" and "tendency toward disorders" as measured by the Minnesota Multiphasic Personality Inventory. *J. abnorm. soc. Psychol.*, 1952, *47*, 159–165.

99. Cass, Loretta K. Parent-child relationships and delinquency. *J. abnorm. soc. Psychol.*, 1952, *47*, 101–104.

100. Weltman, Naomi, and Remmers, H. H. Pupils', parents', and teachers' attitudes—Similarities and differences. *Purdue Univ. Stud. higher Educ.*, 1946, No. 56.

101. Redl, F., and Wineman, D. *Children who hate.* Free Press, 1951.

102. Nowlis, V. A search for significant concepts in a study of parent-child relationships. *Amer. J. Orthopsychiat.*, 1952, *22*, 286–299.

103. Whiting, J. W. M., and Child, I. L. *Child training and personality: a cross-cultural study.* Yale University Press, 1953.

104. Orlansky, H. Infant care and personality. *Psychol. Bull.,* 1949, *16,* 1–48.

105. Liu, C. H. The influence of cultural background on the moral judgment of children. From Carmichael, L., ed. Chap. 13. Character development in children—an objective approach (Jones, V.).

106. Eaton, J. W., and Weil, R. J. Culture and mental disorders. Free Press, 1955.

107. Engle, T. L. Personality adjustments of children belonging to two minority groups. *J. educ. Psychol.,* 1945, *36,* 543–560.

108. Shaw, C. R., and McKay, H. D. *Social factors in juvenile delinquency.* U.S. Nat. Comm. on Law Observ. & Enforcem. Report on the causes of crime. U.S. Government Printing Office, 1931.

109. Carroll, Rebecca E. Relation of social environment to the moral ideology and personal aspirations of Negro boys and girls. *Sch. Rev.,* 1945, *53,* 30–38.

110. Lindzey, G., ed. *Handbook of social psychology.* Addison-Wesley, 1954. Chap. 26. National character: the study of modal personality and socio-cultural systems (Inkeles, A., and Levinson, D. J.).

111. Farber, M. L. English and Americans: values in the socialization process. *J. Psychol.,* 1953, *36,* 243–250.

112. Mussen, P. H. Differences between the TAT responses of Negro and white boys. *J. consult. Psychol.,* 1953, *17,* 373–376.

113. Hammer, E. F. Frustration-aggression hypothesis extended to social-racial areas: comparison of Negro and white children's H–T–P's. *Psychiat. Quart.,* 1953, *27,* 597–607.

114. Gray, J. S., and Thompson, A. H. The ethnic prejudices of white and Negro college students. *J. abnorm. soc. Psychol.,* 1953, *48,* 311–313.

115. Goff, Regina M. Problems and emotional difficulties of Negro children. *Teach. Coll. Contr. Educ.,* 1949, No. 960.

116. Super, D. E. The Bernreuter Personality Inventory: A review of research. *Psychol. Bull.,* 1942, *39,* 94–125.

117. Shuey, Audrey M. Personality traits of Jewish and non-Jewish students. *Arch. Psychol.,* N.Y., 1944, No. 290.

118. Metfessel, M., and Lovell, Constance. Recent literature on individual correlates of crime. *Psychol. Bull.,* 1942, *39,* 133–164.

119. Moses, E. R. Differentials in crime rates between Negroes and whites, based on comparisons of four socio-economically equated areas. *Amer. sociol. Rev.,* 1947, *12,* 411–420.

120. Lindzey, G., ed. *Handbook of social psychology*. Addison-Wesley, 1954, Chap. 28. Effects of the mass media of communication (Hovland, C. I.).

121. Lewin, H. S. Facts and fears about the comics. *Nation's Schs.*, 1953, *52*, 46–48.

122. Hoult, T. F. Comic books and juvenile delinquency. *Sociol. soc. Res.*, 1949, *33*, 279–284.

123. Heisler, Florence. A comparison between those elementary school children who attend moving pictures, read comic books and listen to serial radio programs to an excess, with those who indulge in these activities seldom or not at all. *J. educ. Res.*, 1948, *42*, 182–190.

124. Ricciuti, E. A. Children and radio: A study of listeners and nonlisteners to various types of radio programs in terms of selected ability, attitude, and behavior measures. *Genet. Psychol. Monogr.*, 1951, *44*, 69–143.

125. Witty, P. Comparative studies of interest in TV. *Educ. Adm. Superv.*, 1954, *40*, 321–335.

126. Maccoby, Eleanor E. Why do children watch television? *Publ. Opin. Quart.*, 1954, *18*, 239–244.

127. Zajonic, R. B. Some effects of the "space" serials. *Publ. Opin. Quart.*, 1954, *18*, 367–374.

128. Peterson, Ruth C., and Thurstone, L. L. *Motion pictures and the social attitudes of children*. Macmillan, 1933.

129. Lindzey, G., ed. *Handbook of social psychology*. Addison-Wesley, 1954, Chap. 27. Prejudice and ethnic relations (Harding, J., and others).

130. Aiken, W. M. *The story of the eight year study*. Harper, 1942.

131. Sells, S. B., Loftus, J. J., and Herbert, L. Evaluative studies of the activity program in the New York City public schools: A preliminary report. *J. exp. Educ.*, 1941, *9*, 310–322.

132. Jersild, A. T., and others. A further comparison of pupils in "activity" and "nonactivity" schools. *J. exp. Educ.*, 1941, *9*, 303–309.

133. Jersild, A. T., Goldman, B., and Loftus, J. J. A comparative study of the worries of children in two school situations. *J. exp. Educ.*, 1941, *9*, 323–326.

134. Mensh, I. N., and Mason, Evelyn P. Relationship of school atmosphere to reactions in frustrating situations. *J. educ. Res.*, 1951, *45*, 275–286.

135. Taylor, E. A. Some factors relating to social acceptance in eighth grade classrooms. *J. educ. Psychol.*, 1952, *43*, 257–272.

136. Kinney, Elva E. A study of peer group social acceptability at the fifth grade level in a public school. *J. educ. Res.*, 1953, *47*, 57–64.

137. Adams, J. J. Achievement and social adjustment of pupils in combination classes enrolling pupils of more than one grade level. *J. educ. Res.*, 1953, *47*, 151–155.

138. Lotz, H. R. The relationship between emotional and social adjustment of individuals and their attendance at coeducational and single-sex schools. *Dissertation Abstr.*, 1953, *13*, 517–518.

SUGGESTIONS FOR FURTHER READING

For some important material on the relation of body build to delinquency see:

1. Glueck, S., and Glueck, Eleanor. *Unravelling juvenile delinquency.* Commonwealth Fund, 1950.

2. Sheldon, W. H. *Varieties of delinquent youth.* Harper, 1949.

The books by Garrett and Barker deal with the personality of the physically handicapped. Garrett is a brief account. Barker is more complete.

3. Garrett, J. F., ed. *Psychological aspects of physical disability.* Fed. Sec. Agency, Rehabilitation Series No. 210. U. S. Govt. Printing Office, 1952.

4. Barker, R., and others. *Adjustment to physical handicap and illness.* Bull. 55, revised, Social Science Research Council, 1953.

5. Keys, A., and others. *The biology of human starvation.* Vol. II, University of Minnesota Press, 1950.
    A report of some drastic experiments on volunteer subjects during World War II.

6. Lightfoot, Georgia F. Personality characteristics of bright and dull children. *Teach. Coll. Contr. Educ.*, No. 969, 1951.
    Emphasizes the basic needs of the two groups.

7. Carmichael, L., ed. *Manual of child psychology.* Wiley, 1954.
    Chap. 12. Research on primitive children (Mead, Margaret).
    Chap. 17. Psychological sex differences (Terman, L. M., and Tyler, Leona E.).
    Detailed accounts of sex differences and differences related to child rearing.

8. Eysenck, H. J., and Prell, D. B. The inheritance of neuroticism. *J. ment. Sci.*, 1951, *97*, 441–465.
    A summary of previous studies. Somewhat technical.

9. Kallman, F. J. *Heredity in health and mental disorder*. Norton, 1953.
Includes much work on insanity and other disorders.

10. Whiting, J. W. M., and Child, I. L. *Child training and personality: a cross-cultural study*. Yale University Press, 1953.
Treats the same problem as Mead (above) but more specialized. Freudian approach.

11. Bossard, J. H. S. *The sociology of child development*. Harper, 1954.
This book treats the relation of personality to family background and to the family's position in the community.

12. Auld, F. The influence of social class on personality test responses. *Psychol. Bull.*, 1952, *49*, 318–332.
See for references to earlier studies.

13. Stolz, Lois M., and others. *Father relations of war-born children*. Stanford University Press, 1954.
A detailed report on an important specialized problem.

14. Goff, Regina M. Problems and emotional difficulties of Negro children. *Teach. Coll. Contr. Educ.*, No. 960, 1949.
Results of interviews with selected children in New York and St. Louis.

15. Eysenck, H. J. Primary social attitudes: a comparison of attitude patterns in England, Germany, and Sweden. *J. abnorm. soc. Psychol.*, 1953, *48*, 563–568.
For one representative study on national differences in personal traits.

16. Lindzey, G., ed. *Handbook of social psychology*. Addison-Wesley, 1954.
Chap. 26. National character: The study of modal personality and sociopolitical systems (Inkeles, A., and Levinson, D. J.).
A theoretical and analytical treatment of national character. Comprehensive, but difficult in spots.
Chap. 28. Effects of the mass media of communications (Hovland, C. I.).
Chiefly on methods of persuasion, but some material on the effects of radio, television and movies.

17. Coffin, T. E. Television's impact on society. *Amer. Psychologist*, 1955, *10*, 630–641.
An excellent summary of research. This entire number of the *American Psychologist* is given over to the various aspects of television, including television in education.

Exercises and Questions for Discussion

1. What aspects of physical development are most closely related to personal adjustment?

2. Outline a talk on "Sex Differences in Interests."

3. Suppose you are convinced that the school's stress on middle-class values creates a hardship for lower-class students. What would you recommend?

4. What is the meaning of identification between parent and child? What is its significance?

5. Discuss the rival hypotheses that may be used to explain the relation between home conditions and child adjustment.

6. In the public press there is considerable argument about the effect on character of such things as the movies, comics, television, and radio. What does the evidence seem to indicate? How can you account for the confusion?

20

Guiding Personal and Social Growth: The Problem and the Goals

I N PART THREE we considered the part the teacher plays in directing scholastic or academic growth. In that discussion we learned something of the processes by which academic growth proceeds and the means by which it may be directed and managed. Growth in this field constitutes the chief day-by-day responsibility of the teacher. It is in this field, moreover, that we walk with most assurance, since in this field we have both a large number of data and also an approximation to a group of principles tested under classroom conditions. Consequently, in this limited area of scholastic growth, we are able to construct a fairly neat picture of one phase of our problem.

It is perhaps fortunate that we have this fairly neat picture, confined though it may be to one limited aspect of growth. For now we are about to undertake the study of the new area of personal and social growth, and this area is much larger and is more diffuse and nebulous. In this new area of personal and social growth we lack the many landmarks and the well-established facts that we used in our study of scholastic growth. In considering the new larger field, therefore, it will be convenient to start, tentatively at least, with the outline of concepts we have thus far developed in the smaller field of scholastic growth and to see if this miniature system will help us organize our ideas in the larger area of personal and social growth. Certainly we shall expect to modify this miniature system in some particulars, perhaps even radically. It will be easier, however, to use the pattern of this system as a first-trial pattern for the larger areas than to attempt to study that larger area with no tentative lines of exploration.

In a basic sense, perhaps, there is no unique problem of personality development. Essentially, perhaps, personality development is no different from regular scholastic development. Teaching a child to return the property of others may not be different from teaching him to clear an equation of fractions before transposing. Helping him to know when to stand up for his rights and when to withdraw in favor of others is not entirely different from helping him to know when to solve the quadratic by factoring and when to solve by completing the square. Encouraging him to look boldly and unashamedly at his unorthodox desires and fears is not essentially different from encouraging him to go over partisan arguments with an eye for the lurking fallacy.

In academic trait and in nonacademic trait alike, we are dealing with tendencies which have some basis in heredity and which are susceptible to modification through the action of such environmental forces as the home, the community, and the school. It is to be expected, moreover, that the principles already put forward as general guides to the modification of academic tendencies will also act as general guides to the modification of nonacademic traits.

Teaching for Adjustment: Doubts and Difficulties To Be Faced

When about to undertake an important venture, it is not wise, of course, to concentrate chiefly on the difficulties and hazards that might be encountered. A morbid preoccupation with such matters might keep us from the attempt or at least reduce our zest and enjoyment. But, even so, it would be foolish to ignore those hazards completely, or to try to hide them from our thoughts. As mature and well-adjusted people we should take a good look at these matters, decide on some way of dealing with them in reasonable fashion, and then put them to one side and be on our way.

Fears of Limited Success

Presumably teachers have always taught the "whole child" and, incidentally or by direct effort, have done much in the field of personal adjustment. As a topic of discussion, however, this area is now becoming much more important, and we may feel that we are rapidly taking on a more formal commitment or obligation in the field of personal adjustment. What risks do we face in this old mission that we are now taking on as a more formal obligation? Are there any difficulties that may be unique or especially troublesome in the area on which we are now focusing our attention?

Curriculum Difficult to Control. In the field of academic development, the school has almost complete control of the tasks which confront the child. The school decides whether the child shall face problems in the addition of numbers at the age of seven or at the age of nine. It can also decide whether or not the student will ever face problems in bank discount. In many areas, the school tasks to which the student is required to react constitute an entirely arbitrary series which would never be encountered in actual life until much later. For this reason, the school sets the tasks to be met and does not merely guide the student in problems which he faces in his day-by-day life.

When we turn to the area of personal and social development, we find a very different story. Problems of personal and social adjustment confront the child in an unending series, whether the school arranges such problems or not. There can be no nicely graded series of problems by which the student moves from a fairly easy personality task to another of somewhat greater difficulty. Some of the tasks which the child encounters as a three-year-old may be more difficult (and even more consequential) than those which confront him fifteen years later. To a great extent, the teacher is powerless to regulate the presentation of these tasks. The teacher cannot make sure that each one appears at a time when the student is able to cope with it.

In the field of personality, then, the teacher is less of an instructor and more of a guide. The course of instruction is by no means under his control. He is merely an older, wiser, more mature individual who happens to be around part of the time while the student reacts to the personality situations which he encounters. Consequently, much of what we have had to say about many topics (e.g., the arrangement and distribution of practice) will have little application in this new field.

Maturation and Heredity More Partisan. There are some traits in which heredity or instinct or genetic make-up is relatively neutral. In factoring $a^2 - b^2$, for instance, the child is by sheer genetic constitution no more disposed toward thinking $(a - b)(a - b)$ than toward thinking

$(a-b)$ $(a+b)$. Heredity gives him no strong bias in either direction. Heredity would be equally neutral in determining a child's opinion of the results of the War of 1812. In some other traits, however, the school may have to contend against strong hereditary or instinctual pressure. In teaching a child to own up to his own misdoings and to take the consequences, the school may be working against a strong inherent urge to avoid unpleasantness. In teaching him to keep a definite hour for home study, we may have to counteract strong gregarious tendencies. In teaching sexual restraint or prudence, we encounter powerful instinctual forces. In still other traits, hereditary tendencies may be our allies. In encouraging children to play active games during recess or in encouraging adolescents to develop an interest in members of the opposite sex, we may merely be the handmaid of fairly prevalent and dependable tendencies.

It is clear that the problems of teaching vary as the role of heredity varies. If heredity is neutral we have a fairly free hand. If heredity provides tendencies which oppose our efforts, we have a complicated problem on our hands, as we always do when we seek to modify strong, well-developed tendencies. If heredity works for us, our task is simplified. And, in all this, we must face the possibility that heredity is less likely to be neutral in character development than in academic development.

Interference of Other Social Agencies. Just as heredity may work for us or against us or stand in a neutral corner, so may the many nonscholastic social agencies aid us, hinder us, or leave us unaffected. In teaching the correct factoring of $a^2 - b^2$ most other social agencies, such as the home, the community, or the church, will have little to say. In teaching the results of the War of 1812, on the other hand, we may find the home taking a hand, perhaps contributing to the notion that we have always fought just and successful wars. In other tasks, the influence of the home or community may be something we can utilize or it may be something we must counteract. In teaching the child what we think is a wholesome attitude toward sex, we are almost bound to find that other social agencies also have something to say. The home, the gang, the church, all may have definite views on these matters. Those views may reinforce the tendencies we try to develop, or they may run counter to our efforts. Certainly they are not apt to be neutral. As in sex, so in many other traits, we are only one of many agencies. In attempting to make a child less shy or more sociable, for instance, we may be aided or hindered by countless forces at work in other environments.

It seems only reasonable that the teacher faces one problem when he works on tendencies that he alone (for the time being) attends to, and that he faces an entirely different problem when he works on tendencies that other agencies also act on. In this matter, again, it seems entirely possible that the home, the community, and the church are more likely to play an active day-by-day part in the field of character development than in the field of academic development.

Varying Prestige of Teacher. There are other factors which may reduce our net influence in the field of character training. We as teachers may not have the same prestige in the field of character education as we have in more academic subjects. In the latter area we are acknowledged authorities. It would be a brave parent indeed who would challenge our decisions as to the correct chemical formula or the correct translation of a Latin poem. And if we were challenged by such an incautious parent, we would still stand a fair chance of winning out in the mind of the child. In character education, on the other hand, we do not always hold undisputed sway. The home, the gang, the community may feel free to doubt our opinions on the ethics of "fixing" a parking ticket, on voting the party line, or on sex mores. And if such dissenters do appear, it may be that their opinion of such matters may carry more weight than ours. After all, who are we to offset the opinion or example of Uncle Jim, the local cop, or Marlon Brando?

From what has been said, we must not be surprised if as we move from academic traits to traits of character, personality, and social adjustment, we find ourselves more and more embroiled with other powerful forces acting on the same individuals, either as allies or as enemies, as a help or a hindrance.

Evidence Regarding the School's Success. The difficulties seem formidable. Are we foredoomed to failure? This would be a rash and unduly pessimistic conclusion. These difficulties, after all, are not necessarily insurmountable obstacles. Moreover the evidence, although extremely spotty and often based on studies devoid of control groups, does suggest that the school can make some contribution to personal adjustment(1, 2). There is even some evidence that teachers given special training in this field may accomplish more than teachers who lack the special training(3). In many areas, however, the evidence is still quite confusing. Some studies, for instance, report a definite resemblance between personality traits of teachers and students(4, 5), but in other cases we find no increase in resemblance during the school year(6). One careful investigation finds definite personality differences between young children taught by authoritative teachers and those taught by more democratic or "integrative" teachers(7).

Success in character education can best be described as precarious(8). In teaching arithmetic or history some improvement is the rule, and we would be surprised not to find any. In teaching honesty or citizenship, however, sometimes we get an improvement and sometimes we do not. In teaching attitudes, we also get some successes and some failures. Failures are fairly frequent in teaching such broad attitudes as scientific attitude or tolerance(9). Successes are frequently reported in the task of changing opinions about more specific matters, such as the parsimony of the Scotch or the advantages of private enterprise. More recently, as we shall see, some success has also been reported in the reduction of prejudice.

In summing up, we must conclude that the evidence is extremely fragmentary and not conclusive enough to justify a firm conviction. The general trend, however, goes more to justify a reasonable hope for moderate success than to support any fear of complete failure.

Fears of Working in the Wrong Direction

Not only do some people fear that the school may fail in the task it undertakes but there is also some fear that, in some cases, the school may actually attempt or stress the wrong things.

Difficulty in Defining the Goals of Personal Growth. Compared to academic objectives, the goals of personal development are extremely difficult to determine. When a child faces a situation such as "7 + 6 = ?" or "Influence of the frontier" or "Results of the Industrial Revolution" or "Arma virumque cano," we have a fairly definite idea of the proper or acceptable response. Within limits, most teachers would agree as to the type of reaction they would try to induce. When a child faces social or ethical problems, on the other hand, we may be less likely to be certain about the desirable response. Let us suppose, for instance, that a child is playing with a toy and another child tries to take it away from him. What is the proper response to that situation? Or an older child, while engrossed in an exciting novel, is asked by a friend to come over and help with some project. What should be done? Another child is confronted with the desire to be elected to a fraternity. Should he deliberately cultivate the important people, "polishing apples" whenever possible and expressing interest which he does not feel, or should he continue to be natural and sincere and let the chips fall where they may? Another child is enraged at undue parental control of his activities. What is the proper response to this situation?

Considering all these uncertainties, it would be tragically easy to make the wrong decision. However sure we may be about the exports of Malay or the square on the hypotenuse, we can have no comparable certainty of our answers in problems of self-denial, filial devotion, or a way of life. Shall we transform our pupil into a gullible enthusiast who will rush off to the nearest barricade at the first call instigated by selfish warmongers? Or shall we have him turn out to be a sophisticated cynic to whom any call of a stricken nation, or any threat of evil, is just more propaganda? Would we, even if we had the power, work toward a world devoid of the Micawbers, the Falstaffs, the Tam O'Shanters, or the host of less renowned but amiable rogues who have added color to our lives? Who of us, on the other hand, would deliberately earmark certain of our charges for these unenviable but diverting roles?

It is ironical to note that as certainty becomes less possible there is more and more at stake. It is important to be right in teaching the principle of Archimedes or the laws of Gay-Lussac. It is even more important, however, to be on the right course in teaching a child what he should do about his hatred for his brother, or his suspicions of his associates, or his haunting fear of inferiority, or his confusion about the claims of compromise on the one hand and the rigid adherence to principle on the other.

When we think of the inevitable uncertainty of our goals in personal development, together with the overwhelming importance of this area, we may forgive the teacher for being reluctant to take complete responsibility. Let us suppose, for instance, that the average citizen says to the teacher of history, "You should know much more than I do about the terms of the Peace of Westphalia. Anyway, if you should be wrong it would not be a fatal matter. Why don't I give you complete responsibility in this area?" The teacher might agree to such a proposition. Now, however, the average citizen says, "You should have a much better idea than I have about what constitutes good fellowship, the full life, and a well-balanced personality. Anyway if you should be wrong, it would not be so very serious. Why don't you take the major responsibility for this area?" Here the teacher may challenge both premises. First, he is not sure that teachers have more than average competence in judging these matters. Second, he thinks a mistake in this area might be disastrous. We might forgive him if he thought that responsibility for this area should not be left to one specialized group with no proved expertness in the field.

Handicaps in the Traditional Approach of the School

Some people have feared that there may be an inherent conflict in the values traditionally stressed by the school and the values typically emphasized by those interested in mental adjustment. As Symonds(10) has pointed out, the school must often be exacting and demanding. The school has not been able to take a free and easy attitude about the date of the Norman invasion or the square root of 225. Many clinicians, on the other hand, believe that the essence of their craft is to be permissive, to accept the most illogical fears and most improper urges, and not to sit in judgment. And from this contrast, there may be trouble when the school sets about promoting mental adjustment.

At one time teachers and mental hygienists were very far apart in their views of child behavior. The teachers were botherd by stealing, sex play, and other overt violation of the mores. They indicated less concern about timidity, nervousness, or various minor tics. For the mental hygienists, of course, the emphases were reversed. They saw great significance in the evidence of repression, but regarded the naughtiness as merely a passing nuisance having no hidden meaning. The early studies have been repeated many times(11, 12) and the more recent studies show less difference than that first reported. The difference is still there, however, and the more modern teachers attach considerable weight to the things that interfere with the progress of the lesson, whatever the hygienist thinks of the significance of those things from his point of view(13). The teachers who express the most modern or enlightened attitudes toward behavior problems, however, do not always behave accordingly when they actually encounter those problems in the classroom(14). There is some suggestion, by the way, that it is the teachers who themselves have the poorest adjustment who agree most closely with the mental hygienists(15). We cannot say for sure what this means. It may come from the fact that the more troubled people have more insight into the difficulties of others. Certainly teachers feel more confidence in their judgments of work habits and academic performance than in their judgments of personal relations. They are more accurate in judging the overt, "acted-out" behavior problems of boys than in judging the quieter or more restrained evidence of behavior problems in girls.

Offhand it would seem that this problem could be solved very easily if teachers could be educated to take a more balanced view of these matters and could learn to stress the mental hygiene approach. Insofar as the two tasks may be antithetical, however, we would run some risk in this approach. We must be on our guard against the possibility that in concentrating on the more vital area of personal adjustment the teacher might come to neglect the less vital but important area of academic growth. Suppose, for instance, that the teacher of Latin is properly impressed about the relative long-range importance of a moderate amount of self-confidence as compared to a knowledge of the role of the caesura in Vergil's poetry. Suppose, further, that the teacher keeps the relative importance of these things clearly in mind in his hour-by-hour teaching activities. Is there not a danger that the caesura will be neglected almost completely? It may be better for the teacher to admit frankly that self-confidence is more important than the caesura, but at the same time to realize that the caesura is *his* job. Many other people, such as parents, friends, and club directors are interested in self-confidence, but if the Latin teacher does not teach the caesura, no one else will.

The Broad General Goals of Personal Development

Although it is difficult to decide in detail on the ideal personality for any given child, we must not assume that there can be no agreement whatever in the matter of positive personality goals. On the contrary, the many students of the problem have reached a surprising amount of agreement on the broad outlines of a desirable program of personality development.

The School Should Not Cause Harm to Personality Development

There is one goal over which there will be little disagreement. Everyone would agree that the school should avoid positive damage to the developing personality. The school should operate in such a way as to minimize any harm it might tend to bring to the developing personality. To the extent that the school may constitute a menace to wholesome personality, we should all agree that we are obliged to control that menace and keep it within bounds.

Does the school constitute a menace to wholesome personality development? Very probably. In the exercise of its academic function, the school is forced to present obstacles of considerable magnitude and to impose restrictions which may be galling in the extreme(16). These obstacles and restrictions cannot fail to develop many forms of indirect learning, and some of these, in turn, may readily lead to devices and personality twists which almost anyone would deplore. It is not too much to suppose that many a man has become embittered, discouraged, or intimidated as a result of his scholastic experiences. Many another person, on the other hand, has been led to prolong the unnatural dependence which the school may have provided.

Since the school utilizes instruments capable of serious damage, there is a clear obligation to exercise every precaution and to restrict the damage to the absolute minimum.

Balance between Drive and Control

This is one of the great goals in personal guidance. The happiness and effectiveness of the student will depend in large measure on his achievement of some sort of balance between the drives which activate him and the control which gives direction to those drives. He must avoid controls which govern by seeking to eliminate all bothersome drives. He must be equally careful to avoid drives which are subject to no control. The balance must be maintained without ruling out either the powerful drive or the salutary control.

Contrary to views which may have been prevalent some years ago, the wholesome personality is endowed with strong urges or drives. The happy, admirable person is well-equipped with vigorous appetites and a full quota of needs. Some of these needs may act in relatively primitive form. Others may appear greatly modified. In either case, however, these drives still exist and for the most part constitute a considerable source of satisfaction. The happy and effective person has a rich emotional life. He has enthusiastic likes and loyalties. He may have equally vigorous aversions and dislikes. All in all, he is distinguished from his less fortunate colleague, not by a dearth of natural drives, but by an abundance of them.

It is not difficult to persuade people of the need for effective control of drives. The need for such control has been recognized throughout man's long history. No group would welcome a society in which each individual was governed only by the whim which acted on him at the moment. Few people, moreover, will approve the man who gives free rein to his aggressive drive. We have no use for the man who gives out with violent attacks or a flood of abuse at the slightest interference with his activity. We regard him as unsocial and immature. But we are also reluctant to approve the man who has controlled his aggressive tendencies to the point of complete suppression. Ordinarily we do not admire the man who lets people walk all over him, who never talks back, or who never protests unfair treatment. Such a man does not give the picture of balanced control.

Balance, of course, calls for an avoidance of the extremes. In addition to this obvious requirement, there are some characteristics which, if not an inherent part of balance, at least are very often associated with the attainment of balance. First of all, we know what sort of balance we do not want. We do not want a balance which represents a frantic oscillation between control and impulse. Nor do we want a balance resulting from a complete stalemate of opposing forces by which the person himself is reduced to a quivering mass of nullification.

In a proper balance between drive and control there should be evidence of a happy and spontaneous energy. The balanced individual goes joyfully and zestfully to his task. He does not move reluctantly before a nagging conscience nor does he rush ahead in frenzy as if to escape some fearful panic. If the control is efficient and not too restricted, there is breadth and smoothness to his actions. He does not move ahead with awkward pedantic caution, but proceeds at an even and unhurried rate, taking minor obstacles in his stride, giving major obstacles the attention they deserve and no more. The balanced person is strongly oriented to the present. He is not over-preoccupied with fighting yesterday's battles or in fearing tomorrow's hypothetical problems. The foreseeable problems he faces and takes steps to meet. The vague possibilities he tends to dismiss with very little attention.

Acceptance of Reality

In discussing the problem of a balance between control and drive, we have already mentioned the importance of facing the real nature of the conflict. Facing reality, however, is also an important goal in its own right. The ability to face reality is one of the goals most frequently stressed by students of personality(17). These students would add, moreover, that sheer acceptance of reality is not enough. A grim and grudging acceptance would not represent a wholesome adjustment. We should learn, on the contrary, to face reality with courage and optimism. We should come to look facts squarely in the face and, for the most part, be happy or calm about what we see. There are times, of course, when the particular area of reality which we contemplate at the moment is such as to preclude any great amount of happiness. This despondency, however, should not cloud our view of the large number of facts which are encouraging. And even when reality, or a given segment of it, is too gloomy to permit happiness, it can be faced with courage and with plans for a hopeful program of action.

What is this reality which must be faced? Or, to state it differently, what aspects of reality are likely to prove difficult to face? First of all, we may be reluctant to face our own drives, desires, and limitations. The desires may be so unworthy as to offend our self-esteem. Your wish to "get even" with the boss may appear to you as a childish desire wholly unworthy of a person of your development. A mother's drive to attract the attention of her daughter's boy friends may seem equally horrifying to her. Serious limitations are always hard to face. The failing student cannot bring himself to realize that he is undertaking a task beyond his powers. These things we hate to face, and yet there are times when such things must be faced if any satisfactory solution is to be found or if a satisfactory adjustment is to be made.

One interesting illustration of unwillingness to face reality is our attitude toward our own indispensability. We all see someone else leave a group. We see that the ranks close and the world goes on without a great deal of disruption. Yet, in spite of such clear evidence, it is natural for each of us to think of himself as more or less indispensable. It is hard for a man to realize how little readjustment would be necessitated if he were to withdraw from any activity. He feels that his withdrawal may wreck the activity. Facing such a withdrawal, he prepares elaborate notes and briefs his successor, in spite of the fact that much of what he prepares will be neither necessary nor useful. For most people, the realization that we are not indispensable is a bitter pill to swallow. Yet it is one aspect of reality which must be faced.

In addition to facing our own desires and limitations we must face the outside world without distorting its important characteristics. We must not let our wishes persuade us that there are plenty of jobs in the field of commercial art if the harsh fact remains that the field is very crowded. We must not believe that two can live as cheaply as one if the facts show that this is not so. We must not believe that any ordinary student can attain success in whatever field he chooses, provided he has the ambition, industry, and perseverance.

The fact that we must face reality, and especially the unpleasant features of reality, does not mean that we must quail, helpless and inactive, before that reality. It is true that we must face our antagonist, and that we would do well to obtain a very realistic account of his powers and resources. But that does not mean we must retreat or call off the contest. Even though the odds are against us, we may still decide to go on. Even though there are only a few opportunities in the field of commercial art, we may decide that we are going to make a bid for one of them. Even though two cannot live as cheaply as one, and though marriage would involve certain sacrifice and some risk, the happiness to be had may be worth that sacrifice and risk. Facing reality merely means taking a long, clear look at the obstacles in our way. It does not necessarily mean that we must give in to those obstacles. After taking that look, we may, of course, decide not to go on. But that is not a necessary decision. We may decide instead to take a calculated risk.

Facing reality means moving out of the world of fantasy. While few of us can give up entirely all the solace of the imaginary world, such escape should be kept within bounds. It should be restricted first of all as to amount. We should not spend too much time in flights of fantasy. It should also be restricted as to significance. One should not solve a conflict by fantasy if there is any possibility of solving it by a program of action. More important, one should make sure that the fantasy does not become too real, that there is no confusion as to where the real world stops and the world of fantasy begins.

Maturity

In the minds of the general public and of the specialized students alike, maturity is usually accepted as an essential goal of personality development. Such phrases as childish, adolescent, or immature invariably imply regrettable traits or characteristics.

Maturity, of course, is rather a vague term, and one cannot be too sure just what is meant. It could refer to sort of an age scale in the Binet sense. In this view, a trait would be indicative of maturity if it were more likely to be found in older than in younger people. Thus, if refraining from weeping were more typical of older than of younger people, then such a trait would be an index of maturity. It is questionable, however, if this meaning would be adequate. Vandalism, for instance, may be more prevalent among fourteen-year-olds than among ten-year-olds. Yet this fact would not serve to establish vandalism as an index of maturity. At the older end of the scale, boring repetition of anecdotes would not ordinarily mean maturity merely because it is more typical of older people.

Sheer occurrence of a trait among older people is probably not enough to establish that trait as an aspect of maturity. What then is required in addition?

Change in Drive. Maturity suggests a change in the character of the drive. Many of the drives become stronger with maturity. Some of the ego drives, some aspects of the sex drive, and some of the gregarious or social drives may increase considerably. Other drives, on the other hand, may lose some of their strength. In most respects, however, maturity would imply more abundant drive and a richer emotional life.

One of the striking features of maturity is the modification which drives undergo. Ordinarily drives become more socialized. They seek expression through social groups and by means of socially accepted channels. The drives also become organized around different things. The mature person fears different things. He fears more valid menaces, such as disease or breakdown of international negotiations. His fears, by the way, are more adapted to the menace. His fear of disease may lead him to take a physical examination. It does not reduce him to unreasoning panic. His aggressive drives, too, are modified. He hates more serious offenders. His aggression is less likely than formerly to be evoked by minor slights or inconsequential disparagement. He is more likely to feel the need for action against an unscrupulous political gang or an international bully. Whereas the twelve-year-old may fall in love with some movie queen, the more mature person fixes his affection on some more attainable sweetheart. His affectional and sex drives change markedly. The friendships of the mature person are formed on a different basis and perhaps involve more discrimination or selection than he exercised while younger. His interests are more complex, more productive, and better wearing. All in all, it would appear that the mature person is motivated by types of drives different from those which act on the less mature.

Change in Control. Even more than by change of drives, the mature person is characterized by a change in the control of his drives. Maturity calls for more control. One of the aspects of maturity is the ability to withstand the claims of some immediate imperious drive in order to attain the future satisfaction of a more important but less immediate need. Maturity also calls for better control. The control is more directed and more efficient. Faced with a suspicion of disease, for instance, the mature person does not try frantically to suppress the idea. He does not try to handle his fear by frenziedly thinking of something else. He brings the idea clearly out into the open in all its horror and then if it seems wise, he consults a doctor.

The wisdom of a clear-eyed appraisal of the disturbing drive is clear in such a mild case as the urge toward aggression. Suppose the boss has angered you. The first few moments of silent fury have passed. But there is still a lurking desire to have it out with him, to tell him off. Against this urge there is set all the claim of prudence and all the demands of politeness, all the need to think of yourself as a reasonable person. In the panic aroused by the conflict you may readily say, "This is unworthy of me. I mustn't feel this way toward him. I must be above such childishness." If the aggressive urge is strong, however, it may still rankle and may express itself in unconscious or peculiar methods. Whatever the specific nature of the conflict, to achieve balanced control you must look your anger squarely in the eye. Ask yourself, "What do I really want to do to him? What should I really like to do if I were not afraid of my job, or afraid of appearing cheap or common?" Such close and searching scrutiny may reveal the fact that your hate is not so great as it seemed when you merely saw glimpses of it out of the corner of your eye. But whether closer inspection shows that resentment to be less or greater than you first feared, that closer inspection is one very essential step toward a rational control of the aggressive urge.

Once we have achieved the difficult step of looking realistically and fearlessly at our troublesome drives or desires, what is the next step toward a rational control or direction of the drives? The next step is an attempt to work out an integration of the conflicting drives. No control would be adequate unless the possibility of integration had been explored. How can we "tell the boss off" and yet not get fired or not feel like a rowdy fishwife? Perhaps we can inform the boss of our feelings in an acceptable way. While still using an ordinary tone of voice, while still being in control of ourselves, we may be able to state quietly, "You know, I found that incident awfully hard to take." Such an integration might accomplish both ends. If integration is not possible, compromise should be tried. Perhaps if we cannot announce our annoyance to the boss, we can at least proclaim it to a crony, and in this case we can abandon some of the restraint. Either integration or deliberate compromise represents fairly effective ways of controlling, yet expressing, a powerful urge.

Semi-automatic Control. So far it has been assumed that all balanced control of drives must be at the conscious level. The control discussed so far is the control which the individual exerts over himself from moment to moment. But there is another type of control or direction. This is the control by education or training whereby drives may be given direction and may be provided with acceptable means of expression with a minimum of immediate conscious control. Thus, by training, the child may have learned to express his resentment by a playful, exaggerated complaint. Now, when the need for aggression acts on him, he may automatically tend to express it in this semiplayful way. At the moment of such expression he may feel no need for exercising effortful control. He may merely let his training take its course. In the same way, one may learn socially accepted outlets for sexual needs, for the need of avoiding danger, and for other needs which call for a large measure of control. And again when these needs press, they may find an outlet almost automatically with little need for conscious or deliberate control at the moment.

Control by the socialization of drives, of course, is an excellent device and one of the chief devices to which the school should address itself. Everything that the school can do in this direction will be well worthwhile. We must not expect, however, that the success in socializing drives will eliminate the need for the more deliberate and painful type of conscious control.

Acceptance of Responsibility. One of the clearest indicators of maturity is the willingness to accept responsibility. The mature person accepts responsibility for his own decisions. He is willing to make such decisions when decisions are necessary. He is certainly willing to make decisions about his own life. In making any decision, of course, he is anxious to obtain information and perhaps advice. There are times, too, when the information or advice which he may receive will remove all need for the decision. If the tourist service says the road is closed, or if the doctor says that an operation is the only hope, then the matter may well be closed. But many times there is still a decision to be made after the information is all in and after all the advice has been heard. And when the information is in and when the advice has been submitted, there must be no doubt that the decision is being made by the individual concerned. The high-school student, for instance, may, and should, consult the vocational counselor. The latter should present information and should call attention to the many features which ought to be considered. But the student should make the decision and should be prepared to meet the consequences courageously. The same relation should hold in a host of other enterprises, major and minor. In all important matters, the mature person is anxious for advice and suggestions, but he makes his own decisions and takes the responsibility for the consequences of those decisions.

In addition to taking responsibility for his own decisions, the mature individual will take his share of responsibility for group activities. As team captain, leader, manager, parent, executive, he must accept responsibility for the welfare and activities of others. Under these circumstances, however, the amount of responsibility to be accepted may vary. One who genuinely distrusts his abilities along a certain line may properly reject responsibility on occasion. A decision such as this, if made with a clear view of all the circumstances, does not necessarily indicate an immature attitude.

Improved Group Relations. Maturity is indicated by the individual's relation to the groups to which he belongs. The mature person "gets along" with the other members of the group. He may argue and contest some of the decisions. He may have temporary disagreements or may be party to a long-standing rivalry. But these do not preclude his feeling of belongingness to the group. Nor do such conflicts lead the other members of the group to reject him. They may regard him as cantankerous and disputative, but in their minds, he still belongs.

The balance between general belongingness to the group, on the one hand, and freedom to disagree with the group, on the other hand, is typical of many other group relations. It is typical of the necessity for a balance between independence and normal dependence. With increasing maturity, we are better able to attain this desirable balance. We are able to accept happily a considerable dependence on the group. We are also able to keep from being completely dependent. We can assert our independence in certain matters without having to disavow the group altogether. In similar fashion, increasing maturity enables us to accept help and support from the group with grace and appreciation. At the same time, we are more willing to accept the obligation to contribute to the group, again graciously and happily. It is only the unstable individual, whose self-esteem is tottering badly, who feels injured or threatened by having to accept group support. It is only the immature person who is happy to accept aid continuously and who feels no need to contribute to the group.

With increased maturity we gain the ability to identify with larger groups. As children we must attain a close identity with our parents. Later we must include age mates, gradually feeling less emotional dependence on parents and other adults. Still later we must identify with a community, a profession, or the members of a crusade.

Sympathy and compassion are acquired with maturity. As we grow older, moreover, we must come to regard each person as important in his own right. We must give up our idea that these other people only have significance insofar as they help us or add to our egos.

Along with the increasing realization of the importance of other people in their own right, there should come a general belief in the essential goodness of others. This belief should be resilient enough to prevent us from being shocked when we see unmistakable evidence of lack of goodness. It should also be elastic enough to permit that general belief to re-form after each disappointment. The mature person, that is to say, can accept the fact of individual exceptions, but in spite of those exceptions, he can see that on the average, and most of the time, people tend to be very worthwhile and very likable organisms.

Frustration Tolerance

Since frustration and conflict are the inevitable accompaniments of all living, it is of the utmost importance that children acquire a tolerance for those unpleasant conditions. The child should learn to accept a certain amount of frustration. When he experiences that frustration, he should regard it as a very frequent condition which he can try to overcome but which temporarily he must accept. He should accept this suffering or distress without feeling abused or feeling sorry for himself. Ideally he should learn to achieve a certain amount of serenity or equanimity in spite of the frustration. This he should achieve, not by a blind distortion of the facts of frustration, but by seeing it as one feature of a life that has many other features. He should accept the important fact that frustration is part of the story and it is also necessary that he accept the important fact that frustration is not the whole story.

This problem of meeting frustration honestly and yet rising above it is illustrated at an extreme level by a person facing a tragic disability such as the onset of blindness. At first there is a temptation to refuse to face the possibility. He tells himself that he *will* get better, he *will*, he *will*. In his frantic unwillingness to face the tragedy, he becomes enraged at the nurse, the physician, and the psychological counselor who tells him of his ailment. Clearly he must be helped over this attitude. He must be led to face this terrific frustration. But that is only part of the story. When he first comes to accept the fact of blindness, that fact becomes his whole life. Having faced that fact, he now cannot think of anything else. To complete his adjustment, he must gradually come to see that this limitation or frustration, tragic as it is, is not his whole life. He is not just a blind man. He is a person with many attributes, one of which happens to be blindness. He must not forget this last attribute. It is of too much practical importance. But by the same token, he must not let this deficiency dominate his whole life. He must face the handicap and then, with all the help and skill he can obtain, he must try to work out some way of meeting it.

Fortunately, few of us are called on to meet the degree of frustration just described. The basic problem, however, is similar for the mild type of frustration we meet day in and day out in our ordinary lives. The problem calls for a clear-eyed admission of the facts of the frustration— the girl who has no dates, the employee who is passed over by younger men. After frank admission of the nature of the frustration should come a rational plan of attack. While the frustration continues, however, there must be an ability to tolerate it and to be reasonably happy in spite of it.

Summary

In attempting to guide students toward a more adequate personal adjustment, we should be able to use what we have learned about directing academic growth. There are some differences, however, and these must be taken into account. The teacher has less control over the personality curriculum. As compared to academic development, character traits may be less amenable to schooling because of the more specific role of heredity, because of the greater part played by outside agencies, or because of the teacher's reticence in the face of the overwhelming importance of the subject.

Although the detailed goals of personality are hard to establish, there is much agreement on the broad over-all characteristics of the well-adjusted person. Such a person should show a reasonable balance between his drives and the control he maintains over those drives. He has strong drives and he controls those drives by reasonable methods, facing them honestly and directing them into socially acceptable channels. The well-adjusted person faces reality fearlessly and optimistically. He faces his own unorthodox wishes and his own limitations. The well-adjusted person shows more signs of emotional maturity. His drives are more socialized and more realistic. They are also subjected to a more reasonable type of control. He accepts responsibility for himself and for the results of his own actions. To some extent also, he accepts responsibility for other people. He gets along with the group, being able to disagree on occasion without losing his sense of belongingness. He has a reasonable balance between dependence on the group and a degree of independence. He regards other members of the group as individuals in their own right. Above all, as he grows older, the well-adjusted person is more able to tolerate frustration without distorting his view of the world.

SPECIFIC REFERENCES

1. Flory, C. D. Classroom teachers improve the personality adjustment of their pupils. *J. educ. Res.*, 1944, *38*, 1–8.
2. Kelley, H., and Pepitone, A. An evaluation of a college course in human relations. *J. educ. Psychol.*, 1952, *43*, 193–209.
3. Fleming, R. S. Psychosomatic illness and emotional needs. *Educ. Leadership*, 1951, *9*, 119–123.
4. Boynton, P. L., Dugger, Harriet and Turner M. The emotional stability of teachers and pupils. *J. juv. Res.*, 1934, *18*, 223–232.
5. Amatoro, Sister M. Similarity in teacher and pupil personality. *J. Psychol.*, 1954, *37*, 45–50.
6. Ash, E. F. The effect of teacher adjustment on pupil adjustment. Univ. of Iowa Doctoral dissertations abstracts and references (1940 and 1941), Iowa City, Iowa, 1944, *4*, 76–79.
7. Anderson, H. H., and Brewer, J. E. Studies of teachers' classroom personalities, II. Effects of teachers' dominative and integrative contacts on children's classroom behavior. *Appl. Psychol. Monogr.*, 1946, No. 8.
8. Carmichael, L., ed. *Manual of child psychology.* Wiley, 1954, Chap. 13. Character development in children—an objective approach (Jones, V.).
9. Lichtenstein, A. Can attitudes be taught? *Johns Hopk. Univ. Stud. Educ.*, No. 21, 1934.
10. Symonds, P. M. Education and psychotherapy. *J. educ. Psychol.*, 1949, *40*, 1–32.
11. Stouffer, G. A. W. Behavior problems of children as viewed by teachers and mental hygienists. *Ment. Hyg.*, 1952, *36*, 271–285.
12. Schrupp, M. H., and Gjerde, C. M. Teacher growth in attitudes toward behavior problems of children. *J. educ. Psychol.*, 1953, *44*, 203–214.
13. Ullman, C. A. The socially maladjusted. *Rev. educ. Res.*, 1953, *23*, 432–452.
14. Slobetz, F. How elementary school teachers meet selected school situations. *J. educ. Psychol.*, 1951, *42*, 339–356.
15. Clarke, S. C. T. The effect of teachers' adjustment on teachers' attitudes. *Canad. J. Psychol.*, 1953, *7*, 49–59.
16. Gates, A. I., and others. *Educational psychology.* Macmillan, 1948, pp. 713–720.
17. Menninger, W. C. Attributes of mental health. *Nat. Parent-Teacher*, 1953, *48*, 10–12.

SUGGESTIONS FOR FURTHER READING

1. Havighurst, R. J. *Developmental tasks and education*. Longmans, 1950.
   An account of some of the things a child is called upon to do at different ages, and of the school's responsibility with respect to these tasks.
2. Menninger, W. C. Attributes of mental health. *Nat. Parent-Teacher*, 1953, *48*, 10–12.
   A leading psychiatrist gives a nontechnical description of goals in mental hygiene.
3. Carmichael, L., ed. *Manual of child psychology*. Wiley, 1954.
   Chap. 13. Character development in children—an objective approach (Jones, V.).
   See for a description of the difficulties of teaching for character.
   Chap. 14. Emotional development (Jersild, A. T.).
   A clear statement of the goals of adjustment.
4. National Society for the Study of Education. *Mental hygiene in modern education*. Fifty-fourth Yearbook, Part II, 1955.

Exercises and Questions for Discussion

1. Compare the various forces at work which may affect the teacher's success (a) in teaching the gerundive construction in Latin and (b) in teaching ten-year-old boys not to fight.

2. Outline your own "speculations" regarding the special problems that may arise in the teaching of character.

3. What are some of the dangers that may result from the wrong methods of controlling drives? List some of the indications of balanced control.

4. What aspects of reality may students be reluctant to face? Can you see any new problems that may arise if teachers are successful in getting students to face all troublesome matters?

5. List some of the mental health hazards that may actually be created by the school.

21

Improvement in Adjustment and Attitudes: Mental Hygiene in the Classroom

Now that we have considered the goals of personal adjustment, the next step, of course, is to see how these goals may be realized by the busy teacher as he goes about his workaday tasks in the classroom. How can he teach so as to bring about these goals? What reasonable steps may he take in addition to his regular teaching to further the personal and social adjustment of his students.

Much of what is about to be said has already been covered, at least by implication, in the sections devoted to the management of learning and in the sections on the general problem of desirable personal growth. It is still necessary, however, to bring together in more pointed fashion some of the general rules for guiding pupils into acceptable and satisfactory adjustments in the general field of personality. These rules are based partly on fairly adequate experimental evidence and partly on the opinions of those who have given much thought to the field. At the best, they represent dependable guides not likely to be discredited in the near future. At the worst, they represent merely the best guesses available at the present moment. In any case, they are worthy of serious consideration.

Making Reality Easier for the Child to Face

In previous sections we have discussed many mechanisms by which we delude ourselves and by which we often lead ourselves to unfortunate and harmful maladjustments. Most of these mechanisms are devices for escaping reality. It follows that if reality were easier to take, if there were less need to escape reality, there would also be less need to employ the mechanisms which lead to inadequate adjustment. From this fact we derive one of the basic rules for reducing or preventing maladjustment: *do not make reality unnecessarily harsh. Whenever possible, try to make sure that the reality which you ask the child to accept is not too hard to accept at his level of maturity and experience.* There is no question that some maladjustment is due to the fact that at one time or another the reality which confronted the child was too severe (and needlessly severe) for him to take at that particular time. Insofar as it was needlessly severe, the difficulty could have been avoided by a more reasonable arrangement of the demands acting on the child.

Notice that the rule just enunciated has several limitations or qualifications. These are most important. First of all, the rule says, "*Try* to make sure. . . ." The emphasis on *try* points to the fact that the circumstances are not always under the teacher's control. In spite of the best efforts of the teacher, the child may still confront a situation which is beyond his power to accept. Second, the rule talks about reality that is *needlessly* harsh. This emphasis, of course, shows that each child must face some unpleasant aspects of reality. The rule does not call for the elimination of all the grim or unpleasant features from the life of the child. It merely asks us not to make those features any worse than we have to. The third qualification refers to the reality which the child can accept *at his stage of development.* This limitation suggests that the protection which we provide now does not have to be continued forever. The harshness which we shield him from now we may ask him to accept later on when his increased maturity and greater experience may give him more chance of dealing successfully with the more difficult situation.

Consider the rule and its qualifications in a simple example: a pupil has clumsily spilled a bottle of ink. The other children laugh derisively. The pupil's handwork is spoiled. The teacher feels annoyed. In this situation the teacher might well ask himself these questions:

1. "Is there any likelihood that the pupil may be tempted to refuse to face the reality of this situation?" Yes, definitely. He may blame the

child in front of him, or he may attack his deriders, or he may revert to fantasy.

2. "Might the addition of my disapproval make the reality of culpable clumsiness too hard for this child to accept at his age?" Yes.
3. "Is my overt disapproval necessary to help him avoid accidents like this in the future?" No.
4. "Is that disapproval necessary for any other important purpose?" Probably not.

At some stage, it is true, the student must learn that such clumsiness probably will elicit the disapproval of his elders or superiors. But if the child is still young this adjustment could be left until later. All in all, there seems no doubt that the teacher's overt disapproval would violate our rule. It would make the reality needlessly hard for the child to accept at his stage of development. Under different circumstances, of course, the rule would permit the overt disapproval. If, for instance, the disapproval seemed necessary to correct the undesired clumsiness, the decision might be reversed. Or if the child is at a stage where he should be able to absorb such disapproval, the teacher might permit himself the luxury of an admonition or expostulation.

Is the rule under discussion merely a truism? Is it superfluous to ask teachers not to make reality unnecessarily harsh? The answer, unfortunately, is "No." Many teachers facing the upset ink bottle situation would add a scolding(1), a reprimand, or some expression of annoyance to the already grim picture which the child must face. They would do this even though the added discomfort would do no good and even though it might be the deciding straw which prevented the child from looking the facts squarely in the face. As teachers, in other words, we need the continual warning not to make reality needlessly grim or forbidding if we are to encourage children to face that reality clearly and honestly.

General Acceptance of the Child

There are several ways in which the teacher can help children face reality. One way, as we have seen, is to try to arrange the situations so that they do not press too harshly at any time. Obviously, however, this is only part of the story and not the most important part at that. Whether or not reality will be too formidable to face depends partly on the nature of that reality itself. It depends even more, however, on the person and on how well he is fitted to handle that external reality. This important fact was clearly brought out by the reactions of children to wartime bombing and evacuation(2, 3). Surely these two problems represent reality in its most grim and formidable aspects. Danger, fire, destruction of homes, death of parents, or a sudden move to a new environment and to life with strangers—these are pictures of reality which are exceedingly difficult to face. It is not surprising if children facing these ordeals should break down. Some children did. But some did not. And this is the important fact; the breakdown did not depend primarily on the severity of the shock or danger or on the extent of the separation. The children who adapted to these serious menaces were the children who had acquired a strong sense of security, especially of family security. The children who could not adjust themselves to those sudden terrors were those who lacked this strong sense of family security. They were the children who were secretly or openly worried about their status in the family. They were the children who were not sure that they were loved or wanted or that they really belonged. These factors of security and acceptance were much more important than the external stress to which the child was subjected.

Because of the overwhelming importance of the basic sense of security, it is clear that our task is less than half done if we concentrate entirely on protecting the child from problems that are too severe. We must try to do this, of course, but we must try even more to build the individual up to the point where he can meet problems that are more and more severe. More specifically, we must help him develop that basic sense of security or acceptance which has been shown to be so important in determining adjustments to serious problems.

How much can the teacher do to help build the all-important feeling of security? Well, not so much as the home, of course. But the teacher can provide a warm, human, receptive atmosphere. This does not necessarily mean a sweet, sentimental, overtly solicitous approach. Many a teacher can be hearty, jovial, even rough, and yet give the child a feeling of acceptance and belonging. The teacher does not have to say to each child, "You are sweet and wonderful and perfect," but he should say *by his manner and by his approach,* "You are an important person and your wishes and problems are real wishes and real problems, and even though you are often a young devil, and even though I may have to smack you down, you count no end with me."

A warm accepting attitude is especially important for pupils who have already come to think of the world as hostile, critical, and exacting. And there are many children who acquire this unfortunate attitude early in life and who come to school with all the apprehension, fearfulness, and even defiance which such an attitude engenders. For this child who has had to accept more criticism than he can absorb, or who has had to face standards which he does not know how to meet, the teacher must lean over backward to relax standards somewhat(4). When in doubt, err on the side of accepting too much even at the risk of lowering standards. The child must come to know that you are on his side even when he makes mistakes.

The advice just given may be very difficult to carry out. Ironically enough, it is fairly easy to adopt this permissive, accepting attitude with bright, well-behaved children. Anyone seeing us teach in this situation would find us to be democratic, integrative, and helpful. Let us change to a more difficult section, however, and we tend to change to a more dominative and demanding attitude(5). The children who are in most need of acceptance and liking are not those who are easy to like. If we follow our inclinations, we prefer the students who are already fairly popular(6). When we do surmount these difficulties we will often find our efforts rebuffed. Try to be friendly with children who have experienced extreme rejection over a long period and you will find that your advances are met with suspicion and distrust(7).

Naturally enough, the teacher's own feeling of security will have much to do with the ease of accepting the pupils. If you, yourself, are unsure and frightened, you will find it much harder to accept the pupils in warm, human fashion and to make them feel that you are on their side. The writer, in his early teaching experience, narrowly escaped serious trouble because of oversuspicion. On taking over a new job, he was told of the serious disciplinary problems he would face and was regaled with tales of the things the high-school boys had done to his predecessor. As a result of this unfortunate indoctrination, he began the year on the defensive and regarded even mild irregularities as the beginning of outright rebellion. It was only by extremely good luck that he came to "drop his guard" and to accept the students for what they were, an exceptionally fine bunch of boys, although typically thoughtless and with an ordinary flair for obstreperousness.

Just how can the teacher rid himself of his own insecurity? Preferably he should get some help. He could get much help from an understanding older teacher or principal who himself has acquired a measure of security. His knowledge of mental hygiene should also help him. He should be able to see that a surly or defiant attitude on the part of a pupil is often an expression of the need for acceptance and not a genuine challenge to the teacher. He should be normally alert, of course, to deal with ordinary high spirits or with irregularities which might interfere with the proper objectives of the class. He should not read too much into those irregularities, however. He should not regard them as a personal affront or as a challenge to his authority or esteem.

It is obvious that the teacher's own insecurity may readily prevent him from giving the student a measure of security. Extreme lack of security—anxiety—is desperately infectious. Children, especially, prove to be affected by anxiety in parents or older associates. Children facing severe ordeals will often react more to the attitude of the parents than to the actual objective facts. Even in the face of a genuine tragedy such as the father's loss of a job or a serious financial reverse, the children will be more affected by the anxiety of the parents than by the objective misfortune.

It is possible that even very subtle indications of anxiety on the part of parents may have a disturbing effect on the child. Fleeting expressions of concern or doubt or worry may easily be interpreted as anxiety, especially on the part of a child who is already overapprehensive.

The teacher's anxiety may readily be as infectious as that of parents. If the teacher is terrified of the imminent city-wide examinations or by the visit of the supervisor, the students may well acquire his apprehension and regard these events as psychological catastrophes.

In the simple process of counseling or giving advice, the teacher's anxiety or lack of confidence can readily show itself. By the time the consultation or conference is finished, you should convince the student that you are confident he will make a wise choice or achieve a wise solution to his problem. This conviction should come from your manner rather than from an overt statement. Try to *feel* confident. Try not to be anxious or dubious about the wisdom of the choice which the student will finally make. Anxiety on this point will reduce the general sense of acceptance. Obviously it betokens a certain lack of confidence. And even though your feeling of uncertainty applies only to the ability of the student to master some minor detail, the suggestion may spread to imply a lack of confidence in him as a person. Your anxiety, in other words, may be regarded as a lowering of your general esteem for the student being counseled.

Symptoms of Insecurity. A sense of insecurity or of being rejected may show itself in many ways. Defiance or surliness have already been mentioned. Rejection by other children is also a sign. Not only does it show that the person in question is not accepted by those other children, but it is also a sign of a more general lack of acceptance. Ironically enough, his very feeling of rejection may lead to behavior which will result in actual rejection. An undue urge for privacy may involve the same general mechanism. At any rate, it is true that children who are very prone to solitary activities are often those who have a marked feeling of general unacceptability. The child who feels rejected is also likely to make very obvious and persistent bids to gain adult attention. These bids may consist of showing off, tale bearing, acquiring injuries or ailments, or acting as the teacher's special assistant.

Role of Basic Needs (Maslow's Hierarchy)

In attempting to make reality easier for the child to accept, the teacher will do well to keep in mind the hierarchy of needs. A person is better able to deal with frustration of a higher need if the more primitive needs are taken care of. Conversely, it is harder to deal with frustration of a higher need if one is forced at the same time to adjust to a lower-order need. In the Maslow hierarchy, the physiological needs are considered the most primitive. Then come the needs to avoid pain or danger, then love, then the need for esteem, and finally the need for self-expression. Now a child who has to undergo a threat to his need for safety (e.g., to let the doctor administer a hypodermic) will be better able to manage this conflict if he is not already tired or hungry. Similarly, a person who is asked to forgo his need for the esteem of a certain group will find the frustration easier to bear if he already feels sure of the love or affection of his family or of another close group.

The moral of the hierarchy principle is obvious. If a child is to be asked to deal with deprivation of a higher-level need, be sure that the more basic needs are satisfied. If you can help it, do not ask him to look squarely at his unfulfilled need for aggression or revenge while he still feels the need to avoid danger. Before he is required to face honestly the loss of esteem, be sure that at the same time he does not feel the loss of affection or of fundamental acceptance. In general, the moral of the hierarchy could be likened to the modifications of a building. Before we subject the upper part of the building to any great stress, we would want to be sure that the basic portions were strong and well-bolstered. Similarly, in dealing with needs, we should be reluctant to apply stress to a higher need if a more basic need should be under a critical strain at the same time.

The Maslow hierarchy, or some modification of it, may also help us visualize how a very minor threat might assume serious proportions. The teacher in administering a casual reprimand may intend only a very mild and a quite temporary deprivation of esteem. In effect, the teacher

says, "In this particular respect you are not all that you might be."
There is always the possibility, however, that this mild threat to the
student's esteem may also spread to more fundamental needs. It may
act as a permanent threat to his need for esteem. It may appear as a
very real threat to his need for affection and in some vague way may
threaten his general security.

The possibility of a spread of a reprimand points again to the need of
reducing the stress at the lower levels. If the lower level needs are already
enduring critical deprivation, the additional glancing stress of an un-
intentional threat may be serious. If, on the other hand, these other needs
are well satisfied, they can easily absorb any accidental threat which
spreads to their level.

The teacher, of course, should not be content with bolstering up the
fundamental needs to the point where they can stand the occasional
accidental buffet. In administering any necessary reprimand, he should
try to restrict its influence to the very temporary loss of esteem which he
intends. As pointed out in an earlier section, he can often do this by an
offhand manner and by refusing to make too much of the incident. On
occasion, however, especially when dealing with a very insecure pupil,
he may have to take more definite steps. He may have to point out
deliberately that the pupil has suffered no permanent loss of esteem nor
any loss of acceptance whatever.

Securing Partial Outlet for Drives in Some Acceptable Manner

In trying to make reality easier for the child to accept, we should try
to provide for as much expression of any drive as circumstances will
permit. It stands to reason that insofar as some expression of a drive is
permitted, the degree of stress or frustration will be reduced, and as this
frustration is reduced, there will be less need to escape from the reality
of the frustration. A child may be induced not to cry upon being hurt.
Later on, however, upon receiving a second hurt, he may cry unusually
hard. Conversely, there is plenty of empirical evidence for the fact that
even partial outlet of a need or emotion makes that need or emotion
much easier to tolerate. People in the throes of terrific fear, as an air
crew making a bomb run through flak, or civilians sitting huddled in a
bomb shelter, find some measure of relief in talking about their fears.
The sheer act of telling someone how desperately frightened you are may
take some of the edge off the fear and thus make it easier to face. The
same thing is true of other strong needs or emotions. Describing your
anger may partially reduce your need for aggression. Describing your

affection for some unobtainable dream companion may make the need
for that person a trifle less urgent.

The importance of some outlet for emotions is suggested by the fact
that many emotions normally unpleasant may become pleasant if a
regular outlet is permissible. Fear, for instance, when experienced in
mild doses can be quite exhilarating if free expression is permitted or
encouraged. A roller coaster can induce a very real fear, and yet the
total experience is not entirely unpleasant, partly because some expression of the fear is part of the game. Even more genuine menaces such
as a forest fire which calls for headlong and uninhibited flight may induce an excitement which has its pleasurable aspects. The fear which we
must endure while sitting absolutely quiet, like the bombardier on the
bomb run, or the civilian in the bomb shelter—that fear has no exhilara-
tion. Anger, too, which can be expressed in an uninhibited fight or brawl
is very pleasurable to some people. For some men, the favorite Saturday
night entertainment is to get drunk and stir up some kind of brawl or
fight.

Enough has been said to show that as the amount of expression increases, the feeling of frustration decreases. It happens, however, that
pure natural expression, such as running or fighting, is seldom practicable. Indeed, it is the impracticability of these modes of conduct that
leads to the necessity for frustration. But if natural spontaneous expression is out of the question, what sort of expression can be arranged? Very
often some form of sublimation or of socially acceptable modification
can be found. Aggressions can be expressed in games. Sex needs can
achieve some expression in parties, dancing, songs, and in artistic productions.

Encourage the Conscious Acceptance of the Drive, Need, or Emotion.
Frustration will be handled more comfortably and more efficiently if we
are able to allow the frustrated idea to rise to consciousness. Frustration
is harder to take and more dangerous to experience if we refuse to admit
to ourselves that the frustrated urge actually exists. This admission to
consciousness is one sort of outlet which should be available to all drives
and emotions no matter how impractical, unflattering, or ugly they may
be.

As was pointed out in the previous chapter, there are many times when
we feel the need to protect our sense of self-esteem by refusing to acknowledge that we possess a certain urge or drive which we regard as wicked
or ridiculous. This is especially likely to happen when we begin to wish
for death or harm to parents or close relatives. It is also likely to happen

if any irregular sex interests, such as a homosexual urge, should be suspected. Such repression or refusal to admit the wish may also occur when we suspect ambitions which are merely ridiculous or fantastic, as when the staid minister may catch himself in an unguarded moment, dreaming of himself as a Don Juan or swashbuckler, or when a responsible man may catch a fleeting glimpse of a strong desire to return to a condition of childish dependence.

Repressions such as those mentioned often lead to undesirable behavior and certainly they constitute an added strain. To help the child avoid the danger and the strain which they entail, we should do our best to encourage him not to repress *ideas* or *wishes,* however ridiculous or improper. Suppose, for instance, that a child has become annoyed at a playmate and among other manifestations of aggression he has shouted, "I hate you. I hate you. Some day I'll kill you." We are called on to deal with this situation. What should we do? In our long-range objective for the child, we wish of course to modify this behavior. We do not wish him to go through life reacting to minor annoyances in this extreme way. We should gradually encourage him to change this manner of expression. But we should not try to talk him out of his feelings. We should not try to convince him that he did not hate his tormentor or the one who crossed him. It should not be too hard to point out to the child that it is natural for him to feel the way he does, that almost anyone in a similar situation would feel very much the same way. We can then go on to suggest that things would be better if he expressed himself in a different way.

This same attitude of modifying the expression, but not the thought, should prevail when we deal with a child who has spoken too freely of sexual matters. We should first make it clear that there is nothing wrong with the thought or the idea, that these are very interesting matters, and that they occupy a fairly important place in the minds of many people. We can then go on to point out that some people do not think as we do, and these people may become worried if sexual matters are discussed too openly. Even a very young child can make a fairly adequate adjustment to a problem put in this way. Parents who discuss sexual matters with young children as freely as they discuss other activities are often able to make even the four-year-old adopt a "live and let live" attitude. A child of this age can understand that "We talk about these things and find them interesting, but some parents don't, and it would bother them if we spoke this way in their house, or when their children are around." It is not at all unusual to see one four-year-old "protecting" the neighbor's four-year-old from the facts of life in this fashion. In the same way, the child who has discovered the truth about Santa Claus may take pains to prevent the disillusionment of a younger brother.

In developing the attitude that the wish is natural but that the expression should be controlled, there are two rules to follow. In the first place, avoid the suggestion that one is wicked to entertain unorthodox ideas, that nice people do not think of such things. But this negative approach is not enough. Even if we refrain from the suggestion that the child is unworthy because of his ideas, he may still acquire a feeling of guilt. The sheer fact that we discourage the outward expression of the wish or drive may convince him that the wish or drive itself makes him guilty. Consequently when trying to dissuade a child from the overt expression of an antisocial drive, we should take positive steps to indicate that there is nothing wrong with the wish itself.

We should strive mightily to encourage children to tolerate unpleasant ideas. Some psychiatrists advocate the universal study of anatomy and sociology to enable people to look upon some of the grim and unpleasant, but important, realities without undue squirming. But in spite of our best efforts, we should not expect to be 100 percent successful. By the time we get him, the child has already become used to feeling guilty because of unorthodox thoughts or emotions. This attitude becomes so habitual that any remonstrance over a way of behaving is likely to induce a feeling of guilt not only for the behavior but for the ideas which accompanied the behavior.

Protection against Undue Stress

Competition. Another way to ease the unpleasant aspects of the reality which presses on the child is to reduce the emphasis on competition. Undue competition, of course, makes for strained group feelings(8). More serious, perhaps, there is probably no greater blow to self-esteem than competition in which one continually fails. And loss of esteem is one of the harshest aspects of reality and an aspect which we are often driven to ignore. Try, then, not to carry competition too far. Be especially zealous to play down competition for a child who is already having a difficult time collecting his necessary quota of self-esteem. As his strength and sturdiness and general security increase, be sure that he learns how to compete and to enjoy it. But do not force the more grim features of competition on him too rapidly.

Punishment or Discouragement. In other places, we have learned that punishment and reprimands are often needlessly harsh and elaborate.

One of the simplest means of making reality easier to take is to employ only simple, short, casual reprimands as far as possible. Save the prolonged or elaborate disapproval for the obdurate cases.

The Problem of Failure

The problem of failure in schoolwork has received a good deal of attention. It has been held that the crushing effect of this frustration could readily threaten the child's mental adjustment. It is also claimed that this is an unnecessary frustration since a child seldom profits from being held back in school(9, 10). Both are matters of contention(11) and it would be wise not to be too dogmatic at this stage of our knowledge. With respect to mental adjustment we do know that failure following a clear expectation of success will lead a child to dislike the subject in which he failed(12) and also to refuse to accept the clear fact of failure. Under these conditions he will tend to see success where none really exists(13). It has also been held that such failure, in addition to forcing the child to turn his back on reality, will lead him to regress to a more childish way of doing things. This is a serious matter. The one hopeful thing about failure has been the possibility that we may learn from our mistakes and go on to a better way of behaving. According to this view(14), however, failure does not lead to improvement but to deterioration. Not everyone accepts this view, of course, and there is some claim that frustration merely leads to a great variety in ways of behaving and only some of these will be more childish(15). There can be no question, however, that failure can be extremely hard to face. Whenever the amount of failure can be reduced, reality, to that extent, should be easier to meet.

Protection Must Not Become the Rule. Much of what is to follow will deal with the problem of when to shield the child from the harsher features of reality and when to let him "take it." Before we leave this particular topic, however, we should point out that failure is most devastating when it violates our expectations of success. A continual series of successes, moreover, is one way of building up an expectation of future success(13). Consequently, by maneuvering things so as to bring about a long series of successes we may be setting the stage for serious distress later on.

In general it is most important to remember that protection cannot be supplied indefinitely. We should only try to be sure that the reality is within the tolerance of the child at this particular time. One of our goals, of course, is to increase his power of tolerating frustration and unpleasant reality. As that power increases, we should withdraw our solicitude to a degree. We should concentrate on teaching him how to meet reality, and we should gradually turn him loose to deal with it on his own.

Training in Solving Problems of Personal Adjustment

The primary rules of learning hold for the acquisition of adequate adjustments. Unless these new ways of behaving come from sheer maturation, they must be acquired either through direct practice and reinforcement of ways of behaving or else by means of transfer from other practiced and reinforced ways of behaving. Consequently if we are to go about teaching these new adjustments in a realistic manner, we must arrange either for direct practice or must seek some reasonable chance of transfer from some other activity.

Direct Practice

In many areas of personal adjustment, there is almost continual practice. In those areas the child is almost constantly encountering situations which call for a certain type of response. Daily, he meets physical interference or frustration. Daily, he must deal with physiological needs which are only partially satisfied. Daily, he feels the need for more affection and appreciation. Daily, he strives with almost pathetic intensity for a richer harvest of esteem. Consequently there is no dearth of situations which call for adjustment. For many areas there is no problem about the lack of practice.

Although there are abundant opportunities for practice, that practice is far from ideal as far as the teacher is concerned. The casual practice which comes from the ordinary experience of living is largely beyond the teacher's control. It cannot be administered in a neatly graded series of tasks arranged in increasing difficulty and presented so as to produce a minimum of undesirable spread. This haphazard curriculum may throw the child into *personal* "long division" before he has studied the corresponding *personal* "addition." It may call right now for subtle discriminations which should not be expected until much later in the game. Conversely, it may keep a child on a diet of easy personal problems when he is really well prepared for more strenuous adjustments.

In the face of this haphazard practice, the teacher must rely chiefly on the flexibility of his methods of reinforcement. As will be pointed out later, he will apply very lenient standards to behavior which is really beyond the powers of the child. He will be more exacting with regard to behavior which readily falls within the child's competence.

For some areas, practice, haphazard though it may be, is always at hand. There are some important areas, however, in which little practice will ever occur, and which for practical reasons the teacher cannot supply. The ability to withstand strong temptation to steal, for instance, is of vast importance. Yet it may not occur frequently enough to provide any considerable practice. The teacher, moreover, will hardly be able to supply genuine practice in this problem. The same is true for practice in dealing with intense fear, strong sex drives, or the obligations of parenthood.

Transfer

When direct practice is not feasible, some sort of transfer is the only hope. And as we have suggested, much of personality teaching must be accomplished in this way since direct practice may not be available or may be too unsystematic to be depended on. It is most important, therefore, to utilize transfer as effectively as possible in teaching children adequate personal adjustments.

The fact that transfer may be our only remaining device does not guarantee that it will be an effective device. No one knows for sure just how much transfer can be expected from the tasks which can be practiced in the school to the tasks in personal adjustment which the student will face when he is away from the school. Courses aimed at developing attitudes frequently find much greater gain in information than in the actual practices the information was intended to change(16). But whether completely satisfactory or not, it is the only remaining device, and we must use it as best we can. If it is not adequate, we will merely have to take comfort from the fact that there are many other social agencies working toward the same general goals, and these may be able to provide guidance when the real practice does occur.

Use of Examples from Many Fields. If transfer is to be effective, we must teach for transfer. If, for instance, we wish a piece of literature to develop general tolerance for other religions or for other ways of life, we must make sure that the general principle is applied to several specific illustrations. There should be applications to a variety of other cultures and to a variety of aspects of those cultures. If we wish the experience in running the class shop to transfer to general responsibility, we must point the moral in one instance after another. If we hope that the lesson in analyzing propaganda will work when the child confronts other kinds of propaganda, again we will have to apply this principle to a large number of concrete examples.

Encouraging Children to Generalize. Transfer is more effective if the children themselves can work out general rules which are learned in this lesson and which can be applied to other situations. After presenting two or three examples of the need for community responsibility, for instance, the children should be encouraged to derive a general rule which could be applied to similar cases. After seeing a revival of a movie such as *The Best Years of Our Lives,* they should be encouraged to work out the general rules which facilitated the increased adjustment of the handicapped veteran.

Problem of Priggishness. There is a possibility that some very desirable personal traits cannot be acquired by direct practice. This may be especially true for such traits as spontaneity, vivacity, a touch of devilishness, or other elusive but endearing traits. Perhaps deliberate practice in spontaneity is almost a contradiction in terms. Indeed, the whole problem of practicing desirable behavior may have some dangers. We may fear that any great amount of deliberate practice in worthy conduct may induce a touch of priggishness or self-conscious virtue. Perhaps, however, there may be enough resentment against this sort of thing in the general community or among the students themselves to prevent this problem from reaching serious proportions.

Guidance and Reinforcement of Weak and of Strong Tendencies

It is most important to adjust the application of reinforcement to the status of the tendency. As in the acquisition of academic subject matter, weak transient tendencies call for one type of treatment while stronger or well-established tendencies call for a quite different treatment. Consequently, we should be on the alert to try to judge the strength status of a tendency and to arrange the type of reinforcement accordingly. Alertness and care in this matter is most important, since the teacher cannot always control the arrangement of practice. To make up for the lack of control of practice, we must rely on skill in the application of reinforcement.

As in the case of practice, it is true there are some types of reinforcement which are not under the teacher's control. The approval or disapproval of schoolmates, friends, and relatives is something which will go on in spite of anything the teacher can do. His own overt approval or disapproval the teacher can largely control, although even here his control is not always complete. And it is in the employment of these means of reinforcement that he should have most care.

Weak Tendencies

It is safe to assume that a tendency is weak or transitory (a) when the student reacts to a new situation for the first time or (b) when the reaction to a recurring situation varies markedly from time to time. Such a weak tendency would be expected, for instance, if a child were dealing for the first time with the emotional stress involved in making a talk to a larger group. A weak tendency would also be indicated if the child were anxious to perform at one time and at another time should be near panic at the idea of appearing in public.

Be Sure of Basic Security and Acceptance. When the student is about to encounter a stress situation for the first time (or while the tendency being practiced is still weak), do everything you can to ensure his feeling of acceptance and security. Be sure he realizes that you are on his side and that he belongs to this crowd. He should never feel an acceptance that is merely conditional. He should never believe that he will be accepted and well regarded if he succeeds but that he will be rejected or scorned if he fails. He should take his acceptance for granted. His success is another pleasant ornament which will please everyone, but it is not his passport to acceptance.

Easy Problems First if Possible. Whenever possible be sure that the first situation encountered is not too tough. In his first public-speaking task, for instance, try to find a situation where the stress is not too great. For some children this may mean speaking before strangers—for whose esteem he is less concerned. For other children, a group of friends may seem less formidable. Or to take another instance, in teaching control of aggressive tendencies, try to make sure that the initial provocation to be met is not too great.

Provide Positive Guidance when Possible. In learning how to deal with stress, as in other kinds of learning, it is most important to get off on the right foot. In one experiment(17), for instance, boys were "steered" toward constructive activities by being rewarded for this sort of work prior to the onset of stress. Another group, in contrast, was rewarded and praised for aggressive acts. Later both groups were subjected to stress and frustration. Each group reacted to the frustration by the behavior to which they had been guided. Students who, in the absence of such guidance, prematurely blunder into erroneous attitudes about other people, will be slow to acquire a more appropriate attitude. Guidance is most important in preventing these incorrect approaches from becoming fixed and thus dominating the learning that is to come. Whenever possible, take some active step to guide or direct or maneuver the student into the appropriate response. Suppose, for instance, that a student has just been defeated in a tennis game and seems about to sulk or behave in some childish way. If you can help it, do not give him a chance to do this. Rush over to him, and while you are commenting on the good points in his play, unobtrusively push, guide, or maneuver him over to his opponent, so that he is almost forced to shake hands. If a younger child has fallen in a puddle and is hovering between tears and laughter, lead him to laugh, if you can, by your manner. Laugh *with* him and not *at* him.

The Importance of Praise and Early Success

When dealing with weak tendencies in the initial stages of learning, do not be afraid of liberal praise. Free and generous praise for *general* behavior may help to get a student to give up an early inadequate way of responding that threatens to become permanent(18). Typically, of course, praise is in order only when you can detect some success. For this and for other reasons it is important to arrange for some success in the early trials. This is not so easy, of course, in teaching people to deal with emotions. We cannot always arrange things so that facing an audience, for instance, will be followed by telling a joke, and that this in turn will be followed inevitably by genuine appreciative laughter. Lacking this control, we must seek other expedients, such as presenting tasks in which success is very probable.

Insofar as success is determined by the opinion of the teacher, the problem of guaranteeing success is fairly easy to meet. We can always find something to commend enthusiastically, and we should do so at this early stage of learning. Young children can profit by lavish praise. Older children may blush at praise when it is too effusive and too overt, but they can still absorb a good deal of praise with profit if it is a little more subtle and somewhat more restrained. This praise can often be introduced in incidental fashion. In discussing a new problem, for instance, a teacher might say, "Have you thought of trying to handle this as you did last week when . . . ?" At any rate, appreciation and praise should be very free in these early trials. Do not be afraid to accept and commend behavior which is merely in the right general direction, even if it is far from adequate in many details.

When success is not chiefly determined by the attitude of the teacher, the problem of ensuring success is more difficult. Suppose, again, that we are dealing with the conflict in which the child wants to be able to speak effectively and yet fears the lack of esteem which might follow should he fail. Actually, if he did fail it would be easy for the child to convince himself that he really does not want to speak before a group. Discouragement would push him further toward the repression of this drive. To ensure the success of the early attempts, the teacher will applaud freely whenever there is any excuse whatsoever. Perhaps his applause may lead other students in the audience to applaud, and this should help to bring about a picture of success.

Arranging for initial success in the early stages of learning is one of the most important tasks which faces the teacher. Not only is this initial success necessary for the actual tendency being practiced, but it affects the child's expectations about future success. As we pointed out earlier, a prolonged, unbroken series of successes can arouse expectations that are unrealistic and perhaps dangerous. In the initial stages of learning, however, we seldom have to worry about that problem. At this stage we often have difficulty in attaining any success whatsoever.

A child who has had a reasonable amount of success in his early efforts shows signs of realistic aspiration. When asked to estimate the "score" which he will make on the next attempt, he selects a score just a little above that just made. This, of course, is the reasonable thing to expect. The child who has failed on his initial trials, however, makes no such reasonable estimate. He may set his expectations at a very low failing level—a lower level than he actually attained on his first trial. Or he may set an impossibly high score, determined, apparently, by fantasy. From this it is seen that early success not only enables the child to deal more adequately with the tendency being practiced, but it enables him to face the future in a more realistic fashion(19, 20).

Changing Techniques as Tendencies Get Stronger

As tendencies become stronger, more and more difficult problems may be presented. The potential speaker can face larger and more critical groups. He accepts more vigorous competition. The child who is learning to control the outward expression of aggressive drives can come up against stronger and stronger provocation. He can enter into games with a fair amount of rough bodily contact where aggressive urges are likely to be aroused.

As the problems increase in severity and in the degree of adjustment demanded, it is very important to maintain the basic security already stressed. While the growing youngster may need less overt assurance of affection and acceptance, he must never have any doubt that as a person he counts with the teacher and with the group.

For tendencies which are becoming fairly well established and which still require some modification, it will be necessary to use discouragement or symbolic punishment. Discouragement or disapproval is perfectly in order if the basic reaction is well established but some minor feature still leaves something to be desired. One of the boys, for instance, has made a fairly good adjustment to the rough and tumble of the playing field. He actively seeks this sort of play. He can take his failures fairly casually and expresses his aggression in acceptable form. If, however, we should see him begin to play the man instead of the ball or seek too hard for some chance to "get even," we would be perfectly in order to administer an "Oh! Forget it," or some other casual reprimand.

Symptoms of Too Rapid Change in Method of Applying Reinforcement. In learning any one task, the child must move from the stage of being protected and guided to the stage of being on his own and meeting more exacting standards. It stands to reason, however, that such a transition should be gradual rather than abrupt. Be ever on guard, moreover, to see that we are not asking for too rapid a transition. Such an unduly abrupt transition would reveal itself by a definite increase in the evidence of frustration. In young children, this frustration might express itself in unprovoked weeping or generalized anger. Faced with a specific task which is too frustrating at the moment, the child may loiter or postpone his start on the task. Other evidences of distaste may appear, or he may work around the task with a show of token movements or other useless reactions. Frustration may also reveal itself, however, in undue expenditure of energy. The child may attack an ordinary task almost aggressively. In severe frustration, even more serious behavior problems may develop. Ailments, exhibitionism, or showoff tendencies may appear.

When any of the many signs of frustration reach a point at which serious stress is suspected, ease up in the rate of transition. Provide more guidance and move back for the time being to a less exacting attitude.

In doing this, it would be well if there were not too obvious a connection between, say, the temper tantrum and our "retreat." It would be well if we could change the intensity of the stress and do it in our stride without seeming to alter our approach. But this is a secondary matter. When behavior problems or other evidences of frustration appear, the important thing is to reduce the frustration. Just how gracefully we can arrange the reduction is another and a lesser problem.

Welcoming Opportunities to Develop Frustration Tolerance

This point, already suggested in the previous section, must not be overlooked. Adult life is continually characterized by frustration and stress. The child who first meets the realities of adult responsibility with no experience in enduring frustration is pathetically unprepared. The man of adult years who expects the same protection and guidance which he received as a child is pathetically unhappy and a nuisance to his fellows. There is some evidence, moreover, that one of the distinctive characteristics of some deviates (especially alcoholics) is the fact that they were subjected to very little frustration as children(21). All in all, we render a child a very dubious service if we prolong the period of protection and guidance longer than necessary.

Just what the teacher can do actually to arrange for practice in frustration is difficult to say. Athletics and competitive sports have often been advocated for this purpose. At times, too, children might be encouraged to strive for desirable goals just at the limit of their powers, so that there is some risk of failure. After all, the only way anyone can find out how high a student can actually jump is to try higher and higher settings until he fails. The only way he can find out how much college work he can carry is to carry heavier and heavier loads until he gets a low grade. There is much to be said for encouraging youngsters to try themselves out once in a while, even to the point of failure.

Perhaps, however, the teacher has no great need to concoct occasions for frustration. The regular experiences of life will provide much practice in dealing with stress of that kind. The teacher, then, need merely be prepared to withdraw his protection and guidance gradually but consistently to the point where the student occasionally takes the full brunt of frustration on his own.

A Student May be a Beginner in Some Tasks and Experienced in Others. At any given age a student may be at the stage where he needs guidance in the development of one tendency and at the same time be ready for an independent attack on another problem. The six-year-old may have had little experience in facing the fact that he rides to school in a smaller car than Jimmy does. In facing this situation he needs guidance and reward. Even at this age, however, he may be an old hand at spending a few hours away from home, and he may be asked to accept frustration of this sort with very little protection. Similarly, the sixteen-year-old girl may have readily adjusted to the limited family bank account. In this area, she can meet new slights or stress on her own with very little guidance. She may still be a timid beginner, however, in meeting the frustration caused by her parents' disapproval of a new boy friend. In facing this unpleasant frustration, she may need as much guidance as she needed as a six-year-old in facing other problems.

The Direct Approach: Classes in Adjustment

So far, we have discussed the things that a teacher might do in the course of the ordinary school day. The devices described are those that might be sandwiched in with lessons and with informal playground activity. It is possible, however, that these incidental techniques, important as they are, should be supplemented by a frontal attack and that we should organize classes frankly aimed at more adequate adjustment. There is, of course, a suggestion of priggishness in taking a course in "how to become a better adjusted person," and this may bother some people. Other people, however, will feel no qualms about this direct approach, and in any case, we should consider it on its merits.

Bullis(22) and his colleagues see great promise in the Human Relations Club that they have used for some years. In these classes there is much group discussion of interpersonal tensions, worries, and stresses. In such courses there is an opportunity to use some of the films available for this purpose. Many of these present a clear picture of adjustment difficulties. In such courses we can also introduce books and booklets(23) written for students in various grades. Along with these approaches, we learn of the use of psychodrama or role playing in which students are asked to take a part in some play dealing with adjustment difficulties(24, 25). It would seem wise, however, to undertake these more ambitious projects only in cooperation with someone who is in a position to assume some responsibility for psychiatric treatment.

The Special Problem of Anger and Aggressive Tendencies

So far, there has been no separation of the numerous specific personality problems to which pupils must adjust. Unfortunately, moreover, it is not possible to outline the guidance necessary for adjusting to each specific frustration or to each kind of emotional stress. For two specific emotions, or areas of stress, however, a fair number of data have been gathered, and this information should be considered. Obviously in discussing these special cases, we shall repeat much of what has been said about the general problem.

Reducing the Need for Anger or Aggression

In teaching a child to adjust to any frustration or stress, it is wise at the outset of the teaching to avoid overintense experience with the emotion. Accordingly, in helping a child to manage aggressive urges, it is wise to shield him from as much frustration as possible and to avoid provocation or the need for aggression. Several rules may help(26).

1. Enforce Standards Consistently, but not with Complete Rigidity. A child who knows just what to expect in the matter of enforcement of standards is subjected to much less stress than the child who must face an inconsistent, capricious method of enforcement. To be punished for an action at one time and to be applauded for the same action at a different time is disconcerting in the extreme. It is better for standards to be enforced somewhat severely but consistently than to face an unpredictable vacillation between severity and indulgence.

The emphasis on consistency, of course, should never reach a point where the rule or the standard is more important than any human consideration whatsoever. The standards are set to help in the guidance of people. They are not ends in themselves which people must be made to serve.

2. Avoid a Fussy or Worrisome or Overmoralistic Attitude. A teacher who is always agitated or disturbed over some triviality is more likely to induce anger or aggressive behavior in pupils. Guidance should not use too tight a rein. So long as the child is proceeding in the right direction he should be "given his head" as far as possible. It is also true that the continual application of standards of a generalized "good" or "bad" will cause insecurity which in turn will lead to anger. Young children, especially, are already too much concerned with whether or not they are "good" (in general) or "bad." Such labels cause great distress and do no good. The emphasis should be on the conduct, on the specific act. Did it accomplish the desired result? Did it make you happy? Did it make your friends happy? Try to avoid an appeal to such a vague, nebulous, but frightening standard as general good or general bad.

3. Help the Child Increase His Skill in Dealing with Worrisome Problems. Increased competence should reduce the frustration in many activities. Increased competence in athletics, for instance, should reduce the need for aggression.

4. Find or Create Some Opportunity for Praise or Acceptance if the Situation Is Becoming Tense. Often the storm of aggression gives much warning before it breaks. An alert teacher can detect these warnings and can head off the storm. When there is some hint that the frustration acting on a child is becoming more than he can stand, be sure to add to his general security and his general feeling of acceptance by praise or some other evidence of kindly interest.

Anger Should Not Lead to Success

We must try to reduce the need for anger and to lessen the provocations which the child will encounter. In spite of our best efforts, however, many provocations will arise and many children will give way to unacceptable expressions of aggression. Be careful to see that these do not "pay off." Be sure that the student is not able to solve his problems or to get his own way by a display of temper. If, through accident or mistaken judgment, he has already been pushed to the point of temper tantrum, do not give way at that point in any important matter. Be sure, of course, not to add unnecessary further provocation. Use a conciliating tone. But do not reward him by giving him the toy for which he is screaming.

Providing Acceptable Outlets for Aggression

In our discussion of the general problem of handling frustration and anger, we considered the desirability of finding an acceptable outlet whenever possible. This is very important for unsocial or impractical aggressive drives.

Aggressive Urges without Undue Disturbance or Shame. Clear, frank admission of the existence of aggressive needs will greatly facilitate the

adequate adjustment to the frustrated need. It will also protect the individual from the danger arising from repression. Whenever possible,
facilitate this admission or acceptance of the urge. Facilitate it in the first
place by never implying that the child is unworthy or evil or bad because of his impractical aggressive wishes. To wish to hurt or to wreak
revenge or to kill does not make him evil. Carrying out those wishes,
of course, would be evil. The mere negative approach, however, is not
enough. To help the child, we may have to go to some trouble to point
out that it is natural for him to hate this person (temporarily we hope)
and to point out that almost anyone else in his situation would feel the
same. If time permits, he might even be encouraged to talk out in some
detail the exact line of conduct he would like to follow if circumstances
permitted.

As soon as the child is convinced that you do not condemn him for
hating his rival or superior, it is safe to go on to discuss the sensible
thing to do about it. Get him to see the rival claims of revenge, on the
one hand, and of the need for esteem of others or esteem of self or the
need to avoid punishment, on the other. Do not leave the matter until
the claims of prudence and social obligations have been clearly recognized.

Announcement of Anger.

> I was angry with my friend,
>   I told my wrath, my wrath did end.
> I was angry with my foe,
>   I told it not, my wrath did grow.

Blake's pithy summary of this problem has been supported by sober
investigation(27). Two students, strangers to each other, were asked to
cooperate in the solution of a problem. They faced each other through
a glass partition and all communication was in the form of notes passed
back and forth. As it happened, one "student" was really a stooge for
the experimenter. As the work went on he became more and more
abusive, finally writing a vicious, personal attack. This was repeated with
the same stooge with a number of different students. Some of these students were permitted to reply to the personal attack; others were not.
Some days later, those who had been permitted no outlet were still
bothered by the situation and felt acute resentment against the attacker.
Those who had been permitted to reply had more often dismissed the
whole thing.

It is true, of course, that we cannot always reply "in kind." Under the lash of an unfair reprimand from the boss, we cannot afford to let our blind anger express itself in all its fury. Later on, however, if the boss is reasonably human, we can announce in a matter of fact way that the experience was very hard to accept. Often this may lead to a quiet discussion of the whole matter on the part of both parties concerned, and this may provide release. Even the mere fact that we made the announcement may provide some release and may reduce the need for prolonged fantasies in which we seek an unrealistic and pathetically inadequate outlet for our pent-up rage.

It is true that even a quiet unemotional announcement of annoyance or past hostility may not remain quiet and dignified. In spite of our original decision and in spite of our best efforts, it may end up in an emotional blowoff. Ordinarily, however, the risk is worth taking. An emotional scene is not inevitable. Even if it does occur, it may be better than the alternatives of sustained suppression.

There are some people who advocate an occasional violent quarrel-reconciliation as a wholesome feature of social relations. The pattern is most clear perhaps in the lover's quarrel, followed by "making up." This may be true for some people, but it should not be applied universally. A violent outburst is not the worst thing that can happen. Ordinarily, it is preferable to keeping a grudge or trying to pretend that there is no hostility. But although the lesser of two evils, such an outburst may be undesirable. For most people it may be most disturbing and devastating to the sense of self-esteem. The restrained, jocular, or casual mention of annoyance is to be preferred.

Games or Contests. The device of unemotional announcement is one which older students may properly practice. For younger children, however, it may require a grasp of relations which are somewhat too complicated. This is especially true if there is no clear insight as to the exact nature of the aggressive need. In the face of such vague, poorly directed, aggressive needs, we may turn to games, contests, or general physical activity to provide a considerable measure of release. These activities should make the general frustration less pressing. Such devices, however, should not replace the more deliberate and rational expression of those aggressive needs which are clearly understood.

Play Therapy. Some children who are really very disturbed by unrelieved aggression have been helped by play therapy(28). In this activity, a child uses dolls or puppets to act out a story. He finds it easy to project his own urges into these dolls. A competent therapist, seeing these urges as they are expressed in play, may lead the child to enter a more complete discussion of the problem, in terms of the dolls. He can ask, "What would this doll like to do to his mother (or little sister)?" He can then ask, "What should he do?" As will be pointed out later, therapy of this type should be undertaken only under the close supervision and direction of a competent psychiatrist.

One's Own Aggressive Needs and the Aggressive Needs of Others

It is wise to encourage a child to bring his aggressive needs to the surface and then to deal with them in a rational manner. The chief advantage for this procedure is the fact that it permits a more adequate adjustment than could be made any other way. There is still another reason. Through a clear-eyed view of his own aggressive needs, a child can be led to deal more intelligently with the aggressive needs of others. It is too much, of course, to expect that this transfer will be automatic for all children. But by skillful guidance, the teacher can facilitate such transfer. Suppose that a child has made some sort of adjustment to one of his own aggressive needs and is now able to laugh in the pleasant release which comes from such an adjustment. Once he is bolstered by this feeling of near-exhilaration, it would be safe, and in order, to speculate about how the other fellow felt, what he really wanted, "what was *really* eating him when he jumped on you that day?"

An increased ability to understand the aggressive needs of the other fellow would be an inestimable advantage in smoothing out social relations at all levels. At the simplest level, it would improve the relations between two friends. At the most complex level, it would simplify the dealings between nations. At any level, we would be able to reason more clearly about our relations with the other person if we had a sympathetic understanding of his aggressive needs and of the sources of his hostility.

The Special Problem of Fear

Fear, like anger, is one of the important primitive emotions which, unless well controlled, is likely to complicate life as it is presently lived and to reduce our happiness and efficiency. It is all the more in need of control or management because of the fact that, in many instances, it is superfluous as well as harmful.

By control we do not mean elimination. Fear has proved one of the most valuable of the emotions which have helped us along our evolutionary journey. Even now, it is of great practical importance in the life of each of us. But in some of its manifestations, it serves no useful purpose and may cause great suffering and harm.

Reducing or Preventing Unnecessary or Undesirable Fear

Building Up General Security. The fear of any new menace will be less if the child is not already fearful of a large number of things. If, then, a child is about to encounter a new menace such as absence from home or his first boat trip, he will be better able to deal with this if he is not already frightened of losing affection or esteem, or if he is not already dealing with frustrations at a more basic physiological level. Small children in the hospital, for instance, will handle their inevitable fears much better and recover from the anxiety much sooner, if they have had daily visits from parents and have received general psychological support(29).

Forewarning and Explanation. When a child is about to undergo serious stress, such as an operation, mere forewarning or explanation cannot be expected to abolish fear or greatly to reduce it(30). When dealing with milder stress, however, it often helps to have a moderate length of time to consider the oncoming menace(31). Not only does this permit practical defenses, but it gives us a chance to erect psychological barricades. We can figure out ways of reacting to the danger and can at least brace ourselves against it. Certainly children who are warned to expect a loud noise, or who know that the boat will soon move, are often much less agitated than other children to whom the new stimulus is a complete surprise.

At times an understanding of the mechanics of the menace may help. It may help to know what rattlesnakes can do and what they cannot do. By knowing what the menace can do and what it cannot do, we tend to localize its menacing qualities. Unexplained, it is a vast general "threat," perhaps to everything that we value. Explained, it is a limited menace, serious enough perhaps, but demanding our attention at only certain points.

Advance Acquisition of Skill in Dealing with Menace. An oncoming menace is less severe if we have acquired some confidence in our ability to handle it. If we have never encountered a rattlesnake, we will naturally be perturbed by the possibility of such an encounter. That concern will be reduced, however, even if we have merely watched an expert deal with a rattlesnake. Our concern should be reduced even further if we are given specific instructions. Children about to encounter the steam whistle on the boat could be told to put their hands over their ears when the man reaches for the cord and to remove them a little at a time.

Example of Other People. It may help to watch other people deal with the menace and to see them come off safely. This certainly gives a measure of intellectual reassurance. It cannot, of course, be guaranteed to effect a reduction of emotional stress. It works sometimes, however, and is always worthwhile, since the sheer presence of other people is often reassuring in itself.

Gradual Initiation to the Menace. This is a most effective device and should be used whenever feasible. A brief absence from home should precede the prolonged visit. Experience with subdued steam whistles would be a valuable introduction to the more vigorous real article. Successful adjustment to rattlesnakes may be facilitated if the individual has had some preliminary dealing with harmless snakes.

Permit an Active Approach. Fear is usually less if the learner himself can control the intensity of the stimulus which he encounters. It is better if he can approach or retreat at will, if he can turn the volume up or down as he chooses, if he can go close to the caged snake or withdraw from it when frustration develops, if he can move to the deep end of the swimming pool or back to the shallow end. This approach to a new and somewhat formidable situation should be used whenever practicable.

Dealing with Existing Fears

As in anger, our best efforts in preventing fear will not always be successful. No child can entirely escape the frustrations which come from fears. Some of those fears will be organized around genuine menaces. Other fears will be set off by objects which have no objective menace at all but which, even so, have some very real psychological threat. How should we help children deal with fears?

Provide an Acceptable Outlet for Fear. This is one of the steps for making a fear more tolerable. As mentioned in the general discussion of emotions, a fear which can be expressed freely is much easier to bear than one for which no expression is possible. The very real trepidation encountered on roller coasters or other "rides," for instance, is made endurable, if not actually enjoyable, by the freedom (if not the obligation) to shriek and scream. Similarly, children enjoy games in which someone playing "bear" springs from around a corner and gives chase. This quasi-fear is expressed by uninhibited running and squealing. There is much evidence that genuine intense fear is more easy to endure when one is not required to inhibit the normal expression of fear.

One form of expression which is theoretically always available and which is most effective is the admission of fear to ourselves. Children should be encouraged to admit to themselves that they are afraid and should be further encouraged to admit to themselves the real nature of the fear. Furthermore, they should be encouraged to feel no shame for being afraid. One precept of mental hygiene employed in World War II was to encourage soldiers to feel no shame at the horrible panic which racked them in the stress situations which they encountered.

A further valuable outlet consists of the unemotional, matter-of-fact, often humorous announcement of fear to other people. Experiments on morale in bomb shelters showed this to be the most dependable means of reducing the tremendous tension. This description of just how desperately frightened one is, provided a very definite measure of release. In the bomb shelter it proved to be a better morale builder than such things as singing or playing games.

Even unrelated vigorous physical activity can often make fear easier to take. Keeping busy often helps, either by taking one's mind off the fear or by using up some of the physiological preparation for action.

Adaptation. As most people have observed, we often become accustomed to objects which at one time were very fearful indeed. We learn to walk at ease in the midst of the whirring machinery and noisy crashes which terrified us when we first started work in the factory. We become adjusted to fearful heights, to the ordeal of appearing in public, and to the tirades of the boss.

If such adaptation is to be effective, it is important that the early exposures be harmless and do not involve any sudden increase in the intensity of the situation. If the fear is reinstated upon each exposure, the program of adaptation may do more harm than good.

Emotional Adjustment: The Teacher's Opportunities and Limitations

A teacher does not need to be a pediatrician to notice a persistent cough, a rash on a child's face, or the squinting and peering of another child as he looks at the blackboard. Similarly, the teacher does not need to be a psychiatrist to detect some very ordinary signs of possible personality disturbance. Many of these danger signals have been mentioned throughout the previous discussion. Do not confine your concern, by the way, to the noisy, obstreperous, unruly child. He is a problem all right, but you are bound to notice him and probably no one will have to urge you to refer him to a clinic or to anyone who may be able to influence him. You are not equally prone, however, to notice the unduly shy, timid, frightened child. And this child who is exceptionally docile, cooperative, and "good" may have more need for help in making her adjustments than does her more aggressive brother. The traditional signs of excessive "nervousness" are, of course, very easy to notice. These include habitual nail biting, uncontrolled urination, stuttering, and various tics or compulsive movements.

When serious disturbances are suspected, refer the child to someone who is competent to diagnose and treat the difficulty. There may be a clinic for such cases. If there are no more formal facilities, try to see that the child's physician is informed.

Resist the Temptation to Play the Psychiatrist. The teacher should throw off, at all costs, any lingering suspicion that he is qualified to treat serious personality defects. Like other people, he may be strongly tempted to meddle in this interesting field of mental therapy. But it is a complex and dangerous field, and the temptation must be resisted. The amateur psychiatrist, be he the teacher or the fellow who has just read a book, is one of the new evils which afflict society. True, his remedies, as those of any quack, may succeed at times, since most patients are fairly durable and resilient. There are times, however, when the quack or the amateur may aggravate the very condition which he sets out to correct. At times, a direct attack on a superficial behavior symptom will lead a sufferer to retreat still further from reality and to hide behind an even more impregnable barrier. For these reasons the amateur psychiatrist is a menace to society and must be restrained. For the teacher, that restraint must be self-imposed. It should, none the less, be stringently enforced. Mental therapy is not for us.

Developing Social Adjustment

Social Acceptance

For a great many reasons it is most important to help the rejected child attain a measure of acceptance or liking from his classmates. In the first place, there is the human need to help him avoid a condition that brings distress if not outright tragedy. There is also the need to reduce his temptation to turn his back on this unpalatable reality. More important, however, is the need to help him acquire ways of acting that are more acceptable to others. The causes of his rejection, of course, lie largely in him and in his conduct. The ultimate objective is to secure some improvement in these respects. But meanwhile he must achieve some success in his initial efforts.

Here is a problem of rejection as described by one teacher:

In many ways William would be an excellent example of the average child. His IQ was 95. He was not especially troublesome to his teachers. In Grade 5, where I met him, his school work was fair. In class he did his work but rarely volunteered to take part in class discussion. He would respond briefly when called on. He was one of the taller boys in the class, pale, and moved about the room quietly.

There was little communication between him and the other children. He came into the room in the morning, unpacked his books, put them in his desk, then went to the back of the room to examine the bulletin board. After this he would return to his desk and look at a library book. He spoke to no one. No one spoke to him. This same thing happened over and over again.

Recess: The boys were playing "Defending Fort McHenry." William did not have many turns at throwing the ball. He made an attempt to get the ball but was easily out-maneuvered by the other boys. Once he raised his foot and pretended he was going to kick another boy but he drew back his foot before he touched the boy. The boys took no notice of the action.

William walked to and from school each day with his brother who was in the second grade. No one else walked with them. They walked slowly and did not appear to be carrying on a conversation.

Lunchtime: One rainy day when the children finished their lunch they were playing quiet games in groups. William sat by himself watching some children across the room playing "Tick-Tack-Toe" on the board. Then he went to the cupboard and got a checker game. When another boy returned to the room from cafeteria, William asked him to play checkers. (The checker board was usually in demand.) The boy shook his head "No" and went to watch the children at the board.

One day the children brought their hobbies to school and talked about them. William brought a stamp album and talked about some of his stamps. He said a friend helped him with his collection. (The friend was an adult, a friend of his father's.) There were other stamp collections, but William's was best and he had more information about his stamps. Later several boys asked me where they could get stamps to start a collection. I referred them to William. For the next few days William had a group around him in free times. They showed stamps and talked about stamps.

After the stamp episode, William was accepted just a little more by the group. For example, about a week later, one of the boys grabbed William's arm and pulled him. They got into a friendly tussle.

Reports from his sixth-grade teacher showed that William was still pretty much of an isolate and was just about passing in his work.

As we have been warned repeatedly, a single case such as this cannot be used to prove anything. It does illustrate a few points, however, that can be supported by other evidence. In the first place, we must not expect miracles in the matter of reform. At the end of the story, William was only a little more popular. Careful studies(32) confirm this suggestion. Success may be the exception and not the rule. In the second place, the device adopted by the teacher has support from general principles if not from specific experiments. Bringing out some special but unpublicized skill may do something toward an increase in acceptance.

In dealing with the rejected child we would, of course, fall back on the principles of guidance toward success and gradation in the severity of the tasks. At first, put the rejected student in a situation where popularity is easier to attain and success more likely. Seat him near the students who resent him least. Put him on committees where his objectionable traits will not be so obvious.

To bring out and display any special skill he may have, try to be sure that he participates in a variety of tasks. One of these may happen to be his "line." Some teachers may even go so far as to help him develop some new ability that may evoke a degree of admiration.

Finally, if you are skillful in these matters, you may decide to encourage a group discussion of popularity and its aspects. With luck and good management this may ventilate some of the unacknowledged fears and worries that lead us to reject others. Susie may come to realize that she dislikes Bill partly because something about him makes her think of parts of her own home life that she would prefer to forget. This is high-powered medicine, however, and you should feel no obligation to try it unless you have considerable confidence that you and your group can avoid the obvious dangers.

Leadership

Teaching is not only a process of helping the misfits attain a near-normal status. At the opposite pole, we face the task of helping as many people as possible to develop better-than-average talents. Along with our attempts to secure better acceptance for the rejected student, can we do anything to develop talents for actual leadership in a larger number of students? To some extent leadership can be induced in a person by assigning him a position in which essential information passes through his hands. A student committee, for instance, is planning a yearbook, or a display, or some other project. One student is selected at random to act as a clearinghouse. He is not the chairman, and he is not given any genuine responsibility. He is the one to whom certain kinds of information are given. He is the one to go to for certain information. In many such cases, this arbitrarily selected student will be more of a leader after his experience. In many cases, again, he will show more of a flair for leadership than his equally capable classmate who was not assigned this position(33). This method does not work in all cases. There may be many students who have no aptitude for leadership and who would not be happy in positions of leadership. But if the interest and capacity are potentially there, this seems a fairly simple way of bringing it out.

Changes in Attitudes and Prejudice

Should the teacher try to bring about changes in attitudes or beliefs? This is a most important and vexing question, but it is primarily a question for the philosopher. On this matter the psychologist has little to say. The psychologist must assume that different teachers will have reached different answers to this question and that the same teacher may answer the question one way in considering one issue and in another way in considering a different issue. There will be times when he does not have any single view that he wants his students to accept. He will be content with any belief or conviction that the student adopts provided it is based on a thoughtful study of the materials. There are other times, however, when the teacher will greatly prefer that the students adopt one view rather than another and will try to present the material in a manner that will support the favored opinion. In dealing with the arguments about private versus public development of water power, for instance, he may work hard not to influence the students one way or the other. In teaching about democracy versus totalitarianism, on the other hand, he may feel that this neutral approach is ridiculous. He might feel he had failed unless his students came to see the advantages of democracy. In discussing religions of the world, one teacher might studiously avoid any attempt to sway his class toward one belief or another. In discussing prejudice, however, he may have in his mind the definite purpose of increasing the student's tolerance for his fellow citizens. Whenever you decide that you have the obligation, or at least the right, to try to swing beliefs one way or the other, you will want to know which techniques have been effective. Some of these techniques, of course, you may reject. No matter how effective it is, for instance, you may refuse to distort data or to suppress facts in order to persuade people to change their views. Other techniques, however, may be quite acceptable.

Even when you decide that it is immoral or improper to try to foist certain views upon students, you may still want to know about the techniques of persuasion and the conditions under which people are likely to be influenced. Even though you may adopt a neutral attitude, you can be sure some other agencies will not. During the time they are in school or after they leave, your students will be subjected to terrific pressure to vote this way or that, to buy one product rather than another, to believe this doctrine, to think well of one nation, and, yes, to hate this minority group. You may wish to know about the pressures that will be acting on your students. Perhaps, as we shall see, you can do something to help them meet these pressures. Here, then, are the techniques that have been tried out in various circumstances. Some of them you may wish to use. Others you may reject but may wish to understand.

Techniques of Persuasion. As many people have suspected, there is no assurance that a rational appeal will be better than an appeal to emotion, loyalty, or prejudice. The contrary seems to be the case(34). An appeal to group loyalty will lead people to accept beliefs favorable to the group or to reject unflattering ideas irrespective of the logical appeal of the arguments. Fear can also persuade, although in the field of health advertising, for instance, the emphasis on fear can be overdone. If people become excessively afraid they will be less likely to accept the frightening conviction than if they are only moderately afraid. Prestige can persuade and so can apparent freedom from bias. A speech favoring private development of power sites, for instance, will be quite effective if presented by the author of a book on the subject. The same speech will be less effective if presented by "a man in the street." It will also be less effective if presented by the manager of a private power company or someone else who has something to gain from the policy he advocates(35). Direct suggestion can persuade. The speaker is likely to be convincing if he clearly points the moral or brings out the conclusion to be derived from the facts he has presented. He is less likely to be convincing if he merely lets the facts or analyses speak for themselves.

What happens when we hear both sides of the question? The results are complex but in line with common sense. Hearing a vigorous partisan debate tends chiefly to strengthen the view we had before the debate began. Hearing an impartial summary of the two sides tends to moderate our views if those views originally were somewhat extreme(36). As far as immediate persuasion is concerned, an avowed advocate of one view cannot be sure that he will gain anything by presenting the "other fellow's" case along with his own. This may have some advantage for well-educated people but most results show little advantage. Presenting the other fellow's argument, however, may have some effect in building up resistance against that argument when it is presented later.

This process of building up resistance to a forthcoming argument or statement can be carried to surprising lengths. Shortly before President Truman announced the existence of a Russian A-bomb, for instance, it happened that a group of students, selected at random, had heard a talk showing how it would be impossible for Russia to achieve such a bomb for many years to come. These students were notably skeptical of the President's announcement—much more so than the students who had not heard the earlier talk.

One way to persuade a student is to assign him the task of trying to persuade others(37). Whenever a student is required to repeat, or act out, or present an argument that he has heard, he is more likely to be affected by the argument. This, of course, has its dangers. As might be expected, many students may resent having to expound a view that is not their own. And those who resent it the most, change the least. But they all change to some extent.

Susceptibility to Persuasion. Obviously some students are more easily persuaded than others. As we have suggested, those with strong loyalties to an institution such as a church, or a political party, are unlikely to accept a view that is unfavorable to the institution. Other factors also play a part. Intelligence, as we might suspect, works both ways. It permits the student to understand what is being said. But it often makes him a more critical listener as well. The intelligent student will more readily grasp your point, but he will also question it more readily. If you are presenting material that permits little disagreement once it is comprehended, you will have more success with the brighter people.

If the material permits several different interpretations, however, you will have more difficulty in persuading the intelligent people to adopt the interpretation you endorse.

Personality also plays a part. Anyone setting out to gain adherents to his view will have more success with the timid, depressed person who feels socially inadequate and who keeps his impulses in close check. He will have less success with the outright neurotic or the person overwhelmed by resentment or suspicion.

Attitude Change Apart from Persuasion. Persuasion is a force to be taken into account. On occasions it may be an instrument we may wish to use. In any case it is something that the student can seldom escape. Outright persuasion, however, is by no means the only method by which people are led to modify their attitudes. As we have already seen, attitudes toward food or working conditions may be changed more readily by a group discussion than by a persuasive lecture. Groups that are organized informally do more along this line than groups that are managed on a formal basis. In most of these discussions, moreover, the leader takes an active part and does not merely referee or "chair" the meeting. When the leader merely acts as a supervisor, changes in attitude are less likely to occur(38).

From our earlier discussion of the nature of prejudice and of its correlates, it is clear that the school cannot be the only agency for reducing or preventing intolerance and the rejection of minority groups. In such matters as housing arrangements(39), for instance, or in the intimate realm of parent-child relationships, the school may have little to say. Obviously, however, there is much that the school may attempt.

In many school systems, the study of the local community places considerable stress on the variety of people in the community, their origins, their contribution, and the values that they hold(40, 41). At the national level there are also books(42) that make much of our diversity and present the various groups in a realistic and attractive light.

In some cases, there is an attempt to teach the regular content subjects (biology, English, history) in such a way as to promote group understanding and sympathy for group differences. One study(43) has reported some success.

It is most important, of course, that children should be informed of the worthwhile attainments and contributions of other groups. It is still too soon, however, to decide whether such information also reduces prejudice. In one experiment(44), a course on the Psalms, emphasizing the Jewish contribution to literature, did little or nothing to reduce anti-Semitism. Using the Psalms, however, as a springboard for an open discussion of anti-Semitism did seem to reduce anti-Jewish feeling.

We must not generalize from one or two experiments. It is possible, however, that here again we cannot take it for granted that the evidence will speak for itself. It is possible that we must make our point in fairly direct fashion if we expect to change attitudes in this respect. It is all very well to organize our course in biology or English to bring about more understanding of various groups. But perhaps we had better not be too subtle. We may find it necessary to be sure that the students see how the material applies(43) to anti-Negro feeling or to prejudice against Mexicans. Although the evidence in these matters is far too spotty to give us a great deal of confidence, there is some suggestion that this direct, head-on approach may help with young children(45). With older students there may be something to be gained from bringing the unflattering stereotypes into the open and taking a good look at them(46).

If we do decide to make a direct attack on the problem of prejudice, there is still the question of the best medium or technique to use. Unfortunately there can be no certainty on this point, but there is some suggestion that the face-to-face discussion or lecture is more effective than written statements or materials presented by film or records. One group of investigators, it will be remembered, consider prejudice to arise from deep-rooted repression brought on by unwholesome parent-child relations. If this should be true, we would expect that in some cases direct therapy(47) would be in order. Here, as in other types of severe emotional disturbance, we should refer the matter to someone competent to assume the responsibility.

Summary

In guiding the student toward the well-adjusted life, the teacher, first of all, should make reality easier for the child to face. He should try not to ask the child to cope with problems which are too difficult at the present stage of maturation. He should make it obvious that he likes the children under his care and that he regards them as important people in their own right. To do this adequately, the teacher may have to increase his own feeling of security. Anxiety on the part of the teacher may induce anxiety in the children.

Before asking a child to undergo deprivation of a higher-order need, such as the need for the approval of the gang, the teacher should try to be sure that the student's lower-order needs are well satisfied.

Besides trying to make reality easier for the child to face, the teacher will try to help him find some outlet for his frustrated drives. Even partial expression of fear or anger may help the student deal with these needs. Certainly the student should be encouraged to acknowledge the existence of these drives without any sense of shame. Toward the same end the teacher can avoid excessive use of competition and can keep his reprimands at a mild and casual level.

It is not enough to protect the student from undue stress. It is also necessary to teach him how to handle the stress which he is bound to encounter. To accomplish this, the teacher must provide either direct practice and reinforcement or effective transfer. Successful transfer calls for the use of examples from many fields of behavior. It is aided when students are encouraged to formulate general rules of their own. Direct practice is abundantly present in nature but is not always under the complete control of the teacher. Because of this fact, the teacher must rely on a facile use of reinforcement, being careful to provide one kind of reinforcement for weak transitory tendencies and a different kind for tendencies that are more strongly entrenched. As in other areas, weak desirable tendencies should receive positive guidance and lavish reward. Weak undesirable tendencies should be ignored when possible. Strong undesirable tendencies can be subjected to casual brief reprimand.

Since anger and fear often lead to a good deal of unrelieved frustration, it is wise to consider them in special detail. The likelihood of anger can be reduced by enforcing standards of conduct consistently (but not rigidly), by avoiding a fussy overmoralistic attitude, and by providing general acceptance when the situation is beginning to get tense. When anger does arise, it should not result in the child getting his own way. Encourage the child to find some outlet for the anger (such as talking about it) and admitting it to himself, or, if a psychiatrist is available, through play therapy. Use his insight into his own aggressive needs to help him understand the aggressive behavior of others.

Fear can be prevented to some degree by increasing the student's general feeling of security and acceptance, by advance forewarning and explanation of a new menace, by advance acquisition of skill in dealing with the menace, and by the example of other people. Fear is less likely to occur if the menace is introduced gradually and if the student is free to control the intensity of the stress at will (when he can move freely from deep to shallow water). When fear does arise, try to help the student find some permissible outlet, such as talking about it, certainly admitting it to himself. Often vigorous activity helps.

Much can be done in this area by incidental acts and expressions in the ordinary course of teaching. Beyond these incidental activities, it is possible to establish courses in mental hygiene and to set up formal courses for the change of attitudes. Sheer rationality seldom succeeds against appeals to emotion or group loyalty. The appearance of freedom from self-interest seems to help. Playing an assigned role may lead a student to believe in the role he played. In most cases, the "persuader" cannot afford to be too subtle. If our lessons in history are to reduce anti-minority feeling, we had better be sure to make our point in overt fashion.

SPECIFIC REFERENCES

1. Slobetz, F. B. Elementary teachers' reactions to school situations. *J. educ. Res.*, 1950, *44*, 81–90.

2. John, Enid M. A study of the effects of evacuation and air raids on children of preschool age. *Brit. J. educ. Psychol.*, 1941, *11*, 173–182.

3. Jersild, A. T., and Meigs, Margaret F. Children and war. *Psychol. Bull.*, 1943, *40*, 541–573.

4. Symonds, P. M. *The dynamics of human adjustment.* Appleton-Century, 1946, p. 105.

5. Wandt, E., and Ostreicher, L. M. *Variability in observed classroom behaviors of junior high school teachers and classes.* N. Y. Office of Research and Evaluation, Division of Teachers Education, College of the City of New York, 1953, IV.

6. Gronlund, N. E. Relationship between the sociometric status of pupils' and teachers' preferences for or against having them in class. *Sociometry*, 1953, *16*, 142–150.

7. Redl, F., and Wineman, D. *Children who hate.* Free Press, 1951.

8. Stendler, Celia, Damrin, Dora, and Haines, Aleyne, C. Studies in cooperation and competition: I. The effects of working for group and individual rewards on the social climate of children's groups. *J. genet. Psychol.*, 1951, *79*, 173–197.

9. Goodlad, J. I. Some effects of promotion and nonpromotion upon the social and personal adjustment of children. *J. exp. Educ.*, 1954, *22*, 301–328.

10. Goodlad, J. I. Research and theory regarding promotion and nonpromotion. *Elem. Sch. J.*, 1952, *53*, 150–155.

11. Russell, D. H., and others. The influence of repetition of a grade and of regular promotion on the attitudes of parents and children toward school. *Calif. J. elem. Educ.*, 1952, *21*, 29–41.

12. Gebhard, Mildred E. Changes in the attractiveness of activities: the effect of expectation preceding performance. *J. exp. Psychol.*, 1949, *39*, 404–413.

13. Nuttin, J. *Tâche, réussite et échec; théorie de la conduite humaine.* Publications Universitaires de Louvain, 1953.

14. Barker, R. G., Dembo, Tamara, and Lewin, K. Frustration and regression. An experiment with young children. *Univ. Iowa Stud. Child Welfare,* 1941, Vol. 18.

15. Child, I. L., and Waterhouse, I. K. Frustration and the quality of performance: I. A critique of the Barker, Dembo, and Lewin experiment. *Psychol. Rev.,* 1952, *59,* 351–362.

16. Gillies, D. V., and Lastrucci, C. L. Validation of the effectiveness of a college marriage course. *Marriage Fam. Living,* 1954, *16,* 55–58.

17. Davitz, J. R. The effects of previous training on postfrustration behavior. *J. abnorm. soc. Psychol.,* 1952, *47,* 309–315.

18. Cowen, E. L. Stress reduction and problem-solving rigidity. *J. consult. Psychol.,* 1952, *16,* 425–428.

19. Frank, J. D. Recent studies of the level of aspiration. *Psychol. Bull.,* 1941, *38,* 218–226.

20. Escalona, Sibylle K. An application of the level of aspiration experiment to the study of personality. *Teach. Coll. Contr. Educ.* No. 937, 1948.

21. Marshall, Helen. A study of the personality of alcoholic males. *Amer. Psychologist,* 1947, *2,* 289.

22. Bullis, H. E. Are we losing our fight for improved mental health? *Progress. Educ.,* 1953, *30,* 110–114.

23. Menninger, W. C. *Understanding yourself.* Science Research Associates. 1948.

24. Rosenberg, Pearl R. Experimental analysis of psycho-drama. (Doctor's Thesis) Harvard University, 1952.

25. Weinreb, J. Report of an experience in the application of dynamic psychiatry in education. *Ment. Hyg.* (N.Y.), 1953, *37,* 283–293.

26. Goodenough, Florence L. *Anger in young children.* University of Minnesota Press, 1931.

27. Thibaut, J. W., and Coules, J. The role of communication in the reduction of interpersonal hostility. *J. abnorm. soc. Psychol.,* 1952, *47,* 770–777.

28. Chittenden, Gertrude E. An experimental study in measuring and modifying assertive behavior in young children. *Monogr. Soc. Res. Child Developm.,* 1942, *7,* No. 1.

29. Prugh, D. G., and others. A study of the emotional reactions of children and families to hospitalization and illness. *Amer. J. Orthopsychiat.,* 1953, *23,* 70–106.

30. Jessner, L., Blom, G. E., and Waldfogel, S. Emotional implications of tonsillectomy and adenoidectomy on children. *Psychoanal. Stud. Child,* 1952, *7,* 126–169.

31. Carmichael, L., ed. *Manual of child psychology.* Wiley, 1946. Chap. 15. Emotional development (Jersild, A. T.).

32. Singer, A. Certain aspects of personality and their relation to certain group modes, and constancy of friendship choices. *J. educ. Res.,* 1951, *45,* 33–42.

33. Leavitt, H. J. Some effects of certain communication patterns on group performance. *J. abnorm. soc. Psychol.,* 1951, *46,* 38–50.

34. Lindzey, G., ed. *Handbook of social psychology.* Addison-Wesley, 1954. Chap. 28. Effects of the mass media of communication (Hovland, C. I.).

35. Hovland, C. I., and Mandell, W. An experimental comparison of conclusion-drawing by the communicator and by the audience. *J. abnorm. soc. Psychol.,* 1952, *47,* 581–588.

36. Jarrett, R. F., and Sherriffs, A. C. Propaganda, debate, and impartial presentation as determiners of attitude change. *J. abnorm. soc. Psychol.,* 1953, *48,* 33–41.

37. Janis, I. L., and King, B. T. The influence of role playing on opinion change. *J. abnorm. soc. Psychol.,* 1954, *49,* 211–218.

38. Hare, A. P. Small group discussions with participatory and supervisory leadership. *J. abnorm. soc. Psychol.,* 1953, *48,* 273–275.

39. Lindzey, G., ed. *Handbook of social psychology.* Addison-Wesley, 1954, Chap. 27. Prejudice and ethnic relations (Harding, J., and others).

40. Denver City Schools. *The people of Denver.* Denver Board of Education, 1952.

41. Silverman, A. J., ed. *Baltimore, City of Promise.* Baltimore City Department of Education, 1953.

42. Jaworski, Irene D. *Becoming American.* Harper, 1950.

43. Hayes, Margaret L., and Conklin, Mary E. Inter-group attitudes and experimental change. *J. exp. Educ.,* 1953, *22,* 19–36.

44. Kagan, H. E. *Changing the attitude of Christian toward Jew: a psychological approach through religion.* Columbia University Press, 1952.

45. Trager, Helen G., and Radke-Yarrow, Marian. *They learn what they live: prejudice in young children.* Harper, 1952.

46. Centers, R. An effective classroom demonstration of stereotypes. *J. soc. Psychol.,* 1951, *34,* 41–46.

47. Axline, Virginia M. Play therapy and race conflict in young children. *J. abnorm. soc. Psychol.*, 1948, *43*, 300–310.

SUGGESTIONS FOR FURTHER READING

1. Redl, F., and Wattenberg, W. W. *Mental hygiene in teaching.* Harcourt Brace, 1951.
    A textbook on the problem of this chapter.
2. Menninger, W. C. *Self understanding: a first step to understanding children.* Science Research Associates, 1951.
    A brief, nontechnical discussion.
3. National Society for the Study of Education. *Mental hygiene in education.* Fifty-fourth Yearbook, Part II, 1955.
4. Greenhill, M. H., and others. *Evaluation in mental health.* Public Health Service Publications No. 413, U. S. Govt. Printing Office, 1955.
    An excellent source of references and brief abstracts bearing on evaluation.
5. Lindzey, G., ed. *Handbook of social psychology.* Addison-Wesley, 1954. Chap. 27. Prejudice and ethnic relations (Harding, J., and others). Includes a discussion of experimental attempts to reduce prejudice. Chap. 28. Effects of the mass media of communication (Hovland, C. I.). A comprehensive account of experiments in the changing of attitudes.
6. Hovland, C. I., Janis, I. L., and Kelley, H. H. *Communication and persuasion.* Yale University Press, 1953.
    A detailed account of the Yale experiments in influencing groups by various methods.
7. Lindgren, H. C. *Mental health in education.* Holt, 1954.
    A complete discussion of the problem treated briefly in this chapter. An excellent combination of research and practical application.

Exercises and Questions for Discussion

1. How can the teacher make up for the fact that direct practice in personal development is not completely under his control?

2. A child of two years is about to visit in a home where there is a large, affectionate, and lively dog. The child has had little experience with dogs of any kind. What suggestions would you offer to his parents to keep him from becoming unduly frightened?

3. Show how you could use the various mechanisms of learning to teach a ten-year-old boy to become more resourceful in building mechanical models of

machines. What could you do to help his increased resourcefulness transfer to other kinds of problems?

4. What steps might you take to improve the plight of a child who is largely rejected by his classmates?

5. What steps could you take to increase a student's chance to show his powers of leadership?

6. Under what circumstances do you think a teacher is justified in using the techniques of persuasion? When do you think this would be questionable?

22

The Teacher and His Own Adjustment

THE TEACHER'S own personal adjustment is important in two different ways. It is important in that his adjustment may affect his competence as a teacher. It is equally important as a problem in its own right. Some attention has already been given to the effect of the teacher's own adjustment on the development of his students. Now we consider the more direct problem of the teacher's own personal welfare as a most important end in itself.

Any discussion at this level is directed to the vast majority of teachers who fall within the normal range of adjustment. It is intended to cover those frustrations and sources of worry which may plague us in our teaching but which cause most of us only minor disturbance and unhappiness. This discussion is not intended for the less fortunate minority who may temporarily experience severe disturbance(1). It is not to be recommended to friends whom you believe to be in need of specialized help. Do not lean on such general discussions yourself if you suspect that you are losing your grip; or if your friends have advised you to see a doctor; or if in odd moments you feel that your suspicions of your colleagues are somewhat too intense or extend to an excessive number of people; or if, again at odd moments, you wonder if your sudden tremendous burst of energy is quite normal. Under circumstances such as these, do not "read a book," but seek professional advice and do so without delay.

It is difficult to know whether or not teachers have unusual problems in adjustment. According to one summary(2), one out of five of us could do with some help and one out of twenty needs that help in substantial amounts. Whatever may be the case in other professions, it is obvious that we have our share of problems. Our own adjustment calls for some thought.

The Satisfactions of Teaching

Teaching has many rewards that are rich and substantial(3). The importance of teaching is recognized on all sides. And the teacher has the very comforting satisfaction of cooperating in an enterprise that may spell the salvation of civilization. It is, in fact, not given to the members of many professions to be so completely sure of the essential worth of their efforts.

This reassurance of the essential contribution of one's profession is a wonderful anchor to windward. It is something from which we can take comfort when things are otherwise black and gloomy. This background assurance, however, lacks something in the way of immediate, day-by-day reward. One has to be exceptionally dedicated to one's work and unusually sensitive to the claims of distant goals to be able to get a full quota of reward from sheer knowledge of participating in a worthy enterprise.

Fortunately, the teacher is not limited to the rewards which arise from these general, background assurances. In his immediate daily work, the teacher also tastes many of the warmer, earthier joys that are needed by all but the most devoted workers. The teacher, after all, works with people. During his working hours, he is immersed in contacts with children, with colleagues, with parents, and with members of the community. He could not, even if he chose, escape the warm, natural rewards that come from the interplay of human personalities.

The teacher's rewards from his many human contacts are all the more intense from the fact that he can be unusually sure of the purity of his own intentions. He seldom needs to be plagued by a nagging conscience which questions whether he is really helping these people or merely exploiting them. True enough, in his relations with his colleagues or his superiors there may be occasions when he should question his own motives; but in his direct relations with his students he is in an unusually favorable position.

In satisfying the very human need for esteem, the teacher has a somewhat ambiguous position. As we point out later, he often feels lack of appreciation on the part of the general public. In many respects, however, the teacher has a fair opportunity to meet the need for the esteem of others. He is in a good position to secure the good opinion of his students. True, he cannot work directly toward this goal, but very often in the course of his daily work he may find incidental evidences of high regard from his students. This may come from subtle indications in everyday contacts, or it may come more formally in the overt statements of former students or even in the much rarer form of a testimonial meeting. Such evidence is most rewarding no matter how much the teacher may protest to the contrary. In this respect, the teacher probably has a slight advantage over the members of many other professions.

In addition to the esteem of those directly in our charge, there is esteem (or lack of it) to be had from our colleagues and from our superiors. To the true craftsman, this is usually the esteem that counts most. The praise from our fellow worker is a source of rich satisfaction. The criticism of our peers is something to be reckoned with. In this important matter, the teacher is probably on a par with people in most other professions. Gradually he is bound to achieve some sort of reputation (good or bad) in the eyes of his colleagues and superiors, and to some extent this will become evident to him.

This recital of the blessings of our craft would be incomplete without some mention of the more mundane advantages that we can expect. In the matter of working hours, we are still a privileged group *in one respect*. Our working day (and night) is excessively long and is perhaps becoming longer. But to an unusual extent our schedule of hours is flexible and is under our own control. Although we must put in many hours, it is very often true that we can arrange those hours to suit ourselves. The long week ends and the summer vacations are not all free time, but they can be organized so as to give us fairly large blocks of free time if that is what we wish.

In the matter of health, the teacher is exceptionally fortunate. In the eyes of the life insurance companies, he is clearly a preferred risk. In spite of his close contact with large numbers of children, he is exceptionally free from disease(4, 5) and accident. Just what causes what in this respect, we do not know. But statistically, we have an enviable health position.

In economic affairs, as in the matter of prestige, we are in an ambiguous position. Obviously we are underpaid. Those in the profession admit the fact. The more enlightened citizenry deplore it. But there are some advantages. *Beginning* salaries are very favorable compared to many professions. We do not face unpredictable layoffs. We do not face day-to-day uncertainty about our income. More and more of us are acquiring some tenure, and pensions of one kind or another are very frequent.

The Frustrations of Teaching

Like any other worthwhile undertaking, teaching is not without its irritations and its headaches. This unlovely fact is to be expected and is taken for granted by all mature people. Any realistic view of a profession must include these obstacles and frustrations as well as the positive satisfactions to be gained.

The intelligent student will not be disturbed, of course, by the fact that more space is devoted to frustrations than to satisfactions. The prospective wayfarer needs only slight instruction to permit him to enjoy the satisfactions of his trip. With a minimum of briefing and sensitization, these rewards will be appreciated as soon as they are encountered. The obstacles to be faced, however, constitute a different story. Very often, much instruction is necessary if these are to be dealt with adequately.

Let us remember, then, that the frustrations are merely minor obstacles to be overcome in an otherwise exciting and satisfying project. Let us remember, too, that ordinary skill in meeting these frustrations will greatly increase the rewards we will experience from our undertaking.

Dealing with the Frustrations: General

In the previous chapters we have stressed the various methods by which students can be taught to deal with troublesome frustrations. Let us quickly review these points and see how they apply to the general frustrations of teaching. Suppose, for instance, we are worried about the "low prestige" of the teaching profession. We feel that the public does not place us on a par with other professions, and this fact acts as a gnawing frustration to our very natural need for esteem. How can we deal with frustrations such as these?

Face the Fact of Frustration. First of all, if this real need is not adequately met, we must be willing to face the fact. We may be tempted to deny that we have any need for prestige. We may also be tempted to talk ourselves into believing that the prestige of the profession is much higher than it is. Both these steps should be avoided. We must face the fact of our need, if it is really there. We must also face the fact that the need is not really being met, if that is the case. If objective evidence points to our lowly prestige (and, remember, this is an "if" statement), then we must accept the evidence and not try to gloss over it, or try to search for pathetic exceptions which will blind us to the general picture.

Consider the Feasibility of Remedial Action. Having faced the fact of our unsatisfied need for more public esteem, our next step is to decide if there is some reasonable means of remedying the situation. If we think that there is something that can be done about it and that the effort is worthwhile, the logical thing to do is to take action. We should realize, by the way, that there is little objective evidence to guide us in this decision. It is highly unlikely, for instance, that we can command prestige merely by clamoring for it or by complaining that people do not "do right by us." There may be indirect methods of attaining this goal, however, and at present different teachers will reach different conclusions as to whether or not an increased measure of prestige is attainable.

Place the Frustration in its Proper Perspective. For some frustrations, remedial action may be impossible or impractical. In other cases a good deal of frustration may remain after we have done all that we can to remedy the situation. What then? Then we must accept the facts and learn to live with them if we cannot change them. If we believe, for instance, that teaching is fated to receive less than its share of prestige, then we must try to accept the situation as one of the many unpleasant facts of life, such as disease, pain, ingratitude, and death. It is there; we must live with it, and moreover, we must try to be happy in spite of it. This should not be too difficult in our case. Every profession has its disadvantages and even has its ludicrous aspects. People poke fun at bankers, lawyers, plumbers, and undertakers. They also poke fun at us. Our profession has other handicaps which we must accept. It lacks glamor and physical adventure. It lacks the opportunity to make a financial "killing." We must accept these other limitations when we enter the profession, and it is possible that we should be similarly prepared to accept lack of prestige.

In learning to live with frustration that does not lend itself to remedial action, we can make use of the device of symbolic expression. It may help us to admit unpleasant facts to ourselves if we discuss those facts with others. For people under stress, as we have stated so often, one of the simplest forms of relief is the sheer act of talking about the stress. Those teachers, for instance, who are really uncomfortable because of lack of prestige, might do well to express themselves freely to discreet and understanding colleagues or friends.

For many teachers, humor will prove to be a tremendous palliative in dealing with frustration that refuses to yield to direct remedy. Almost every situation, no matter how trying, has its ludicrous aspects that are good for a laugh. The disparity, for instance, between our own idea of our worth and the community's impression of our importance may be tragic in its over-all significance, but it is also raw material for many a joke, bitter or good-natured, as the case may be.

Dealing with Specific Frustrations

Increasing Demands on Time. Earlier we pointed out that the teacher is relatively free in budgeting the time he spends on his profession. It would be foolish to deny, however, that the total amount of time that he must spend on his work is often very great. Certainly as the profession has become more complex and elaborate, it seems that the teacher's working day may readily come to extend to unreasonable lengths. In recent years, for instance, the teacher has been expected to spend some of his leisure in attending summer schools, institutes, and "in-service" training courses. He has been expected to spend much outside time attending parent-teachers' meetings and in visiting the homes of his students. More recently, he has been expected to spend long hours writing individual letters about each student under his care.

It would be ridiculous to suggest that lack of leisure or overwork always brings serious frustration. Actually, if a person is engrossed in his task he may feel resentment when he is advised to leave his work and to secure leisure. When the task has obvious importance and makes a clear demand on our time, it is also fairly easy to accept the fatigue and lack of leisure. The busy physician, for instance, may be keenly aware of his excessive hours and of his longing for sleep, rest, or for a day of fishing. Yet he may experience only slight resentment, provided, of course, that he feels that the work is clearly important and, second, that he considers that his actions spring largely from his own decisions.

Similarly, the teacher may be only moderately disturbed at the demands on his time if he thinks of these activities as genuinely important and as expressing his own decisions. He may readily lament the shortness of the day or the weariness of the flesh, but he will feel little downright resentment. If, on the other hand, the teacher should feel that the many extracurricular activities imposed on him have little intrinsic worth, then the situation may be irritating in the extreme. If, in addition, he feels that he has been forced or subtly maneuvered into performing these excessive tasks, his sense of frustration may reach serious proportions.

Restrictions on Social Life. Socially, we may be under some scrutiny. If we live up to the expectations of our high-school students we will lead a virtuous but semimonastic life. Even marriage during the school term would be improper in the minds of one third of our students. Another third are against smoking, and over half would not have us drink. Regular church attendance is taken for granted(6). Young people can be exceedingly stern, of course, in the conduct they demand from their elders, and many of us will understand this list of requirements but feel somewhat amused. The written expectations of the community, however, cannot be dismissed so lightly, and in many cases the code for teachers, especially for women, has been very severe(7, 8, 9) Many forms of social activities, such as dancing, social drinking, or attendance at night clubs, are not considered proper for teachers. In certain communities, too, there are restrictions on the type of person with whom the teacher may associate. These restrictions may be very galling and irritating. They are likely to become serious if the teacher comes to feel sorry for himself or to be annoyed with himself for submitting to such infringements on his freedom.

Low Prestige of Teaching. In our general discussion, we used this worry as an illustrative frustration. There is some evidence that it may be a very real source of irritation for many members of the teaching profession. Actually many people, when asked, do profess to think that teachers are important people(10) and that teaching ranks high among the professions. Our leaders often claim that this is merely lip service, however, and that the public does not act as if it took us seriously. Among our high-school students, moreover, we clearly do not rate with the lawyer or the doctor. The college professor is rated sixth from the top with high-school students. But the high-school teacher stands tenth, just above the secretary or bookkeeper, and the elementary-school teacher even lower(11). Along with this lowly opinion of our students is the fact that for generations the teacher has been a stereotype(12). The very words pedagogue or pedant carry mild connotations of opprobrium. According to many literary presentations, we are often considered to be serious, humorless, graceless, and given to offering gratuitous corrections to the mistakes of others. We must face the possibility that we simply do not elicit the same deference, the same claim to be considered seriously, as doctors or lawyers.

As an allied source of irritation there is some evidence that the young men going into teaching are not so bright as those going into other professions. The most startling results along this line have come from the selective service qualifying examinations given to many thousands of male college students(13). It is quite possible, of course, that these results do not hold for women who plan to teach.

In dealing with this frustration, we should use all the devices earlier suggested. In this particular frustration, moreover, we must be prepared to adopt a live-and-let-live attitude. Even though many people may not take our profession so seriously at we think they ought, we ourselves need not be any less sure of its essential worth. Fortunately it is not necessary to equate the opinion of the general public with the opinion of the individual worker. There are many occupations which society in general regards lightly but which may be most satisfying for the individual engaged in them. He can realize that most people would not relish his job, but for him it is a very fine thing. It is true, of course, that there are many others who cannot adopt such an attitude. Some people cannot be content merely with the very rich rewards that come to a successful salesman. They cannot be happy unless they think that everyone else would also like to be a salesman if he could, that even Shakespeare was a salesman at heart.

As teachers, we should be prepared to accept differences in opinion regarding the worth of different jobs. Most of us in the profession naturally regard teaching as a most important and worthy activity. Having reached that personal conclusion, however, we should not feel that everyone else is bound to regard it in the same light. If the other fellow dismisses teaching with an airy wave of his hand, we should not feel that one of us must be wrong. Both of us may be right.

The Implications of Unmanliness. Many male teachers may at times worry over the fact that the profession is not always considered as especially manly(3). This concern, if it is present, cannot merely be pushed aside or pooh-poohed out of existence. Trivial as it may seem, it could be a genuine source of trouble. It should be faced, and it calls for as much intelligent handling as any other frustration.

The Clash between Ideals and Practice. For most people, teacher or nonteacher alike, the discrepancy between ideals and practice produces only moderate stress. Most people can profit from the Sabbath-day inspiration to higher things and then go back, without undue disturbance, to the less idealistic workaday world for the remainder of the week. Such fortunate people can see that the lofty ideals are seldom realized and can still see that those unrealized ideals exert a very valuable influence on everyday affairs. No matter how sharply our practices may contrast with our professed hopes and aspirations, those practices seem farther along and more enlightened than they would be if the seldom-realized ideals were not held before us.

An extreme discrepancy between ideals and practice, of course, may readily cause resentment or frustrations when it suggests irresponsibility or hypocrisy. Some of the more exuberant educational orators, for instance, have been accused of exhorting the rest of us to attitudes and performances which are clearly impractical. A high-school teacher, for instance, is told that he should have a "complete understanding" of each of his two hundred students. This strikes us as a ridiculous suggestion when we realize that few parents, or psychoanalysts, would dream of pretending that they approached a complete understanding of even one child. The hard-working teacher, fresh from some of the grim realities of the classroom, may feel annoyance at the easy picture painted by the supervisor who has no direct classroom responsibilities. The same teacher may also resent the glib advice of the textbook writer. The teacher may be somewhat annoyed even if he feels that the exhorter is merely a well-meaning soul, strong in good will but short in discernment and judgment. He is even more likely to be resentful if he feels that the expounder of ideals is actually insincere.

In dealing with the frustrations induced by the unrealistic picture painted by some of our leaders, there is always the possibility of direct action. You may be a genuine skeptic and may think that your view of education is sound and honest, whereas that of the theorist is either hypocritical or confused by a sentimental "see-no-evil" blindness. In that case, say so. Collect together those who think as you do and campaign for a more realistic, a more down-to-earth view of education.

If an overt attack on the situation does not seem feasible, work out ways to live with the situation. Do you need to argue with the theorists? Could you not go your theoretical way and let them go theirs? If a certain amount of superficial acquiescence is required of you, deal with that conflict openly too. If an out-and-out showdown is too much or unwise or fruitless, you may have to work out some sort of compromise.

Meeting the Need for Self-expression. The need for self-expression, although perhaps the least primitive of the needs we have considered, is still an important problem for most people. There is the drive to do things and see things happen, to get a certain kind of result, to create or achieve a certain effect. Is the teacher handicapped in respect to this need? Probably so. As teachers, we are handicapped by the fact that the results of our activities are seldom immediate and definite(14). Compare our work, for instance, to that of the machinist at the lathe. The results of his efforts are immediate and almost dramatic. As he manipulates the lathe, the wood or metal changes almost immediately. It changes, too, in a way that could not be mistaken. There is satisfaction from such immediate and definite results that must not be ignored.

The satisfactions available to the machinist are also to be had by most people who work with their hands. The carpenter, the dressmaker, and the typist can all see the results of their labor after only a moderate delay and in a fashion which needs little interpretation. Even when the results are not immediate, as in the case of the gardener, they are usually definite in character.

Some of the most important results of the teacher's work are neither immediate nor definite. Certainly those results do not make their presence felt automatically. We must search for them. We must give examinations or tests. We must send out follow-up questionnaires. Ordinarily, we must take some deliberate and perhaps elaborate step to see if we have achieved any results. Often, too, we wait for a considerable period of time. It is only at the end of the unit, of the term, or the year, or at the end of many years that we know what we have accomplished. Those results, moreover, often lack the conviction and definiteness of the results granted to the painter or the plowman or the businessman. Often we do not completely trust the examination results or the ratings of other observers. We feel, and properly so, that the thing we have accomplished is deep within the children and is only imperfectly revealed by the various devices at our disposal.

This feeling of working in the dark deprives the teacher of many sources of satisfaction and, to that extent, leaves the creative needs partially unfilled. Fortunately this frustration is one that invites direct action. Much has already been said about the methods of testing and of obtaining dramatic records of growth. Insofar as these devices can be adopted and automatically incorporated into regular practice, this need for self-expression will be partially met.

Making the Most of Teaching

Adjustment as a teacher, of course, consists of much more than merely meeting the frustrations of teaching in an efficient manner. In our journey or expedition it is not enough merely to overcome obstacles and to master difficulties. The thing of real importance is to get somewhere or to accomplish something. Obstacles, of course, will be met; and, if we are to get anywhere, they must be overcome. But they are mere incidents which hinder our expedition. They are not our main concern.

Is there, then, anything in our psychology which will help the teacher in his main enterprise? Can we help him in actually completing his expedition apart from suggesting how to overcome the detailed frustrations and difficulties?

The Importance of a Definite Motive or Goal. Motivation or goal-set, so important for the student, is also important for the teacher. To make the most effective use of motivation, set yourself a definite goal as a teacher. Keep the goal in mind. Break it down into subgoals. Know what you want to accomplish.

The goal that you set must be justifiable and acceptable to you. It is not necessary that it be completely acceptable to everyone else. The problem of acceptable goals, of course, is a matter for the philosopher and not for the psychologist. As far as the psychologist is concerned, you could properly accept any one of a number of goals. For you, perhaps, the chief object of the teacher may be to bring your students closer to God. Or you may be impelled by a need to help students live their immediate lives as fully and richly as possible. Or you may feel a terrific drive to help students so that they will become more effective members of society when they are older. Or you may merely have a sort of blind, inarticulated hunch that things will be better all around if children have some competence in these academic matters that have intrigued people for so many generations. Whatever your goal, if you have thought it through, if it fits in with your over-all view of life, and if it is compelling to you, then it should be a most effective motive.

Your goal, of course, should be in harmony with the important goals of those for whom you work. It would obviously be unethical to occupy a position of trust in which you were working directly counter to the main purposes of those who support you. But, fortunately, you can find a variety of goals among employing authorities, and you will encounter someone whose main purposes are in general harmony with your own.

To say that your goals must be in harmony with those of your employer does not mean that the goals must be identical. You may be strongly moved, for instance, to help children live their present lives as effectively as possible. Your superintendent or headmaster, on the other hand, may be concerned about producing future citizens. Yet there may be no conflict whatever between these two statements. In working toward your objective, you may also be working toward his.

Seek Guidance at the Outset. As you first begin your teaching, do not hesitate to seek guidance at every reasonable opportunity. An experienced, intelligent, and understanding supervisor or older teacher can be of inestimable value to you. Many successful teachers attribute much of their professional happiness and effectiveness to the early guidance provided by an older hand. For the beginner, even an ordinary guide is often better than none. The ordinary guide has been over the path and has survived thus far. That is at least something in the way of recommendation.

Do what you can for yourself, of course, and steadily work toward the point where you can get along with less and less guidance. For a little while, however, when you are still learning the ropes, do not be ashamed even of playing the sedulous ape. When traversing especially difficult terrain, you may be forgiven if, like the inexperienced mountain climber, you deliberately place your feet in the precise tracks of your guide. On less treacherous paths, of course, you will be more free, and as you acquire competence, you will use your own judgment.

With the Growth of Competence, Let Yourself Go. As you branch out on your own and as you come to dispense with guidance except for the most treacherous tasks, try to let yourself go. After all, sheer effort and energy and good will, even with faulty techniques, will get you somewhere, however inefficiently. And perfect techniques, lacking energy or drive, will get you nowhere. Keep in mind the relative importance of these two aspects. Sheer effort with inefficient techniques is wasteful and falls short of what it might accomplish. But techniques without drive or effort are not merely wasteful: they are nothing.

Let yourself go as an educational reformer. There is room for reform. There is need for a host of enthusiastic voices calling attention to our lacks and urging their remedy.

Let yourself go as a student of education. Perhaps more than anything else, we need an insightful, lucid view of the essential nature of the educational process. Speculate, read, discuss. Announce your hypotheses. If you are cautious, you will announce them as hypotheses which need to be tested. But at any rate, publicize your hunch.

Let yourself go as a skeptic. We need more and more people who can pierce through wordy statements and see the assumptions that lie therein and the hypotheses that must be tested before the statements can be accepted. If this is your strong suit, exercise it.

Above all, let yourself go as a teacher. In plunging on toward your objective, of course, you will make whatever use you can of the many techniques and minor devices that you may remember. Do this by all means. But these devices are your servants and not your master. They are merely minor refinements of the general process of teaching. Look at it this way. Most of the hundreds of "do's" and "don't's" in this textbook, for instance, were developed from experiments performed since the year 1900. What did people do before they knew about these many restrictions? Was there any effective teaching prior to 1900? Assuredly so. The suggestions or restrictions set forth in this book are merely minor aids to a process that is much more fundamental than the minor suggestions.

The moral is obvious. Go ahead and teach. Use the many minor suggestions when you can. They are useful aids when they are kept in their place. You should not stop the main process of teaching while fumbling for unobtainable perfection in the complete use of these rules. If you have forgotten some of these rules on occasion, do not feel guilty. Do not feel that your lesson has been a failure just because in the excitement of teaching you used white chalk instead of yellow chalk, or because your blackboard work failed to achieve the desired standards of neatness, or because you did not allow enough time for the required pupil-summary. True, these defects may have injured your lesson somewhat. They may have reduced the effectiveness by as much as 1 percent. But these defects are at the 1 percent level. The other things are much more important. "Whittle away" at that 1 percent while you can, but do not feel guilty if you neglect it occasionally in favor of the 99 percent of teaching.

Permit Others to Let Themselves Go. If, as events march on, it becomes your lot to supervise or direct the work of others, try to give them the same freedom that you should ask for yourself. The same basic principles which call on you to go ahead—efficiently when you can, but to go ahead anyway—those same principles demand that you encourage others to proceed in similar fashion. There are many ways to teach long division. There are many ways to create an atmosphere of warm, human acceptance. There are many ways to be a good teacher. Let your teachers be successful *their* way.

Summary

Over and above its bearing on his effectiveness, the teacher's adjustment is a most important problem in its own right. Naturally he will do everything he can to handle his frustrations and conflicts in an effective manner.

Fortunately, the teacher has many substantial satisfactions to give meaning and support to his professional activities. His work is universally accepted as important. In his day-to-day duties, he is immersed in human contacts. He has a good chance to experience the esteem of his students and of his colleagues. In health and freedom from accident, the teacher is clearly a preferred risk. Although his hours are long, they are largely under the teacher's own control. In spite of limited opportunity for a large income, the teacher has a measure of financial security denied to many other professions.

Like every other profession, teaching has its frustrations, and these must be met and handled if we are to make the most of the larger satisfactions. Frustrations must be faced. We cannot afford to ignore or to belittle our unfulfilled needs. When possible, remedial action should be taken. Failing that, we must live with the frustrations but keep them in their proper perspective. In so doing, we can often profit from free discussion with others and from the gift of humor.

The specific frustrations with which the teacher must contend include many items both trivial and important. There are many demands on his time, and these may be growing. This is not likely to be a serious frustration unless, at the same time, the teacher feels imposed upon. Restrictions on social activity, likewise, are more likely to be irritating if the teacher feels he is unjustly treated. Although education is universally acknowledged to be important, there is often a feeling that teachers themselves are taken for granted and lack their proper prestige. Insofar as this is true, it may well rankle in the background of our minds. Here we should be able to tolerate a difference of opinion regarding the worth of different professions. In some quarters, male school teachers have been regarded as a "third sex," and this imputation may be troublesome to many men.

Certain teachers have been disturbed by what they regard as insincere or unrealistic preachments on the part of those who have few direct classroom responsibilities. This may well cause irritation. If it is merely a matter of difference in views, the skeptic should feel free to speak his piece. If it is a matter of deference to authority, a more serious problem presents itself. Finally, with respect to creative needs, teachers may be under a handicap, not because they fail to create, but because the results of their efforts are not immediately and dramatically apparent.

More important than merely meeting frustrations, it is important to make the most of the many positive satisfactions of teaching. Remembering the lessons in the preceding chapters, the teacher will clarify and dramatize his goals or objectives. As a beginner in any task, he will seek and use as much guidance as he can. As he acquires competence, he will depend more and more on his own efforts and will let himself go in his professional relations and above all in his classroom activities. He will use techniques and suggestions when he can, but he will not substitute these minor tools for the more important forces of drive, energy, and effort. As a supervisor, he will take this same attitude toward those under his charge.

SPECIFIC REFERENCES

1. Snyder, W. U. Recent investigations of mental hygiene in the schools. *Educ. Res. Bull.,* 1945, *24,* 231–248.
2. Blair, G. M., Jones, R. S., and Simpson, R. H. *Educational psychology.* Macmillan, 1954.
3. Kline, Frances F. Satisfactions and annoyances in teaching. *J. exp. Educ.,* 1949, *18,* 77–89.
4. Dowell, Anita S. The physical disability of teachers in the white elementary schools of Baltimore, Maryland. *Johns Hopk. Univ. Stud. Educ.,* No. 24, 1936.
5. Wayland, L. C. N. School nurse, school physician, and teacher health. *Publ. Hlth. Nursing,* 1946, *38,* 555–561.
6. Cobb, P. R. High school seniors attitudes toward teachers and the teaching profession. *Bull. nat. assoc. second. Sch. Principals,* 1952, *36,* Bull., No. 183, 140–144.
7. Crowder, F. Educational strait jackets. *Survey Graphic,* 1947, *36,* 617–619.
8. Lichliter, Mary. Social obligations and restrictions placed on women teachers. *Sch. Rev.,* 1946, *54,* 14–23.
9. Kaplan, L. New horizons in teacher-community relationships. *J. educ. Sociol.,* 1948, *21,* 417–427.
10. Anderson, W. F., Jr. Attitudes of parents of differing socio-economic status toward the teaching profession. *J. educ. Psychol.,* 1954, *45,* 345–352.
11. Richey, R. W., Phillips, B. N., and Fox, W. H. Factors that high school students associate with selection of teaching as a vocation. *Bull. Sch. of Educ.,* Indiana Univ., 1952, *28,* No. 2.
12. Charles, D. C. The stereotype of the teacher in American literature. *Ed. Forum,* 1950, *14,* 299–305.
13. Educational Testing Service. *Annual report to the board of trustees,* 1951–52, 1952.
14. Peterson, H. A., Marzolf, S. S., and Bayley, Nancy. *Educational psychology.* Macmillan, 1948, p. 347.

SUGGESTIONS FOR FURTHER READING

Clark, D. L., and Burke, A. J. Economic, legal, and social status of teachers. *Rev. educ. Res.*, 1955, 25, 239–251.

Exercises and Questions for Discussion

1. Imagine that you are a high-school teacher and one of your students asks you about teaching as a career. You think he would like to teach but is somewhat worried about the conditions he will find. List some of the points (favorable and unfavorable) that he should consider. Try to add some points that are not mentioned in the chapter.

2. Go over some of the "needs" mentioned in Chapter 16. Which of these do you consider especially important in your own make-up? To what extent do you think teaching will help you meet these various needs?

AUTHOR INDEX

Numbers in parentheses give the reference number of a publication. Separate publications are divided by a semicolon, e.g., 289(12); 326(18). Separate citations of the same publication are divided by a comma, e.g., 289(18), 326(4). Numbers not followed by parentheses refer to mentions in the text.

Aberle, D. F., 610(62)
Aborn, M., 326(7)
Abrahamson, S., 226(85)
Ackerson, L., 546(44)
Adams, D. K., 329(7)
Adams, F. J., 177(21)
Adams, G. S., 179(11)
Adams, J. J., 472(27), 615 (137)
Adcock, C. J., 104(9)
Adkins, D. C., 139(11); 179 (13)
Adler, A., 260
Adler, M. J., 17(6)
Adorno, T. W., 547(4)
Aikin, W. M., 474(48), 614 (130)
Alexander, C., 66(3)
Alexander, H. B., 224(62)
Allison, H. W., 608(21)
Allison, S. G., 608(21)
Allport, G. W., 493, 514 (11); 547(3)
Almy, M. C., 225(73)
Alper, T. G., 326(9), 450 (23); 327(26)
Alschuler, R. H., 515(21)
Alt, P. M., 607(4)
Amatora, M., 637(5)
Ammons, C. H., 543(2)
Ammons, R. B., 543(2)
Amster, W. W., 104(15), 607(12)
Anastasi, A., 141(2), 516 (5); 141(7)
Andersen, E. M., 544(10)
Anderson, G. L., 262(2)
Anderson, H. H., 637(7)
Anderson, J. E., 546(40), 576(1)
Anderson, W. F., Jr., 696 (10)
Andrews, T. G., 452(4)
Angell, G. W., 326(14); 326(17)

Arnoult, M. D., 452(58)
Ash, F. E., 637(6)
Atkinson, J. W., 415(11); 610(60)
Auble, D., 349(6)
Auld, F., 616(12)
Ausubel, D. P., 576(12)
Axelrad, S., 546(52)
Axline, V. M., 680(47)

Babitz, M., 439, 451(44)
Baernstein, H. D., 291(19)
Bagley, W. C., 17(5); 224 (65)
Bain, A., 178(29)
Baker, G. D., 474(52)
Baker, K. E., 452(55)
Baldwin, A. L., 612(94)
Baldwin, B. T., 102(2)
Baller, W. R., 127
Barker, L. S., 102(13)
Barker, R. G., 227(1), 607 (10), 615(4); 678(14)
Barnes, C. A., 515(33)
Barr, A. S., 45(3); 459; 471 (14)
Barron, F., 515(32)
Bartlett, E. R., 546(41)
Bartlett, F. C., 450(21)
Bass, B. M., 580(68); 580 (69)
Bauernfeind, R. H., 543(4)
Bayley, N., 128, 140(24); 223(50); 696(14)
Beach, F. A., 227(8)
Bean, K. L., 179(16)
Bedoian, V. H., 576(8); 576(9)
Beechley, R. M., 612(88)
Beito, E. A., 451(36)
Belknap, G., 578(38)
Bell, R. Q., 140(32)
Benda, C. E., 142(8); 222 (18)
Bendig, A. W., 472(17)

Benne, K. D., 580(2)
Bennett, M. E., 467, 473 (46)
Bernard, H. W., 17(1)
Biel, W. C., 166, 178(31)
Biersdorf, K. R., 514(18)
Bills, R. E., 579(64)
Bilodeau, E. A., 349(9)
Bilodeau, I. M., 415(7)
Binet, A., 109-10
Birch, H. G., 384(15)
Birch, L. B., 516(40)
Bird, C., 545(37)
Blair, G. M., 17(1); 17(2), 696(2)
Blom, G. E., 679(30)
Bloom, B. S., 384(21)
Blue, J. T., Jr., 611(75)
Boles, R. C., 471(5)
Bonney, M. E., 515(23); 576(6); 576(15); 612(89)
Bookwalter, K. W., 103 (19)
Borgatta, E. F., 579(53)
Boring, E. G., 263(12)
Bossard, J. H. S., 616(11)
Boynton, P. L., 637(4)
Breed, F. S., 451(40)
Brett, G. S., 262(9)
Brewer, J. E., 637(7)
Brickman, W. W., 547(9)
Brill, M., 226(96)
Broder, L. J., 384(21)
Brody, D. S., 576(11)
Brogden, H. E., 515(29)
Bronner, A. F., 608(30)
Brouda, L., 91, 93, 103(16)
Brown, S. B., 223(36)
Brownell, W. A., 383 (5)
Brueckner, L. J., 451(36)
Brunswik, E., 262(6)
Bullis, H. E., 659, 678(22)
Bunch, M. E., 419-20, 449 (4)
Burdick, H., 545(37)

Burgemeister, B. B., 221 (15)
Burke, A. J., 63(3); 612 (87), 697(1)
Burks, B. S., 142(11); 223 (45); 611(72)
Buros, O. K., 180(19)
Burt, Sir C., 177(16)
Burton, A., 450(22)
Burtt, H. E., 420, 425, 449 (5)
Buxton, C. E., 449(9)
Byrd, E., 576(4)
Byrns, R., 451(50)

Campbell, A., 578(38)
Campbell, D. T., 349(14); 545(30)
Campbell, W. J., 225(71)
Cantor, N., 579(57)
Carlson, H. B., 226(98)
Carmichael, L., ed., 103 (1); 178(34)
Carrol, R. E., 602, 613 (109)
Carter, H. D., 609(37)
Carter, L., 579(52)
Carter, R. S., 223(37)
Cason, H., 327(34)
Cass, L. K., 546(46), 612 (99)
Cattell, R. B., 104(10); 515 (25); 516(8)
Cava, E. L., 612(97)
Centers, R., 679(46)
Challman, R. C., 17(2)
Charles, D. C., 140(23); 696(12)
Chassel, C. F., 608(31)
Chein, I., 547(2)
Child, I. L., 613(103), 616 (10); 678(15)
Childs, G. B., 471(2)
Childs, J. L., 17(7)
Chittenden, G. E., 678(28)
Christie, R., 547(5)
Clark, D. L., 612(87), 697 (1)
Clark, J. H., 608(29); 609 (50)
Clarke, S. C. T., 637(15)
Clarke, W. J., 473(37)
Class, E. C., 177(7)
Clay, H. M., 141(41)
Cobb, P. R., 696(6)
Coch, L., 578(41)
Coffin, T. E., 616(17)
Cohen, M. R., 45(1)

Coladarci, A. P., 17(3), 262(2), 262(3), 611(86)
Coleman, J. C., 327(37)
Collins, S. D., 103(14)
Collister, E. G., 576(10)
Combs, A. W., 262(8)
Commins, W. D., 17(4)
Conklin, M. E., 679(43)
Conrad, H. S., 140(33); 514(14)
Conway, P., 221(10)
Cook, W. W., 177(18)
Coomer, A., 544(9)
Corman, B. R., 545(23)
Cornett, S., 611(77)
Corsini, R. J., 141(40)
Cosand, J. P., 178(37)
Coules, J., 678(27)
Courtenay, M. E., 578(35)
Courtis, S. A., 167, 178(35)
Cowen, E. L., 384(18); 678 (18)
Cowen, P. A., 226(100)
Cox, C., See also Miles, C. C., 140(22), 142(11)
Craig, R. C., 349(10)
Crandall, E. B., 609(44)
Crane, A. R., 577(28)
Crawford, P. L., 546(54)
Cronbach, L. J., 17(5); 141 (3), 516(6); 452(4)
Crook, M. N., 515(38)
Crowder, F., 696(7)
Cruickshank, W. M., 607 (16)
Crutchfield, R. S., 578(39), 580(5)
Cruze, W. W., 166, 178 (30); 419-20, 449(3)
Cunningham, R., 581(9)
Cureton, E. E., 139(4)
Cureton, T. K., 103(18)

Dahl, M. H., 66(1)
Damrin, D., 578(43), 677 (8)
Darcy, N. T., 225(75)
Darley, J. G., 578(44); 609 (45)
Dashiell, J. F., 327(25)
Davenport, K. S., 224(64); 471(6)
Davidson, H. H., 544(21)
Davie, J. S., 225(78)
Davis, A., 223(51); 594, 611(79)
Davis, B., 225(72)
Davis, F. B., 176(4)
Davis, R. A., 45(3)

Davitz, J. R., 678(17)
Deese, J. E., 293(10), 329 (9), 349(19), 415(14), 452 (1); 329(5)
Delys, L., 140(39)
Dembo, T., 678(14)
Dennis, W., 223(43)
Denver City Schools, 679 (40)
Desing, M. F., 472(20)
Dexter, L. A., 176(2)
DiCarlo, L. M., 104(15), 221(12), 607(12)
Diggory, J. C., 610(54)
Dinsmoor, J. A., 349(20)
Dolansky, M. P., 178(38)
Dollard, J., 291(13), 293 (11), 350(2)
Dolphin, J. E., 607(16)
Domas, S. J., 471(11)
Douglass, H. R., 177(8); 451(46); 451(48)
Dowell, A. S., 696(4)
Dressel, P., 328(49)
Drought, N. E., 609(46)
Drucker, A. J., 611(76)
Dugger, H., 637(4)
Dumpson, J. R., 546(54)
Dunbar, D. S., 580(70)
Duncan, C. P., 452(59)
Dunkelberger, G. F., 473 (41)
Dunkerly, M. D., 578(34)
Dymond, R. F., 577(21)

Eaton, J. W., 613(106)
Eaton, M. T., 471(4); 472 (31)
Ebbinghaus, H., 419-20
Eber, H. W., 579(59)
Eckenrode, C. J., 546(47)
Edgren, R. D., 222(30)
Edwards, A. S., 222(27); 473(33)
Eells, K., 213, 225(80); 225 (81)
Eglash, A., 579(63)
Eisenson, J., 221(7)
Elliott, F. R., 328(44)
Ellis, A., 514(14); 612(88)
Ellis, R. S., 17(6)
Emmons, W. H., 326(5)
England, O. C., 473(34)
Engle, T. L., 473(36); 613 (107)
English, H. B., 293(15); 449(10)
Epps, P., 607(2)
Eriksen, C. W., 415(12)

Escalona, S., 263(22); 678 (20)
Estes, W. K., 293(6); 293 (9)
Eustice, D. E., 471(14)
Exline, R. V., 576(13)
Eysenck, H. J., 104(8); 177 (23); 515(26), 516(9); 611 (70), 615(8); 616(15)

Fagin, B., 17(4)
Fahey, G. L., 473(47)
Farber, I. E., 325(1), 328 (4); 349(15)
Farber, M. L., 613(111)
Farris, L. P., 221(14)
Fassett, K. K., 141(40)
Faust, W. L., 579(51)
Ferrell, G. V., 226(89)
Festinger, L., 577(24); 580 (6)
Fifer, G., 222(33)
Finch, F. H., 226(86); 472 (28)
Findley, W. G., 180(22)
Fink, M., 472(21)
Fischer, L. K., 223(40)
Fitch, M. L., 326(13)
Fleishman, E. A., 103(21)
Fleming, R. S., 637(3)
Fleming, V. V., 515(34)
Flory, C. D., 140(35); 637 (1)
Floyd, W., 471(9)
Flügel, J. C., 263(10)
Foley, J. P., 141(7)
Forbes, J. K., 224(67)
Ford, C. F., Jr., 610(58)
Forlano, G., 349(12); 348 (4), 349(13), 350(3); 515 (39)
Fox, C., 17(7)
Fox, W. H., 696(11)
Frank, J. D., 678(19)
Frank, L. K., 610(56), 611 (78)
Fransden, A. N., 609(38)
Fraser, R. J. A., 139(20)
Frazee, H. E., 612(93)
Frazier, A., 607
Freeman, F. N., 176(5); 223(44); 224(58)
Freeman, F. S., 141(1), 516 (4)
French, J. R. P., Jr., 578 (41)
French, J. W., 158, 177 (17); 507-08, 515(30)

Frenkel-Brunswik, E., 532, 547(4); 545(29)
Freud, S., 15, 256
Friedman, K. C., 451(48)
Fritz, M. F., 221(5); 222 (20)
Fulk, B. E., 226(91)
Fulkerson, G., 471(12)
Furfey, P. H., 544(15)

Gable, F., 326(15)
Gadson, E. J., 222(16)
Gage, N. L., 179(3); 576 (13)
Gagné, R. M., 452(55)
Gallagher, J. R., 91, 93, 103(16)
Galton, F., 182
Gardner, D. E. M., 474(49)
Garn, S. M., 102(8); 607(5)
Garrett, H. R., 178(26)
Garrett, J. F., 227(2), 607 (11), 615(3)
Garrison, K. C., 18(8)
Garrison, S. C., 140(37)
Gaskill, H. V., 221(5)
Gasser, E. B., 576(12)
Gates, A. I., 17(2), 637(16); 221(11); 263(15); 451(41)
Gates, M. F., 607(15)
Gebhard, M. E., 677(12)
Gerberich, J. R., 179(4); 328(39)
Gertler, M. M., 607(5)
Gesell, A. L., 140(26)
Gibb, C. A., 577(31), 580 (1)
Gibbs, P. K., 611(85)
Gibson, E. J., 114(2)
Gillette, A. L., 449(6)
Gillies, D. V., 678(16)
Gilliland, A. R., 226(93)
Givens, P. R., 609(39)
Gjerde, C. M., 637(12)
Glaze, J. A., 222(26)
Glick, S. J., 546(52)
Glueck, E., 546(48), 607(1), 615(1)
Glueck, S., 546(48), 607(1), 615(1)
Goff, R. M., 613(115), 616 (14)
Goldman, B., 474(51), 614 (133)
Good, C. V., 67(5)
Goodenough, F. L., 141 (8); 203, 224(55); 678(26)
Gooderich, H. B., 472(18)

Goodlad, J. I., 677(9); 677 (10)
Goodman, M. E., 545(35)
Gordon, T., 579(55)
Gough, H. G., 545(31); 546(49); 577(19)
Grace, G. L., 326(19)
Gray, H., 515(28); 610(53)
Gray, J. S., 18(8); 613(114)
Green, B. F., Jr., 608(35)
Greene, E. B., 179(3)
Greene, H. A., 179(4)
Greenhill, M. H., 680(4)
Gronlund, N. E., 576(3); 677(6)
Gross, N., 578(44)
Guetzkow, H., 222(31), 384(14); 579(65)
Guilford, J. P., 515(27), 577(26); 544(7); 610(55)
Guilford, R. B., 515(27), 577(26)
Guthrie, E. R., 270-71, 280, 283, 284-85, 291(6); 291(7), 296

Haffter, C., 612(90)
Haggard, E. A., 610(61)
Haines, A. C., 578(43), 677 (8)
Hall, C. S., 263(16)
Hamley, H. R., 452(52)
Hammer, E. F., 613(113)
Hammond, W. H., 102 (10)
Handy, L. M., 610(67)
Hanley, C., 102(4)
Harding, J., 547(2), 614 (129), 679(39), 680(5)
Hare, A. P., 578(45); 679 (38)
Harlow, H. F., 327(32); 327(33); 329(7); 450(30); 450(31)
Harrell, R., 222(17)
Harrell, T. W., 226(91)
Harrell, W., 177(24)
Harris, A. J., 514(12)
Harris, D. B., 546(41)
Hartley, D., 241
Hartley, R. E., 577(16)
Hartmann, G. W., 263(13); 263(14)
Hartung, M. L., 451(34)
Harvey, O. J., 576(7)
Hathaway, S. R., 546 (51)
Hattwick, L. B. W., 515 (21)
Havel, J., 545(29)

Havighurst, R. J., 223(51); 610(61); 638(1)
Hayes, C., 140(31); 452(60)
Hayes, K. J., 452(60)
Hayes, M. L., 545(38); 679 (43)
Hays, W., 608(27)
Healy, W., 608(30)
Heathers, L. B., 178(36)
Hebb, D. O., 262(7)
Heisler, F., 614(123)
Heisler, F. A., 473(39)
Helfant, K., 545(24)
Helson, H., 262(2)
Henderson, N., 226(98)
Hendrick, I., 514(9)
Hendrix, G., 452(53)
Hendrix, O. R., 178(41)
Henmon, V. A., 451(50)
Henry, A. F., 579(53)
Herbart, J. F., 241, 256
Herbert, L., 474(53), 614 (131)
Herr, W. A., 473(35)
Hewitt, J. E., 103(17)
Hicks, J. A., 178(33)
Hieronymus, A. N., 611 (80)
Hildreth, G. H., 179(17); 179(18)
Hilgard, E. R., 222(30); 262(3); 291(4), 292(28), 292(1); 327(30); 383(6)
Hilgard, J. R., 178(32)
Hinkleman, E. A., 608(23)
Hoff, A. G., 451(47)
Hoffman, M. L., 578(40)
Hoffman, M. N. H., 349 (12)
Hoffman, W. S., 177(25)
Hofstaetter, P. R., 546(39)
Hollenberg, E., 612(95)
Hollingworth, H. L., 291 (9)
Hollingworth, L. S., 122, 123, 139(14), 142(10); 182; 221(4)
Hollinshead, M. T., 104 (15), 607(14)
Holzinger, K. J., 223(44); 224(58)
Homans, G. C., 578(36), 580(1)
Horn, E., 451(39)
Horrocks, J. E., 103(1), 547(1), 577(22); 576(5); 577(17)
Horwitz, M., 576(14), 580 (3)

Hoult, T. F., 614(122)
Hovland, C. I., 414(1); 415 (3), 452(3); 614(120), 616 (16), 679(34), 680(5); 679 (35); 680(6)
Howells, W. W., 102(9); 102(11)
Hughes, A. S., 577(21)
Hull, C. L., 15, 17(8), 262 (5), 291(12), 348(5); 276-79, 281, 282, 284, 285, 291(11); 291(14); 291 (15); 291(19), 296, 335, 402
Humphrey, G., 384(1)
Hunt, E. E., 103(22)

Inkeles, A., 613(10), 616 (16)
Irion, A. L., 328(2), 415 (15), 452(2)
Irvine, R. P., 222(30)
Irwin, O. C., 140(28)

Jahoda, M., 547(5)
James, W., 243
Janis, I. L., 679(37); 680 (6)
Jarrett, R. F., 383(10); 679 (36)
Jaworski, I. D., 679(42)
Jellinek, E. M., 222(23)
Jenkins, M. D., 226(92)
Jenkins, R. L., 540, 546 (50); 612(91)
Jenkins, W. O., 349(7); 414(4)
Jensen, D., 142(11)
Jensen, K., 103(4)
Jensen, M. B., 383(7)
Jenson, R. E., 178(39)
Jersild, A. T., 17(2); 474 (50), 614(132); 474(51), 614(133); 514(3), 516(1), 544(6), 547(1), 638(3); 677(3); 679(31)
Jessner, L., 679(30)
John, E. M., 677(2)
Johnson, B. C., 545(34)
Johnson, D. M., 384(3); 579(61)
Johnson, G. R., 608(32)
Johnson, P. O., 45(3)
Johnston, A., 384(11)
Jones, A. W., 547(7)
Jones, H. E., 104(14); 140 (25); 140(33); 516(42)
Jones, R. S., 17(2), 696(2)
Jones, S., 177(12)

Jones, V., 547(1), 613(105), 637(8), 638(3)
Jordan, A. M., 451(42)
Jorgensen, A. N., 179(4)
Judd, C. H., 443, 473(32)

Kagan, H. E., 679(44)
Kallmann, F. J., 228(9), 610(68), 616(9); 611(69)
Kallner, A., 102(7)
Kao, D., 328(48)
Kaplan, L., 696(9)
Kaplan, O. J., 516(42)
Katona, G., 383(3)
Keislar, E. R., 577(30)
Kelley, D. M., 514(15)
Kelley, H., 637(2)
Kelley, H. H., 577(25), 580 (1); 680(6)
Kelley, T. L., 139(8)
Kelly, E. L., 579(65)
Kendler, H. H., 292(25)
Kephart, N. C., 471(9)
Keys, A., 615(5)
Keys, N., 439, 450(19); 451 (44)
King, B. T., 679(37)
Kinney, E. E., 615(136)
Kinsey, A. C., 514(13)
Kinzer, J. R., 178(42)
Kinzer, L. G., 178(42)
Kirk, S. A., 139(19), 608 (26)
Klebanoff, S. G., 221(1)
Klein, A., 608(33)
Klein, V., 610(66)
Kline, F., 696(3)
Klineberg, O., 215, 224 (56); 224(57); 228(14)
Klopfer, B., 514(15)
Klubeck, S., 580(69)
Kluckhohn, C., 226(101)
Knapp, R. H., 472(18)
Koch, H. L., 139(3)
Koch, S., 262(5); 291(16)
Koffka, K., 247, 291(5)
Köhler, W., 247, 263(18), 282
Kolstoe, O. P., 139(19), 608(26)
Kremer, A. H., 546(42)
Kretschmer, E., 84
Kuhlen, R. G., 576(10)
Kutner, B., 547(2)

Lacy, L. D., 227(103)
Lahey, M. F. L., 449(12)
Lambert, W. E., 578(49)
Landis, C., 608(18)

Landreth, C., 545(34)
Langfeld, H. S., 222(25)
Lanmon, M., 577(18)
Lashley, K. S., 246-47
Lastrucci, C. L., 678(16)
Lawrence, E. M., 225(77)
Lawrence, W. C., 226(90)
Lawson, J. V., 450(19)
Laycock, S. R., 18(9)
Lazarus, R. S., 327(22), 329(5)
Leahy, A. M., 224(61)
Leal, M. A., 544(20)
Learned, W. S., 177(19)
Leavitt, II. J., 679(33)
Leeper, R., 263(15), 291 (3); 384(4)
Lehman, H. C., 178(28)
Leighton, D., 226(101)
Leipold, L. E., 609(41)
Lemaire, A., 383(7)
Leuba, C. J., 327(29)
Levinson, D. J., 547(4); 613(110), 616(16)
Levit, G., 578(37), 580(2)
Levitt, E. E., 545(33)
Lewin, H. S., 614(121)
Lewin, K., 247, 251, 252, 254-55, 260, 263(22); 282, 290(2); 678(14)
Lewis, D. K., 221(13)
Lewis, W. D., 139(15)
Lichliter, M., 696(8)
Lichtenstein, A., 472(23); 637(9)
Light, B. H., 514(19)
Lightfoot, G. F., 608(22), 615(6)
Lindgren, II. C., 680(7)
Lindzey, G., 680(5)
Lippitt, R., 577(32)
Lisonbee, L. K., 607(6)
Liu, C. H., 613(105)
Loftus, J. J., 474(51), 614 (133); 474(53), 614(131)
Logan, F. A., 291(17)
Long, W. F., 544(17)
Longstaff, H. P., 328(41)
Lorge, I., 578(48); 608(24)
Lorr, M., 540, 546(50); 612 (91)
Lotz, H. R., 615(138)
Louise, M. F., 140(36)
Lovell, C., 546(45), 613 (118)
Low, C. M., 292(30)
Lowell, E. L., 327(31)
Luckiesh, M., 222(28)
Lund, F. H., 225(70)

Lyness, P. I., 544(13)
Lyon, D. O., 328(44)
Lysgaard, S., 611(81)

McAllister, D. E., 452(56)
McBean, D., 544(9)
McCall, W. A., 471(10)
McCandless, B. R., 223 (39); 261(1); 545(30)
McCarthy, D., 140(27); 141(8); 223(35)
McClearn, G. E., 327(33)
McClelland, D., 327(24), 481, 541(4), 610(57); 328 (1), 516(11)
McConnell, T. R., 17(2)
McCorquodale, K., 293(7)
McCurdy, H. G., 578(49); 579(59)
McCurry, W. H., 140(28)
McDougall, W., 254-55, 263(19)
McFann, H. H., 415(6)
McFarland, R. A., 222(23)
McGeoch, J. A., 326(6), 349(11), 349(17), 383(2), 449(1), 449(8), 450(13), 450(28); 328(2), 415(2), 415(15), 452(?)
McGraw, M., 167, 178(24)
McGuire, C., 577(18); 577 (23)
McGurk, F. C. J., 225(83)
McKay, H. D., 613(108)
McKeachie, W. J., 579(65)
McKillop, A. S., 609(40)
McKinnon, K. M., 509, 515(35)
McNamara, W. J., 179 (14)
McNemar, O., 384(17), 385 (9), 578(47), 580(7)
McNemar, Q., 139(13)

Maas, H. S., 611(84)
Maccoby, E. E., 611(85); 614(126)
Mace, C. A., 262(4)
Maier, N. R. F., 291(22); 579(54); 579(56)
Malamud, D., 546(54)
Maller, J. B., 327(27)
Malone, A. J., 516(41)
Malpass, L. F., 608(34)
Maltzman, I., 384(16)
Mandell, W., 679(35)
Mandler, G., 327(23)
Marcuse, F. L., 514(18)
Marron, J. E., 139(10)

Marshall, H., 222(24); 678 (21)
Martin, C. E., 514(13)
Martin, H., 610(55)
Martin, W. C., 578(44)
Martin, W. E., 140(29)
Marzolf, S. S., 696(14)
Maslow, A. H., 483, 514 (5); 514(6); 517(12)
Mason, E. P., 614(134)
Mason, J. M., 326(14)
Massler, M., 516(41)
Matin, L., 139(11)
Mauldin, W. P., 224(53)
Maxwell, J., 139(12)
Mead, M., 228(12), 615(7)
Mech, E. V., 327(36); 349 (8)
Meer, B., 384(17)
Meigs, M. F., 677(3)
Mellone, M. A., 139(20)
Melton, A. W., 449(2), 450 (16)
Menninger, W. C., 637 (17), 638(2); 678(23), 680 (2)
Mensh, I. N., 614(134)
Meredith, G. P., 451(51)
Meredith, H. V., 224(69)
Merrill, M. A., 141(5)
Merrill, R. M., 178(36)
Metfessel, M., 546(45), 613 (118)
Meyer, G., 177(9)
Meyerson, L., 104(15), 221 (18), 607(13)
Miles, C. C., 142(8)
Mill, J., 241
Mill, J. S., 241
Miller, J., 545(36)
Miller, K. D., 102(6)
Miller, N. E., 292(33); 291 (13), 293(11), 348(1), 350 (2)
Mintz, A., 327(28)
Misbach, L., 290(1)
Mitchell, B. C., 223(44)
Mitchell, R., 546(55)
Monachesi, E. D., ed., 546 (51)
Monroe, R. L., 263(17)
Monroe, W. S., 66(4); 180 (20); 452(4)
de Montmollin, G., 579(50)
Mooney, R. L., 466, 473 (44)
Moraes, A. M. de M., 222 (32)
Morgan, A. B., 384(22)

Morgan, C. L., 18(12), 179 (15)
Morgan, C. T., 514(1)
Morgan, L.D., 450(20)
Morgan, W. J., 384(22)
Morrisett, L., Jr., 384(16)
Morse, W. C., 18(10)
Moser, H. E., 383(5)
Moses, E. R., 613(119)
Moss, F. K., 222(28)
Mowrer, O. H., 286, 291 (21); 293(13); 293(14)
Mudge, E. L., 438-39, 451 (43)
Mull, H. K., 544(22)
Munn, N. L., 104(13), 385 (6)
Murchison, C., 327(25)
Murphy, F. J., 546(43)
Murphy, G., 263(11)
Murray, H. A., 514(16)
Mursell, J. L., 18(11); 179 (1)
Mussen, P. H., 613(112)

Naegel, K. D., 610(62)
Nagel, E., 45(1)
Neilon, P., 515(36)
Nemzek, C. L., 221(10); 226(86); 472(28); 472 (29); 609(47)
Newcomb, T., 577(24)
Newland, T. E., 226(90)
Newman, H. H., 224(58)
Newman, S. C., 466, 473 (43); 473(44)
Nicolson, A. B., 102(4)
Nisbet, J., 226(88)
Noble, C. E., 383(1), 450 (14)
Noe, E. J., 471(14)
Noel, D. I., 225(74)
Noll, V. H., 326(12)
Norris, E. B., 415(13)
Northway, M. L., 576(2), 581(11)
Norvell, G. W., 548(11)
Nowlis, V., 612(102)
Nuttin, J., 678(13)
Nyssen, R., 140(39)

Odell, C. W., 179(8)
Oden, M., 140(21)
Ojemann, R. H., 472(19)
Olander, H. T., 437, 451 (35)
Olds, J., 292(29)
Orata, P. T., 440, 451(33)
Orlansky, H., 613(104)

Ormiston, M., 177(14)
Orr, H. K., 471(7); 471(8)
Ort, R. S., 611(83)
Osgood, C. E., 292(26); 415 (5)
Osler, S. F., 329(5)
Ostreicher, L. M., 579(66), 677(5)
Outhit, M. C., 223(49)
Owens, W. A., Jr., 140(38)
Oxtoby, T., 225(76)

Parke, L. H., 544(8)
Parnell, R. W., 607(2)
Pasamanick, B., 227(104)
Pastore, N., 514(7)
Pattie, F. A., 611(77)
Pauly, F. R., 223(34)
Pavlov, I. P., 269-70, 284, 285-86
Peak, H., 328(50)
Penfold, D. J., 226(102)
Penrose, L., 227(5)
Pepitone, A., 577(24), 637 (2)
Pepitone, E. A. B., 326(8)
Perlmutter, H. V., 579(50)
Peters, H. C., 178(43)
Peterson, H. A., 696(14)
Peterson, R. C., 614(128)
Phillips, B. N., 696(11)
Phillips, E. L., 577(27)
Pinneau, S. R., 223(41)
Pintner, R., 221(7); 221 (11); 515(39)
Plesset, I. R., 610(67)
Poffenberger, A. T., 327 (35)
Polansky, N., 577(32)
Pomeroy, W. B., 514(13)
Pope, B., 611(82)
Portenier, L. G., 226(97)
Porter, E. H., 325(2)
Postman, L., 291(15), 415 (17), 453(5); 350(4); 383 (10)
Potter, E. H., 327(21)
Poull, L. E., 222(19)
Powell, J., 576(6)
Powell, M., 222(22)
Powers, E., 547(56)
Prell, D. B., 611(70), 615 (8)
Prentice, W. C. H., 415 (9); 415(10)
Pressey, S. L., 547(7)
Proshansky, H., 547(2)
Prugh, D. G., 678(29)
Putnam, T. J., 221(15)

Raabe, V. L., 577(21)
Rabinowitz, H. S., 384(15)
Radke-Yarrow, M., 545 (36); 679(45)
Raush, H. L., 612(97)
Ray, A. M., 545(27)
Redl, F., 612(101), 677(7); 680(1)
Reed, H. B., 383(4)
Reeder, C. W., 473(43)
Reid, T., 240
Remmers, H. H., 18(12), 179(15), 610(59); 179(3); 224(64), 471(6); 472(30); 473(42); 543(4); 611(76); 612(100)
Revitz, P., 577(27)
Reynolds, E. L., 103(23)
Ricciuti, E. A., 473(38), 544(14), 614(124)
Richardson, J., 415(16), 450(27)
Richey, R. W., 696(11)
Riecken, H. W., 578(36), 580(1)
Riley, D. A., 450(15)
Rinsland, H. D., 177(13)
Roberts, K. E., 515(34)
Roe, A., 611(72)
Roff, M., 576(11)
Rogers, J. F., 73, 102(1)
Rogers, M. L., 103(20)
Rohrer, J. H., 226(99)
Rolfe, J. F., 472(22)
Rosanoff, A. J., 610(67)
Roseborough, M. E., 580 (4)
Rosen, S., 577(32)
Rosenberg, N., 544(18)
Rosenberg, P. R., 678(24)
Ross, C. C., 179(12)
Rostker, L. E., 472(15)
Rotter, J. B., 384(20)
Ruja, H., 328(38), 572, 579 (60), 580(8)
Rulon, P. J., 176(3)
Russell, D. H., 327(30); 385(8); 677(11)
Ryan, T. A., 452(54)
Ryans, D. G., 452(61); 472 (16)
Ryden, E. R., 18(12), 179 (15)

Saltzman, I. J., 326(4)
Sandiford, P., 263(13); 443-44, 452(4); 452(64)
Sanford, G. A., 224(54)
Sanford, R. N., 547(4)

Sarason, S. R., 326(11), 327 (23)
Scates, D. E., 67(5); 100 (21)
Schehr, F., 452(54)
Scheinfeld, A., 228(10); 610(65)
Scherer, I. W., 221(3), 608 (20)
Schiff, H. M., 576(12)
Schlosberg, H., 385(5), 415 (7), 416(4), 453(6)
Schmidt, H. O., 326(18)
Schneider, L., 611(81)
Schneirla, T. C., 291(22)
Schoeppe, A., 610(61)
Schofield, W., Jr., 609(51)
Schonfeld, W. A., 607(8)
Schroder, H. M., 384(20)
Schrupp, M. H., 637(12)
Schultz, D. G., 608(35)
Scott, R. B., 226(94)
Sears, P. S., 543(1), 609(52)
Sears, R. R., 514(10); 612 (96)
Segal, D., 516(2)
Seidman, J. M., 18(13)
Sells, S. B., 474(53), 614 (131)
Selover, M. S., 177(22)
Sessions, A. D., 609(38)
Seward, J. P., 328(3)
Shaffer, R. H., 609(49)
Shaw, C. R., 613(108)
Shears, L. W., 580(67)
Sheffield, F. D., 414(4)
Sheldon, A., 544(22)
Sheldon, W. H., 82-84, 90, 102(5); 103(6); 104(7); 582, 607(3), 615(2)
Shenker, S., 577(27)
Sherriffs, A. C., 679(36)
Shields, J., 611(71)
Shimberg, M. E., 224(52)
Shirley, M. M., 546(43); 597, 612(92)
Shoben, E. J., Jr., 292(24)
Shuey, A. M., 613(117)
Shultz, I. T., 608(19)
Shuttleworth, F. K., 102 (3); 103(2)
Sills, F. D., 102(12)
Silverman, A. J., 679(41)
Simon, C. W., 326(5)
Simpson, R. H., 17(2), 696 (2); 179(9)
Sims, V. M., 176(6)
Singer, A., 679(32)
Singer, J. L., 221(1)

Skeels, H. M., 223(46)
Skinner, B. F., 279-80, 291 (18); 293(16), 335
Skinner, C. E., 18(14)
Skodak, M., 223(48)
Slobetz, F. B., 637(14); 677 (1)
Smith, A., 241
Smith, A. B., 180(22)
Smith, C. A., 451(49)
Smith, F. V., 262(3)
Smith, H. C., 579(61); 580 (70)
Smith, H. L., 471(4); 472 (31)
Smith, H. P., 18(15)
Smith, M. E., 450(17)
Smith, Mary E., 451(46)
Smoke, K. L., 414(3)
Snyder, W. U., 696(1)
Snygg, D., 262(8)
Sobel, F. S., 223(38)
Solem, A. R., 579(56)
Solomon, H., 578(48)
Solomon, R. L., 292(31); 292(32)
Sommers, V. S., 607(17)
Sones, A. M., 450(24)
Sopchak, A. L., 612(98)
Sorenson, H., 18(16); 451 (45)
Spache, G. D., 609(48)
Spearman, C., 107, 115, 117, 119, 139(1)
Spence, K. W., 292(5); 293 (8); 349(15)
Spence, R. B., 17(3)
Sperry, M., 612(95)
Spinelle, L., 609(47)
Spitzer, H. F., 472(26)
Springer, D., 140(30)
Sprol, S. J., 471(3)
Stagner, R., 609(42)
Stanley, J. C., Jr., 179(12); 349(7)
Stanton, M., 221(5)
Stedman, M., 221(9)
Stein, M., 384(19)
Stellar, E., 514(1)
Stendler, C. B., 225(79); 578(43), 677(8)
Stephens, A. L., 348(2)
Stephens, J. M., 224(60), 472(25); 291(20); 291 (23); 348(3); 349(18); 471(1); 472(23)
Stephenson, W., 179(2)
Stevens, S. S., 384(4)
Stevenson, H. W., 326(3)

Stewart, N., 224(63)
Stogdill, R. M., 578(33)
Stolurow, I. M., 292(3)
Stolz, H. R., 103(5); 607 (7)
Stolz, L. M., 103(5); 607 (7); 616(13)
Stone, G. R., 349(21)
Stouffer, G. A. W., 637(11)
Stoughton, M. L., 545(27)
Strang, R., 473(40); 473(45)
Strong, E. K., 530, 544(19)
Stroud, J. B., 223(47); 328 (43); 328(40), 450(18); 450(24)
Stuit, D., 178(40)
Sullenger, T. E., 544(8)
Sullivan, C., 529, 544(16)
Super, D. E., 613(116)
Sutton, R. S., 326(10)
Swanson, G. E., 578(42)
Symonds, P. M., 514(17); 514(8), 677(4); 543(3); 637(10)

Taba, H., 514(2), 516(7)
Taft, R., 450(26)
Tanser, H. A., 226(95)
Tate, M. E., 225(84)
Taylor, D. W., 384(17), 385(9), 578(47), 580(7); 579(51)
Taylor, E. A., 614(135)
Terman, L. M., 140(21); 141(5); 142(11); 182, 142 (8), 228(12), 610(64), 615 (7)
Terry, P., 177(10)
Tetlow, H., 17(4)
Thelen, H. A., 578(46); 581(10)
Thibaut, J. W., 577(25), 580(1); 678(27)
Thiele, C. L., 451(37)
Thistlethwaite, D., 384 (13)
Thomas, R. M., 179(6); 515(22)
Thompson, A. H., 613 (114)
Thompson, G. G., 326(20); 577(17)
Thompson, H., 103(1); 140(26)
Thompson, R., 452(60)
Thomson, G. H., 104(11)
Thorndike, E. L., 242, 263 (20); 271, 319(16), 402. 443

Thorndike, R. L., 140(34); 224(68); 385(7)
Thorpe, L. P., 544(5)
Thurstone, L. L., 117, 118, 119, 139(5); 139(7); 614(128)
Tiedeman, D. V., 471(11)
Tinker, M. A., 222(29)
Tizard, J., 579(58)
Tolman, E. C., 256, 260, 262(4); 263(21); 280-81, 282, 284, 285, 335, 361, 415(17), 453(5)
Torgerson, T. L., 179(11)
Townsend, A., 177(20)
Trager, H., 545(36); 679 (45)
Travers, R. M. W., 227(7)
Traxler, A. E., 177(22); 179(10)
Triggs, F. O., 178(27)
Trow, W. C., 18(17)
Trumbull, R., 608(25)
Tryon, C. M., 545(26)
Tuddenham, R. D., 610 (63)
Tueller, R., 450(22)
Tufts, E., 546(53), 547(8)
Turner, G. H., 226(102)
Turner, M., 637(4)
Tyler, F. T., 213, 225(82); 515(31)
Tyler, L. E., 45(2), 141(6), 224(59); 142(8), 228(12), 610(64), 615(7); 610(58)
Tyler, R. W., 449(11)

Ullman, C. A., 548(10), 637(13)
Underwood, B. J., 292 (25); 415(8), 450(25); 415 (16), 450(27); 449(7)

Vallance, T. R., 177(11)
Various authors, 516(42)
Varon, E. J., 139(2)
Vernon, P. E., 104(12), 139(9); 177(15); 262(4); 516(3)

Veroff, J., 610(60)
Verplanck, W. S., 291(16)
Vinacke, W. E., 384(2)
Voeks, V. W., 291(8); 328 (47)
Vosk, M., 545(32)

Waldfogel, S., 679(30)
Walk, R. D., 383(9)
Walker, H., 103(3)
Walker, H. M., 472(24)
Waller, C. H., 473(47)
Wallin, W. K., 544(8)
Walther, E. C., 328(42)
Wandt, E., 579(66), 677 (5)
Wapner, S., 327(26)
Warburton, F. W., 226(87)
Ward, L. B., 135, 150(92)
Warner, K. O., 328(39)
Warren, J. M., 450(31)
Waterhouse, I. K., 678(15)
Watson, A., 451(38)
Watson, G., 17(3); 579(62)
Watson, J. B., 246
Wattenberg, W. W., 680 (1)
Watters, W. A., 471(13)
Wayland, L. C. N., 696(5)
Wear, B. A., 576(5)
Weber, R. J., 221(6), 607 (9)
Weiden, R., 326(16)
Weigand, G., 609(36)
Weil, R. J., 613(106)
Weinreb, J., 678(25)
Weitzman, E., 179(14)
Weltman, N., 612(100)
Wertheimer, M., 247
Wheat, H. G., 18(18)
Wheelwright, J. B., 515 (28)
White, G. D., 577(18)
Whiting, J. W. M., 613 (103), 616(10)
Whitney, P. F., 67(7)
Wickens, D. D., 450(29)
Wilcox, S., 610(60)

Wilensky, H., 221(1)
Wilkinson, F. R., 472(19)
Willerman, B., 577(20)
Willgoose, C. E., 103(20)
Williams, H. M., 608(28)
Williams, J. R., 226(94)
Wilson, C. C., 103(15)
Wilson, F. T., 139(16)
Wineman, D., 612(101), 677(7)
Wingo, G. M., 18(10)
Witherington, H. C., 18 (19)
Witmer, H. L., 546(43); 546(53), 547(8); 547(56)
Witty, P., 139(17); 544(9); 544(11); 544(12), 614 (125)
Wolf, S. J., 609(13)
Wolff, C., 240
Wolfle, D., 225(76); 515(24)
Wolman, B., 577(29)
Wood, B. D., 177(19)
Woodruff, A. D., 329(8)
Woodworth, R. S., 262(3), 292(27); 383(8), 384(12); 385(5), 416(4), 453(6)
Woody, G., 611(74)
Wrenn, C. G., 547(6); 609 (44)
Wrightstone, J. W., 176(1)
Wyatt, D. F., 349(14)
Wynne, L. C., 292(31)

Yarrow, see Radke-Yarrow
Yates, A. J., 221(2)
Young, N., 225(79); 545 (23)

Zahl, P. A., 104(17)
Zajonic, R. B., 614(127)
Zelen, S. L., 545(33)
Zeligs, R., 545(25)
Zimmerman, F. T., 221 (15)
Zimmerman, W. S., 139(6)
Zingg, R. M., 223(42)

SUBJECT INDEX

Abbreviations, journal titles, 50
Abstractions, dangers in, 371-72
Academic growth, limits of, 162-63
Academic values, possible neglect of, 625-26
Acceleration, and achievement, 464
Acceptance, of aggressive urge, 661-62; of child, home, 597—teacher, 641-44—dealing with anger, 661—dealing with weak tendencies, 654; of drive, in adjustment, 647-49; into group, process, 557; of reality, as adjustment goal, 628-30; of responsibility, in maturity, 633-34; social, and IQ, 585-86—leadership and, 569-70 —promoting, 668-70
Accomplishment quotient, 169, 171-72
Accuracy, in science, 27
Achievement, scholastic, constancy, 160-61 —development, 161—factor analysis, 158-59—high school vs college, 160-61—individual differences, 159—and intelligence, 169-72—observing, 145—and teachers' ratings, 588-89
Achievement need, 307; as motive, 481
Acne, see pimples
Active approach, in reducing fear, 666
Activity, in reading or listening, 311-13; of students, effects on transfer, 441
Activity in progress, as motive, 306-07
Activity schools, achievement and adjustment, 468
Adaptation, in reducing fear, 667
Adjustment, classes in 659; cultural differences, 600-01; goals of, 626-36; inadequate, persistence, 598-99; and physical defect, 583-85; racial and national differences, 602-03; school hazards, 626-27; of teacher, 682-83; teaching for, problems, 618
Administrative factors, and adjustment, 605
Adolescent crowd, 558
Adolescent spurt, 78
Adopted children, heredity-environment, 201
Adult achievement, intellectual, 164-65
Adult intelligence, 136
Adventure, spirit of, in teaching, 693-94
Affection, development, 524

Age changes, personality, 511-12; scholastic achievement, 165-68
Aggression, age changes, 519-22; in children, 520—home conditions, 597; dealing with, 660-64
Ailments, as defense mechanism, 492-93
Alcohol, psychological effects, 187-88
Alcoholism, heredity, 593
Amish, 601
Amount of material, in learning, 316-17; in retention, 431
Analogies, of teaching process, 387-88
Analysis, preliminary, transfer, 442-43
Anger, acknowledging, 661-62; age changes, 519-22; announcement of, 662-63; causes of, 519-22; dealing with, 660-64
Animal psychology, in connectionism, 242
Animals, children reared with, 198-99; curiosity in, 307-08
Annual Review of Psychology, 49
Anthropology, in study of adjustment, 600-01
Anti-Semitism, Freudian base, 260
Anxiety, in adults, effects on children, 644; effects of praise and blame, 303; in learning, 300; in learning theory, 286
Appearance, physical, and intelligence, 184—and popularity, 554; worry over, 583
Application of rules, transfer, 441-42
Aptitude tests, and scholastic achievement, 174
Arbitrary material, use of structure, 357
Arithmetic, transfer in, 437
Aspiration, level of, 650
Associationism, 240-41; dynamic, 241—and Freudianism, 256
Athletic ability, test, 94-5
Atmosphere, classroom, democratic-autocratic, 571-72; of school, and adjustment, 605
Attendance, and achievement, 462-64
Attitude to school, and achievement, 587; class differences, 212-13
Attitudes, age changes, 531-32; change, group dynamics, 563-64—incidental forces, 674-75; developing, 671-74; parent-child, 598; of teacher, achievement,

459-60; teaching of, efficacy, 622-23; un-intentional learning, 298-99
Auditory vs visual learning, 315-16
Autocratic classroom, 570-74
Averages, use of, 58

Backward association, 298
Bain, A., illustration of maturation, 165
Balance, dependency, in group relations, 634; in personal adjustment, 627-28
Barriers, in psychology, 252
Basal metabolism, age changes, 92; and intelligence, 184
Beauty, and intelligence, 183-84
Behavior problems, teacher vs clinician, 624-25
Behaviorism, 246
Benzedrine, psychological effects, 189
Beta hypothesis, 929-21
Bilingualism, and intelligence, 211
Binet Tests, 109-11
Blacky Tests, 499, 514(20)
Blake, W., on suppression, 662
Blame, as a motive, 302-03
Blood pressure, age changes, 92-3
Bluffing, objective and essay tests, 150, 154
"Boners," from lack of experience, 366-67
Boredom, in plateau, 321
Brain, and intelligence, 183; and person-ality, 585
Broken homes, child adjustment, 596; de-linquency, 539-40

Caffeine, psychological effects, 189
Calculated risks, in education, 22
California Study, prejudice, 532-33
Capacity, view of intelligence, 169
Causal-comparative method, in study of education, 32, 37
Character education, 623-24; and the school, 622-24
Cheating, and SES, 594
Chi square, 64
Child, only, adjustment, 596
Child-rearing, cultural differences, 600-01
Childhood group, 557-58
Childhood memories, 420, 425
Children's Apperception Test, 499
Class, social, adjustment, 594-96—intelli-gence, 209—sex role, 592—and teachers, 595-96
Class size, 461-62
Classroom, group-centered, 570-74
Classroom activities, and connectionism, 244
Climate, emotional, of home, 596-97
Clinic referrals, age changes, 511-12
Clinical attitude, and teaching, 624-25
Clique, in student groups, 558-59

Coefficient of correlation, 59
Cognitions, 280-81
Cognitive maps, 281
Collecting (hobby), 528-29
College achievement, sex differences, 194-95
College students, intelligence of, 123
College teaching, directive vs student-cen-tered, 572-74
Combination theories, effect and substitu-tion, 276-80
Comics, and adjustment, 604
Common cause, pitfall, 37, 39
Communication, in attitude change, 672-73
Community factors, 602; and adjustment, 600-01, 621-22; and delinquency, 600-01
Compensation, defense mechanism, 490-91
Competition, effects, achievement, 304-05—adjustment, 649, 657
Composition, English, testing, 148-49
Concepts, abstract, extraneous learning, 401-02—teaching, 368-69
Concrete examples, teaching for adjust-ment, 652-53; in teaching meaning, 366-71
Conditioned response, in classroom, 337-38; as form of guidance, 336; historical, 269-70; trace, 398
Conduct, age changes, 537-38
Conflict, ego needs, 486-88; surface needs, 484-86
Conformity, in children, 536; controlling, 564; group pressure, 562-63; individual urge, 563; pressure toward, problem solving, 568
Connectionism, description, 236, 242-46
Consensus, group decisions, 561-62
Constancy, geometric forms, 249, 250; lead-ership, 560-61; maladjustment, 598-99; patterns of experience, 248; of personal-ity, 509-10; of result produced, 255; size, 250; vocational interests, 530
Context, as guidance, 368
Continuity vs discreet groups, intelligence, 120-21
Control, of drives, automatic, 632-33—change with maturity, 631—personal ad-justment, 627-28; statistical, methods of, 39
Control group, necessity of, 28
Controversies, psychological, 234-35; deal-ing with, 286-89; educational reform, 287-88
Conversational interests, 526-27; sex dif-ferences, 590-91
Cooperative play, early stages, 549-50
Correlation, coefficient of, 59
Correspondence courses, 456

Cost of school, and achievement, 457
Criminals, heredity, 593
Crippled children, intelligence, 184-86
Critical ratio, 62
Criticism of studies, impersonal approach, 40
Cross education (transfer), 435
Cross-sectional method, intelligence, 135-36
Crowd, adolescent, 558
Crying (infant), as language, 131
Cue reduction, 271
Cultural patterns, personality and adjustment, 600-02
Cultural role, sex differences, 591-92
Cumulative Book Index, as source of data, 48
Curiosity, as motive, 307-08
Curriculum, in personal development, 620, 651-52
Curves of learning, 317-20; see also Learning curves

Darwin, C., childhood IQ, 126
Day dreaming, defense mechanism, 491
Death rate, and age, 89
Decision, delayed, problem solving, 379-80
Decreasing returns, 318; learning curve, 319-20
Defects, physical, prevalence, 88—achievement and intelligence, 186-87
Defense mechanisms, description, 488-93; and negative reinforcement, 390
Deferred practice, advantages and disadvantages, 165-68
Definitions, function of, 106-07; intelligence, 107-09; of maturity, 630; personality, 493-96
Delay, in problem solving, 379-80
Delinquency, 538-41; age changes, 538-39; body build, 583; city neighborhood, 600-01; heredity, 593; and intelligence, 540, 586; parental rejection, 597; personality, 540; racial and national factors, 603; remedial programs, 540-41; sex differences, 590
Delinquents, ethical knowledge, 537
Democratic atmosphere, in home, 597
Democratic classroom, 570-74
Dependency, in group relations, 634
Desegregation, armed forces, and prejudice, 535; housing, and prejudice, 535
Desultory reading, 51
Development lesson, 355
Deviation score, intelligence tests, 114
Diet, psychological effects, 186, 189-90
Differential Aptitude Tests, as intelligence tests, 119
Diminishing returns, academic growth, 162-63; and administrative factors, 455; learning curve, 318, 319-20
Direct attack, teaching for adjustment, 659
Discipline, teacher's attitude, 643-44
Discussion method, vs lecture, 314-15—group process, 571-74; management of, 314
Disease, and intelligence, 184; and personality, 584-85; teacher's detection of, 72
Distraction, effects on learning, 308
Disuse, in forgetting, 418
Doll play, therapy, 663-64
Double classes, 462
Drawings, children's and personality, 500
Drill, 315
Drive, in adjustment, 477-83; change with maturity, 630-31; and control, personal adjustment, 627-28; nature of, 478-79
Drives, troublesome, dealing with, 647-49
Drop-out, as extraneous learning, 389
Dull students, 123-25
Dunlap, K., 324

Earning while studying, 465-66
Eclectic attitude, psychological theories, 286-89; in views of tests, 157-58
Ectomorph, description, 83
Education, income and, pitfalls, 21; problems in understanding, 20
Educational Index, as source of data, 50
Educational age, from standard tests, 156
Educational growth, nature and significance, 3
Educational psychology, as applied psychology, 9-10; contributions to general psychology, 10-11; limitations of, 11; role of, 5-7
Educational quotient, from standard tests, 156
Effect, principle of, 271-76
Ego, in conflict of needs, 486-88; force in Freudianism, 257-58, 259; resisting conformity, 563
Ego involvement, in learning, 299-300; problem solving, 379; and retention, 428, 431; retroactive inhibition, 408-09
Ego needs, in adjustment, 480-81; indirect satisfaction, 488-93
Eleven-year systems, 464
Emitted responses (Skinner), 279-80
Emotional climate, home, 596-97
Emotional expression, development of, 518-19
Emotional problems, teacher's role, 667-68
Emotions, development, 518-25; differentiation, 519; need for outlet, 646-49
Empirical relations, in study of education, 30-32

Encyclopaedia of Educational Research, as source of data, 48

Endomorph, description, 82

Energy *vs* technique, teaching, 693-94

Engineer, contrasted to teacher, 15

Enthusiasm, in teaching, 693-94

Environment, abnormal, and intelligence, 198; and intelligence, 198-201

Environment-heredity, problem, 197-98

Error, in investigations, 24

Essay tests, achievement, 148-52; advantages, 148-49; disadvantages, 149-52

Established structure, use with new material, 356

Ethical behavior, and intelligence, 586-87

Ethical knowledge, development, 537

Example of others, in fear, 666

Examples, concrete, in teaching concepts, 370

Existing interests, as motive, 306-07

Expectations from transfer, 444-45

Expenditure for schools, regional differences, 208-09

Experience, as a basis for meanings, 366-68; harmful types, in learning, 295; influence on test, 110; in intelligence tests, 119; and success of teacher, 460; types of, in learning, 310-15

Experimental method, in study of education, 31; pitfalls, 35

Explanation, in reducing fear, 665

Extracurricular activities, and achievement, 464-65

Extraneous learning, classroom problem, 389-90; role of practice, 400-01; significance, 399-400

Extraneous stimuli, in learning, 398-99

Extrinsic motives, 305-06

Extroversion, 505-06; praise and blame, 303

F-test, 63

Facilitation, learning, 405-09

Facing reality, in frustration, 635-36; teachers, 685-86; useful aids, 640-51

Factor analysis, achievement tests, 158; body build, 84-6; delinquency, 540; description, 84-5, 117; intelligence, 115-19; interests, 525; parental behavior, 596; personality, 505, 507-08; prejudice, 532; successful students, 587-88

Faculty psychology, description, 240

Failure, effects, teaching for adjustment, 650, 656; as a motive, 302-03

Fallacies, role of concrete experience, 370-72

Family, size, adjustment, 596—intelligence, 214

Family conditions, in adjustment, 596-600; in delinquency, 539-40

Fantasy, defense mechanism, 491; *vs* reality, 630

Fatigue, in plateau, 321-22; and spaced practice, 413

Fear, announcement of, 667; in children, 522-23; dealing with, 664-67; parent-child resemblance, 598; and SES, 594

Feeble-minded children, adult adjustment, 127-28

Feeble-mindedness, 124-25

Field psychology, description, 237; nervous system in, 282

Fitness (physical), test, 94

Fitness index (physical), 91

Flexibility, problem solving, 380; *see also* Rigidity

Follow-up studies, intelligence, 136

Forces, psychological, Lewin, 252

Forewarning, in reducing fear, 665

Forgetting, curve of, 425-26; differential, spaced practice, 412; in learning theory, 283-85; qualitative changes, 426-27

Freedom, for teacher, 692-93

Frequency distributions, characteristics of, 56; interpretation of, 53

Frequent tests, as motive, 300-01

Freudianism, as explanation of prejudice, 533

Friendships, 555-56; associated factors, 554-55

Frustration, childhood, and adjustment, 600-01; ego involved, 486-88; felt by teacher, 685-91; from physical barrier, 484; in problem solving, 374; surface, treatment, 485-86; symptoms, 657-58; tolerance for, 635-36, 649, 658; types of, 483-88

Furfey Scale, 529

g (general factor), intelligence, 115-17

Games, child, 550; outlet for feelings, 663; and SES, 594

Gang, childhood, 558

General impression, achievement testing, 147; in study of education, 23, 25

Generalization, teaching for adjustment, 653; transfer, 443-44

Genius, intellectual, 122, 126; and physique, 182; *see also* Gifted

Gestalt psychology, description, 237-38, 247-51; learning in, 268

Gifted adults, age and achievement, 164-65

Gifted child, characteristics of, 122-23

Gifted men, childhood IQ, 122, 126

Glands, factor in growth, 98

Goal, use in psychological theory, 255-56

Goals, legitimate, in attitude change, 671-72; problem in personal adjustment, 623-24; in teaching, 692
Goethe, childhood intelligence, 127
Grade scores, from standard tests, 156
Graded tasks, reducing extraneous learning, 391-92; in reducing fear, 666; teaching for adjustment, 620, 651-52—weak tendencies, 654
Graphs, interpretation of, 54
Graphs of learning, see Learning curve
Group, as an entity, 556-57
Group differences, educational significance, 216-18
Group dynamics, 561-70
Group factor, intelligence, 116
Group pressure, 562; attitude change, 563-64
Group process, 556-60
Group relations, changes with maturity, 634-35
Group size, efficiency, 565-66; problem solving, 567-69
Group solidarity, 564-65, 566-67
Group structure, in developing leadership, 671
Group tests, intelligence, 111
Groups, spontaneous, 557-58
Growth pattern, revealed in physical growth, 73
Guessing, essay tests, 149; objective tests, 154
Guidance, in adjustment teaching, 654-57; classroom procedure, 330, 337-38; in developing leadership, 671; in early stages of learning, theory, 273-74; learning in absence of, 332; limitations, 340; manual, 337; problem solving, 378-81; and reinforcement, overlapping, 338-40, 392-94; in social acceptance, 670; for teachers, 643-44, 693; in teaching meaning, 365-66; with weak tendencies, 341-43

H-T-P Test, 499
Hand books, as source of data, 47
Handicap, physical, and personality, 583-85
Happiness, age changes, 523-24
Health, and intelligence, 182; regional differences, 207-08; school hazards, 72; of teacher, 684
Height, age differences, 75; individual differences, 74, 75; sex differences, 75
Heredity, effects on teaching for adjustment, 620-21; intelligence, 204-07; personality and adjustment, 593
Hierarchy, Maslow's, 483, 487; in promoting security, 645-46
High-school students, intelligence of, 123

High-school subjects, and college success, 439-40
Hobbies, 528-29
Home, influence of, teaching for adjustment, 621-22
Home-study courses, 456
Homosexuality, heredity, 593
Hopes, human, problem for scientist, 22
Hormones, factor in growth, 98
Hostility, in adolescents, 521-22
How-to-study courses, 466-67
Human Relations Club, 659; and social acceptance, 670
Humor, and teacher's frustrations, 687
Hutterites, adjustment among, 601
Hypocrisy, as teacher irritant, 690
Hypotheses, in problem solving, 373, 376-77; in study of education, 32, 33, 35, 36, 37

id, 257, 258
Ideals, age changes, 531-32; vs reality, in teaching, 689-90
Ideas, responses to, 311-12
Identical elements, transfer, 443-44
Identical twins, vs fraternal twins, adjustment and criminality, 593—intelligence, 204-05; reared apart, 200-01
Identification, defense mechanism, 492; group, changes with maturity, 634; parent-child, and adjustment, 598, 600
Idiot, 125
Illness, age changes, 90; as defense mechanism, 492-93; prevalence, 88
Illogical behavior, problem solving, 375, 380-81
Illumination, effect on achievement, 190
Imbecile, 125
Incidental learning, 297-98
Income, and education, fallacies, 21; of teacher, 684-85
Increasing returns, learning curve, 317, 319
Incubation, problem solving, 381
Indispensability, feeling of, 629
Individual differences, achievement, in a single class, 159-60; athletic ability, 94; intelligence, 120-25; personality, 503-04; sexual maturity, 79; weight, 80
Individuality, as personality, 495
Infant, intellectual development, 129
Infant personalities, persistence, 509-10
Information, factual, in combating prejudice, 674-75
Inhibition, in learning, 405-09
Insecurity, symptoms, 644-45
Insight, from aggressive needs, 664; learning, classroom, 360-63—prevalence, 361; use in transfer, 440-41, 442

Instructor, student-centered approach, 571-73
Instrumental avoidance, in learning theory, 285-86; persistence of, 286
Integration, of conflicting drives, 632
Intellectual tasks, age level, 135
Intelligence, and achievement, data, 172— theory, 169-72; of adults, 136; and body size, 183; as capacity for learning, 169; as general achievement, 170-72; infant, 129; normal range, 123; and personality, 585-87; prospective teachers, 688-89; and suggestibility, 673-74; of teacher, 458
Intelligence quotient, constancy, 126-29; fluctuations in, 128; nature of, 112-14
Intelligence tests, administering, 111, 120; American Council, 114; and aptitude tests, 119; Binet, 110; Davis-Eells, 119; Stanford-Binet, 110-11; Wechsler, 110-11
Intention to learn, as motive, 297-98
Interests, age changes, 529; description, 525-30; factor analysis, 508, 525; vocational, 529-30
Interference (learning), combating, 409-10—and retention, 431; and forgetting, 418-19
Intervening variable, 256
Interview, personality testing, 496-97
Intrinsic motives, 305-06
Introversion, 505-06
Inventory, personality, 498-99
Iowa Studies, intelligence, 199-200
IQ, see Intelligence quotient
Irregularities in growth, 77
Irreversibility, maladjustment, 598-99
Isolated communities, intelligence, 209

Journals, technical, citing, 50
Joy, occasions for, 523-24

Knowledge of results, devices, 302; as motive, 301-02; in teaching, 684, 690-91

Language, child vs chimpanzee, 134; development, 131-34—sex differences, 193; in infancy, 130; and intelligence, 130, 134
Latin, high school and college success, 439; transfer from, 438
Leader, classroom, functions, 570-71; emergent, 559-61—problems of, 569—qualities for different ages, 560; qualities of, 559-61; tasks of, 562; training of, 570
Leadership, promoting, 671; size of group, 566; in spontaneous groups, 559-60
Learning, in connectionism, 245; extraneous, classroom problem, 389-90; in field theory, 250-51; speed of and retention, 422-23

Learning curves, 317-20; as motives, 322-23
Learning to learn, 435-36
Learning set, 435-36
Lecture, vs discussion, achievement, 314-15—group feeling, 570-74; as educational experience, 311-13; requirements, 313
Lewinian psychology, 251-55; and learning, 266-67; and nervous system, 282
Life space, 251; in learning, 266-67
Lighting, effect on achievement, 190
Limits, academic growth, 162-63; of learning, 322
Listening, nature of, 311-13; vs reading, 315-16
Logic, and problem solving, 375, 380-81
Longitudinal method, intelligence, 135
Love, age changes, 524
Loyalty, group, in conformity, 563

Machover Draw-a-Person Test, 499
Man-to-man scales, 501-02
Manipulation, as motive, 307-08
Manipulatory needs, in adjustment, 480
Maslow's heirarchy, in promoting security, 645-46
Maturation, and administrative influences, 445; animals, 166; motor skill, children, 166-67; in scholastic achievement, 164-68; in teaching for adjustment, 620-21
Maturity, lack of, in plateau, 320; personal adjustment, 630-35; social, scale, 551-52
Maturity (interests), tests of, 529
Maxims, as insights, 362-63
Meaning, as goal of teaching, 355-56, 363-67; in reducing interference, 409-10; and retention, 427-28; in teaching, limitations of, 354-56
Meaningful material, reminiscence in, 423; retention in, 425
Mediation theories, learning, 276-80
Memory, and connectionism, 244; meaningful material, 353-54
Mental age, 112-14
Mental hygiene, in classroom, 639-75
Mental hygienist, and teachers, views of child behavior, 625-26
Mental vs motor tasks, retention, 434
Mesomorph, description, 83
Metabolism, age changes, 92; and intelligence, 184
Method, inefficient, in plateau, 320
Methods of study, suggested, 445-47
Middle class, attitude to schools, 212-13
Middle-class values, and school, 214
Mill, J. S., childhood IQ, 126
Misconceptions, from lack of experience, 366-67

Mnemonic aids, 358
Model, for search, problem solving, 374-75; of teaching process, 387-88
Models, in psychological theory, 251, 280
Mongolism, 125
Moral standards, age changes, 537
Morale, student, and success, 587-88
Morals, and intelligence, 586-87
Moron, 125
Motivation, excessive, achievement, 309-10; learning, relation to other mechanisms, 296; with minimal reinforcement, 394-95; in reducing interference, 409-10; and retention, 428; school learning, general problems, 309-10; in teaching meaning, 364-65; undesired, from reinforcement, 396-98
Motive, in learning theory, 282-83; performance or learning, 309; for teachers, 692; see also Need
Motives, in classroom use, 297
Motor control, infancy, 130
Motor fitness test, 94
Motor skill, growth in, 97, 98; sex differences, 98
Movie preferences, 528
Movies, and attitude formation, 604-05
Multiple factor theories, intelligence, 117

Nail biting, age changes, 510-11
National differences, intelligence, 216—selective migration, 203-04; personality and adjustment, 602
Need, in adjustment, 477-83; deprivation of, 645-46; psychological vs educational usage, 282-83; security, in adjustment, 481-82
Needs, bright children, 585; catalogues of, 482; of child, parental awareness, 598; ego, in adjustment, 480-81; manipulatory, in adjustment, 480; physiological, in adjustment, 479; relation between, 482-83; social, in adjustment, 479-80
Negative practice, 323-24
Negativism, children, 536-37
Neighborhood, city, adjustment and delinquency, 600-01
Nervous system, in connectionism, 245-46; learning theory, 280-82
Nonscholastic forces, interference by, 7; prevalence, 4; in teaching for adjustment, 621-22
Nonsense syllables, learning, 352
Norms, in achievement tests, 156; intelligence tests, 112
Number of cases, in investigations, 25
Nursery school, effects on intelligence, 200

Objective tests, see Short-answer tests

Objectives, educational, affected by tests, 157—meaningful description, 145—tests to fit, 145
Objectivity, achievement tests, 151
Observation by others, as motive, 304
Occupations, differences in intelligence, 211
Omomorph, description, 86
Oral tests, achievement, 147-48
Orientation, problem solving, 373-74
Outlet, for anger, 661-62; for drives, 646-49; for fear, 666-67
Over-concern, and anger, 660-61
Overlapping, group differences in intelligence, 217
Overlearning, 428-29

Pacing, as motive, 304
Paintings, children's, and personality, 500
Parallel play, children, 549
Parent-child similarity, attitude, 533, 598; fears, 598; intelligence, 205-06; interpretation of, 201
Parental education, intelligence of children, 211
Parents, and child hostility, 520-21; understanding of child, 598
Participant, class discussion, personality, 572
Participation, group decisions, 562
Pattern, see Structure
Patterns in experience, 248; see also Structure
Percentile rank, in intelligence tests, 114-15
Perception, importance in field theory, 250
Performance tests, personality, 502
Permissiveness, parental, child adjustment, 596—class differences, 595
Persistence, problem solving, 378-79
Personal adjustment, goals of, 626-36
Personality, adolescent girl, 591; age changes, 510-12; cultural differences, 600-01; definitions, 493-94; in effects of praise and blame, 303; as individuality, 495; as integration, 494; racial and national differences, 602-03; as social impact, 494-95; successful students, 587-88, 589-90; and susceptibility to persuasion, 674; of teacher, achievement, 458-59; (teachers' ratings) academic success, 588-89; as whole person, 494
Personality tests, academic success, 589-90; use of, 502-03
Persuasion, susceptibility to, 673-74; techniques of, 672-73
Perversion, sexual, as ego threat, 259
Physical appearance, worry over, 583
Physical defects, prevalence, 88

Physical growth, illustration of general growth, 73
Physical handicap, and intelligence, 184-85; and personality, 583-85
Physical performance, growth in, 95, 96; sex differences in, 95, 96; tests of, 94
Physiological efficiency, age changes, 92, 93; measure of, 90; sex differences, 93
Physique, and personality, 582-83
Pimples, 99; worry over, 583
Plateaus, learning, 320-22
Play, parallel, 549; and SES, 594; sex differences, 590; "turn about," 550
Play interests, age changes, 525-26
Play therapy, 663-64
Pleasant materials, retention, 430-31
Popularity, in children, 553-54
Positive transfer, 434-35
Power test, 159
Practice, distributed, 410-13; extraneous learning, 400-01; in learning, 323; negative, 323-24; teaching for adjustment, 651-52; types of, 310-15; see also Spaced practice
Practice periods, length of, 410
Praise, academic learning, 303-04; teaching for adjustment, 655-56
Predicting scholastic achievement, from aptitude tests, 174; from earlier achievement, 173-74; from intelligence, 172-73
Preidentification, transfer, 442
Prejudice, 532-36; associated factors, 534-36; combating, 535-36, 674-75; development, 534; nature of, 532-33
Preparation for examinations, essay vs objective, 149
Prestige, in attitude change, 672-73; of teacher, 688-89—in adjustment teaching, 622
Priggishness, 653
Proactive facilitation, 407-08; and transfer, 432
Proactive inhibition, 408; and transfer, 432
Problem check list, 498
Problem solving, process, 373-77—groups, 567-69; sex differences, 193; teaching, 373-80
Productivity, intellectual, at different ages, 164-65
Professional training, teachers, and success, 460-61
Profiles, personality, 508-09
Progressive schools, achievement and adjustment, 467-68
Projection, defense mechanism, 492
Projective tests, 498-99
Promotion, continuous, adjustment, 650

Proportion, physical, 82—age and sex factors, 86, 87—factor analysis, 84
Protection, from reality, effects, 650-51
Proverbs, as insights, 362-63
Psychiatrist, and teacher, 659, 667-68
Psychoanalytic theories, 256-60
Psychodrama, 659
Psychological Abstracts, as source of data, 51
Psychological Bulletin, as source of data, 49
Psychologist, and educational aims, 671-72
Psychology, facts vs principles, 14
Puberty, onset of, 79
Pulse rate, age changes, 92, 93
Punishment, effect on adjustment, 649-50; in home, 597; in learning, strong tendencies, 345-46—weak tendencies, 342; in teaching for adjustment, 657; see also Reprimands
Purposive psychology, 238, 255-256

Quality scales, achievement tests, 155
Quarreling, 520
Questionnaire, personality, 497-98

r (coefficient of correlation), 59
Race, intelligence and achievement, 215-16; personality and adjustment, 602-03
Race awareness, development, 534
Radio listening, and achievement, 464; and adjustment, 604
Radio preferences, 528
Rating scales, 500-01
Rationalization, defense mechanism, 491-92
Reactive inhibition, description, 284; in spaced practice, 412
Readiness for learning, 167
Reading, activity for learning, 311-13; vs listening, 315-16
Reading interests, development, 527
Realism, in educational leaders, 689-90; increase with maturity, 632
Reality, acceptance of, goal, 628-30; facing, in frustration, 635-36; unduly harsh, 640
Reasoning, effects of transfer, 436-37
Recall, measure of retention, 419
Recitation, vs rereading, 337-38—strong tendencies, 344-45
Recognition method, retention, 421
Reconstruction method, retention, 421
Recovery, from physical exertion, 91
Reflex arc, psychological theory, 243
Reflex reserve, 279
Regional differences, 207-08
Regression effect, intelligence, 126; physical growth, 99, 100

Reinforcement, in adjustment teaching, 656-58; automatic, 332; casual, 333; in classroom, 330; deliberate, 333-34; and guidance, overlapping, 331, 339-40, 392; in Hullian theory, 276-77; insightful, 360-62; in later stages of learning, 274-75; partial, 334-35; Pavlovian use, 270; secondary, 286; spread of, 402; in teaching meaning, 365; time relations, 279—in classroom, 334; undesired, 393, 394-96

Rejected child, security for, 642-43; and teacher, 641-45

Rejection, social, example, 669-70

Relations, empirical, place in study of education, 30

Relearning method, retention, 419-20

Reliability, achievement tests, 155

Religious attitudes, age changes, 531

Remedial action, in teacher frustrations, 686

Remedial programs, delinquency, 540

Reminiscence, 423-24

Repression, as defense mechanism, 489-90; in forgetting, 418-19; harm from, 648; of negative reinforcement, 390; see also Suppression

Reprimands, 396-398

Rereading vs recitation, 338; strong tendencies, 344-45

Research reports, critical interpretation, 53, 65; selective use of, 52

Resentment, and demands on time, teacher, 687-88

Resonance theory, problem solving, 375-76

Response generalization, as transfer, 435

Responsibility, acceptance of, maturity, 633-34; age changes, 551-52

Rest periods, length of, 410-11; problem solving, 381; rote learning, 410-13

Retention, method of measuring, 419-22; and speed of learning, 422-23

Retroactive facilitation, 408

Retroactive inhibition, 408-09

Reversed causality, pitfall, 40-41

Review, in retention, 429-30

Review of Educational Research, as source of data, 49

Reward, with weak tendencies, 342

Rhetorical questions, as guidance, 338

Rigidity, in outstanding scientists, 378; and prejudice, 533; problem solving, 378, 380

Role, sex, 592

Role playing, attitude change, 673

Rorschach Test, 498-99

Rural-urban differences, intelligence, 208; personality, 601

Sampling, as source of error, 60

Saving method, retention, 419-20

Schizophrenia, home conditions, 597

Scholastic achievement, and personality, 587-90

School, hazard to adjustment, 626-27; and other forces, 4; philosophy of, and achievement, 467-68—and adjustment, 605; success in character education, 622-23

School cost, 457

School factor, achievement tests, 158

School quality, 457

School size, 456-57

School year, length of, 464

Science, high school, and college success, 439-40; nature and limitations, 14; transfer from, 438-39; values and limitations in education, 22, 24

Scientists, intelligence of, 123; outstanding, flexibility in, 378—teachers of, 459

Scott, Sir W., childhood IQ, 126

Search, in problem solving, 374-76

Search model, 374-75

Secondary reinforcement, learning theory, 286

Security, child, and acceptance, 641-42; feelings, in teachers, 643-44; lack of, symptoms, 644-45; need, in adjustment, 481-82; in reducing fear, 665; with weak tendencies, 654

Selected cases, pitfall, 26

Selective migration, 196-97; and intelligence, 202-03

Selective Service Qualifying Test, occupational differences, 211; regional differences, 208

Self-control, 537-38

Self-esteem, indirect enhancement, 488-93

Self-expression, need for, teachers, 690-91

Sensory avenue, effect on learning, 315-16

Sensory generalization, 399

Sentences, in infant language, 133

Serial learning, interference in, 403-05

Set, for learning, 435-36; problem solving, 377-78—groups, 568

Setting, physical, retroactive inhibition, 408

Severity, parental, class differences, 595

Sex differences, achievement, 193-95; body proportions, 87; friendships, 555-56; intelligence, 192-93; motor skill, 98; occasions for joy, 523-24; personality, 590-92; physical proficiency, 95, 96; physiological efficiency, 93; quarreling, 521; weight, 80

Sex hormones, factor in growth, 98

Sex role, 592

Sexual maturity, 79

Short-answer test, advantages and disadvantages, 154; vs essay, 148; types, 153
Sign learning, 280-81
Significance, statistical, 60
Size, body, and intelligence, 183; of class, 461-62; of family, adjustment, 596; of groups, efficiency, 565-66—problem solving, 567-69; of school, and achievement, 456-57
Skill, acquisition of, reducing fear, 665-66; and social acceptance, 670
"Skipping" grades, 464
Sleep, learning during, 298; loss of, psychological effects, 190
Social acceptance, description, 552-54; promoting, 668-70
Social class, vs socioeconomic status, 210
Social distance scales, 502
Social factors, motivation, 303-05
Social life of teacher, 688
Social participation, 554
Social rejection, example, 669-70
Social sensitivity, age changes, 550-51
Socialization, of drives, 632-33
Socioeconomic status, and adjustment, 594; and attitudes, 602; and intelligence, 210-12; and prejudice, 535
Sociogram, 552-53
Somatotype, athletic ability, 95; description, 83; disease and, 90; factor analysis, 86; and temperament, 582-83
Spaced practices, 410-13; advantages for, 412-13; limitations, 411-12
Speech, development, 131-32
Speed, factor in achievement tests, 158-59
Speed set, problem solving, 379
Speed test, achievement, 153
Spelling, transfer in, 437-38
Spontaneous groups, as working groups, 561
Spread of effects, 402
Spurt in height, adolescence, 78
Stammering, sex differences, 193
Standard error, 62
Standard tests, advantages and disadvantages, 155-56
Standard to be met, as motive, 305
Standards, arbitrary, and anger, 660; class differences, 594-95
Stanford-Binet Test, description, 110-11; and Wechsler, 125
Statistical method, see Causal-comparative method
Stimulation, unintentional, 393
Stimulus generalization, classroom, 399
Stimulus-response, 236, 242-46
Strong tendencies, treatment, 343-46; vs weak tendencies, 346-47
Structure, aid in learning, 352-54; artificial, 357-58; in experience, classroom use, 351-52; in Gestalt psychology, 247; and retention, 427-28; use with new material, 354-55
Student-centered teaching, 570-74
Study, effective methods, 445-47
Study hall, efficiency, 303
Subconscious (Freud), 258
Subjectivity, essay tests, overcoming, 151-52
Sublimation, defense mechanism, 488
Substitution principle, 270-71; advantages and disadvantages, 273-76; and reinforcement, classroom relations, 331
Success, as a motive, 303-04; need for, in adjustment, 655-56
Suggestibility, children, 536-37
Suggestion, in attitude change, 672-73
Summer camp, leadership behavior, 559
Summer vacation, forgetting, 426
Super-ego, 258-59
Supervising teachers, flexibility, 694
Support of schools, regional differences, 208-09
Suppression, of anger, 661-63; change with maturity, 631-32; Freudian, 258; harmful, 646-49; see also Repression
Swaddling, infant, and adjustment, 601
Syllogism, use of concrete experience, 370-71
Sympathy, change with maturity, 634
Symptoms, frustration, 657-58; maladjustment, detection, 667-68
Synapse, in connectionism, 245
Synthesis, psychological theories, 238-39
Systematic study, in education, 23

t-test, 63
Teacher, attitude of, student achievement, 459-60; autocratic vs democratic, 570-74; class origins of, 595; and clinician, 625-26; energy vs caution, 693-94; engineer, 15; guide vs instructor, 620; intelligence of, and student achievement, 458; permissive vs demanding, 625-26; prestige of, adjustment teaching, 622; and psychiatrist, 667-68; and psychological theory, 223; ratings by, and student achievement, 588-89; responsibility, character education, 623-24—scholastic growth, 144; security feelings, 643-44; social life, 688; and therapy, 675; working hours, 687-88
Teachers' marks, sex differences, 194-95
Teachers' views, importance of, 9
Teaching, art vs applied science, 11-12; complexity of, 387-88; frustrations of, 685-91; satisfactions of, 683-85—making most of, 691-94

Teaching success, factor analysis, 459; factors associated with, 459-61
Television preferences, 528
Television viewing, and achievement, 464; and adjustment, 604
Temperament, and body build, 582-83
Tendencies, strong vs weak, academic teaching, 346-47—adjustment teaching, 653-54
Test favoritism, class differences, 213-14; and intelligence test results, 196, 201-02
Testing, frequency of, motivation, 300-01; practice exercises in, 436
Tests, personality, use of, 502-03; of race awareness, 534; unannounced, as motive, 301; see also Specific tests
Thematic Apperception Test, 499
Theories, controversial, and educational reform, 287-88; eclectic attitude, 224; in learning, 265; possible synthesis, 238-39; tested in schools, 288-89
Theorizing, urge toward, 8
Therapy, and teacher, 667-68
Time spent in study, 466
Tobacco, psychological effects, 189
Topological psychology, 251-55
Tough-mindedness, sex differences, 591
Trace conditioned response, in serial learning, 403-04
Transfer, in adjustment teaching, 652-53; effect on learning curve, 319-20; enhancing, achievement, 440-41; expectations from, 433-34; high school to college, 439-40; individual differences, 443; in lay thought, 432-34; prevalence of, 436; theories, 443-44
Trial-and-error learning, 271-76; advantages and disadvantages, 273-76; description, 271-72; illustration, 332
Truancy, as extraneous learning, 389
Tuition (guidance), 337
Twins, identical, reared apart, 200-01—vs fraternal, adjustment and delinquency, 593—vs fraternal, intelligence, 204-05
Two-phase theories, learning, 276-80
Types, personality, 504

Unconscious solutions, problem solving, 375-76

Unpalatable evidence, administrative factors, 468-69
Urges, autonomous, Freudianism, 257-60

Vacation forgetting, 426
Valence, 252
Validity, achievement tests, 146-47
Values, class differences, 594-96; educational psychology and, 13; middle class, and the school, 595-96; personality dimension, 506-07; and psychological controversy, 235
Variable, dependent and independent, 31
Variability, intelligence, sex differences, 192; and uncertainty, 61
Variance, measure of, 62
Ventilation, effects, achievement, 190-91
Vineland Scale of Social Maturity, 551-52
Visual aids, combating prejudice, 675
Visual vs auditory learning, 315-16
Visual defects, see Defects, physical
Vitamins, and intelligence, 186-87
Vocabulary development, 132
Vocalizations in infant, 132

Ward-Hovland effect, 424-25
Weak tendencies, adjustment learning, 654-56; distinguished from strong, 346-47; treatment, academic learning, 340-43
Wechsler-Bellevue Test, 110-11
Wechsler Intelligence Scale for Children, 111; deviation scores in, 114; and Stanford-Binet, 114, 125
Weight, growth in, 80
Wetzel grid, 84
White House Conference, 516
Whole vs part learning, 358-60
WISC, see Wechsler Intelligence Scale for Children
Wishes, guilty, expressing, 647-49
Wishful thinking, pitfall, 21
Working group, 561-70
"Working" student, 465-66
Worries, age changes, 522-23

Youthful achievement, gifted adults, 164-65